Drone Law and Policy

Drone Law and Policy describes the drone industry and its evolution, describing the benefits and risks of its exponential growth. It outlines the current and proposed regulatory framework in Australia, the United States, the United Kingdom and Europe, taking into consideration the current and evolving technological and insurance landscape.

This book makes recommendations as to additional regulatory and insurance initiatives which the authors believe are necessary to achieve an effective balance between the various competing interests. The 23 chapters are written by global specialists on crucial topics, such as terrorism and security, airport and aircraft safety, maritime deployment, cyber-risks, regulatory oversight, licensing, standards and insurance.

This book will provide authoritative reference and expert guidance for regulators and government agencies, legal practitioners, insurance companies and brokers globally, as well as for major organisations utilising drones in industrial applications.

Anthony A. Tarr is Senior Consultant, Clyde & Co, Brisbane; Director, Robyn Ashton Consulting Pty Ltd; formerly Vice Chancellor, University of the South Pacific; Dean & Professor of Law, Indiana University—Indianapolis; Dean & Sir Gerard Brennan Professor of Law, The University of Queensland and Dean & Foundation Professor of Law, Bond University; author of ten books/treatises including *Insurance Law in New Zealand* and *Australian Insurance Law*.

He has been Chairman, Managing Director or Non-executive Director of various commercial and resource sector companies; formerly Chief Executive Officer of the Queensland Law Society; Director of the Indiana Bar Foundation and Chairman of the Fiji Law Reform Commission.

Julie-Anne Tarr is Senior Consultant, Clyde & Co, Brisbane, and Professor of Commercial Law, Queensland University of Technology. She has held professorial and senior executive roles in the United States, South Pacific and Australia including at Indiana University, University of the South Pacific, the QIMR Berghofer Medical Research Institute, and Queensland's Litigation Reform Commission. Specialising in insurance and risk management, emerging technologies and complex contracting, she has authored six books/treatises including *Disclosure and Concealment in Consumer Insurance Contracts and The Laws of Australia Insurance*. She has published more than 100 articles and law reform reports and is the Insurance and Transport Editor for the Australian Business Law Review.

Maurice Thompson is Senior Equity Partner, Clyde & Co, Melbourne and Perth. He is Founder and Chair of Clyde & Co's International Drones Group, and he has been engaged by insurance majors, corporates, governments and regulators to assist in compliance, policy creation, registration, regulation and insurance policy wordings with regard to drones. Maurice also heads Clyde & Co's Australian "Energy, Marine, Natural Resources Group" (EMNR) and the firm's Australian "Aviation Group". He is a member of the firm's EMNR Global Executive.

He qualified in 1992 and has 28 years of experience advising clients in the shipping, offshore oil and gas, resources and mining, commodity trading, aviation, insurance and ports industries both domestically and internationally.

Jeffrey Ellis is Partner, Clyde & Co, New York. He focuses his practice on aviation, insurance, products liability, commercial, litigation and appellate matters. Jeff represents airline carriers in connection with the various liability and regulatory issues confronting the aviation industry on both the domestic and international fronts. He represented the interests of United Airlines in the litigation arising from the 9/11 terrorist attacks. He also represented the interests of Delta Air Lines in the Swissair/Delta Flight 111 crash, Continental Airlines in the Air France Concorde crash, Delta/Northwest in the litigation arising out of the Underwear Bomber incident, General Aviation Manufacturers Association (GAMA) in product pre-emption litigation and the Association for Unmanned Vehicle Systems International (AUVSI) and the Consumer Technology Association (CTA) in drone pre-emption litigation.

Drone Law and Policy

Global Development, Risks, Regulation and Insurance

Edited by Anthony A. Tarr, Julie-Anne Tarr, Maurice Thompson and Jeffrey Ellis

Routledge
Taylor & Francis Group
LONDON AND NEW YORK

First published 2022
by Routledge
2 Park Square, Milton Park, Abingdon, Oxon OX14 4RN

and by Routledge
605 Third Avenue, New York, NY 10158

Routledge is an imprint of the Taylor & Francis Group, an informa business

British Library Cataloguing-in-Publication Data
A catalogue record for this book is available from the British Library

Library of Congress Cataloging-in-Publication Data
Names: Tarr, A. A. (Anthony A.), editor. | Tarr, Julie-Anne, editor. | Thompson, Maurice, editor. | Ellis, Jeffrey (Jeffrey John), editor.
Title: Drone law and policy: global development, risks, regulation and insurance / edited by Anthony A. Tarr, Julie-Anne Tarr, Maurice Thompson and Jeffrey Ellis.
Description: Abingdon, Oxon; New York, NY: Routledge, 2022. | Includes bibliographical references and index.
Identifiers: LCCN 2021006309 (print) | LCCN 2021006310 (ebook) | ISBN 9780367463021 (hardback) | ISBN 9781032050270 (paperback) | ISBN 9781003028031 (ebook)
Subjects: LCSH: Drone aircraft—Law and legislation.
Classification: LCC K4105.D76 2022 (print) | LCC K4105 (ebook) | DDC 343.09/75—dc23
LC record available at https://lccn.loc.gov/2021006309
LC ebook record available at https://lccn.loc.gov/2021006310

ISBN: 978-0-367-46302-1 (hbk)
ISBN: 978-1-032-05027-0 (pbk)
ISBN: 978-1-003-02803-1 (ebk)

Typeset in Sabon
by Apex CoVantage, LLC

Contents

About the contributors

Robert S. Barrows Director of Legal Operations and Projects for the New York City Police Department, New York, USA Bob has worked for the NYPD for over nine years. In his role, he provides legal guidance and direction on a variety of subjects impacting the Department's operations, including its unmanned aircraft systems programme. He earned a Bachelor of Arts degree from Manhattan College and his JD from Albany Law School.

Christopher Carlsen Partner, Clyde & Co US LLP, New York, USA. Chris has focused his practice on the trial, litigation and arbitration of a variety of matters involving products liability, aviation, insurance coverage and general commercial disputes. He began his legal career as a Captain in the United States Marine Corps where he was a criminal trial attorney. He also spent three years as a Senior Litigation Counsel with The Coca-Cola Company where he was responsible for its international products liability litigation. He graduated from the University of Notre Dame in 1980 and from the University of Notre Dame Law School in 1983.

Javaan Chahl Professor, University of South Australia, Adelaide, Australia. Javaan Chahl is DST Group Joint Chair of Sensor Systems, a joint appointment between the University of South Australia and Defence. His research programme creates new sensing and detection technology in defence, medical and agricultural applications. Javaan leads an active research programme on aerospace design, flight dynamics, navigation, control and UAV platform autonomy. Javaan has filed 15 patents and has published over 140 full-length refereed publications on topics including insect behaviour, optics, planetary exploration and aircraft avionics.

Tom Chamberlain CUO Aviation—Global Project Manager and Senior Business Analyst, Allianz Global Corporate & Specialty, London, UK. Tom Chamberlain graduated from Oxford University with a Master of Mathematics in 2001 and later qualified as a General Insurance Actuary. Since 2016, as Underwriting Manager General Aviation and Aerospace, London Region, he has been leading a team of senior underwriters, managing the P&L for the region and developing a digital strategy for aviation globally. More recently, he has moved into the CUO area, where he is responsible for global projects across aviation. He is currently the Chair of the International Underwriting Association's (IUA's) Developing Technologies Monitoring Group.

Cameron Chell, CEO and co-founder of Draganfly Inc. an award-winning, industry-leading drone manufacturer and systems developer and the oldest operating commercial drone manufacturer in the world. Recognized as being at the forefront of technology for over 22 years, Draganfly is an award-winning, industry-leading manufacturer and technology developer serving the public safety, agriculture, industrial inspections, security, and mapping and surveying markets. He is the Chairman and co-founder of CurrencyWorks, a financial technology blockchain pioneer and alternative digital payments provider. CurrencyWorks has been at the forefront of NFTs and was instrumental in the 27 Hour Sell-Out of $100,000 of Digital Collectibles for the Topps Company on the WAX Blockchain.

Cameron is also co-founder of Business Instincts Group, a venture growth lab. He has co-founded multiple companies with his focus on market development and product architecture.

Reece Corbett-Wilkins Partner, Clyde & Co, Sydney, Australia. Reece regularly advises clients globally on cyber incident and crisis response, data protection and privacy issues, including incident response management and vendor coordination; ransomware response and recovery; extortion negotiations and threat intelligence; payment misdirection fraud, funds tracing and funds recovery; email and social media account takeover response; communications strategy and stakeholder management; data breach assessment and notification, including coordination of global and multi-party data breaches across over 100 jurisdictions; e-safety, image-based abuse and cyberbullying; regulatory responses across more than 50 jurisdictions; third-party disputes; recovery litigation against wrongdoers; and class action risk relating to privacy breaches. He is recognised for contributions to the cyber insurance industry.

James M. Cooper Special Counsel, Clyde & Co, Melbourne, Australia. James specialises in aviation, maritime and trade and is experienced in contentious and non-contentious matters in Australia and internationally. He has previously been recognised as a "rising star" in Transport by "Doyle's Guide to the Australian Legal Profession". In 2020 he was recognised by Chambers and Partners for his work in Aviation in Australia.

Professor Martin Davies Senior Consultant, Clyde & Co, New Orleans; Admiralty Law Institute Professor of Maritime Law, Tulane University Law School, and Director of the Tulane Maritime Law Center, New Orleans, USA. Martin holds MA and BCL degrees from Oxford University and an LLM from Harvard Law School. Before joining Tulane, he was Harrison Moore Professor of Law at The University of Melbourne in Australia, and before that he taught at Monash University, The University of Western Australia and Nottingham University. He has also been a visiting professor at universities in China, Italy, Azerbaijan and Singapore. In 2019, he was elected to be Titulary Member of the Comité Maritime International (CMI). He has authored (or co-authored) books on maritime law, international trade law, conflict of laws and the law of torts. He has also published many journal articles on these topics. He has extensive practical experience as a consultant for over 30 years on maritime matters and general international litigation and arbitration, in Australia, Hong Kong, Singapore and the United States.

Jeffrey Ellis Partner, Clyde & Co, New York, USA. Jeff focuses his practice on aviation, insurance, products liability, commercial, litigation and appellate matters. He represents airline carriers in connection with the various liability and regulatory issues confronting the aviation industry on both the domestic and international fronts. He represented the interests of United Airlines in the litigation arising from the 9/11 terrorist attacks. He also represented the interests of Delta Air Lines in the Swissair/Delta Flight 111 crash, Continental Airlines in the Air France Concorde crash, Delta/Northwest in the litigation arising out of the Underwear Bomber incident, General Aviation Manufacturers Association (GAMA) in product pre-emption litigation and the Association for Unmanned Vehicle Systems International (AUVSI) and the Consumer Technology Association (CTA) in drone pre-emption litigation. He has a BA degree from Albany Law School and JD from St John's University.

Sam Golden Head of Marketing, Flock, London, UK. Sam Golden is a trained journalist with ten years of experience working in strategy and communications for some of the world's fastest-growing tech companies. Combining in-depth analysis with strategic storytelling, Sam specialises in taking disruptive tech to market. He is currently Head of Marketing at Flock, a UK insurtech reinventing insurance for a connected and autonomous world. Sam graduated from the University of Sheffield and spent the last decade working with companies including BuffaloGrid, the BBC, Google, DocuSign, GoCardless, Pusher and Pleo.

Jess Harman Associate, Clyde & Co LLP, London, UK. Jess has a broad practice across non-contentious and contentious aviation matters. Her main areas of practice include commercial disputes in a range of aviation-related matters, cross-border debt recovery, advising airlines and insurers in relation to licensing, aviation consumer law, conditions of carriage, ground-handling, airport slot trading, package travel regulations, contractual matters, aircraft lease disputes, passenger claims, environmental issues and consumer claims. Jess also advises stakeholders regarding the development and operation of unmanned aircraft systems. She is a qualified Australian legal practitioner with an Advanced Master's (LLM) degree in Air & Space Law from Leiden University.

Alan Kells Senior Associate, Clyde & Co, Manchester, UK. Alan is an experienced regulatory crime lawyer working in Clyde & Co's nationally recognised Safety, Health and Environment (SHE) Regulatory Team and is noted as a "Rising Star" in legal directories. He represents businesses and individuals across a wide range of sectors including aviation, which are the subject of criminal regulatory investigations, prosecutions and associated inquests providing strategic and pragmatic advice throughout. This includes assistance with crisis management in the immediate aftermath of an incident and undertaking sensitive internal investigations for clients who include household names, PLC's, and national and international businesses. He is an experienced court advocate with higher rights of audience in the criminal courts and significant experience acting as advocate before the criminal and coroner's courts. He has acted in a number of high profile corporate and gross negligence manslaughter cases.

Yuen Gi Ko Associate, Clyde & Co, Melbourne, Australia. Yuen Gi specialises in maritime and trade disputes and has extensive experience in both dry and wet shipping litigation after having worked in Singapore and Tokyo, Japan previously. He represents and advises P&I Clubs and shipowners in collisions, salvage, pollution and charterparty dispute matters. He gained his LLB degree from King's College London and is qualified to practise in England & Wales and Singapore. He is fluent in Korean, English and Mandarin Chinese.

Alastair Long Senior Associate, Clyde & Co, Hong Kong. Alastair is a Hong Kong-based aviation lawyer, acting for various service providers, such as airlines, aircraft operators, ground handlers and maintenance organisations on commercial and regulatory legal matters. He also assists multinational clients with cross-border commercial dispute resolution (pre-litigation) and non-insurance-related claims between aviation stakeholders from time to time. He also advises on aviation safety, security and economic regulatory compliance matters as well as discrete competition law issues. His practice also involves broader advisory work on intellectual property, data privacy and cyber security within the aviation industry. Alastair is a member of the Royal Aeronautical Society and admitted as a solicitor in Hong Kong and England & Wales.

Chris Morrison Partner, Clyde & Co, Manchester, UK. Chris is Head of Clyde and Co's UK Safety, Health & Environment (SHE) Department and for several years has been recognised as one of the United Kingdom's leading Health & Safety lawyers, consistently ranked in the legal directories including as a "Leading Individual" in Legal 500, 2021. Typically splitting his work between "upstream" compliance and post-incident regulatory investigations, he has a keen interest in autonomous technologies designed to improve the safety of workers at the workplace. Chris has been instructing in a number of criminal health and safety investigations acting for aircraft manufacturers, ejection seat manufacturers and airlines, as well as advising and representing numerous organisations with warehousing, distribution and logistics functions where automation plays an ever-increasing role in employee safety. Clients include those in the retail, logistics, mining, chemicals, energy, aviation and manufacturing sectors.

Inês Afonso Mousinho Associate, Clyde & Co, London, UK. Inês qualified in Portugal and is in Clyde & Co's aviation team. Her practice covers a wide range of both contentious and non-contentious matters for a range of airlines, MRO Organisations, UAS manufacturers and operators and other aviation stakeholders. Her non-contentious practice includes various aviation consumer law issues, commercial drafting and aviation regulatory advice. Inês also assists with a broad range of aviation liability claims (insured and uninsured), including attritional aviation claims, consumer rights litigation and major losses, with a particular focus on Portuguese-speaking countries. She holds an LLM degree in Air & Space Law from Leiden University.

Professor Enrique Navarro Partner, Clyde & Co, Madrid, Spain. Enrique specializes in aviation (airlines, airports, cargo, accidents and incidents, regulatory issues, passengers, product liability), transport (road, train) and shipping. His practice also includes insurance and reinsurance, professional indemnity, arbitration and competition law. He is a professor of International Private Law at the University Rey Juan Carlos of Madrid, and his education includes a PhD in law. Enrique has written numerous publications (books and articles) on Insurance Law and International Trade Law. He regularly lectures on national and international forums.

Titilayo Ogunwa Titilayo holds a Bachelor in Engineering degree in Aerospace Engineering from Universiti Putra Malaysia, Malaysia. Currently, a Graduate Research Student at the University of South Australia, Titilayo has published several papers in areas including insect behaviour and flight dynamics.

Diego Olmedo Legal Director, Clyde & Co, Madrid, Spain. Diego is a qualified lawyer and also a qualified Air Accident and Incident Investigator. He joined Clyde & Co in 2014 as part of the team in charge of launching the Aviation Department. He has defended the interests of insurers and airlines in three major losses that occurred in Spain in the last 20 years. Additionally, Diego, as an expert in Spanish Aviation regulations, uses his knowledge to act for airlines managing the team of the Clyde & Co. Madrid office in charge of the defence of thousands of claims brought mainly by passengers under international regulations and also defends clients in various administrative proceedings.

Masha Ooijevaar Associate, Clyde & Co, Dubai, United Emirates. Masha is in Clyde & Co's Middle East commercial, intellectual property and technology, media and telecommunications (TMT) group. She has been based in Dubai since 2019 after relocating from London, where she trained in-house at one of the largest global entertainment companies and later worked at several leading international law firms. Masha's clients include both public and private sector entities in the healthcare, automotive, financial, education, media and entertainment sectors, as well as some of the world's largest technology companies. Masha has a BA degree from Columbia University and an LLM degree from the University of California, Los Angeles in Media, Entertainment and IP Law and an LLM in European Law from Leiden University, Netherlands. Masha was admitted as a solicitor in England and Wales in September 2016 and qualified to the State Bar of California in April 2016.

Kirsty Paynter Assistant Editor, Drone Law and Policy: Global Development, Risks, Regulation and Insurance. Kirsty has completed various legal qualifications including a Bachelor of Laws (Hons), a Postgraduate Diploma in Commercial Law, a Postgraduate Diploma in Legal Practice and a Graduate Certificate in Future Law Technologies. Kirsty has extensive experience in governance, strategic planning and regulatory compliance review. She is a sessional lecturer and senior research assistant in the Faculty of Business and Law at Queensland University of Technology. She is currently enrolled as a PhD student.

Antton Peña Founder and CPO, Flock, London, UK. Antton is the Founder of Flock, a London-based insurtech on a mission to make the world a safer, smarter place. Antton's background is in engineering, design and product development, with extensive experience in the mobility and transportation industry. After working for Audi and Seat, he moved into academia to research how emerging technology could be safely integrated into society and it was there that Flock and its mission was born. Antton graduated from Imperial College and the Royal College of Art (MSc and MA in Masters in Global Innovation Design). Prior to founding Flock, Antton was the co-founder of Farewill, the world's first digital will writing platform.

Dr Asanka G. Perera Research Associate, University of South Australia, Adelaide, Australia. Asanka's research interests include signal processing, machine learning, computer vision and robotics. His research has attracted worldwide media attention including ABC Australia, Scientific American and BBC. He has a Bachelor's degree in Electrical and Electronic Engineering and a Master's degree in Industrial Automation. Asanka did his PhD at the University of South Australia on human motion analysis from drones.

Christopher Pettersen Associate, Clyde & Co, Melbourne, Australia. Chris works in the Marine, International Trade and Energy team at Clyde & Co in the Melbourne office. He contributes to Clyde & Co with past experience in litigation, finance, project management and cross-border work. He completed a Bachelor of Arts degree at the University of Melbourne, followed by JD at Melbourne Law School.

Olivia Puchalski Associate, Clyde & Co, Melbourne, Australia. Olivia is an associate in the Australian maritime, aviation and trade team. She has experience in contentious and non-contentious matters both in Australia and internationally and has also previously contributed an article in the internationally recognised journal *Air and Space Law* concerning air carrier's liability from an Australian perspective. She holds both a BA degree and JD from Monash University.

Gema Díaz Rafael Aviation Legal Adviser, Madrid, Spain. Gema Díaz is a lawyer who has specialized in Aviation and Space Law and International Commercial Arbitration. In these respects, she has worked with prestigious law firms, and she currently advises international groups and large companies in relation to aircraft finance, aviation regulatory issues and commercial law. She is the author of the monographs *Discover Aviation Law, Air Navigation Legislation* and numerous articles in specialised journals. She has participated as a speaker and lecturer in international conferences, seminars and scientific meetings.

Simon Ritterband Managing Director, Moonrock Drone Insurance, London, UK. Simon currently sits on a number of key government advisory panels in the United Kingdom along with the Department for Transport (UK), the Civil Aviation Authority (UK) and other key stakeholders within the industry. He also sits on the British Standards Institute Committee (BSI). He regularly consults with national authorities on the drone industry, and Moonrock is firmly established as a leading drone insurance provider in the market. With policies developed in partnership with Hiscox, Moonrock drone insurance policies cover areas previously unavailable such as invasion of privacy cover, cyberattack cover and mandatory public liability insurance.

Nick Sharpe Chief Executive Officer, Modini Ltd, London, UK. Modini is a specialist programme delivery company that focuses on projects which are niche, complex and often ambiguous. Initially focusing on the aviation, maritime and defence sectors, Nick has broadened the scope of the company to include renewable energy and digital infrastructure at the request of clients who operate in this space. Currently, Modini's Keystone programme is the delivery of large Unmanned Air Systems, for an international client operating in the maritime domain. The challenge of utilising UAS which are over 150 kilograms brings regulatory and operational challenges that have significant complexity; not just in flying, but training, engineering, continuing airworthiness and demonstrating that they are safe to operate.

Patrick Slomski Partner, Clyde & Co, London, UK. Patrick's principal areas of practice relate to complex and technical aerospace matters. His practice is split between contentious and non-contentious work. Contentious work includes aviation catastrophe work, complex insurance coverage, major commercial disputes (including lease and finance disputes), acting for maintenance and repair organisations and subrogation recoveries. Patrick specialises in English Commercial Court proceedings, multi-jurisdictional litigation and international arbitration. His clients have noted his ability to advise on, and synthesise strategies in, cases involving complex engineering and scientific issues. In recent years, his non-contentious practice has increasingly involved supporting major aerospace design and development programmes (civil and military) and advising on legal risk aspects of terrestrial and space systems. His work on unmanned aircraft systems includes regulatory and legal risk advice to systems developers and operators across various jurisdictions. Patrick became a Partner in 2000, is a past examiner for the Chartered Insurance Institute and a Fellow of, and the Honorary Solicitor to, the Royal Aeronautical Society.

Darryl Smith Partner, Clyde & Co, Melbourne, Australia. The majority of Darryl's practice involves conducting the defence of D&O, professional indemnity and liability insurance claims. He has a particular interest in new and emerging risks. In addition to contentious work, Darryl provides coverage advice and assists his clients with compliance and regulatory issues unique to the insurance industry. He also provides corporate clients with advice in relation to the insurance and indemnity aspects of disputes and transactions.

Merinda Stewart Associate, Clyde & Co, Melbourne, Australia. Merinda holds a PhD from Leiden University on the topic of coastal state jurisdiction in international airspace. She also holds an LLB and a BA from the University of Melbourne and an LLM from Leiden University, with a thesis on privacy aspects of drones. During her PhD appointment, Merinda lectured in air law at Leiden University and was Managing Editor of the journal *Air & Space Law* (Wolters Kluwer). Prior to completing her LLM, Merinda undertook a graduate programme with the Australian government in Canberra, Australia, and worked in The Hague, the Netherlands, for the TMC Asser Institute, in research and project management and as an intern at the International Criminal Tribunal for the Former Yugoslavia (ICTY).

Dr Anthony A. Tarr BA, LLB (Natal), LLM (Cambridge), PhD (Canterbury), PhD (Cambridge) Senior Consultant, Clyde & Co, Brisbane, Australia Director, Robyn Ashton Consulting Pty Ltd; formerly Vice Chancellor, University of the South Pacific; Dean & Professor of Law, Indiana University—Indianapolis; Dean & Sir Gerard Brennan Professor of Law, The University of Queensland; Dean & Foundation Professor of Law, Bond University; author of ten books/treatises including *Insurance Law in New Zealand* and *Australian Insurance Law*. Chairman, Managing Director or Non-executive Director of various commercial and resource sector companies, formerly Chief Executive Officer of the Queensland Law Society, Director of the Indiana Bar Foundation and Chairman of the Fiji Law Reform Commission.

Professor Julie-Anne Tarr BA (Wisconsin), JD (Cornell), LLM (Monash), PhD (Queensland) Senior Consultant, Clyde & Co, Brisbane, Australia Professor, Commercial Law, Queensland University of Technology; formerly Professor of Law, Indiana University—Indianapolis; Director of the Asia Pacific Law Institute; Chief

Operating Officer, Queensland Institute of Medical Research; Director, Litigation Reform Commission. Specialising in insurance and risk management, emerging technologies and complex contracting, she has authored six books/treatises including *Disclosure and Concealment in Consumer Insurance Contracts* and *The Laws of Australia: Insurance* and more than 100 articles and law reform reports. She is Editor, Insurance and Transport section, *Australian Business Law Review*.

Maurice Thompson LLB (Bond), LLM (Shipping)(Hons)(Cape Town), LLM (Admiralty)(Distinction)(Tulane) Senior Equity Partner, Clyde & Co, Melbourne and Perth, Australia. Maurice is Founder and Chair of Clyde & Co's "International Drones Group", and he has been engaged by insurance majors, corporates, governments and regulators to assist in compliance, policy creation, registration, regulation and insurance policy wordings with regard to drones. Maurice also heads Clyde & Co's Australian "Energy, Marine, Natural Resources Group" (EMNR) and the firm's Australian "Aviation Group". He is a member of the firm's EMNR Global Executive. He qualified in 1992 and has 28 years' experience advising clients in the shipping, offshore oil and gas, resources and mining, commodity trading, aviation, insurance and ports industries both domestically and internationally.

Dino Wilkinson Partner, Clyde & Co, Abu Dhabi. Dino is recognised as one of the leading technology lawyers in the Middle East and was named in The Legal 500's Hall of Fame for his work in technology, media and telecommunications law. Dino has advised clients throughout the region on technology contracting, data protection and cybersecurity for more than ten years. He has also worked with regional governments and regulatory authorities on a number of significant legislative developments in this area, including the drafting of electronic commerce laws, data sharing regulations and privacy legislation. Dino's expertise spans all types of technology-related contracts, including data processing agreements, software development and licensing, outsourcing, research and collaboration agreements. He has worked on projects of both regional and international significance, including mobile app and internet product launches, national digital wallet schemes and ICT infrastructure rollouts. Dino's clients include government departments, state-owned entities and private sector organisations in the Middle East. He also helps international clients to navigate legal and regulatory issues in the region.

Part A

Introduction

1 New horizons

Anthony A. Tarr, Julie-Anne Tarr and Maurice Thompson

Overview

The exponential growth[1] in the use and deployment of Unmanned Aircraft (UA) and Unmanned Aircraft Systems (UAS),[2] or Remotely Piloted Aircraft (RPA) and Remotely Piloted Aircraft Systems (RPAS),[3] (hereafter "Drones"),[4] as well as the technology underpinning their scope and operation is delivering enormous opportunity, economic advantages and societal benefits for various users, operators and the community at large.

Drones are now in widespread use in mining, remote exploration works and repair, geological survey, agricultural land management, urban transport and delivery, aerial photography, media and more. Increasing recreational use continues to fuel market growth of drones globally, and their increasing use in areas like law enforcement, search and rescue and emergency relief is evolving very rapidly. Viewed by the European Union (EU) as a new tool to reduce Europe's carbon footprint and protect natural resources, drones offer numerous societal benefits.[5] As the Australian Senate

1 At present there are nearly 1.3 million registered drones in the United States and more than 116,000 drone operators. Officials say there are hundreds of thousands of additional drones that are not registered. See, for example, David Shepardson, 'US Agency Requires Drones to List ID Number on Exterior' (*Reuters*, 13 February 2019) <www.reuters.com/article/us-usa-drones/u-s-agency-requires-drones-to-list-id-number-on-exterior-idUSKCN1Q12O9>; The commercial and civilian drone market is expected to grow at a compound annual growth rate of 19 per cent over a five-year period according to a new research report by Global Market Insights, Inc. See 2018 report, Ankita Bhutani and Preeti Wadhwani, 'Commercial Drone/Unmanned Aerial Vehicle (UAV) Market' (Report, February 2018) <www.gminsights.com/industry-analysis/unmanned-aerial-vehicles-UAV-commercial-drone-market>.

2 The term Unmanned Aircraft (UA) is used to describe the aircraft itself, whereas the term Unmanned Aircraft System (UAS) is generally used to describe the entire operating equipment including the aircraft, the control station from where the aircraft is operated and the wireless data link. See, for example, Federal Aviation Administration, 'Unmanned Aircraft Systems' (*Federal Aviation Administration*, 5 January 2021) <www.faa.gov/uas/>.

3 The International Civil Aviation Organization (**ICAO**) employs the acronym RPAS (standing for Remotely Piloted Aircraft System) or RPA (Remotely Piloted Aircraft). The term RPAS appears to be the preferred terminology used by international aviation-related agencies like ICAO, Eurocontrol, the European Aviation Safety Agency (**EASA**), the Civil Aviation Safety Authority (**CASA**—Australia) and the Civil Aviation Authority (CAA—New Zealand).

4 In this book, unless the context demands more "jurisdiction specific" language, unmanned aircraft and remotely piloted aircraft will be referred to as "drones".

5 SESAR Joint Undertaking, 'European Drones Outlook Study, Unlocking the Value for Europe' (Report, November 2016) <www.sesarju.eu/node/2951>.

Committee of Inquiry stated in 2018 around contemporary forecasts: "any list will not be exhaustive, as the range of applications continues to grow at a rapid pace, with RPAS having become the fastest growing segment of the civil aviation market".[6]

PwC in a global report[7] on the commercial applications of drone technology assessed the value of the global market at over US$127 billion in 2020, with the drone revolution disrupting industries ranging from agriculture to filmmaking.[8] Goldman Sachs, in a research report titled "Drones reporting for work",[9] predicted a $100 billion market opportunity for drones helped by growing demand from the commercial and civil government sectors.[10] Predictions for future growth vary, but all reports predict continuing growth across the world.[11] This is not surprising as drones have proved their worth in the commercial and industrial environments, helping businesses and organisations improve safety, collect fast and accurate data and improve efficiency and profitability. Moreover, they are increasingly demonstrating their indispensable applications in law enforcement and in healthcare and humanitarian contexts.

The global health challenge that the COVID-19 pandemic has precipitated brings this growth phenomenon into very sharp focus. When the COVID battle recedes and 2020, the year the world stayed home, is put into broader perspective, one area exhibiting positive outcomes will be that of drone use and innovation in a health crisis. The rapid adaptations of drones in managing COVID-19 outbreaks in real-world practices will inevitably be incorporated into emergency services and future law enforcement frameworks as well as spur greater recognition of drone technology capacities.

6 Regulatory requirements that impact on the safe use of Remotely Piloted Aircraft Systems, UAS and associated systems, Rural and Regional Affairs and Transport References Committee, *Current and Future Regulatory Requirements that Impact on the Safe Commercial and Recreational Use of Remotely Piloted Aircraft Systems (RPAS) Unmanned Aerial Systems (UAS) and Associated Systems* (The Senate, July 2018) para 1.15.

7 PwC, 'Clarity from Above: PwC Global Report on the Commercial Applications of Drone Technology' (Report, May 2016) <www.pwc.pl/pl/pdf/clarity-from-above-pwc.pdf>. The predicted value of drone-powered solutions in key industries is (global view): Infrastructure: US$45.2bn; Agriculture: US$32.4bn; Transport: US$13bn; Security: US$10bn; Media & Entertainment: US$8.8bn; Insurance: US$6.8bn; Telecommunication: US$6.3bn; Mining: US$4.4bn.

8 ibid. The predicted value of drone-powered solutions in key industries is (global view): Infrastructure: US$45.2bn; Agriculture: US$32.4bn; Transport: US$13bn; Security: US$10bn; Media & Entertainment: US$8.8bn; Insurance: US$6.8bn; Telecommunication: US$6.3bn; Mining: US$4.4bn.

9 Haye Kesteloo, 'Drones Reporting for Work—Goldman Sachs Forecasts $100B Drone Market by 2020' (*Drone DJ*, 28 January 2019) <https://dronedj.com/2019/01/28/drones-reporting-for-work-goldman-sachs/>. See also Deloitte, 'InFocus: Insurance Industry Drone Use is Flying Higher and Farther' (*Deloitte*) <www2.deloitte.com/us/en/pages/financial-services/articles/infocus-drone-use-by-insurance-industry-flying-higher-farther.html>, who similarly project the value of drone solutions by 2020 to be US$100 billion across all industries.

10 ibid. Goldman Sachs observes that drones got their start as safer, cheaper and often more capable alternatives to manned military aircraft. Their research indicates that defence will remain the largest market for the foreseeable future as global competition heats up and technology continues to improve.

11 See, for example, Mordor Intelligence, 'Drones Market—Growth, Trends and Forecasts (2020 2025)' (Report, March 2020) <www.mordorintelligence.com/industry-reports/drones-market>. Variances in predicted growth outcomes often are attributable, at least to some degree, on what is included (such as defence expenditure) and geographical assessment (global versus regional); Grand View Research, 'Commercial Drone Market Size, Share & Trends Analysis Report by Application (Filming & Photography, Inspection & Maintenance), by Product (Fixed-wing, Rotary Blade Hybrid), by End Use, and Segment Forecasts, 2019–2025' (Report, June 2019) <www.grandviewresearch.com/industry-analysis/global-commercial-drones-market#>.

As Michael Richardson observes:

> As COVID-19 restrictions tighten around the world, governments are harnessing the potential of drones. From delivering medical supplies, to helping keep people indoors—drones can do a lot in a pandemic. Since the outbreak began, China has used drones to deliver medical supplies and food, disinfect villages, and even provide lighting to build a hospital in Wuhan in nine days. Drone medical deliveries have cut transit times, reduced the strain on health personnel and enabled contactless handovers, reducing the risk of infection. It's clear drones are helping combat COVID-19, as governments use them to control and monitor.[12]

In the delivery of emergency medical supplies in a crisis, where the main message is "stay at home", or in harsh environments like war zones or during environmental disasters,[13] drones can provide practical assistance in several ways, such as collecting samples for testing,[14] delivering vaccines which require refrigeration in areas without such facilities[15] and delivering food.[16] Drones can not only deliver these supplies and treatment, but at the same time they help prevent the movement of potentially sick people.[17]

Accordingly, the current COVID-19 crisis serves to highlight benefits of enhanced drone use and innovation, and it is increasingly clear that the use of drones in the transport of people and goods will be one of the key areas fuelling market growth of drones globally. As the New South Wales government observes in its report "Transport for NSW: Future Transport Strategy 2056",[18] the next 40 years will see more technology-led transformation than the past two centuries did, with rapid innovation bringing increased automation,[19] including the use of drones to support future transport in areas like rapid point-to-point services that could transform emergency services and deliveries.[20]

12 Michael Richardson, '"Pandemic Drones": Useful for Enforcing Social Distancing, or for Creating a Police State?' *The Conversation* (Melbourne, 31 March 2020) <https://theconversation.com/pandemic-drones-useful-for-enforcing-social-distancing-or-for-creating-a-police-state-134667>.

13 See, for example, CBS News, 'How Drones are Playing a Vital Role in Disaster Scenarios' (*CBS News*, 7 June 2019) <www.cbsnews.com/news/drones-are-being-deployed-in-disaster-scenarios-heres-how/>.

14 See, for example, Katie Prescott and Sarah Treanor, 'Drones in Africa: How They Could Become Lifesavers' (*BBC News*, 6 April 2020) <www.bbc.com/news/business-51837296>.

15 See, for example, Chloe Kent, 'Moving Medical Supplies: Enter the Drone' (*Medical Technology*, 4 December 2019) <https://medical-technology.nridigital.com/medical_technology_dec19/moving_medical_supplies_enter_the_drone>.

16 An Irish start-up in the United Kingdom claims it could produce as many as 2,000 drones a day to deliver medicine and food to the elderly, Hannah Boland and Michael Cogley, 'Thousands of Drones Could be Deployed to Deliver Medicine and Food to Elderly' *The Telegraph* (London, 19 March 2020) <www.telegraph.co.uk/technology/2020/03/19/thousands-drones-could-deployed-deliver-medicine-food-elderly/>.

17 See, for example, Simon Chandler, 'Coronavirus Delivers "World's First" Drone Delivery Service' (*Forbes*, 3 April 2020) <www.forbes.com/sites/simonchandler/2020/04/03/coronavirus-delivers-worlds-first-drone-delivery-service/#40685bb04957>; and Jess White, 'How Drones Could Revolutionise Care Delivery at Your Hospital' (*Healthcare Business & Technology*, 7 June 2019) <www.healthcarebusinesstech.com/drones-care-hospital/>.

18 See New South Wales Government, 'Transport for NSW: Future Transport Strategy 2056' (March 2018).

19 ibid 10.

20 ibid 66.

Job creation, job change, job destruction and job shift are all being facilitated by drones.[21] Where drones disrupt industries and take over manual tasks, productivity and sustainability are often increased, and prices are lowered. Routine work replaced by drones will have an impact on the daily tasks of employees, and this new form of work, with drone-complementing labour, could make the jobs safer and more fulfilling. As expressed in "The great job-creating machine" paper from Deloitte:

> Improvements in living standards, which have been felt by most, from generation to generation, and an accumulation of life-changing innovations, from the steam engine to antibiotics, to mass travel, TV and communication, have made progress tangible.[22]

The paper highlights the fact that in the United Kingdom over the last 150 years technology has created more jobs than it has destroyed. Historical evidence demonstrates that when a machine replaces a human, the result, paradoxically, is faster growth and, in time, rising employment.

Jobs such as information technology managers, programmers, software developers and of course, drone pilots are soaring. The processes and activities that are required to support the drone industry are large, and include

> the development of hardware components for drones; assembly of drones; software that supports the operation of drones; software and technology to support value added services delivered by the drones—such as specialised cameras or sensors; infrastructure requirements; and associated services such as legal and training requirements.[23]

This varied work is likely to be attractive to the younger generation. It is this adoption of technology which is helping to accelerate the deployment of drones. Indeed, the FAA expects certified remote pilots will soon outnumber private and commercial pilots combined.[24] Job prospects in manned aviation have fallen steeply for newly qualified pilots due to the coronavirus crisis and the catastrophic impact this has had on the airline industry. This has, in part, led to the increase in certification of drone pilots. In some areas, newly qualified pilots are moving straight to Beyond Visual Line of Sight (BVLOS) training courses to give themselves wider opportunities for employment.[25]

21 This phrase is taken from Christophe Degryse, 'Digitalisation of the Economy and its Impact on Labour Markets' (2016) European Trade Union Institute Research Paper—Working Paper 2016.2 <http://doi.org/10.2139/ssrn.2730550>.

22 See Ian Stewart, Debapratim De and Alex Cole, 'Technology and People: The Great Job-creating Machine' (Report, 2015) <www2.deloitte.com/tr/en/pages/technology/articles/technology-and-people.html>.

23 See, Australian Government Department of Infrastructure, Transport, Regional Development and Communications, 'Emerging Aviation Technologies, National Aviation Policy Issues Paper' (September 2020).

24 See, Federal Aviation Administration, 'FAA Aerospace Forecast, Fiscal Years 2019–2039' (Report, 2019) <www.faa.gov/data_research/aviation/aerospace_forecasts/>.

25 See, sUAS News, 'How Newly Qualified Airline Pilots will Become Tomorrow's Pioneering Drone Pilots' (*sUAS News*, 17 July 2020) <www.suasnews.com/2020/07/how-newly-qualified-airline-pilots-will-become-tomorrows-pioneering-drone-pilots/>.

Global growth, development and applications

The second part of this book, comprising Chapters 2–6, examines key areas in relation to the global growth, development and application of drones. Detailed consideration is given to drones' usage in key commercial areas such as infrastructure, transport, mining, oil and gas, maritime deployments and agriculture. These chapters canvass also the public or societal benefits deriving through applications in law enforcement and humanitarian relief operations and describe recreational uses where drones are flown as a hobby or sport.

An appreciation of the wide diversity and ever-expanding operations and circumstances in which drones are deployed or are used is essential for (a) understanding the risks associated with their use and (b) informing the regulatory regime appropriate to these diverse contexts.[26]

For example, some of the factors highlighted as important considerations in the development of regulatory responses include:

- Where the drone is deployed or operating. Increased deployment through transport and delivery services in high-density population areas will increase personal injury and property damage risks. Operation in this complex urban environment, as compared to more remote and less densely populated areas, requires a more intense focus on considerations of risk (personal injury and property damage), technological protections and mitigations, management of very low-level airspace and its traffic, as well as aviation regulation, planning law and the rights of individuals to their privacy and peace.
- The drone operator. Licensing and certification requirements for drone pilots and operators are centred on safety issues. Minimum standardised training and education obligations are imposed to ensure that individuals ultimately in control of the drones in our skies have a clear understanding of the authorised operating conditions, the limits on where and in what circumstances a drone can be flown and the potential dangers associated with unlawful activity.
- Technological advances. Overcoming certain technology challenges is essential for drones to be safely integrated into airspace and coexist with other air traffic. Detect and avoid technology and improving land-based command and control concepts are required to enable the broad range of drone capabilities to be carried out accurately and safely.
- The regulator. This question has caught most governments and regulators completely off-guard. The age of drones is breaking the classic stereotype of "aviation" and bridging into other sectors. From a maritime perspective, for instance, a classic aviation regulator would have little or no knowledge of the risks associated with (i) offshore oil rigs, (ii) ocean going vessels, (iii) port operations, (iv) confined tanks, (v) climate environments inside cargo holds and storage

26 Generally, see Julie-Anne Tarr, Anthony Tarr and Kirsty Paynter, 'Transport, Drones and Regulatory Challenges: Risk Accountability Meets COVID Fast Tracking of a Critical Industry' (2020) 48 Australian Business Law Review 202; Julie-Anne Tarr, Maurice Thompson and Anthony Tarr, 'Regulation, Risk and Insurance of Drones: An Urgent Global Accountability Imperative' (2019) 8 Journal of Business Law 559; Julie-Anne Tarr and others, 'Drones in Australia—Rapidly Evolving Regulatory and Insurance Challenges' (2019) 30 Insurance Law Journal 135.

tanks and facilities loaded with various commodities, (vi) deep-sea mining at three kilometres below the ocean's surface or (vii) maritime law. With drones now used so heavily in sectors such as maritime, offshore oil and gas, natural resources, mining and transport, it could be argued that drones should be regulated separately from classic aviation or, at the very least, consideration should be given to some dual regulatory oversight. There are a number of good examples internationally.[27]

- Risk and regulatory intervention. A significant challenge faced by regulators is to appropriately assess the risk and to introduce a regulatory framework commensurate with that risk. The regulatory intervention ideally needs to tread a path that does not stifle innovation and is not so "heavy handed" as to unduly impact commercial and recreational uses of drones. This is no easy task because the rapid development of drone technology in the industry requires active and ongoing regulatory attention, and regulators are still trying to assess the various risks. By providing tangible examples of drone applications, Chapters 2–6 highlight the delicate balancing act required of regulators, where strong economic or public interest considerations dictate rapid expansion in drone deployment.

Risks

Notwithstanding the new horizons in efficiency ushered in through drone usage, there is a growing need for well-thought-out and properly integrated regulation. This is easy to state and to recognise, but the rapid growth in the use and deployment of drones creates significant challenges to regulators and the community at large—both practical and regulatory. Detailed justification for this statement is provided in the third part of this book, comprising Chapters 7–12, but a few illustrations are provided here to give some context.

A primary and growing concern of aviation authorities and experts is the number of incidents where drones have come into contact with or caused hazards to aircraft. For example, Gatwick Airport,[28] the United Kingdom's second largest airport and busiest single runway airport in the world, was brought to a standstill in December 2018 through the illegal operation of drones within the airport's airspace.[29] This disrupted the travel plans of 125,000 people and cost the airlines an estimated US$63 million. The Federal Aviation Administration (**FAA**) in the United States reports that

27 For example, offshore oil and gas rigs in Australia are regulated by two authorities: the National Offshore Petroleum Safety and Environmental Management Authority (NOPSEMA) and the Australian Maritime Safety Authority (AMSA), with the jurisdiction between the two grey, to say the least, but competently dealt with via an MOU between the two authorities to cooperate in their dealings with such "maritime" and "offshore" assets and services. A similar obvious example is the FAA, which entered into an MOU with the Occupational Safety and Health Administration (OSHA) to jointly regulate in respect of airport ramp safety issues.

28 Gatwick Airport has operated since 1936 and survived World War II, when it served as a base for R.A.F. night fighters flying missions against Nazi Germany but was brought to a standstill by a drone. See Your London Airport Gatwick, 'History' (*Your London Airport Gatwick*) <www.gatwickairport.com/business-community/about-gatwick/company-information/our-history/>.

29 James Cooper, Patrick Slomski and Maurice Thompson, 'Gatwick Meltdown: Drones in a No-go-zone' (*Clyde & Co*, 21 December 2018) <www.clydeco.com/en/insights/2018/12/gatwick-meltdown-drones-in-a-no-go-zone>.

unmanned aircraft sightings (**UAS**) from pilots, citizens and law enforcement have increased dramatically over the past two years.[30] The FAA now receives more than 100 such reports each month.[31] The agency has sent out a clear message that operating drones around airplanes, helicopters and airports is dangerous and illegal. Unauthorised operators may be subject to stiff fines and criminal charges, including possible jail time.[32]

The use of a drone in the commission of a terrorist act is another major concern. The Sana'a Center for Strategic Studies[33] reports that particularly in 2019 Houthi forces deployed explosive-laden drones on long-range kamikaze missions against the Yemeni government, and in that same year a drone guided by satellite technology was flown 800 kilometres to attack a Saudi Arabian pipeline.[34] Even more recently, the Houthis claimed responsibility for the attacks on Saudi Arabian oil plants, affecting more than half of Saudi oil output and more than 5 per cent of the global supply.[35]

Injury to persons and property damage are very real concerns arising out of the use of drones.[36] Given the increasing sophistication of these aircraft, the veritable explosion in their usage, their capacity to carry payloads and their ability to travel vast distances, the potential for such injury or damage is ever increasing.[37]

The increasing use of drones also gives rise to privacy concerns. As Matthew Koerner[38] observes:

> Drones have gained notoriety as a weapon against foreign terrorist targets; yet, they have also recently made headlines as an instrument for domestic surveillance. With their sophisticated capabilities and continuously decreasing costs, it is not surprising that drones have attracted numerous consumers—most notably, law enforcement.

Yet, these privacy concerns extend beyond law enforcement. There is also the potential for unauthorised collection of data and industrial espionage. Additional drone

30 FAA, 'UAS Sightings Report' <www.faa.gov/uas/resources/public_records/uas_sightings_report/>.

31 ibid.

32 Federal Aviation Administration, 'Reported UAS Sightings (October 2018–December 2018)' (Report, 28 July 2020) <www.faa.gov/uas/resources/public_records/uas_sightings_report/>.

33 SANA'A Center for Strategic Studies, 'Drone Wars—The Yemen Review' (Report, June 2019) <https://sanaacenter.org/publications/the-yemen-review/7665>.

34 See Alex Gatopoulos, 'Houthi Drone Attacks in Saudi "Show New Level of Sophistication"' (*Al Jazeera*, 15 May 2019) <www.aljazeera.com/news/2019/05/houthi-drone-attacks-saudi-show-level-sophistication-190515055550113.html>. Interesting questions arise in this context as to the potential liability of a satellite service provider and its responsibility to secure its network and to prevent malfeasance.

35 See Reuters, 'US Points Finger at Iran over Saudi Oil Drone Attack that Could Cause Energy Prices to Spike' (*ABC News*, 16 September 2019) <www.abc.net.au/news/2019-09-15/us-lays-the-blame-for-saudi-oil-drone-attack/11514992?section+technology>.

36 See, for example, Pam Stewart, 'Drone Danger: Remedies for Damage by Civilian Remotely Piloted Aircraft to Persons or Property on the Ground in Australia' (2016) 23 Torts Law Journal 290.

37 Jacinta Long and Sarah Yau, 'Drone Damage: What Happens If a Drone Hits You?' (*Clyde & Co*, 13 December 2017) <www.mondaq.com/australia/aviation/655664/drone-damage-what-happens-if-a-drone-hits-you>.

38 Matthew R Koerner, 'Drones and the Fourth Amendment: Redefining Expectations of Privacy' (2015) 64 Duke Law Journal 1129.

risks unrelated to safety include potential damages arising from private law claims (such as trespass, nuisance, invasion of privacy) and possible damage to a company's goodwill or reputation.

As with any rapidly evolving technology, drone use is revealing new vulnerabilities and cybersecurity threats. No organisation is immune from the risks and associated costs of tackling cyber threats. Loss of reputation, monitoring and notification costs and network interruptions associated with breaches all need to be considered. Attacks such as exploiting drones' software or firmware vulnerabilities to take over the drone and gain access to other networks and systems of an organisation, or malware embedded in drone software that could compromise the device where it is located and allow data sent to and from the drone to be exfiltrated and reviewed are real concerns. These risks need to be mitigated with improvements in technology, regulation and appropriate insurance.

In this regard, it must be acknowledged that the risk attached to drones is a 21st-century problem requiring a 21st-century response. As former US Secretary of State Madeleine K. Albright explains:

> Citizens are speaking to their governments using 21st century technologies, governments are listening on 20th century technology and providing 19th century solutions.[39]

Although this observation is related to disinformation, it is valid for all emerging technologies.

Regulation

The fourth part of this book, comprising Chapters 13–19, examines the evolving regulatory environment in which drones operate.

Unlike earlier fundamental changes and evolutions—such as the automobile, the airplane, the train[40]—the drone industry has unique aspects that make it less well placed to evolve along the same regulatory trajectory and timeframes of these industries—or to adopt their existing frameworks in entirety. Although all of these industries have had take-up of registration and tracking requirements that lagged behind their evolutions with limited consequences, the approach of employing common law principles such as *Rylands v Fletcher*[41] in the process as gap fillers is flawed in relation to the drone liability market for several reasons.

(1) Early iterations of protypes in relation to motor vehicles and airplanes, for example, were expensive, industry oriented and limited in distribution. Drones conversely arise out of inexpensive technology that has already been positioned most broadly as a consumer "toy" of sorts with recent enhancement of this technology "flowing up" to commercial sector uses. They are cheap to produce, reverse

39 See, Atlantic Council, '#DisinfoWeek' (29 June 2017) <www.youtube.com/watch?v=oJQRckFCWZw>.
40 Perhaps even the currently emerging driverless car.
41 *Rylands v Fletcher* [1868] UKHL 1, (1868) LR 3 HL 330.

engineer and/or procure second hand.[42] The revolution of drones is different due to the extensiveness of its scope and global distribution.

(2) The aforementioned forerunner industries did experience lag times in relation to registration and liability around registration/operational requirements, but on the basis of direct nexus between operators and vehicles, it was possible in most instances to rely on classic tort liability principles to determine and to affix liability as to trespass, negligence and injury. The ownership of a drone, or the identification of its operator, can be much more difficult to ascertain, thereby rendering general liability principles less susceptible to the application, particularly where operators choose to use them for nefarious purposes.[43] Indeed, analogising drones to handguns in this limited respect could be argued as those who have licences and operate legitimately are not the users of concern to society. It is the unlicenced guns with remote accountability that cause damage.[44]

(3) As damages go, the capacity of drones dramatically exceeds these other industries in nascent contexts not only because of prolific use and availability but also because of the magnitude of damages capable of being inflicted. To date concerns have focused primarily on privacy invasion or limited physical impact injuries. However, recent events such as the capacity to close down airports, bomb oil fields and cause wider scale disaster—while unregistered and potentially unattached to any recognisable operator for liability purposes—mean that a measured, graduated timeline of simultaneous evolution and regulation is a level of leisure taxpayers can ill afford. Taxpayers at present constitute the safety net for injuries or property damage arising out of the use of drones where the owner or operator of the drone causing injury or damage does not have private liability cover, cannot be found or is impecunious. This may be because the drone in question was not properly registered and insured—intentionally or unintentionally—or because many of the users of this inexpensive type of technology may prove to be judgement proof at the end of the day even if found liable.[45] The drone, is, in other words, a new beast of a very different liability hue.[46]

42 Consumers can purchase a brand-new drone such as the Kogan VultureX with a Wi-Fi camera for less than US$50 and much less on the second-hand market.

43 After the Gatwick Airport incident, the policing operation and subsequent investigation cost over US$1 million, but the police failed to identify who was flying the drones. See BBC News, 'Gatwick Airport Drone Attack: Police Have No Lines of Inquiry' (*BBC News*, 26 September 2019) <www.bbc.com/news/uk-england-sussex-49846450>.

44 According to a US Department of Justice special report, only 7 per cent of prisoners who carried or possessed a firearm during their offence had purchased it under their own name from a licenced firearm dealer. See Mariel Alper and Lauren Glaze, 'US Source and Use of Firearms Involved in Crimes: Survey of Prison Inmates, 2016' (Special Report, U.S. Department of Justice, January 2019) <www.bjs.gov/index.cfm?ty=pbdetail&iid=6486>.

45 The FAA concludes that recreational aircraft is almost 34 per cent higher than ownership registration. The figure is based on comparing industry sales with other data and this calculation involves taking into account retirement, redundancy and loss of craft corresponding to ownership registration. As craft becomes sturdier and operators situationally aware, we expect this rate to change dynamically over time. Furthermore, with FAA regulations increasingly encouraging recreational drones to be registered, as opposed to ownership, registration would soon come to represent equipment like commercial counterpart. See, Federal Aviation Administration, 'FAA Aerospace Forecast 2020–2040: Unmanned Aircraft Systems' (Report, 23 July 2020) <www.faa.gov/data_research/aviation/aerospace_forecasts/>,

46 See Tarr and others (n 26).

Although drone activity around the world is increasing exponentially, many countries are struggling with how to regulate. Regulations vary from a total absence[47] to outright ban and everything in between.

Traditional regulatory structures are complex, risk-averse and adjust slowly to shifting social circumstances. Emerging technologies such as drones can lead to unforeseeable outcomes where clear regulations and ethical guidelines are absent. Regulatory approaches need to strike a balance between private sector interests such as profits and public interests such as trust, safety, nature preservation and climate change.

Furthermore, the proposed regulatory approach needs to cover the complex web of airspace integration, safety, security, noise, environment, privacy, safe and efficient electric take-off and landing vehicles, infrastructure, technology trials and central coordination.[48] These are all important issues and are integral to the development of a comprehensive national policy that will allow countries to benefit from the considerable opportunities provided by emerging aviation technologies.

Insurance

The fifth part to this book, comprising Chapters 20–22, examines the evolving insurance environment in which drones operate.

In addition to the development of bespoke policies, insurers have used innovative solutions to meet the demand in relation to the recreational proliferation of drones and to meet the demand in industries which have expanded their business activities to include drone operations. These include developing on-demand "pay as you fly" products and providing add-on or write-back cover within existing product lines. By leveraging Big Data to intelligently identify and quantify flight risks, innovative products have been developed for the drone market to provide tailor-made policies based on individual risk profiles.

In a recent Policy Issues Paper, the Department of Infrastructure, Transport, Regional Development and Communications in Australia[49] observes that "most commercial drone operators make the business decision to hold insurance to cover for any damage or injury caused as part of managing the risk of their operations". The same might be said for recreational drone users who obtain appropriate insurance to manage their risk exposures.

However, not all jurisdictions are willing to leave the issue of appropriate insurance cover in the hands of individual operators, commercial or recreational.

For example, in the European Union certain drone operators and operations must have public liability insurance to protect against legal liability for third-party property damage or injury whilst using a drone.[50]

47 According to several websites, the Central African Republic, for example, does not have any published regulations regarding drones. See, for example, UAV Coach, 'Drone Laws in the Central African Republic' (*UAV Coach*) <https://uavcoach.com/drone-laws-in-central-african-republic/>.

48 See, Australian Government Department of Infrastructure, Transport, Regional Development and Communications (n 23). See also, Tarr, Thompson and Tarr (n 26); Tarr and others (n 26).

49 Australian Government Department of Infrastructure, Transport, Regional Development and Communications (n 23) 25.

50 Regulation (EC) No 785/2004 required all commercial drone operations to carry third-party liability insurance with the minimum third-party insurance requirement being based on the mass of the aircraft on take-off. New Drone Regulations 2019/947 and 2019/945, effective 31 December 2020, place the emphasis on what type of drone is being operated and associated risks, rather than upon a commercial versus non-commercial distinction. See full discussion in Chapter 22.

In addition, the International Civil Aviation Organization ICAO UAS Toolkit,[51] described by ICAO as a helpful tool to assist states in realising effective UAS operational guidance and safe domestic operations, Chapter 2.8 states:

> The operator shall have adequate insurance in the event of an incident or accident. Some States require a minimum third-party liability insurance to be in effect for all UAS operations.

The insurance chapters consider the current and evolving insurance landscape as the industry looks to address the risks posed by drones and provides an overview and commentary on compulsory third-party liability insurance.

Concluding comments

The final part of this book, Chapter 23, concludes with recommendations on additional regulatory and insurance initiatives that are necessary to achieve an effective balance between the various competing interests.

The exponential growth in the use and deployment of drones globally and of the technology underpinning their scope and operation dictates that the regulatory framework and associated security and commercial arrangements such as insurance will continue to evolve. This edition of this book therefore represents a marker or place maker for the status of the evolution at the end of 2020. Subsequent editions will describe the journey as it unfolds.

The adequacy of insurance requirements has been considered in the United Kingdom: Lloyds, 'Drones Take Flight: Key Issues for Insurance, Emerging Risk Report, Innovation Series' (Report, 2015) <www.lloyds.com/news-and-risk-insight/risk-reports/library/technology/drones-take-flight>.

51 ICAO, 'The ICAO UAS Toolkit' (*ICAO*) <www.icao.int/safety/UA/UASToolkit/Pages/Narrative-Regulation.aspx>.

Part B

Global growth, development and applications

2 Drones—delivering value to the economy

Anthony A. Tarr and Kirsty Paynter

Introduction

Widespread use of drones is now in place around natural resource management, shipping, construction, mining, remote exploration works and repair, geological surveys, agricultural land management, urban transport and delivery, aerial photography, media and more. This chapter focuses upon some of these applications that add significant value to the economy and, as was explained in the introductory chapter, endeavours to provide an insight into the wide diversity and ever-expanding operations and circumstances in which drones are deployed or are used. This is essential to (a) understand the risks associated with their use and (b) to inform the regulatory regime appropriate to these diverse contexts.

The technological capabilities of drones have surged forward in recent years. Drones are now small enough to fit in a backpack and large enough to transport goods. New applications of drones are being developed with each improvement to the hardware and software. The improvements in technological software such as detect and avoid, robustness in the hardware to fly through difficult conditions and major upgrades to the cameras used to capture images are helping to make drones a vital technological tool. Businesses trying to improve safety, decrease costs, speed up services or simply to find innovative ways to expand their business models are looking to drones to provide the answer. In the coming years, drones will be used in areas we have not even thought of yet.

Each type of drone has benefits and drawbacks. For example, multirotors have tremendous control and can more easily survey vertical faces or confined spaces without the need for a landing strip. Conversely, fixed wings cannot easily survey confined or other unusual spaces but have excellent duration and can cover larger areas. Hybrid models are providing further options for use. By leveraging the new technology and using the right drone, the applications are seemingly endless and often novel. In this chapter, some of the industrial and commercial applications of drones are briefly outlined.

Oil and gas

Drones are becoming an indispensable tool in the mining, oil and gas, and other resource sector industries. Companies are finding new ways of moving their staff out of "dull, dirty and dangerous" environments by allowing drones to take their place.[1]

1 See, for example, Jeremiah Karpowicz, 'UAVs as Solutions to Dull, Dirty, and Dangerous Jobs' (*Commercial UAV News*, 14 September 2016) <www.commercialuavnews.com/construction/uavs-solutions-dull-dirty-dangerous-jobs>.

Dr Joseph Barnard provides two cogent examples:

> As exploration activities move to the more hostile regions of the Earth, such as the Arctic Ocean, and to more politically unstable areas, expect to see a growing use of Unmanned Aircraft operating in areas where it would be irresponsible to expect pilots to fly: low level, night flights over the Arctic Ocean; flights over regions in which there is low level strife, where the larger manned survey aircraft provide target practice and some excitement for the locals.[2]

For example, consider the oil and gas industry. In the United States alone, there are approximately three million miles of mainline and other pipelines that link natural gas production areas and storage facilities with consumers,[3] half of which were built in the 1950s and 1960s. Add to that 218,956 miles of oil pipelines, and the vast work involved in inspections is put into perspective.[4] Often, the task of inspecting the lines is handled by pilots flying in small aircraft. Monitoring by air is expensive and can be risky as often the pilots are flying at low altitude and in mountainous regions. Some of the largest oil and gas companies around the world now use drones to address a wide variety of operational challenges. DroneDeploy observes that this rapidly improving technology, along with advances in big data and artificial intelligence, is poised to transform the oil and gas industry in the coming years.[5] The aerial intelligence provided by drones offers several key benefits, including safer inspections and assistance to companies in complying with regulatory requirements—while saving millions of dollars in labour, remediation and other costs.[6]

Drones are the perfect solution for conducting visual inspections of infrastructure and gathering extensive data. An increasing number of oil and gas companies use drones to perform three basic industry functions—pipeline inspection and monitoring, oil well and rig inspection and surveying and construction monitoring—at a significantly lower cost than ground, manned aircraft or helicopter inspection crews. By taking photos and videos of above-ground pipelines, drones allow inspectors in the field or engineers in a remote location to view pipes, either in real time or later. The operator can zero in on areas of concern to gather additional information and, if necessary, recommend that a ground crew visually check the area.[7] Systematic surveys of extensive areas are better completed with fixed-wing platforms and automatic

2 Joseph Barnard, 'UAS for Pipeline Inspection and Exploration' (ESA/EDA Workshop—New Capabilities for Unmanned Aerial System, ESTEC, Noordwijk, 11–12 May 2010) <https://business.esa.int/sites/default/files/Presentation%20on%20UAS%20for%20pipeline%20inspection%20and%20exploration.pdf>.

3 See US Energy Information Administration, 'Natural Gas Weekly Update' (*U.S. Energy Information Administration*, 5 December 2019) <www.eia.gov/naturalgas/weekly/archivenew_ngwu/2019/12_05/>.

4 See data set Excel for 2018: Bureau of Transportation Statistics, 'U.S. Oil and Gas Pipeline Mileage' (*United States Department of Transport Bureau of Transportation Statistics*) <www.bts.gov/content/us-oil-and-gas-pipeline-mileage>.

5 See DroneDeploy, 'Pushing the Boundaries of Aerial Inspection with Drones' (*Medium*, 7 February 2019) <https://medium.com/aerial-acuity/pushing-the-boundaries-of-aerial-inspection-with-drones-c2bd7b4bb9a7>.

6 See interview with Cyberhawk's Chris Fleming on oil and gas inspection with drones: Ian Smith Podcast, '#050—Oil and Gas Inspection Drones with Cyberhawk's Chris Fleming' (*Commercial DronesFM*, 19 July 2017) <https://commercialdrones.fm/?s=chris+fleming>.

7 See DroneDeploy (n 5).

flight design, whilst multirotor platforms provide flexibility in shorter and localised inspection missions. The type of sensor carried by an aerial platform determines the sort of data acquired and the obtainable information; sensors also determine the need for specific mechanical designs and the provision of energy on-board required from the system.[8] To detect potential underground leaks, drones take photos along pipeline routes and user-friendly software, combine these images, create high-resolution vegetation maps that identify plant kill-off zones, which may indicate a leak. Equipping a drone with an infrared camera provides an additional way to inspect pipelines: thermal imagery of pipeline routes reveals hotspots, which may indicate potential defects in pipeline insulation or leaks invisible to the human eye. Drone images also detect anomalies along a pipeline network or any encroachments, such as construction or roadwork, on a right-of-way that could threaten the integrity of the pipeline. In case of significant leaks, explosions or other emergency situations, drones provide real-time video to help emergency response teams assess the situation before sending in crews.[9] Oil and gas companies also use drones to photograph oil wells and offshore rigs throughout the initial drilling process, and their uses in the maritime context are discussed in Chapter 5 of this book.

Mining

Dangerous and monotonous work, mining often generates a high return, and drones are delivering significant value to the mining industry.

BHP, a global mining company, estimated that they were saving $5 million a year in one part of Australia alone by using drones to inspect cranes, towers and roofs and to ensure areas are clear before a blast is carried out and to track fumes post-blast.[10]

Drones which are capable of delivering samples from sites, allow surveyors to spend less time gathering data in the field and more time interpreting it. Temperature and fume sensors can be attached to drones, so when a geologist is using drones to identify or map outcrop, the drone is collecting environmental baseline data at the same time.[11] Water management with accurate management of tailing dams, watersheds, drainage basins assessment and mapping the potential flow of water base on-site current topography can all be improved with the use of a drone.

New algorithms in image processing allow identification of the type of rocks, strike, faults and dips which decrease the manual workload significantly. All of these assist operators when blasting to make safer, better-informed and more cost-effective decisions.

Drones are now equipped with technology which can assist to navigate in dark underground mining tunnels. A dangerous task usually performed physically by inspectors, drones can survey rock mass in place of a person and can also reach

8 Cristina Gomez and David R Green, 'Small Unmanned Airborne Systems to Support Oil and Gas Pipeline Monitoring and Mapping' (2017) 10:202 Arabian Journal Geosciences <https://doi.org/10.1007/s12517-017-2989-x>.

9 See DroneDeploy (n 5).

10 See BHP article, Franx Knox, 'How Drones are Changing Mining' (*BHP*, 19 April 2017) <www.bhp.com/media-and-insights/prospects/2017/04/how-drones-are-changing-mining/>.

11 See article by Steven Micklethwaite, 'Drones in Mining: The New Possible' (*AUS IMM*, October 2018) <www.ausimmbulletin.com/feature/drones-mining-new-possible/>.

previously inaccessible areas to gain valuable data. The data from the drones can help predict rock mass stability, ventilation modelling, hazardous gas detection and leakage monitoring. Forward-looking infrared (FLIR) imagery can be used to recognise areas of loose rock which normally remain unnoticed until it becomes a hazard.[12] Drone technology is continuing to improve with proposals for autonomous spherical micro-drones for underground mine safety inspection to overcome some of the challenges of flying underground with reduced visibility, air velocity and dust concentration.[13] The proposed encased drone will be able to recognise obstacles in mines and work in these GPS denied environments. As the technology develops, drones underground can help assess viability of mining and provide vital and timely assistance to workers who may be trapped or injured in mines.

Time lapse photography can monitor sites and provide accurate timelines to make future predictions on the time it takes to mine and move the minerals. Digital models of open pits can also help detect irregularities in the mine and help timely assessments for better planning.

Analysis of drone images can greatly improve the safety at the coal face. Insight into the current conditions and geometry of the haul roads can assist teams to investigate problem areas and improve worksite efficiency. Safety berms[14] and block heights can be detected with compliance values calibrated to in-site equipment via drone surveys. This enables monitoring of a bench nearing a non-compliant height, early action can be taken, minimising shutdowns.

Drones can perform volumetric surveys to calculate stockpile volumes using cameras to take hundreds of images to provide a 3D model of the stockpile with enough detail that bulldozer tracks can be seen.[15] Conventional surveys can involve surveyors using GPS and climbing over stockpiles. This is slow, hazardous and often produces less accurate results than drones can supply. Terra Drone estimates that volumetric surveys by drones is up to 60–80 per cent faster than by conventional survey methods.[16] The process can assist inventory management, improve safety and efficiency for stockpiles of aggregates and minerals.

The dynamic oversight afforded by drones can be safely produced by on-site workers at a fraction of the cost of traditional survey methods, helping to identify potential problems early and improving the efficiency and health and safety of the mine.

Drones can also assist to reduce the risks of abandoned mines. In the United States, over 50,000 sites have abandoned mines.[17] Abandoned mines pose environmental

12 R M Turner and others, 'Geotechnical Characterization of Underground Mine Excavations from UAV-Captured Photogrammetric & Thermal Imagery' (52nd US Rock Mechanics/Geomechanics Symposium, Washington, 17–20 June 2018).

13 Javad Shahmoradi, Pedram Roghanchi and Mostafa Hassanalian, 'Drones in Underground Mines: Challenges and Applications' (2020 ASEE Gulf-Southwest Annual Conference, Albuquerque, 29 April 2020).

14 A horizontal shelf or ledge built into the embankment or sloping wall of an open pit or quarry to break the continuity of an otherwise long slope and to strengthen its stability or to catch and arrest slide material. A berm may be used as a haulage road or serve as a bench above which material is excavated from a bank or bench face. Mindat.Org, 'Definition of Berm' (*Mindat.Org*) <www.mindat.org/glossary/berm>.

15 Terra News, 'Major Wood Chip Exporter Now Prefers Drones to Calculate Stockpile Volumes Rather than Conventional Survey Methods' (*TerraDrone*, 30 October 2019) <www.terra-drone.net/global/2019/10/30/wood-chip-stockpile-drone-volumetric-survey-australia/>.

16 ibid.

17 According to the US Department of the Interior, Bureau of Land Management 52,200 mines are abandoned on public lands as of 5 January 2017, at US Department of the Interior, Bureau of Land Management,

risks and drones can assist by mapping these vast areas in a cost-efficient way for areas which have no commercial value. The mapping can help create a subsistence inventory map and create digital models to calculate the amount of soil required for recultivation of a closed mine.[18]

Revisiting abandoned mines to scope the prospect of reopening the mine to access valuable materials is now possible with the use of drones. In Philadelphia, drones collected data from a previously inaccessible area in a historic gold mine that had been inactive since the 1940s. Procedures were too costly, and conditions were potentially too dangerous for human surveyors to perform.[19] Data retrieved from the drones allowed a report of existing mine openings and helped determine how much gold remained to be mined on-site to present to potential investors.

Construction

Deloitte estimates that the global construction industry's revenue will reach $15 trillion by 2025.[20] Recent research into the utilisation of multirotor drones in the construction industry shows extensive use in land surveying, logistics, on-site construction, maintenance and demolition. The results reveal that the main contributions are work safety, cost-effectiveness and carbon-emission reduction.[21]

The logistics of construction can be increased by monitoring deliveries and offering real-time updates on any changes or improvements that may be necessary. A drone flyover during construction can provide progress reporting, project milestone completion validation, quality control and safety inspections and logistics planning for easier project management and stakeholder oversight. Construction companies can use the progress reports at the end of a project to better plan for future projects, environmental impact verification and reporting. Contractor engagement can be regularly monitored and real-time images can provide documentation that can be used to provide factual evidence to settle disputes.

Naveed Anwar, Muhammad Amir Izhar and Fawad Ahmed Najam describe the following innovation:

> The technological progress in the design and navigation of low-weight and autonomous drones and UAVs can be efficiently used in a dynamic manner to result in more practical and cost-effective operations in the fields of construction management and monitoring. In the presented approach, the data in terms of drone images from multiple locations and point clouds (from 3D scanning of construction site) can be used to construct 3D models using the photogrammetry techniques. These

---

'Abandoned Land Mines—AML Inventory' (*U.S. Department of the Interior, Bureau of Land Management*) <www.blm.gov/programs/public-safety-and-fire/abandoned-mine-lands/blm-aml-inventory>.

18 Javad Shahmoradi and others, 'A Comprehensive Review of Applications of Drone Technology in the Mining Industry' (2020) 4(3) Drones 34 <http://doi.org/10.3390/drones4030034>.

19 See Robotics Business Review, 'How a Drone Mined Data from a 70-Year-Old Gold Mine' (*Robotics Business Review*, 21 November 2019) <www.roboticsbusinessreview.com/energy-mining/how-a-drone-mined-data-from-a-70-year-old-gold-mine/>.

20 Deloitte, 'GPoC 2019 Global Powers of Construction' (Report, July 2020) <www2.deloitte.com/global/en/pages/energy-and-resources/articles/deloitte-global-powers-of-construction.html>.

21 Yan Li and Chunlu Liu, 'Applications of Multirotor Drone Technologies in Construction Management' (2019) 19(5) International Journal of Construction Management 401 <https://doi.org/10.1080/15623599.2018.1452101>.

drone models can be compared to the Building Information Model (BIM) at various construction stages to monitor the construction progress. Beside construction scheduling and costing, this comparison can be expanded to include real-time recording, reporting, billing, verification and planning. Using the example of a case study construction project, the effective use of drone data is demonstrated in terms of smart construction monitoring and comparisons between drone model and BIM model. It is shown that this fully automated system can significantly reduce the effort required in traditional construction monitoring and reporting procedures. The system not only provides convenient and smart ways of site supervision and management but also results in better operations, planning and effective on-site adjustments.[22]

Construction compliance officers use drone photos to compare actual conditions to pre-construction designs, as well as to detect and correct plan defects and deviations and spot any potential safety issues. This information also helps streamline decision-making throughout the project. Companies can even create, document and share a visual timeline with all stakeholders. Once construction is finished, drones provide a digital 3D representation of structures to use as a baseline reference.[23]

Agriculture

Drones provide a myriad of benefits to agriculture with PwC estimating the market for drone-powered solutions in agriculture at US$32.4 billion.[24] Drones offer the potential for addressing several major challenges in agriculture. With the world's population projected to reach nine billion people by 2050, experts expect agricultural consumption to increase by nearly 70 per cent over the same time period. In addition, extreme weather events are on the rise, creating additional obstacles to productivity. Agricultural producers must embrace revolutionary strategies for producing food, increasing productivity and making sustainability a priority. Drones are part of the solution, along with closer collaboration between governments, technology leaders and industry.[25]

The European Commission identifies the following avenues whereby drones may improve upon existing agricultural processes.[26]

22 Naveed Anwar, Muhammad Amir Izhar and Fawad Ahmed Najam, 'Construction Monitoring and Reporting using Drones and Unmanned Aerial Vehicles (UAVs)' (The Tenth International Conference on Construction in the 21st Century (CITC-10), Colombo, 2nd–4th July 2018) <www.researchgate.net/publication/326264559_Construction_Monitoring_and_Reporting_using_Drones_and_Unmanned_Aerial_Vehicles_UAVs>.

23 DroneDeploy (n 5).

24 Michal Mazur, 'Six Ways Drones Are Revolutionizing Agriculture' (*MIT Technology Review*, July 20 2016) <www.technologyreview.com/2016/07/20/158748/six-ways-drones-are-revolutionizing-agriculture/>.

25 ibid.

26 Laurent Probst, Bertrand Pedersen and Lauriane Dakkak-Arnoux, 'Digital Transformation Monitor—Drones in Agriculture' (Report, European Commission, January 2018) <https://ec.europa.eu/growth/tools-databases/dem/monitor/content/drones-agriculture>.

Soil and field analysis

Drones are able to produce 3D maps, quickly and cheaply, which are then used for the design of seed-planting patterns and the generation of a wide range of data types with many applications, for example, nitrogen-level management.

Crop monitoring

Satellite imagery was previously the most advanced form of crop monitoring, but it suffers from some major drawbacks:

- Satellite imagery is very costly.
- Images must be ordered in advance and can be imprecise.
- Poor weather impedes data quality.

Drones however can monitor crops much more accurately, frequently and affordably, delivering higher quality data that is updated regularly to provide insight into crop development and highlight inefficient or ineffective practices. According to SenseFly (a drone manufacturer specialising in agriculture), the utilisation of drones by the Ocealia group resulted in a 10 per cent average increase in crop yields.[27]

Health assessment

Drones can also be used to generate multispectral images of crops (based on the amounts of green and infrared light reflected), which are then analysed to track changes in health and maturity.[28] The ability to assess the health of a crop quickly and precisely can be invaluable for farmers. If for example, a bacterial or fungal infection is identified, early detection allows for quick action to be taken in order to remedy the issue.

Irrigation

Agriculture accounts for the vast majority (70%) of water used in the world—more than twice that of industry (23%).[29] Aside from being wasteful, excessive water usage is increasingly unsustainable as competition for the planet's finite resources intensifies in the face of rapid population growth. Leaky irrigation systems and wasteful field application techniques are two of the factors contributing to inflated agricultural water use figures, and both can be addressed by drones. Drones equipped with special monitoring equipment can be used to identify parts of a field experiencing "hydric stress" (inadequacy of water of sufficient quality). They use infrared and thermal sensors to provide snapshots of entire fields, allowing targeted diagnosis of areas receiving too much or too little water. These drones also allow for the vegetation index

27 See, senseFly, 'Farming High—How a French Farming Cooperative Used Drones to Boost its Members' Yields' (Case Study, 2016) <www.sensefly.com/industry/agricultural-drones-industry/>.

28 Len Calderone, 'How Do Drones Help Farmers?' (*AgriTech Tomorrow*, 28 December 2017) <www.agritechtomorrow.com/article/2017/ 08/how-do-drones-help-farmers/10153>.

29 World Wildlife Fund, 'Farming: Wasteful Water Use' (*World Wildlife Fund*) <wwf.panda.org/what_we_do/footprint/agriculture/impacts/water_use/>.

(density and health of the crop) to be calculated while the crop is growing, enabling and informing better crop management.

Crop spraying

The ability of drones to easily adjust their altitudes and flight paths according to the surrounding topography and geography comes from the use of increasingly sophisticated equipment (radar, LiDAR, etc.). This makes drones well suited for crop spraying, as they can scan the ground and apply liquids quickly and with great precision. Some experts argue that crop spraying by drones may be up to five times faster than with regular machinery.[30]

Aerial planting

Drone-planting systems are under development with the goal of drastically reducing labour costs by using compressed air to fire seed pods directly into the ground. This avoids the significant labour costs traditionally associated with planting activities.[31] The importance of drones in the agricultural context cannot be overstated. As the Food and Agricultural Organisation (FAO) explains: "In the current milieu, use of sustainable information and communication technology in agriculture in not an option. It is a necessity".[32]

The aforementioned applications identified by the European Commission serve to highlight the potential of drones to move less efficient traditional farming methods into more technical and efficient farming. Drones are used to assist landowners and farmers by mapping[33] and collecting data to monitor the health and needs of the soil beneath it. Drones in agriculture facilitate continuous crop health monitoring by targeting pesticide operations,[34] nutrient management, irrigation management efficiency—water saving and soil and field analysis to plan planting. Access to satellite imagery data can assist farmers to monitor animal grazing patterns and increase the efficiency and utilisation of their land. Smart planting, where drone software can count plants shortly after they emerge from the ground, can help determine if areas need to be replanted. All of these are key to growing crops more efficiently, effectively and reducing the use of pesticides.[35] As National Drones state:

30 Mazur (n 24).

31 Probst, Pedersen and Dakkak-Arnoux (n 26).

32 Gerard Sylvester, 'E-Agriculture in Action: Drones for Agriculture' (Report, *Food and Agriculture Organization of the United Nations and International Telecommunication Union*, 2018) <www.fao.org/family-farming/detail/en/c/1200079/>.

33 India TV News, 'Maharashtra Updates Decade-old Agricultural Maps, Uses Drones for Efficient Water Management' (*India TV News*, 10 May 2019) <www.indiatvnews.com/news/india-maharashtra-uses-drones-for-efficient-water-management-updates-decade-old-agricultural-maps-519122>.

34 See, for example INP, 'China Gifts 12 Drones to Pakistan to Fight Locusts' (*The Nation*, 24 July 2020) <https://nation.com.pk/24-Jul-2020/china-gifts-12-drones-to-pakistan-to-fight-locusts 24 July 2020>; Vikash Aiyappa, 'In a First Drones Used to Drive Away Locusts in Rajasthan' (*One India*, 28 May 2020) <www.oneindia.com/india/in-a-first-drones-used-to-drive-away-locusts-in-rajasthan-3095538.html>.

35 See, for example, Jason Reagan, 'Agricultural Drone Speeds Chinese Rice Seeding' (*DroneLife*, 28 May 2020 <https://dronelife.com/2020/05/28/agricultural-drone-speeds-chinese-rice-seeding/>.

> Previously, farmers relied on historical records of seasonal rain and temperatures to predict crop yields. Today, drones provide a more accurate, real time analysis of crop yields and potential threats, including disease, weed and pest activity.[36]

In addition to crops, drones can count and take stock of herds of animals. They can contrast the temperatures of individual animals in herds and identify and treat sick animals before the spread of a disease. Drones can survey the land faster, more accurately and likely cheaper than planes or satellites and provide high value and effective results. Studies testing the viability of herding sheep with a drone[37] are proving successful with barking drones moving livestock faster and with less stress using a dog, reducing a two-hour job for two people with two dogs to 45 minutes for a single drone.[38] The same drone can also save time by allowing the farmer to monitor water and feed levels and check on livestock health without disturbing animals.

Drone spray applications also provide massive benefits for farmers in countries with developing agriculture. In countries like China and India, drones have enabled farmers to leap from handheld applicators, skipping vehicle-mounted boomed machines and going straight to drones. At the same time, drones improve application timeliness, reduce the need for skilled labour and cut handheld sprayer operators' exposure to harmful pesticides. In 2020, DJI Agriculture claimed that DJI Agriculture pilots had provided drone spraying services for more than 6.67 million hectares of farmland.[39]

Governments are demonstrating their support for the adoption of modern agricultural techniques with grants and subsidies. For example, in the Netherlands grants are available for small drones to help greenhouse growers control synthesis better.[40] Some states in Australia are providing farmers with a rebate for the purchase of drones as a flying farm management tool, driven by the safety benefits in addition to the likely increase in production.[41] Cross-border projects such as "Remote Sensing Based Information and Insurance for Crops in Emerging Economies (RIICE)" have made significant impacts in countries like Vietnam and the Philippines in terms of rice monitoring,

36 National Drones, 'Improve Crop Health, Crop Yields and Overall Decision Making with Drones' (*National Drones*) <https://nationaldrones.com.au/industries/agriculture/>.

37 BBC News, 'University Studies Benefits of Herding Sheep with Drone' (*BBC News*, 23 March 2019) </www.bbc.com/news/av/uk-england-shropshire-47672206/university-studies-benefits-of-herding-sheep-with-drone>.

38 Peter Holley, 'New Zealand Farmers Have a New Tool for Herding Sheep: Drones that Bark Like Dogs' *The Washington Post* (Washington, 7 March 2019) <www.washingtonpost.com/technology/2019/03/07/new-zealand-farmers-have-new-tool-herding-sheep-drones-that-bark-like-dogs/>.

39 DJI Agriculture also claimed their drones have covered more than 520 million mu of farmland globally, DJ Agriculture (@DJI Agriculture), "In less than half a year, DJI Agriculture pilots have used the MG_IP series and T16 to provide drone spraying services for more than 6.67 million hectares (100 million mu) of farmland. To date, DJI agricultural drones have covered more than 520 million mu of farmland globally" (28 May 2020) <https://twitter.com/DJIAgriculture/status/1265976851001835520>; see also Yuka Obayashi, 'Drones Offer High-Tech Help to Japan's Aging Farmers' (*Reuters*, 23 August 2018) <www.reuters.com/article/us-japan-farming-drones/drones-offer-high-tech-help-to-japans-aging-farmers-idUSKCN1L80TX>.

40 See René Koerhuis, 'Subsidy to Develop Fully Automated Drone Workforce' (*Future Farming*, 26 May 2020) <www.futurefarming.com/Machinery/Articles/2020/5/Subsidy-to-develop-fully-automated-drone-workforce-587840E/>.

41 See New South Wales Farmers, 'New Heights for Quad Bike Safety Rebate' (*NSW Farmers*, 27 February 2019) <www.nswfarmers.org.au/NSWFA/NSWFA/Posts/News/mr.19.29.aspx>.

mapping and forecasting.[42] The benefits of accurate information on rice growth from drone mapping can help governments to adapt their economic policies on rice import and export. Replacing satellite imagery with drones can provide substantial cost reductions, improve imagery and crop simulation models. Heavy investment supporting farmers or rural cooperatives to buy agricultural drones is occurring in China with increasing subsidies for machine and tool purchases.[43]

Finally, in relation to this brief overview of drone applications in the agricultural environment, it should be mentioned that there are significant financial and insurance-related advantages deriving from drone deployment. Drones, for example, can help to assess the creditworthiness of a farmer which can be better justified on a digitised farm. This allows farmers to more quickly borrow funds which are set at the right amount for their assets. Similarly, crop insurers can also use drones to assist in insurance claims to help speed up the assessment, timing and accuracy of any payment, and indemnities payable under prevented planting provisions in certain agricultural insurance policies have been expedited through aerial surveillance and mapping by drones.[44]

While the potential for drone-use in agriculture is significant, there are still several notable impediments to their progression beyond the niche market they occupy today. Difficult financial situations of many farms are likely to hamper adoption. Agriculture remains a difficult, low-margin business for many farmers, with governments providing assistance in the form of bailouts and subsidies when adverse weather or market conditions arise. Despite their savings potential, drones still require substantial capital investment and technical expertise to be acquired and properly utilised, making their purchase difficult to justify for many small-to-medium sized farms that are less likely to benefit from economies of scale.[45] Moreover, drones are now commonly deployed in tandem with traditional farming methods, as a complementary tool, until such time as the technology is mature enough to act as a replacement for existing methods. This requires the rapid integration of newer sensors, cameras and processing technologies to constantly improve the quality of data captured.[46] Finally, there are regulatory

42 The project was funded by the Swiss Agency for Development and Cooperation (SDC) and was a public–private partnership aiming to reduce the vulnerability of smallholder farmers engaged in rice production. For further details, see achievements: RIICE, 'What RIICE Achieved' (*RIICE*) <www.riice.org/what-riice-achieved/what-riice-achieved/>.

43 See Wendy Ye, 'Chinese Agriculture Drone Makers see Demand Rise Amid Coronavirus Outbreak' (*CNBC*, 9 March 2020) <www.cnbc.com/2020/03/10/chinese-agriculture-drone-makers-see-demand-rise-amid-coronavirus-outbreak.html>; Li Jianhua, 'Agricultural Drones Used in Rural China to Replenish Farm Labor' (*China Global Television Network*, 2 November 2019) <https://news.cgtn.com/news/2019-11-01/Agricultural-drones-used-in-rural-China-to-replenish-farm-labor-LgP7blQMsE/index.html#:~:text=The%20Chinese%20government%20%E2%80%93%20in%20hopes,rural%20cooperatives%20buy%20such%20drones>.

44 See, for example, Sara Wyant, 'Crop Insurance Industry Looks Back on Eventful 2019 and Forecasts 2020 Changes' (*Agri Pulse*, 19 February 2020) <www.agri-pulse.com/articles/13205-crop-insurance-industry-looks-back-on-eventful-2019-and-forecasts-2020-changes>; PrecisionHawk, 'How Crop Insurers are Using Drones to Improve the Claims Cycle' (*PrecisionHawk*, 22 February 2019) <www.precisionhawk.com/blog/how-crop-insurers-are-using-drones-to-improve-the-claims-cycle>; Sara Wyant, 'Crop Insurance Industry Celebrates Successes, But Looks to Future Challenges' (*Agri Pulse*, 20 February 2019) <www.agri-pulse.com/articles/11923-crop-insurance-industry-celebrates-successes-but-looks-to-future-challenges>.

45 Probst, Pedersen and Dakkak-Arnoux (n 26).

46 ibid.

barriers to realising the full potential of drones in some regions—principally driven by safety considerations and discussed in detail in Part D of this book. For example, regulations impose limitations such as operations not being permitted to occur beyond an operator's visual-line-of-sight (BVLOS)[47] and must occur at a maximum groundspeed of 100 mph and at a maximum altitude of 400 feet.[48] Goldman Sachs reports that a drone operating within these constraints is able inspect up to 1,000 acres of farmland a day, but if regulators were to increase the maximum flight height by just 40 per cent, the drone inspection coverage could double.[49] The cost of regulation to society is evident in examples such as this, as safety and risk are balanced against the economic rewards of using drones.

Transport

Drone-to-door delivery is one of the most widely publicised applications of the drone. Delivery of any supply is a costly service to research and launch, but after more than a decade of research, along with tentative government support, the drone has launched into the city and countryside and is ready to take on the "last mile delivery" to consumers.[50]

The potential market for drones as delivery vehicles is vast, but it is still in a nascent stage. With the arrival of COVID-19 and the now ubiquitous need for "social distancing", the use of drones in the retail market will expand as consumers embrace contact-free technology.

The last mile delivery market is the movement of goods from a transportation hub to the final delivery destination. ECommerce has evolved into a huge global market,[51] where increasingly the default demand from customers is that they "need it now". They want faster, cheaper delivery with greater control over their experience. The need to deliver more parcels faster and at a lower cost to meet customer expectations is increasing the pressure on retailers, delivery providers and their wider supply chain as the "last mile"—the final phase in the delivery process when the parcel reaches the end customer—is the most expensive and time-consuming step of the fulfilment process.[52] According to *Statista*, in 2019, the autonomous last mile delivery market (worldwide) was sized at US$12 billion and is expected to grow to US$91.5 billion by 2030.[53] Delivery drones lead the way in the growth of the autonomous last mile

47 Discussed in the section Transport later in this chapter.

48 See, for example, in the United States the FAA operational rules for commercial use of small (weighing less than 55 pounds) "unmanned aircraft systems" (UAS) or drones in 14 C.F.R. §107.

49 Goldman Sachs, 'Insights—Overview—Drones—Reporting for Work' (*Goldman Sachs*) <www.goldmansachs.com/insights/technology-driving-innovation/drones/index.html>.

50 Jean-Paul Rodrigue, Claude Comtois and Brian Slack, 'The "Last Mile" in Freight Distribution' in *The Geography of Transport Systems* (2nd edn, Routledge 2009) 212.

51 In 2019, retail e-commerce sales worldwide amounted to US$3.53 trillion and e-retail revenues are projected to grow to US$6.54 trillion in 2022. Online shopping is one of the most popular online activities worldwide, Statista, 'Retail E-commerce Sales Worldwide from 2014–2023' (*Statista*) <www.statista.com/statistics/379046/worldwide-retail-e-commerce-sales/>.

52 Accenture, 'How Could Last Mile Delivery Evolve to Sustainably Meet Customer Expectations?' (Report) <www.accenture.com/_acnmedia/pdf-96/accenture-postal-last-mile-delivery.pdf>.

53 Statista, 'Autonomous Last Mile Delivery' (*Statista*) <www.statista.com/statistics/1103574/autonomous-last-mile-delivery-market-size-worldwide/>.

delivery.[54] As time of delivery is a critical factor in consumer decision-making, speeding up the process is crucial to maintaining a competitive position in the market. Drone delivery for retail delivery is one of the most significant ways that the public can interact with drone technology on a routine basis.

Global growth in the deployment of delivery drones has been slower than might have been anticipated. The principal reason for this is discussed in detail in the chapters dealing with regulation in Part D of this book; namely, those countries that have promulgated drone regulations have focused upon safety with operations such as flights over populous areas (crowds and public gatherings), in an urban environment, in unsegregated airspace, in close proximity to airports and helipads and operations beyond visual line of sight (BVLOS) only permitted in limited instances by the granting of approvals or exemptions by aviation regulatory authorities and then only on a case-by-case basis. Regulations requiring a human pilot to have control of a drone during flight makes implementation of large-scale drone delivery challenging, if not impossible. Approvals and stifling regulations were described by the Flytrex co-founder and CEO Yariv Bash: "Before the company can scale, however, it must ace an approval process that's essentially the same as what a Boeing 787 jetliner would need to clear."[55]

However, many countries are beginning to allow drone delivery trials whilst they try to decide how and when trials will develop into an everyday commercial business. Croatia Post successfully delivered parcels in heavy winds while flying completely autonomously on a pre-programmed route in recent testing.[56] In France, the Civil Aviation Authority permitted La Poste to start using the drones for deliveries to remote villages in the Alps mountains where roads can become icy and blocked by snow, saving time and reducing risk, and as the drones are powered by electric, their use provides an added benefit to the environment.[57]

Another recent example is that of Wing Aviation, the drone delivery company owned by Google's parent company Alphabet, licensed by the Australian Civil Aviation Safety Authority (CASA) in 2019,[58] to provide public drone delivery services in Canberra and certain regions in Queensland. By partnering with local businesses such

54 Figures released July 2019, Statista, 'Projected Market Size of the Autonomous Last Mile Delivery Worldwide from 2021 to 2030' (*Statista*) <www.statista.com/statistics/1103574/autonomous-last-mile-delivery-market-size-worldwide/#statisticContainer>; see also United States Department of Transport, Bureau of Transportation Statistics, 'Transportation Statistics Annual Report, Chapter 5, Transportation Economics' (Report, June 2017) <www.bts.gov/archive/publications/transportation_statistics_annual_report/2016/chapter_5>.

55 See interview with Karen Webster on PMYNTS.com, Simon Barker Podcast, 'How To Decentralize Vendor Spend Without Losing Control' (29 July 2029) <www.pymnts.com/spend-management/2020/how-to-decentralize-vendor-spend-without-losing-control/>.

56 Croatian Post, 'Croatian Post Successfully Delivered Shipment by Drone' (*Croatian Post*) <www.posta.hr/hrvatska-posta-uspjesno-dostavila-posiljku-dronom-8167-8168/8168?drone-posta>; see video hrvatskaposta, 'Hrvatska posta testira dostavu dronom (24 January 2020) <www.youtube.com/watch?v=MlCrMeQmb18>.

57 See Press Release, '2nd Line for Parcel Delivery by Drone in France' (*DPDgroup*, 7 November 2019) <www.dpd.com/group/en/2019/11/07/2nd-line-for-parcel-delivery-by-drone-in-france/>.

58 Australian Government Civil Aviation Safety Authority, 'Drone Delivery Systems' (*Australian Government Civil Aviation Safety Authority*, 19 March 2020) <www.casa.gov.au/drones/industry-initiatives/drone-delivery-systems>.

as pharmacies and coffee shops to deliver their products "in minutes",[59] aerial delivery of groceries, coffee (Kickstart Expresso), breakfast burritos (Guzman y Gomez), fashion (The Iconic) and golf equipment (Drummond Golf) has become a reality.[60] Wing has had further success in the United States, where it finally received approval for drone delivery trials in July 2020 along with Flytrex and Uber. Wing is trialling in Virginia delivering coffee, books, meals and gifts,[61] as well as pastries and cakes to residents in Helsinki, Finland.[62]

The US Federal Aviation Administration (FAA) commenced an FAA pilot programme in 2017[63] and also included Uber and UPS. The pilot programme was a major leap in the United States from prototype mock-ups, to PR stunts in supervised areas, to patent filings. The programme brought together state, local, and tribal governments together with private sector entities, such as Unmanned Aircraft Systems (UAS) operators or manufacturers, to test and evaluate the integration of civil and public drone operations into the US national airspace system. Although this testing is scheduled to continue until September 2023,[64] some major advances have already been made with Wing delivering goods on demand to specified test neighbourhoods with a typical time from order to delivery of less than ten minutes.[65] Emphasis is given to community feedback where the drone companies and industry partners spend months understanding the community's expectations and hopes for the drone industry. This slow start may assist with longer term acceptance and support by the general public for drones and their applications. The trial looks to be a success with over 1,000 deliveries in a one-week period made across the communities during a COVID-19 lockdown where essentials such as medicine and baby food were delivered.[66]

The United Kingdom is set to lead the charge in bringing commercial drone deliveries on a mass scale, according to a new European aerospace study by Protolabs. Protolabs's "Horizon Shift" report involved 325 aerospace business leaders from across Europe and notes an increased interest in "low space" innovation as well as more investment into the fast-track testing of robots and drones. Depending on EU

59 See Jon Porter, 'Google's Wing Drones Approved to Make Public Deliveries in Australia' (*The Verge*, 9 April 2019) <www.theverge.com/2019/4/9/18301782/wing-drone-delivery-google-alphabet-canberra-australia-public-launch>.

60 Jennifer Dudley-Nicholson, 'Drone Deliveries: Wing to Launch New Home-delivery Drone Service for Australia, Offering Flying Food' *Courier Mail* (Brisbane, 7 September 2019) <www.couriermail.com.au/lifestyle/food/qld-taste/drone-deliveries-wing-to-launch-new-homedelivery-drone-service-for-australia-offering-flying-food/news-story/d1e23bd13fbf12eb4cccc817dfa73e79>; See also Dave Lee, 'Amazon to Deliver by Drone "Within Months"' (*BBC News*, 19 June 2019) <www.bbc.com/news/technology-48536319>.

61 Wing, 'Wing—United States—Virginia' (*Wing*) <https://wing.com/en_au/united-states/virginia/>.

62 Wing, 'Wing—Finland—Helsinki' (*Wing*) <https://wing.com/en_au/finland/helsinki/>.

63 Federal Aviation Administration, 'UAS Integration Pilot Program' (*Federal Aviation Administration*, 30 October 2020) <www.faa.gov/uas/programs_partnerships/integration_pilot_program/>.

64 Federal Aviation Administration, 'UAS Test Site Program' (*Federal Aviation Administration*, 6 May 2020) <www.faa.gov/uas/programs_partnerships/test_sites/>. The FAA website explains: The original five-year programme was extended for two more years under FESSA 2016, then extended for another four years under the FAA Reauthorization Act of 2018 (FRA 2018) and is scheduled to continue until September 30, 2023.

65 Virginia Tech Daily, 'Drone Delivery Launces in Southwest Virginia' (*Virginia Tech Daily*, 18 October 2019) <https://vtnews.vt.edu/articles/2019/10/ictas-wingdronedeliverylaunch.html>.

66 India Block, 'Google's Wing Drones Delivery Essentials during Coronavirus Pandemic' (*Dezeen*, 15 April 2020) <www.dezeen.com/2020/04/15/google-wing-drone-delivery-coronavirus-virginia/>.

legislation and advances in technology, last mile delivery of products by drones could eventually reach up to 30 per cent of EU citizens, and the study also suggests that over half of people surveyed expect drone deliveries to be commonplace by 2023.[67]

Tests are proving that drones have the technical capability for delivery, but the airspace, privacy and safety issues are still outstanding. Technology limitations, inhibitory regulations and method of implementation are just a few questions surrounding delivery drone investment. Delivery drones as a constructive technology, where they are deployed from the delivery trucks to make that last mile more efficient, is likely to be the outcome in the short term at least. When drones are able to conduct more complex multiple deliveries, supported by regulation, their uses will really expand as the drones have the capacity to reduce ground traffic congestion and make parcel delivery truly efficient. With longer range drones, delivery time and cost reductions could also benefit rural areas. Fast delivery of online retail is one of Amazon's major aims with products such as fresh groceries being delivered in under two hours. Amazon has even built a series of small warehouses closer to big US cities to reduce delivery times. Supporting this infrastructure with drones will reduce ground traffic. A record of two minutes 47 seconds from order to delivery by Wing in Australia[68] is the speed and service that consumers most desire.[69] A recharge reduction from 30 minutes to just five minutes and positioning close to parcel centres can all help the drones to take first place in parcel delivery.[70] A cost analysis of the Prime Air delivery system proposed by Amazon.com, Inc., which uses drone technology to deliver packages to customers' doorsteps, demonstrates a cost advantage of one-third or more per package over ground delivery.[71] Delivery times which were once unimaginable or cost prohibitive can now be a reality, and with the positive early feedback from the trials along with regulatory support and public acceptance, the drones will most certainly be part of everyday delivery.

When drones become a normal part of a delivery service, the logical next step is drone pick-up services to fast-track a two-way system. In China, fashion retailer Vanci allows customers to try on clothing delivered to their door by hand and immediately return any items they do not wish to keep.[72] Drones could also provide this service with delivery and return in one transaction.

Asset and infrastructure inspections

Performing asset and infrastructure inspections can entail high risk, and maintaining adequate health and safety standards is expensive. Drones can inspect and monitor

67 Jean-Philippe Aurambout, Konstantinos Gkoumas and Biagio Ciuffo, 'Last Mile Delivery by Drones: An Estimation of Viable Market Potential and Access to Citizens across European Cities' (2019) 11:30 European Transport Research Review <https://ec.europa.eu/jrc/en/publication/last-mile-delivery-drones-estimation-viable-market-potential-and-access-citizens-across-european>.

68 Wing, 'How it Works—Wing' (*Wing*) <https://wing.com/en_au/how-it-works/>. In 2019 Wing achieved a delivery time of 2 minutes 47 seconds from order to delivery.

69 See survey and report by AlixPartners, Alix Partners, 'Opening New Doors For Home Delivery' (Report, May 2019) <www.alixpartners.com/insights-impact/insights/opening-new-doors-for-home-delivery-2019/>.

70 See StoreDot, 'In the News' (*StoreDot*) </www.store-dot.com/news> where Storedot is promising a new technology called Flashbattery which can allow for a full recharge in five minutes.

71 Adrienne Welch Sudbury and E Bruce Hutchinson, 'A Cost Analysis of Amazon Prime Air (Drone Delivery)' (2016)16(1) Journal for Economic Educators 1.

72 See survey and report by AlixPartners (n 69).

buildings and telecommunication towers and reduce the need for risky work by employees with scaffolding, lifts and ladders. Drones can help businesses monitor their assets more regularly and source and find problems such as faults, corrosion and other types of deterioration as they arise, saving significant costs.

A further advantage of drones in this context is that data can be captured and used in the following years or months to provide side-by-side comparisons by years, across similar assets and across similar sites. Where inspections are performed manually, the same employee may not perform the next inspection and the value of a comparison such as whether an asset's small defect has worsened is lost. When using a drone, previous data is readily available.

In addition to the asset and infrastructure inspections outlined in the resources sector and construction industries, drones are making a strong impact within the renewable energy sector. For example, in the solar energy environment drones can provide one technological solution to drive down the costs and increase the efficiency of solar panels. Drones can track leaks, cracks and damaged solar cells. Ground-based maintenance can be time-consuming and, with the preponderance of solar panels installed on rooftops, physical inspections dangerous. Drone inspections can be used to detect defects early and provide proof to manufacturers for warranties if relevant or be used for insurers in a claim assessment. The accuracy of drone inspections is reported to save significantly and to identify repairs commonly missed by a manual inspection.[73]

Similarly, in relation to wind energy work often carried out by pilots and helicopters or on ropes can now be completed by drones. Offshore wind development is increasing worldwide at a 13 per cent compound annual growth rate (CAGR) from 2020 to 2029.[74] The levellised cost of energy of offshore wind has been rapidly declining in recent years as technology improves, with higher capacity turbines, larger rotor diameters and the ability to build turbines further from the shore. The decreasing cost of this energy will make it market competitive, and drones are the key technology to help monitor and maintain these hard-to-access wind turbines. China, Taiwan and Europe are the leading markets in this area. The United States is entering this market with recent offshore wind installations off the east-coast with a forecast that offshore winds can supply energy to more than ten million homes.[75] As drones are developed to better handle windy conditions, they will play an increasing role in ensuring that wind energy generation infrastructure is kept in better repair, thereby reducing offline time and maximizing energy generation. This will help countries meet those ambitious renewable energy targets. Future improvements will see teams of drones near wind farms which are programmed to do routine inspections on a frequent schedule as well as unscheduled flights after weather events. With the cost of wind turbine blades being around US$600,000, the added value of drones to keep these blades running safely and efficiently is enormous.[76]

73 Measure, 'The Case for Drones in Energy' (White Paper) 15 <www.measure.com/the-case-for-drones-energy-download>.

74 Guidehouse Insights, 'Steady Growth Ahead for the Global Wind Power Market' (*2Q20*, 2020) <https://guidehouseinsights.com/reports/steady-growth-ahead-for-the-global-wind-power-market>.

75 Gregory Mayer, 'US Offshore Wind Power Spending Has Oil in Its Sights' (*Financial Times*, 8 July 2020) <www.ft.com/content/93950d29-fa91-434e-8791-ee2d0d998481>.

76 P Bortolotti and others, 'A Detailed Wind Turbine Blade Cost Model' (Report, National Renewable Energy Laboratory, 2019) <www.osti.gov/biblio/1529217-detailed-wind-turbine-blade-cost-model>.

Rail and road inspections are increasingly being conducted with the assistance of drones. For example, drones are utilised for railroad inspections to assist with maintenance and evaluation after weather events and other incidents in addition to surveying areas for development of new railroads. The British rail infrastructure Network Rail uses drones for track inspection and to monitor difficult to reach areas like cliff faces where the railway runs directly underneath.[77] Safety is also improved as engineers spend less time on the tracks. In France, Thales has started to develop drones as eyes for autonomous trains to fly ahead to monitor the tracks to assist with a safe trip. With their ability to see ahead, drones could signal any problem or obstacle, including at road crossings, so that fast-moving trains would be able to react in time.[78] By monitoring the high-voltage electrical lines above and the safety of the tracks below, drones can keep trains running safely and on time and allow a greater number of trains to run on the track at peak times with huge economic benefits.

Road surveys are also relying on drones to provide substantial reductions in cost and time. To support Norway's goal of reaching zero-fatalities or severe injuries on its roads, having earned the title of having the safest roads in Europe, drone surveys are assisting with road creation and inspection.[79] Field time was cut from five days for traditional inspections to about an hour using a drone. One of the key ways drone accuracy proves its cost-effectiveness is in its ability to help reconcile contractor estimates. The administration hires contractors to build roads. With drone data, it is easier, faster and more accurate to compare work estimates with what is actually happening and how much money is to be paid for it. Details down to how much debris was moved can be logged and analysed. With rough terrain to be reviewed, a helicopter survey could cost up to US$11,000 more than a drone survey for a five-kilometre stretch of road.[80] Immense savings are achieved by surveying with drones.

Another example is that of dam inspections in risky areas with limited accessibility. The 3D models the drone imagery can generate allow a more proactive and predictive maintenance model and improves the safety of downstream populations. A study of the Ridracoli dam in Italy which has reduced accessibility would require considerable safety inspections work (involving climbers) and the simultaneous sharing of information would not always be possible.[81] The study concludes that the use of drones enhances effective maintenance practices and can significantly reduce costs.

In a more general context, inspections, mapping and field data collection by drones are assisting authorities to plan for the future. For example, a new mapping initiative in Africa is becoming a model for other parts of the continent in a project supported

77 See Network Rail, UK, 'How We Use Drones' (*Network Rail*) <www.networkrail.co.uk/running-the-railway/looking-after-the-railway/our-fleet-machines-and-vehicles/air-operations/drones-or-unmanned-aircraft-systems-uas/>.

78 Thales Group, 'How Drones Will Change Future Railways' (*Thales*, 11 November 2019) <www.thalesgroup.com/en/worldwide/transport/magazine/how-drones-will-change-future-railways>.

79 Statens Vegvesen, 'National Plan of Action for Road Safety 2018–2021 for Norway' (Report) <www.vegvesen.no/_attachment/2322975/binary/1261865?fast_title=National+Plan+of+Action+for+Road+Safety+2018-2021+%28short+version%29.pdf>.

80 Figures retrieved from a Wingtra case study, Wingtra, 'Norwegian Government Saves Time and Money on Road Surveys with VTOL Drone Data [ROI Study]' (*Wingtra*) <www.wingtra.com/case_studies/road-surveys-with-vtol-drone-data/>.

81 Giulia Buffi and others, 'Survey of the Ridracoli Dam: UAV-based Photogrammetry and Traditional Topographic Techniques in the Inspection of Vertical Structures' (2017) 8(2) Geomatics, Natural Hazards and Risk 1562 <https://doi.org/10.1080/19475705.2017.1362039>.

by the World Bank.[82] Town planners are sending out drones daily to map vast areas. For example, with the Tanzanian archipelago of Zanzibar growing around 4.5 per cent each year, the pace of demand on infrastructure cannot be met. The same applies for other rapidly urbanising areas in Africa. Maps generated by drones can help resolve these issues by showing authorities what is going on, so that they can better plan in terms of economic development and infrastructure. Elevation data can assist town planners to predict potential flood areas and adapt their plans according to this. Similarly, the World Bank is also exploring innovative field data collection approaches using drones for school infrastructure information. A highly detailed database of the educational infrastructure facilities—consisting of geographic coordinates, aerial imagery, orthophoto maps and 3D models of the school buildings has been created by KazUAV,[83] aiming to inform better decision-making for relevant stakeholders to improve the safety and functional conditions of schools. Using drones, a complete picture of the current condition of the school façade is achieved, including the presence of potential loss of integrity in the wall and roof structures. Inspecting the surrounding area of the schools also helps to determine the ease of access for emergency transport services. This application could be utilised in relation to buildings globally.

Challenges and opportunities

All of these applications, while bringing new horizons in efficiency, also hasten the growing need for well-thought-out and properly integrated regulation. Injury to persons and property damage are, of course, very real concerns arising out of the use of drones,[84] and these concerns will become more acute as the use of drones expands to include routine freight delivery and point-to-point transport of people in high-density population environments. Furthermore, the increasing use of drones in these contexts also give rise to very real privacy and noise concerns.[85] Also, increasing investment in infrastructure to support drone use will be needed.[86]

But these obstacles are being addressed and the imperatives to ensure drone deployment are very compelling. As is elaborated upon in the chapters addressing regulation in Part D of this book, considerable research and development time is being devoted to address some of the risks associated with the use and misuse of drones. This work is being conducted by national aviation authorities, such as the FAA, the CAA, bodies such as the European Union Aviation Safety Agency (EASA)[87] and numerous commercial entities.

82 See video, BBC News, 'Africa's Drone Mapping Experts' (*BBC News*, 11 January 2019) <www.bbc.com/news/av/business-46831522/africa-s-drone-mapping-experts>.

83 See Terra News, 'Terra Drone Group Company Kaz UAV Supports the World Bank in Exploring Opportunities to use Drones to Collect Data about School Infrastructure' (*Terradrone*, 17 January 2020) <www.terra-drone.net/global/2020/01/17/terra-drone-kazuav-world-bank-aerial-3d-mapping/>.

84 See, for example, Pam Stewart, 'Drone Danger: Remedies for Damage by Civilian Remotely Piloted Aircraft to Persons or Property on the Ground in Australia' (2016) 23 Torts Law Journal 290.

85 See, for example, Julie-Anne Tarr, Maurice Thompson and Anthony Tarr, 'Regulation, Risk and Insurance of Drones: An Urgent Global Accountability Imperative' (2019) 8 Journal of Business Law 559; Matthew R Koerner, 'Drones and the Fourth Amendment: Redefining Expectations of Privacy' (2015) 64 Duke Law Journal 1129.

86 New South Wales Government, 'Transport for NSW: Future Transport Strategy 2056' (March 2018) 66.

87 Discussed in detail in Chapter 14 <www.easa.europa.eu/>.

The integration of drones into unsegregated airspace requires a balance between effective enforcement measures, such as sufficient penalties, registration and restricted flight zones, with that of technology-based solutions. In this regard, there are an array of technologies currently being developed to enhance the safety mechanisms built into drones, including geofencing, collision avoidance and other transponder-based systems such as Automatic Dependent Surveillance Broadcast (ADS-B).[88]

88 See discussion in Chapters 6, 8 and 19.

3 Drones—healthcare, humanitarian efforts and recreational use

Anthony A. Tarr, Asanka G. Perera, Javaan Chahl, Cameron Chell, Titilayo Ogunwa and Kirsty Paynter

Introduction

As outlined in Chapter 1, the enormous global health challenge precipitated by the COVID-19 pandemic has highlighted a myriad benefits that deployment of drones can deliver to various users and operators and the wider community. For example, in the following case study Draganfly[1] and scientists at the University of South Australia describe the development of health diagnosis technology and deployment onto specialised drones to combat COVID-19 and future health emergencies.

Deployment of drones in the medical environment has been growing rapidly over the past decade from delivery of medical supplies like defibrillators, medicines and vaccines through to the remote diagnosis and treatment of patients by means of telecommunications technology.[2] Drone use in these contexts can be very beneficial for several reasons; for example, the use of drones can facilitate access in remote areas without electricity to medicines and vaccines requiring refrigeration and to the rapid delivery of emergency medical supplies.

Similarly, drones make the perfect first responder to an area hit by a natural disaster such as a tsunami, earthquake, volcanic eruption, or flooding. They are quick, expendable, not delayed by blocked roads and can provide vital and real-time information to rescue teams. Drones can survey the damaged areas immediately after the disaster, assist with the disaster logistics and cargo delivery and continue to provide post-natural disaster assessment.[3] Producing images of a disaster area quickly after the event maximises the recovery phase and can save the lives of people trapped and injured by scanning for victims.[4]

Another area where drones are making a big difference is in search and rescue missions. Drones can provide so much detailed data quickly and efficiently that

1 Draganfly, 'About Us' (*Draganfly*) <https://draganfly.com/about-us/>.

2 Discussed later.

3 For a paper detailing the technical requirements and efficacy of drones in natural disasters see, Mario Arturo Ruiz Estrada and Abrahim Ndoma, 'The Uses of Unmanned Aerial Vehicles—UAV's—(or Drones) in Social Logistic: Natural Disasters Response and Humanitarian Relief Aid' (2019) 149 Procedia Computer Science 375.

4 For an interesting application of drones which are used to survey areas to allow its citizens to ensure that their historical memories are not lost so that cultural heritage can be preserved. Massimiliano Lega, L d'Antonio and Rodolfo Maria Alessandro Napoli, 'Cultural Heritage and Waste Heritage: Advanced Techniques to Preserve Cultural Heritage, Exploring Just in Time the Ruins Produced by Disasters and Natural Calamities' (2010) 140 WIT Transactions on Ecology and the Environment 123.

they directly impact the decision-making process that any incident commander or search coordinator goes through to conduct the search. As Gene Robinson describes it:

> With drone imagery, all parties involved know there is a stream, fence, cliff, hill, obstacle or something that will require special equipment or skill. This precludes sending a team out blind and having them encounter said obstacle unprepared. All this can impact the time to find when minutes matter![5]

Accordingly, in relation to the delivery of emergency medical supplies, in a crisis where the main message is "stay at home", or in harsh environments like war zones or during environmental disasters and in search and rescue missions, drones can provide practical assistance in several ways such as collecting samples for testing, delivering medical supplies, delivering food and vital information and intelligence.

Medical environment

Deliveries

As is noted in Chapter 2, the global growth in the deployment of drones in the transport sector has been slower than might have been anticipated. Regulatory requirements focusing upon safety inhibit or prohibit operations such as flights over populous areas (crowds and public gatherings), in an urban environment, in unsegregated airspace, in close proximity to airports and helipads and operations beyond visual line of sight (BVLOS) in the absence of approvals or exemptions by aviation regulatory authorities and then only on a case-by-case basis.[6]

However, in 2020 regulators worldwide have issued waivers and provided dispensations to support the use and deployment of drones into airspace to provide support in the medical environment, including the transport and delivery of medical supplies. Some of these developments are described later, but given the relatively slow integration of drones for retail delivery, drones as a tool for delivering healthcare, including lifesaving equipment is likely to boost the integration of drone delivery into the retail market further with both facing the same regulatory and technological challenges. Delivering to urban, suburban and rural markets each has its own benefits and challenges, and these need to be addressed in both retail and healthcare delivery. Where profit may be the driving factor for the service provider and speed for the consumer in retail delivery, saving a life or many lives is often the driving factor with drone delivery of medical supplies.

Unprecedented times in 2020 due to the COVID-19 pandemic led to an increase of waivers being granted in relation to drones in the United States. In May 2020, the FAA granted an emergency COVID-19 waiver to Novant Health to partner

5 Angad Singh, 'How Drones are Used in Search and Rescue [Interview]' (*Pix4d*, 5 March 2020) <www.pix4d.com/blog/drones-search-and-rescue>, Interview with Gene Robinson, the "grandfather of search and rescue drone operations".

6 See Part D Regulation, Chapters 13–19 of this book.

with Zipline[7] to use drones to drop off medical supplies by parachute on two designated routes.[8] This waiver is particularly notable as it is the first waiver to be granted by the FAA which allows a drone in these circumstances to be operated beyond visual line-of-sight. If proven to be successful and accident-free, the results of this significant waiver with other similar waivers will help to provide a blueprint for the safest way to expand drone deployment in other delivery contexts in the United States.

The need for medical supplies coupled with the global mandates to socially distance from one another during the COVID-19 pandemic have generated multiple examples of governments fast-tracking ways in which industry could use drones within their regulatory framework or as part of trials where drones are allowed to operate in the same airspace as aircraft. For example, the United Kingdom allowed the trial of a new drone service which reduces delivery times from 30 minutes to ten minutes for urgent medical supplies to a hospital on the Isle of Wight, which lies about eight kilometres off the south coast of England.[9]

In another trial in Ireland, Manna Aero is working with the Irish Health Service Executive to deliver medicines and other essential supplies to vulnerable people in a small rural town.[10] The drone company was aiming to receive support for a trial for fast-food delivery. The BBC explains that in the trial, local health practitioners write medical prescriptions for their patients and drones then drop off the prescription supplies at patients' homes.[11] For those remaining at home, essential supplies like bread and milk can also be delivered as part of this service. In Chile, a similar trial is allowing drones to deliver medications, masks and hand sanitiser to elderly inhabitants in remote areas.[12]

While the COVID-19 pandemic has served to enhance the visibility of drones within the medical environment, their deployment in this context already had a very strong pedigree. Zipline is one of the success stories of drones which has spearheaded vital, on-demand delivery throughout the world. Ranking seventh in the CNBC Disrupter

7 Discussed later.

8 The details of the waiver granted: Federal Aviation Administration, 'Certificate of Waiver Issued To: Novant Health COVID-19 Response' (*Waiver*, 14 May 2020) <www.faa.gov/uas/commercial_operators/part_107_waivers/waivers_issued/media/107W-2020-02083_Rob_Zawrotny_CoW.pdf>. The waiver states: "This Certificate of Waiver is effective from May 14, 2020 to October 31, 2020, or until all COVID-related restrictions on travel, business, and mass gatherings have been lifted for the State of North Carolina, whichever date occurs first, and is subject to cancellation at any time upon notice by the Administrator or an authorized representative."

9 The first delivery took place on 9 May 2020, University of Southampton, 'Drone Successfully Completes First Delivery of Medical Equipment to the Isle of Wight' (*University of Southampton*, 13 May 2020) <www.southampton.ac.uk/news/2020/05/drone-trial-delivery.page>.

10 David Molloy and Jen Copestake, 'Drone to Door Medicines Trial Takes Flight in Ireland' (*BBC News*, 30 April 2020) <www.bbc.com/news/technology-52206660>.

11 ibid.

12 Reuters Staff, 'Chilean Seniors Look to the Sky for Medicine and Masks' (*Reuters*, 21 April 2020) <www.reuters.com/article/us-health-coronavirus-chile-drone/chilean-seniors-look-to-the-sky-for-medicine-and-masks-idUSKBN2222PJ>—The small Chilean beach enclave of Zapallar is using high-tech drones to deliver medications, masks and hand sanitizer to its elderly in remote areas as the coronavirus continues its advance across the largely rural South American nation.

list 2020,[13] the private company Zipline started in 2014 with a mission to "Provide every human on Earth with instant access to vital medical supplies".[14]

Zipline operates from distribution centres placed at the centre of each region of service. Part medical warehouse, part drone airport, each distribution centre can make hundreds of deliveries each day to any point in a 22,500-square kilometre (8,750 square mile) service area.[15] By 2016 Zipline was already delivering blood and blood platelets in Rwanda earning the comment from Margaret Chan, Director General of the World Health Organization, that: "This visionary project in Rwanda has the potential to revolutionize public health, and its life-saving potential is vast".[16]

The early integration of drones in Rwanda's healthcare system was largely due to the Rwandan government's recognition of the practical significance and benefits that deployment of drones in the medical environment could afford and their liberal and progressive approach to the adoption of the technology.

Rwanda partnered with the World Economic Forum (WEF) and provided and continues to provide access to airspace to drone companies who meet safety requirements.[17] The crucial aspect of this access to airspace is that it is granted in a timely manner. The WEF explains:

> The government specifies the safety standard of the mission, and the drone operators specify how they are going to meet it. This regulation is agile. It enables the government to keep up with the rapid development of the technology. Certification takes time, and technology is moving faster than governments.[18]

Other countries such as Switzerland[19] have sought to accelerate the deployment of drones in these contexts through the adoption of an agile and progressive regulatory

13 CNBC (a US pay television news channel) which identifies private companies whose breakthroughs are influencing business and market competition at an accelerated pace. See details: CNBC.com Staff, 'These are the 2020 CNBC Disruptor 50 Companies' (*CNBC*, 16 June 2020) <www.cnbc.com/2020/06/16/meet-the-2020-cnbc-disruptor-50-companies.html>. Zipline moved from 39th position in 2019 to 7th in 2020.

14 See Zipline's company mission on their website, Zipline, 'Our Mission: Provide Every Human on Earth with Instant Access to Vital Medical Supplies' (*Zipline*) <https://flyzipline.com/company/>.

15 Zipline claims that each Zipline distribution centre can make hundreds of deliveries per day anywhere across an 8,000 square mile area. This allows health systems to precisely target the distribution of more than two tons of critical and lifesaving health products, each and every day. If a health worker needs a single mask, they can cost-effectively deliver it within minutes. See Zipline, 'Zipline's Covid-19 Response' (*Zipline*) <https://flyzipline.com/covid-19/>.

16 See Will Knight, 'Why Rwanda is Going to Get the World's First Network of Delivery Drones' (*MIT Technology Review*, 4 April 2016) <www.technologyreview.com/2016/04/04/71244/why-rwanda-is-going-to-get-the-worlds-first-network-of-delivery-drones/>.

17 For further details, see the World Economic Forum in Focus with further details: Amanda Russo and Harrison Wolf, 'What the World Can Learn from Rwanda's Approach to Drones' (*World Economic Forum*, 16 January 2019) <www.weforum.org/agenda/2019/01/what-the-world-can-learn-from-rwandas-approach-to-drones/>.

18 ibid.

19 Advanced regulation in Switzerland has attracted advanced pioneers in the integration of drones into the economy. See Mireia Roca-Riu and Monica Menendez, 'Logistic Deliveries with Drones—State of the Art of Practice and Research' (19th Swiss Transport Research Conference (STRC 2019), Ascona, 15–17 May 2019) <https://doi.org/10.3929/ethz-b-000342823>. Although it is noted that EU drone Regulations, when in force will take precedence.

framework, and the European Commission[20] recently declared that it fully supports the deployment of drones and unmanned aircraft in the transport sector generally and will put in place favourable conditions for the further development of this technology and its regulatory and commercial environment.[21]

The medical supplies drones can deliver are almost limitless—from oral rehydration salts to children suffering from potentially life-threatening diarrhoea, to life-saving blood matched to mothers in labour and HIV diagnostic kits.[22]

Each of these can be delivered easily and help to reduce wastage of limited supplies. Sample testing can also be carried out quickly whilst reducing human contact when drones are utilised to fly samples to laboratories for testing.

One of the major benefits of drone use is the reduction in time it takes to deliver a product. In some instances, this time saving can save lives. This is clearly demonstrated by drone delivery of automated external defibrillators. The time from collapse to defibrillation is crucial for survival. According to a recent study in Sweden, a drone can deliver a defibrillator for use by a bystander up to 16 minutes before an ambulance arrives.[23] Trials are being conducted, and if the regulators can work with the technology to allow full integration of this service, countless lives could be saved.[24] For every minute that passes without CPR and defibrillation, the chances of survival decrease by 7–10 per cent.[25] In remote areas of Canada, BVLOS trials of defibrillator deliveries are also proving successful where drones have shown to provide more than a seven-minute advantage in delivering shocks with the defibrillator before paramedics arrive via ambulance.[26] With results such as these, considerable pressure is placed upon regulators to create frameworks facilitating the use and deployment of drones in everyday medical practice. Further, lifesaving deliveries can include an oxygen mask to someone trapped in a fire, an insulin injection to a diabetic, epinephrine for anaphylaxis or naloxone for opioid overdose. Drones can be pre-positioned at despatch centres throughout the community to give a time advantage in life-threatening situations and support paramedic response.

---

20 Commission to the European Parliament, The Council, The European Economic and Social Committee and the Committee of the Regions, 'Sustainable and Smart Mobility Strategy—Putting European Transport on Track for the Future' COM (2020) 789 final, paras 64–66.

21 See also recent initiatives in the United States. In 2019, UPS and CVS made the first revenue-generating drone delivery of prescription medication to a residential home in North Carolina, Lisa Baertlein, 'UPS Drone Makes First Home Prescription Deliveries for CVS' (*Reuters*, 6 November 2019) <www.reuters.com/article/us-ups-drones/ups-drone-makes-first-home-prescription-deliveries-for-cvs-idUSKBN1XF2JC>.

22 UNICEF, 'News Note: Malawi Tests First Unmanned Aerial Vehicle Flights for HIV Early Infant Diagnosis' (*UNICEF*, 14 March 2016) <www.unicef.org/media/media_90462.html>.

23 J Sanfridsson and others, 'Drone Delivery of an Automated External Defibrillator—A Mixed Method Simulation Study of Bystander Experience' (2019) 27:40 Scandinavian Journal of Trauma, Resuscitation and Emergency Medicine <https://doi.org/10.1186/s13049-019-0622-6>.

24 See Piers Ford, 'Drones Join Emergency Care Front Line in Sweden with Defibrillator Drops' (*mobihealth news*, 19 May 2020), where it states that <www.mobihealthnews.com/news/europe/drones-join-emergency-care-front-line-sweden-defibrillator-drops> "the drone will use GPS technology and advanced camera systems to navigate to the scene of the incident, delivering the AED exactly where it is needed—lowered by a winching device while the drone hovers 30m above."

25 M P Larsen and others, 'Predicting survival from out-of-hospital cardiac arrest: a graphic model' (1993) 22(11) *Ann Emerg Med* 1652.

26 See Buckley Smith, 'Renfrew County Uses Drones to Deliver Defib Units 7 Minutes Faster than Ambulances' (*IT World Canada*, 15 October 2019) <www.itworldcanada.com/article/renfrew-country-uses-drones-to-deliver-defib-units-7-minutes-faster-than-ambulances/422627>.

Vaccines

Globally, drones are demonstrating that they are helping to revolutionise public health and save lives. Distributing vaccines, including those to babies in remote locations,[27] is a game changer for bridging the last mile to reach every child.[28] Drones can reach remote locations, access areas in conflict and fly above poor terrain. In Vanuatu, only a third of its inhabited islands have airfields and proper roads.[29] Delivering medical equipment to these areas is expensive and difficult, especially vaccines which are often required to be carried at specific temperatures. Drones, equipped with a temperature logger, can transport these vaccines safely and quickly by using an electronic indicator which is triggered if the temperature of the vaccines swings out of acceptable range. Drones can reach even remote areas quickly and vaccines can be administered immediately where there is no electricity or access to refrigeration.

Vaccinations against life-threatening viruses are often the only way to keep pandemics from occurring. The most efficient way of bringing the COVID-19 pandemic under control is likely to be widespread global vaccination. Drone flying of vaccines in batches may be the safest, fairest and most efficient way to help distribute millions of vaccines. With the global economy losing more than $10 billion each day, any way of speeding up transport of the vaccine to the population will bring with it countless savings.[30] In the fight against COVID-19, Coldchain Technology Services, a vaccine supply chain management company, selected Draganfly to immediately develop and provide flight services of a robust vaccine delivery payload for use in critical regions for drone delivery of the COVID-19 vaccine. The payload to be developed by Draganfly is a sustainable thermal management system with capability to carry a minimum of 300 multi-doses or 100 single doses. It is being designed as part of a comprehensive delivery and logistics platform which Draganfly will operate.[31]

27 A one-month-old, Joy Nowai became the world's first child to be given a vaccine delivered commercially by drone in a remote island in the South Pacific country of Vanuatu. See UNICEF, 'Child Given World's First Drone-delivered Vaccine in Vanuatu—UNICEF' (*UNICEF*, 18 December 2018) <www.unicef.org/press-releases/child-given-worlds-first-drone-delivered-vaccine-vanuatu-unicef>. The company responsible for the delivery was Australian company Swoop Aero.

28 ibid. Henrietta H Fore, UNICEF Executive Director said: "Today's small flight by drone is a big leap for global health. With the world still struggling to immunize the hardest to reach children, drone technologies can be a game changer for bridging that last mile to reach every child".

29 See World Bank, 'Project Information Document—Integrated Safeguards Data Sheet—Vanuatu Climate Resilient Transport Project—P167382 (Report, 13 November 2018) <http://documents1.worldbank.org/curated/en/402161542854905069/pdf/Concept-Project-Information-Document-Integrated-Safeguards-Data-Sheet-Vanuatu-Climate-Resilient-Transport-Project-P167382.pdf>.

30 See the World Economic Forum Report, Seth Berkley, Richard Hatchett and Soumya Swaminathan, 'The Fastest Way Out of the Pandemic' (*World Economic Forum*, 21 July 2020) <www.weforum.org/agenda/2020/07/covid19-vaccine-global-distribution-manufacturing-lockdown-social-distancing>, where over 1,000 organisations are working together in response to the pandemic.

31 Drone companies are attracting huge investment during the pandemic with many partnering with technology services and drug makers to find the quickest and most efficient way to distribute vaccines. See, for example, 'Draganfly Selected to Immediately Develop Vaccine Drone Delivery Payload System' (*Global Newswire*, 22 December 2020) <www.globenewswire.com/news-release/2020/12/22/2149481/0/en/Draganfly-Selected-to-Immediately-Develop-Vaccine-Drone-Delivery-Payload-System.html>; Mark Vartabedian, 'Drone Startups Aim to Carve Out Role in Delivery of Potential Covid-19 Vaccine' (*Wall Street Journal*, 1 November 2020) </www.wsj.com/articles/drone-startups-aim-to-carve-out-role-in-delivery-of-potential-covid-19-vaccine-11604239201>.

Telemedicine and monitoring

Telemedicine, the remote diagnosis and treatment of patients by means of telecommunications technology is another promising use of drones. Telementoring is the provision of remote guidance by an experienced surgeon or proceduralist to a less experienced colleague with emerging procedures using computers and telecommunications. Using this concept, Harnett et al. demonstrated how drones can be used to establish a wireless communication network between the surgeon and a robot to perform telesurgery—the performance of surgical procedures using a robot, with the operator being located remotely from the site of the patient.[32] In the study, the surgeon and robot were placed in tents about 100 metres apart. The surgeon was able to successfully operate the robotic arms to perform exercises simulating surgical manoeuvres.[33]

Economic pressures often result in care centres and facilities for the aged, being understaffed, with an increasing number of patients suffering from Alzheimer's disease. Trials are being conducted using drones to track down the elderly who go missing from home or a facility.[34] The "lifesaver" drone will help find people much faster than by foot or car.[35] With the first six hours being the most critical to finding a patient alive and well, drones can provide the vital low-cost assistance to authorities.[36] In further research, drones are being tested to autonomously navigate inside the house and recognise a person lying on the floor.[37] Healthbuddy is designed to navigate around the house at regular intervals trying to detect the person/patient using image, sonar and voice recognition (VR) strategies. Once located, the drone starts a wireless communication with a server and receives further instructions based on queries. Health-based queries are designed to require simple yes/no responses; VR strategies are used to classify the speech responses extracted from surrounding noise; using the collected information, the server provides patient analysis; and finally, the Healthbuddy system as a whole determines what is the most appropriate line of action in the given situation.

Software developed at the University of South Australia in conjunction with Canadian drone manufacturer Draganfly could see drones used to monitor the health of people, including spotting sneezes and tracking whether they have a fever. The so-called Pandemic Drones can detect heart rates within eight metres and a cough from 15–20

32 Brett Harnett and others, 'Evaluation of Unmanned Airborne Vehicles and Mobile Robotic Telesurgery in an Extreme Environment' (2008) 14(6) Telemedicine Journal and E-Health 539.

33 James C Rosser Jr and others, 'Surgical and Medical Applications of Drones: A Comprehensive Review' (2018) 22(3) Journal of The Society of Laparoscopic & Robotic Surgeons e2018.00018 <https://doi.org/10.4293/JSLS.2018.00018>.

34 See, for example, George Diaz, 'Drone Technology Will Track Alzheimer's, Autism Patients in Orange County' *Orlando Sentinel* (13 September 2018).

35 ibid. The technology is provided by Project Lifesaver, which will provide tracking devices for those with cognitive disorders. The device can be placed on a person's foot or ankle. Working with 911, deputies will be able to find the person using a frequency emitted from the device with a drone.

36 Meredeth Rowe, 'People with Dementia Who Become Lost' (2003) 103(7) American Journal of Nursing 32.

37 Radosveta Sokullu, Abdullah Balcı and Eren Demir, 'The Role of Drones in Ambient Assisted Living Systems for the Elderly' in Ivan Ganchev and others (eds), *Enhanced Living Environments* (Lecture Notes in Computer Science, vol 11369, Springer 2018) <https://doi.org/10.1007/978-3-030-10752-9_12>.

metres away.[38] The main purpose of this drone is to collect data on a large scale and track patterns of behaviour to paint a broad picture of the spread of a virus such as COVID-19 in a city rather than monitor individuals. Technology originally developed to monitor the heart rate of premature babies in incubators will now be used to understand health trends if regulatory hurdles around privacy and safety can be overcome.

An interesting and comprehensive description of the development of the technology underpinning pandemic drones is provided in the following case study.

Case study: Draganfly/UNISA COVID-19 pandemic drone usage[39]

Draganfly produced the first commercial multirotor drone, appearing in 1998 at the beginning of this innovative period in drone technology.[40] The earliest models had options suited to hobby applications which did not have a GPS unit[41] and could be carefully flown using remote control through the onboard stability augmentation system, a basic autopilot focused on limiting uncommanded rotations. There were also models that were GPS equipped that could hover in position and follow waypoint missions. The comparatively small size of the systems, less than 900 millimetre diagonally from blade-tip to blade-tip was unique and the key to commercial viability. The earliest Draganfly drones suffered from the limitations of older battery technologies and brushed DC motors leading to light but fragile structural designs using foam and fibre composites to save weight and thereby increase endurance to around ten minutes. Modern multirotor drones using lithium-based batteries can fly for over 45 minutes and have robust plastic and carbon fibre chassis.

The mathematical complexity, development of user experience and complex behaviour possible from the multirotor have ensured that they have been the subject of continuous improvement and research since their beginning. Reliability and usability have progressed the drones into the hands of young children and to users with no ability to fly any sort of aircraft. Swarms and formations of drones,[42] light shows with drones,[43] and construction by drones[44] have all been possible due to precise and

38 University of South Australia, 'UniSA Working on "Pandemic Drone" to Detect Coronavirus' (Media Release, 26 March 2020) <www.unisa.edu.au/Media-Centre/Releases/2020/unisa-working-on-pandemic-drone-to-detect-coronavirus/>.

39 This case study is contributed by Asanka G Perera, Javaan Chahl, Cameron Chell and Titilayo Ogunwa.

40 The multirotor is truly a modern flying machine, born from advances in solid state electronics, electromagnetics and energy storage that have occurred only since the 1990s.

41 The United States military deployed the Global Positioning System (GPS) in the 1980s, a constellation of satellites that orbit the earth providing a coded radio frequency signal to ground receivers that they use to solve for their position. Suddenly drones, weapons, robots and aircraft could escape the physical limitations imposed by large inertial navigation systems. At around the same time, there were rapid advances in solid state inertial measurement devices using silicon microelectromechanical systems. Within a few years, during the 1990s, it became possible to make a GPS and inertial package small enough to put in aircraft the size of model aeroplanes.

42 Anam Tahir and others, 'Swarms of Unmanned Aerial Vehicles—A Survey' (2019) 16 Journal of Industrial Information Integration 100106 <https://doi.org/10.1016/j.jii.2019.100106>.

43 Intel, 'Intel Drone Light Show' (*intel*) <www.intel.com/content/www/us/en/technology-innovation/aerial-technology-light-show.html>.

44 Yan Li and Chunlu Liu, 'Applications of Multirotor Drone Technologies in Construction Management' (2018) 19(3) International Journal of Construction Management 401.

reliable flight. Decrease in the size of avionics components (sensors and computers for managing flight and payload) has allowed drones to become smaller and thus, safer around humans. A drone from 1998 would not be considered safe 30 metres from a person not involved in the operation, yet small drones in 2020 are often in quite close proximity to bystanders. Indeed, some small but capable commercial drones are designed specifically for taking "selfies" at very close range.[45] Safe operation in proximity to people opens a range of new applications.

A scientific demonstration of measurement of heart rate and breathing rate from over 50 metres of a group of individuals using a conventional video camera was done in 2017 by Chahl and Al-Naji.[46] Shortly afterwards, a demonstration was done by Al-Naji, Chahl, and Perera using a video camera mounted on a commercial drone. The demonstration was the first of its kind, showing that the signal was visible and could be extracted[47] with accuracy within one breath or one beat per minute, similar to that of hospital instrumentation. Progressing technology from a scientific paper to an application in the real world is never straightforward, but these experiments have been done in the real world, with real equipment. The work attracted significant attention for the technological achievement and possibilities, but also the beginning of concerns about privacy.[48]

When the COVID-19 outbreak emerged, early indications were mixed, with some reports suggesting that up to 2 per cent of the population might perish. At the time of this writing, it has become clear that the virus is particularly lethal to specific populations of frail elderly and subjects with particular combinations of pre-existing ailments.[49] Governments started to deploy hospital ships, build field hospitals, establish triage centres in car parks and commenced locking down entire towns.

Debate raged about how the virus might be transmitted between people. Was it airborne? Droplet borne? Surfaces only? How close was too close? Medical staff were becoming infected at an alarming rate that was directly impacting capability and survival rates.[50]

It became apparent that there was a dearth of means to safely assess subjects' health in a situation with large numbers of infectious cases. Draganfly had already started to consider the role of drones in a human landscape as a natural progression from their experience with mapping physical landscapes with drones. The crisis grew in China and Europe, and the world watched in bemused horror, bracing themselves for the inevitable arrival of the virus in their own communities. Discussions with defence and medical experts in Canada, the United States and Australia were held to try to

45 DJI, 'DJI Spark' (*DJI*) <www.dji.com/spark>.

46 Ali Al-Naji and Javaan Chahl, 'Contactless Cardiac Activity Detection based on Head Motion Magnification' (2017) 17(1) International Journal of Image and Graphics 1750001 <https://doi.org/10.1142/S0219467817500012>.

47. Ali Al-Naji, Asanka G Perera, and Javaan Chahl, 'Remote Monitoring of Cardiorespiratory Signals from a Hovering Unmanned Aerial Vehicle' (2017) 16(1) Biomedical Engineering OnLine 101<https://doi.org/10.1186/s12938-017-0395-y>.

48 Angela Lavoipierre, 'Drone Technology: What Happens When Good Tech Falls into the Wrong Hands?' (*ABC News*, 8 March 2018) <www.abc.net.au/news/2018-03-08/drones-what-happens-when-good-tech-falls-into-the-wrong-hands/9524130>.

49 World Health Organization, 'COVID-19: Vulnerable and High-risk Groups' (*World Health Organization*) <www.who.int/westernpacific/emergencies/covid-19/information/high-risk-groups>.

50 The Lancet, 'COVID-19 Transmission—Up in the Air' (2020) 8(12): P1159 The Lancet Respiratory Medicine <https://doi.org/10.1016/S2213-2600(20)30514-2>.

understand what a government response might entail and where a drone might fit in. It became clear that in the nightmare scenario, the most achievable and useful capability would be to detect vital signs such as heart rate, breathing rate, temperature and blood oxygen saturation from a safe distance.

The nightmare scenario, still faced by the world, needs some definition. The worst case would have been a virus as infectious as the measles (R0 of more than 10),[51] with the mortality rate of the Marburg virus (more than 50%).[52] Faced with such a virus, the economy would almost immediately grind to a halt as individuals refuse to go out for legitimate fear of the virus. The less affluent or well prepared would eventually run out of food. Services such as electricity and water would not be maintained due to abandonment of posts or outbreaks among workers. To provide any aid services, multiple layers of screening for signs of the virus would be needed, possibly starting hundreds of metres away from the point of service. Surveillance for symptoms and delivery of aid and test kits by drone would be one way to push the safe perimeter out and keep essential personnel away from the virus.

Draganfly had a history with Chahl's laboratory which had purchased one of their early models of drone in 1999. After 20 years of research on various topics, his group had almost stumbled into measuring vital signs from the onboard camera of a drone in a well-publicised world first.[53] They had also attracted attention for publishing the results of a race between a drone and an ambulance for provision of first-aid supplies in the cluttered streets of Mosul in Iraq.[54] Draganfly began to work with the University of South Australia on implementing their experimental work as a fieldable capability.[55] There was significant interest in the project from the international media, with a combination of curiosity, hope, terror and another emotion that took the technologists involved completely by surprise—suspicion! Little were the team to know that things were about to become much more complicated than solving a technology problem and defining a viable business case for a well-identified customer.

The aim of the team was to achieve drone based capability to help with potential scenarios should the worst reports about lethality that were circulating at the time be accurate.[56] At the time of this writing, there remains a possibility of a lethal mutation of COVID-19 that could change all of the risk calculus. Indeed, in November 2020, the government of South Australia believed that a new highly transmissible strain had been

51 Fiona M Guerra and others, 'The Basic Reproduction Number (R0) of Measles: A Systematic Review' (2017) 17(12) The Lancet Infectious Diseases e420–e428 <https://doi.org/10.1016/S1473-3099(17)30307-9>.

52 Anne Harding and Nicoletta Lanese, 'The 12 Deadliest Viruses on Earth' (*Livescience*, 4 March 2020) <www.livescience.com/56598-deadliest-viruses-on-earth.html>.

53 University of South Australia (n 36).

54 Megan Scudellari, 'Drone Beats Ambulance in Race to Deliver First Aid to Patients' (*IEEE Spectrum*, 16 August 2019) <https://spectrum.ieee.org/the-human-os/biomedical/devices/drone-vs-ambulance-drone-wins>.

55 University of South Australia, 'Disease-fighting Drones' (*University of South Australia*) <www.unisa.edu.au/research/covid-19/disease-fighting-drones/>.

56 Jasper Fuk-Woo Chan and others, 'A Familial Cluster of Pneumonia Associated with the 2019 Novel Coronavirus Indicating Person-to-Person Transmission: A Study of a Family Cluster' (2020) 395(10223) The Lancet 514 <https://doi.org/10.1016/S0140-6736(20)30154-9>.

discovered when a series of deceptions by patients led contact tracers to believe that a pattern of transmission from pizza boxes was occurring.[57]

Infection causes the body to react with elevated temperature and elevated heart rate,[58] COVID-19 was no exception. Further, the disease affects the lungs and limits their ability to absorb oxygen, which might lead to an elevated breathing rate, but very often a reduced blood oxygen saturation. Measurement of temperature required a camera sensitive to long-wave infrared, commonly available on drones. These four variables became the focus of a crash research and development effort by the University of South Australia (UniSA) and Draganfly. The strategy rapidly evolved towards ensuring that the technology had the robustness to function on a drone, in terms of reliability and stability, while working to ensure that any suitable installation of cameras could be used to achieve vital signs measurements.

It also became clear that there is a stage of prevention that can break the chain of transmission, which is to avoid physical contact, wear masks and keep a safe distance. It was initially described as "social distancing" although it is increasingly being called "physical distancing", possibly because the term does not carry the full implications of these social changes.

There was no objective means for staff and law enforcement to inform people that they were standing too close to others. Some physical altercations ensued, culminating in stabbings and shootings.[59] To assist with this, Draganfly and UniSA created the first aerial social distancing software over a busy week in April 2020. A demonstration video with drone footage of an informal soccer game was picked up by syndicated television news throughout the world.[60] The video showed a circle under each person's feet, the circle was green when they were more than 1.5 metres away from other people's circles and red if they were closer. The concept is effective even on handheld and stationary cameras, yet the drone is a hard test of a concept, with movement, long distances and uncontrolled outdoor lighting. The decision was taken to release the concept because it was a pressing need globally and a relatively a simple idea. Subsequently, other companies including Amazon have implemented the concept in their own software to keep work sites safe.[61]

57 Eugene Boisvert, 'Coronavirus Spread to a Teenager Picking Up a Pizza—So Why Isn't SA Back in Lockdown?' (*ABC News*, 26 November 2020) <www.abc.net.au/news/2020-11-26/student-got-coronavirus-ordering-a-pizza-but-no-lockdown-in-sa/12924252>.

58 Safiya Richardson and others, 'Presenting Characteristics, Comorbidities, and Outcomes among 5700 Patients Hospitalized with COVID-19 in the New York City Area' (2020) 323(20) JAMA 2052 <https://doi.org/10.1001/jama.2020.6775>.

59 Codi Wilson, 'Man Gunned Down Outside Toronto LCBO After Alleged Social Distancing Dispute Identified' (*CTV News*, 27 October 2020) <https://toronto.ctvnews.ca/man-gunned-down-outside-toronto-lcbo-after-alleged-social-distancing-dispute-identified-1.5160344>; Jacob Pucci, 'DA: Social Distancing Argument Led to Syracuse Woman's Stabbing Death' (*Syracuse.com*, 14 June 2020) <www.syracuse.com/crime/2020/06/da-social-distancing-argument-led-to-syracuse-womans-stabbing-death.html>.

60 Les Steed, 'EYES IN THE SKY: Drones Detecting Body Temperature and Monitoring Social Distancing Could Soon Be Coming to Hardest Hit Cities in US' *The Sun* (London, 22 May 2020) <www.thesun.co.uk/news/11690216/drones-detecting-body-temperature-monitoring-social-distancing-coming-cities-us/>.

61 Brad Porter, 'Amazon Introduces "Distance Assistant"' (*Amazon*, 16 June 2020) <www.aboutamazon.com/news/operations/amazon-introduces-distance-assistant>; Intel, 'How Safer Shopping Gets Done' (*intel*) <www.intel.com.au/content/www/au/en/corporate-responsibility/covid-19-response-sensormatic-article.html>.

While this was happening, Cameron Chell was being contacted by public safety officials from all over the world who could see the potential need to maintain order in a virus-induced pandemonium. Amongst them was West Port Connecticut Police, who had long been early adopters of advanced technology, including drones, to support their operations. In April, Draganfly and West Port Police began a pilot programme, exploring what could be done with aerial footage from West Port.[62]

Shortly after the announcement, the suspicion that had been expressed from time to time about the role of drones, combined with the involvement of police, escalated into a social media conversation about civil liberties.[63] The pilot programme had achieved some very promising results, with all of the technology performing as expected, but it was time to re-evaluate appropriate scenarios where the technology could add value. It also helped that COVID-19 revealed itself to be highly contagious, but only highly lethal amongst certain populations who already had compromised health, unlike the Ebola virus and others. With the case fatality rate well under 1 per cent, the prospect of mass casualties and chaos on a large scale diminished. Strictures on freedom of movement, gatherings, lockdowns and curfews created an environment where angels would fear to tread, let alone a start-up company working on medical software.

Research and development for implementing the technology on drones continued to completion without further exposure of the company and UniSA to controversy. A good intention to provide a capability to save lives had been interpreted in some quarters as sinister, which was quite a shock to the technology developers.

The technology continued to have many applications in businesses and institutions across the United States. The tendency of COVID-19 sufferers to have extremely mild symptoms created a need to detect more subtle symptoms than just having a temperature of 100.4 degrees Fahrenheit. Heart rate and blood oxygen saturation turned out to be critical variables for detecting mild symptoms and detecting those individuals medicating themselves to reduce their fever and slip into workplaces. Commercial applications of the Draganfly technology shifted towards stationary cameras, providing remote measurement of vital signs to augment thermal screening for the virus. Yet, the drone application of the technology in mid-2020 has created questions about privacy, imagery, drone surveillance, data retention and government power that continue to the current day.

Drones and natural disasters

Drones make the perfect first responder to an area hit by a natural disaster such as a tsunami, earthquake, volcanic eruption or flooding. They are quick, expendable, not delayed by blocked roads and can provide vital and real-time information to rescue

62 Stephanie Pagones, 'Connecticut Town Using Drones for Coronavirus Symptom-Monitoring' (*Fox Business*, 22 April 2020) <www.foxbusiness.com/technology/connecticut-drones-coronavirus-symptom-monitoring>; NBC Connecticut, 'Westport Police to Test "Pandemic Drone" that can Sense Fevers, Coughing' (*NBC Connecticut*, 21 April 2020) <www.nbcconnecticut.com/news/local/westport-police-to-test-pandemic-drone-that-can-sense-fevers-coughing/2258746/>.

63 Doha Madani, 'Connecticut Town Reverses Course on "Pandemic Drones" amid Privacy Concerns' (*NBC News*, 24 April 2020) <www.nbcnews.com/news/us-news/connecticut-town-reverses-course-pandemic-drones-amid-privacy-concerns-n1191051>; ACLU Connecticut, 'Statement Regarding Westport Drone Covid-19 Pilot Program' (*ACLU Connecticut*, 22 April 2020) <www.acluct.org/en/press-releases/statement-regarding-westport-drone-covid-19-pilot-program>.

teams. Drones can survey the damaged areas immediately after the disaster, assist with the disaster logistic and cargo delivery and continue to provide the post-natural disaster assessment.[64] Producing images of a disaster area quickly after the event maximises the recovery phase and can save the lives of people trapped and injured by scanning for victims.[65] Modern drones can endure high temperatures, low visibility and dangerous winds. They can assist firefighters to pinpoint areas of quickly progressing fire, assess flood damage quickly which can help predict areas of future flood risk and pinpoint victims by using thermal imaging software. Rescue teams are then better prepared to locate trapped victims or warn others moving towards dangerous areas such as fires.

The Heliguy provides six examples of drone usage in a natural disaster context ranging from huge fires to major earthquakes. One example provided is as follows:

> In November 2018, California's deadliest and most destructive fire on record broke out, scorching more than 150,000 acres and raging for more than two weeks. Before containment, the blaze tore through urban areas across Paradise, Chico, Oroville, Magalia and other cities, taking almost 100 lives and leaving many more missing. The inferno destroyed nearly 14,000 homes, 528 commercial structures and close to 4,300 buildings. Although an unwanted record, the fire also prompted the largest UAV disaster response to date, with emergency crews using unmanned aircraft to collect aerial insights in the wake of the disaster. Drone data software package, DroneDeploy, was used to help map the destruction to aid the recovery process in the days leading up to the fire's containment. Over three days, 16 teams of public safety professionals completed more than 500 drone flights, capturing 70,000+ images of the areas surrounding Paradise and Magalia. Drones footage captured 360° videos and photographs of the devastated neighbourhoods and helped to create 3D maps of the affected areas. The result: Close to 500GB of drone data which DroneDeploy turned into 26.5 square miles (15,000 acres) of high-res aerial maps to help state agencies and the public assist in the recovery efforts. This data was used to aid search and rescue operations, assist with the planning and response to potential mudslides, issue FEMA (Federal Emergency Management Agency) relief funds and help process insurance claims faster so that wildfire victims can get back on their feet. The images have since been transformed into maps that are highly accurate, geo-referenced, dated, timestamped and overlaid with street names. These maps were critical tools in the recovery process as neighbourhoods were no longer recognisable. he drones were also used to provide 360° imagery, which allowed for an interactive way to view a scene—being able to look around, zoom in and look in all directions. This type of data, aided by the app Hangar, quickly provides useful situational awareness. The victims of the fire were also able to put the maps to good use. With entire neighbourhoods mapped, homeowners were able to submit the imagery to insurance providers to process claims immediately—a process that traditionally could

64 For a paper detailing the technical requirements and efficacy of drones in natural disasters see, Estrada and Ndoma (n 3).

65 For an interesting application of drones which are used to survey areas to allow its citizens to ensure that their historical memories are not lost; so that cultural heritage can be preserved see, Lega, d'Antonio and Napoli (n 4).

take days or weeks. Many used the imagery to gain access to FEMA relief funds for the families affected by the fires.[66]

Areas that are prone to large-scale disasters such as earthquakes and flooding benefit greatly from visual imaging and 3D mapping. Manned aircraft are often too expensive to use, satellite mapping does not meet high-resolution needs, and both take too much time during emergency situations.[67] The use of drones to map disaster areas provides greater advantages in costs and in rapid response times when compared to traditional methods. Drones can be deployed quickly, generate high-resolution and 3D mapping, identify hotspots that have sustained the most damage and upload the data in real time to coordinate relief efforts. In the aftermath of the 2015 Nepal earthquake, drones assisted in creating 3D maps and models through image processing software. These aided in assessing the widespread damage, operating search and evacuation missions, reconstructing buildings and preserving areas of the city.[68]

Drones also can reduce and, in some circumstances, eliminate the risks faced by firefighters, pilots, first responders and others. For example, because aircraft must fly at low altitudes to fight wildfires, pilots and crew are put in serious danger. They are made to endure high temperatures, low visibility, dangerous winds and high stress. With drones one can eliminate the risks that pilots face and increase the effectiveness of battling fires including flying in low visibility and dropping fire retardants more accurately and safely. Deploying drones provides greater situational awareness. Outfitted with communication systems, they add the benefit of sustaining contact between the command centre and firefighters on the ground.[69] With aircraft and helicopter crashes accounting for up to 24 per cent of wildland firefighter deaths, drones can help save the lives of firefighters by replacing the need for firefighters on the ground or identifying a quick escape route if fire starts to close in on the crew.[70] Looking ahead, swarms of drones may be able to drop flammable balls to set small, controlled fires. The balls ignite on the ground and burn up vegetation lying in the wildfire's path; when the wildfire arrives, there's no fuel left. By flying autonomously, these drones could negate the need for drone pilots on the ground and share information with each other and with firefighters on the ground.[71]

Drones can also help to shift from reactively managing crises to proactively reducing risks by providing data which can assist with planning, decision-making and risk analysis. For example, while drones cannot necessarily improve storm forecasting, they

66 James Willoughby, 'Six Times Drones Have Helped with Disaster Response' (*Heliguy.Com™*, 22 March 2019) <www.heliguy.com/blog/2019/03/22/six-times-drones-have-helped-with-disaster-response/>.
Other examples given in the article describe drone usage and deployment during Hurricane Irma (Caribbean 2017), Mexico City Earthquake (2017), Genoa Bridge Collapse (Italy, 2018), Liverpool Echo Arena Multi-Storey Car Park Fire (United Kingdom, 2017) and Balkans flooding (2014).

67 EKU Online, '5 Ways Drones are Being Used for Disaster Relief' (*EKU Online*) <https://safetymanagement.eku.edu/blog/5-ways-drones-are-being-used-for-disaster-relief/>.

68 ibid.

69 Airborne Drones, 'Natural Disasters: Drone Technology for Natural Disasters' (*Airborne Drones*) <www.airbornedrones.co/natural-disasters/>.

70 See Kate Baggaley, 'Drones are Fighting Wildfires in Some Very Surprising Ways' (*NBC News*, 17 November 2017) <www.nbcnews.com/mach/science/drones-are-fighting-wildfires-some-very-surprising-ways-ncna820966>.

71 Burchan Aydin and others, 'Use of Fire-Extinguishing Balls for a Conceptual System of Drone-Assisted Wildfire Fighting' (2019) 3(1) Drones 17 <https://doi.org/10.3390/drones3010017>.

can help with measurement and tracking as evidenced by the US National Oceanic and Atmospheric Administration (NOAA) launching drones into the eye of hurricanes to collect atmospheric data for better storm tracking.[72] James Van Meter comments further that drones' contribution is even more significant in wildfire management by tracking fires, identifying hotspots for better deployment of resources and personnel and even for the prescribed burning as already described.[73]

The American Red Cross, leading private sector companies, United States federal agencies, including the FAA, the US Department of Homeland Security and the US Coast Guard, coordinated by Measure, a 32 Advisors Company, produced a detailed report titled "Drones for Disaster Response and Relief Operations" in April 2015.[74] The executive summary of their key findings and views is very instructive:

> Aerial drones are one of the most promising and powerful new technologies to improve disaster response and relief operations. Drones naturally complement traditional manned relief operations by helping to ensure that operations can be conducted safer, faster, and more efficiently.

When a disaster occurs, drones may be used to provide relief workers with better situational awareness, locate survivors amidst the rubble, perform structural analysis of damaged infrastructure, deliver needed supplies and equipment, evacuate casualties and help extinguish fires—among many other potential applications.

In advance of an emergency, drones are able to assist with risk assessment, mapping and planning of risk-prone areas. When individuals, businesses and communities are able to understand and manage risks and plan effectively, they reduce overall damage and losses. Rebuilding and recovery are then able to begin more quickly, ultimately strengthening the resiliency of communities.

Drones have long been described as optimally suited to perform the "3D" missions, often described as dirty, dull and dangerous. They can provide needed aerial data in areas considered too hazardous for people on the ground or for manned aircraft operation, such as sites with nuclear radiation contamination or in close proximity to wildfires. Drones can also deliver needed supplies and relay Wi-Fi and cellular phone service when communications are needed the most.[75]

Other humanitarian drone activities

Since 2006, drones have been used to assist in peacekeeping measures.[76] Since then, unarmed drones are at the front line protecting civilians by providing real-time pictures of situations as they develop on the ground. Drones help peacekeeping missions

72 See James Van Meter, Allianz Global Corporate & Specialty, 'Drones and Natural Catastrophes: Flying Masters of Disasters' (*Allianz*, 12 September 2019) <www.allianz.com/en/press/news/commitment/environment/190912_Allianz-drones-and-hurricanes-flying-masters-of-disasters.html>.

73 ibid.

74 Measure, 'Drones for Disaster Response and Relief Operations' (Report, April 2015) <www.issuelab.org/resources/21683/21683.pdf>.

75 ibid 4.

76 Aimee van Wynsberghe and Tina Comes, 'Drones in Humanitarian Contexts, Robot Ethics, and the Human–Robot Interaction' (2020) 22 Ethics and Information Technology 43 <https://doi.org/10.1007/s10676-019-09514-1>.

act more quickly and more decisively with aerial vision. They also provide better security and can inform teams if an attack is imminent. In the conflict zones of areas like Mali and the Central African Republic, drones may be the only option to safely monitor situations on the ground.[77] It is acknowledged that where drones displace peacekeepers on the ground, this can have a negative effect on the refugees who may need that human interaction. However, drones may be the only practical, safe and cost-efficient tool in a war zone or volatile area.

Drones are also proving themselves as an effective wildlife protector and researcher—from counting wildlife (more accurately and more precisely than humans according to research),[78] to helping catch or deter poachers,[79] and even catching whale mucus to provide a snapshot of whales' health.[80] While helicopters have long been the chosen vehicle for wildlife monitoring, they are expensive and low-level flying stresses animals and can be dangerous for the humans involved.[81] Electric drones are much quieter, operate at a fraction of the cost, offer a safer way for scientists to observe their subjects and are more precise than traditional approaches.[82] There are challenges in relation to their deployment in wildlife management and ecological research with, for example, reported disturbance effects of drones on birds, reptiles and mammals.[83] However, on balance, drones are starting to realise their potential to assist with cost-effective and innovative solutions to handle a wide variety of conservation and environmental problems that threaten biodiversity in protected areas.

Accidents, search and rescue

As a first responder, drones can provide the first pictures of an accident, relay those pictures back to a central team to help guide critical decision-making. The most efficient traffic routes, the number and type of on-ground first responders required and images of the immediate aftermath of an accident are vital to saving lives and closing and reopening roads efficiently. Take for example, a study by the Department of

77 See interview with Hervé Ladsous, the United Nations under-secretary-general for peacekeeping operations: Masimba Tafirenyika, 'Drones are Effective in Protecting Civilians—Hervé Ladsous' (*United Nations*, April 2016) <www.un.org/africarenewal/magazine/april-2016/drones-are-effective-protecting-civilians>.

78 See J C Hodgson and others, 'Drones Count Wildlife More Accurately and Precisely than Humans' (2018) 9(5) Methods in Ecology and Evolution 1160 <https://doi.org/10.1111/2041-210X.12974>.

79 Samuel G Penny and others, 'Using Drones and Sirens to Elicit Avoidance Behaviour in White Rhinoceros as an Anti-poaching Tactic' (2019) 286 Proceedings of the Royal Society B 20191135 <http://doi.org/10.1098/rspb.2019.1135>.

80 Hover UAV, 'Collecting Whale Snot from Humpback Whales' (*Hover UAV*, 12 March) <www.hoveruav.com.au/news-1/collecting-whale-snot-from-humpback-whales>.

Collecting whale snot from humpback whales, the company leading the collaborative project explains that when the whale decides to come to the surface and exhale, it blows biological mucus from deep inside its lungs. This exhale condensate can be collected via a drone fitted with a series of six to eight petri dishes and sent to the laboratory to check aspects of the whale's health including viruses, hormone levels and DNA.

81 Barbara Cozzens, 'How Drones are Playing a Role in Wildlife Conservation' (*Sciencing*, 29 March 2018) <https://sciencing.com/how-drones-are-playing-a-role-in-wildlife-conservation-13710359.html>.

82 Nancy Averett, 'Drones Take Off as Wildlife Conservation Tool' (*Audubon*, July–August 2014) <www.audubon.org/magazine/july-august-2014/drones-take-wildlife-conservation-tool>.

83 Jesús Jiménez López and Margarita Mulero-Pázmány, 'Drones for Conservation in Protected Areas: Present and Future' (2019) 3(1) Drones 10, para 3.2.2 <www.mdpi.com/2504-446X/3/1/10/htm>.

Transport, North Carolina which simulated a two-car crash. It took the reconstruction team an hour and 51 minutes to collect the data using a laser scanner.[84] It took 25 minutes using drones. The time saved meant that the scene of the collision could be cleared more than an hour earlier allowing traffic to start moving. Crucially, where drones replace people on the ground after accidents, they can significantly reduce the risk posed to those involved including investigators and emergency services.

Looking to the future, drone designs large enough to carry casualties from accidents are being considered. Tactical Robotics have proposed a "drone ambulance" version capable of carrying up to two injured soldiers.[85] The US design company Argodesign has also produced a concept for a flying ambulance drone capable of carrying a single patient that could be deployed to an accident scene.[86] A single pilot who would usually fly a single helicopter could manage a whole fleet of drone ambulances remotely, relying on autopilot through the skies and taking over manual controls only during more complicated take-offs and landings. The drone is designed to land almost anywhere, as it has a footprint the size of a compact car. With estimates of up to 30 per cent of deaths due to slow emergency responses, the benefits of time reduction are high where a flying ambulance could land, the emergency worker stabilises and loads up the patient and quickly flies back to the hospital for further treatment.[87]

Recreational use

Drones being operated for recreational use is perhaps the best-known application to the general public. Recreational drones are commonly observed in operation within a family and friends' environment, during school vacations, taking photographs and even in a racing environment.[88]

The FAA defines a person as a recreation drone user if you "fly your drone for fun",[89] and very distinct laws and regulations have been developed in numerous jurisdictions for recreational and "hobby" fliers.[90]

84 See details of the study N.C. Department of Transportation, 'Use of Drones in Collision Reconstruction Studied' (*NCDOT*, 6 September 2017) <www.ncdot.gov/news/press-releases/Pages/2017/Use-of-Drones-in-Collision-Reconstructio.aspx>.

85 Argodesign, 'Drone Ambulance: A Visionary Solution to Speed Emergency Care' (*Argodesign*) <www.argodesign.com/work/drone-ambulance-argodesign.html>.

86 ibid.

87 Anita Acha George and others, 'Golden Aid an Emergency Ambulance System' (2017 International Conference on Networks & Advances in Computational Technologies (NetACT), Thiruvananthapuram, 20–22 July 2017) <https://doi.org/10.1109/NETACT.2017.8076818>—the articles state that according to *Times of India* about 146,133 people were killed in road accidents in India in the year 2016 with delayed ambulance services contributing to 30 per cent of the deaths.

88 news.com.au, 'Aussie Teenager Rudi Browning becomes World First FAI Drone Racing Champion' (*news.com.au*, 7 November 2018) <www.news.com.au/sport/sports-life/aussie-teenager-rudi-browning-becomes-worlds-first-fai-drone-racing-champion/news-story/083ccf7d135ce958c5ab246e63132fbb>.

89 Federal Aviation Administration, 'Recreational Flyers & Modeler Community-Based Organizations' (*Federal Aviation Administration*, 2 December 2020) <www.faa.gov/uas/recreational_fliers/>.

The recreational or consumer drones market describes the market for unmanned aerial vehicles used for the purposes of entertainment and which have simple-to-use controls targeted for general public usage rather than for commercial purposes.

90 See discussion in Part D Regulation, Chapters 13–19.

Regulators have a delicate balancing act to perform to ensure that regulatory requirements imposed upon recreational drone use is commensurate with the risks they pose and are not so heavy-handed as to stifle such use or participation in hobby groups. The fundamental challenges in navigating regulatory options are making sure drone users are educated, have basic training and that where accidents occur due to recklessness or bad luck, innocent bystanders who may be injured or have their property injured are protected.

The drone market for recreational users is growing rapidly with strong competition among drone manufacturers pushing down costs for these types of consumer drones—particularly among higher-end models that can shoot photos and live stream video.[91] The rising popularity of aerial photography is a significant factor in driving the recreational drones market. The Business Research Company (TBRC) reports that the global consumer drones market was valued at about US$2.09 billion in 2018 and is expected to grow to US$4.05 billion at a compound annual growth rate (CAGR) of 18.0 per cent through 2022.[92] TBRC comments further that:

> [P]hotography enthusiasts are increasingly using drones to capture photographs and videos from a birds-eye view which would otherwise require high-end video cranes. This increase in popularity has led consumers to purchase hobbyist drones and use them for photography purposes, thus driving market growth.[93]

The decreasing cost and increasing availability of recreational drones have resulted in a significant increase in the number of recreational drones and commensurate increases in the number of arrests and fines reported for inappropriate and unsafe use. Alex Fitzpatrick[94] points out that learning to build and fly a drone or remote-controlled aircraft was once a time-consuming, arduous process, factors that kept the hobby from spreading. Now, new technologies like user-friendly quadcopter designs, equipped with smaller, high-powered motors and batteries mean that pilots can have their aircraft ready to go in minutes instead of days, greatly enhancing the appeal of the hobby. And while the old-school pilots often met in clubs, which enforced flight rules as a social norm, the "newbies" are buying their gear off Amazon and heading out solo. He also points out that:

> [T]he real issue here is that many of the new designs come with cameras attached, a feature that has fundamentally changed why people fly model aircraft. Though some old-school remote controlled aircraft hobbyists experimented with DIY digital camera hookups, they mostly viewed building and flying their aircraft as

91 Business Insider Intelligence, 'Drone Market Outlook: Industry Growth Trends, Market Stats and Forecast' (*Business Insider*, 4 March 2020) <www.businessinsider.com/drone-industry-analysis-market-trends-growth-forecasts?r=AU&IR=T>.

92 The Business Research Company, '2020 Drones Market (Commercial & Consumer) Growth, Trends, Market Size and Forecasts' (*Cision PR Newswire*, 9 March 2020) <www.prnewswire.com/news-releases/2020-drones-market-commercial-consumer-growth-trends-market-size-and-forecasts-by-tbrc-301019687.html>.

93 ibid.

94 Alex Fitzpatrick, 'Here's Why So Many Drone Pilots Are Getting in Trouble' (*Time*, 8 July 2014) <https://time.com/2966246/drone-pilots-arrest-fine-law/>.

> the endgame of their project. They generally avoided risky flying, as that could cost their club permission to use the local park, or could damage their expensive, intricate model aircraft that took hours to build. The new wave of hobbyists see their GoPro-equipped drones less as remote-controlled aircraft and more as flying cameras, set to embark on a cinematic adventure. Flying for the sake of flying is no longer the point—the point is getting awesome YouTube footage, which leads to riskier behavior.[95]

Membership of drone clubs, groups and organisations can be very helpful to recreational drone users. For example, the Australian Miniature Aerosports Society Inc,[96] in accordance with their motto, "Safety is no Accident", provides assistance to persons operating recreational drones including guidance as to where, how, and when? Additionally, membership of an organisation such as FPV UK, the UK association for radio control model and drone flying, carries with it £5 million public liability insurance for drone and model flying included within the range of membership benefits for a modest annual membership fee. Finding a drone group that resonates with a recreational user's needs and interests is not difficult, for example, there are even sites enabling individuals join Drone groups around the world, such as Drone Meetup,[97] which has 49,850 members and 190 groups around the world, with nine of the ten largest drone groups being located in the United States.

Concluding comments

Drones are making substantial contributions in relation to healthcare and humanitarian efforts. They are also extensively used and enjoyed by the public at large in recreational environments. In these diverse contexts, they deliver benefits to society and to the community at large that augment their more commercial and industrial applications.

By responding to demand surges and preventing stock-outs, hovering over hospital construction sites at night,[98] disinfecting hospital rooms and delivering medications and equipment, drones can make medical deliveries safe, fast and efficient. Drones are even saying thank you to health workers in high-tech light shows.[99] Being a friend not a foe by saving lives, replenishing stocks of medical equipment and doing so safely is moving drones in public perception from a sci-fi or military weapon or recreational toy to a much wanted, needed and valued technology. For governments, supporting drone delivery of medical equipment is essential. As the examples provided in the chapter show, speeding up access to remote areas, maintaining social distancing,

95 ibid.

96 Australian Miniature Aerosports Society (AMAS), 'Recreational Drones' (*AMAS*) <www.amas.org.au/wspDrones.aspx>.

97 Meetup, 'Drone' (*Meetup*) <www.meetup.com/topics/drone/>.

98 Mohit Sagar, 'How Drones are Assisting Government in China Fight COVID-19' (*OpenGov Asia*, 11 March 2020) <https://opengovasia.com/how-drones-are-assisting-government-in-china-fight-covid-19/>.

99 Erin McCarthy, 'A Drone Light Show Lit Up the Philly Skies to Thank Health Workers amid the Coronavirus Pandemic' (*The Philadelphia Inquirer*, 30 April 2020) <www.inquirer.com/health/coronavirus/coronavirus-philadelphia-penn-drone-light-show-verge-aero-covid-19-20200430.html>—in Philadelphia, fast-flying drones formed images of medical symbols, a flattening curve, a waving American flag, a ringing Liberty Bell, the LOVE sign, and the message "Thank u heroes".

monitoring health and replenishing stocks in a timely manner with medical supplies are growing priorities for governments globally. Drone usage and deployment in these contexts are likely to gain growing support by governments who are looking for efficiencies in the medical services environment with the added benefit that enhancing healthcare with drones will be a popular choice among many voters. It naturally flows that as drones prove themselves to be effective in medical delivery, so too will they take over more of the last mile in retail delivery.

Drones are also proving to be invaluable in improving disaster response and relief operations by helping to ensure that those operations can be conducted safer, faster and more efficiently. Natural and man-made disasters destroy environments, often making conditions so difficult that relief workers are unable to access areas and provide assistance. Drones have the ability to take on roles where relief workers and manned vehicles fall short and to perform the "3D" missions often described as dirty, dull and dangerous.[100] When a disaster occurs, drones may be used to provide relief workers with better situational awareness, locate survivors amidst the rubble, perform structural analysis of damaged infrastructure, deliver needed supplies and equipment, evacuate casualties and help extinguish fires—among many other potential applications. In advance of an emergency, drones are able to assist with risk assessment, mapping and planning. When individuals, businesses and communities are able to understand and manage risks and plan effectively, they reduce overall damage and losses. Rebuilding and recovery are then able to begin more quickly, ultimately strengthening the resiliency of communities.[101]

100 Measure (n 74).
101 ibid 12–33.

4 Drones and law enforcement

Robert S. Barrows[*]

Introduction

Drones[1] have dramatically changed the public safety arena. This "classically disruptive"[2] technology offers significant opportunities to improve public safety outcomes for law enforcement officers and other first responders as well as the communities they serve. Drones have been used by the US military in overseas operations since at least 2000,[3] and in subsequent years, many police and sheriff departments have acquired drones and used them for a variety of operations, such as search and rescue missions, disaster response, crowd monitoring, traffic collision reconstruction, crime scene reconstruction, as well as providing a bird's eye view in dangerous active shooter and hostage situations.[4] As one local police chief said about law enforcement's deployment of drone technology: "the use of drones is limited only by one's creativity."[5]

Generally, there are two central issues when exploring the intersection of law enforcement and drones. The first is how law enforcement can use drones to advance public safety. As noted above, there are many operational, as well as financial benefits, to police agencies that utilise drones. Nonetheless, drones are perceived by some as potent law enforcement tools that can potentially erode the public's privacy and expand intrusive surveillance. In fact, public suspicion and fear surrounding the use of drones by law enforcement have motivated some municipalities to forbid drone use by law enforcement completely,[6] essentially denying local law enforcement agencies

* Any opinions either expressed or derived from this chapter are solely those of the author and do not reflect the official position(s) of the New York City Police Department.

1 For consistency, the more informal term "drone" or "drones" to refer to unmanned aerial vehicles (UAV), unmanned aircraft systems (UAS), and small unmanned aircraft (sUAS). The term UAS refers to the entire system for using a drone, including the aircraft and the ground control unit, while UAV refers only to the vehicle itself.

2 Timothy M Ravitch, 'Grounding Innovation: How Ex-Ante Prohibitions and Ex-Post Allowances Impede Commercial Drone Use' (2018) Columbia Business Law Review 495, 501.

3 Police Executive Research Forum, 'Drones: A Report on the Use of Drones by Public Safety Agencies—And a Wake Up Call About the Threat of Malicious Drone Attacks' (2020) xv <www.policeforum.org/free-online-documents> [hereinafter "PERF Report"].

4 See generally, 'Use of Department Unmanned Aircraft Systems' Patrol Guide of the New York City Police Department Section 212-124 (Effective, 4 December 2018) <www1.nyc.gov/site/nypd/about/about-nypd/patrol-guide.page> [hereinafter "NYPD Patrol Guide"].

5 PERF Report (n 3), at xv.

6 Laura L Myers, 'Seattle Mayor Grounds Police Drone Program' (*Seattle Times*, 7 February 2013) <www.seattletimes.com/seattle-news/seattle-grounds-police-drone-program>.

the ability to take advantage of a beneficial technology that could assist in a variety of critical operations—including dangerous and rapidly evolving situations. Confronted with these duelling interests, law enforcement agencies are faced with a series of challenges. Notably, law enforcement agencies must make strategic decisions about the purposes for which drones will be used. These agencies must navigate a veritable labyrinth of laws and regulations that span the federal, state and local levels of government, including proper certification, licensure, and training of personnel. Furthermore, they must also acknowledge the legitimate privacy concerns from the public, balancing operational needs with sensible oversight and transparency.

Second, despite the vast benefits that this disruptive technology provides, equally significant are the concerns that unauthorised drone operations can cause in local jurisdictions. A critical issue is the role of law enforcement, particularly that of front-line responders, to detect and mitigate drone use that threatens public safety. These threats include terrorism, reconnaissance to further criminal activity, and reckless or negligent use that may result in serious physical injury to the public.[7] Most of the international communities rely on the central or federal government to address errant drone detection and mitigation. Such reliance may prove problematic, as most federal or central agencies do not have the authority, capital, or human resources to invest in and operate drone detection and mitigation on a frequent or daily basis.[8]

Drone technology, however, has evolved at an astounding rate in the last ten years; the legal and regulatory state of play has not kept pace. In the United States, only four federal agencies have the authority to engage in counter-drone actions, and this authority does not allow for persistent counter-drone coverage in major cities.[9] Federal agencies can certainly assist their local law enforcement partners by exercising this authority to help police major events in large cities, such as the Super Bowl or the World Series, but every day there are innumerable routine events in US cities that draw crowds of thousands of people, and it is simply impractical for federal law enforcement to be involved in all such events. Moreover, despite having express authorisation to detect and mitigate unauthorised uses, US federal agencies generally rely on local law enforcement to be the first line of response to deter and investigate such incidents.[10] The lack of local law enforcement's participation in mitigation and detection technology, particularly in major cities, provides a limited toolbox for local law enforcement to address this errant drone use.

Examining drone use by law enforcement at the same time as detection and mitigation casts a disingenuous light on law enforcement's drone use given that law enforcement wants to use it, but at the same time it should be able to prevent others from

7 PERF Report (n 3) 65–67 (quoting John Miller, NYPD Deputy Commissioner of Intelligence and Counterterrorism, who notes that most drone incidents involving the NYPD are "hobbyist playing with drones, and they fall out of the sky"); see also 'Protecting Against Rogue Drones, Congressional Research Service' (September 2020) <https://fas.org/sgp/crs/homesec/IF11550.pdf>.

8 Blue Ribbon Task Force on UAS Mitigation at Airports, 'Final Report of the Blue Ribbon Task Force on UAS Mitigation At Airports' (2019) 10 <https://uasmitigationatairports.org/wp-content/uploads/2019/10/BRTF-Report2019.pdf> [hereinafter "BRTF Report"].

9 Preventing Emerging Threats Act of 2018, Pub. L. No. 115–254, §§ 1601–1603, 132 Stat. 3522–3530 (2018).

10 Federal Aviation Administration, 'Law Enforcement Guidance for Suspected Unauthorized UAS Operations' (2018) 5 <www.faa.gov/uas/public_safety_gov/media/FAA_UAS-PO_LEA_Guidance.pdf>. [hereinafter "FAA Guidance to Law Enforcement"].

doing so. Such an assessment, however, is inexact. Disruptive technologies such as drones present benefits and causes of concern for those using them. No party, whether it is a law enforcement agency or a member of the public, should have unfettered use. Use should be subject to careful consideration and the imposition of critical and sensible safeguards. The depth and level of that examination and those safeguards will always be subject to debate.

The chapter will discuss the operational and financial benefits that drone technology presents to law enforcement as well as an overview of common and extraordinary uses by law enforcement. Focus will also be on the consortium of federal laws and regulations addressing law enforcement's use of drones as well as an acknowledgement of state and local laws which seek to regulate this area. The chapter also addresses concerns that law enforcement drones raise regarding privacy and surveillance as well as common approaches police agencies have taken to address them.

The last section of this chapter will provide an in-depth discussion about the legal landscape surrounding law enforcement's ability to detect and mitigate malicious drone use as well as potential considerations geared towards addressing the legal gaps that exist.

Use of drones by law enforcement agencies to advance public safety

Operational and financial benefits

In general, law enforcement agencies seek to leverage the benefits of new and improving technology as it enables their officers to be more responsive to the communities they serve and to carry out the agency's critical work in ways that are more effective, efficient, and safe for all. Technology has rapidly changed the face of modern policing. Most police departments now have computers in patrol cars and communicate with their officers via cell phone. They use new technologies to gather licence plate data and focus on crime hotspots. New DNA testing capabilities are closing cold cases, offering the chance to bring finality to an investigation, and in some cases, reverse a wrongful conviction. The embrace of technology by law enforcement can conserve or better deploy critical resources and staffing levels.[11] It also has the potential to reduce some in-person engagements between the public and the police which in turn can limit negative interactions.

Undoubtedly, drones present unique capabilities to law enforcement as they are affordable, manoeuvrable, not bound to a road structure, and pose little risk of harm to the pilot. The cost of buying and operating, as well as maintaining manned aircraft is considerable. Prior to the arrival of drone technology, law enforcement agencies were relegated to carrying out aerial operations via airplanes or helicopters. For most local police departments, the use of these vehicles was cost prohibitive. Helicopters and airplanes are not widely available to local police agencies, and they are costly to operate and maintain.[12] The cost of a drone, however, is significantly less. For example, the New York City Police Department (NYPD) was able to purchase its fleet

11 Jean-Paul Yaacoub and others, 'Security Analysis of Drones Systems: Attacks, Limitations, and Recommendations' 11 Internet of Things 79 (2020) <https://doi.org/10.1016/j.iot.2020.100218>.

12 See generally U.S. Dep't of Justice: Bureau of Justice Statistics, 'Aviation Units in Large Law Enforcement Agencies 2007' (2009).

of 14 drones at a cost of about US$480,000,[13] a fraction of the base price of a typical helicopter outfitted for police use.[14] For other police agencies, the costs of a drone programme are even less.[15] Moreover, drones can travel in some cases over 100 miles per hour, potentially allowing first responders to arrive at a scene sooner. Put simply, this technology enables departments to conduct aerial operations more readily than before, due to the lower impact upon funding and resources.

Law enforcement has been using drones for a variety of purposes, such as survey damage or search for survivors following natural disasters, observe and reconstruct crime scenes and vehicle collisions, search for missing persons, assist at hostage or barricaded situations, view hazmat incidents, as well as monitor vehicular and/or pedestrian traffic at large events.[16] A recent survey of 860 law enforcement agencies on their use of drone technology found the most common purposes were search and rescue (90.82%), crime scene photography and reconstruction (84.69%), disaster response (83.67%), and traffic collision reconstruction (80.61%).[17] In fact, the largest percentages of drone use by local law enforcement are for non-surveillance purposes. When it comes to search and rescue or disaster response, drones can be utilised where it may be too dangerous to send in officers or volunteers. The Hampton (Virginia) Police Department, a low-lying jurisdiction with a serious hurricane risk, noted that its drone programme assists its disaster preparedness efforts because drones can fly into flood zones that cannot be reached by cars or trucks.[18] In New York City, during the annual Times Square New Year's Eve celebration, drones serve as a non-invasive complement to other security measures employed by the NYPD, such as bomb-sniffing dogs, radiation detection teams, heavy weapons squads, and plain-clothed officers.[19] The technology provides a "birds-eye" view of a large area and can inform personnel deployment regarding pedestrian congestion in large areas.[20]

Given their functions, drones are well placed to photograph crime scenes and reconstruct and document vehicle collisions. In some jurisdictions, drones have been used to take crime scene videos. These videos not only benefit investigations but are also used for review by juries in criminal proceedings so that the scene can be viewed in its entirety—rather than being confined to still photographs.[21] The New York State Police have used drones to reconstruct vehicle collision scenes "in less time than other

13 Ashley Southall and Ali Winston, 'New York Police Say They Will Deploy 14 Drones' (*N.Y. Times*, 4 December 2018) <www.nytimes.com/2018/12/04/nyregion/nypd-drones.html>.

14 Jay Stanley, 'We Already Have Police Helicopters, So What's Big Deal Over Drones?' (*ACLU*, 8 March 2013) <www.aclu.org/blog/smart-justice/mass-incarceration/we-already-have-police-helicopters-so-whats-big-deal-over>.

15 See PERF Report (n 3) 24 (noting that the cost of a basic police department drone programme was approximately $35,000–$55,000 based on the programme costs of the Scottsdale (AZ) Police Department).

16 See, for example, NYPD Patrol Guide (n 4), for the limited purposes where NYPD will deploy a drone.

17 See PERF Report (n 3) 5.

18 ibid 12.

19 Justin Rohrlich, 'Everything We Know About the Drones Watching Over Times Square on New Year's Eve' (*Quartz*, 31 December 2019) <https://qz.com/1777469/what-we-know-about-the-drones-watching-times-square-on-new-years-eve/>.

20 ibid. (citing comments from Asst. Chief Martine Materasso, Commanding Officer of the NYPD's Counterterrorism Division, on the advantages of drone technology during the celebration).

21 See John Tufts and others, 'Jury Sees Images of San Angelo Woman's Body, Drone Footage on First Day of Murder Trial' (*Des Moines Register*, 16 September 2019) <www.desmoinesregister.com/story/news/

methods, reducing the time that roads are closed for investigations."[22] Moreover, in 2019, the NYPD's most common reason for deploying drones was for collision and crime scene documentation.[23] At crime scenes, drones can satisfy the need to survey an area quickly, which is particularly important where environmental disturbances such as wind or an incoming tide could ruin valuable evidence. The technology can hone in on a piece, or pieces, of evidence and record it from multiple angles exactly as found.

More recently, during the COVID-19 pandemic, local law enforcement agencies have deployed drones to disperse crowds in order to enforce social distancing rules, have been equipped with loudspeakers to communicate public health messages and have been used to monitor people's movements to enforce lockdown and quarantine orders.[24] This, however, has not occurred without controversy. In France, the Paris Police's deployment of drones to detect large gatherings in violation of local lockdown measures drew litigation from privacy advocates. The Council of State, the highest administrative court in France, held that such uses by the Paris Police were legitimate for purposes of detecting unlawful outdoor gatherings during the pandemic, but that the cameras equipped with the drone could not activate the zoom function or maintain a memory card so that personal identifying data could not be captured or stored.[25]

Regulatory considerations

A labyrinth of laws and regulations impact law enforcement's ability to deploy drone technology in the United States. While many of these are centralised at the federal level, several states and municipalities have entered the arena to explicitly, or more commonly implicitly, address drone use. The US Supreme Court has affirmatively stated that Congress has "exclusive sovereignty of airspace in the United States." In 1944, the US Supreme Court explicitly distilled federal oversight of the national airspace:

> Congress has recognized the national responsibility for regulating air commerce. Federal control is intensive and exclusive. Planes do not wander about the sky like vagrant clouds. They move only by federal permission, subject to federal inspection, in the hands of federally certified personnel and under an intricate system of federal commands. The moment a ship taxies onto a runway it is caught up in an elaborate and detailed system of controls. It takes off only by instruction from the

---

crime/2019/09/16/ jury-sees-grisly-evidence-san-angelo-murder-trial-camille-garcia-body-dumpster-andres-ramirez/2342830001/>.

22 Governor Andrew M Cuomo, 'N.Y. State, Governor Announces Deployment of First State Police Aerial Drone Systems' (Press Release, 10 January 2018) <www.governor.ny.gov/news/governor-cuomo-announces-deployment-first-state-police-aerial-drone-systems#:~:text=Certain%20Emergency%20Situations-,Governor%20Andrew>.

23 'NYPD Unmanned Aircraft Systems (UAS) Operations Report' <www1.nyc.gov/site/nypd/stats/ reports-analysis/uas-drones.page> [hereinafter "NYPD Quarterly Drone Report"].

24 See PERF Report (n 3) iv.

25 Jérôme Philippe and others, 'French Court Rules on Use of Drones by Paris Police' (*Lexology.com*, 11 June 2020) <www.lexology.com/library/detail.aspx?g=e81fdeeb-b669-456a-a600-b220129e57e7>. (Noting that the Council of State decided that since drones are equipped with a zoom and can fly lower than current police practice, drones can still collect data that can identify an individual. The court followed that monitoring by drones amounts to personal data collection and subject to French and European Union data protection regulations.)

> control tower, it travels on prescribed beams, it may be diverted from its intended landing, and it obeys signals and orders. Its privileges, rights, and protection, so far as transit is concerned, it owes to the Federal Government alone and not to any state government.[26]

Such pronouncements, however, do not preclude states or municipalities from regulating other elements of aviation consistent with their police powers such as land use, zoning, privacy, and trespass.[27] While federal laws govern navigable airspace, state and cities have the power to enact laws that impact the use of local property, such as the designation of take-off and landing spaces,[28] as well as the privacy interests of their constituents. Common state and local ordinances that regulate drones within their local police powers include requirements for police to obtain a warrant prior to using a drone for "surveillance"; laws prohibiting the operation of a drone for "unlawful surveillance" or "voyeurism"; prohibitions on using drones for hunting or fishing or to interfere with those who are hunting or fishing; or statutes that prohibit the attachment of weapons to drones.[29] While exemptions may exist, law enforcement agencies must be aware of federal, state, and local criminal laws that regulate conduct that could implicate drone flights. These can include laws involving eavesdropping, unlawful collection of personal and identifying information, as well as criminal nuisance. Thus, the deployment of drone technology by local law enforcement agencies in the United States requires a diligent understanding of applicable regulations at all levels of government.

At the federal level, drones are regulated by the Federal Aviation Administration (FAA), although this regulatory power is limited. The FAA oversees drone regulations and safety standards for all drones, whether flown by hobbyists, commercial entities, or federal, state, or local government offices.[30] While there are separate regulations for recreational drone operators, law enforcement agencies have a number of regulatory options available in order to fly a drone. Agency personnel can obtain a remote pilot certificate under 14 C.F.R. Section 107, commonly referred to as a Part 107 licence or a remote pilot certificate.[31] To receive a remote pilot certificate, each drone pilot for the agency must pass the FAA's Aeronautical Knowledge Test.[32] A Part 107 licence allows operations of drones under 55 pounds at or below 400 feet above ground

26 *Northwest Airlines v. State of Minnesota*, 322 U.S. 292, 303 (1944) (Jackson, R., concurring).

27 *Singer v. City of Newton*, 284 F. Supp.3d 125, 129 (D. Mass. 2017) (citing 49 U.S.C.A. § 40103(a)(1); *Braniff Airways v. Neb. State Bd. Of Equalization & Assessment*, 347 U.S. 590, 595 (1954)).

28 See, for example, Timothy M. Ravitch, 'Airports, Droneports, and the New Urban Airspace' (2017) 44 Fordham Urban Law Journal 587, 602; NYC Admin. Code § 10-126(c) (stating "[i]t shall be unlawful for any person navigating an aircraft to take off or land within the limits of the city other than places of landing designated by the department of transportation or the port of New York authority.").

29 Federal Aviation Administration, 'State and Local Regulation of Unmanned Aircraft Systems (UAS) Fact Sheet' (2015), 3 <www.faa.gov/uas/resources/policy_library/media /UAS_Fact_ Sheet_Final.pdf>.

30 See Federal Aviation Administration, 'Unmanned Aircraft Systems (UAS) Frequently Asked Questions' <www.faa.gov/uas/resources/faqs/>.

31 See 14 C.F.R. § 107 (2017); Federal Aviation Admin, 'Fact Sheet—Small Unmanned Aircraft Regulations (Part 107)' (Press Release, 23 July 2018) <www.faa.gov/news/fact_sheets/news_story.cfm?newsId=22615>.

32 ibid.

level—for visual line of sight operations only—and contains some flight restrictions such as forbidding night-time flights absent a separate waiver.[33]

The FAA also issues certificates of authorisation (COA) that allow agencies to "self-certify UAS and operators for flights performing government functions."[34] Agencies can set standards for determining whether someone is qualified to be a pilot, rather than taking the FAA Aeronautical Knowledge Test. A "blanket" COA is available under federal law which permits operators to fly in or outside their jurisdiction, except in restricted airspace, at an altitude of 400 feet or less during daylight hours for line-of-sight operations.[35] Many law enforcement agencies also opt for a jurisdictional COA which allows the agency to operate within their jurisdiction at higher altitudes and at night, in addition to the blanket COA.[36]

The decision of what certification to seek is dependent on the individual agencies. Part 107 licences are often attractive as they are perceived to be less burdensome than obtaining a certificate of authorisation and allows the agencies to expediently begin testing drones and establishing a programme.[37] Nonetheless, it is beneficial for agencies to consider a COA as it allows for flexibility of operations, especially for jurisdictions near or within highly controlled airspace.[38]

Privacy considerations

As noted, far down on a recent law enforcement survey for the most common purposes for deploying a drone are "surveillance" or "general surveillance of high crime areas."[39] Only 26 per cent of the respondents in the survey acknowledged the deployment of this technology for such a purpose.[40] The tension between security and privacy interests is certainly not new, but it has been accentuated by the explosion of new technology embraced by law enforcement. Nearly all of the criticism surrounding law enforcement's ability to use drone technology centres around public suspicion and fear over the enabling or expansion of "surveillance" or "mass surveillance", or "warrant-less surveillance." The US public strongly recognises that the use of drones by law enforcement for mitigating various types of security challenges is beneficial, but a pervasive concern with this technology is privacy—that the technology could pose an infringement to individual privacy through unauthorised aerial footage of homes and property and the tracing of one's movements.[41]

33 ibid.
34 See generally, 49 U.S.C. §§ 40102(a), 40125.
35 ibid.
36 ibid.
37 See PERF Report (n 3) 6–7.
38 ibid 6–8 (citing Tim Herlocker, former Director of the FDNY Emergency Operations Center, who stated that "[t]here are advantages of using a COA for a place like New York City, where about 65 percent of the airspace is highly restricted. . . . The COA gives us the ability in advance to work out the rules in which we will fly in that airspace. It also gives me the ability to decide the skillset that my pilots need, as opposed to being a [part] 107[—licensed] pilot and just needing to pass the FAA exam. I can set my own standards as to how we train them.").
39 ibid 5.
40 ibid.
41 Ariel Rosenfield, 'Are Drivers Ready for Traffic Enforcement Drones?' (2019) 122 Accident Analysis and Prevention 199, 200.

Concerns also exist over mission creep as well—that the police will enlarge the use of this technology beyond what it first intended.[42] Where drones are initially presented for relatively innocuous purposes like disaster response, or search and rescue, legislators, advocates, and members of the public often imagine more controversial ways that law enforcement can use this technology, ranging from general crime control, to writing traffic tickets,[43] or policing First Amendment activities. Despite all of their benefits, some argue that the main utility of drones for law enforcement purposes is derived from serving as a platform for surveillance technology.[44]

The results of these concerns have had a mixed impact on law enforcement's use in the United States, ranging from sensible safeguards to extreme prohibitions. For example, the debate over privacy concerns prompted the NYPD to publicly disclose the agency's drone policy, in advance[45] impose reporting requirements on their usage,[46] and conduct in a methodical process of explaining their plans publicly and engage with local legislators, advocates, and community members to address their legitimate trepidation. Conversely, such concerns over privacy have led to extreme results such as outright bans on law enforcement use[47] (resulting in categorically negating all of the non-investigative, and mostly unobjectionable, benefits this technology presents), to creating a heightened Fourth Amendment warrant requirement (even where footage is to be captured in public areas where no expectations of privacy exists)[48] simply because of the use of "this technology" as opposed to other legal technologies and investigative tactics.[49] Aerial observations by the police in a public space, and even the curtilage of a home, are generally not prohibited by the Fourth Amendment so long as the police are conducting the observations from public, navigable airspace, in a non-physically intrusive manner, and such conduct does not reveal intimate activities, traditionally associated with spaces where a reasonable expectation of privacy

42 Southall and Wilson (n 13).

43 See generally, Rosenfield (n 41)199.

44 Jennifer M Bentley, 'Policing the Police: Balancing the Right to Privacy Against the Beneficial Use of Drone Technology' (2018) 70 Hastings Law Journal 249, 257.

45 See NYPD Patrol Guide (n 4).

46 See 'NYPD Unmanned Aircraft Systems (UAS) Operations Report' (2020) <www1.nyc.gov/site/nypd/stats/reports-analysis/uas-drones.page>. This is a quarterly report published by the NYPD which captures each drone use disaggregated by reason for usage and geographic borough in machine-readable format.

47 Laura L Myers, 'Seattle Mayor Grounds Police Drone Program' (*Seattle Times*, 7 February 2013) <www.seattletimes.com/seattle-news/seattle-grounds-police-drone-program/>.

48 See generally, *Calif. v. Ciraolo*, 476 U.S. 207 (1986) (holding that the "[t]he Fourth Amendment was not violated by the naked-eye aerial observation of respondent's backyard."); *Dow Chemical Co. v. United States*, 476 U.S. 227 (1986) (deciding that the taking of aerial photographs of an industrial plant complex from navigable airspace is not a search prohibited by the Fourth Amendment).

49 See, for example, Gregory McNeal, 'Drones and Aerial Surveillance: Considerations for Legislatures' (*Brookings Institute*, 2 November 2014) <www.brookings.edu/wp content/uploads/2016/ 07/Drones_Aerial_Surveillance_McNeal _FINAL.pdf>. (noting that such "legislation is rarely tailored in such a way to prevent the harm that advocates fear. In fact, in every state where legislation was passed, the new laws are focused on the technology (drones) not the harm (pervasive surveillance). In many cases, this technology-centric approach creates perverse results, allowing the use of extremely sophisticated pervasive surveillance technologies from manned aircraft, while disallowing benign uses of drones for mundane tasks like accident and crime scene documentation, or monitoring of industrial pollution and other environmental harms.").

exists (such as a home).[50] Nevertheless, nearly 20 states have enacted laws requiring law enforcement to obtain warrants prior to using drones to conduct "surveillance."[51] Over 30 states have attempted to enact laws requiring law enforcement to obtain a warrant in all cases absent exigent circumstances.[52] While warrants are appealing to privacy advocates, as well as required for the police to search or inspect areas where there is a reasonable expectation of privacy, broad restrictions on drone use can conceivably hamper public safety while also denying law enforcement a tool to deploy its personnel more efficiently and streamline its operations. Such proposals either assume that deployment of a law enforcement drone will always take place in areas where there is a reasonable expectation of privacy, or they create new expectations of privacy in areas where historically there have not—such as in a public park. This new, heightened expectation of privacy only attaches when drone technology is used. The park can literally be surrounded by legally installed police pole cameras and closed-circuit cameras with no court order required, but if law enforcement seeks to use a drone, then a warrant must be procured even though the public's privacy interest does not change. More disconcerting for law enforcement, it is unclear from these proposals how law enforcement would be able to obtain a court-issued warrant in advance of deploying drones and what the legal standard would be for issuance. Drones are often deployed by law enforcement prospectively, such as for monitoring pedestrian traffic at a major event, or retrospectively, such as photographing a vehicle collision that has already occurred. Probable cause of criminality, the typical standard for the issuance of a warrant in the United States is usually not present for prospective or retrospective uses. The hurdles just to deploy a drone under such proposals are in many ways tantamount to a prohibition on their use.

In deploying drones for law enforcement purposes, earning the confidence and trust of the public may be a greater challenge than the technological, financial, and regulatory ones. Regardless of the jurisdiction, law enforcement agencies that either utilise, or seek to utilise, the benefits of drone technology must acknowledge and recognise this public debate and be ready to be an active contributor.

Community outreach models used by law enforcement

Now, more than ever, the ability for police departments and other law enforcement agencies to build strong relationships of trust with the communities they serve is a critical component to policing. This notion permeates throughout most major city police departments, particularly when instituting new initiatives impacting the public—transparency and cooperation between the police and the community are a common theme and objective. Recognising concerns over privacy and surveillance, law enforcement agencies have developed comprehensive community outreach strategies during the implementation stages of their drone programmes. These strategies include, but are not limited to, a clear explanation of the agency's planned approach and reasons for the uses of drones; assurances, explanations, and discussions with stakeholders about privacy, accountability, and other issues of concerns with an eye towards memorialisation in policy and a process to address questions and concerns.

50 ibid 5.
51 See Bentley (n 44) 268.
52 ibid 270.

Some have argued that despite efforts to conduct community outreach, however well-intentioned, the police should not be left to police themselves.[53] Assurances and ostensible offerings of transparency are not satisfactory—and agency programmes should be strictly legislated. Some have advocated that with the absence of granular federal regulations on law enforcement drone use, states, rather than cities, are best suited to legislate and safeguard privacy.[54] Whatever the approach, municipalities and the interests of local police agencies have to be a large part of the equation when regulating law enforcement drone use. While some are concerned that local legislation would simply create an "inconsistent patchwork of regulations,"[55] municipal involvement actually can account for the unique needs of their localities—this is especially true in major American cities like New York City. States such as New York have cities, towns, and villages with diverse populations, topographies, infrastructures, resources, and interests within its own border. Standards and expectations for drone flights by law enforcement are indubitably different in New York City versus a town like Malone, NY.[56] From a legislative standpoint, the patchwork of local regulation, whether through law, resolution, or agency policy, may be necessary to account for each municipality's unique needs and interests.

Engagement through public forums and community stakeholders

Rulemaking authority also exists within state and local executive agencies in the United States.[57] Agency rules are often promulgated as a result of legislative delegation or because a new agency policy materially impacts a benefit or service that is offered to the public.[58] For example, state or local legislation may authorise the creation of street vendor licences to sell foods and goods on public streets, but may delegate the authority to designate the streets where vendor sales can take place to a state or municipal agency. Generally, the rulemaking process involves publication or promotion by the agency of this new rule/initiative, a public comment period on the new rules/initiative, as well as a public hearing at a fixed date and time, and then a review period by the agency to consider input before finalising the rule.[59]

Over the last several years, law enforcement agencies have sought to mirror this process when it comes to the pre-launch of new initiatives or the use of new technologies such as drones. Agencies have placed a premium on public input before starting a new programme.[60] With drones, several police departments engaged in public

53 ibid 263.

54 Jay Stanley and Catherine Crump, 'Protecting Privacy from Aerial Surveillance: Recommendations for Government Use of Drone Aircraft' (ACLU, 2011) <www.aclu.org/files/assets/protectingprivacyfromaerialsurveillance.pdf>.

55 Bentley (n 44) 290.

56 For reference, the Town of Malone, NY has a population of 14,139. The population of the City of New York is 8.4 million people. Both numbers are based on recent figures provided by the United States Census Bureau, 'Data Commons' (2018) <https://datacommons.org/place/geoId/3651000>.

57 See, for example, 'Official Compilation of the Rules of the City of New York' <https://rules.cityofnewyork.us/codified-rules>.

58 See, for example, N.Y.C. Charter §§ 1041-47, which outlines New York City's executive rulemaking procedure.

59 ibid.

60 See PERF Report (n 3) 11–12.

forums before the launch of their programmes.[61] These forums generally involved a presentation by the agency that outlined its intentions, the technology's benefits and capabilities, as well as efforts to address security, privacy, and appropriate safeguards. Some agencies went further by conducting smaller focus groups to provide more precise commentary.[62] While engagement by the public varies in each jurisdiction, most departments have reported that the process is productive not only from the perspective of obtaining valuable insight but also as a gesture of goodwill to signify that the agency recognises the concerns associated with the use of this technology.[63]

Other agencies have opted to target involvement by specific community stakeholders and advocates. These involve a series of meetings between agency officials and elected officials, members of the local legal community, privacy advocates, and other community groups and associations. Generally, the process involves sharing the proposed drone policy in advance with these stakeholders and providing an opportunity either during the in-person meeting(s), or post-meeting, to provide comments before finalisation. While in many cases these stakeholders will be reticent to "bless" the agency's policy or programme in full, due to political affiliations or policy positions, the process is valuable in gaining input and addressing concerns at the outset, before final decisions on the policy are made. From a community policing standpoint, the process is important because, as one police chief noted, "[y]ou are showing respect to their viewpoint. If you never reach out, you never open that communication."[64]

After completing these processes, several agencies have engaged in further transparency measures surrounding their programmes. These have included posting drafts and final versions of the drone policies on the agency website to reflect changes that occurred as a result of the public input process, releasing video on drone deployments, and/or publicly posting periodic data regarding frequency of flight use and the purposes.[65]

NYPD's drone programme—a short case study on stakeholder engagement

The NYPD's drone programme was launched in December 2018. The Department had been considering the use of drone technology since at least 2014 but opted gradually to develop its plans to gather best practices and policies from jurisdictions that had already begun using the technology.[66] By the time the Department had launched its programme, approximately 900 state and local police, fire, and emergency units were deploying drone technology. At the time of this writing, the Department's drone programme is operated by its Technical Assistance Response Unit (TARU). While not solely dedicated to performing drone operations, the unit was selected because it

61 See, for example, Kate Mather, 'LAPD Becomes Nation's Largest Police Department to Test Drones After Oversight Panel Signs Off on Controversial Program' (*LA Times*, 17 October 2017) <www.latimes.com/local/lanow/la-me-ln-lapd-drones-20171017-story.html>; Jason Tidd, 'Wichita Police are Buying a Drone and They Want Public Input on its Use' (*Wichita Eagle*, 2 July 2018) <www.kansas.com/news/local/article214032819.html>.

62 For discussion, see PERF Report (n 3) 22–23.

63 ibid 11–12.

64 ibid 15.

65 ibid 18.

66 See Southall and Winston (n 13).

was already providing specialised investigative equipment and tactical support to all bureaus within the NYPD. The unit had already developed expertise in audio/visual technology and used their skills to help recover surveillance video footage during investigations, record police action at large-scale demonstrations and arrest situations and provide live-video feeds to NYPD commanders during emergency situations.[67] Several members of TARU obtained their Part 107 licences from the FAA, and the Department was issued a COA from the FAA as well.

The gathering and research stage was critical as it helped the Department narrow how such technology would be used to support NYPD operations. Additionally, in drafting its proposed drone policy, the Department consulted a model policy put forth by the American Civil Liberties Union.[68] Throughout the process, the Department was cognisant of the privacy concerns that would inevitably be raised upon announcement of its interest in using drone technology.[69]

In essence, the Department's drone policy, which was ultimately incorporated into the Department's larger Patrol Guide, delineated specific, limited circumstances in which an NYPD drone would be utilised in the field: search and rescue operations, documentation of collisions and crimes scenes, evidence searches at large or inaccessible scenes, hazardous material incidents, monitoring of vehicular traffic and pedestrian congestion at large-scale events (as noted earlier, this could include events such as the Macy's Day Thanksgiving Parade or NYC Marathon); visual assistance at hostage/barricaded suspect situations, as well as rooftop security observations at shooting incidents.[70] The policy also explicitly states what drones cannot be used for: routine foot patrol by officers, traffic enforcement, immobilising a vehicle or suspect, and the technology cannot be equipped with a weapon or facial recognition software.[71] Notably, the Department's policy largely adhered to the ACLU's and other privacy advocate recommendations (see Table 4.1).

The Department also engaged in targeted engagement with community stakeholders and held multiple meetings with members of the state legislature, the city council, as well as advocacy organisations. Of particular concern at these sessions was the Department's potential use of drones to police protests and First Amendment activity in New York City. On any given day in New York City, there are multiple protests or demonstrations taking place. The filming of protests and First Amendment activity by NYPD officers is governed by the *Handschu* consent decree which stemmed from litigation surrounding NYPD investigations involving political activity in the 1970s.[72] Generally, the guidelines only permit filming by NYPD personnel when it reasonably appears that unlawful conduct is about to occur, is occurring, or has occurred during

67 'NYPD Unveils New Unmanned Aircraft System Program' (Press Release, 4 December 2018) <www1.nyc.gov/site/nypd/news/p1204a/nypd-new-unmanned-aircraft-system-program#/0>.

68 'Domestic Drones' (ACLU, 2020) <www.aclu.org/issues/privacy-technology/surveillance-technologies/domestic-drones>.

69 See Southall and Winston (n 13).

70 NYPD Patrol Guide (n 4).

71 ibid.

72 *See Handschu v. Special Services Division*, 605 F. Supp. 1384 (S.D.N.Y. 1985); See also, 'Guidelines for the Use of Video/Photographic Equipment By Operational Personnel At Demonstrations' NYPD Patrol Guide Section 212–71 (Effective, 19 July 2016) <www1.nyc.gov/site/nypd/ about/about-nypd/patrol-guide.page>.

Table 4.1

Advocate Recommendations	*NYPD Policy*
Drones should be deployed by law enforcement only:	
• with a warrant in areas with an expectation of privacy, or	The policy allows for use in these circumstances without a warrant if there are exigent circumstances. This is consistent with the 4th Amendment and criminal procedure case law. Also, it further specifies no use for routine patrol, traffic enforcement, or immobilising vehicles or suspects.
• where there are specific and articulable grounds to believe they will collect evidence of a specific instance of criminal wrongdoing in areas with no expectation of privacy, or	The policy goes further to include monitoring traffic and pedestrian congestion at large-scale events and for rooftop security observation during shootings and large-scale events.
• for a geographically confined and time-limited emergency situation where lives are at risk, or	The policy further specifies the kinds of emergencies.
Images retained only where there is a reasonable suspicion that they contain evidence of a crime or are relevant to an ongoing investigation or trial	The Patrol Guide limits retention to 30 days but may be extended if they contain evidence of a crime or at the request of its legal bureau.
Publicly available written policies and procedures for drone use, except details of particular investigations	The entire policy and quarterly data on use are posted on the NYPD's website.
No weaponisation or facial recognition technology used	**The policy explicitly states that drones are never to be used as a weapon and facial recognition technology is not used.**

the demonstration.[73] Thus, drones cannot be used by the NYPD to aimlessly capture footage of a protest or demonstration absent some indication that criminal activity is about to, or has, taken place. While drones are deployed at large-scale events such as the Macy's Thanksgiving Day Parade to monitor pedestrian traffic, it is usually done from a fixed location, where the drone elevates to a height where it can obtain an expansive, bird's-eye view of the event and cannot focus on specific individuals.

Additionally, stakeholders were critical of what is perceived to be a catch-all use for drone deployment by the NYPD. The policy permits deployment to public safety, emergency, or other situations, not otherwise enumerated in the policy, with the approval of the Chief of Department. The Chief of Department is the highest uniform member of the NYPD.[74] In developing a policy related to law enforcement operations,

73 ibid.

74 As per NYC Charter §§ 431, 434, the Police Commissioner of the New York City Police Department is a civilian title.

it is incredibly challenging to confine the use of technology or tactic to a singular, limited list. The roles that police departments play are dynamic. Their mission to protect public safety pulls in multiple directions and it is difficult to account for all of these dynamics. While the concerns raised by stakeholders were legitimate, elasticity has to exist that balances these concerns about broad exceptions and overuse with other public safety considerations that can evolve—and the responsibility of when to deploy a drone given unique circumstances that may not be foreseen or prescribed in policy has to be charged to a major decision-maker within that department. To date, the NYPD has not deployed a drone for this use.[75]

While not able to appease every concern, direct engagement with the Department was well received by the stakeholders.[76] In order to address concerns surrounding privacy and mission creep, the Department publicly posted its finalised drone policy on its website[77] and has provided a quarterly report to the public of aggregate data surrounding the Department's drone use, broken down by reason for usage and geographic borough.[78]

Conclusion

Implementing and devising a significant advancement in law enforcement technology such as drones is not a programme around simple and uncomplicated process. Though the technology offers obvious and valuable benefits to law enforcement, it also requires a great deal of preparation, training, understanding of various laws and regulations, as well as outreach and community involvement in developing a programme. Given their nearly limitless abilities, drones can be the technological partner to the common police officer—but this will not happen unless the public trusts that this technology is also working for their benefit. Community concerns, privacy, and other civil rights issues must be factored into any agency's programme from the beginning. The public must believe that drone usage will not only enhance the work of those who are sworn to protect them but also that the technology will not be a potent tool to invade their privacy. The police profession must be able to convey to the community the benefits of drones while making clear that privacy and civil liberties can be protected.

Issues with detection and mitigation

The rapid availability and affordability of small drones and their legal operation by hobbyists and commercial operators has opened low-altitude airspace above every community, in every country, to countless new users and uses. The operation of drones by the public raises new and valid concerns surrounding public safety. The FAA projects the integration of over seven million drones into the airspace in the near future. The question of who and how drones can fly safely in a national airspace originally designed for airplanes and helicopters is both formidable and essential.

75 NYPD Quarterly Drone Report (n 23).

76 See Southall and Winston (n 13) (noting that Donovan Richards, the Chairman of the New York City Council's Committee on Public Safety, said "the police were right to seek outside input before launching the drones.").

77 NYPD Patrol Guide (n 4).

78 NYPD Quarterly Drone Report (n 23).

The advent and availability of this technology not only benefits the objectives of law enforcement, but they also provide new capabilities for criminals and terrorists. Drones can be used by criminals to facilitate crimes such as robberies or thefts. They have been used to drop contraband into restricted areas such as correctional facilities.[79] More harrowing, terrorists can use this technology to drop a bomb, shoot firearms, or spray chemical agents over large crowds.[80] They are remarkably adept for criminal reconnaissance because they can bypass security structures such as bollards, checkpoints, and other mechanisms. With a few simple modifications, a standard, "off-the-shelf" consumer drone or hobby kit aircraft can be converted into a rudimentary but veritable lethal missile or other attack systems.[81] As the Director of the FBI noted before a Congressional hearing in 2019,

> [W]e do know that terrorist organizations have an interest in using drones. We've seen that overseas already . . . the expectation is that it's coming here. They are relatively easy to acquire, relatively easy to operate, and quite difficult to disrupt and to monitor.[82]

Myriad technologies have been developed and continue to be tested for the purpose of detecting, disrupting, or disabling threatening drones. The technology ranges from identification technology that detects the presence of a drone based on radio frequency or non-radio frequency methods and even the location of the operator, to devices that can intercept and jam a drone's transmission, essentially blocking communication signals between a drone and its pilot, to taking control of drones in flight by hacking its on-board computer system.[83]

Many of these technologies, however, are not available for purchase to American local law enforcement agencies. Currently, law, policy, and regulations limit local law enforcement's use of these various technologies to counter drones that may be used to harm and threaten the public. Federal restrictions prohibit local law enforcement from operating mitigation technology, and some detection technology, which was previously available for purchase, has since had its legal status questioned by recent case law and federal guidance.[84]

The legal gap is significant. While the ability to deploy technology that can detect and mitigate malicious drone use is generally confined to federal agencies, local law

79 See, for example, Lauren M Johnson, 'A Drone Was Caught on Camera Delivering Contraband to an Ohio Prison Yard' (*CNN Online*, 26 September 2019) <www.cnn.com/2019/09/26/us/contraband-delivered-by-drone-trnd/ index. html>.

80 Zak Doffman, 'Warning Over Terrorists Attacks Using Drones Given by EU Security Chief' (*Forbes*, 4 August 2019) <www.forbes.com/sites/zakdoffman/2019/08/04/europes-security-chief-issues-dire-warning-on-terrorist-threat-from-drones/#37e9f55c7ae4> (noting the European Union's Security Commissioner's that the real fear from a drone attack is that a chemical or biological payload could be delivered into the midst of a crowded space with relative ease).

81 Arthur Holland Michel, 'Counter-Drone Systems' (2nd edn, *Center for the Study of the Drone*, 2019) <https://dronecenter.bard.edu/files/2019/12/CSD-CUAS-2nd-Edition-Web.pdf>.

82 Doffman (n 80).

83 Michel (n 81).

84 See *Joffe v. Google*, Inc., 764 F.3d 920, 928–29 (9th Cir. 2013), *cert. denied*, 134 S.Ct. 2877 (2014); see also Dep't of Justice: Office of Public Affairs, 'Advisory on the Acquisition and Use of Technology to Detect and Mitigate Unmanned Aircraft Systems' (August 2020) <www.justice.gov/file /1304841 / download> [hereinafter "DOJ Guidance"].

enforcement officers are usually the front-line responders to such incidents. A drone incident that draws the attention of local, state, and even federal and central government agencies will usually be reported first in the form of an emergency call to the authorities—in the United States, this is a 911 call.[85] Those calls are almost exclusively answered by local authorities—and while local agencies generally have the ability to address threatening conditions where exigent circumstances exist, the legal landscape when it comes to detection and mitigation leaves these agencies nearly beholden to federal counterparts to address chronic issues.

Moreover, since local law enforcement generally responds to emergency and quality of life calls regarding drones, and may not have a ready ability to know whether such use is legal, what the intentions of the operators are, an awareness of federal regulations that have been violated, and be able to enforce them, such agencies are naturally resistant to wider drone use in their jurisdictions. When errant drone use does occur in large American cities, the operator is generally in violation of several FAA regulations, in addition to other local criminal or administrative laws. While the FAA has committed to assisting local law enforcement, most patrol police officers are unfamiliar with aviation regulations—and even if they were, they do not have the authority to enforce them. As a result, these agencies are put in a position to stretch criminal and administrative statutes that they are empowered to enforce beyond their intention and purposes to address local security concerns. The current legal environment surrounding drone use in the United States has yet to produce a regulatory system capable of rapid response and enforcement. Similar challenges exist in Canada, where their aviation regulatory system very much mirrors that of the United States.[86] Such an environment is deleterious as it prevents innovation and deprives many urban and even rural economies from embracing the benefits of this technology. This is particularly salient as commercial use continues to expand in the United States and among the international community. Localities are concerned that their airspace will become drone canyons with little local input, with no real-time enforcement capability for those that violate aviation regulations, and no practical and legally sound way to separate good actors from bad actors.

Counter-drone systems

Air defence systems that have traditionally been deployed to protect the airspace have mostly been designed for the purpose of addressing conditions created by manned aircraft.[87] They were intentionally constructed to detect, track, and disable large accelerating objects. These systems are inadequate to detect small, adaptable, low-flying objects like drones. Additionally, drones are not required, at this time, to be equipped with transponders, so there is limited ability to detect and recognise this kind of aircraft with existing air traffic control systems. Alternatively, a reliance on visual observation to track drones is ineffective. The technology can be operated at a considerable distance from the pilot.

85 See PERF Report (n 3) 65 (quoting remarks of John Miller, Deputy Commissioner of Intelligence and Counterterrorism for the NYPD, who notes that in 2014, the NYPD responded to 82 drone incidents, in 2016, it responded to 416, and in 2018, it had responded to 1,649).

86 See BRTF Report (n 8) 5.

87 See generally Michel (n 81) 2.

In the United States, the FAA is in the process of implementing a remote identification rule to address concerns regarding unauthorised or malicious drone use.[88] A remote identification system detects the presence of a drone in the airspace by reading the particular drone's "electronic signature" which is shared with the FAA. The system can provide information, when shared with local law enforcement,[89] about the drone and its current location and ground control station, which will facilitate real-time law enforcement response. If a drone operates in the airspace without this automatic identification system, it can alert law enforcement that the drone is unregistered, which can be considered when determining whether the drone represents a threat to the public. While the technology is promising and will indeed address some of the worries about detecting malicious drone use, concerns do exist when compared to other available detection technology—specifically, the effectiveness and reliability of both broadcast and network systems which will be critical components for low-altitude drone system traffic management. In dense jurisdictions like New York City and other urban centres, these systems could provide a false sense of reliability in environments that are notorious for radio frequency interference and saturation due to dense building construction, urban canyons, and a dense population utilising similar radio frequency bands. Furthermore, the technology is premised upon actors who are willing to comply with the federal regulatory scheme. Remote identification will not detect drones manufactured by companies that have not provided their electronic signatures to allow easy detection. Additionally, criminals, including terrorists, may hand-build drones that do not have a radio frequency signature and will thus escape detection by radio frequency-based systems. It is an encouraging development, but not a panacea.

A variety of technologies have been created to provide security defences against errant drone use. The systems continue to evolve, and a variety of legal and technological barriers exist before broader use by law enforcement agencies will be possible. The systems rely on a variety of methods and techniques for detecting and mitigating drones and are available in ground-based fixed and mobile, as well as handheld platforms. Several research and industry experts in the drone sector have distilled these methods and techniques.[90] Tables 4.2 and 4.3 are derived from the former Center for the Study of the Drone, which was affiliated with Bard College in Upstate New York.

Technological challenges to detection and mitigation technology

With an emerging market and technology, the technical challenges facing drone detection and mitigation have not been fully realised. The challenges range from effectiveness to practicality and safety. For detection technology, whether the system utilises radar, radio-frequency, or cameras, struggles with tracking small drones flying close to the ground or confusion with other flying objects such as a bird or toy aircraft are common.[91] Some systems require a direct line of sight with the offending drone in

88 See PERF Report (n 3) 62–63.

89 It is uncertain whether information from the system will indeed be shared with local law enforcement.

90 Both the former Center for the Study of the Drone at Bard College and the Blue Ribbon Task Force on UAS Mitigation at Airports have done an admirable job in outlining and summarising the capabilities of these systems. See Michel (n 81) 3–4; BRTF Report (n 8) 42–45.

91 ibid 7–11.

Table 4.2 Detection, Tracking, and Identification Methods[1]

Radar	Detects the presence of small unmanned aircraft by their radar signature, which is generated when the aircraft encounters radio frequency pulses emitted by the detection element. These systems often employ algorithms to distinguish between drones and other small, low-flying objects, such as birds.
Radio Frequency (RF)	Detects, locates, and in some cases identifies nearby drones by scanning for the frequencies at which most drones are known to operate. Some systems are also able to detect the operator's location.
Electro-Optical	Identifies and tracks drones based on their visual signature.
Infrared	Identifies and tracks drones based on their heat signature.
Acoustic	Detects drones by recognising the unique sounds produced by their motors. Acoustic systems rely on a library of sounds produced by known drones, which are then matched to sounds detected in the operating environment.
Combined Sensors	Many systems integrate a variety of different sensor types in order to provide a more robust detection, tracking, and identification capability.

[1]See generally Michel (n 81) 3–4.

order to make such detection.[92] In urban areas, this can be particularly problematic because a drone may appear in the system's line of sight for only a fleeting moment. The technology can also be myopic, as some systems can detect drones by specific manufacturers only.[93]

With mitigation technology, hazards over deployment as well as questions of effectiveness are abound. Technology that can interrupt a drone flight through kinetic or radio frequency jamming may result in the aircraft falling from the sky, presenting an obvious risk to the public and infrastructure below. Such technologies also have to ensure that they will not interrupt or interfere with the flight of nearby manned aircraft. In the United States, this has been the primary motive for confinement of the ability to mitigate a drone to four federal agencies.[94] The concern is that broader use of this technology in turn increases the risk of irresponsible deployment.

The effectiveness of current mitigation systems is also of concern. Radio frequency jamming systems are unable to interdict drones that do not have an active radio frequency link—a development that is becoming much more common at the time of this writing.[95] The jamming range is extremely limited and they can struggle against drones that are moving quickly or in unpredictable patterns. The cost of these systems also appears to be prohibitive. While manufacturers are reticent to advertise their pricing for various detection and mitigation systems, they appear to be beyond the reach of smaller law enforcement agencies. Following an incident where errant drone flights resulted in the closing of London's Gatwick Airport in 2018 for 27 hours, it

92 ibid.
93 ibid.
94 See generally, PERF Report (n 3) 67.
95 Jen Colton, 'The Problems and Limitations of RF Jammers for Stopping Rogue Drones' (*Fortem Technologies*, 26 March 2019) <https://fortemtech.com/blog/rf-jamming-limitations-rogue-drones/>.

Table 4.3 Mitigation Methods[1]

RF Jamming	Disrupts the radio frequency link between the drone and its operator by generating large volumes of RF interference. Once the RF link, which can include Wi-Fi links, is severed, a drone will usually either descend to the ground or initiate a "return to home" manoeuvre.
GNSS Jamming	Disrupts the drone's satellite link, such as GPS or GLONASS, which is used for navigation. Drones that lose their satellite link will usually hover in place, land, or return to home.
Spoofing	Allows one to take control of or misdirect the targeted drone by feeding it a spurious communications or navigation link. (For our purposes, we include within this category a range of measures such as cyberattacks, protocol manipulation, and RF/GNSS Deception.)
Dazzling	Employs a high-intensity light beam or laser to "blind" the camera on a drone.
Laser	Destroys vital segments of the drone's airframe using directed energy, causing it to crash to the ground.
High-Power Microwave	Directs pulses of high-intensity microwave energy at the drone, disabling the aircraft's electronic systems.
Nets	Designed to entangle the targeted drone and/or its rotors.
Projectile	Employs regular or custom-designed ammunition to destroy incoming unmanned aircraft.
Collision Drones	A drone designed to collide with the adversary drone.
Combined Interdiction Elements	A number of C-UAS systems also employ a combination of interdiction elements to increase the likelihood of a successful interdiction. For example, many jamming systems have both RF jamming and GNSS jamming capabilities in the same package. Other systems might employ an electronic system as a first line of defence and a kinetic system as a backup measure.

[1]See generally Michel (n 81) 3–4.

was reported that the airport spent over US$6 million to install counter-drone technology to prevent similar occurrences.[96]

Legal barriers to local law enforcement's use of counter-drone technology

In the United States, Congress has exclusively authorised the federal Departments of Defense, Energy, Justice, and Homeland Security to engage in limited mitigation activities to counter drones presenting a credible threat to public safety.[97] While this exclusive authority was legislated in 2018,[98] it does not contemplate any role for local law enforcement to utilise this technology. These federal agencies do not have the authority to approve non-federal public and private use of drone detection or mitigation capabilities, nor do they conduct legal reviews of commercially available

96 Josh Spero, 'Gatwick Spends £5m on Airport Anti-Drone Measures' (*Financial Times*, 3 January 2019) <www.ft.com/content/cdaa19e6-0f97-11e9-a3aa-118c761d2745>.

97 See 10 U.S.C. § 130i, 50 U.S.C. § 2661, and 6 U.S.C. § 124n.

98 Preventing Emerging Threats Act of 2018, Pub. L. No. 115–254, §§ 1601–1603, 132 Stat. 3522–3530 (2018).

products' compliance with those laws.[99] Aside from mitigation technology, the federal government has grown increasingly concerned about local law enforcement's use of drone detection technology—which unlike, mitigation technology—is not expressly prohibited by statute. The federal government has increasingly cautioned that local law enforcement's use of detection technology may not comply with applicable laws related to eavesdropping, wiretapping, and the interception of electronic communications, and local agencies could be risking both civil and criminal liability.[100] These laws were drafted well before the development of drones and counter-drone systems to address other technologies.

Jamming, spoofing, and hacking technologies all implicate various federal laws that seek to protect communication and computer systems. Title 18 of the United States Code contains multiple sections prohibiting acts that implicate drone mitigation strategies.[101] These sections include prohibitions against damaging or destroying an aircraft, wilful or malicious interference with US government communications, and intentional or malicious interference with satellite communications.[102] Under the US Computer Fraud and Abuse Act, criminal penalties exist for gaining access to computers without authorisation or exceeding authorised access.[103] These acts are crimes even if the unauthorised access is for the purpose of countering or preventing the unauthorised activities of others. Title 49 of the US Code prohibits "seizing or exercising control of an aircraft . . . by force, violence, threat of force or violence, or any form of intimidation, and with wrongful intent."[104] All of these statutes can implicate mitigation and detection technology if they were to be used by local law enforcement.

Systems that detect, monitor, or track drones often rely on radio-frequency, radar, electro-optical, infrared, or acoustic capabilities, or a combination thereof. These capabilities detect the physical presence of a drone or signals sent to or from the drone. In general, whether a detection or tracking system implicates federal criminal surveillance laws, such as the federal Pen/Trap Statute and the Wiretap Act, depends on whether it captures, records, decodes, or intercepts, in whole or in part, electronic communications transmitted to and from a drone and/or controller and the type of communications involved.[105] The federal Wiretap Act prohibits the intentional interception of communications or disclosing or using the contents of such communications.[106] Recent exemptions from this prohibition pertain to certain federal agencies only under specific circumstances. The federal Pen/Trap Statute generally prohibits the installation or use, without a court order, of a device that "records or decodes" signalling and other information transmitted by electronic communications, or any device capable of identifying information that identifies the source of an electronic communication.[107] These laws carry significant criminal and civil penalties. Thus, the liability for purchasing and operating this technology, absent specific authorisation in federal law, is significant. The availability of this technology to local law enforce-

99 See DOJ Guidance (n 84) 1.
100 ibid.
101 See 18 U.S.C. § 1362; 18 U.S.C. § 1367(a); 18 U.S.C. § 32; 18 U.S.C. § 2511.
102 ibid.
103 18 U.S.C. § 1030.
104 49 U.S.C. § 46502(a)(1)(A).
105 See 18 U.S.C. §§ 3121-3127.
106 See 18 U.S.C. §§ 2510 *et seq.* (also known as Title III).
107 18 U.S.C. §§ 3121-3127.

ment has not gone unnoticed. In 2020, as drone detection and mitigation technology has become more sophisticated, the US Department of Justice has increasingly issued stricter guidance to local law enforcement advising that such equipment could violate a host of federal laws such as the Federal Pen Register and Trap and Trace Device Statute ("Pen/Trap Statute") and the Wiretap Act.[108]

Concerns over civil and criminal liability are shared internationally. In the United Kingdom, countering a drone in any way may violate portions of the Aviation Security Act and the Criminal Damage Act.[109] The mitigation and jamming of a drone can implicate the Wireless Telegraphy Act and the Electromagnetic Compatibility Regulations.[110] In Europe, some counter-drone technology that collects personally identifiable information may involve the General Data Protection Regulation.[111]

Local law enforcement's confounding role

As noted earlier, aviation regulation is generally a federal or national concern. In the United States, as more and more drones take to the skies, the FAA has been explicit that it has exclusive authority conferred by Congress to regulate the navigable airspace. Congress has also authorised just four federal agencies to deploy mitigation technology to protect the public and critical infrastructure, and it has been issuing guidance to local law enforcement on their limited ability to use detection technology. The federal government has also been equally explicit that it does not have the resources or manpower to deploy this technology on a daily basis throughout the country. It has acknowledged that local law enforcement is the first-line of response to a malicious drone attack—even though they would be facing civil and criminal penalties if they were to use mitigation technology and some forms of detection technology. Consequently, local law enforcement lacks both the authority and the ability to mitigate malicious and errant drone use in real time. The state of play paints a picture where local law enforcement is expected to respond to unauthorised drone use but does not have the legal tools to do so. When it comes to responding to dangerous drone operations, local American police agencies play a puzzling role in the drone regulatory structure.

Despite the FAA's explicit primacy of the navigable airspace, it has taken the stance that state and local law enforcement agencies are in the best position to deter and investigate unauthorised or unsafe drone operations.[112] In fact, federal authorities will not deploy resources to a local drone incident until local law enforcement resources are exhausted.[113] The FAA is a civil regulatory agency. Its general enforcement capabilities are limited to warning and demand letters, letters of correction, and civil penalties.[114] Nonetheless, since FAA aviation inspectors are often "unable to immediately

108 See generally DOJ Guidance (n 84).

109 See Michel (n 81) 12 (the author further notes, however, that "a number of British laws might likewise provide legal cover for [counter-drone] actions, depending on the context, including the Criminal Law Act, the Police and Criminal Evidence Act, the Criminal Justice and Immigration Act, and the Investigatory Powers Act.").

110 ibid.

111 ibid.

112 See FAA Guidance to Local Law Enforcement (n 10) 6.

113 See BRTF Report (n 8) 12.

114 See FAA Guidance to Local Law Enforcement (n 10) 6.

travel to a location of an incident,"[115] the agency has provided guidance to local law enforcement to assist with its mission in regulating drone use. This can include law enforcement identifying witnesses at a specific incident, identifying operators, video or photo recording of the incident and aircraft, as well as evidence collection, etc.[116]

This structure places local law enforcement in a bewildering predicament. First, local police departments are criminal law enforcement agencies, they generally do not enforce civil violations—much less federal civil aviation violations. These are esoteric to routine patrol officers. They almost always do not have the authority to enforce these rules, as well as the legal ability to seize or detain the operators for that purpose. Thus, in order for law enforcement to deter and investigate unauthorised or unsafe drone operations, these agencies must take criminal enforcement. Such enforcement can be straightforward where the intent of the operator to inflict harm is clear.[117] Local laws criminalising assault, property damage, unlawful surveillance, and obstructing justice may be applicable. But what about unauthorised operations that are the result of recklessness or carelessness of the operator? What is the proper deterrent? In most cases, identification of the pilot along with a demand to ground the drone with an admonishment may be sufficient. Other incidents, however, may call for stiffer penalties. Examples include incidents where a drone crashes in a public place due to pilot error or malfunction which then causes panic and possible evacuation of the area.[118] When this occurs, local law enforcement is often left stretching the bounds of local criminal laws that did not contemplate errant drone flights. These could include criminal statutes that prohibit reckless conduct that poses a risk of injury to the public, improper take-offs and landings, or nuisances. While probable cause may exist in order to make a lawful arrest—and this has occurred—prosecution and conviction beyond a reasonable doubt against the reckless operator may prove dubious.[119]

Such a system calls into question the proper response and deterrent. When it comes to local law enforcement's ability to respond to unsafe drone operations, there is an imbalance between responsibility and authority; namely, that the first-line responders do not have the authority to regulate against such uses nor the technical abilities to address threats in real time.

Future Considerations: Gradual use of mitigation technology by local law enforcement

In the United States, recent federal legislation has not provided any new authority to state and local police to disable malicious drone use. Given that local police are often the front-line responders to malicious drone use, as well as the primary enforcement arm at major events and gatherings in their jurisdictions, federal legislation should

115 ibid.

116 ibid.

117 Although in practice, knowledge on the intent of the operator is almost never clear.

118 See, for example, Julia Talanova, 'Drone Slams into Seating Area at U.S. Open; Teacher Arrested' (*CNN.com*, 5 September 2015) <www.cnn.com/2015/09/04/us/us-open-tennis-drone-arrest/index.html>.

119 Arthur Holland Michel and Dan Gettinger, 'Drone Incidents: A Survey of Legal Cases' (*Center for the Study of the Drone*, 2017) 6 <https://dronecenter.bard.edu/drone-incidents/>.

either be amended or introduced to open up the possibility that local law enforcement can utilise this technology. This needs to be done gradually as the technology continues to evolve and address understandable concerns related to its use. While drone mitigation technology seeks to disable a present threat that has already been located, local law enforcement's interest in detection technology is preventative, including identifying and locating threats in advance. Understanding that not all police departments are created equal, this could be done on a case-by-case basis. Due to long-standing partnerships, federal agencies are in a position to assess whether a local police department can capably and responsibly handle this technology. In large urban centres, task forces between federal and local law enforcement agencies could also be established which solely focus on drone detection and mitigation. Such cooperative agreements create a dedicated stream of resources from each of the participating agencies. In addition to authorising such use, amendments would need to be made to federal laws surrounding wiretaps, trap and trace devices, hacking, and communication interference in order to account for the legitimate deployment of this technology.

A similar process is already taking place in Europe. The European Union has designated a manufacturer to develop and provide counter-drone technology to participant police departments. The technology will be procured by local police departments with ample oversight.[120]

Local input into local drone operations

The introduction of drones has raised questions as to who is the proper authority to regulate the immediate airspace over property, public gathering spaces, and around critical infrastructure. Should it be a responsibility of national concern, local concern, or both? This is an especially salient issue for large urban areas that have multiple assets attracting both malicious and reckless drone operations. In the United States, the FAA does issue temporary flight restrictions (TFRs) and other administrative tools to safeguard sensitive locations of state and municipal concern. TFRs are tools that restrict aircraft operations, including drones, in a designated area. For national security, they have been widely used to restrict over-flights in certain airspace. Local input is part of this process. Additionally, the FAA has implemented the Low Altitude Authorization and Notification Capability (LAANC) programme to permit operators to fly in controlled airspace under 400 feet as long as airspace authorisation is obtained from the FAA. As more drones begin to fill the airspace, and as commercial use expands, programmes such as these need to be leveraged between national and local agencies. Some have advocated that agencies such as the FAA should simply delegate their regulatory authority over the immediate airspace (generally 200 feet or below) to local law enforcement.[121] Regardless of the approach, discussions between national and local agencies about drone traffic management and avoiding the creation of drone canyons in municipalities and other populous areas, the identification of

120 See Imelda Cotton, 'DroneShield Wins EU Police Force Contract to Improve National Security' (*SmallCaps*, 21 May 2020) <https://smallcaps.com.au/droneshield-eu-police-force-contract-improve-national-security/>.

121 Chris Mills Rodrigo, 'Republican Lawmaker Proposes Transferring Drone Authority to Local Government' (*The Hill*, 16 October 2019) <https://thehill.com/policy/technology/466143-republican-lawmaker-proposes-transferring-drone-authority-to-local>.

frequency "dead-zones", and the establishment of geofences around sensitive locations (in addition to general airspace restrictions) will be necessary.

Public education

Most drones are flown safely by responsible pilots and hobbyists. In making an effort to constantly improve and ensure safety, law enforcement agencies can educate drone operators and enthusiasts about the dangers of operating outside of airspace restrictions and other critical regulations. Local law enforcement can leverage data on recent incidents and detect locations and other hotspots to provide a targeted safety message to the general public. The objective of public education is to have hobbyists and recreationalists aware of relevant regulations thereby reducing the volume of unauthorised drones in the airspace during large-scale events where law enforcement seeks to focus on actual threats.

Conclusion

Assessing and addressing criminal and malicious conduct on the ground are the primary responsibility of local law enforcement agencies. Responding to those conditions and ameliorating a threat is the responsibility of the police, and local police departments, worldwide, mostly accomplish this goal every day. The roles and responsibilities of other law enforcement agencies are well established by statute and regulatory authority, and they provide agencies and the public with clear direction as to who carries out the enormous responsibility of keeping everyone safe and secure.

When it comes to the threat of unauthorised drones, however, the state of play is mixed. Currently defined roles by the national and federal government are unclear, as are state and local law enforcement agencies and they are statutorily constrained from using technology to mitigate threats posed by unauthorised drone operations. As technology evolves, so too must the roles and responsibilities of those responding to the threats posed by drones.

5 Maritime uses of drones

Maurice Thompson and Martin Davies

Introduction

Drone technology is already used in many different ways by a variety of maritime industries, and more potential uses are currently in active development. The wide variety of different uses of drone technology in the maritime world means that it is convenient to divide this chapter into three main sections, dealing with three different physical strata of the use of autonomous and remotely controlled equipment, namely:

On the surface. This section deals with autonomous and remotely controlled surface ships, which the International Maritime Organization (IMO, an agency of the United Nations) has decided to call MASS: Maritime Autonomous Surface Ships.[1] As explained later, the IMO is currently engaged in a 'scoping exercise', examining international legal instruments that may need to be amended to accommodate the increasing commercial use of MASS. That is obviously a painstaking exercise, given the number of international conventions governing shipping business, particularly in relation to the safety of navigation. Nevertheless, it cannot possibly cover all legal issues raised by the use of MASS technology. Space does not permit even a cursory examination of all other possible legal questions, so focus is given to two issues—piracy and criminal law and pilotage—to give context to the legal issues to be addressed.

Under the surface. This section deals with the use of drone technology under the surface of the sea. Here, in contrast to the high degree of regulation in relation to surface craft, there is a dearth of legal guidance about what can and cannot be done legally.

Above the surface. This section deals with the use of drones that fly above the surface of the water or above the deck of a ship—or, indeed, inside the holds of a ship. It deals with a number of the legal conundrums that arise when flying drones ('aircraft' as currently defined in many jurisdictions) in a maritime context.

Each stratum poses very different issues in relation to legal regulation.

On the surface

General

Since 2018, the IMO has been engaged in a 'scoping exercise' in relation to what it calls 'MASS' (Maritime Autonomous Surface Ships). The purpose of the exercise is

1 Readers might fairly assume that all ships must be maritime whether or not they are autonomous. The otherwise superfluous adjective 'maritime' is necessary to avoid what would be a rather unfortunate acronym.

to assess the degree to which the existing regulatory framework of IMO instruments may need to be modified to make them applicable to MASS.[2] The IMO's definition of 'MASS' is unfortunately broad, encompassing everything from futuristic robotic drones to ships that are plying the seas right now:[3] 'A ship which, to a varying degree, can operate independent of human interaction'.[4] The IMO has also prescribed four provisional 'degrees of autonomy',[5] the first of which describes many ships already at sea at the moment, and the last of which describes ships that will not see operational service until sometime in the perhaps-distant future.

(1) Ship with automated processes and decision support. Seafarers are on board to operate and control shipboard systems and functions. Some operations may be automated and at times be unsupervised but with seafarers on board ready to take control.
(2) Remotely controlled ship with seafarers on board. The ship is controlled and operated from another location, but seafarers are on board to take control and to operate the shipboard systems and functions.
(3) Remotely controlled ship without seafarers on board. The ship is controlled and operated from another location. There are no seafarers on board to take control and to operate the shipboard systems and functions.
(4) Fully autonomous ship. The operating system of the ship is able to make decisions and determine actions by itself.

The Maritime Safety Committee's scoping exercise is considering: the Safety of Life at Sea Convention (SOLAS);[6] the Collision Regulations (COLREGs);[7] ship loading and stability (Load Lines);[8] training of seafarers and fishers (STCW,[9] STCW-F);[10] search and rescue (SAR);[11] tonnage measurement (Tonnage Convention);[12] safe containers

2 IMO Maritime Safety Committee, *Framework for the Regulatory Scoping Exercise for the Use of Maritime Autonomous Surface Ships (MASS)* MSC 100/20/Add.1, Annex 2 (hereafter 'MSC Framework'), para 2.
3 Robert Veal, 'Regulation and Liability in Remoted Controlled and Autonomous Shipping: A Panoptic View' (2020) 45 Tulane Maritime Law Journal (101) (hereafter Veal, 'Panoptic view').
4 International Maritime Organization, *Report of the Maritime Safety Committee on its Ninety-Ninth Session* (16–25 May 2018) MSC 99/WP.9, Annex 1, para 3.
5 MSC Framework (n 2) para 4.
6 International Convention for the Safety of Life at Sea (opened for signature 1 November 1974, entered into force 25 May 1980) 1566 UNTS 401 (hereafter SOLAS).
7 Convention on the International Regulations for Preventing Collisions at Sea (opened for signature 20 October 1972, entered into force 15 July 1977) 1050 UNTS 16 (hereafter COLREGs).
8 International Convention on Load Lines (opened for signature 5 April 1966, entered into force 21 July 1968) 640 UNTS 33 (hereafter Load Lines Convention).
9 International Convention on Standards of Training, Certification and Watchkeeping for Seafarers (opened for signature 7 July 1978, entered into force 28 April 1984) 1361 UNTS 190 (hereafter STCW).
10 International Convention on Standards of Training, Certification and Watchkeeping for Fishing Vessel Personnel (opened for signature 7 July 1995, entered into force 29 September 2012) (hereafter STCW-F).
11 International Convention on Maritime Search and Rescue (opened for signature 27 April 1979, entered into force 22 June 1985) 1405 UNTS 118 (hereafter SAR).
12 International Convention on Tonnage Measurement of Ships (opened for signature 23 June 1969, entered into force 18 July 1982) 1291 UNTS 3 (hereafter Tonnage Convention).

(CSC);[13] and special trade passenger ship instruments (SPACE STP, STP).[14] The IMO's Legal Committee and Facilitation Committee is conducting similar 'scoping exercises' in relation to instruments under their purview, including some for which the IMO shares joint responsibility with other UN bodies such as UNCTAD.[15]

This intense and focused activity will, no doubt, produce recommended amendments to the 'scoped' international instruments to make them amenable to the particular issues raised by autonomous and remotely controlled vessels. That will be a laudable and very significant improvement to the international regime governing shipping operations, but, predictably, it will not be the end of the legal questions raised by MASS. To be fair, the IMO does not pretend otherwise. To consider only two of the very many remaining issues, this chapter describes two very different areas that clearly call for amendment to existing laws, but which are not dealt with by the IMO's 'scoping exercise': piracy and pilotage. In relation to both, the necessary solutions may not lie in international activity at bodies like the IMO, but in national legislation.

Piracy and criminal law[16]

The IMO's scoping exercise is obviously focused on the lawful use of MASS, but it can be expected that criminals, pirates, and terrorists will make increasing use of the new technologies to transport illicit cargoes or to conduct unmanned attacks on naval or civilian vessels. Little thought has yet been given to the amendments to legal instruments that will be necessary to accommodate the possibility of use of MASS in criminal activity. The ship-architects of the MASS of the future have paid considerable attention to the vulnerability of MASS to pirate attacks—piracy *against* MASS—but little thought has been given to the legal consequences of possible piracy *by* MASS.

Although piracy is usually thought of as an act of violent theft or kidnapping committed for financial gain, terrorist attacks from one ship against another also constitute piracy under international law. Article 101(a) of the United Nations Convention on the Law of the Sea (UNCLOS) defines piracy as:[17]

> [A]ny illegal acts of violence or detention, or any act of depredation, committed for private ends by the crew or the passengers of a private ship or a private aircraft, and directed: (i) on the high seas, against another ship or aircraft, or against persons or property on board such ship or aircraft; or (ii) against a ship, aircraft, persons or property in a place outside the jurisdiction of any State.

13 International Convention for Safe Containers (opened for signature 2 December 1972, entered into force 6 September 1977) 1064 UNTS 25 (hereafter CSC).

14 These are the instruments in the scoping exercise as identified at International Maritime Organization, *Report of the Maritime Safety Committee on its One Hundredth Session* (3–7 December 2018) MSC 100/20/Add.1, Annex 2, Appendix 1.

15 The full list of instruments being considered by the IMO during the 'scoping' exercise can be seen at: <www.imo.org/en/MediaCentre/HotTopics/Pages/Autonomous-shipping.aspx>.

16 See generally, Anna Petrig, 'Autonomous Offender Ships and International Maritime Security Law' in Henrik Ringbom, Erik Røsæg and Trond Solvang (eds), *Autonomous Ships and the Law* (Routledge 2020) Chapter 3.

17 United Nations Convention on the Law of the Sea (opened for signature 10 December 1982, entered into force 16 November 1994) 1833 UNTS 397 (hereafter UNCLOS) Art 101.

'Depredation' is usually understood to mean 'plunder, pillage or robbery', the acts traditionally associated with piracy.[18] 'Detention' is the kind of kidnapping for ransom that Somali pirates did in the early 2010s. 'Illegal acts of violence' include terrorist acts such as those of Houthi rebels, who have been using remotely controlled, explosive-laden boats to attack naval and commercial ships in the Red Sea since 2017.[19] All three kinds of activity are 'piracy' according to the definition in Art 101(a)—or would be, but for the obvious textual problem that the relevant acts must be committed by people, namely the crew or passengers of a ship. If an attack is mounted using remotely controlled vessels, it can only amount to piracy, and the remote controller can only be regarded as a pirate under Art 101(a), if he or she can be said to be part of the 'crew' of the attacking MASS.

There are purely textual arguments for and against reading Art 101(a) to include a shore-based remote controller as a member (presumably the sole member) of 'the crew'. On the one hand, Art 101(a) uses the composite phrase 'the crew or the passengers' of the attacking ship, and one must necessarily be on the ship itself to be a 'passenger', which suggests that one must also be on board the ship to be a member of 'the crew'.[20] On the other hand, the only reference to people being 'on board' a ship is in relation to the attacked ship, not the attacking ship, which would suggest that someone can be a member of 'the crew' of the attacking ship without being on board.[21]

It might be thought that Art 101(b) of UNCLOS solves this textual problem in relation to Art 101(a) by providing that an alternative way of committing piracy is to perform: '[A]ny act of voluntary participation in the operation of a ship or of an aircraft with knowledge of facts making it a pirate ship or aircraft'.[22] A remote controller clearly participates voluntarily in the operation of the ship, knowing the activities in which it is engaged, which satisfies the first part of the paragraph, but could a crewless attacking MASS properly be called a 'pirate ship' for purposes of the second half of the paragraph? Article 103 of UNCLOS provides that: 'A ship or aircraft is considered a pirate ship or aircraft if it is intended by the persons in dominant control to be used for the purpose of committing one of the acts referred to in article 101'.[23] It is quite possible for the person in 'dominant control' of the ship to be on land and intend the ship to be used for piracy, which would make it a pirate ship. That was the case with many of the Somali pirate attacks of the early 2010s, where the masterminds of the operation stayed on shore and the attacks themselves were committed by conscripts, often very young. That is also the case with the Houthi rebel attacks by remotely controlled MASS. However, Art 103's reference back to Art 101 creates something of a definitional feedback loop when applied to MASS. The mastermind or dominant controller intends for bad things to happen at sea, but does he or she intend the MASS to be used 'for the purpose of committing one of the acts referred to in article 101', acts which suppose that they are committed by a person at sea? Article 101(b) refers

18 Douglas Guilfoyle, 'Article 101: Definition of Piracy' in Alexander Proelss (ed), *United Nations Convention on the Law of the Sea: A Commentary* (Beck/Hart Publishing 2017) 740.
19 Petrig (n 16) 23.
20 ibid 32–33.
21 ibid.
22 UNCLOS (n 17) Art 101(b).
23 ibid Art 103.

to voluntary and knowing participation in the operation of a 'pirate ship', which takes us to Art 103, which refers back to Art 101, and so on.

It is more difficult to imagine traditional 'depredation' piracy being committed using MASS, but not impossible. An autonomous or remotely controlled vessel could be used to disable the target vessel, making it vulnerable to boarding by humans to perform the traditional tasks of theft or kidnapping. Here, too, the wording of UNCLOS Art 101(a) raises doubts about whether that kind of attack would constitute piracy. Article 101(a) refers to an attack by 'the crew or the passengers of *a* private ship' (emphasis added). If the attack is done by the MASS and the theft is done by humans arriving on another vessel later once the target ship (and possibly also its crew) is disabled, does either attacking ship commit piracy?[24] The MASS makes a violent attack but has no crew; the follow-up vessel has crew but no need to commit violence. Or do both vessels commit piracy, the MASS by committing an act of violence in which others are knowingly involved and the crewed ship by committing an act of depredation?

Even if the remote controller of a MASS could be regarded as a pirate according to international law as stated in UNCLOS, another possible problem arises. Piracy is the paradigm example of universal jurisdiction in international law, the concept that any country has jurisdiction to prosecute a pirate, regardless of where the offence was committed or the nationalities of the offender or the victim, because pirates are 'enemies of all humanity'.[25] If the remote controller is on some kind of pirate mother ship on the high seas, he or she might still be a proper subject for universal jurisdiction, amenable to prosecution by any country that might lay hands on him or her. If, however, the remote controller is on land, within the sovereign territory of a particular country, it is much less obvious that universal jurisdiction is appropriate. Piracy must take place on the high seas or otherwise outside the jurisdiction of any country in order for it to be piracy—Art 101(1)(a) says as much very clearly. Acts of 'violence . . . or depredation' taking place within territorial waters are not piracy, but crimes of theft or assault as defined by the law of the coastal state. Acts of 'violence . . . or depredation' *committed* on land but *effected* far away at sea look even more like crimes against the law of the country where the remote controller sits, rather than piracy. It seems that it would be better for countries to amend their domestic laws to criminalise such behaviour than to try to fit them within the straitjacket of the definition of piracy under international law.[26] However, leaving the solution to national legislation means that the solution, if any, will not be internationally uniform. That is exactly the problem in relation to the very different issue of pilotage, which is considered in the next section of this chapter.

Pilotage[27]

Although pilotage of MASS may seem to be much less important than the fundamental safety-related issues dealt with by the IMO's 'scoping exercise', the regulation

24 Petrig (n 16) 36.

25 Kenneth Randall, 'Universal Jurisdiction under International Law' (1988) 66 Texas Law Review 785, 788.

26 Petrig (n 16) 35.

27 See generally, Martin Davies, 'Pilotage of Autonomous and Remotely-controlled Ships' in Henrik Ringbom, Erik Røsæg and Trond Solvang (eds), *Autonomous Ships and the Law* (Routledge 2020) Chapter 17.

of pilotage may actually prove to be a profound legal obstacle to the introduction of autonomous and remotely controlled ships. Even if technical accommodations could be made, perhaps at the instigation of the IMO, at an international level, by amendments to SOLAS and other conventions, a profound legal obstacle still remains in relation to pilotage of autonomous and remotely controlled ships, which is that there is no international regulation of pilotage. Indeed, in many countries there is not even *national* regulation of pilotage, which is regarded as an essentially local matter, regulated by local legal instruments. Thus, there is no single international instrument that could be amended to bring international uniformity to the legal treatment of pilotage of autonomous and remotely controlled ships. Hundreds, if not thousands, of legal instruments in ports all over the world will have to be amended if autonomous and remotely controlled ships are to be able to move freely from a port in one country to a port in another.

In 2003, the IMO published recommendations on the training of, and operational procedures for, maritime pilots other than deep-sea pilots.[28] Many training institutions around the world follow the IMO's recommendations which means that there is at least some level of international uniformity in relation to standards of pilot licensing and competence, but that is only the beginning of the many legal issues in relation to pilots and pilotage.

National regulation of competency standards for pilots is common; national regulation of compulsory pilotage areas and the grant of pilotage exemption certificates is much less so. Countries differ considerably in the level at which such matters relating to pilotage are handled.

Some countries regulate all aspects of pilotage at a national level, with national standards and also national designation of pilotage areas and the grant of pilotage exemptions. That is the case, for example, in Australia, Norway, and Korea, where the designation of compulsory pilotage areas, the requirements for pilot qualifications, and the conditions for pilotage exemption certificates are all done at a national level.[29]

In contrast, some countries have national regulation of pilotage competency standards but delegate to local authorities such matters as the designation of compulsory pilotage areas and the grant of pilotage exemption certificates. For example, in China, the China Maritime Safety Administration is responsible for the certification of maritime pilots through the testing and assessment of experience, qualification, and suitability of applicants,[30] but local harbour administrations are responsible for the supervision of the safety of marine traffic in the coastal waters under their supervision, including regulation of pilotage.[31] Similarly, in Canada, there is national regulation

28 Resolution A.960(23), *Recommendations on Training and Certification and on Operational Procedures for Maritime Pilots other than Deep-Sea Pilots*, IMO A 23/Res.960(23) (5 December 2003).

29 For Australia, *see* Navigation Act 2012 (Cth), ss 163 (compulsory pilotage areas), 164 (licensing of pilots), 172–3 (exemptions). Marine Order 54 (Coastal Pilotage) 2014 (Cth), Div 2 deals with the grant of licences to private pilotage providers. For Norway, see Norwegian Coastal Administration, 'Pilot Services' <www.kystverket.no/en/EN_Maritime-Services/Pilot-Services>. For Korea, see Pilotage Act (Korea), Arts 4 to 9 (licensing), 17 (pilotage areas), 20(2)(pilotage exemptions).

30 Weifeng Li, Jiagen Yu and Robert Desrosiers, 'Introduction and Overview of China's Pilot Training Regime' (2016) 10(4) International Journal on Marine Navigation and Safety of Sea Transportation 543.

31 Maritime Traffic Safety Law of the People's Republic of China, Art 3 provides that local Harbour Superintendency Administrations are 'the competent authorities solely responsible for the supervision of the

of competency standards and the grant of pilotage certificates,[32] but such matters as the responsibility for designating compulsory pilotage areas and the grant of pilotage exemptions are delegated to four regional pilotage authorities.[33]

In other countries, the regulation of pilotage is delegated almost completely to local authorities which control the licensing of pilots, the designation of compulsory pilotage areas, and the grant of pilotage exemption certificates. For example, the UK legislation creates 'competent harbour authorities', which have power in relation to the regulation of shipping movements and the safety of navigation within their harbours.[34] The 'competent harbour authorities', of which there are at least 90,[35] regulate all matters in relation to pilotage, including: whether pilotage services are required in their respective harbours and whether pilotage should be compulsory; the licensing of pilots; the designation of compulsory pilotage areas; and the grant of pilotage exemption certificates.[36] Similarly, there is no national pilotage law in Turkey, where pilotage services are provided in a cooperative structure of public institutions, private port companies, and pilotage companies in 38 different pilotage regions, which regulate pilot competency, training and certification, as well as the provision of pilotage services.[37]

Similarly, pilotage in the United States is largely a matter of state regulation. Apart from two fairly small exceptions where federally licensed pilots must be used (coastwise and Great Lakes trade),[38] federal legislation provides that 'pilots in the bays, rivers, harbors, and ports of the United States shall be regulated only in conformity with the laws of the States'.[39] As a result, regulation of pilot licensing, compulsory pilotage areas, and pilotage exemptions in the United States is almost entirely a matter of state law. Thirty-six of the 50 US states touch on an ocean or a navigable waterway (excluding the Great Lakes), such as the Mississippi River system, including its navigable tributaries.[40] Thus, each one of those 36 states may regulate pilotage in relation

safety of traffic', and Art 13 provides that no foreign-flagged vessel may enter or leave a Chinese port, or navigate or shift berths in port without a pilot being sent on board 'by the competent authorities'. Port Law of the People's Republic of China, Art 6 provides that 'The local people's governments shall . . . decide on the administration of the port situated within their own administrative areas', and Art 39 provides that 'The specific measures for pilotage shall be formulated by the competent department of communications under the State Council'.

32 General Pilotage Regulations SOR/2000-132 (Can).

33 Pilotage Act, RSC 1985, c P-14 (Can), s 20(1)(a), (c) (regional Authorities may make regulations 'establishing compulsory pilotage areas' and 'prescribing the circumstances under which compulsory pilotage may be waived'). The four regional authorities are: Atlantic Pilotage Authority; Laurentian Pilotage Authority; Great Lakes Pilotage Authority; Pacific Pilotage Authority—see Sch 3.

34 Pilotage Act 1987 (UK), s 1(1).

35 UK Ports, 'Major UK Ports' <www.ukports.com/ports-directory>.

36 Pilotage Act 1987 (UK), ss 2(1)(a)(whether pilotage compulsory), 3 (licensing), 7 (designation of compulsory pilotage areas), 8 (exemptions).

37 Özkan Uğurlu, Mehmet Kaptan, Serdar Kum and Serdar Yildiz, 'Pilotage Services in Turkey; Key Issues and Ideal Pilotage' (2017) 16(2) Journal of Marine Engineering & Technology 51, 54.

38 46 USC § 8502 (coastwise trade), § 9302 (Great Lakes trade). The US Coast Guard is responsible for issuing federal pilot licences: see 46 USC § 7101(a),(b),(c)(2).

39 46 USC § 8501(a).

40 The states touching the ocean or a navigable waterway other than the Great Lakes are: Alabama, Alaska, Arkansas, California, Connecticut, Delaware, Florida, Georgia, Hawaii, Illinois, Indiana, Iowa, Kentucky, Louisiana, Maine, Maryland, Massachusetts, Minnesota, Mississippi, Missouri, New Hampshire, New Jersey, New York, North Carolina, Ohio, Oklahoma, Oregon, Pennsylvania, Rhode Island, South Carolina, Tennessee, Texas, Virginia, Washington, West Virginia, Wisconsin.

to its ports or navigable waterways, as may the US territories of Puerto Rico, the US Virgin Islands, Guam, the Northern Mariana Islands, and American Samoa. Some of the larger states have regional pilotage authorities with their own regulatory provisions relating to pilotage: Texas alone has six.[41] Wide latitude is given to the states and territories in determining the waters in which a vessel must procure a state-licensed pilot. Thus, there are dozens of different pilotage authorities within the United States, each with considerable power to impose its own requirements in relation to such matters as the definition of compulsory pilotage areas, certification of pilots, and the grant of pilotage exemptions.

Many other examples could be given, but it should be obvious already that in many countries, regulation of pilotage is very much a local matter. There is no international instrument that could be amended to accommodate pilotage of autonomous or remotely controlled ships.

Of course, fully autonomous ships will be controlled entirely by computers, with little or no input from shore-based operators (SBOs). It is difficult to imagine what role a local pilot could play in the navigation of such a ship, unless the ship's computer systems make it possible for a manual override in some circumstances, either from onboard the ship itself or by SBOs (or remote pilots). Without the possibility of manual override of the ship's autonomous systems, the only conceivable alternative would be to exempt fully autonomous ships from local requirements of mandatory pilotage. The role of the local pilot (or pilotage authority) would then presumably be limited to initial vetting of the ship for port state control purposes.

It is too soon to tell how pilotage of autonomous or remotely controlled ships will be handled in technical terms, but even this brief examination of the possibilities suggests that two matters will be of particular significance in the future: (1) communication between the pilot (whether on board the ship or ashore) and the ship and its SBO and (2) the scalability of the ship's navigational systems to allow intervention by many different shore-based systems at ports and straits so that the pilots can operate the ship remotely, if necessary. It may well be necessary for internationally uniform technical standards to be developed for these and similar issues relating to the interaction between the pilot and the ship. If a remotely controlled ship's navigational systems can accept input from a port-based controller at one end of its voyage but not from a port-based controller at the other end, its ability to make that voyage will obviously be compromised, unless the port without the means of control is prepared to let the ship enter without any effective means of local oversight.

Pilotage is a matter of localised regulation because of the understandable concern that coastal communities have about retaining some degree of local control over the safe navigation of ships entering and leaving their ports. The technological developments associated with MASS may diminish the ability of local authorities representing those communities to exercise that control. Quite apart from the understandable local concerns about the safety of crewless ships entering and leaving port, there may be other political objections to modifying local pilotage laws to accommodate MASS. Pilotage providers, whether governmental or private, are usually powerful local monopolies able to charge monopoly prices in compulsory pilotage areas. They will

41 The Texas Transportation Code makes provision for six 'navigation districts', each of which has its own 'pilot board': see VTCA Transportation Code, §§ 62.001, 62.021.

be able to defend their territory—and, thus, the stream of income produced by pilotage services—by raising perfectly legitimate concerns about the safety of bringing ships into or out of berth without anyone on board, much less a local pilot.

If pilotage is to remain a requirement for MASS at all, rather than being abolished completely, it will be necessary to amend hundreds, if not thousands, of local pilotage laws. It is highly unlikely that the amendments needed for pilotage laws to accommodate MASS will be made in uniform fashion or at a uniform speed. Even if some international body such as the IMO were to publish a model law or template for reform that would not solve the problem because the pace of its adoption would most probably vary significantly among countries and regional pilotage districts, leaving a patchwork of pilotage laws, some of which would be able to accommodate MASS but many of which would not. In short, although pilotage of MASS might seem like an afterthought, an 'and also' problem to be addressed after the principal issues of safety and security have been worked out, it actually has the potential to be a major legal obstacle to the practical implementation of these technological advances, as it will impede the ability of MASS to move freely from one country to another in compliance with the legal requirements of both.

Under the surface

There is surprisingly little law relating to subsea craft, and what little regulation exists is not at all well suited to the increasingly widespread use of 'unmanned underwater vehicles' (UUVs), which is the term used to refer generically to both remotely operated vehicles (ROVs) and completely autonomous underwater vehicles (AUVs). UNCLOS contains only one short provision on underwater vehicles, Article 20, which states simply:[42]

> In the territorial sea, submarines and other underwater vehicles are required to navigate on the surface and to show their flag.

Apparently, this obligation was drafted with military submarines in mind, and it is obviously breached far more often than it is observed when it comes to commercial UUVs. The catch-all phrase 'and other underwater vehicles' is surely broad enough to apply to the kind of ROVs that are widely used in offshore oil and gas exploration and production but which neither 'navigate on the surface' when used in territorial waters nor 'show their flag' when working. Indeed, as we shall soon see, most ROVs are regarded as equipment of the ship from which they are operated and have no flag of their own that could be shown. The only part of the provision that seems apt to refer to UUVs is the word 'vehicles', which was used in preference to 'vessels', which is the term used throughout the rest of UNCLOS—unfortunately so, as it means that Art 20 therefore fairly clearly applies to all kinds of UUVs and not merely those that might otherwise qualify as 'vessels'.

The very fact that the word 'vehicle' is used to refer to this underwater equipment, both in general usage and in UNCLOS, implies that these things are not 'ships' or 'vessels' by any of the various definitions of that term for different purposes. For example, the Federal Court of Australia has recently held that an ROV is not a

42 UNCLOS (n 17) Art 20.

'ship' for purposes of the Australian statutory provisions relating to ship arrest.[43] The Admiralty Act 1988 (Cth) defines 'ship' very broadly, to mean 'a vessel of any kind used or constructed for use in navigation by water, however it is propelled or moved'.[44] In the Federal Court, Colvin J said that that definition might include submersible vehicles because: 'A structure that moves through the water may be described as undertaking navigation by water',[45] but held that the particular ROV in question was not a ship because (among other reasons) it could not float on or below the water, it remained tethered to a launch apparatus, and it could not move from one site to another by its own navigation or by being towed but was loaded onto a ship and transported as cargo.[46] Of particular significance in relation to the question of arrest was the fact that the ROV was 'unable to leave the jurisdiction by its own effort and thereby readily evade claims'.[47] Importantly, Colvin J made no mention of the fact that the ROV had no people aboard. All of this implies that some UUVs might be regarded as 'ships' according to the Australian definition, particularly untethered robotic AUVs that can travel far from shore without the need for any support ship nearby, such as, for example, the AUVs used to conduct seabed mapping operations under the Arctic ice.[48]

Although the definition of 'vessel' in the US Code is similarly broad—'every description of watercraft or other artificial contrivance used, or capable of being used, as a means of transportation on water'[49]—it was interpreted by the US Supreme Court to include only such objects that 'a reasonable observer, looking to the [object]'s physical characteristics and activities, would consider it designed to a practical degree for carrying people or things over water'.[50] Both the words '*on* water' in the statutory definition and the Supreme Court's reference to transporting 'people or things *over* water' suggest that no UUV could qualify as a 'vessel' in the United States. Consistent with that, it has been held that an ROV operator is not a 'seaman' despite having the 'direction and command' of an ROV, because an ROV is not a vessel but 'superficially attached machinery' of the support vessel.[51] Conversely, before the Supreme Court adopted its 'reasonable observer' test, it was held that a remotely controlled hull-cleaning device known as a SCAMP could qualify as a 'vessel' and its operator as a 'seaman',[52] with the court noting that: 'Strange looking, special purpose craft for the

43 *Guardian Offshore AU Pty Ltd v Saab Seaeye Leopard 1702 Remotely Operated Vehicle Lately on Board the Ship 'Offshore Guardian'* [2020] FCA 273, [2021] 1 Lloyd's Rep 201 (hereafter *Guardian Offshore*).

44 Admiralty Act 1988 (Cth), s 3(1).

45 *Guardian Offshore* (n 43) [79] (Colvin J).

46 ibid [83–86].

47 ibid [88].

48 A Kukulya and others, 'Under-Ice Operations with a REMUS-100 AUV in the Arctic' *2010 IEEE/OES Autonomous Underwater Vehicles* 1–8.

49 1 USC § 3. This section appears in the Rules of Construction Act (1 USC §§ 1-8), so the definition applies whenever the word 'vessel' is used anywhere in the US Code.

50 *Lozman v City of Riviera Beach, Fla* (2013) 568 US 115, 121 (SCUS).

51 *Halle v Galliano Marine Service LLC* (2017) 855 F 3d 290, 2017 AMC 913 (5th Cir).

52 *Estate of Wenzel v Seaward Marine Services Inc* (1983) 709 F 2d 1326 (9th Cir). It should be noted that the Ninth Circuit did not hold that the SCAMP *did* constitute a vessel, but merely denied a motion for summary judgement brought by the employer of a deceased worker whose estate alleged that he had been a seaman.

oil and gas business, far different from traditional seafaring ships have sometimes been held to be vessels'.[53]

Although the vessel status of UUVs obviously remains unsettled under US law, it does seem clear that American courts would agree with Colvin J of the Federal Court of Australia that the mere fact that an object is submersible is not enough in itself to preclude it from being a 'vessel'. There is long-standing authority in the United States that submersible objects such as drilling barges are 'vessels' for purposes of US law, largely because they have to be towed to the relevant location before being submerged.[54] If a UUV were to be transported across the surface, perhaps by towing but in any event by some means other than as cargo or 'superficially attached machinery' of a transporting vessel before being submerged, it might be a 'vessel' even under the narrow American definition.

Whether or not UUVs constitute 'vessels' under the sometimes-idiosyncratic definitions of national law, it is also important to determine whether they constitute 'vessels' under the international instruments governing safety of navigation. That question has attracted some debate with, perhaps predictably, considerable differences of opinion.[55] The obvious problem is that the relevant international instruments were all drafted with surface vessels in mind, despite the fact that submarines have existed for a very long time. To take the International Regulations for Preventing Collisions at Sea (COLREGs)[56] as an example, the definition of 'vessel' sounds as though it will apply to UUVs—until one arrives at the end of the sentence. Rule 3(a) defines 'vessel' to include 'every description of water craft, including non-displacement craft, WIG craft and seaplanes, used or capable of being used as a means of transportation on water'. The troublesome word is, of course, 'on'. Similarly, Rule 1(a) provides that 'These Rules shall apply to all vessels *upon* the high seas and in all waters connected therewith navigable by seagoing vessels' (emphasis added). A purposive interpretation of the COLREGs would apply them to submersibles such as UUVs, but that generous spirit might well achieve too much, as several of the rules make little or no sense in relation to vessels (if they are vessels) under the water. To take just one simple example, Rule 5 requires all vessels to 'at all times maintain a proper look-out by sight and hearing', which might conceivably be possible for ROVs equipped with cameras and sonar but presumably not for AUVs—unless 'sight and hearing' are to be extended to include the computer-driven sensing equipment on a fully autonomous UUV.

Collision avoidance in subsea navigation is clearly important, but more significant than the COLREGs for the commercial (and military) use of UUVs are the sovereignty provisions of UNCLOS. UNCLOS refers to 'vessels' throughout its text but does not define the term. The international law right of coastal states to regulate the activities of UUVs outside the territorial sea is questionable, even if they do constitute 'vessels' (and particularly if not).

53 ibid 1328.

54 *Gianfala v Texas Co* (1955) 350 US 879 (SCUS); *Producers Drilling Co v Gray* (1966) 361 F 2d 432 (5th Cir); *McCarty v Service Contracting Inc* (1970) 317 F Supp 629 (ED La); *Hicks v Ocean Drilling & Exploration Co* (1975) 512 F 2d 817 (5th Cir).

55 Andrew Henderson, 'Murky Waters: The Legal Status of Unmanned Undersea Vehicles' (2006) 53 Naval Law Review 55, 66–67 argues that 'free-swimming' UUVs are likely to be considered vessels. Daniel Vallejo, Note, 'Electric Currents: Programming Legal Status into Autonomous Unmanned Maritime Vehicles' (2015) 47 Case Western Reserve Journal of International Law 405 argues that they are not.

56 COLREGs (n 7).

Within the territorial sea, the sovereignty of a coastal state extends to the 'adjacent belt of sea' as well as to the airspace over it and its bed and subsoil,[57] with the result that a coastal state would be entitled to regulate the activities of UUVs in the water column of the territorial sea. Beyond the 12 nautical miles of the territorial sea, however, the sovereign rights of coastal states over the water column above the seabed are much more limited, and UNCLOS specifically preserves the rights of other states to navigation within the Exclusive Economic Zone (EEZ).

Article 56 (1) of UNCLOS provides that a coastal state has sovereign rights within its EEZ:

> [F]or the purpose of exploring and exploiting, conserving and managing the natural resources, whether living or non-living, of the waters superjacent to the seabed, and with regard to other activities for the economic exploitation and exploration of the zone, such as the production of energy from the water, currents and winds.

Article 56(1) might just be broad enough to give a coastal state the right to regulate the use of UUVs in relation to oil and gas exploration and fisheries in the EEZ but clearly not for other purposes including, perhaps importantly, military, recreational, or commercial purposes not related to natural resource exploration or fisheries. Furthermore, when exercising its rights under Art 56(1), a coastal state must 'have due regard to the rights and duties of other states'.[58] This limited sovereignty over the water column beyond 12 nautical miles would seem to call into question the extent to which the private law of the coastal state might apply more generally to the activities of UUVs. Imagine, for example, that the lessee of a subsea drilling lease has installed an expensive and innovative piece of equipment on the seabed in the EEZ using commercially sensitive proprietary equipment in the process of oil and gas exploration. Imagine also that a competing oil and gas company from another country sends an ROV to take close-up photographs of the equipment in an attempt to learn about its operations. Could the equipment-owning company invoke the law of the coastal state to complain of a violation of its rights?

There is a small but well-established body of tort law to the effect that the owner of property on land may complain of trespass to the airspace above the land, at least if the incursion occurs at a height that might interfere with any ordinary use of the land by the property-owner.[59] This body of law may well be relevant to overflight by airborne drones, but should incursion into the water column around and over a subsea lease properly be regarded as analogous?[60] If the incursion occurs outside the territorial sea, the answer seems quite clearly to be No. The analogy of airborne overflight breaks down because of the limited nature of a coastal state's sovereignty over the water column beyond its territorial sea. Every country has complete and exclusive sovereignty over the airspace

57 UNCLOS (n 17), Art 2.

58 ibid Art 56(2).

59 Compare *Bernstein of Leigh (Baron) v Skyviews and General Ltd* [1978] QB 479 (no trespass by flying over plaintiff's land); *Schleter (t/as Cape Crawford Tourism) v Brazakka* (2002) 12 NTLR 76 (SCNT) (same) with *Janney v Steller Works Pty Ltd* (2017) 53 VR 677 (SC Vic) (trespass to airspace by overhanging crane jib).

60 This issue receives extensive consideration in Annie Brett, 'Secrets of the Deep: Defining Privacy Underwater' (2019) 84 Missouri Law Review 47.

above its territory.[61] Consistent with that complete sovereignty, countries may (and do) regulate overflight and can quite properly apply other laws, such as the law of torts, to activities in airspace, such as trespass by overflight. As we have seen, though, countries do not have similarly 'complete and exclusive sovereignty' over the water column in the EEZ and must respect the rights of other states in relation to it. Among those rights are the freedom of navigation in the EEZ of other countries, including 'other internationally lawful uses of the sea related to these freedoms'.[62] If the coastal state in our example of the snooping ROV were to apply its tort laws to make it unlawful to enter the water column above the subsea lease, it would be denying the ROV's freedom of navigation (if such freedom applies to a UUV) and probably asserting jurisdiction that goes far beyond what is permitted by UNCLOS Art 56(1). Attempting to steal trade secrets and other intellectual property is unlawful by the domestic law of most countries, but it is doubtful whether it would be an *internationally* unlawful use of the seas—unless it is made so by future amendments to the various international instruments.

This surely cannot mean, however, that *no* country's laws apply in the water column above a country's EEZ—or above the seabed of the high seas, for that matter. After all, collisions between surface ships on the high seas are routinely regarded as giving rise to liability in tort, producing large awards of damages. However, courts are usually rather more vague about *which* country's laws apply to torts occurring at sea. Most countries assume jurisdiction to hear a claim arising from a high seas or EEZ collision, as most apply their admiralty jurisdiction to all claims, wherever in the world they arise, without reference to the flag of the ship.[63] The US Supreme Court held long ago that the law to be applied to high-seas collisions between foreign ships is 'the general maritime law, as understood and administered in the courts of the country in which the litigation is prosecuted'.[64] More recently, a majority of the High Court of Australia said much the same thing, observing, obiter, that a court should apply its own law (the *lex fori*) to a maritime tort occurring on the high seas[65] but including 'the general principles of maritime law or the maritime law of the world'.[66] As a Full Court of the Federal Court of Australia later explained, this is not international law, but Australian municipal law, taking into account the international nature of events on the high seas.[67] The Full Court stated, again obiter, that Chinese law would not apply to a collision beyond Chinese territorial waters but within China's EEZ, because China has no sovereign right to regulate navigation there but only limited sovereignty in relation to the matters stated in Art 56 of UNCLOS.[68]

61 Convention on International Civil Aviation (opened for signature 7 December 1944, entered into force 9 April 1947) 15 UNTS 295 (hereafter the Chicago Convention), Art 1. The Chicago Convention has 191 parties: see <www.icao.int/publications/Documents/chicago.pdf>.

62 UNCLOS (n 17), Arts 58(1), 87(1)(a).

63 See, for example, Admiralty Act 1988 (Cth), s 5; Senior Courts Act 1981 (UK), s 20(7); High Court (Admiralty Jurisdiction) Act c 123 (Sin), s 3(4); *The Belgenland* (1885) 114 US 355 (SCUS).

64 *The Belgenland* (n 63) 369.

65 *Blunden v Commonwealth* [2003] HCA 73, (2003) 218 CLR 330 [23] (Gleeson CJ, Gummow, Hayne, Heydon JJ).

66 ibid [13] (Gleeson CJ, Gummow, Hayne, Heydon JJ).

67 *CMA CGM SA v The Ship Chou Shan* [2014] FCAFC 90, (2015) 224 FCR 384 [91]–[92] (Allsop CJ, Besanko, Pagone JJ) (hereafter *The Chou Shan*).

68 *The Chou Shan* (n 67) [87]–[90] (Allsop CJ, Besanko, Pagone JJ), cited with approval in *Bright Shipping Ltd v Changhong Group (HK) Ltd (The CF Crystal and the Sanchi)* [2019] HKCA 1062, [2020] 2 Lloyd's Rep 1 [23]–[24] (Kwan VP).

Because torts allegedly committed by UUVs are unlikely to be concerned with the 'internal economy of the vessel'[69] (if, it should be repeated, they are 'vessels' at all), and because UUVs may not be registered on any country's registry of ships and so may have no law of the flag, it would seem to follow that this rather vague reference to 'the general maritime law' as recognised in the forum country is the best that can be done. Of course, the problem with applying 'the general maritime law' is that it has always been of very uncertain content, as has been pointed out by judges from Oliver Wendell Holmes[70] to Lord Diplock.[71] More particularly, there are obviously no 'ancient traditions of maritime law'[72] in relation to UUVs, no 'acceptance by common consent of civilized communities'[73] about the rules that should be applied to these new machines with new capabilities. To return to the example of the snooping ROV, the general maritime law has very little to tell us about whether it was acting unlawfully by taking photographs hundreds of feet below the surface of international waters.

Above the surface

General

One of the greatest juxtapositions in risk profiles consequent on the advent of the increased usage of aerial drones can be seen in the maritime sector, where users, operators, and regulators (e.g. aviation, maritime, classification and offshore oil & gas) are faced with the potential for the effective collision between national and international laws that relate to the 'aviation' sector and national and international laws that apply in respect of the 'maritime' sector. To date, this reality has not been fully appreciated by the respective national and international organisations that regulate or seek to represent the aviation and maritime sectors. As is explained earlier, for instance, the IMO is currently engaged in a 'scoping exercise' examining which international legal instruments may need to be amended to accommodate the increasing commercial use of MASS. The development of MASS has been ponderously slow as compared to the development of drones and for obvious reasons; the R&D in respect of a potentially unmanned 400-metre-long and 550,000-DWT-vessel needs meticulous detail, and prototypes of that size are expensive and could take years to build. While the IMO's 'scoping exercise' is essential, they and other similar representative maritime organisations would be wise to look to the skies with the same diligence to assess and take advantage

69 The idea that the law of the ship's flag should be applied to matters of 'internal economy' derives from *Mali v Keeper of the Common Jail (Wildenhus' Case)* (1887) 120 US 1 (1887) (SCUS) (habeas corpus). See also *McCulloch v Sociedad Nacional de Marineros de Honduras* (1963) 372 US 10 (SCUS) (labor relations laws); *Re Maritime Union of Australia; Ex parte CSL Pacific Shipping Inc* [2003] HCA 43, (2003) 214 CLR 397, 417–19.

70 See Holmes J's famous complaint in *The Western Maid* (1922) 257 US 419, 432 (SCUS): '[H]owever ancient may be the traditions of maritime law, however diverse the sources from which it has been drawn. . . . There is no mystic over-law to which even the United States must bow'.

71 *The Tojo Maru: Owners of MT Tojo Maru v NV Bureau Wijsmuller* [1972] AC 242, 290–91 (HL(E)): '[T]he fact that consequences of applying to the same facts the internal municipal laws of different sovereign states would be to give rise to similar legal rights and liabilities should not mislead us into supposing that those rights and liabilities are derived from a "maritime law of the world"'.

72 *The Western Maid* (n 70) 432 (Holmes J).

73 *The Lottawanna* (1874) 88 US 558, 572 (SCUS).

of the impact of drones on maritime commerce. Similarly, while the International Civil Aviation Organization (ICAO) and individual countries' aviation regulators are busy seeking to lay the foundations for the safe development of the drones sector, none to date, that these authors are aware of at least, have been looking to the seas, or indeed the land, to consider any possible overlapping of the necessary legal and regulatory environments. This is an oversight that requires urgent attention, because without a coordinated approach between the 'maritime' and 'aviation' sectors, much of the effort that is currently being expended by governments and sector-specific regulators and international representative organisations could well be wasted if what is planned and implemented is not compatible with an obviously overlapping sector.

Make no mistake; drones will revolutionise global transportation, supply chains, and indeed global commerce like no change we have witnessed in history, more so than when merchant ships changed from sail to steam or steam to combustion engines. In 1956, Malcolm McLean invented the modern shipping container.[74] That simple metal box of principally two sizes provided the necessary vehicle to standardise the shipment of cargo globally and provided shipping with the ability to scale. That simple container and the desire to scale matters up in the maritime industry have heavily influenced the design of vessels and ports, stevedoring infrastructure, rail rolling stock and even truck size over the last 70-odd years. It was a disrupter, reducing the costs associated with international trade and increasing its speed. It was revolutionary. With drones, we are on the precipice of another revolution in the maritime and broader transport industries.

This section of the chapter will identify some of the ways in which drones are being used in the maritime sector 'above the surface' and some of the legal conundrums that will need to be addressed.

Drones as a disrupter and inertia

Many of those who read this chapter will begin with a prejudice. Certain readers will already be participants in the aviation sector and will have assumed that matters concerning drones that fly will be matters pertaining to aviation alone. Others will be involved in the maritime sector and will be using drones in their delivery of maritime services above, on, and below the ocean surface, and assume that the drone is nothing more than a tool for the delivery of those maritime services. The one group will likely know very little about the laws as they relate to the other group's sector, largely because there has really been no need to do so to date. For example, an airline's general counsel or the airline's insurance broker or underwriter will have had no reason to know anything about how a court might assess the legal 'seaworthiness' of a vessel. Likewise, a shipowner's general counsel or its marine insurance broker or the suite of different insurers involved in any marine venture will not have had cause to consider matters pertaining to international aviation conventions or aviation laws in the multiple legal jurisdictions their vessels may traverse. One of the aims of this chapter is to shake up that perspective and provide stakeholders in each sector, as well as governments, regulators, and international representative bodies, with a means of at

74 There were many admirable predecessors in various countries, but McLean's version was the one that gained global uptake.

least recognising some 'red flags' as these two worlds of aviation and maritime come together with the use of drones.

To begin with, it will be useful to briefly canvass the relative weight of legal history in these diverse sectors.[75] This will provide some perspective as to tensions that may come to the fore when seeking to harmonize or even simply discuss laws across both sectors; the weight of inertia can be heavy and needs to be recognised to then be addressed.

The maritime sector can be as savage financially for its participants as the seas that are thrown at the vessels at its heart. Commercial margins are typically tight and considerable risk pervades every marine venture. So it has been for some 5,000 years when the first major maritime trade routes were established in the Arabian Sea between modern-day India/Pakistan and Kuwait/Iraq.[76] From roughly 1775 BC, the Babylonian King Hammurabi had carved onto a massive black stone pillar the 'Hammurabi Code',[77] one of the earliest written legal codes. Among others, it permitted the transfer of risk from sea merchants to moneylenders so that if goods were lost at sea, then the loans to the moneylenders would be expunged.[78] That was one of the earliest forms of marine insurance, with modern marine insurance as we now know it based off those roots and practices developed in the 13th and 14th centuries AD in Italian and mid-European cities fringing the North Sea and the Baltic.[79]

The development of these concepts of affraying risk ran in parallel with the development of the distinct legal jurisprudence of 'admiralty'. Early origins can be traced back to the ancient Mediterranean region, the most famous being the 'Rhodian Sea-Law' dating to the Eastern Roman or the Byzantine Empire, between AD 600 and AD 700 [80] itself based on maritime customary law originating from the island of Rhodes in even more ancient times in roughly 900 BC.[81] Following the age of the Viking seafarers from the late 8th to the late 11th centuries AD and the Norman conquest of England by William the Conqueror in 1066, in the 12th century AD, maritime law began to develop further from a base of European customary sea law. A collection of

75 As the primary author of this section of this chapter, I should point out that my co-author for this chapter, Professor Davies, confesses to have, as he puts it 'as little patience for references to the Rhodian Sea Law and the Rolls of Oléron as Hermann Göring supposedly did for culture'. No analysis of the history of maritime law, however, would be complete without it. Professor Davies points out that the Göring quotation he cites to is generally given as: 'When I hear the word "culture", I reach for my revolver'. He heartily explains, however, that the quotation is both apocryphal and mistranslated. He informs that it is also occasionally attributed to Heinrich Himmler or Joseph Goebbels, but if any of them ever said it, it was only by way of quotation. He points out that it is actually from a line from Act 1, Scene 1 of Hanns Johst's pro-Nazi play Schlageter, written in 1933, delivered by the character Friedrich Thiemann. The exact quotation is: 'Wenn ich Kultur höre . . . entsichere ich meinen Browning!' ('When I hear the word "culture", I remove the safety catch on my Browning!') That said, while Professor Davies may have grown weary of reading about the history of maritime law, I considered for the reasons stated herein that it provides some solid context for those who may be reading from an 'aviation' background. So, while Professor Davies may leapfrog these few paragraphs in any future reading, I hope you don't.

76 Stephen Gosch and Peter Stearns, *Premodern Travel in World History* (Routledge 2007) 12.

77 History.com Editors, 'Code of Hammurabi' <www.history.com/topics/ancient-history/hammurabi>.

78 'History of Insurance' <thismatter.com/money/insurance/insurance-history.htm>.

79 Dionysos Rossi, Robin Squires and Graham Walker, 'Marine Insurance' in Aldo Chircop, William Moreira, Hugh Kindred and Edgar Gold (eds), *Canadian Maritime Law* (2nd edn, Irwin Law 2016) 393–94.

80 Damien Cremean, *Admiralty Jurisdiction* (5th edn, Federation Press 2020) 2.

81 Robert Benedict, 'The Historical Position of the Rhodian Law' (1909) 18 Yale LJ 223, 223.

these laws committed to written form was known as the 'Rolls of Oleron', which were promulgated by Eleanor of Aquitaine in France in around 1160 and began to gain broad influence.[82] Her son, the English king Richard I (Richard the Lionheart), then adopted that collection of maritime laws in England at the end of the 12th century AD.[83] They were later codified in the 'Black Book of Admiralty' in England in 1336 in the reign of King Edward III.[84] At that time, Edward III was having difficulties with foreign sovereigns in connection with matters of state-backed piracy and spoil and is said to have created the English 'High Court of Admiralty' in about 1340 to deal with these matters outside of the jurisdiction of the English common law courts.[85] That jurisdiction derived not from the King but from the 'Lord High Admiral' who exercised the jurisdiction of the Crown over the seas.[86]

For the next 400 years, the admiralty jurisdiction in England grew separately from, and indeed in competition with, the jurisdiction of the common law courts. Jurisdictional clashes between the two were rife, leading to various legislated restrictions and re-directions of both jurisdictions over the centuries.[87] The Napoleonic Wars, culminating in the Battle of Waterloo in 1815, established England as the world's predominant maritime nation at that time. That fuelled the desire by England to have an established set of maritime laws to better serve its trading desires across the British Empire at the time.[88] As a result, modern maritime law in many countries, and not just those that were ever part of the British Empire, or latterly the Commonwealth, was based on England's early maritime laws. To this day, English maritime jurisprudence has a persuasive influence in courts exercising admiralty jurisdiction all over the world.

This is an embarrassingly brief discourse on matters pertaining to the rich history of maritime law[89] and might well seem out of place in a text dealing with drones as 'aircraft'. Indeed, many would be quick to point out that it is also somewhat biased to English maritime law, and there would be some truth in that. In a similar fashion, one could chart the evolution and impact of certain maritime law from China and France. Any deeper analysis of maritime law history would be out of place here, but the brief review provided here makes a point and sets some perspective, particularly for those reading with a classic 'aviation' perspective, namely that 'maritime' law is steeped in history with some of its origins literally carved into stone. To describe the commonality of 'maritime' law internationally as exhibiting 'harmonization' is to forget that the history of its development and spread has been charted over the centuries through crusades, wars, and naval battles that are household names, even if their significance to maritime law may not be known to many. Where the use of drones may result in a clash between classic 'aviation' law and 'maritime' law, care should be taken when

82 William Tetley, 'Maritime Liens in the Conflict of Laws' in James Nafziger and Symeon Symeonides (eds), *Law and Justice in a Multistate World: Essays in Honor of Arthur T von Mehren* (Brill 2002), 443.

83 Michael White, *Australian Maritime Law* (3rd edn, Federation Press 2014) 2.

84 ibid.

85 Cremean (n 80) 3.

86 ibid., and *The Longford* (1889) 14 PD 34, 37 (Lord Esher MR).

87 White (n 83) 2–4.

88 ibid 4.

89 Mirroring the depth of maritime history is the depth of truly scholarly works detailing that history. To provide a bit more context to this scant historical review, readers can find excellent and manageably short summaries in Cremean (n 80) 1–5 and White (n 83) 1–9.

addressing where change may be required. In essence, we are now only in the early stages of any established history of dedicated laws and regulation in respect of drones. While drones in some form or another have certainly been around for a few decades, and there has been some law promulgated in some countries concerning their operation for a short while, where we are now in terms of that law and regulation, even in countries such as England, Australia, and the United States, pales as compared to what will be required moving forward. When considering how to legislate and regulate drones in the maritime context, governments, regulators, and international representative organisations should carefully assess how any new laws with regard to drones will interact, not just with the body of 'aviation' law that dates largely from the first flight by the Wright brothers in 1903[90] but with 'maritime' law with its origins reaching back millennia.

A degree of harmonisation of laws internationally is clearly possible, as it has been separately with both maritime and aviation law to date. The work and thought leadership that has been done by the likes of ICAO in the aviation sector and the IMO in the maritime sector over decades is creditworthy. However, the challenge moving forward with the proliferation of the use of drones in the maritime sector is for both classic maritime and aviation sectors to come together in an attempt to chart a way forward that is acceptable to both. Even such cross-sector discussion itself is a considerable challenge, because at present, both sectors could be forgiven for thinking that the other sector already has matters under its classic bailiwick in hand. The reality is that it is not an accurate assumption one can make. That is not a criticism, rather an observation based on this author's experience operating simultaneously in both of these sectors and having engaged with government, regulators, insurers, brokers, and large commercial stakeholders in respect of issues arising with the use of drones. In the previous sections, we opined on the work being conducted by the IMO with regard to MASS and the need to amend numerous international legal instruments to accommodate the increasing commercial use of such vessels. A similar 'scoping exercise' should also urgently be commenced relative to the growing use of drones 'above the surface' in the maritime sector.

Use of drones in the maritime sector

The principal attraction of the use of drones to the maritime sector is no different to the attraction to many other sectors, but as discussed here, may be amplified. It is fuelled by three key benefits that the use of drones can achieve: (i) improvements to safety; (ii) reductions in risk; and (iii) the ability to reduce costs and/or create new revenue streams.

These key benefits perversely fuel some of the challenges. That is, taken at a global level, none of the inventors of drone technology, none of the users of that technology, and none of the corporates pivoting into the use of drones technology are bothering to wait for the promulgation of laws and regulation concerning that usage. By using drones, they are cutting their risks and improving safety, and it is positively impacting their financial bottom lines. As far as they are concerned, provided they are not

90 While aviation law had its earliest origins in France in 1784 in connection with the flights of balloons and the like, for the most part, significant legislation and regulation only followed the introduction of commercial flights circa 1919.

breaking any laws that is all they need to know. So, the current development of drones in the maritime sector, not dissimilar from most other sectors, is taking place in a vacuum of little applicable regulation.

Some of the ways airborne drones are being used in the maritime sector are:

(a) search and rescue, and shark monitoring;
(b) oil spill response;
(c) emissions and other environmental monitoring;
(d) detection of illegal fishing and drug trafficking;
(e) inspections and surveys of port structures, maritime navigational aids and offshore oil & gas and renewables infrastructure;
(f) vessel classification surveys;
(g) ship-to-shore transfers;
(h) pilotage;
(i) navigation;
(j) stevedoring;
(k) logistics

It is beyond the scope of this chapter to explore each of these topics in detail. That said, while the *uses* may vary and each may have certain unique challenges, there are certain broad underlying challenges that have the potential to impact them all. In the following, we will explain some of these uses and address some of the common themes in the legal challenges ahead.

Drones in ports

To state the obvious, ports are to global shipping and trade like international airports are to aviation. They are at its heart and they are big business. Many port operators globally are incorporating the use of drones into their operations to drive operational efficiencies and increase safety. Indeed, along with the use of MASS and other land-based autonomous vehicles, drones are revolutionising how ports will operate in the future. The use of drones in ports will provide a host of legal challenges and it would be prudent to start to consider these now.

Ship-to-shore transfers

In managing any large commercial vessel, it will often be necessary to order various deliverables from shore. This might include 'last mile deliveries' such as spare parts, parcels from the ship owners or documents, or other marine products. If a vessel is in the geographical limits of the port, this would normally be achieved by hiring a launch vessel and crew from the port for the delivery/pick-up. That requires scheduling time and can involve significant costs. Indeed, a call at port may not otherwise have been needed at all but for that deliverable, such that the entire visit could cost a significant sum, particularly when charter hire and running costs are considered. Various shipping agents are now offering to conduct these types of ship-to-shore services via the use of drones. While the size of the items being transported by drone between ship and shore has started small, the ambitions of the early movers in this space are large. One Singapore-based market leader, F-Drones, is developing a 'hyperlaunch heavy' drone that will be able to deliver a 100-kilogram payload over distances of up to 100 kilometres with the stated ambition of 80 per cent savings on cost, time, manpower, and carbon emissions for aerial transportation services to vessels and offshore platforms.[91] Another company, China-based Ehang, already has a drone for the logistics sector that can carry a payload of 200 kilograms for a distance of 35 kilometres.[92] Another company taking initiative in this space is Wilhelmsen, having successfully trialled ship-to-shore services in the Port of Singapore in 2018 and having completed hundreds of deliveries since.[93] Indeed, Singapore provides an example of where it has been necessary for aviation regulators to coordinate the use of drones with their maritime counterparts and where they have done so to date with aplomb.

As most readers would appreciate, there is a need to have drone exclusion zones around any airport site. The Wilhelmsen service was trialled from Marina South Pier Terminal in Singapore, which was originally in an aviation zone in which certain limited aviation such as kiters and parasails were permitted. It is only in proximity to a number of port anchorages. A good number of other anchorages, however, are located below airspace that is otherwise restricted due to its proximity to Changi International Airport and other air and military bases on the island. Some of these port anchorage sites are located in the direct flight path to Changi International Airport, with some within two kilometres of the end of the runway.[94] As the closure of Gatwick Airport due to a reported drone infringement in December 2018 evidenced, any airport closure as a result of the use of drones has the capacity to cause chaos and significant losses. The losses resulting from the closure of a major airport can quickly amount to tens of millions and could hit over US$100 million in just a couple of days. Indeed, Singapore also experienced its own airport interruptions from drones when Changi Airport was forced to close one runway for ten hours between 18 and 19 June 2019 with delays to 37 scheduled flights.[95]

Singaporean aviation regulators have been quick to recognise the increased usage of drones delivering maritime services in its restricted airspace and have been an early mover to embrace a cooperative approach with their maritime regulator counterparts and commercial stakeholders. In early 2019, this saw the Maritime and Port Authority of Singapore join with the Civil Aviation Authority of Singapore to create a 'Maritime Drone Estate' near Marina South Pier to permit the testing of maritime applications of drones in proximity to restricted airspace. The Singapore government referred to the estate as providing a 'regulatory sandbox' for the development of regulatory and safety standards for maritime drone applications.[96]

91 Harry McNabb, 'This Singapore Drone Company Wants to Reinvent Ship to Shore Delivery' <dronelife.com/2020/05/11/this-singapore-drone-company-wants-to-reinvent-ship-to-shore-delivery/>; F-Drones, 'F-Drones: Drones for Maritime Logistics' <f-drones.com>.

92 Ehang, 'Ehang's Smart Logistics Ecosystem' <www.ehang.com/Logistics/>.

93 Wilhelmsen, 'Pilot Launch in Singapore: Autonomous Drone Delivery of Parcels from Shore to Ship' <www.wilhelmsen.com/ships-agency/maritime-drone-delivery/>.

94 These risks were highlighted by Maurice Thompson in a presentation given in Singapore on 6 May 2019 titled 'Drones in the Maritime Sector: Enablers and Disrupters'.

95 Civil Aviation Authority of Singapore, 'Response to Media Queries on Drone Sightings in the Vicinity of Changi Airport' <www.caas.gov.sg/who-we-are/newsroom/Detail/response-to-media-queries-on-unauthorised-drone-sightings-in-the-vicinity-of-changi-airport>.

96 Zhaki Abdullah, 'Maritime Drone Testing Area to Be Set Up Near Marina South Pier' <www.straitstimes.com/singapore/transport/maritime-drone-testing-area-to-be-set-up-near-marina-south-pier>.

Singapore will not be alone in facing these challenges, with literally countless airports globally located within close proximity to major ports and commercial shipping channels. Indeed, many airport precincts worldwide actually abut port precincts.[97] The reason for the proximity may be related to the construction of airport precincts on reclaimed land near ports, or zoning and town-planning done decades ago when drones as we now know them were not even part of science fiction. It is also somewhat of a safety issue in itself, as having water close by mitigates somewhat against losses in the event of aircraft crashes in proximity to the airport.

Port facility inspections

One area in which drones have been widely used in ports and shipping is with regard to inspections. In order to maintain the safety and integrity of various port infrastructure and machinery, and indeed to comply with requirements for its insurance, frequent inspections and data collection are necessary. Typical structures or machinery may include wharves, piers, docks, sea walls, anchorage buoys, navigation beacons, ship building gantry cranes, ship-to-shore container cranes, etc. In a large port there could be tens of kilometres of wharves and sea walls and the area of the port itself might be from a few hundred square kilometres to the staggering 3,619 square kilometres of the Port of Shanghai. The size of some of the machinery used at ports also makes physical inspections time-consuming and dangerous. For example, gantry cranes large enough to straddle an entire container vessel or a newly built ship are simply massive. The largest of these are aptly named 'mega-ship cranes' with heights of up to 80 metres and spans of up to 140 metres. Large commercial ports may have 30–40 of these 'mega-ship cranes'. Because of the size and location of this infrastructure and machinery, carrying out physical inspections and collecting necessary data via 'boots on the ground' can be both dangerous and time-consuming. Furthermore, it is costly not just to account for the labour-hours and risk, but also because the machinery may need to be shut down for the duration of the inspection which can have significant financial implications in the 24/7, year-round commercial operations of a busy port. Drones are increasingly being used in ports to meet some of these challenges. Fitted with the necessary sensors and cameras, drones can capture pictures and videos in a fraction of the time, for a fraction of the cost, and with no risk to human life in its collection. This is also not restricted to above the water. Many of the port structures will have components both in and out of water and the technology is already available to deploy a single drone that can transition from aerial flight to underwater navigation in one continuous operation.[98] As will be dealt with later, such hybrid drones create further unique legal challenges consequent on whether they are deemed an 'aircraft' or a 'vessel/ship'.

Notwithstanding their positive uses, the use of drones in ports in certain scenarios can create new risks and dangers. An example is with regard to the storage or warehousing of some materials that can give off combustible dusts. These combustible

97 Readers may wish to look up the following airports on Google Maps to note the proximity: Brisbane Airport (Australia), Hong Kong International Airport, Dubai International Airport, Hamad International Airport (Doha), Aberdeen Harbour (Scotland), Belfast Harbour (Northern Ireland). There are countless more.

98 See SubUAS, 'Exploring a New Frontier: The Naviator' <https://thenaviator.com/>.

dusts can originate from a large number of organic or metal solid materials when they are ground into small particles, fibres, chips, fines, or chunks. Examples are dusts from some powdered metals, coal, coffee, cocoa, flour, grain, sawdust, and sugar. When these dusts are suspended in air with the right temperature and confinement, they can explode if exposed to a sufficient ignition source. Apart from a fire itself, ignition could be via a hot surface, machinery, friction, or electrostatic charge. Similar explosive atmospheres can arise in connection with the build-up of flammable gases like methane within a warehouse or tank. In some instances, there may be the potential for a mixture of both flammable gases and combustible dusts, such as with the storage of wood and agricultural products. Drones will have sources of ignition with their motors, electronics, and batteries and could cause the necessary friction for combustion if coming in contact with any metal structure, be it the walls of a wharf-side warehouse or the tank walls of the hold of a vessel. Most people globally today would have an appreciation of the risks of storing large quantities of combustible product at a port, following the devastating losses arising from the 4 August 2020 explosion of what is said to have been 2,750 tonnes of ammonium nitrate stored in a port warehouse in Beirut, which resulted in the death of 204 people, leaving 6,500 others injured, 300,000 homeless, and causing US$15 billion in property damage.

The British Ports Association (BPA) and Associated British Ports (ABP) are two other early movers to focus their attention on the future use of drones in their members' ports. BPA produced a significant whitepaper in November 2020 addressing the need to manage the risks and opportunities associated with the use of drones in ports,[99] while ABP has successfully embedded drone technology into its asset management practices and policies.[100]

Vessel surveys

Commercial shipping is one of the most regulated industries in the world and one of the earliest to implement international safety standards. By its nature, commercial shipping needs to be as international in its regulation as possible. If matters concerning navigational rules, standards of crew competence, and ship construction and maintenance were not subject to international regulation it would be detrimental to world trade. Key stakeholders would need to navigate countless potentially conflicting national regulations from the port at the commencement of a marine voyage in one country, potentially via multiple ports in multiple other countries, before the voyage was concluded perhaps in another country yet entirely. Equally, it would duplicate policing those standards to a degree that would be counterproductive. Cruise ships and cargo vessels on scheduled liner services internationally are quintessential examples.

99 Sara Walsh, 'Aerial Drones and Ports: Managing the Risks and Opportunities: A British Ports Association Briefing Paper' <mcusercontent.com/9fa5533f9884aad39ffc18f0e/files/184dac57-38d3-42e4-a298-186ff7bf9303/Aerial_drones_and_ports_BPA_briefing_paper_Nov_2020.pdf>.

100 Associated British Ports, 'New Drone Technology Transforms ABP's Asset Management, in Partnership with PWV and Aerodyne' <www.abports.co.uk/news-and-media/latest-news/2020/new-drone-technology-transforms-abp-s-asset-management-in-partnership-with-pwc-and-aerodyne/>; Dronelife, 'Drones in Ports and Shipping: The Next Big Market for the Industry?' <dronelife.com/2020/07/28/drones-in-ports-and-shipping/>.

To meet this international focus, the maritime industry is regulated by a number of international bodies including the aforementioned IMO, which is tasked as an agency of the United Nations to regulate the safety of vessels and the protection of the marine environment. The IMO sets standards via international diplomatic conventions which its member states then adopt and enforce via their national laws. Given the potential geographic range of service of any vessel over its lifetime and the possible myriad nationalities of its owners, despondent owners, and other charterers, all of which will likely be subject to multiple changes over the life of the vessel, responsibility for the enforcement of IMO regulations primarily rests with the vessel's 'flag state', the country in which the vessel itself is registered at any given time, as opposed to the nationality of its owner etc. A secondary layer of responsibility rests with 'port state control', which is the control that a country may exert on foreign vessels that enter or traverse its sovereign waters. Both the flag state and the port state will police these IMO requirements and the principal method of doing so is via regular mandated, and often directly ordered inspections and surveys of vessels. These surveys are typically undertaken by 'classification societies' or similar organisations. There are 12 of the former in the company of the 'International Association of Classification Societies' (IACS), and roughly 30 others offering various marine classification services, with the IACS member organisations classifying in the order of 90 per cent or more of the world's commercial shipping fleet.

While the layers of standard oversight provided by the likes of the IMO and port states rely on classification societies to assist in 'policing' these standards, the classification societies themselves do not enforce any rules or standards. It is a nuanced relationship in that the classification society will make recommendations to vessel owners on matters of maintenance and safety etc., which the vessel owner will need to comply with in order to ensure that the vessel will be confirmed to remain 'in class'. It is the vessel owner, however, who holds a non-delegable duty to maintain a 'seaworthy' vessel.[101] Without that endorsement from the classification society, the vessel's insurance may be compromised, or insurance may then be difficult or even impossible to obtain both for the vessel and any cargo to be carried on it. The lack of class certification could also be a breach of any charterparty itself, giving rise to the right of a charterer to terminate the charter party and sue the vessel owner or counterparty up the charter chain for damages. Further, failure to evidence class certification could result in access to ports and a country's territorial waters being limited or indeed prevented. Accordingly, classification surveys are vital to the maritime industry, shipping, modern trade and commerce. Classification societies and other organisations providing certain surveying services are increasingly using drone technology which has the potential to raise some legal issues.

Historically, inspections conducted on vessels have required the surveyor to be so close to the surface he is inspecting that he could nearly touch it. When contemplating an inspection of the bowels of a VLCC vessel, that requirement comes at a significant cost.

First, there may be rafting costs incurred in discharging oil-contaminated water from cargo tanks and ballasting the vessel by filling certain cargo tanks up with sea

101 *Koch Marine Inc v D'Amica Società di Navigazione ARL* (The Elena D'Amico) [1980] 1 Lloyd's Rep 75, 76 (Robert Goff J).

water, permitting surveyors to navigate the internal structure by raft. That initial discharge and the discharge after a rafting-based inspection are both sources of pollution which some port states will not permit. As a consequence, a vessel may need to empty those tanks in the open sea away from ports and shore, so that can add further days out of operation. It may also be necessary to ventilate tanks to permit surveyors to safely enter them. In LNG/LPG vessels, this might involve having to empty tanks of any methane gas and substituting with inert gases and oxygen.

Then there may be staging costs. These may involve constructing scaffolding within the tank and painstakingly moving that scaffolding around the structure or the placement of a cherry-picker vehicle within the structure itself. Staging costs will vary, of course, but could be in the vicinity of US$200,000 just for one tank in a VLCC. If a dry dock is involved, there will be yard costs as well. The costs of any single survey can therefore very quickly exceed US$1 million.

Then there is the risk of damage to the vessel's tank coatings and the like from the staging itself. That can lead to clean-up and reparation costs, noting that to take most cargoes on board the vessel will first need to present 'clean' tanks. All these steps involve manpower of differing expertise which is another cost, and finally, there are significant safety risks to all persons involved. Falling accidents are commonplace, rafting accidents can occur when the vessel is rolling, oxygen shortage or gas build-up can prove deadly, as can overheating with temperatures inside tanks frequently exceeding 50°C in the summer months in Middle Eastern ports in particular.

Safely preparing for and conducting such inspections can take considerable time which effectively adds to the cost when one considers the daily hire the vessel could otherwise be commanding or the demurrage costs being incurred during the inspection. These costs and risks can escalate even further when one is inspecting offshore vessels and structures. Consider, for example, the challenges in inspecting the underside of the main deck of a semi-submersible oil-rig, drillship, or jack-up rig. While day rates will vary, even on today's depressed rates, a day's downtime on such vessels could cost hundreds of thousands of dollars and the inspection could give rise to downtime of days, weeks, or even months. These vessel surveys give confidence to the vessel owners, any charterers, their respective financiers and any insurers, in addition to cargo interests and their insurers, as well as port states. That confidence enables the continuation of international trade and offshore exploration and exploitation. That said, as explained, they can be very expensive and attract significant risks to both the vessel and those involved in preparing for and conducting the inspection.

Enter drones, as a disruptive technology. IACS member DNV has been working with drones and drones technology companies since 2015 in an effort to utilise drones technology to improve the safety and efficiency of the inspection process.[102] Following test surveys in November 2015 on-board various classes of vessels (e.g. oil, chemical, gas, and bulk) and training surveyors in piloting drones, DNV conducted the first production survey on-board a chemical tanker in Norway in June 2016, shortly followed by a drone test survey of a jack-up unit in Dubai in January 2017, and then the first offshore drone survey of a semisubmersible off the coast of Norway in July 2017.

Since then, they and various other classification societies have conducted and overseen hundreds of drone production surveys around the world. The cost savings can

102 <www.dnvgl.com/services/drone-surveys-the-safer-and-smarter-way-103018>.

be significant, with the ability to do in a few hours with drones what might otherwise have taken days, or in a few days what might otherwise have taken weeks or months. Another benefit of using drones is that their movement and performance can be accurately tracked and logged, which means that the inspection process is more transparent.

The concept would appear simple enough: adapt a drone's software and hardware so that rather than having it physically configured to shoot video footage downwards, it can record footage in front of and above it, then add high-resolution zoom cameras and powerful lighting systems and encase it all in protective gear for the benefit of both the drone's payload and the structure being surveyed. However, while risks to both vessel and inspectors have been reduced along with survey times, staging costs, and environmental impact, and at the same time the quality of inspections has increased, as with the adoption of any new technology it has come with its own challenges.

One of the main challenges concerns the environments in which the drones must be operated in. For example, if inspecting the inside of the cargo hold of a large oil tanker, the drone would need to be flown possibly 30 metres away from the pilot in the dark and surrounded by thousands of tonnes of steel. That amount of steel can render useless the GPS, magnetic compass, and positioning support on many standard drones. When surveying offshore structures, there will be additional environmental factors, with the pilot often being in the order of 180 metres away from the drone and having to deal with severe wind and weather.

Now, consider the possibilities of autonomous drones; effectively the disrupter of the disruptive drones technology. The development of autonomous drones installed with artificial intelligence (AI) has the potential to yet again transform the quality assurance sector by stepping around the limitations of human pilots. Companies such as ADRASSO,[103] SwarmX,[104] and Scout Drone Inspection,[105] along with classification societies like DNV and ABB among others, and various universities worldwide,[106] are focussed on providing fully autonomous drone solutions. In June 2020, Scout Drone Inspection, working with DNV, was successful in inspecting a 19.4-metre-high oil tank on-board an FPSO vessel with the use of an autonomous drone fitted with AI.[107] The video footage captured by the drone was then interpreted in real time by an algorithm to detect cracks in the structure. Autonomous drones can also be fitted with Light Detection and Ranging (LiDAR) to navigate inside vessel tanks, where GPS navigation is problematic if not impossible when requiring the degree of precision necessary to conduct these inspections. DNV has also been developing AI to interpret video footage to not only identify cracks but also to detect anomalies below the surface such as corrosion and structural deformations. Autonomous drones, loaded with a 3D model of a vessel, could be tasked with conducting vessel sweeps without human intervention, programmed to stop at designated way points to take hi-resolution video

103 <www.dnvgl.com/research/review2018/featured-projects/adrasso-autonomous-drone-ship-surveys.html>.

104 <https://swarmx.com/>.

105 <www.scoutdi.com/>.

106 Notably the University of Bristol in the United Kingdom and the University of Trondheim in Norway.

107 DNV, 'Autonomous Drone Inspections Move Step Closer after Successful Test' <www.dnvgl.com/news/autonomous-drone-inspections-move-step-closer-after-successful-test-177264>.

footage and analyse it before the sweep itself has been completed.[108] All of a sudden, the need for staging with scaffolding or using rafts or climbing ropes to conduct inspections seems positively primitive.

The development of autonomous drones creates a further conundrum for regulators. First, they were expected to play 'catch-up' to grasp the need for different pilot competencies for flight in vastly different environments and to then regulate those pilots. Most regulators worldwide are still some distance from that level of development. Yet, before they are able to adapt to even meet that challenge, they are now faced with the disrupter that as quickly as they can mobilise to regulate pilot competencies, such efforts may be largely obsolete if autonomous drones are already a reality and growing in use.

With the development of this technology to facilitate autonomy and harness AI, the use of drones in the maritime sector will be but one development in many within the wholesale digitisation of the entire maritime industry. Evidence of the drive towards that goal can be seen in the June 2020 announced partnership of DNV and ABB to collaborate in developing a 'digitisation roadmap' to examine how the maritime industry can benefit from the greater availability of data, interconnectivity of systems, data analysis, and new technologies such as AI and machine learning.[109] A sector renowned for its resilience, the developments to date are already having positive impacts permitting more secure and sustainable operations.

Classification society challenges

While classification societies have been early movers in the adoption of drone technology, it could come at a price. Classification societies had their origins in the late 18th century, when marine insurers based at Lloyd's in London developed a system for the annual independent inspection of vessels' hulls and equipment presented to them for insurance cover.[110] Their origins were rooted in the notion that a vessel's seaworthiness was central to most vessel-related transactions.[111] Being in class does not imply, however, nor expressly warrant, the safety, fitness for purpose, or seaworthiness of a vessel.[112] It is merely an attestation that the vessel is in compliance with the standards that have been developed and published by the society issuing the classification certificate.

Originally, classification societies were independent, self-regulated organisations that worked with shipowners, shipbuilders, insurance companies, and flag states in matters relating to the construction, maintenance, and repair of vessels. As regards their independence, it was usually the case that they had no commercial interests related to ship design, ship building, ship ownership, ship operation, ship management, ship maintenance or repairs, insurance, or chartering. That classic role slowly

108 ibid.

109 Naida Hakirevic, 'DNV, ABB Team Up to Advance Maritime Digitalisation' <www.offshore-energy.biz/dnv-gl-abb-team-up-to-advance-maritime-digitalisation/>.

110 IACS, 'What are Classification Societies?' <www.iacs.org.uk/_pdf/Class%20monograph.pdf>.

111 Hannu Honka, 'The Classification System and its Problems With Special Reference to the Liability of Classification Societies' (1994) 19 Tulane Maritime Law Journal 1, 2.

112 *Sundance Cruises Corp v The American Bureau of Shipping (The Sundancer)* 7 F 3d 1077 (2nd Cir 1994).

evolved, however, to the point that whether a classification society was acting in a non-profit or profit-making capacity could impact what, if any, duties it owed to both those that engaged it and to third parties. That evolution saw many classification societies create succinct profit-making subsidiaries that provided, among others, consultancy services in connection with the requirements of classification. The benefit to shipowners in taking advantage of these classification consultancy services was they could take steps in advance of any required classification survey, to monitor and maintain their vessels pursuant to recommendations from the classification society, and therefore reduce the possibility that significant repairs or other action may be needed subsequent to the official survey. The impact of this development was that despite the early contention that classification societies were non-profit organisations that existed to provide services for the 'public interest', the financial interest often being developed brought their independence into some question.

That was a significant development, because classification surveys had been viewed as being of such importance to the maritime industry, shipping, modern trade and commerce that internationally there has been a historic reluctance on the part of courts to conclude that classification societies could owe a duty of care to principals or third parties in respect of its discharge of services.

The seminal English legal authority is *Marc Rich & Co AG v Bishop Rock Marine Co Ltd (The Nicholas H)*.[113] In *The Nicholas H*, the House of Lords was faced with the question of whether a classification society owed a duty of care to a third-party cargo interest arising from the alleged careless performance of a survey of a damaged vessel by a classification society which resulted in the vessel sailing and subsequently sinking.[114]

The court held that it would not be fair, just, and reasonable to impose such a duty of care on a classification society. Among others, the court held that:

(1) the recognition of such a duty would 'disturb the balance created by the Hague Rules and Hague-Visby Rules as well as by tonnage limitation provisions, by enabling cargo owners to recover in tort against a peripheral party to the prejudice of the protection of shipowners under the existing system'.[115]
(2) classification societies act in the public interest and were created 'for the sole purpose of promoting the collective welfare, namely the safety of lives and ships at sea', filling a role that would otherwise need to be fulfilled by States.[116] Recognition of such a duty could adversely affect the willingness of classification societies to continue providing their services;[117] and
(3) further to (2), recognition of such a duty would result in classification societies becoming potential defendants in many cases,[118] which would necessitate a further layer of insurance, complicate otherwise straightforward claims procedures between (for example) cargo interests and shipowners, and, again, could

113 [1996] AC 211 (hereafter *The Nicholas H*).
114 ibid 240 (Lord Steyn).
115 ibid 241.
116 ibid 242.
117 ibid.
118 The Court stated that NKK conducts approximately 14,500 surveys per year worldwide: ibid 241.

result in the classification societies becoming unwilling to conduct the necessary surveys.[119]

The approach adopted by the English courts was not born overnight in response to any particular set of facts or in respect of classification societies generally. It had its origins in the three-pronged interpretation developed via the judgements in *Anns v Merton London Borough Council*[120] through to the milestone English cases of *Donoghue v Stevenson*,[121] *Hedley Byrne & Co Ltd v Heller & Partners Ltd*[122] and *Dorset Yacht Co v Home Office*,[123] then affirmed and developed further in *Caparo Industries Plc v Dickman*.[124] That is, as held by the English Court of Appeal in *Reeman v Department of Transport*,[125] 'foreseeability, proximity of relationship and the question of whether it is fair, just and reasonable to impose a duty of care are matters which overlap and are really facets of the same thing'.

Nevertheless, *The Nicholas H* is not authority for the proposition that a duty of care will never be owed by a classification society towards a third-party claimant. The key to the English approach is that the public policy arguments militating against imposing a duty of care upon a classification society will always need to be balanced with the reasonable imposition of such a duty in any particular circumstance. As far as claims by third parties were concerned, the US courts took a different approach, with the United States Court of Appeals for the Fifth Circuit deciding, in *Otto Candies LLC v Nippon Kaiji Kyokai Corporation* (*Otto Candies*),[126] to hold a classification society liable to a third party for negligent misrepresentation. As *Otto Candies* was the first such successful claim in the United States, it was thought that it could result in a proliferation of claims in the United States against classification societies for alleged negligence and/or negligent misrepresentation. While that proved not to be the case, it goes to show the differing views internationally as to the original perceived effective immunity of classification societies.

The adaptation and use of drones by classification societies could see a further erosion of that bubble of immunity. Indeed, with this possibility in mind, some classification societies are rethinking their strategies of implementation of this technology.

One of the problems faced by classification societies globally has been the lack of sufficient regulation of the drones sector to date. This is a problem because while one can safely assume that a classification society will have expert marine surveyors, as it pivots into services utilising drones, various questions may be raised. For example: (i) will it also have expert drones pilots?; (ii) will those drones pilots be employees or contractors?; (iii) which body is responsible for certifying the pilot and the analyst?; (iv) who is certifying the safety and integrity of the drone itself?; (v) are those certification companies themselves being appropriately regulated?; (vi) what is the competency of the analyst reviewing any drones survey footage (noting that 2D video

119 *The Nicholas H* (n 113) 241.
120 [1978] AC 728, 751.
121 [1932] AC 562, 580.
122 [1964] AC 1129.
123 [1970] AC 1004, 1027.
124 [1990] 2 AC 605, 617.
125 [1997] 2 Lloyd's Rep 648, 677.
126 346 F3d 530 (5th Cir 2003).

visuals, no matter the clarity, will suffer from a lack of depth)?; (vii) alternatively, is the video being analysed by AI algorithms, and if so, who has certified that as an analytical tool? Questions of this type should be kept in mind by all, including classification societies. Particularly, at this early stage of the drones revolution when companies are popping up everywhere claiming to have a point of difference over their many competitors. Basically, absent appropriate levels of regulation, assessing competencies becomes very difficult.

Accordingly, seeking to pivot into this 'aviation' type scenario, alien to the 'marine' scenario can raise further challenges for classification societies. While the likes of DNV and ABB might be market leading and well tested in their use of drones in their services, what of the capabilities of other classification societies not as advanced in their development in this space? In an attempt to pivot their 'marine' offering to absorb these 'aviation' opportunities, some classification societies could expose themselves to contractual and tortious duties of care they may not previously have been exposed to.

Drone-assisted pilotage

As explained earlier, the lack of any harmonised regulation of pilotage, either nationally within many countries or internationally, may prove to be a profound legal obstacle to the introduction of autonomous and remotely controlled ships. There is a further overlay of possible difficulties when contemplating the use of drones in the provision of pilotage services to any vessels, let alone MASS.

As anyone who has boarded a large bulk carrier or container vessel via a Jacob's ladder while at sea will attest, be they a vessel pilot, a marine surveyor, a maritime lawyer, or other, it can be fraught with life-threatening danger. For the uninitiated, it can involve having to jump from the bow of a pilot boat onto a wood and rope Jacob's ladder loosely resting against the side of the vessel to be boarded. The jump must be timed precisely to take account of the rise and fall of the pilot vessel on the ocean swell relative to the vessel to be boarded. That can be precarious enough, and when you do get onto the ladder, you might then have a 10–20 metre vertical climb in the elements. It can be physically challenging for the most able-bodied. It is labour-intensive and costly. The pilot boat will typically have a crew of two, and the vessel to be boarded will need to deploy crew to assist in the receipt of the pilot. That cost and risk needs to be taken even before the pilot actually commences to provide the actual pilotage services. Traditional pilotage services are also challenged by limitations in visibility. The pilot will usually operate from the vessel's bridge or bridge wing and could be some 200–300 metres from the vessel's bow on a large vessel. Visibility may be further impaired by the vessel's cargo, particularly on a container vessel. The pilot may also need to contend with fog or heavy smog. Accordingly, notwithstanding their local knowledge of the port they are operating in, manoeuvring a large vessel into port and onto its berth can be difficult. Add to this, that while the size of vessels has continued to increase, most ports (or at least their channels) have not grown in proportion. As a result, margins of error decrease. The importance of pilotage services cannot be overemphasised. When errors are made, the impact can be significant. Leaving aside the possibility of loss of life and damage to property, if a large vessel runs aground in a main channel in or approaching a port, it could result in the suspension of all shipping traffic to and from the port with significant economic consequences.

Various ports have been trialling the use of shore-based pilotage services with the assistance of drones. Fremantle Port in Australia has been at the forefront of seeking to embrace these innovations. In recent years, it has permitted companies such as leading classification society DNV NDMS and global marine and engineering consultancy London Offshore Consultants to test various shore-based pilotage services. Both companies independently engaged with specialist drones service company Global Unmanned Systems. The results are impressive and plain to see from the high-resolution drone video footage they both provide access to online.[127] Situational awareness for the pilot and vessel's master is greatly improved with the drone providing live streaming to the drone pilot and marine consultant from their shore station, as well as to the vessel's master and any tug. The live streaming provided to any tug also enables it to better anticipate in advance when its services may be required. Taking up a position high above the stern, the drone is able to deliver a 'bird's eye view', but can then be moved off to provide a more 'profile' view to showcase the space forward and aft of the vessel. Any changes in clearance can be quickly noted and countermeasures can be adopted where needed. The drone footage also enables the tug to better balance the provision of the necessary pushing forces. The improved communications, with visuals, mean that blind estimations can be greatly reduced. When margins for error are so small, these developments are welcomed. The video can then be automatically saved for training purposes or as a record of evidence in the event there should be an incident requiring investigation. Challenges with the vast array of vessel operating and communications systems can be combatted by delivering (again via drone) a communications package to the vessel (e.g. iPad, GNSS, communications headsets, etc.).

While reducing certain risks and costs, however, drones-assisted pilotage would not be infallible. Most current drones have operating and manoeuvrability limitations in certain weather events such as rain, wind, extreme heat and cold, and visibility. The drones would ordinarily incorporate two cameras to enable them to maintain position relative to the vessel while simultaneously providing live streaming to the drone pilot. Both cameras would have their own limitations in terms of the previously mentioned weather events and their own design and manufacturing limitations. The batteries used in the drones (as with all current-generation batteries) would have limitations such that there would need to be procedures for the ready identification of failing power and an ability to manually change batteries while maintaining coverage. Communications would also be dependent on the strength and integrity of Wi-Fi and radio links.

The development of drones-assisted pilotage and the aforementioned limitations raise some legal issues for the vessel owner. A tenent of maritime law in most countries is that while the pilot may provide the vessel's master with advice, the master remains responsible for the vessel's navigation and handling. Historically, as a matter of common law at least, vessel owners were liable for the negligence of a pilot that had been engaged voluntarily[128] but not if the use of the pilot was compulsory.[129] As ports developed into important commercial businesses in their own right, facilitating

127 London Offshore Consultants in conjunction with Global Unmanned Systems <www.youtube.com/watch?v=GZbrknKXCmc&feature=youtu.be>; DNV NDMS in Conjunction with Global Unmanned Systems <https://dnvgl-15.wistia.com/medias/zrfof5ggoi>.

128 *The Eden* (1846) 2 W Rob 442; 166 ER 822; *Steamship Beechgrove Co Ltd v Aktieselskabet Fjord of Kristianaia* [1916] 1 AC 364 (HL).

129 *The China* 74 US 53; 2002 AMC 1504 (1868).

trade, this distinction was removed in many countries in the 19th and 20th centuries. As a consequence, if damage was caused by a vessel during compulsory pilotage, the vessel owner would also be held liable.[130]

In begrudgingly accepting this position, one would imagine that vessel owning interests would have noted that most modern ports, operating as sophisticated commercial or government-controlled enterprises, would have well-experienced local marine pilots and systems. However, similar to the earlier discussion with regard to classification societies and the use of drones, questions may be raised as to the acceptability of drones-assisted pilotage when those services may be provided by either port employees or contractors who do not have the same level of expertise as the common marine pilot discharging pilotage services in the classic manner. Whereas limitations on pilotage in the classic sense centre largely around the pilot's training and experience of the port, communication abilities, eyesight, and judgement, with drones-assisted pilotage, one is introducing variables not previously contemplated that have their own limitations. For instance, the design and manufacture of the drone; the training of the drone pilot with regard to both the flight of the drone and the ability to understand communications that may have an 'admiralty' slant; the adequacy and integrity of Wi-Fi and batteries, etc. Notwithstanding the eventual potential positives of drone-assisted pilotage, the negatives for a vessel owner could be in these considerable new variables. In circumstances where the vessel owners will be liable for losses caused by any negligence in the provision of the pilotage services, it will be interesting to see how this potential increased risk to the vessel owner is dealt with.

Drone-assisted pilotage could also impact time charterers. Unless the charterparty provides otherwise, the obligation to send the vessel to a safe port or berth is an absolute one on the part of the charterer, which is breached if the port or berth is unsafe, whether or not the charterer was aware of that fact, or could have done anything about it. Some charterparties will alternatively impose the lesser obligation to exercise due diligence to ensure the vessel is sent only to safe ports, but if the port ultimately proves unsafe, the question of due diligence does not arise. Consider the classic definition of 'safe port' made by Sellers LJ in *The Eastern City*:[131]

> A port will not be safe unless, in the relevant period of time, the particular ship can reach it, use it and return from it without, in the absence of some abnormal occurrence, being exposed to danger which cannot be avoided by good navigation and seamanship.

An event will be 'abnormal' unless it happens sufficiently frequently for it to be regarded as a normal characteristic of the port.[132] Safety is also a relative term, in the

130 For example, in Australia the distinction was removed by the introduction of s.410B(2) in the *Navigation Act 1912* (Cth) by s.195 of the *Navigation Act 1958* (Cth), modelled on s.15(1) of the *Pilotage Act 1913* (UK). The Australian position is now consolidated by s.326(3) of the *Navigation Act 2012* (Cth).

131 *Leeds Shipping Co v Societe Francaise Bunge (The Eastern City)* [1958] 2 Lloyd's Rep 127 at 131, quoted with approval in *Kodros Shipping Corp of Monrovia v Empresa Cubana de Fletes (The Evia) (No 2)* [1983] AC 736 at 749, 750, 756, 768.

132 *K/S Penta Shipping A/S v Ethiopian Shipping Lines Corp (The Saga Cob)* [1992] 2 Lloyd's Rep 545 at 550–51 (CA); *Gard Marine & Energy Ltd v China National Chartering Co Ltd (The Ocean Victory)* [2017] UKSC 35, [2017] 1 Lloyd's Rep 521.

sense that it is concerned with the safety of the port for the particular vessel that has been chartered. A port may be safe for some ships, but not for others, depending on their size and other characteristics. Where shore-based drone-assisted pilotage services are provided in circumstances where the provision of pilotage services is compulsory, then given the possible limitations mentioned earlier, the question could well be asked in the future as to whether such services provided by a port might render the port a danger to certain vessels.

Competing limits of liability

This topic has the potential to impact many uses of drones in the maritime sector and will likely cause some consternation amongst vessel owners, charterers, and the full suite of marine insurers who underwrite any marine venture. Simply put, by engaging drones in their operations could see them lose their current limitations of liability.

For the benefit of readers from each of the 'aviation' and 'maritime' sectors, some context will assist. Under various international conventions ratified by signatory nations and, where necessary, adopted into the signatory's legislation, vessel owners are able to limit their liability in a manner connected with the gross tonnage (i.e. the size) of the vessel involved in certain losses.[133] The purpose of the scheme limiting vessel owners' liability can be stated frankly:

> The policy evident in [limitation provisions] is the protection of the owner engaged in the maritime carrying trade from financial ruin where his vessel causes damage of the prescribed kind.[134]

Limitation of this kind is virtually unique to maritime law. The United Kingdom introduced its first statute limiting a ship owner's liability in 1734,[135] and it is clear that the shipping industry was singled out for this overt protectionism because of its importance to the British economy. Invisible exports such as shipping freight and marine insurance accounted for about three-quarters of the value of British-produced exports until well into the 20th century.[136] The importance of shipping trade to the national economy was openly cited as a reason for introducing limitation of liability for ship owners. The preamble to the first limitation statute began:

> [W]hereas it is of the greatest consequence and importance to this Kingdom, to promote the increase of the number of ships and vessel, and to prevent any

133 International Convention Relating to Limitation of the Liability of Owners of Sea-Going Ships 1957 (signed at Brussels on 10 October 1957); Convention on the Limitation of Liability for Maritime Claims 1976 (signed at London on 19 November 1976); 1996 Protocol to amend Convention on the Limitation of Liability for Maritime Claims 1976.

134 *China Ocean Shipping Co v South Australia* (1979) 145 CLR 172 at 185 per Barwick CJ, quoted in *Strong Wise Ltd v Esso Australia Resources Pty Ltd (The APL Sydney)* (2010) 185 FCR 149; [2010] 2 Lloyd's Rep 555 at 561 [31] per Rares J.

135 *Responsibility of Shipowners Act 1734*. See M Thomas, 'British Concepts of Limitation of Liability' (1979) 53 Tulane Law Review 1205 at 1206.

136 See W Ashworth, *An Economic History of England 1870–1936* (Routledge 1969) 153.

discouragement to merchants and others from being interested and concerned therein.[137]

So, the basic tenets of a ship owner's limitation of liability are that the liability will be 'limited' and that the standard will be one of 'negligence'.

This can be contrasted with how limitation of liability developed in the context of aviation law. Following World War I, when the commercial aviation sector slowly started to gather some momentum, concepts of travel by air conflicted with conventional legal principles of privacy and trespass to property. While the *Paris Convention 1919*[138] had recognised the principle of exclusive air sovereignty to nations, there remained tension between the aviation sector wanting the right to fly across private property and the property owners' concerns as to damage to their properties from incidents arising from such overflight. This was born out of even earlier notions that land ownership included rights to the subsoil as well as all airspace above the land. Such notions were eventually dismissed in the United States in 1936[139] and in the United Kingdom in 1978,[140] but before that the international community attempted to address this tension by virtue of a number of conventions, namely the *Rome Convention 1933*,[141] the *Rome Convention 1952*,[142] and the *Montreal Protocol*.[143] None of these enjoyed widespread ratification, with the likes of the United States, China, the United Kingdom, Germany, and Japan being notable abstentions.

Broadly speaking, these conventions provided that an 'operator'[144] of an aircraft would be held strictly liable for damage to property on land caused directly by an aircraft in flight, with such liability limited by a formula depending on the weight of the aircraft. Unlike in the maritime context, the limitation to the liability was in fact what many countries found objectionable as the liability limits were considered to be too low. Two further attempts have been made at convention level in an effort to achieve some degree of harmonisation, with both referred to collectively as the *Montreal Conventions 2009*.[145] The principal changes proposed by the *Montreal Conventions 2009* were that the 'operator' of an aircraft would be required to carry acceptable insurance against such damage and that if negligence was proven, the liability would be unlimited. Unfortunately, 12 years on from those two conventions, the number of ratifications is still a long way off either of them achieving the numbers to formally come into effect.

137 M Thomas, 'British Concepts of Limitation of Liability' (1979) 53 Tulane Law Review 1205 at 1206.

138 Convention Relating to the Regulation of Aerial Navigation (Paris, 13 October 1919).

139 *Hinman v Pacific Air Transport*, 84 F.2d 755 (9th Cir. 1936).

140 *Bernstein of Leigh (Baron) v Skyviews & General Ltd* [1978] 1 QB 479.

141 International Convention for the Unification of Certain Rules relating to Damage Caused by Aircraft to Third Parties on the Surface (Rome, 29 May 1933).

142 Convention on Damage Caused by Foreign Aircraft to Third Parties on the Surface (Rome, 7 October 1952).

143 Protocol to amend the Convention on Damage Caused by Foreign Aircraft to Third Parties on the Surface (Montreal, 23 September 1978).

144 The owner of an aircraft is deemed to be the operator unless it is proved that another party had sole operational control over the aircraft.

145 (i) The Convention on Compensation for Damage by Aircraft to Third Parties in the Case of Unlawful Interference; (ii) The Convention on Compensation for Damage by Aircraft to Third Parties.

Against this persistent backdrop of a lack of international harmonisation, countries have developed their own legislation to deal with the risks of damage done on the surface by aircraft in operation. In many instances, that legislation mirrors the proposed developments in the *Montreal Conventions 2009* or goes one step further. An example is the Australian *Damage by Aircraft Act 1999* (Cth). Pursuant to ss.10 and 11 therein, the concepts of strict and unlimited liability are applied for damage caused on the surface by any impact by an aircraft in operation or by something that is the result of such an impact (e.g. a fire following an aircraft impact).

So broadly speaking, a ship owner's or operator's liability for damage caused by a ship may be 'limited' and with a standard of 'negligence', whereas an aircraft owner's or operator's liability for damage caused by an aircraft will be 'unlimited' and with a standard of 'strict liability'.

This very large potential difference in liability will be a concern to vessel owners, charterers, and their P&I insurers in connection with the use of drones on board vessels, as if a vessel owner or charterer is deemed to fall within the relevant legislation's definition of 'owner' or 'operator', then potentially they could face strict liability and be liable for unlimited liability.[146] By way of example, the Australian *Damage by Aircraft Act 1999* (Cth) adopts definitions that go to the 'use' of the aircraft, with tests dependent on which party retains "control of its navigation" and who has 'an active role in the operation'. Arguably, even if an owner or charterer engaged a third-party provider of drone services, they could still be held liable under the relevant aviation legislation. The authors have noted a number of member alerts from P&I Clubs in which the owners/operators are encouraged to work with any third-party drone service provider to 'draw up a detailed risk assessment' and "apply the necessary controls to mitigate the risk', including 'flight planning and a thorough risk assessment'. The conundrum is that while this would appear eminently sensible, the very act of doing so could see the vessel interests deemed an 'operator' and at risk of being held jointly and severally liable with the third party in the event of losses caused by the drone.

Some may scoff at the suggestion a drone could do any significant damage to warrant this being of any concern. It would be a mistake to limit one's consideration of these risks of damage by drones in the maritime context to the risks posed by the size of drones currently being used for the likes of vessel hold surveys and ship-to-shore transfers. This mirrors a mistake currently being made by governments and regulators internationally. In short, they are not thinking and planning 'big' enough. Further to the previous discussion, consider that commercial drones that can carry payloads of 200 kilograms are already in operation. Also note that companies are already conducting considerable R&D to produce drones that can carry ten-tonne, 40-foot shipping containers distances of some 700 kilometres.[147] That could comprehensively revolutionise the maritime and freight industries. Indeed, it could revolutionise the commercial ports space entirely, as changes to stevedoring could then see 'mega-ship cranes' reduced to scrap metal. Indeed, in 50 years' time there might not be the same need for a container vessel to call at a port to load or unload containers at all. Such developments could significantly impact the current constructs of the international

146 The Australian *Damage by Aircraft Act 1999* (Cth) adopts definitions that go to the "use" of the aircraft, with tests dependent on which party retains "control of its navigation" and who has "an active role in the operation".

147 <http://internationalfreightdrone.org/>.

carriage of goods by sea. Where we have had the ocean carrier's obligations ending first at the ship's rail, and then latterly a container yard, an ability to remove a container from a vessel and seamlessly fly it to the customer's premises perhaps hundreds of kilometres away could then further shake up the current usage of the Hague Rules, Hague-Visby Rules, and Hamburg Rules.

It is also notable that one of the main drones being used to 'sniff-out' sulphur-oxide rule breakers as part of the policing of the IMO 2020 regulations in some of the world's leading ports is the Skeldar V-200 drone, which is 4 metres long, weighs 235 kilograms, and can fly at speeds of 150 kilometres per hour. It is not inconceivable that a drone of that size, let alone those contemplated to carry ten-tonne containers, dropping from a considerable height or colliding at significant speed could cause considerable damage and spark a fire and/or an explosion, etc.

Similar concerns as to how drones could see vessel owners and operators exposed to greater risks are seen in the context of vessel surveys, for classification surveys, and for drone-assisted pilotage.

Conclusion

One of the principal difficulties for the authors in this chapter was to choose what to include and what not to. In the authors' view, the development of autonomous methods of transportation will give rise to many legal issues and it simply has been beyond the scope of this chapter to delve into all of them here. Many countries' governments and various international regulatory bodies and organisations are seeking to examine how this technology will impact their own sectors and care should be taken to seek to ensure that there is some synergy across sectors, lest developments in the laws in respect of one sector cut across or negatively impact another sector. A topic not covered separately in this chapter illustrates one such dilemma: 'splash drones'. That is, drones that can seamlessly transition from flying above the surface, to operating on the surface, to operating below the surface. Such drones are ideal for tasks in the offshore oil and gas and ports sectors among others. The question then becomes whether it is an 'aircraft' or a 'ship' or a 'vessel' or a 'vehicle' at any given time, because aviation law and admiralty law generally developed around law making with regard to the 'object'. It may be that such thinking needs to be altered to think more along the lines of the 'operation' of the object, or broader still, the 'principal venture' in which the object is engaged. Various marine insurance legislation internationally centres around the concept of a 'marine venture' and there will be the need to address how that branch of law is impacted and potentially adapted for the age of the drones and autonomous vehicles.

It is hoped that this chapter may give rise to some collaborative discussions between the relevant thought leaders, governments, regulators, and international organisations in each of the aviation and maritime sectors as to how drones and autonomy should best be managed moving forward. There is currently no clear separation of these issues between the two sectors, and while this chapter may be the first of its kind internationally to raise these issues, it will certainly not be the last.

6 The urban environment

Patrick Slomski and Jess Harman

Introduction

This chapter sets out an overview of the use of drones in the urban environment, focusing on historic and current trends as well as on the opportunities, risks and barriers going forward. This subject is detailed and technically complex, involving a multitude of technical and operational issues. Links and references are provided in the endnotes, which should provide a route into that detail, for the interested reader.

As a starting point consideration of what is to be understood by "urban" in this context must be addressed. While that word is commonly used in discussion of drone activities, some caution is required. In land use and development law,[1] the word and its equivalents may variously connote areas designated by local or national government,[2] areas having certain population densities or agglomerations of buildings or the localities of administrative or commercial importance.[3]

In the field of aviation regulation, "urban" corresponds more closely with those areas designated as "congested"[4] or within which the spacing of buildings and other man-made structures makes the operation of aircraft outside defined separation minima[5] challenging or impossible; unless indicated otherwise in this chapter, "urban" will connote areas having those characteristics. That choice is appropriate not least because many aviation regulations of relevance are widely applicable regardless of the geographical area's status under land use and development law.

As a broad generalisation, the limited capabilities and maturity of drone technology have previously led States (through regulation and their civil aviation authorities) to seek to ensure an acceptable level of safety by means of segregating drone operations from people, vehicles, vessels and buildings (and other man-made structures) on the ground and from other aircraft (manned and unmanned).

1 Including "planning law". See the following discussion.

2 For example, see, 23 U.S.C § 101 (2011) (definitions "Urbanization" and "Urban").

3 For example, see, the definitions used in different States, as summarised in the United Nations, Department of Economic and Social Affairs, 'UN Demographic Yearbook' (70th edn, Report, 2020) <https://unstats.un.org/unsd/demographic-social/products/dyb/index.cshtml#:~:text=Demographic%20Yearbook%20System%20The%20United%20Nations%20Statistics%20Division,social%20statistics%20on%20a%20wide%20range%20of%20topics>.

4 For example, see, in relation to any city, town or settlement, . . . any area which is substantially used for residential, industrial, commercial or recreational purposes, The Air Navigation Order 2016, sch 1.

5 See discussion of the separation minima, later.

Consideration of manned aircraft is relevant in the aforementioned sense, because while cruising passenger aeroplanes will use airspace that is well above buildings, it is not uncommon for helicopters to fly to and from commercial heliports and hospital helipads located within urban areas. Police helicopters and air ambulance flights operate at low levels within such areas. It is also to be noted that there are numerous cities hosting airports, examples including London City Airport in the United Kingdom and Sao Paulo's Conghonas Airport in Brazil. The risks presented by drones at aerodromes and to manned aircraft are discussed in Chapter 8.

The default position in many States has involved prohibition of the operation of drones above an altitude ceiling[6] or near[7] or over buildings, highways and concentrations of people. That tends to restrict drone operation in urban environments. Many civil aviation authorities have discretionary powers to permit drone operations within those areas upon demonstration of a suitable safety case. While the regulatory regimes vary considerably by State and are evolving, typically such permission will be restricted to small volumes of airspace within the urban environment and be limited so as to ensure a small number of drones within those volumes.

These limitations contrast with the aspirations of an increasing number of commercial, State and public authority operators which, taken together, would see a large population of drones across extended areas of the urban environment. The realisation of those aspirations will require the evolution of technology, infrastructure, services (for example, traffic management) and regulation to support the operation of the drone population. This work is written at a time when significant progress has been made, but much remains to be achieved in defining the requirements and developing the technology and infrastructure to meet them.

Drone operation in the urban environment

The opportunities for, and the benefits of, drone use across extended urban areas are too numerous and diverse to list and detail, but include retail and consumables delivery services,[8] healthcare delivery and emergency response services[9] and monitoring

6 Typically set at 400–600 feet from the surface, the precise minimum varying by State and possibly location therein.

7 Typically, within 30–100 metres measured laterally, where the buildings are not under the control of those operating the drone and the people are not involved in the operation of the drone, the precise minimum varying by State and possibly location therein.

8 Some examples: Rakuten Media Room, 'Rakuten Successfully Completes Japan's 1st Drone Delivery Demonstration Flight in Mountainous Region' (*TelecomTV*, 18 September 2020) </www.telecomtv.com/content/emerging-tech/rakuten-successfully-completes-japan-s-1st-drone-delivery-demonstration-flight-in-mountainous-region-39704/>; Ilker Kokal, 'Amazon's Prime Air Drone Delivery Service Gets FAA Approval' (*Forbes*, 31 August 2020) <www.forbes.com/sites/ilkerkoksal/2020/08/31/amazons-prime-air-drone-delivery-service-gets-faa-approval/>.

9 Some examples: Solent Transport, 'Drones Will Be Used to Transport Medical Supplies across the Solent to Support the Response to COVID-19' (*Solent Transport*, 27 April 2020) <https://solent-transport.com/news/item/drones-will-be-used-to-transport-medical-supplies-across-the-solent-to-support-the-response-to-covid-19>; Lora Kolodny, 'Zipline, Which Delivers Lifesaving Medical Supplies by Drone, Now Valued at $1.2 Billion' (*CNBC*, 17 May 2019) <www.cnbc.com/2019/05/17/zipline-medical-delivery-drone-start-up-now-valued-at-1point2-billion.html#:~:text=Zipline%2C%20a%20drone-delivery%20start-up%2C%20is%20now%20valued%20at,of%20hard-to-reach%20health%20clinics%20in%20Rwanda%20and%20Ghana>.

of infrastructure (for example, road or rail). Currently, operations or demonstrations within such use categories take place over rural areas and low-density populations. There is also the prospect of flying taxi services.[10]

Uses within a more contained area include property survey (for example, by estate agents or engineers), cinematography, entertainment and sporting events coverage and localised law enforcement activities. Localised and limited operations of this kind are permitted by numerous (although not all) civil aviation authorities upon demonstration of a suitable safety case.

The advantages promised by drone use are considerable and varied.[11] In general terms, many tasks that traditionally require direct human inspection or manned aircraft may be undertaken by drones more safely, efficiently, at lower financial cost and with reduced environmental footprint. As an example, efficiency gains have led to widespread use of drones in the inspection of elevated and large-scale structures (including power and telephone cables, pylons and large-scale industrial complexes such as oil and gas facilities). A drone may gain closer proximity to a structure than an aircraft and expedite inspections that would otherwise involve human inspectors climbing and navigating their way around the structure.[12]

The localised use of drones by law enforcement agencies for surveillance from the air is becoming routine in many States, at a fraction of the cost of operating manned aircraft and reducing the risk to flying personnel inherent in low-altitude flying in a congested environment.[13]

Considerations such as these point convincingly to commercial and societal benefits attainable by the widespread deployment of a variety of drones for different purposes in the urban environment.

Risks of urban navigation

The risks associated with drone activities in the urban environment relate primarily, but not exclusively,[14] to the increased likelihood of physical collision and the resulting harm to people in buildings or on the ground, as well as property damage. In essence, this increased risk results from the concentration of buildings, other man-made structures and people in that environment. Assuming that drone use will proliferate in this environment, it is also necessary to consider the risk of collision or interference between drones (confliction).

10 See the following discussion.

11 For a discussion on opportunities offered by drone use in the United Kingdom, see Nesta's "Flying High" report published in July 2018: Nesta, 'Flying High: The Future of Drone Technology in UK Cities' (Report, July 2018) <www.nesta.org.uk/report/flying-high-challenge-future-of-drone-technology-in-uk-cities/>.

12 The use on offshore oil and gas industry structures provides a useful illustration. See, for example, John Wood, 'Role of Drones Expanding over Offshore Installations' (*Offshore*, 2 January 2018) <www.offshore-mag.com/field-development/article/16755873/role-of-drones-expanding-over-offshore-installations>.

13 For an interesting discussion of drone use by police in the United States, see Police Executive Research Forum, 'Drones: A Report on the Use of Drones by Public Safety Agencies—and a Wake-Up Call about the Threat of Malicious Drone Attacks' (Report, 2020) <www.policeforum.org/index.php?option=com_content&view=article&id=63:online-documents-alphabetical&catid=20:site-content>.

14 Other risks include radio frequency interference, noise and nuisance. See the following discussion.

Risk of physical collision may materialise from malfunction or failure of the drone in flight resulting in loss of lift and its consequent fall; or because of the drone failing to navigate obstacles (which may be stationary or moving).

The risks following malfunction or failure and the fall of the drone may be addressed by limits on one or more of the drone's mass, speed and altitude, since those limit the kinetic energy of an impact with a person or property.[15] However, such limits may well prove to be too restrictive on the proposed uses, for example, the delivery of retail goods by drone. Some technological mitigations and protections are also available in respect of such risks. The simplest example is perhaps the use of a parachute, deployed by the drone in the event that it loses propulsion (and so lift). Another rather obvious but important technological factor derives from assurance of the reliability of the drone's power and propulsion systems. There are likely to be limitations accompanying an operator's dependence on such mitigations and protections when their reliability has not yet been demonstrated so as to satisfy civil aviation authorities that a sufficient level of safety is assured in this environment.[16]

The risks relating to navigation of the drone through a congested urban environment are potentially more challenging. As noted earlier, there will be areas of the urban environment within which it is either difficult or impossible for the drone to operate in accordance with separation minima. The operator will typically then be required to obtain permission to operate within such minima, resulting in restrictions on the location and scope of operations. Further, flight of drones over an extended urban area will in many instances involve operation beyond visual line of sight (BVLOS) of the pilot.[17]

BVLOS operations have been permitted in segregated volumes of airspace in non-urban environments. In non-segregated airspace, BVLOS operation will require an acceptable form of "detect and avoid" system ("D&A").[18] The first element ("Detect") of such a system must identify potential collision with obstacles (moving or stationary). Drone-based cameras providing a view to the remote pilot have generally not been accepted as providing sufficient situational awareness for these purposes in civil aviation.

15 For example, for the United Kingdom see the Civil Aviation Authority guidance on flight in congested areas: UK Civil Aviation Authority, 'CAP722: Unmanned Aircraft System Operations in UK Airspace—Guidance' (Guidance, 5 November 2020) <https://publicapps.caa.co.uk/modalapplication.aspx?appid=11&mode=detail&id=415>, 2.1.3.3, Chapter 2. It is perhaps worth noting that the kinetic energy of impact is not the only consideration; the structure of the drone is relevant—see Chapter 8 for discussion of the relative harm caused by drones as compared to birds of the same mass. Sharp or rigid parts of the drone will tend to amplify the effect of impact.

16 It is perhaps worth noting that those authorities having safety oversight (the civil aviation authorities and including EASA and the FAA) require not only that the technology fulfils the required function but that (in order to assure sufficient safety) it does so reliably, which is usually assessed by reference to some "acceptable" probability of a harm or hazard materialising. Technologies developed and used outside of civil aviation may offer the prospect of successfully operating and navigating in a complex urban environment but will not necessarily, or immediately, be accepted for use in civil aviation.

17 For the avoidance of any doubt, in this chapter unless we indicate otherwise (e.g. in connection with "auto-pilot"), "pilot" means a *human* pilot.

18 The capability to see, sense or detect conflicting traffic or other hazards and take the appropriate action. International Civil Aviation Organization, 'Manual Doc 10019: Manual on Remotely Piloted Aircraft Systems' (*International Civil Aviation Organization*, 2015).

Some BVLOS operations in non-segregated controlled airspace[19] have been permitted and successfully conducted using radar surveillance and electronic conspicuity ("EC"). EC is an umbrella term for technologies that can help airspace users and air traffic services to be more aware of aircraft operating in the same airspace with the ability to "see and be seen" or "detect and be detected". Full adoption of EC solutions in BVLOS operations means that all users operating in a designated block of airspace can be detected electronically. EC solutions may involve multiple elements including Secondary Surveillance Radar (SSR) transponders[20] or transponders that broadcast the drone's position (ascertained using GPS, for example),[21] installed on the aircraft.[22]

The instances in which BVLOS operations have been conducted in non-segregated airspace have tended to be in relatively remote and low traffic-density volumes of airspace, and the methods of detection used there do not necessarily transpose effectively to the urban environment.

Radar surveillance will in certain urban areas be impossible or impractical for reasons including the presence of multiple obstacles (buildings etc.)[23] The emphasis may then be on drone-based EC (providing identification and positional information), together with accurate mapping of the relevant urban area. Modern mapping methods, including the use of LIDAR,[24] are efficient and accurate, but there remain considerations regarding the real-time accuracy of such maps and whether they capture all potential static obstacles in the urban environment.

The use of drone-based EC equipment, and the means of using this to track and manage a large volume of drone traffic, is the subject of ongoing studies. Initial standards have been and are being developed in this area.[25] In respect of the urban environment,

19 An airspace of defined dimensions within which air traffic control service is provided in accordance with the airspace classification. International Civil Aviation Organization, 'Annex 11—Air Traffic Services' (15th edn, *International Civil Aviation Organization*, 2018).

20 A surveillance radar system which uses transmitters/receivers (interrogators) and transponders. See International Civil Aviation Organization, 'Annex 10—Aeronautical Telecommunications—Volume IV—Surveillance Radar and Collision Avoidance Systems' (5th edn, *International Civil Aviation Organization*, 2014).

21 An example of such a system that is being operated and harmonised across the global aviation industry is ADS-B ("Automatic Dependence Surveillance Broadcast"); see Chapter 8 and 19 for some discussion of its use.

22 UK Civil Aviation Authority (n 15) includes a useful general explanation of the concepts and requirements for BVLOS flight in non-segregated airspace.

23 The use of radar systems in complex and congested environments has been studied and successfully demonstrated for certain use scenarios; for example, at Drone Port facility in Belgium (a drone testing area) and the extended area of the Port of Antwerp, as part of the SESAR "SAFIR" project, see Single European Sky ATM Research (SESAR) Joint Undertaking, 'SAFIR Demos Viable Drone Traffic in Port of Antwerp' (*Single European Sky ATM Research (SESAR) Joint Undertaking*, 30 September 2019) <www.sesarju.eu/news/safir-demos-viable-drone-traffic-port-antwerp>; Aveillant, 'Safir Open Day Proves Ability of Drones to Safeguard Critical Areas' (*Aveillant*, 26 September 2019) <www.aveillant.com/safir-open-day-proves-ability-of-drones-to-safeguard-critical-areas/>; Unmanned Airspace Traffic Management News, 'SAFIR Demonstrator Programme "Shows Integrated U-Space Systems can Support Multiple Drone Operations"' (*Unmanned Airspace*, 26 September 2019) <www.unmannedairspace.info/uncategorized/safir-demonstrator-programme-shows-integrated-u-space-systems-can-support-multiple-drone-operations/>.

24 "Light Detection and Ranging".

25 For examples, see, Single European Sky ATM Research (SESAR) Joint Undertaking, 'Strategic Research and Innovation Agenda (SRIA) for the Digital European Sky' (Report, September 2020) <www.sesarju.eu/sites/default/files/documents/reports/SRIA%20Final.pdf>. With regard to equipment standards,

it will require consideration of the effectiveness and reliability of transmissions to and from the drone for that purpose; the presence of buildings and other structures may have an impact in this respect, and this also raises considerations concerning the use of the radio spectrum and interference.

Even with the mandating of EC equipment on drones, there will remain a risk posed by any non-compliant drones, the presence of which may not be detected and so possibly pose an "invisible" hazard to other drones.

The "avoid" element of D&A is also essential.[26] Considerable research has been invested in drone-based automatic collision avoidance and mass-produced drones with basic functionalities of this are widely available. However, to the authors' knowledge, to date their use over extended (BVLOS) distances in complex or congested environments has not been approved by civil aviation authorities.

The drone's flight must be managed by the remote pilot so as to avoid confliction. At this point, it may be useful to note that as on the date of writing, while there is significant interest and research into autonomous aircraft,[27] it remains an important principle of general application that the drone must be under the command of a (human) pilot. While the aircraft may have functions akin to "auto pilot" (including the prospective drone-based collision avoidance mentioned earlier), the human pilot must be capable of intervening at any time so as to take over the management of the flight.

Such avoidance activity raises considerations that are likely to be all the more important in operations at low altitude and in the urban environment. To be successful, the drone's evasive manoeuvre must be timely. Further, the avoidance action itself may risk damage or injury elsewhere, if it takes the drone into an alternative confliction or causes the pilot to lose control. In the urban environment, considerations arise

---

work has been undertaken by a number of international standards bodies, including EUROCAE, 'Home' (*EUROCAE*) <www.eurocae.net>. See also the FAA's documents in respect of its notice of proposed rulemaking on the subject, Federal Aviation Administration, 'Memorandum: Overview of Remote Identification of Unmanned Aircraft Systems Notice of Proposed Rulemaking for Aviation Authorities in the Middle East' (Memorandum, 20 February 2020) <https://beta.regulations.gov/document/FAA-2019-1100-19638>; and see also, ASTM International, 'ASTM F3411-19, Standard Specification for Remote ID and Tracking' (*ASTM International*, 2019).

26 See, for example, the work undertaken by the Joint Authorities for Rulemaking for Unmanned Systems ("JARUS"): Rules and RPAS Rules & Regulation Information Source, 'JARUS' (*RPAS Rules & Regulation Information Source*) <https://rpas-regulations.com/community-info/jarus/>; and in particular the discussion on—Joint Authority for Rulemaking of Unmanned Systems, 'Working Group 6—Safety & Risk Assessment, Scoping Paper to AMC RPAS.1309, issue 2, Safety Assessment of Remotely Piloted Aircraft Systems' (Scoping Paper, November 2015) <http://jarus-rpas.org/sites/jarus-rpas.org/files/jar_04_doc_2_scoping_papers_to_amc_rpas_1309_issue_2_0.pdf>; and Joint Authority for Rulemaking of Unmanned Systems, 'Working Group 6—Safety & Risk Assessment, AMC RPAS.1309, Issue 2, Safety Assessment of Remotely Piloted Aircraft Systems' (Report, November 2015) <http://jarus-rpas.org/sites/jarus-rpas.org/files/jar_04_doc_1_amc_rpas_1309_issue_2_2.pdf>.

27 An autonomous aircraft is defined as "An unmanned aircraft that does not allow pilot intervention in the management of the flight" International Civil Aviation Organization (n 18); and autonomous operation is defined as "An operation during which an unmanned aircraft operates without the remote pilot being able to intervene", Commission Implementing Regulation (EU) 2019/947 of 24 May 2019 on the procedures and rules for the operation of unmanned aircraft (2019) OJ L152/45. The future use of such systems in civil aviation is not discounted by regulators and civil aviation authorities. For example, see UK Civil Aviation Authority (n 15) ch 3, s 3,9.

as to how much airspace the drone has available to safely avoid collision.[28] It may be possible for that risk to be mitigated by landing the drone, but that itself may create a hazard on the ground.[29]

There are two further key considerations relating to the link between the pilot and the drone, the "C2 link".[30] The first concerns loss of that link. If the C2 link is lost, the pilot is unable to take control of the management of the drone's flight in accordance with the key principle mentioned earlier. In an urban environment, where obstacles may be relatively close to the moving drone, loss of the link for a short time may be sufficient to result in collision. The general approach to loss of C2 link is to include a functionality in the drone that will either keep it in holding pattern or location while it attempts to re-establish the link, or that will take the drone to an area where it can safely land. That in turn requires identification (possibly as part of the pre-flight planning) of safe areas or volumes of airspace to hold or land. It is not too difficult to anticipate potential problems in identifying such volumes or areas within a busy urban environment.

A second consideration concerns the timely communication of information to the pilot and of commands to the drone, so as to ensure that collision is avoided. This raises consideration of whether an adverse delay is introduced through the processes and systems involved in the acquisition and communication of information to the pilot and in the communication to and command of the drone. The concept of delay introduced in this way is often termed "latency". The scale of major cities may mean that latency arising from the travel time along the C2 link is unlikely to become significant. We note however that indirect C2 link pathways, for example, via satellite communications, will increase the time taken for signal travel. Another source of latency is the time taken for equipment to process and react to signals, including that in the pilot's control station, along the signal pathway and in the drone itself.

Radio equipment and spectrum considerations

In general terms radio equipment and transmissions will be needed for the following:

(i) the C2 link, involving radio equipment connected to the pilot's control station and installed on the drone.
(ii) EC purposes, with radio equipment to be installed on the drone as well as the equipment elsewhere used to receive information or interrogate the drone.
(iii) in some instances, radar may be installed on the drone as part of its D&A equipment.
(iv) if the drone is being used for surveillance or data acquisition purposes (for example, optical imaging, sound recording, radar mapping, LIDAR mapping, chemical

28 In civil aviation there are rules for avoidance of collisions which include a basis for avoidance manoeuvres by an aircraft. They may, in some respects, vary according to the block of airspace. Those rules apply to drones operating in blocks of non-segregated airspace. See, for example, Regulation (EU) 923/2012 the Standardised European Rules of the Air (SERA) Chapter 2 (avoidance of collisions), as adjusted by Rule 8 of the Rules of the Air Regulations 2015 (Rules for avoiding aerial collisions); and Annex 2 to the Chicago Convention.

29 For example, by landing in the middle of a road.

30 Command and control (C2) Link: "The data link between the remotely piloted aircraft and the remote pilot station for the purposes of managing the flight." International Civil Aviation Organization (n 18).

sensing/"sniffing"), that may well involve radio transmission of data from the drone payload to the user, as well as radio transmission of payload telemetry to the operator/ user and exchange of control data between operator/user and drone.

(v) there may be volumes of airspace within which radar surveillance is conducted from the ground or other infrastructure, by air traffic services.

This list is by way of example and unlikely to be exhaustive; other radio transmissions may be required in connection with air traffic surveillance and conspicuity as well as in connection with the relay of signals around obstacles. It is then not difficult to see that the proliferation of wide-ranging drone operations across the urban environment may result in a significant expansion of the demand for radio communications within a limited geographical area.

The radio spectrum is a limited and precious (and pressured) resource subject to regulation. The detail of that regulation and its consequences is beyond the scope of this book, but we highlight some key considerations.

In many States there is currently no specific radio spectrum band allocation for use by drones or for drone traffic management. Drone use of radio spectrum is therefore shared with other uses, including bands allocated to manned aviation use. Use is regulated by each State and the details of the regulations, licensing and administration process may differ by State.[31] Licences will often be subject to limitations, for example, on geographical location, frequencies and the transmission power.

A key issue to flag in this respect is that of interference. Radio transmissions used by drones and their related equipment and infrastructure may interfere with equipment and transmissions of importance to others both on the ground and in the air. Also, existing uses of radio equipment and transmissions by others (lawful or otherwise) may interfere with essential radio communications used by drones; we have commented previously on the risks associated with loss of the C2 link.

UTM

The concept of UAS[32] Traffic Management ("UTM") (and the equivalent "U-space"[33] concept) is defined as:

> [A] specific aspect of air traffic management which manages UAS operations safely, economically and efficiently through the provision of facilities and a seamless set of services in collaboration with all parties and involving airborne and ground-based functions.[34]

31 For example, Ofcom in the United Kingdom and the FCC in the United States.

32 Unmanned Aircraft Systems.

33 See, Single European Sky ATM Research (SESAR) Joint Undertaking, 'U-Space Blueprint' (Report) <www.sesarju.eu/U-space>. The U-space concept has been described as "a set of new services relying on a high level of digitalisation and automation of functions and specific procedures designed to support safe, efficient and secure access to airspace for large numbers of drones". See, Single European Sky ATM Research (SESAR) Joint Undertaking, 'U-Space' (*SESAR Joint Undertaking*) <www.sesarju.eu/U-space>.

34 International Civil Aviation Organization, 'Unmanned Aircraft Systems Traffic Management (UTM)—A Common Framework with Core Principles for Global Harmonization' (Report) <www.icao.int/safety/UA/Documents/UTM-Framework.en.alltext.pdf>.

UTM is considered necessary to enable large-scale safe integration of drone operations alongside manned aviation and many aspects of UTM will also be necessary to enable widespread operation of drones in the urban environment. Key aspects of the envisaged UTM concept include the following.

(1) The provision of services and facilities for flight planning (in advance of operation) to manage safety and efficiency; it will also allow advance notification of the planned flight to other airspace users.
(2) Air Navigation Services Providers ("ANSPs"),[35] including traffic control to enable authorisation to use managed airspace and provide situational awareness to the drone.
(3) "De-confliction", meaning the provision information to the drone that identifies potential confliction with other aircraft and facilitates avoidance. It operates both in advance of the flight (through flight planning and notification) and ultimately is envisaged to operate in real time through the use of EC and such other surveillance methods as will be necessary.

UTM will depend upon essential elements including D&A, EC and geofencing. The latter offers a potentially powerful means of protecting critically important volumes of airspace and ensuring segregation. Geofencing will rely upon the definition and publication of details of airspace volumes to which access is prohibited; it is envisaged that software will detect when the drone is approaching such volumes and control the drone so as to prevent entry.[36]

UTM is also envisaged to provide the means of allocating radio spectrum for given drone flights, so providing a tool for management of spectrum and mitigating the risk of radio interference.

There are numerous studies and demonstrations in respect of various aspects of UTM across a multitude of States. While the urban environment presents particular challenges, given the rapid rate of development and the commercial and societal motivations, the authors believe that the necessary basic UTM infrastructure and services for that environment will be implemented in the near future (in the region of five years).

Noise

The proliferation of drone use in the urban environment may give rise to issues concerning noise. There exist detailed regulations and certification requirements for noise in the aviation context which appear unlikely to be relevant to drones. However, we observe that the proliferation of drones in the urban environment may give rise to issues of noise pollution, loss of enjoyment of property and nuisance. Certain developments that would involve the concentration of drone traffic in specific urban areas may amplify those issues.

We comment on some of those aspects here.

35 See Chapter 8.

36 Standards are being developed and published at the time of writing: for example, see the EUROCAE, 'Minimum Operational Performance Standard for UAS Geo-Fencing' (*EUROCAE*, 2 June 2020) <https://eurocae.net/news/posts/2020/june/ed-269-minimum-operational-performance-standard-for-uas-geo-fencing/>.

Privacy

Chapter 10 considers issues of privacy and data protection. Certain of those issues are more likely to be relevant in the urban environment than elsewhere, given the potential concentration of drone activity in densely populated areas.

Drones may acquire images and other data considered as private or subject to protection and may do so intentionally or inadvertently; for example, capturing personal images while surveying a building.

Drones may capture such images and data for the purpose of navigating, controlling or monitoring the drone. Certain legal regimes draw a distinction between data acquired for this purpose and for other purposes.[37] Whether the images and data acquired by the drone are exclusively processed and retained internally (as opposed to being transmitted to the pilot or operator) may be relevant. Some navigation systems capture images which are used and retained within the drone without onwards transmission.

Urban infrastructure for drone and eVTOL operations

Ground infrastructure and support services are crucial enablers of drones in an urban environment. Currently, the lack of existing infrastructure to support drones in urban areas presents a significant challenge to facilitating urban operations. The type of ground infrastructure required to support such operations will depend upon the future evolution of the technology. It will also depend upon:

- the type and size of the aircraft: small unmanned aircraft systems, electric vertical-take-off and landing vehicles (called eVTOL or VTOL aircraft)[38] or horizontal take-off;
- the purpose of the aircraft: such as payload deployment (for example, commercial delivery of items to residences or designated drop-off zones), passenger "air taxis" or other forms of air transport, data gathering, surveillance and communication or recreational;
- network planning;
- integration with other forms of ground transport, air routes and air traffic management.

The following sections of this chapter consider the infrastructure requirements for drones in an urban environment and urban air mobility, the regulatory challenges for urban drone and eVTOL infrastructure including planning issues and issues for landowners or landlords installing "vertiports".

Infrastructure supporting drones in an urban environment

In the near term, the earliest types of infrastructure required to support drone operations in an urban environment are likely to involve facilities for payload deployment.[39] Whilst payload deployment by drones is already being tested in suburban,

37 See Commission Implementing Regulation (EU) 2019/947 (n 27) art 14 (5)(a) ii.

38 Such eVTOL aircraft are being positioned to operate as air taxis similar to helicopter operations, before transitioning to autonomous operations in the longer term.

39 This is on the basis that there has already been testing of delivery drones in regional and suburban settings in numerous countries, and because the regulation of urban air mobility (i.e. eVTOL aircraft as a form of passenger transport) and its supporting infrastructure is likely to be more complex.

regional and rural areas,[40] incorporating drone delivery networks into dense urban settings will require further new infrastructure or structural adaptations to existing buildings.[41] The use of drones for "last mile delivery" of small items in urban areas has the potential to replace millions of kilometres driven by delivery cars and trucks.[42]

Drones may either be despatched using a stationary facility (such as a warehouse) or from a vehicle. Such operations may require a centrally located logistics or distributions centre to/from which to perform deliveries to private residences[43] or certain delivery drop-off and collection points.[44] Drones could then return to a centrally located facility for recharging and collection of further delivery orders.[45] Moreover, despatching drones from vehicles in urban centres has the advantage of covering a wider geographic area.[46] A patent has also reportedly been filed in the United Kingdom for "flying warehouses" equipped with a fleet of drones that would enable rapid delivery to key urban locations.[47] It is clear that the infrastructure required to support drone deliveries is rapidly evolving.[48]

Infrastructure supporting urban transport by eVTOL

In the longer term, there is a significant amount of development in the area of urban air mobility, whereby eVTOL vehicles will be used to supplement existing transport

40 For example, in Australia, small-scale commercial deliveries of pharmaceutical and food and beverage items are being tested in Canberra, Wing, 'Canberra—Australia—Wing' (*Wing*) <https://wing.com/australia/canberra>.

41 Such as a repurposing of existing warehouses or parcel delivery stations.

42 Using electric-powered drones for delivery is estimated to, in many cases, produce less greenhouse gas emissions and energy than traditional road vehicles using petrol or diesel. Australian Government Department of Infrastructure, Transport, Regional Development and Communications, 'Emerging Aviation Technologies, National Aviation Policy Issues Paper' (September 2020) 40.

43 At the time of writing, manufacturers are designing, manufacturing and testing various delivery drones that would enable commercial door-to-door delivery. For example, in 2016 Amazon trialled its first successful Prime Air drone delivery in Cambridge directly to the garden of a nearby customer. Tesco is also trialling home deliveries of "small basket" orders by drone in Ireland.

44 For example, DHL envisages that its existing Packstation network across Europe, which uses self-service booths for collection and despatch of parcels, could be upgraded to accept UAV deliveries. See DHL, 'Unmanned Aerial Vehicles In Logistics—A DHL Perspective on Implications and Use Cases for the Logistics Industry' (Report, 2014) <www.dhl.com/global-en/home/insights-and-innovation/thought-leadership/trend-reports/unmanned-aerial-vehicles.html>.

45 For example, in Rwanda UPS, GAVI and Zipline collaborated on a delivery-by-drone project involving the delivery of medical products. The project involved infrastructure including launching and landing stations for delivery up to emergency deliveries of medical supplies. See Zipline, 'Vital, On-Demand Delivery for the World' (*Zipline*) <https://flyzipline.com>.

46 It is predicted that in the longer term, despatch vehicles may not be needed due to technological improvements to drone operating distances and battery life.

47 See BBC News, 'Amazon Files Patent for Flying Warehouse' (*Amazon*, 29 December 2016) <www.bbc.com/news/technology-38458867>.

48 There was significant testing and regulatory development for drone delivery tests in 2019: with Wing making its first delivery in Virginia, United States and also launching an air delivery service for food, coffee and other over-the-counter items via an app in Canberra, Australia. UPS also received certification from the FAA in the United States for its 'drone airline'. UPS, 'UPS Flight Forward™ Drone Delivery' (*UPS*) <www.ups.com/us/en/services/shipping-services/flight-forward-drones.page> and Wing (n 40).

options in a city.[49] The capabilities of "air taxis" are among the most intensely discussed developing technologies. Landing pads that allow vertical take-off are referred to as "vertiports" (where they have multiple take-off and landing pads, charging infrastructure and support personnel) or "vertistops" (a single landing pad without support facilities, appropriate for stopping for deliveries or to drop off and pick up passengers).[50] Vertiports may also allow various UAS operations such as cargo-UAS operations.

Transport operations by eVTOL will place a greater demand on ground infrastructure and support services.[51] In order to operate in urban centres, air taxi drones may require (amongst others) landing and take-off pads, charging facilities, parking and storage, support personnel, areas to support and accommodate passengers (for example, security areas or lounges) and/or cargo and maintenance locations. Facilities will also be needed to accommodate and process passengers using the vertiports.

Whilst there are no existing commercial operations from a vertiport at present, trials and planning for eVTOL operations have been announced in Singapore,[52] Florida,[53] Los Angeles, Dallas and Melbourne.[54] Skyports, a mobility company developing and operating landing infrastructure for drones, and Volocopter, a German air taxi manufacturer, have partnered with the Singapore government to launch an air taxi network by 2022.[55] In 2019, the companies unveiled the first full-scale passenger air taxi vertiport, named the "VoloPort", at the Intelligent Transport Systems World Congress in Singapore.[56] The VoloPort design includes landing and take-off facilities, as well as charging capabilities and passenger processing areas.

49 The Australian government estimates that eVTOL aircraft will be integrated with the UTM system and operate in regional areas in with five to ten years, and that autonomous eVTOL and drone operations will be commonplace and fully integrated into the aviation system within 15 to 30 years.

50 For example, Uber envisages that passenger drones will transport commuters from the suburbs into city centres, where there would be a network of vertiports or vertistops. Uber, 'Fast-Forwarding to a Future of On-Demand Urban Air Transportation' (White Paper, 27 October 2016) <www.uber.com/elevate.pdf>.

51 In comparison to drone operations that do not involve carriage of passengers.

52 Skyports is a ground infrastructure developer for drone operations. It partners with landlords, governments and property owners to locate appropriate sites, design and develop and then operate vertiports. The UK company is working together with Volocopter, a German aircraft manufacturer and air taxi pioneer, to launch an air taxi network by 2022. The two companies partnered to building the first full-scale air taxi vertiport prototype in Singapore in October 2019, named the "VoloPort". The VoloPort is still in its prototype phase, and Skyports have identified that the major aspects that need to be in place to make urban air mobility a reality are "the aircraft, the infrastructure, and the necessary regulation for both". Alex Brown, 'World's First Full-Scale Air Taxi VoloPort Unveiled in Singapore' (*Skyports*, 21 October 2019) <https://skyports.net/2019/10/worlds-first-full-scale-air-taxi-voloport-unveiled-in-singapore/>.

53 Lilium, a German flying taxi start-up, has also recently designed a modular vertiport which it plans to build in Orlando, Florida. Lilium aims to commence operations using its five-seater passenger aircraft, the Lilium Jet, taking regional trips beginning in 2025. Andrew J Hawkins, 'Flying Taxi Startup Lilium will Build a Hub for Its Electric Aircraft in Florida' (*The Verge*, 11 November 2020) <www.theverge.com/2020/11/11/21558670/lilium-jet-flying-taxi-orlando-vertiport-hub-evtol>.

54 Los Angeles, Dallas and Melbourne have all been announced as pilot cities for Uber Air's testing of eVTOL air taxis in urban centres. eVTOL, 'Melbourne is First International Pilot City for Uber Air' (*eVTOL*, 11 June 2019) <https://evtol.com/news/melbourne-is-first-international-pilot-city-for-uber-air/>.

55 Skyports, 'VoloPort' (*Skyports*) <https://skyports.net/projects/volo-port/>.

56 ibid.

Investors have also started to secure sites for landing pads in preparation for when the vehicles are ready.[57] Vertiports are anticipated to use far less space than airports, and it is possible that existing heliports could be transformed into vertiports or vertistops to accommodate drone operations.[58] Suitable locations may include airports, heliports or existing building rooftops with a clear approach and departure paths free from obstacles (such as shopping centres, concert venues or sports stadia with big, flat surface areas or office roofs, particularly those buildings with elevators to the rooftop). Vertiports located close to other transport modes are likely to be ideal locations for eVTOL operations. Some cities may also support floating barge vertiports over the water, which would likely reduce noise complaints and risk of personal injury to third parties compared to infrastructure among densely populated buildings.

Whilst it may be possible to convert existing infrastructure to support drone and eVTOL operations, the scale of existing infrastructure is likely to be lacking in most cities. eVTOL take-off and landing operations are anticipated to generate moderate levels of noise, meaning that vertiports and vertistops may be better suited to areas with higher background noise, rather than residential areas.[59]

Cities or regions with urban drone operations will also require maintenance locations (separate to vertiports) for vehicles to be serviced, inspected and parked when not in operation. These will need to be centrally or conveniently located to enable support personnel to recover the aircraft in the event of emergency landings or equipment failure.

Other unique challenges for the operation of vertiports for passenger travel include the types of passenger security requirements and regulatory oversight. It is not yet clear whether transit through a vertiport and embarking on an eVTOL flight will more closely reflect the experience of getting a bus or taxi with relatively lower security requirements or getting on an aircraft.[60] If the latter, airport safety rules or helicopter regulations could be considered for processing passengers at vertiports.

57 Mike Cherney, 'Drones to Carry People Have Yet to Take Off, but They Will Have a Place to Land; Interest in Landing Pads, Even at an Early Stage, Underscores How Investors See Big Opportunity Despite Risks' *Wall Street Journal* (New York City, 11 June 2019) <www.wsj.com/articles/drones-to-carry-people-have-yet-to-take-off-but-they-will-have-a-place-to-land-11560267249>.

58 German fly taxi manufacturer Lilium has described its proposed vertiport as "something between an existing heliport today and an airport". See Ilaria Grasso Macola, 'Who Will Govern the Urban Vertiports of the Future?' (*Airport Industry Review*, October 2020) <https://airport.nridigital.com/air_oct20/vertiport_regulations_air_taxis>.

59 See Doug Creighton and others, 'Advanced Aerial Mobility and eVTOL Aircraft in Australia: Promise and Challenges' (White Paper, September 2020) <www.deakin.edu.au/iisri/_nocache>. If this is the case, then eVTOL operations are more likely to support travel between transportation hubs, rather than door-to-door operations.

60 Uber's whitepaper, 'Fast-Forwarding to a Future of On-Demand Urban Air Transportation', envisages a boarding process through a vertiport which more closely resembles an airport experience: "(w)e will clearly direct passengers where to go and what to do to embark or disembark on their VTOL journey. . . . On the way to that departure door, we imagine a rapid and seamless process whereby the rider's identity, security checks and even the weighing of the rider and their luggage (if necessary) can all be done. . . . When the VTOL is ready at the takeoff/landing pad, the confirmed rider would be invited into the aircraft area by means of an automatic door, and she would walk the short distance on a marked pathway to the VTOL". Uber (n 50).

Who will regulate vertiports and other ground infrastructure?

Countries with existing drone regulations continue to grapple with the question of who will be responsible for regulating drone and eVTOL ground support. Regulations or guidelines will be required to cover a wide array of topics. For example, regulatory mandates or policy guidance for vertiports will need to take into account design standards, fire codes, building codes or best practices and operational standards specific to eVTOL operations.[61]

There is undoubtedly a role to be played by national civil aviation authorities regarding approvals and management of aircraft and infrastructure facilities. It is also clear that approvals for the construction of urban infrastructure will involve local city councils, government and other local authorities. In order to reduce the regulatory burden for industry, coordination and consistency will be needed between numerous government regulators for the approvals and ongoing oversight of ground infrastructure supporting drones in an urban environment.[62] Developing appropriate regulations and safety standards for urban settings is further complicated by the current limited amount of evidence regarding the nature and magnitude of the risk posed by drone operations to other people and property on the ground.

In Europe, EASA has issued the Special Condition VTOL,[63] which is a set of dedicated technical specifications for the type certification of eVTOL aircraft. At this point, vertiport requirements do not yet exist. However, it is reported that EASA has started to develop regulations for ground infrastructure and vertiports.[64]

The UK Civil Aviation Authority has invited participation from industry organisations to explore the regulatory requirements of urban air mobility and support ground infrastructures.[65] It is not yet clear whether the CAA will follow EASA and harmonise its standards for vertiports with those in Europe.

61 See National Air Transportation Association, 'Urban Air Mobility: Considerations for Vertiport Operation' (White Paper, June 2019) <www.nata.aero/pressrelease/nata-releases-urban-air-mobility-whitepaper>.

62 For example, the Australian government has proposed to adopt a national 'whole-of-government policy approach' to emerging aviation technologies and supporting infrastructure which is aimed at reducing the scope of the regulatory burden on industry. Australian Government Department of Infrastructure, Transport, Regional Development and Communications (n 42).

63 European Union Aviation Safety Agency, 'SC-VTOL-01 Special Condition for small-Category VTOL Aircraft' (2 July 2019) <www.easa.europa.eu/document-library/product-certification-consultations/special-condition-vtol>. See also European Union Aviation Safety Agency, 'Proposed Means of Compliance with the Special Condition VTOL' (25 May 2020) <www.easa.europa.eu/document-library/product-certification-consultations/special-condition-vtol>.

64 See Harry Plested, 'Vertiport Regulations and Standards: Creating the Rules Framework for UAM Infrastructure' (*Skyports*, 23 July 2020) <https://skyports.net/2020/07/vertiport-regulations-and-standards-creating-the-rules-framework-for-uam-infrastructure/>.

65 See UK Civil Aviation Authority, 'Future Air Mobility Regulatory Challenge' (Report, 18 May 2020) <https://publicapps.caa.co.uk/modalapplication.aspx?appid=11&mode=detail&id=9627>. In relation to ground infrastructure, the CAA is seeking input regarding the following questions: (1) What should the infrastructure requirements be to enable safe ground operations? This includes considerations on bird strikes, dangerous goods, rescue and firefighting services, etc. (2) How should aircraft be refuelled/recharged? What are the implications on the safety of both ground and air operations? What are the implications of operating in an urban environment? (3) How can the safety and security of landing areas be assured?

In other countries with existing drone regulations, it is not yet clear whether the CAA will approve new vertiports.[66]

It is an understatement to say that this is a difficult area for regulation. Gaining regulatory approval for ground infrastructure supporting drones and eVTOL is new territory for governments and regulators alike. Aviation regulations, building and planning regulations and approval mechanisms must adapt. On the one hand, rule-makers and regulations need to be dynamic to evolve as technology changes in this emerging sector. However, the operation of drones and supporting infrastructure in an urban environment presents increased risks to persons and property which must be effectively managed by regulators and governments.

Urban infrastructure planning

Local planning authorities in urban centres face numerous challenges of integrating urban air mobility and supporting ground infrastructure into existing planning practice. One of those biggest obstacles is undoubtedly community acceptance of drone and eVTOL operations in a congested urban environment. Planning authorities will have to provide assurances of safety, sustainability, security and resilience regarding infrastructure, support services and operations.[67] Governments will also need to consider land use planning along flight paths, management of take-off and landing facilities and the impact of potential noise exposure upon zoning.[68]

The location of charging and depot facilities will also be a key determinant of designing delivery routes. Distribution of ground infrastructure will also influence the longer-term sustainability, efficiency and profitably of urban drone deliveries, and the planning phase will therefore be critical to ensuring long-term viability.

One of the primary issues of building drone landing and take-off infrastructure in an urban setting will be ensuring the avoidance of overflight of neighbouring property at low altitudes in accordance with local law. This presents a planning challenge of striking a balance between conflicting interests of operators and neighbouring properties in an urban setting.[69] Whilst there is generally no precise altitude at which private ownership above a property ends and public airspace begins, vertiports in densely built areas will need to take into account that drones and eVTOL must be able to operate whilst respecting the legal rights of other property owners and bystanders on

66 For example, in the United States it has not yet been determined whether the FAA would approve new vertiports. Certain types of finance which are available to airports will require FAA oversight and approval. On the other hand, private helipads do not always require the approval of the FAA and are instead subject to oversight by the city council, firefighting departments and building permits, and FAA guidance may be sought as a supplementary safety measure. See Cherney (n 57); and Macola (n 58).

67 See Creighton and others (n 59).

68 ibid.

69 For example, English law provides that an owner has rights in the air space above his land to "such height as is necessary for the ordinary use and enjoyment of his land and the structures upon it": *Bernstein of Leigh v Skyviews & General Ltd* [1978] QB 479, [1977] 2 All ER 902 at 907, Griffiths J. Above this height, the landowner has no greater rights in the air space than any other member of the public. Similarly, low-altitude overflight over private property is prohibited in the United States. *United States v. Causby* 22 Ill.328 U.S. 256, 66 S. Ct. 1062, 90 L. Ed. 1206 (1946). This case establishes the principle that the air is a public highway, but that private property ownership includes the airspace immediately above the property and that low-altitude flights are "a direct invasion of the landowner's domain".

the ground. Locations for vertiports may therefore need to be surveyed and registered for arrival and departure routes.

Landowners or landlords installing vertiports

Landowners and landlords considering installing a vertiport at their premises, whether in a commercial or residential context, will have numerous practical and legal issues to consider. Necessary approvals will need to be obtained from local councils and civil aviation authorities. Contractual and construction arrangements will need to be negotiated with the infrastructure provided, including responsibility for aviation authority and planning issues.

Landlords will also need to maintain flexible leasing arrangements with tenants to allow for the installation and operation of a vertiport at their building. For example, existing leasing arrangements may create issues for those operating and/or accessing a vertiport to have access to common parts and services. Access to the vertiport may only be possible by going through areas that have already been demised to existing tenants. In that case, there would need to be sufficient reservations in the lease to permit such access. Whilst it would be ideal for buildings to have separate access to the roof for vertiport operations to avoid disrupting other tenants within the building, there may be physical restrictions in existing buildings or legal restrictions under leases which prevent such access.

Tenants disrupted by vertiport operations may have a possible claim for breach of quiet enjoyment due to the noise of construction or operation of the vertiport. One way to mitigate such issues would be to include a specific acknowledgement of the vertiport (or potential construction and operation of a vertiport) within the leases.

Landlords and building owners installing vertiports will also be concerned with the risk of activities associated with the vertiport causing injury to third parties or damage to property. Owners have a duty of care to tenants and certain other third parties using the building. A rigorous health and safety assessment and ensuring compliance with the relevant health and safety legislation will be critical to managing risk in this regard. Property owners should also check that insurance arrangements provide the appropriate cover for liability.

As outlined in this chapter, the prospective benefits of extensive drone operations point to an expansion of commercial operations in the urban environment over the coming decade.

This complex environment requires a more intense focus on considerations of risk (personal injury and property damage), technological protections and mitigations, management of very low-level airspace and its traffic, as well as aviation regulation, planning law and the rights of individuals to their privacy and peace. With the proliferation of "air taxis", this will further intensify the need for discussion, thought and planning to allow the integration and expansion of new forms of transport into urban environments.

Part C
Risks

7 Global terrorism and security

Jeffrey Ellis and Robert S. Barrows

Introduction

Terrorist and criminal misuse of unmanned aerial vehicles (interchangeably UAS, UAV and drone) is a major concern of the military, police and intelligence communities. As is the case with the development of an overall regulatory scheme for authorised UAV operations,[1] the law and law enforcement are struggling to keep pace with this new technology and the purposes for which it can be used and misused. While there is always an initial inclination to use existing law and law enforcement techniques to respond to issues related to new technologies and the threats they pose, there are also instances where the law and law enforcement must adapt to both authorised and unauthorised use and misuse of technological advancements.

This chapter focuses on the issues arising out of intentional misuse of UAV technology. It provides an overview of the nature of the threat posed by terrorist and criminal misuse of drones and what is being done to prevent such attacks. The emphasis is on (1) publicly available information describing the terrorist threat and capabilities (2) and non-sensitive information relevant to the technology required to detect potentially malicious drones as well as the means to interdict and mitigate this threat and (3) the legal and jurisdictional authority to implement these measures.

Military development of UAVs[2]

The starting point for understanding the nature of terrorist threats related to the use of drones and the risks they pose is the way the military has advanced this technology. Terrorists pick up on these developments and look to exploit it for nefarious purposes just like they turned airplanes and the means of peaceful commerce into flying bombs on 9/11. Terrorists also learn from military tactics and strategic capabilities and, in this regard, they have witnessed American drone use during the so-called war on terror first hand and came away armed with knowledge that they tried to exploit. Military drone technology is quite advanced and has been used effectively in armed combat.

Military use of drones dates back to the First World War when Orville Wright and his company constructed an unmanned aircraft designed for military use and equipped with an explosive payload. It had a crude "guidance" system that relied

1 See Chapter 4 Drones and Law Enforcement and Chapter 13 Regulatory Overview.

2 For a detailed description of the history of military development and use of drones, see Ron Bartsch, James Coyne and Katherine Gray, *Drones in Society* (Routledge 2017), chapter 2 'From Battlefield to Backyard', 19–34.

upon a calculation of wind speed, direction, distance and the number of engine revolutions needed to take the unmanned aircraft to its target.[3] It functioned by determining the amount of time to reach the target, the engine then shutting down and the aircraft plunging to the earth and detonating the explosives on board.[4]

Military development continued after World War I, and during World War II both sides developed far more effective means of using unmanned aircraft to deliver explosive payloads. Nazi Germany developed the V-1 "flying bomb"[5] to rain terror on London, while the British developed their own unmanned aircraft to support their war efforts.[6]

Following the war, military development of unmanned aircraft increased dramatically, and by 1952 the Australian Government Aircraft Factories had developed the technical expertise to construct a target drone called the Jindivik. That name is derived from an Aboriginal word meaning "the hunted one."[7] The drone's performance was quite remarkable, being capable of high-speed flight ranging in altitude from 50 feet to 70,000 feet.[8]

Over the next several decades, drone technology continued to develop, with an emphasis on using drones for military and intelligence surveillance. The United States took the lead in this area and developed a highly efficient drone called the Predator. It was equipped with cameras that provided operators with a 60-mile panorama from a platform that could stay airborne more or less permanently, with vehicles flown in 12-hour shifts.[9] The Predator also played an instrumental role in both the lead up to and post incident response to the 9/11 attacks and foreshadowed the current state of drone warfare.

Prior to 9/11,[10] al Qaeda had been tied to the 1993 World Trade Center bombing and the 1998 bombings of two US embassies in Africa. Osama bin Laden was indicted for those attacks in the United States and efforts were undertaken to locate him in Afghanistan. It was ultimately agreed to use the Predator drone to provide surveillance in the search for bin Laden. The imagery provided by the Predator's first

3 See, for example, Larry Holzwarth, 'The Story of the Kettering Bug, the World's First Aerial Drone' <https://historycollection.com/the-story-of-the-kettering-bug-the-worlds-first-aerial-drone/>.

4 National Museum of the United States Airforce, 'Kettering Aerial Torpedo Bug' (7 April 2015) <www.nationalmuseum.af.mil/Visit/Museum-Exhibits/Fact-Sheets/Display/Article/198095/kettering-aerial-torpedo-bug/>.

5 V-1 missile, German in full Vergeltungswaffen-1 ("Vengeance Weapon 1"), also popularly called flying bomb, buzz bomb, or doodlebug, German jet-propelled missile of World War II, the forerunner of modern cruise missiles. See, for example, Britannica, 'V-1 Missile' <www.britannica.com/technology/V-1-missileBundesarchiv,Bild146-1975-117-26/Lysiak/CC-BY-SA 3.0>.

6 See, for example, War History Online, 'The Early Days of Drones—Unmanned Aircraft from WW1 & WW11' (12 May 2018) <www.warhistoryonline.com/military-vehicle-news/short-history-drones-aircraft.html>.

7 D Crotty, 'GAF Jindivik Target Aircraft in Museums Victoria Collections' (2010) <https://collections.museumsvictoria.com.au/articles/3668>.

8 Australia's Museum of Flight, 'GAF Jindivik Mk.3B' (N11806) (30 May 2005) <https://web.archive.org/web/20070830035113/www.museum-of-flight.org.au/site/index.php?option=com_content&task=view&id=39&Itemid=65>.

9 Mark Bowden, 'How the Predator Drone Changed the Character of War' (*Smithsonian Magazine*, November 2013) <www.smithsonianmag.com/history/how-the-predator-drone-changed-the-character-of-war-3794671/>.

10 The 11 September 2001 terrorist attacks upon the United States.

flight was apparently quite detailed and subsequently described by the US Director of National Intelligence as "truly astonishing."[11]

The surveillance imagery that was provided of Osama bin Laden has been stated to have shown the following:

> [A] tall man in a white robe at Bin Laden's Tarnak Farms compound outside Kandahar. After a second sighting of the "man in white" at the compound on September 28, intelligence community analysts determined that he was probably Bin Laden.[12]

As detailed further in 9/11 Commission Report,[13] various logistical and diplomatic considerations played into the analysis of this surveillance imagery and what to do in response to it. It was ultimately decided not to act due to the time lapse and uncertainty resulting from doing so.[14] However, the lack of an immediate response capability spurred discussions as to whether the Predator could be equipped with hellfire missiles and used as an offensive weapon.[15] The magnitude of the 9/11 attacks quickly silenced those wishing to proceed cautiously and, in that regard, it was only weeks after 9/11 that the Predator was outfitted with missile launching capability and this technological advancement was used to kill al Qaeda's military commander in Iraq.[16]

Thus, it came to be that the same drone that provided the passive surveillance information that some claimed should have enabled the United States to kill bin Laden and prevent the 9/11 attacks was transformed into a key offensive weapon in the United States' response to those attacks. The effectiveness of this new technology in remote regions caused its use to become so prevalent that it has been reported that between 2010 and 2020, the United States conducted more than 14,000 drone strikes in Pakistan, Afghanistan, Yemen and Somalia.[17] The staggering death toll from these strikes is reported to have been up to 16,000 people, including approximately 2,200 civilians and 450 children.[18]

The strategic use of these drone strikes as well as the collateral harm caused to innocent civilians has clearly been a factor in motivating responsive acts of terrorism and recruitment. However, from a legal perspective, it has also been stated that US drone strikes "represent a significant challenge to the international rule of law."[19]

These concerns arise "not because recent U.S. drone strikes 'violate' international law [but] . . . because they defy straightforward legal categorization."[20] Indeed, this

11 National Commission on Terrorist Attacks, 'The 9/11 Commission Report' (GPO 2004) chapter 6, 189, 190 <https://govinfo.library.unt.edu/911/report/911Report_Ch6.pdf>.

12 ibid.

13 <www.9-11commission.gov/report/911Report.pdf>.

14 ibid.

15 Warren Bass, 'How the US Stumbled Into The Drone Era' (*Wall Street Journal*, 24 July 2014) <www.wsj.com/articles/how-the-u-s-stumbled-into-the-drone-era-1406234812>.

16 ibid.

17 See report prepared by The Bureau of Investigative Journalists <www.thebureauinvestigates.com/projects/drone-war>.

18 ibid.

19 Rosa Brooks, 'Drones and the International Rule of Law' (2014) 28 Journal of Ethics & International Affairs 83–104.

20 ibid.

legal uncertainty was also noted in a Court decision dismissing a wrongful death claim brought by the father of an American citizen who was killed in a targeted drone strike in Yemen while acting as the leader of an al Qaeda affiliate located in that country. The Court's decision began by noting this issue is "not easy" to resolve but then acknowledged that "the danger posed by an individual who is aligned with an enemy of the United States is very real, whether he is a citizen of this or another country."[21] The Court ultimately held that the issue was one for the US Congress to address, not the courts, and the claim was dismissed.[22]

Irrespective of the legal analysis as to whether the targeted killing of identified terrorists is legal, some of those directly involved with these operations have claimed that such strikes played a key role in the increase in terrorist recruitment post-9/11. In that regard, a number of military pilots who operate drones remotely and fire the missiles used in attacks sent an impassioned plea to cease the attacks because they helped ISIS recruitment and, in their words, had become one of the most "devastating driving forces for terrorism and destabilisation around the world."[23]

Terrorist use of drones

Drone use in a military context has not been limited to traditional Western powers like the United States, the United Kingdom and Australia. It was not long after the Islamic Revolution that overthrew the Shah that Iran began to use and develop its own drone technology. This dates back 40 years to the Iran–Iraq war in the 1980s.[24] Additionally, Iran's proxy in the Middle East, Hezbollah,[25] has used drones to fly into Israeli airspace since the early 2000s.[26] More recently, ISIS has also used drones since 2014 and even published photos of ISIS fighters taking drone technology classes in 2017.[27]

The attraction of such groups to using drone technology is quite obvious. Drones can be relatively inexpensive to purchase or construct and easy to launch surreptitiously. Indeed, even small commercially available drones can be modified for explosive delivery. In that regard, ISIS's online publication recently threatened the Eiffel

21 *Al-Aulaqi v. Panetta*, 35 F. Supp. 3d 56, 80 (D.D.C. 2014).

22 ibid.

23 'Obama's Drone War a "Recruitment Tool" for ISIS, Say US Air Force Whistleblowers' (*The Guardian*, 8 November 2015) <www.theguardian.com/world/2015/nov/18/obama-drone-war-isis-recruitment-tool-air-force-whistleblowers>.

24 Michael Rubin, 'A Short History of the Iranian Drone Program' (Report, American Enterprise Institute, August 2020) <www.aei.org/wp-content/uploads/2020/08/A-short-history-of-the-Iranian-drone-program.pdf?x88519>.

25 Claire Parker and Rick Noack, 'Iran has Invested in Allies and Proxies across the Middle East' (*Washington Post*, 3 January 2020) <www.washingtonpost.com/world/2020/01/03/iran-has-invested-allies-proxies-across-middle-east-heres-where-they-stand-after-soleimanis-death/>.

26 Milton Hoenig, 'Hezbollah and the Use of Drones as a Weapon of Terrorism' (*FAS Public Interest Report*, Spring 2014) Volume 67 Number 2 <https://fas.org/wp-content/uploads/2014/06/Hezbollah-Drones-Spring-2014.pdf>.

27 Steven Stalinsky and R Sosnow, 'A Decade of Jihadi Organizations' Use of Drones—From Early Experiments by Hizbullah, Hamas and Al-Qaeda to Emerging National Security Crisis for the West as ISIS Launches First Attack Drones' (*The Middle East Media Research Institute*, 21 February 2017) <www.memri.org/reports/decade-jihadi-organizations-use-drones-%E2%80%93-early-experiments-hizbullah-hamas-and-al-qaeda>.

Tower with a surprise drone attack using a commercially available drone carrying what appears to be an explosive payload.[28]

These threats have not gone unnoticed. During a US Senate Homeland Security and Governmental Affairs Committee, National Counterterrorism Center Acting Director Russ Travers testified:

> We're in the early stages of seeing terrorist use of drones and UASs for swarm attacks, explosive delivery means and even assassination attempts.[29]

To paraphrase the initial finding of the 9/11 Commission, a major drone attack would be a "shock," but it would "not be a surprise."[30]

The Combating Terrorism Center at West Point (CTC) has described the following reasons drones are attractive to terrorists:

> Drones provide a number of benefits and can be used by terrorist entities in five primary ways: for surveillance, for strategic communications, to smuggle or transport matériel, to disrupt events or complement other activities, and as a weapon. This last category includes instances of a drone being piloted directly to a target, a drone delivering explosives, and a weapon being directly mounted to a drone.[31]

The CTC report also noted that in April 2015 what appears to be a Hezbollah UAS airstrip was discovered in Lebanon's Bekaa Valley.[32] A short video that appeared online in early August 2016 reportedly shows Hezbollah dropping two cluster bomblets from a modified commercial UAS onto a rebel position in Syria.[33]

The CTC indicated that existing evidence demonstrates that the potential for terrorist misuse of drones is truly global in scale.[34]

The potential for a dramatic and globally significant attack in the western hemisphere can be readily demonstrated by incidents where drones were used to threaten government leadership in Germany and Venezuela. For example, at a 2013 press conference an activist flew a drone directly in front of German Chancellor Angela Merkel and was able to hover the drone over her head before he was arrested.[35] Commentators noted that if the drone had been equipped with even a small explosive device, it could

28 Phantom Technologies, 'ISIS Threatens Eiffel Tower with a Surprise Drone Attack' <https://phantom-technologies.com/isis-threatens-eiffel-tower-with-drone-attack/>.

29 Wesley Bull, 'Aerial Swarming Threats: Preparing Agencies for the Next Attack' (*Chair of IPSA's UAS Committee*, 12 February 2019) <www.joinipsa.org/IPSA-Blog/7161074>.

30 "The 9/11 Attacks were a Shock, but They Should Not Have Come as a Surprise". The 9/11 Commission Report, 'Final Report of the National Commission on Terrorist Attacks upon the United States' (Executive Summary, GPO, 2004) 2 <https://govinfo.library.unt.edu/911/report/911Report_Exec.pdf>.

31 Don Rassler, 'Remotely Piloted Innovation, Terrorism, Drones and Supportive Technology' (*Combating Terrorism Center, US Military Academy*, October 2016) iv <https://ctc.usma.edu/wp-content/uploads/2016/10/Drones-Report.pdf>.

32 ibid 28.

33 ibid 29.

34 ibid 41.

35 'Drone Crash-lands in Front of Angela Merkel in Pirate Party Protest' (*South China Morning Post*, 17 September 2013) <www.scmp.com/news/world/article/1311206/drone-crash-lands-front-angela-merkel-pirate-party-protest>.

have been an effective weapon.[36] This threat became a reality when a drone attack on live television almost took the life of the Venezuelan president, Nicolas Maduro.[37]

Even more recent drone attacks in Saudi Arabia dramatically illustrate the destructive potential of terrorist drone use. According to *Al Jazeera*, the drone used in the Saudi pipeline attack "flew more than 800 km into Saudi Arabia to successfully attack its target . . . [and] was guided using satellite technology." As Aljazeera further noted, "This implies increasingly sophisticated levels of training."[38]

Couple the foregoing with reports indicating that Houthi drones can fly up to 1,500 kilometres with a 40-pound warhead[39] and a statement by the US Federal Aviation Administration (FAA) that anti-drone security technology is still developing, and it should be apparent that a risk that may have been considered only theoretically now seems to be very real.[40]

Anyone with even a cursory knowledge of risk assessment can readily see the potential dangers posed by a 40-pound bomb capable of travelling up to 1,500 kilometres with GPS targeting capability. But to paraphrase the opening lines of the 9/11 Commission Report, should we be surprised? The answer to that question seems obvious. We know that terrorists innovate and learn from prior attacks. We underestimate them at our peril and increase the attractiveness of a target when we fail to implement measures to deal with the potential disruption and damage that they intend to cause. Implementing such measures is, however, fraught with legal and technological issues that are far from resolved.

Challenges and barriers to counter-drone systems

As described in Chapter 4[41], air defence systems traditionally deployed to protect the airspace have been designed mostly for the purpose of addressing conditions created by manned aircraft.[42] Although remote identification rules can address some concerns regarding unauthorised or malicious drone use,[43] concerns exist when compared to other available detection technologies—specifically, the effectiveness and reliability of both broadcast and network systems, which will be critical components

36 CTC Report, 51.

37 Oli Smith, 'Shock Moment Assassination Drones Explode in Front of Venezuela's Maduro on LIVE TV' (*Daily and Sunday Express*, 6 August 2018) <www.express.co.uk/news/world/999125/Drone-explosive-assassination-plot-Venezuela-Nicolas-Maduro>.

38 Alex Gatopoulos, 'Houthi Drone Attacks in Saudi Show New Level of Sophistication' (*Aljazeera*, 15 May 2019) <www.aljazeera.com/news/2019/5/15/houthi-drone-attacks-in-saudi-show-new-level-of-sophistication>.

39 'Yemen Rebel Drone Attack Targets Remote Saudi Oil Field' (*PBS News Hour Weekend*, 17 August 2019) <www.pbs.org/newshour/world/yemen-rebel-drone-attack-targets-remote-saudi-oil-field>.

40 FAA Statement (7 May 2019) <www.faa.gov/airports/airport_safety/media/Updated-Information-UAS-Detection-Countermeasures-Technology-Airports-20190507.pdf>.

41 See Chapter 4 for discussion of counter-drone systems, detection, tracking and identification methods, mitigation, technological challenges and legal barriers to local law enforcement's use of counter-drone technology.

42 See generally, Arthur Holland Michel, 'Counter-Drone Systems' (*Centre for the Study of the Drone*, 2019) <https://dronecenter.bard.edu/files/2019/12/CSD-CUAS-2nd-Edition-Web.pdf>.

43 See 'Drones: A Report on the Use of Drones by Public Safety Agencies—And a Wake Up Call About the Threat of Malicious Drone Attacks' (*Police Executive Research Forum*, 2020), 62–63 <www.policeforum.org/assets/Drones.pdf> [hereinafter "PERF Report"].

for low-altitude drone system traffic management. Furthermore, the technology is premised upon actors who are willing to comply with the federal regulatory scheme. Technological challenges to detection and mitigation technology range from effectiveness to practicality and safety.[44]

In addition to the technological challenges, legal barriers continue to exist for law enforcement agencies where local agencies may be risking criminal and civil liability for deploying detection technology.[45] Many of these laws were drafted well before the development of drones and counter-drone systems and intended to address other technologies.[46]

Concerns over civil and criminal liability are shared internationally. In the United Kingdom, countering a drone in any way may violate portions of the Aviation Security Act and the Criminal Damage Act.[47] The mitigation and jamming of a drone can implicate the Wireless Telegraphy Act and the Electromagnetic Compatibility Regulations.[48] In Europe, some counter-drone technology that collects personally identifiable information may involve the General Data Protection Regulation.[49]

Conclusion

The terrorist and criminal misuse of drones is both present and continuing to develop. As 9/11 taught us all, the possibility of a catastrophic attack would be shocking but not a surprise. The need for countermeasures to address this clear and present danger is quite obvious but fraught with legal and technological issues that still need to be resolved. As the pre- and post-9/11 use of the Predator demonstrates, governments can act proactively and quickly when motivated to do so. While the legal and technological concerns noted here are understandable, viewing these difficulties with a post-9/11 mindset would expedite the implementation process. As 9/11 demonstrated, cautiousness can sometimes be more of an obstacle than a benefit.

44 See discussion in Chapter 4.

45 See Department of Justice: Office of Public Affairs, 'Advisory on the Acquisition and Use of Technology to Detect and Mitigate Unmanned Aircraft Systems' (August 2020) <www.justice.gov/file /1304841 / download> [hereinafter "DOJ Guidance"].

46 See, for example, Title 18 of the United States Code contains multiple sections prohibiting acts that implicate drone mitigation strategies, see 18 U.S.C. § 1362; 18 U.S.C. § 1367(a); 18 U.S.C. § 32; 18 U.S.C. § 2511.

47 See generally, Arthur Holland Michel, 'Counter-Drone Systems' (*Centre for the Study of the Drone*, 2019) <https://dronecenter.bard.edu/files/2019/12/CSD-CUAS-2nd-Edition-Web.pdf> (the author further notes, however, that "a number of British laws might likewise provide legal cover for [counter-drone] actions, depending on the context, including the Criminal Law Act, the Police and Criminal Evidence Act, the Criminal Justice and Immigration Act, and the Investigatory Powers Act").

48 ibid.

49 ibid.

8 Aerodromes and aircraft safety

Patrick Slomski, James M. Cooper, Inês Afonso Mousinho, Olivia Puchalski and Merinda Stewart

Introduction

The proliferation of drones requires consideration of the risks that they pose to manned aircraft, as well as mitigations and protections. The principal risks in that respect are posed to the occupants of the manned aircraft and people on the ground, as well as to the aircraft and other property.

Assessment of risk involves consideration both of the probability of the hazardous event and of the severity of the resulting consequences. Both elements of that exercise are complex when considering the physical collision or interference of drones with manned aircraft, not least because they are dependent on characteristics that vary widely. The risk will depend upon the number of manned aircraft and of drones in the given airspace, as well as the size, mass, construction, speed and trajectory (flight path) of both the manned aircraft and the drone.

Assessment of the likely consequential losses, liabilities, penalties and sanctions suffered as a result of an event may be far from straight-forward given the far-reaching relationships between the actors and stakeholders, as well as the wider economic dependencies on the commercial aviation industry.

In this chapter, we focus on the immediate risks of physical collision or interference with manned aircraft. We provide an overview of those risks, the key stakeholders and their roles, the potential liabilities and issues raised by mitigation and protection. It is perhaps worth noting at this point that what follows is based on the risk landscape and the study results as they are in late 2020.[1] That risk landscape will surely evolve and possibly do so rapidly. The population of drones is expected to grow and the technology, design and availability will evolve. The infrastructure and services to support the integration of drones into shared airspace (including "UTM" or "U-space")[2]

1 Examples of study results include those of: the Alliance for System Safety of UAS through Research Excellence ("ASSURE") <https://assureuas.org/>; EASA, '"Drone Collision" Task Force Final Report' (4 October 2016) <www.easa.europa.eu/sites/default/files/dfu/TF%20Drone%20Collision_Report%20for%20Publication%20(005).pdf>; UK Military Aviation Authority, British Airlines Pilots Association and UK Government's Department for Transport, 'Small Remotely Piloted Aircraft Systems (Drones): Mid-Air Collision Study' (2016) <https://assets.publishing.service.gov.uk/government/uploads/system/uploads/attachment_data/file/918811/small-remotely-piloted-aircraft-systems-drones-mid-air-collision-study.pdf> [hereinafter "BALPA/MAA/DfT study"].

2 The U-space concept has been described as "a set of new services relying on a high level of digitalisation and automation of functions and specific procedures designed to support safe, efficient and secure access to airspace for large numbers of drones." See: <www.sesarju.eu/U-space>. "UTM" (or "UAS Traffic Management") is the equivalent term used in ICAO nomenclature, discussed later.

are being actively developed at this time and with the aim of reducing those risks. Research continues apace and that will undoubtedly refine the understanding of the risks posed and how to mitigate and protect against them.[3]

Characterising the risk

Broadly speaking, the scenarios to be considered are:

(i) interference, without physical collision between drone and manned aircraft, which may result in loss of control of the manned aircraft or injury to the occupants during evasive manoeuvres;
(ii) physical collision of drones with aircraft, which may impede control of the manned aircraft by the flight crew.[4]

Interference is more likely to cause loss of control of the manned aircraft during the critical flight phase of landing or take-off. That is primarily because of the increased risk of severe injury and damage, should the aircraft experience degraded performance or loss of control at the speeds and altitudes involved in those phases.

A full treatment of this subject requires consideration of both cooperative drone operation as well as uncooperative drone incursions into the airspace. Cooperative operation is authorised and coordinated with manned aircraft traffic. It may be achieved by segregation of the drone(s) from the airspace used by manned aircraft or alternatively by coordination with other air traffic; the latter option will generally depend upon the conspicuity of the drone(s) and cooperation with air traffic control in controlled airspace or other "detect and avoid" capability on the part of the drone.

The confliction between manned aircraft and uncooperative drones presents the most challenging of issues, notably in relation to prevention or deterrence of such confliction, detection of the drones and how to avoid or remove them once they are detected. This category includes drones operated innocently but in ignorance or disregard of legal requirements, as well as those operated maliciously.[5]

Likelihood of confliction

We start by considering the likelihood of a drone being found in proximity to a manned aircraft in flight. The majority of the assessments to date are based on statistics gathered from "air proximity"[6] reports or mandatory occurrence reporting.[7] In

3 Examples include continued work by ASSURE (n 1) and the EASA Horizon 2020 Research Project, 'Vulnerability of Manned Aircraft to Drone Strikes' (2020) <www.easa.europa.eu/research-projects/vulnerability-manned-aircraft-drone-strikes>.

4 It may of course also result in cost and expense of repair to the operator in any event and possibly without any risk of loss of control.

5 The likelihood of malicious operations is not negligible, as illustrated by events resulting in the extensive disruption of operations at London Gatwick Airport in 2018; see 'Gatwick Airport: Drones Ground Flights' (*BBC News*, 20 December 2018) <www.bbc.co.uk/news/uk-england-sussex-46623754>.

6 For example, for the UK scheme, see UK Airprox (2020) <www.airproxboard.org.uk/Learn-more/Frequently-asked-questions/>. "Proximity" in this sense is taken to mean a separation, which in the opinion of the pilot or air traffic services personnel in the circumstances may have compromised the safety of the aircraft involved.

those assessments the definition of "proximity" varies but is often taken to mean that the drone is within visual line of sight of the manned aircraft. The majority, if not all, of those statistics will relate to events involving uncooperative drone operation.

To date, worldwide there have been 12 confirmed collision events between a manned aircraft and a drone.[8] One of those events resulted in critical damage to the manned aircraft, loss of control and two consequent fatalities.[9] As has been noted by the UK CAA, on that basis collisions between drones and manned aircraft at present are statistically unlikely but certainly possible.[10]

In the United Kingdom, there has been an increasing trend in the number of proximity occurrences involving drones reported year on year with the exception of 2019. There were six events in 2014, 29 events in 2015, 71 events in 2016, 93 events in 2017, 125 events in 2018 and 91 in 2019.[11] There have been a number of drone sightings near major airports in proximity to large passenger aircraft. To put that in context, the number of confirmed bird-strike events reported in 2016 was 1,835, and the number of confirmed proximity events between manned aircraft has declined over the same period. A similar trend is observed in other jurisdictions.

The likelihood of a proximity occurrence involving an uncooperative drone and a manned aircraft will vary with geographical location and altitude. The UK CAA's 2018 assessment concluded that the majority of drone proximity events occurred at an altitude below 2,000 feet and 95 per cent of such events occurred below 10,000 feet. The altitude distribution is important for a number of reasons, one of which relates to the typical airspeed of a given type of manned aircraft at those altitudes (see the discussion on severity, later).

The UK CAA assessment estimated[12] that the probability of a large passenger aircraft being in proximity of a drone in the London Terminal Manoeuvring Area (one of the busiest volumes of airspace in the UK) at or below 12,000 feet and at or above typical cruise speed was two per million flights.[13] The probability of collision causing critical damage to such an aircraft will inevitably be very much smaller.

Is the probability of collision with a manned aircraft sufficiently small to provide comfort to the regulators and airspace users? The general consensus appears to be "no".

The probability of mid-air collision between aircraft corresponding to the target level of safety is generally taken to be five per billion flight hours,[14] which is three

7 For example, as applied in the United Kingdom, see <www.caa.co.uk/Our-work/Make-a-report-or-complaint/MOR/Occurrence-reporting/>. The obligation to report arises where there is an incident which endangers (or if uncorrected would endanger) the safety of an aircraft, its occupants or any other person.

8 See Aviation Safety Network Drone Database at <https://aviation-safety.net/database/issue/drones.php>.

9 A collision between a Grob G109B type manned aircraft and a 10-kilogram "Dingo" type drone on 3 August 1997 in Germany; see <www.bfu-web.de/DE/Publikationen/Untersuchungsberichte/1997/Bericht_97_3X306-1-2.pdf?__blob=publicationFile>. The manned aircraft was well below the required minimum altitude and entered the segregated airspace allocated to the drone use.

10 UK CAA, 'Drone Safety Risk: An Assessment' (CAP1627, January 2018) <https://publicapps.caa.co.uk/docs/33/CAP1627_Jan2018.pdf>.

11 See UK Airprox Board Summary Reports for updated statistics at <www.airproxboard.org.uk/>.

12 Using 2017 traffic statistics (UK CAA (n 10)).

13 UK CAA (n 10).

14 ICAO Annex 11, Air Traffic Services.

orders of magnitude smaller than the probability of proximity assessed by the UK CAA, referenced earlier. This probability threshold is equated with what would most likely result in loss of both aircraft and all those on board. The studies conducted to date recognize that the probability of collision will be significantly lower than that of a drone being in proximity with a manned aircraft; and the probability of the collision causing loss of the aircraft is much lower than that. The probability of catastrophic loss due to a drone collision may well be below the target safety level. However, the studies to date are arguably insufficient to estimate the probability of loss of manned aircraft and tend to recognise that they do not address the full spectrum of possible collision scenarios.

Second, the assessments described here are based on scenarios that unintentionally bring drones into proximity with manned aircraft; as we discuss later, there is good reason to be concerned about intentional (mischievous, if not malicious) operation of drones in this context.

Third, to date the majority of studies into the risk have focused on large passenger aeroplanes. As discussed later, the aircraft most likely to be vulnerable upon collision with drones are those of smaller "general aviation" type and helicopters, for which the likelihood of collision appears to be less well characterised.

Fourth, these assessments have been primarily based on reported statistics of proximity events. As has been noted by the UK CAA and others,[15] the risk of collision is a complex issue that depends on the interaction of many factors. The data concerning frequency and the nature of drone use is limited. The relationship between drone ownership and risk of collision is not simple or clear, depending as it does on patterns of operation and adherence to the rules of flying. As technology evolves, the risks will change; for example, in response to factors affecting conspicuity of drones or altitude capability. Taking all such factors into account, it appears currently to not be possible to model future collision risk probabilities and while they may decline with the introduction of technological safety measures, the authors submit that this should not be assumed.

The aforementioned considerations all relate to risks of actual interference or physical collision. At this point it is worth considering a slightly different risk concerning aerodromes and other critical infrastructure.

A number of major airports have closed their runways due to the reported presence of uncooperative drones, resulting in disruption. In 2016, Dubai International Airport's airspace was closed for over an hour due to the presence of a drone, at an estimated cost of US$69 million.[16] London Gatwick Airport closed its runways in 2017 for 13 minutes due to the reported presence of a drone. Operations at the same airport were suspended for 36 hours in 2018 due to the presence of one or more drones apparently operated with intent to cause disruption. The cost of the latter episode to industry and the airport operator has been estimated at £50 million.[17]

15 See UK CAA (n 10), EASA (n 1) and BALPA/MAA/DfT study (n 1) and (n 12) above.

16 See Kelly Clarke, 'Drone Brings Dubai Airport to a Halt for an Hour' (*Khaleej Times*, 12 June 2016) <www.khaleejtimes.com/nation/dubai/dubai-airport-closed-for-over-one-hour>.

17 See 'Gatwick Airport: Drones Ground Flights' (*BBC News*, 20 December 2018) <www.bbc.co.uk/news/uk-england-sussex-46623754>; and Hallie Dietrick, 'Gatwick's December Drone Closure Cost Airlines $64.5 Million' (*Fortune*, 22 January 2019) <https://fortune.com/2019/01/22/gatwick-drone-closure-cost/>.

There have been subsequent incursion events causing suspension of airport operations at Dubai International Airport in 2019 (under 30 minutes), Singapore Changi Airport in 2019 (10 hours of intermittent suspension)[18] and Frankfurt in 2020 (over 1 hour of suspension).[19]

The roles and responsibilities of aerodrome operators are discussed further later. A number of the instances listed above appear likely to have been the result of malicious or at least mischievous operation, and the assessments of likelihood discussed earlier are unlikely to assist in predicting those types of incursion. Further, given the perceived consequences of interference or collision with a manned aircraft, airport operators may well consider themselves compelled to close their runways even where the reported presence of the drone is unconfirmed and where the probability of conflict would be assessed as low. Airport operators may be unable to assess whether and for how long the drone is present, in which case the likelihood of disruption of a given magnitude becomes far more difficult to assess.

Severity

There have been no reported instances of interference by a drone (i.e. confliction without physical collision) that threatened or resulted in loss of control of a manned aircraft or injury to the occupants. It remains plausible that interference may have such consequences, in particular during landing or take-off phases of flight. How likely that is appears not to have been the subject of detailed study.

Conversely, the effect of physical collision with an aircraft has been the subject of a number of studies and the commentary earlier refers to the wide variations in characteristics of potential collision scenarios. The studies to date do not purport to take account of the full extent of those variations and recognise the need for further research.[20]

The vulnerability of a manned aircraft depends upon its construction, which will tend to vary considerably with size and type. When considering passenger aircraft, the design and construction standards required by airworthiness and safety regulations (which we will refer to as type design standards) become relevant. Those standards vary according to the type of aircraft and, in general terms, its size. A large passenger aeroplane is generally taken to be one capable of carrying more than 21 occupants.[21] A smaller passenger aeroplane (capable of carrying 21 occupants or less) will generally be designed and constructed to different type design standards. The same observation applies to the distinction between small and large rotor craft (including helicopters). A large rotor craft is generally taken to be capable of carrying more than 11 occupants.

18 See Civil Aviation Authority of Singapore Press Release, 'Response to Media Queries on Drone Sightings in the Vicinity of Changi Airport' (2019) <www.caas.gov.sg/who-we-are/newsroom/Detail/response-to-media-queries-on-unauthorised-drone-sightings-in-the-vicinity-of-changi-airport>.

19 See Alastair Jamieson, 'Drone Sighting Causes Flight Chaos at Frankfurt Airport' (*Euronews*, 2 March 2020) <www.euronews.com/2020/03/02/flights-grounded-at-frankfurt-airport-after-drone-activity>.

20 See (n 1) and (n 2).

21 The criteria determining the application of the type design standards are more complex than simply referring to occupancy, but a more general approach suffices here. For the more detailed criteria for aeroplanes, see the EASA and FAA certification specifications.

Aircraft of different sizes and types may therefore be constructed to differing type design standards, some of which have a direct bearing on the vulnerability to drone collision, even if they were not originally addressed to such risk.[22]

The studies to date relating to aeroplanes identify the principal vulnerabilities as being associated with the windscreen, engines, wing/tailplane leading edges and the control surfaces (on the wings and tailplane). The principal vulnerabilities for rotor craft relate to the windscreen and rotor assembles.

Critical damage to a windscreen risks injury to flight crew, obscuration of the pilot's field of view and possible loss of control of the aircraft. The type design standards applicable to both large and small passenger aeroplanes require that the windscreen should be capable of withstanding a direct bird strike. In the case of large aeroplanes, the windscreen generally must withstand impact with a bird of mass four pounds (1.8kg), when travelling at the aircraft's typical cruise speed (usually taken to be 340 knots or kts). The equivalent requirement for the smaller category of passenger aeroplanes relates to a two-pound (0.9kg) bird at 140 knots.[23] Smaller "general aviation" aeroplanes (generally taken to be capable of carrying around two people) are usually subject to type design standards that do not include bird strike requirements.

It may be expected that the design and construction standards relating to bird strike may result in some resilience of aircraft components in the event of drone collision. That indeed appears to be the case, although studies have shown that the rigidity of drone components may result in greater damage to an aircraft than a collision with a bird of equal mass.[24]

The studies to date tend to assume that the drone most likely to be encountered by an aircraft will be of mass equal to or less than four kilograms.[25] Taking into account the most commonly available mass-marketed drones, the UK CAA assessed in 2018 that the drones most likely to be found in proximity to large passenger aircraft will have a mass equal to or less than two kilograms.

Testing and simulation of windscreen collisions with drones suggests that at higher altitudes (typically above 12,000 feet) certain types of large passenger aeroplane windscreens may suffer severe damage upon collision with a four-kilogram mass drone. The aircraft will tend to be travelling at around its cruise speed at those higher

22 The standards are set out in "certification specifications" issued by the relevant authority. In Europe that authority is the European Aviation Safety Agency ("EASA") and the EASA specifications of relevance are: CS-25 for large passenger aeroplanes; CS-23 for smaller passenger aeroplanes (generally 21 occupants or less); CS-27 for small rotor craft (generally 11 occupants or less); and CS-29 for large rotorcraft. There are other specifications for aircraft satisfying different criteria. See <www.easa.europa.eu/regulations#regulations-initial-airworthiness>. The certification specifications applied by the FAA may be found at <www.faa.gov/aircraft/air_cert/airworthiness_certification/std_awcert/std_awcert_regs/regs/>.

23 See EASA, 'Certification Specifications and Acceptable Means of Compliance for Large Aeroplanes CS-25' (Amendment 25, 24 June 2020) <www.easa.europa.eu/sites/default/files/dfu/cs-25_amendment_25.pdf> and EASA, 'Certification Specifications for Normal-Category Aeroplanes (CS-23) and Acceptable Means of Compliance and Guidance Material to the Certification Specifications for Normal-Category Aeroplanes (AMC & GM to CS-23)' (Amendment 5/AMC & GM C-23 Issue 3, 24 June 2020) <www.easa.europa.eu/sites/default/files/dfu/cs-23_amendment_5_-_amc_gm_to_cs-23_issue_3_0.pdf>.

24 Discussed in the BALPA/MAA/DfT study (n 1).

25 For example, see the BALPA/MAA/DfT study (n 1) and EASA (n 1).

altitudes. Large and small passenger aeroplane windscreens have been found to retain their integrity upon collision with drones in the mass range up to four kilograms at speeds typical for approach and landing.[26]

There appears to be a greater risk of critical windscreen damage in the case of small rotorcraft and small "general aviation" aeroplanes. Such aircraft generally are not subject to type design standards requiring windscreens that are demonstrated to withstand bird strike. Tests have shown that such windscreens may be critically damaged in collisions with drones (across a wide range of masses below 4kg) at speeds well below the typical cruise speed of the manned aircraft.

While studies have shown that in principle wing/tailplane leading edges and the control surfaces may suffer significant damage upon collision with drones falling within the above mass range,[27] it does not appear to have been studied in detail. It has been noted however that significant collisions with drones will most likely involve impact of the aeroplane structure exposed in the direction of travel (which will not include the location of control surfaces). Also, the design of modern large passenger aeroplanes is such that impact at a single point on a leading edge (wing or tailplane) is unlikely to result in degradation of the aeroplane's systems and control.

The studies also support the conclusion that modern turbo-fan jet engines of the kind installed on large passenger aeroplanes are unlikely to suffer critical damage due to collision (or ingestion) of a drone of mass most likely to be encountered. Such engines are typically subject to type design standards that include the requirement that the engine must be capable of shutting down safely after ingestion of a bird of up to approximately four pounds (1.8kg) mass.[28] Further, multi-engine passenger aircraft are typically capable of landing on one engine in the event of engine(s) loss, and the procedures for doing so are part of commercial pilot training.

However, these studies indicate that rotorcraft rotor assemblies are vulnerable to critical damage upon impact with drones across a wide range of drone masses, well below four kilograms.

The likelihood of encountering a drone of four-kilogram mass at an altitude at which large passenger aircraft is travelling fast enough to result in critical damage would presently appear to be low.[29] Accordingly, the clearest risks of collision identified to date relate to small "general aviation" aeroplane and rotorcraft windscreens and (for rotorcraft) rotor assemblies.

We close this section by reiterating a point made earlier: the studies discussed in this section make assumptions about the mass of drones most likely to be encountered by the aircraft within a given range of altitudes. That may well change as the capability of mass-marketed drones evolves.

Stakeholders

There are a number of stakeholders to be considered in the context of safety. We set out a brief overview of their roles and responsibilities in the following discussion. It

26 See UK CAA (n 10), EASA (n 1), and BALPA/MAA/DfT study (n 1) and (n 2).

27 See ASSURE UAS, 'Airborne Collision Severity Evaluation Final Report' (2017) <www.assureuas.org/projects/deliverables/sUASAirborneCollisionReport.php>.

28 For example, EASA (n 23)—see CS-E. 800.

29 For example, see CAP1627, section 3 for discussion of altitude distribution of airprox reports; and see the discussion of likelihood, above.

is worth bearing in mind that many aspects of these roles and responsibilities were defined before it was necessary to consider drone operations, and in many respects, it may be said that the law and regulation have yet to catch up.

The State

Inevitably, each State has the dominant role in regulating drones and their operation within their territory. The starting point is to consider States' international law obligations in respect of aviation. Those obligations may arise from a number of sources, but of particular note is the Chicago Convention 1944[30] (the "Convention"), which has been ratified or is adhered to by 193 countries (referred to as "contracting States").

The Convention includes an undertaking by the contracting States to provide in their territory airports, radio services and other navigation facilities to facilitate international air navigation.[31] It also includes an undertaking to collaborate in securing the highest practicable degree of uniformity in regulations, standards, procedures and organisations.[32]

The minimum standards to be applied by each contracting State are published by the Convention organisation ("ICAO")[33] and attached to the Convention as Annexes. They include standards and recommended practices relating to the Rules of the Air,[34] Meteorological Service for International Air Navigation,[35] Aeronautical Telecommunications[36] (including radar and collision avoidance systems), Air Traffic Services (including air traffic control),[37] Aerodromes,[38] Aeronautical Information Services[39] and Security.[40] There is as yet no separate Annex concerning drones and drone operation. ICAO is however in the process of drawing up international standards for Remotely Piloted Aircraft Systems ("RPAS") (drones) conducting international Instrument Flight Rules ("IFR") operations.[41] Contracting States undertake to notify ICAO of departures from the standards and procedures required pursuant to the Convention.[42]

The Convention includes the obligation on contracting States to ensure that the flight of pilotless aircraft (which includes drones) in regions open to civil aircraft shall be so controlled as to obviate danger to civil aircraft.[43]

30 'The Convention on International Civil Aviation done at Chicago on the 7th Day of December 1944' <www.icao.int/publications/pages/doc7300.aspx>.
31 Article 28 of the Convention.
32 Article 37 of the Convention.
33 The International Civil Aviation Organisation created pursuant to the Chicago Convention; ICAO is a specialised agency of the United Nations.
34 ICAO Annex 2.
35 ICAO Annex 3.
36 ICAO Annex 10.
37 ICAO Annex 11.
38 ICAO Annex 14.
39 ICAO Annex 15.
40 ICAO Annex 17.
41 See 'ICAO Remotely Piloted Aircraft System (RPAS) Concept of Operations (CONOPS) for International IFR Operations', unedited and not yet approved in final form <www.icao.int/safety/UA/Documents/ICAO%20RPAS%20CONOPS.pdf>.
42 Article 38 of the Convention.
43 Article 8 (part) of the Convention.

Accordingly, States will generally legislate so as to ensure that the minimum standards for safe navigation of airspace are applied in their territory. This is usually regulated in detail through licensing of users of the airspace and providers of facilities and services for air navigation, including air navigation service providers ("ANSPs"; see following section) and aerodrome operators (see following section).

States will also define and enforce limitations on or exclusion of flight over geographical areas or in volumes of airspace for the purposes of safety. One pertinent aspect of this concerns the limitations on operation of drones, which commonly include altitude ceilings, limitation of flight to within visual line of sight (or other limited distance) of the drone pilot and the designation of protected (no-fly) zones around critical facilities and infrastructure, including aerodromes.

Another aspect is the regulation and enforcement of conditions and limitations on the use of airspace or related equipment that may interfere with other legitimate uses. The latter category includes the use of radio equipment which may interfere with radio communications used for air traffic control communications.

The safeguarding role of the State, when considering the use of airspace for civil aviation, is reflected by certain provisions of the European Union's "Basic Regulation" (Regulation (EU) 2018/1139), which provides that European Member States shall take all necessary measures to ensure that aerodromes are safeguarded against activities and developments in their surroundings which may cause unacceptable risks to aircraft using the aerodrome;[44] this is addressed further later.

Usually, the State will be responsible for enforcing restrictions on the use of airspace, including by drone operators. This will usually be pursuant to the State's criminal law regime and effected by way of the State's law enforcement agencies and/or civil aviation authorities. It is to be noted that, generally, the powers to enforce restrictions or prohibitions through physical or other intervention against the drone or actors will lie only with law enforcement agencies.

Similar considerations arise concerning security. While it is not always clear cut, there is a distinction between the safety and security of civil aviation. The latter will include protection against malicious acts, such as attacks by terrorists or state actors. Instances of physical damage resulting from the use of drones by such actors are thankfully few in number and have used drones that are not commonly available. The extent of the security risk posed by commonly available small drones is discussed in Chapter 7. In line with existing civil aviation security procedures and systems, it is likely that in the future States will impose security-related obligations in respect of drone risks on services and facilities providers such as an ANSP[45] and aerodromes operators.

Air navigation service providers

An ANSP may provide a number of services covering diverse activities, including "air traffic services", such as air traffic control (area, approach and aerodrome

44 Article 38(1) of Regulation (EU) 2018/1139 on common rules in the field of civil aviation and establishing a European Union Aviation Safety Agency.

45 Air Navigation Service Provider (ANSP).

control services), information services, alerting services and air traffic advisory functions.[46]

An ANSP may be required at an aerodrome if the traffic volume makes this appropriate and all major commercial hub airports will qualify in that respect. The ANSP responsibilities with respect to air traffic control include preventing collisions between aircraft, including collisions on the manoeuvring area and obstructions on that area, as well as expediting and maintaining an orderly flow of air traffic.[47]

They are regulated in most jurisdictions both in terms of qualification of personnel and equipment to be used. This is put in to effect through the licensing of ANSPs by the applicable State. An entity must have a current valid licence in order to provide those services and in order for other organisations such as aerodrome operators to be able to comply with their obligations through delegation.

The ANSP will typically be responsible for monitoring the aerodrome traffic zone and the exclusion zone (as described for aerodromes, below) and therefore have a crucial role in warning aerodrome operators of identified potential hazards to aircraft using that aerodrome. Similarly, where they provide services over other volumes of airspace, they will have a role in monitoring for and warning of hazards. The extent of that responsibility raises interesting legal questions; for example, concerning the extent of the measures that must be taken to detect drone incursions in a given volume of airspace. In practice, that may be determined by the equipment standards imposed on the ANSP under legislation including the applicable aviation authority's (for Europe, European Aviation Safety Agency's (EASA)) regulations and specifications and in connection with obligations imposed through licensing of the ANSP by the State.

Aerodrome operators

An aerodrome is a defined area on land or water (including any buildings, installations and equipment) intended to be used either wholly or in part for the arrival, departure and surface movement of aircraft.[48] The definition covers "heliports" as well as facilities for arrival and departure of fixed wing aircraft. Aerodromes may or may not be called "airports". The definition covers a spectrum ranging from infrequently used rural landing strips, to international hubs such the airports for London, Dubai and Los Angeles.

The risks presented by drones at or around aerodromes warrant particular consideration for a number of reasons. Aerodromes reside in geographical areas and volumes of airspace where there is a concentration of aircraft traffic at altitudes accessible to mass-marketed drones. Those areas and volumes may be busy and, with their

46 For example, see the definitions in the European Union's Regulation (EC) No. 549/2004 (Articles 2(4), 2(5) and 2(11)).

47 See ICAO Annex 11, Air Traffic Services.

48 ICAO Annex 14- Aerodromes—Volume I—Aerodromes Design and Operations, 8th Edition, July 2018, definitions. Note the slightly more extensive definition used, for example, in Commission Regulation (EU) No 139/2014 ("Definitions" Article 2(1)); and see also the UK instrument, the Air Navigation Order 2016 ("Interpretation", Schedule 1).

air navigation restrictions, controls and installations represent a complex operating environment.

Some aerodromes will be a part of a nation's critical infrastructure, the operation of which is of wide-ranging economic importance.

A civil aerodrome may be owned and operated by a State or, more commonly, by private entities. In the latter case, the aerodrome operator must obtain a licence to operate the aerodrome in question; it is through the requirements of that process and of the licence that the State in question imposes and regulates the detailed requirements, duties and restrictions on the aerodrome operator.

An aerodrome will have a defined and recorded geographical surface boundary. It will also have an aerodrome traffic zone ("ATZ") defined as the "airspace of defined dimensions established around an aerodrome for the protection of aerodrome traffic".[49]

States usually define a UAS[50] geographical exclusion zone; also known by other names, including "Flight Restriction Zone" or "No Fly Zone". Within such an exclusion zone, the flight of drones is generally prohibited unless the aerodrome operator (and typically the local civil aviation authority) has given permission. The dimensions and orientation of such a zone are defined by the State or its agencies (for example, the state's civil aviation authority) and may vary according to location. Typically, such an exclusion zones consists of two elements: the ATZ, being a cylinder centred on the aerodrome extending to 2,000 feet altitude or more and having a radius of a few kilometres (typically around 5 km); and a runway protection zone.

Runway protection zones have previously been in use for reasons independent of drone risks. Drone incursions at airports have resulted in many such runway protection zones being extended. In 2019, following the extensive disruption at London Gatwick Airport, the UK government extended the dimensions of such zones to five kilometres beyond the threshold of each runway in both directions, and to (typically) a width of one kilometre centred on the runway centre-line. The runway protection zones typically extend to an altitude equal to that of the ATZ.

The aerodrome operator will usually be responsible for ensuring the provision of air navigation services appropriate to the level of traffic and the operating conditions at the aerodrome.[51] Where there is a sufficient volume of traffic, air traffic control services will be required. An aerodrome operator may subcontract such services from ANSPs but will remain responsible for ensuring that the services are provided in accordance with the safety standards required by the State.

The aerodrome operator will generally be responsible for activities within the geographical boundaries of the aerodrome. The aerodrome operator will be under a duty to take measures to ensure that no unsafe condition arises at the aerodrome that endangers aircraft using the aerodrome. Likewise, the aerodrome operator will be under a duty to monitor the aerodrome to detect unsafe conditions at the aerodrome and must have procedures in place to mitigate such risks as could impact

49 ICAO Annex 2. Different terminologies may be used in other instruments and legislation, but the concept is common.

50 "Unmanned Aircraft Systems", which include drones.

51 Pursuant to Regulation (EU) No. 139/2014 (Annex III, ADR.OR.C.005(b)(1)); but this reflects similar requirements under other legal regimes in other areas of the world.

safe operations. If an unsafe condition is detected, the part of the aerodrome that is affected (which may be all of the runways) must be closed.[52]

The duty of the aerodrome operator to monitor for risks to aircraft using the aerodrome may extend beyond the boundaries of the aerodrome. The obligation to provide air navigation services appropriate to the level of traffic has been aforementioned; that will usually involve monitoring the airspace in the ATZ or beyond. The scope of this responsibility can raise difficult legal questions and is not always clear.

Additionally, the aerodrome operator may be under legal duties to monitor the surroundings of the aerodrome (surface and airspace) for "safeguarding" purposes. Traditionally, the term "safeguarding" was used to refer to monitoring of the habitual use and development of land surrounding the aerodrome to identify potential risks and it was related to planning law. However, in the authors' view the obligations of "safeguarding" may apply to the more transitory risks represented by drones at aerodromes. That is consistent with provisions under European law (for example, Regulation (EU) No.139/2014 Annex III, ADR.OPS.B.075)[53] and English law (for example, Articles 212(1)(a) and (7) of the Air Navigation Order 2016 ("ANO 2016")).[54]

Drone operators and pilots

Pilots and operators are responsible for the overall operation of the drone and in particular for its safe operation. These limitations are mapped out by States and state agencies (typically the civil aviation authorities). By way of example, in the United Kingdom the ANO 2016 sets out responsibilities and duties for safe operation that apply to drones.[55]

Generally, pilots and operators will be required to ensure a safe flight, and pilots will be required to operate the drones within certain limitations so as to ensure no confliction with manned aircraft. Typically, this involves prohibitions against flying the drone above a certain altitude or beyond a certain distance from the pilot. It also involves the requirement to comply with the airspace restrictions near aerodromes[56] as well as exclusion zones as discussed earlier.

As technology matures and services and facilities are introduced to support drone operations (such as "U-space" and UTM),[57] it is expected that States will widen

52 For example, see Regulation (EU) No. 139/2014 (Annex III, ADR.OR.C.005(d) and ADR.OPS.B.075). Such duties may well arise as a matter of law, independently of express regulation requirements.

53 The [aerodrome operator] shall monitor on the aerodrome and its surroundings . . . (3) hazards related to human activities and land use in order to take action within its competence, as appropriate.

54 The CAA must grant a licence . . . if satisfied . . . "(a) the applicant is competent, having regard to its previous conduct and experience, and its equipment, organisation, staffing, maintenance and other arrangements, to secure that the aerodrome and the airspace within which its visual traffic pattern is normally contained are safe for use by aircraft". (Article 212(1) of the ANO 2016); and [the aerodrome operator] must take all reasonable steps to secure that the aerodrome and the airspace within which its visual traffic pattern is normally contained are safe at all times for use by aircraft (Article 212(7) of the ANO 2016).

55 ibid.

56 See Articles 94A (3) (4) (7) and 94B of the ANO 2016.

57 As previously noted, U-space is a UAS traffic management (UTM) project for Europe that has been developed by SESAR consisting of a set of services to support increasingly complex drone operations in European airspace; see <www.sesarju.eu/U-space>.

opportunities to fly beyond these limitations. Currently, the general pattern is that to fly outside such limitations the operator must provide and evidence a specific (and well-defined and limited) operating scenario and a safety case to the relevant civil aviation authority. That will usually involve the operator supporting a risk assessment and demonstrating sufficient mitigations and protections to reduce the risk (to third parties) to an acceptable level.

The non-compliance with the applicable regulations gives rise to penalties, including fines and in certain circumstances imprisonment. The pilot typically has the primary responsibility for controlling the drone in such a way as to ensure the safety of a flight.

Drone manufacturers[58]

The primary responsibility for safe operation of the drone lies with the pilot and the operator, but it is perhaps not too difficult to foresee that they may increasingly depend upon technological safeguards "built-in" to the drone.[59] Regulators currently contemplate that measures to mitigate the risk of incursion of a drone in to (say) aerodrome airspace or above a certain altitude may be effected through aspects of the drone design.[60] The manufacturer (and if different, the designer) of a drone therefore becomes a "stakeholder" in the real sense.

Technologies such as "geo-fencing" can prevent drones from flying over certain areas and are already contemplated for use, for example, via U-space. "Geo-fencing" systems, UAS traffic management (UTM) and counter-UAS systems must be built and developed alongside both U-space and UTM providers in order to tailor the systems to the established exclusion zones, (also known as "Flight Restriction Zones" or "No Fly Zones") as described earlier.

Technology such as "geo-fencing" software, electronic conspicuity and other built-in safety features is therefore envisaged to result in a design standard that all manufacturers may be required to include in their drones.[61] Much of this safety technology is already available on certain mass-marketed drones and will evolve in the next few years.[62]

The European Commission has referred to the balance between the obligations of drones manufacturers and operators in relation to safety[63] and the Federal Aviation Administration (FAA) has already imposed safety obligations on manufacturers[64]

58 See discussion in Chapter 12.

59 See, for example, EASA, 'Special Condition Light Unmanned Aircraft Systems—Medium Risk' (17 December 2020) this document in EASA's terminology describes the Acceptable Means of Compliance (ACM) and Guidance Material (GM) for the specific category. See <www.easa.europa.eu/sites/default/files/dfu/special_condition_sc_light-uas_medium_risk_01.pdf>.

60 For example, Commission Delegated Regulation (EU) 2019/945 requires altitude limits (or limiters) and "geo-awareness" functionalities by design in certain classes of small drones to be placed on the mass market; and contemplates (although it does not require) functions limiting a drone's access to certain volumes of airspace; see Article 6(1) and the related sections of the Annex thereto.

61 House of Commons Science and Technology Committee, 'Commercial and Recreational Drone Rise in the UK' (Twenty-Second Report of Session 2017–19, HC 2021, 11 October 2019).

62 Generally, see discussion in Chapter 19.

63 See European Commission, 'European Commission Paves the Way for Safe, Secure and Green Drone Operations' (12 March 2019) <https://ec.europa.eu/transport/modes/air/news/2019-03-12-drones_en>.

64 Federal Aviation Authority Reauthorization Act of 2018.

who will be required to self-certify that their products comply with the relevant safety standards.[65] It appears inevitable that the evolution of the safety responsibilities of the manufacturer will increasingly expose them to liability and other sanctions for non-compliance.

Jurisdictional case studies

Having established in the earlier section the stakeholders to be considered in the context of drone safety, this section will address the key regulations in three jurisdictions: the European Union, the United States and Australia. Regulations dealing with both the exclusion of drones from the vicinity of airports and their integration will be considered.

European Union[66]

Drone safety regulation in the EU is governed by two main regulations: Commission Implementing Regulation (EU) 2019/947 and Commission Delegated Regulation (EU) 2019/945. These regulations adopt a risk-based approach in that they focus on the risk posed by a given drone operation as opposed to drawing a distinction based on the purpose of the operation.[67] These regulations have as their foundation EU Regulation 2018/1139 ('EASA Basic Regulation'), which forms the basis for civil aviation safety regulation in the EU. Rules for aerodrome safety in the EU are set out under Commission Regulation (EU) 139/2014. It sets out general rules for management and oversight at aerodromes and so will also be relevant to this discussion.

As a baseline, unmanned aircraft should be considered, ultimately, as being able to operate in the same airspace as manned aircraft: "unmanned aircraft, irrespective of their mass, can operate within the same Single European Sky airspace, alongside manned aircraft".[68] The operator of the drone and the operation itself must be regulated to enable this and the rules applicable reflect the risk of operation. For this purpose, drone operations are divided into three categories (from lowest to highest risk): open, specific and certified.[69] As part of this, member States may in UAS geographical zones[70] "prohibit certain or all UAS operations, request particular conditions for certain or all UAS operations or request a prior operations authorisation for certain or all UAS operations".[71]

Drone operations falling under the "open" category pose the lowest risk. Operations at aerodromes would not fall within this category. They apply to drones that operate beyond and up to the periphery of aerodrome traffic zones and runway

65 ibid s345.

66 See detailed discussion in Chapter 14.

67 EASA, 'Civil Drones (Unmanned Aircraft)' <easa.europa.eu/domains/civil-drones-rpas>.

68 Regulation (EU) 2019/947, Recital 1.

69 Regulation (EU) 2019/947, Article 3.

70 Defined under Regulation (EU) 2019/947, Article 2(4) as: "a portion of airspace established by the competent authority that facilitates, restricts or excludes UAS operations in order to address risks pertaining to safety, privacy, protection of personal data, security or the environment, arising from UAS operations".

71 Regulation (EU) 2019/947, Article 15(1)(a).

protection zones and in this sense, they form the rules that help protect the aerodromes by excluding these drones. Operations within this category do not require prior operational authorisation from the national aviation authority (NAA).[72] They must have a maximum take-off weight of less than 25 kilograms, the drone must not fly over people, it must remain in the visual line of sight (VLOS) and it must not fly at an altitude more than 120 metres or /400 feet,[73] among other regulations.[74]

Drone operations at aerodromes are considered for a range of purposes including but not limited to aerodrome movement area inspection/monitoring, runway pavement inspection, foreign direct object (FDO) detection, wildlife management and parcel delivery.[75] Technological advancements will enable drone operations to be increasingly integrated, safely, at aerodromes, both in terms of equipment at airports to detect, communicate with and counter drones and safety features in the manufacturing of the drones themselves. This is reflected in the regulations, which stipulate that in their decision to allow access of drones at aerodromes, member States may consider whether UAS are "equipped with certain technical features, in particular remote identification systems or geo-awareness systems".[76] On this matter, the U-Space concept,[77] which is to be implemented in stages for the safe inclusion of drones, identifies three key initial elements, all of which are particularly important in the airport environment: (i) registration of drone operator/pilot; (ii) electronic identification (to link the drone in flight to the information on the registry); (iii) geo-awareness and geo-fencing.[78]

Drone operations at aerodromes are included within the "specific" and "certified" categories. Drone operations falling under the "specific category" are those that do not meet one of the elements to be included in the "open" category. The authorisation for this category of operation is issued—or not—with consideration to the risk assessment known as the Specific Operations Risk Assessment (SORA), including whether the UAS will be flown in the vicinity of an aerodrome.[79] For operations under this category, operational authorisation is required,[80] the drone operator must be registered, and their registration number must be displayed on the drone, among other requirements.[81]

Finally, operations in the "certified" category will operate under the rules for manned aircraft, with the necessary amendments to those rules to facilitate this. This reflects the fact that operations under this category are considered to have the same risk level as those of manned aircraft. The category involves operations of drones

72 Regulation (EU) 2019/947, Article 3(a).

73 This altitude is determined based on the fact that, with the exception of take-off and landing, most manned aircraft fly at an altitude above 500 feet, with some exceptions such as police, air ambulance and search and rescue (ACI Europe, 'Drones in the Airport Environment' (2020) 19).

74 Regulation (EU) 2019/947, Article 4(1)(a)–(f).

75 ACI Europe (n 73) 35.

76 Regulation (EU) 2019/947, Article 15(1)(d).

77 SESAR, 'A Preliminary Summary of SESAR U-Space Research and Innovation Results (2017–2019)' <www.sesarju.eu/sites/default/files/documents/u-space/U-space%20Drone%20Operations%20Europe.pdf>.

78 Regulation (EU) 2019/945, Recital 26. See further, Regulation (EU) 2019/945 for application and/or consideration of these elements.

79 Regulation (EU) 2019/947, Article 11(4)(b)(iii).

80 Or, depending on the circumstances, a declaration by the operator.

81 Regulation (EU) 2019/947, Article 5(5), Article 5(b) and Article 14(8), respectively.

involving one or more of: flight over assemblies of people, transport of people and carriage of dangerous goods.[82] The operator must be certified and the (remote) pilot must be licensed. Furthermore, the drone must be certified pursuant to EU Regulation 2019/945, which imposes obligations on, among others, drone manufacturers to meet certain requirements for the purpose of ensuring a minimum standard of safety.[83]

In terms of the obligations on aerodrome operators to ensure safety at aerodromes in the case of drone operations, Article 33 of the EASA Basic Regulation requires that safety-related aerodrome equipment must comply with the requirements set out in the relevant annexes to the Regulation.[84] Certification of aerodromes is dependent upon the safety-related aerodrome equipment meeting these requirements.[85] There are currently no provisions for drone detection or counter-drone equipment in this category.[86] Furthermore, as noted earlier in section 3(A), EU member States have an obligation to take measures to ensure that aerodromes are safeguarded against unacceptable risks.[87] There is a division of responsibility in respect to this obligation, as organisations that have been certified as responsible for the operation of aerodromes have an obligation to monitor and mitigate these risks and, where the latter is not possible, bring them to the attention of the relevant authority within the member State.[88]

United States[89]

In the United States, the FAA is the regulatory body for the operation of drones.

Drones operated for commercial purposes and weighing less than 55 pounds (25kg)[90] are regulated under 14 CFR Part 107. Operational restrictions under these regulations include that the drone must be, for example, flown within VLOS, not operated over people who are not involved in the operation or covered by a structure and that it must not be flown at an altitude higher than 400 feet.[91] The drone must also be registered and the pilot requires a Remote Pilot Certificate.[92]

82 Regulation (EU) 2019/947 Article 6(1)(b)(i)–(iii)). Article 6(2) also includes in this category operations that have been considered under the risk assessment for the "specific" category and where it is considered that operation requires certification of the UAS and UAS operator to mitigate the safety risks.

83 Regulation (EU) 2019/945, Article 6 and Annex. See Aerodrome Operators, which mentions requirements for certain classes of small drones to have altitude limiters and geo-awareness functionalities under this Regulation, as well as contemplating functions limiting drone access to certain airspace (geofencing).

84 That is, Annex VII and, if applicable, Annex VIII. "Safety-related aerodrome equipment" is defined in Article 3(17) as "any instrument, equipment, mechanism, apparatus, appurtenance, software or accessory that is used or intended to be used to contribute to the safe operation of aircraft at an aerodrome". The specifications of this equipment are addressed in Articles 34 and 35.

85 Regulation (EU) 2018/1139, Article 34.

86 See discussion of current detection and countermeasure options later.

87 Regulation (EU) 2018/1139, Article 38(1).

88 Regulation (EU) 2018/1139, Article 38(2), read together with Article 37(1). Further specifications regarding the obligation of the aerodrome operator in this capacity are set out in Regulation (EU) 139/2014, Annex III. See, in particular, ADR.OR.C.005(b)(1) and (d), ADR.OPS.B.075(a) and (b).

89 See also discussion in Chapter 15.

90 14 CFR §107.3.

91 14 CFR §§107.31, 107.39, 107.51(b).

92 14 CFR §107.13 and §91.203(a)(2), and §107.12, respectively.

For the purposes of this chapter, Part 107 provides that drones within its scope are not to be operated in the vicinity of airports or, more precisely, that "no person may operate a small unmanned aircraft in a manner that interferes with operations and traffic patterns at any airport, heliport, or seaplane base".[93] Drone operations in controlled airspace, including "within the lateral boundaries of the surface area of Class E airspace designated for an airport", require prior authorisation from air traffic control.[94] The FAA states, in relation to the restrictions under Part 107, that it is possible to "request a waiver of most restrictions if you can show your operation will provide a level of safety at least equivalent to the restriction from which you want the waiver".[95]

Aircraft flown strictly for recreational purposes[96] are subject to the provisions under 49 U.S.C. 44809. Again, these apply to drones weighing less than 55 pounds, but operation of heavier drones may be approved by the FAA.[97] As with commercial drones, drone operations under these rules must be performed within VLOS and flown at an altitude of not more than 400 feet.[98] The drone must also be registered.[99] If drones within these regulations are operated in airspace other than controlled airspace, including within the lateral boundaries of the surface area of Class E airspace designated for an airport, the operator is required to obtain prior approval from "the Administrator", that is, the FAA, and comply with all regulations that apply.[100]

For both commercial and recreational drone operations, a request for authorisation to fly in areas of controlled airspace can be made through the FAA's Low Altitude Authorization and Notification Capability (LAANC).[101] Drones, as manned aircraft, must be equipped with ADS-B Out [102] to operate in most controlled airspace.

Penalties for non-compliance with US drone laws include civil penalties as well as criminal penalties. Intentionally operating within an airport runway exclusion zone can incur a penalty of up to US$250,000 or imprisonment of up to a year. In the case of serious bodily injury or death resulting, the term of imprisonment could be as high as ten years (for reckless violation) or life (for intentional violation).[103]

Australia[104]

The regulatory body for aviation in Australia is the Civil Aviation Safety Authority (CASA), and the principal legislation governing the safety of drone operations is the

93 14 CFR §107.43.
94 14 CFR §107.41.
95 See Fact Sheet, 'Small Unmanned Aircraft Systems (UAS) Regulations (Part 107)' (6 October 2020) <www.faa.gov/news/fact_sheets/news_story.cfm?newsId=22615>.
96 49 U.S.C. 44809(a)(1).
97 49 U.S.C. 44809(c)(2)(a)(A).
98 49 U.S.C. 44809(a)(3) and (6).
99 49 U.S.C. 44809(a)(8).
100 14 CFR §101.41(e).
101 See, FAA, 'UAS Data Exchange (LAANC)' (2020) <www.faa.gov/uas/programs_partnerships/data_exchange/>.
102 Automatic Dependent Surveillance-Broadcast. See 14 CFR §91.225.
103 Jamie Francesca Rodriguez, Jennifer M Nowak, Joel E Roberson and Jonathan M Epstein, 'Drone Regulation in USA' (10 December 2019) <www.lexology.com/library/detail.aspx?g=4377fd16-93a2-4048-a52e-88a4e884456e>.
104 See also discussion in Chapter 18.

Civil Aviation Safety Regulations 1988 (CASR) Part 101 and the accompanying Part 101 Manual of Standards. This subsidiary legislation falls under the *Civil Aviation Act 1988*.[105]

In Australia, drones are classified by weight,[106] and operations are divided according to their purpose: either recreational or commercial. Commercial operations are required to be registered regardless of the weight of the drone,[107] and recreational operations will require registration if the drone weighs over 250 grams.[108]

There are no-fly zones within three nautical miles (5.5km) of movement areas of controlled aerodromes, as well as over the approach and departure paths.[109] A drone must not be operated within this area unless permission has been granted, the details of which will be discussed later.[110] "Micro-RPAs"—RPAs weighing not more than 250 grams[111]—are permitted to operate without the need to obtain permission but under the condition that they are not operated over the movement area or over the departure or approach path, and that they do not create a collision hazard for other aircraft.[112] Operations at non-controlled aerodromes are not subject to these restrictions and drone operations are permitted when manned aircraft are not operating or about to operate within 5.5 kilometres of the aerodrome or the departure and approach paths.[113] Drone operations must also in general be conducted below 400 feet and within VLOS.[114]

Permission to operate within 5.5 kilometres of a controlled aerodrome must be obtained from the air traffic control service in the case of controlled aerodromes.[115] Airservices Australia is responsible for Australia's air traffic management and explains:

> If an RPAS operation is above 400 feet AGL in controlled airspace or over the movement area, runway or approach/departure path of a controlled aerodrome, ATC is responsible for the safety of other aircraft and the prevention of collisions between other aircraft and the RPAS, through segregation.[116]

Access to airspace surrounding controlled aerodromes is assessed for UAS operations in accordance with three "RPAS fly zones": red, amber and green, which are determined according to the compatibility of the drone operation with other airspace users

105 *Civil Aviation Act 1988* (Cth). The main object of this Act is "to establish a regulatory framework for maintaining, enhancing and promoting the safety of civil aviation, with particular emphasis on preventing aviation accidents and incidents".

106 Micro (<250g), Very small (between 250g and 2kg), Medium (between 25kg and 150kg), large (>150kg).

107 As of 28 January 2021. See, CASA, 'Drone Registration' <www.casa.gov.au/drones/register>.

108 As of 30 May 2022. See, CASA, 'Registration and Accreditation' (2020) <www.casa.gov.au/knowyourdrone/registration-and-accreditation>.

109 Part 101 Manual of Standards, 4.02.

110 CASR 101.075 and 101.080; Part 101 Manual of Standards, 4.03.

111 CASR 101.022.

112 CASA, 'CASR Part 101: Micro and Excluded Remotely Piloted Aircraft Operations—Plain English Guide' (September 2020) 14.

113 'Part 101 (Unmanned Aircraft and Rockets) Manual of Standards 2019 (as amended)' 9.03 and 9.04. See also, CASA (n 113) 15.

114 CASR 101.085 and 101.073, respectively.

115 CASR 101.080.

116 Airservices, 'Management of Remotely Piloted Aircraft Systems (RPAS) in ATM Operations: Operational Concept' (August 2018) 6.

in the zones.[117] Airservices Australia undertakes this assessment and determines if the operation can be facilitated or not.[118]

A certified RPA operator is permitted to operate within the no-fly zone of a controlled aerodrome provided certain requirements are met.[119] To be eligible as a certified RPA operator the person must have an organisation and structure that is appropriate for safe operation of RPA, enough qualified and experienced personnel to undertake the proposed operations safely and facilities and equipment to carry out the proposed operations, among other things.[120] The operation within the no-fly zone must be either conducted indoors or be a "tethered operation", in accordance with Part 101 Manual of Standards.[121] The tethering element imposes certain altitude restrictions depending on where in the zone the operation is conducted.[122]

Contravention of the *Civil Aviation Act 1988* and the subordinate legislation, including CASR and the Part 101 Manual of Standards can result in significant penalties including, in some instances, terms of imprisonment.[123] Most of the aviation laws applying to drones are strict liability offences.[124]

Table 8.1 lists the altitude and distance restrictions in the vicinity of aerodromes by jurisdiction.

Mitigation and protection

The roles and responsibilities held by key stakeholders in safeguarding against the risk of drone activities in and around aerodromes were explained earlier in this chapter. In this section, the measures that are currently employed to protect against that risk, and the legal considerations that drive, and in some cases limit, the use of those measures are considered.

Safeguarding duties

The responsibility for protecting against the risk of drone activity both within the geographical boundary of the aerodrome and its surroundings is a shared one. We have explained earlier that the State has an overarching role to ensure aerodromes are safeguarded against activities which may cause unacceptable risks to aircraft. In the context of drones, this frequently includes placing limitations on the operating conditions for drones, including protected no-fly zones around aerodromes.[125]

117 ibid 7–13.

118 There are three models of facilitation under this concept: segregated, coordinated and integrated operations (Airservices, *Management of Remotely Piloted Aircraft Systems (RPAS) in ATM Operations: Operational Concept* (August 2018) 10).

119 Part 101 Manual of Standards 4.04.

120 CASR 101.335(1) (a)–(c). The other requirements (101.335(1)(d) and (f)) are: suitable documented practices and procedures to do so, and nominated suitable persons to be its chief remote pilot and maintenance controller.

121 Part 101 Manual of Standards 4.04(2).

122 Part 101 Manual of Standards 4.04(3).

123 See CASA, 'Enforcement and Penalties' (2020) <casa.gov.au/drones/rules/enforcement>.

124 Including, for instance, the restrictions on operating within 5.5 kilometres of an aerodrome or above 400 feet (CASR 101.075(5)).

125 See further discussion of The State and stakeholders earlier.

Table 8.1 Altitude and Distance Restrictions in the Vicinity of Aerodromes by Jurisdiction

	Altitude Limit	*Vicinity to aerodromes*
EU	120m/400ft	Not stipulated
Australia	120m/400ft	5.5km
US	120m/400ft	8km

The duty to monitor for and detect drone activity within the boundary of the aerodrome (and potentially surrounding area) will rest with the aerodrome operator in the first instance.[126] That duty is also likely to extend to an ANSP engaged to provide air traffic services at the particular aerodrome (although uncertainty remains as to how far that duty extends and what drone monitoring and detection measures the ANSP must take in practice).[127] Once a drone is detected, the power to actively counteract that activity (through physical or other intervention) normally sits exclusively with the State's law enforcement agencies and/or aviation safety agencies.

What this means in practice is that protection against drone activity in the context of aerodromes is successfully achieved only through collaboration between all of the key responsible stakeholders. Examples of that collaboration are becoming more common worldwide.[128] Regulations are expected to develop further to more clearly define the roles and responsibilities of these stakeholders in the context of drone activities.

Shutdown of aerodrome

The most obvious and immediate step that can be taken in the case of a rogue drone posing a risk in and around an aerodrome is to suspend operations at that aerodrome until the risk has passed or been neutralised.[129] Such a step has been taken in most, if not all, of the well-publicised drone incursion events at major aerodromes in recent years.[130] Indeed, closure of an aerodrome (or part thereof) is legally mandated where drone activity constitutes an unsafe condition.[131]

126 The aerodrome operator's duties include to detect unsafe conditions at the aerodrome and to mitigate such risks as could impact safe operations. That duty may extend beyond the boundaries of the aerodrome.

127 An ANSP has a key role in monitoring for and warning of hazards in the relevant area in and around the aerodrome.

128 In Australia, drone countermeasures have been put in place at 29 major airports through collaboration between CASA (Australia's aviation safety regulator), Defence Department, Airservices Australia (ANSP), and the relevant airport operator. See Department of Infrastructure, Transport, Regional Development and Communications, 'National Aviation Policy Issues Paper on Emerging Aviation Technologies' (September 2020) <www.infrastructure.gov.au/aviation/drones/national-aviation-policy-issues-paper-on-emerging-aviation-technologies.aspx>.

129 The chief operating officer of London Gatwick Airport who oversaw the response to the December 2018 incursion event at that airport observed that, "[w]hat this incident has demonstrated is that a drone operator with malicious intent can cause serious disruption to airport operations". See, Justin Rowlatt, 'Gatwick Drone Attack Possible Inside Job, Say Police' (*BBC News*, 14 April 2019) <www.bbc.com/news/uk-47919680>.

130 See (n 17) (n 18) and (n 19) for further details on recent incursion events causing suspension/shutdown of aerodrome operations.

131 See previous discussion of aerodrome operator duties.

Drone incursion events carry peculiar risks in the context of aerodromes, meaning a temporary shutdown of operations is often a necessary and unavoidable consequence. Specifically:

(1) Given the large geographic spread of an aerodrome, and the constant and dynamic nature of airport operations, it is particularly challenging for airport operators to assess whether an incursion has in fact occurred and for how long it may have continued. That uncertainty can be heightened depending on the characteristics of the drone operator. For instance, the police report into the Gatwick Airport event found that the operator(s) of the drones that caused the airport shutdown "*had detailed knowledge of the airport*".[132] This may have been a factor in the offender's ability to prolong the event by pre-empting the airport's responsive actions.[133]
(2) Drones present an obvious hazard to manned aircraft, whether through the risk of a collision with the drone or via a negative impact on manned aircraft operations as a result of action being taken to avoid a collision. There can also be secondary risks, such as when the operations of emergency response aircraft are hindered through groundings or suspensions of activity.[134]
(3) Large crowds in the vicinity of airport terminals raise particular safety concerns that limit the availability of some targeted countermeasures.[135]

The financial and reputational consequences resulting from an aerodrome shutdown, even for a period of time measured in hours, can be severe.[136] Long-term reputational harm to the aerodrome operator can flow from a number of different sources—passengers (shift to competing aerodromes or alternative transport options), airlines (move business to a competing aerodrome), regulators (increased scrutiny) and employees and associated network of personnel (safety concerns, impacts on employment, etc).[137] Interestingly, while there is a significant loss of revenue for an aerodrome operator when an aerodrome is temporarily closed, often the brunt of the loss is borne by the airlines whose flights have been impacted.[138] An example is the Gatwick

132 See 'People behind Gatwick Drone Chaos had "Detailed Knowledge" of Gatwick' (27 September 2019) <www.theguardian.com/uk-news/2019/sep/27/gatwick-drone-disruption-perpetrators-detailed-knowledge-airport-police-report>.

133 See Justin Rowlatt, 'Gatwick Drone Attack Possible Inside Job, Say Police' (*BBC News*, 14 April 2019) <www.bbc.com/news/uk-47919680>.

134 See National Aviation Policy Issues Paper, 'Emerging Aviation Technologies' (September 2020) <www.infrastructure.gov.au/aviation/drones/national-aviation-policy-issues-paper-on-emerging-aviation-technologies.aspx>.

135 G Lykou, D Moustakas and D Gritzalis, 'Defending Airports from UAS: A Survey on Cyber-Attacks and Counter-Drone Sensing Technologies' (2020) 20(12) Sensors (Basel) 3537 <https://doi.org/10.3390/s20123537>.

136 In 2017, the Emirates Authority for Standardisation and Metrology (ESMA) found that airports in the UAE suffer financial losses of AED350,000 (equivalent to close to US$100,000) a minute due to unauthorised drone activity, 'Shutting Down Dubai International Airport Due to a Drone Costs $100,000 a Minute' (9 July 2017) <www.arabianbusiness.com/content/375851-drone-costs-100000-minute-loss-to-uae-airports>.

137 Willis Towers Watson, 'Drone Disruption at Airports' (31 July 2019) <www.willistowerswatson.com/en-AU/Insights/2019/07/drone-disruption-at-airports-a-risk-mitigation-and-insurance-response>.

138 Airlines use-contracts/licences with airport operators often provide the latter with an opportunity to insulate themselves from liability for interrupted aerodrome operations.

Airport incident in 2018. Out of an estimated total incident cost of GBP50 million, EasyJet reported a loss of GBP15 million (compensation to passengers and associated lost revenue). The airport operator's costs, by comparison, were reported as GBP1.4 million.[139]

Current detection and countermeasure options

The availability and effectiveness of current drone-specific detection technologies in a civil setting is progressing but still limited. Many traditional radar systems in use in civil aviation and elsewhere are of questionable suitability for spotting drones. The relatively small size of drones and the low speeds at which they travel make it difficult for radar systems to detect them or distinguish them from other objects such as birds. The heavy noise and high-frequency environments (e.g. Wi-Fi use) within aerodromes also present challenges for some radio frequency and acoustic detection methods.

Drone-specific detection systems have been developed in the context of military operations and applied in some civil settings, deployed on a temporary emergency basis. Advanced radar systems have been developed with the aim of detecting and distinguishing small slow-moving targets, such as the Aveillant holographic radar system that has been used in UTM demonstrations in Antwerp.

The types of detection sensors currently being employed at aerodromes can generally be categorised as follows.

(1) Radar sensors—this can be active radar (radio signal is sent out and detects signals reflected by objects in the sky) or passive radar (radar receives signals from other sources and can detect when that signal is interrupted by a third-party object such as a drone).
(2) Acoustic sensors—the sensors pick up the unique sound imprints of drones and use that information to identify drone type and location.
(3) Radio frequency sensors—radio frequencies are monitored to detect the specific communication link omitted by a drone, and that information is then used to identify the presence and, in some cases, the specific location, of a drone.
(4) Visual sensors—the use of sophisticated cameras and other imaging systems (including infra-red) to detect a drone.

In practice, a combination of these sensors is needed at aerodromes in order to provide a reliable detection system to protect against potential drone incursions. This may well be on top of any broader drone traffic management system that is ultimately developed.[140]

139 'Gatwick Drone Disruption Cost Airport Just £1.4m' (19 June 2019) <www.theguardian.com/uk-news/2019/jun/18/gatwick-drone-disruption-cost-airport-just-14m#:~:text=The%20drone%20attack%20that%20disrupted,4m%20on%20anti%2Ddrone%20technology>.

140 USA, Europe and other states are planning to develop and implement unmanned aerial system traffic management (UTM) systems and remote identification requirements for civilian drones, which will enable airspace authorities to segregate compliant and non-compliant drones [90]. UTM, as a traffic management ecosystem for UAV operations, will compliment manned aviation Air Traffic Management systems and is intended to allow integration of manned and unmanned aircraft operation.

Countermeasures

Current countermeasures available to seek to neutralise the risks posed by drones (once detected) to manned aircraft and in and around aerodromes are many and varied. They broadly fall under two categories—"kinetic" and "non-kinetic".

Kinetic systems cover all measures designed to physically disable or intercept a drone mid-flight. Examples include:[141]

- (i) the use of nets fired from another drone at close proximity to seize the targeted drone and bring it to ground;
- (ii) trained birds of prey which are used to attack and capture the drone;
- (iii) sophisticated weapons utilising high-energy laser or microwave technology to interfere with key component parts of the drone, rendering it inoperable.

Much of these techniques have, to date, only been employed in a military setting. There are obvious concerns as to their suitability in the airspace around aerodromes, given the high volume of air traffic and the risk a physically damaged or disabled drone is likely to pose to crowded areas. Hurdles also exist in terms of the legality of some of these measures under local laws (an issue which is addressed later).

Non-kinetic, or electronic, countermeasures apply radio frequency or GPS jamming technology to disrupt the link between the drone and the drone pilot/controller. A related technique involves manipulating the drone's command system to effectively take over control of the drone from the actual pilot.[142] In each case, the intention is to override the operations of the drone that have raised the safety risk and allow the drone to be brought to a controlled landing or return to its initial or "home" location.

A consistent and widely adopted approach to drone countermeasures for aerodromes is not yet established. Nevertheless, the risks are well known, and governments and key stakeholders are increasingly taking proactive steps to put in place protective measures to avoid the type of scenario seen at some major international airports in recent years. Following the drone disruption event at London Gatwick Airport in late 2018, operators of a number of the United Kingdom's major aerodromes worked quickly with government authorities to source and invest in drone tracking, detection and deterrent systems.[143] While operators are understandably reluctant to disclose specific details of the systems currently employed, it is understood they include a combination of kinetic and non-kinetic countermeasures. Collaboration between national aviation authorities and airports on drone detection is also becoming more common place.[144]

141 Lykou and others (n 135).

142 See, for example, Counter Drone Solutions Pty Ltd (2020) <https://counterdronesolutions.com.au/technology/counter-drone/>.

143 London Gatwick Airport and London Heathrow Airport were two of the main examples of that. See, for example, Unmanned Airspace, 'How UK Government and Airports Responded to Gatwick Drone Chaos' (14 June 2019) <www.unmannedairspace.info/counter-uas-systems-and-policies/how-uk-government-and-airports-have-responded-to-gatwick-drone-chaos/>.

144 In Australia, it was announced in late 2019 that the Civil Aviation Safety Authority had partnered with Airservices Australia (Australia's chief provider of air traffic control services) on a programme to detect and track drone activity at Australian airports. The programme is said to run at 29 of Australia's busiest airports. See, 'Airservices Partners with CASA on Drone Detection Program' <www.airservicesaustralia.com/airservices-partners-with-casa-on-drone-detection-program/>.

Consultation between stakeholders

It is anticipated that drone detection and countermeasures will become more common and, ultimately, more effective. The measures that do become the norm will almost certainly require close consultation between key stakeholders (aerodrome operators, aircraft operators, and relevant government bodies and local law enforcement agencies), together with potential adjustments to existing privacy, surveillance and/or telecommunications laws.

Limitations on deployment of countermeasures

Given the duties of aerodrome operators, as discussed earlier, and the more general obligations on any entity that may affect aviation safety, they must ensure that equipment operated at the aerodrome does not interfere with essential equipment and services (including air navigation services) or itself create an unsafe condition for air traffic. That may present difficulties not only because the use of countermeasures (and possibly methods of detection) may violate those duties and obligations, but because it may be unclear whether the equipment to be used meets the requisite standard under those duties and obligations. In most jurisdictions, there are legal prohibitions on interfering with third-party property. It is generally accepted that this extends to action that interferes with the operation of a drone. Some countries have gone further by specifically prohibiting action to shoot down or interfere with a drone.[145]

The extent to which aerodrome operators can themselves utilise countermeasures varies. In the United States, the FAA issued a statement to aerodrome operators in May 2019 making it clear that the use of drone counter technologies in and around aerodromes is prohibited under US law other than by US federal departments with explicit statutory authority.[146] Concerns that such technology could pose an aviation safety risk by interfering with aircraft navigation are at the heart of that prohibition. The position is different in the United Kingdom, where a number of airports (including London Heathrow and London Gatwick) have (with the backing of government agencies) sourced and employed drone detection, tracking and deterrent systems.

A limiting factor in the deployment of drone countermeasures is the lack of uniformity with regard to privacy and surveillance legislation relevant to drones in some jurisdictions. This makes compliance challenging from a drone operator perspective but also from a detection or mitigation perspective. This in turn has created hurdles for the implementation of countermeasures, even where designed to enhance public safety and security.

For example, in Australia, most states have enacted surveillance laws prohibiting the use of tracking devices to determine the location of a person or an object without

145 See Australia for instance, where penalties for such action are up to two years in prison and/or a fine of up to $26,640 for an individual. See CASA, 'Enforcement and Penalties' (2020) <casa.gov.au/drones/rules/enforcement>.

146 FAA's statement to 'Airport Sponsors' (7 May 2019) <www.faa.gov/airports/airport_safety/media/Updated-Information-UAS-Detection-Countermeasures-Technology-Airports-20190507.pdf>.

consent.[147] Those laws do not expressly refer to "drones", but the language used may be broad enough to capture the use of drones or the tracking of drones through countermeasures. Significantly, surveillance laws are not consistent across Australia in terms of possible exclusions that may apply and also the effect of any breach.[148] This adds up to a complex and, on one view, outdated, landscape for aerodrome operators seeking to protect themselves.

Equipment standards

The development of drones-specific standards addressing issues such as design, engineering and airworthiness are not discussed in detail here. It is relevant to note that many national aviation authorities have in recent years been working to develop a comprehensive and consistent set of standards unique to drones. That work is occurring in a number of settings; for example, through multilateral forums such as ICAO and the Joint Authorities for Rulemaking on Unmanned Systems (JARUS) and independently.[149] Key considerations include the need for fail-safe functions such as "return-to-home" and forced flight termination. It is expected that such standards will play an important role in minimising the air and ground risks associated with drone activity and aerodromes.[150]

At the time of writing, a detailed and comprehensive set of standards is yet to have been settled on, either internationally or domestically. This work is no doubt a priority for lawmakers. In the meantime, uncertainties remain about the structural and technical reliability of some drones commonly flown for recreational and commercial purposes. Those uncertainties are likely to have a bearing on the protective steps taken at an aerodrome in the event of a drone incursion event, including whether to temporarily suspend operations.

Sanctions and penalties

Most jurisdictions now have well-established regimes to identify and take enforcement action against drone operators who are flying unsafely or breaking prescribed

147 In the state of Victoria, for instance, section 8(1) of the Surveillance Devices Act 1999 (Vic) provides that it is an offence to knowingly install, use or maintain a tracking device to determine the geographical location of a person or an object without consent. "Person" and/or "object" arguably capture "drones" and "drones pilots" (although this is yet to be tested).

148 In Queensland and the Australian Capital Territory (ACT), there is no offence provision applying to tracking and detection devices. In New South Wales, there is no offence where the device is used for a "lawful purpose": section 9(2)(c) of the Surveillance Devices Act 2007 (NSW). That exclusion has been relied on by some institutions such as prisons, where the "lawful purpose" is prison security.

149 In Australia—see CASA, Discussion Paper, 'UAS Airworthiness Framework' (2016) and subsequent public consultation. Rural and Regional Affairs and Transport Committee, Parliament of Australia, 'Report on the Regulatory Requirements that Impact on the Safe Use of Remotely Piloted Aircraft Systems, Unmanned Aerial Systems and Associated Systems' (Report, 31 July 2018) 8 <www.aph.gov.au/Parliamentary_Business/Committees/Senate/Rural_and_Regional_Affairs_and_Transport/Drones/Report> [hereinafter "Australian Senate Inquiry Committee"].

There has been limited further public discussion/consultation in Australia since then.

150 It is reported that 64 per cent of drone incidents between 2006 and 2016 were caused by technical problems with the drone, Graham Wild and others, 'Exploring Drone Accidents and Incidents to Help Prevent Potential Air Disasters' (2016) 3(3) Aerospace.

operating conditions. That includes operating drones in prohibited airspace such as around aerodromes. Enforcement action generally includes fines and, in extreme cases, potential imprisonment.

The core principle underlying these enforcement regimes is to discourage unsafe operations, thereby minimizing the risk of occurrence of unauthorised activities, including around aerodromes. Concerns have been raised in some jurisdictions, though, about whether existing penalties are harsh enough to succeed as a deterrent.[151] There are also challenges in ensuring that enforcement bodies are adequately resourced to identify and investigate incidents. Given the potentially serious consequences of interaction between a drone and a manned aircraft, some countries have put in place specific, harsher penalties where a drone is operated in a way that is hazardous to other aircraft.[152]

Aerodrome operators are, themselves, also at risk of regulatory sanction where they fail to perform duties required of them to safeguard against the risk of drones.[153] That sanction commonly takes the form of a fine to the level prescribed in the applicable domestic legislation. It could also result in the suspension or cancellation of an aerodrome's operating certificate by the relevant authorities.[154] There is also the prospect of a civil claim being brought for damage suffered by an affected third party as a result of an alleged breach of duty by the aerodrome operator. While the author is not aware of specific cases to date involving drones in that context, there are many examples of such claims against aerodrome operators for breach in relation to other more traditional risks such as bird strike.[155]

Concluding comments

As drones have become more available and capable over the years, so too has the threat of drone attacks. One of the biggest challenges for key stakeholders in facilitating safe drone operations is ensuring that the regulations keep up to speed with the rapid development of drone technology. Airports in particular can be seen as attractive targets for attacks because of the potential safety, economic and security consequences that can follow an interruption, as was illustrated by the Gatwick incident.[156] Counter-drone technology is of particular interest to those operating in an aerodrome environment because key stakeholders such as airlines must be aware of any conditions that may impose a risk to safety during flight operations.[157]

151 Australian Senate Inquiry Committee (n 149).

152 See, for instance, in Australia, where such unlawful activity can give rise to a penalty of up to two years in prison and/or a fine of up to AU$26,640 for an individual offender.

153 See previous section re summary of duties.

154 For example, in Australia, the CASA may suspend or cancel an aerodrome operating certificate in certain circumstances, including where the operator has failed to operate or maintain the aerodrome with a reasonable degree of care and diligence (reg 139.035 of the *Civil Aviation Safety Regulations 1998* (Cth)).

155 For example, in *Safeco Insurance Co of America v City of Watertown, South Dakota & Ors* 529 F. Supp. 1220, the airport operator was found negligent for failing to devise a satisfactory system to warn of the danger of bird incursion at the airport. See also *Insurance Company of North America v Asplundh Aviation Inc* 574 F Supp 373 (airport operator has a duty to exercise reasonable care and control to protect against anticipated dangers arising from conditions at the premises).

156 UK Counter-Unmanned Aircraft Strategy (October 2019) 15 <https://assets.publishing.service.gov.uk/government/uploads/system/uploads/attachment_data/file/840789/Counter-Unmanned_Aircraft_Strategy_Web_Accessible.pdf>.

157 ibid.

As highlighted earlier, there are a number of legal hurdles in various jurisdictions that prevent the implementation of counter-drone technology in States. In addition to this, there is no clear consensus as to what constitutes "international best practice" for States to adopt by ICAO, who are the responsible agency for providing safety standards for international civil aviation. The added complication of this is that States vary in the development of their drone regulation policy as some are more advanced than others.[158] What is clear though is that States are now focussing on the safe integration of drones into a shared airspace. Countries such as Australia are recognising the potential economic and social benefits of utilising drone technology in various industries, not just the aviation sector. However, before this technology can be properly implemented, consultation between stakeholders, government and industry is required to effectively manage any risks associated with drone use or anti-drone use.[159]

It is suggested that enabling safe and secure drone operations will require "a balance between effective enforcement measures, such as sufficient penalties, registration and restricted flight zones, with that of technology-based solutions including geofencing, ADS-B and UTM (unmanned traffic management)".[160]

These technology-based solutions are considered in further detail detail in Chapter 19.

158 See National Aviation Policy Issues Paper, 'Emerging Aviation Technologies' (September 2020) <www.infrastructure.gov.au/aviation/drones/national-aviation-policy-issues-paper-on-emerging-aviation-technologies.aspx>.

159 ibid.

160 (n 149) para 6.40.

9 Personal injury, property damage, trespass and nuisance

Anthony A. Tarr and Julie-Anne Tarr

Introduction

The preceding two chapters described the actual and potential use of drones in the commission of terrorist acts and the growing risks of confliction between drones and manned aircraft. Whilst there have not been any major incidents involving drones and a passenger aircraft resulting in a catastrophic loss of human lives at the date of publication, there have been a number of airport closures, flight delays and near-collisions with commercial aircraft involving drones all around the world. These events and acts of terrorism attract worldwide attention.[1]

This chapter focuses more generally on the risks posed by drones to cause damage to persons or property on the ground, whether the cause be illegal or irresponsible use, system failure, equipment malfunction or human error.[2] There are reports globally of accidents and incidents involving drones causing personal injury and property damage, and it is expected that as the frequency of drone usage and the number of drones in operation increase, there will be a commensurate increase in the seriousness and frequency of such incidents. Risks to people on the ground can be from a drone flying into a person or the drone or debris from a drone falling onto a person. Similarly, property damage may be inflicted by such collision or crash. These may have different consequences and require different mitigations which could vary considerably based on the size and design of the drone.

Accordingly, injury to persons and property damage are very real concerns arising out of the use of drones, and these concerns will become more acute as the use of drones expands to include routine freight delivery and point-to-point transport for people in high-density population environments.[3]

The increasing use of drones also gives rise to very real privacy concerns (which will be considered in more detail in the next chapter). As Matthew Koerner observes:

> Drones have gained notoriety as a weapon against foreign terrorist targets; yet, they have also recently made headlines as an instrument for domestic surveillance. With

1 See Chapter 7 Global Terrorism and Security.

2 See, for example, Pam Stewart, 'Drone Danger: Remedies for Damage by Civilian Remotely Piloted Aircraft to Persons or Property on the Ground in Australia' (2016) 23 Torts Law Journal 290.

3 Julie-Anne Tarr, Anthony Tarr and Kirsty Paynter, 'Transport, Drones and Regulatory Challenges: Risk Accountability Meets COVID Fast Tracking of a Critical Industry' (2020) 48 Australian Business Law Review 202.

their sophisticated capabilities and continuously decreasing costs, it is not surprising that drones have attracted numerous consumers—most notably, law enforcement.[4]

These privacy concerns extend beyond law enforcement considerations and encompass issues such as the unauthorised collection of data and industrial espionage.

Other real drone risks of a non-safety nature include potential damages arising from private law claims (for example, such as trespass, nuisance, invasion of privacy) and possible damage to a company's goodwill or reputation.[5]

Personal injury and property damage

Numerous examples of personal injury and damage to property are already emerging through drone accidents. For example, there are recorded instances of drones having crashed into individuals in parks and public spaces, into runners during athletic events and of drones crashing into trains, buildings and even onto the lawns of the White House.[6] There was a widely publicised incident of personal injury on the ground by a drone at the Geraldton Endure Batavia Triathlon in Western Australia in April 2014. On that occasion, Raija Ogden, a triathlete competitor, was struck on the head by an RPA that fell from the air while being used to film the race.[7] One submission to the Australian Senate Inquiry Committee[8] demonstrated how the lack of registration and insurance has previously resulted in a bystander footing the bill for a drone operator's mistake when in August 2016 a DJI Inspire 1 RPAS collided into the front of a new Mercedes GLS as it was being driven across the Sydney Harbour Bridge. The impact left part of the RPAS embedded in the car bodywork and other debris scattered across the road. Because of heavy traffic the vehicle was travelling at a slow speed; had the traffic been moving faster the incident could have affected several vehicles and resulted in greater damage in general. Because the operator of the drone remains unknown, and despite police investigations, the owner of the motor vehicle has been left with the repair bill.[9]

4 Matthew R Koerner, 'Drones and the Fourth Amendment: Redefining Expectations of Privacy' (2015) 64 Duke Law Journal 1129.

5 See, for example, Des Butler, 'Drones and Invasions of Privacy: An International Comparison of Legal Responses' (2019) 42(3) UNSW Law Journal 1039.

6 Michael D Shear and Michael S Schmidt, 'White House Drone Crash Described as a US Worker's Drunken Lark' *The New York Times* (New York, 27 January 2015) <www.nytimes.com/2015/01/28/us/white-house-drone.html?_r=0>.

7 Stewart (n 2) 293.

8 Australian Certified UAV Operators, Submission No 73 to the Senate Standing Committee on Rural and Regional Affairs and Transport, 'Regulatory Requirements that Impact on the Safe Use of Remotely Piloted Aircraft Systems, Unmanned Aerial Systems and Associated Systems' (30 December 2016) 31.

9 See also Edgar Alvarez, 'Drone Camera Almost Takes out a Skier on Live TV' (*ENGADGET*, 21 December 2015) <www.engadget.com/2015/12/22/drone-camera-almost-crashes-into-skier/> (malfunctioning drone almost hits World champion skier at race in Italy); Steve Miletich, 'Drone Operator Charged with Knocking Out Woman at Pride Parade' (*The Seattle Times*, 28 October 2015) <www.seattletimes.com/seattle-news/crime/drone-operator-charged-with-knocking-out-woman-atpride-parade/> (drone crashes into building and knocks a woman unconscious during the Pride Parade in downtown Seattle); Julia Talanova, 'Drone Slams into Seating Area at U.S. Open; Teacher Arrested' (*CNN*, 5 September 2015) <www.cnn.com/2015/09/04/us/us-open-tennis-drone-arrest/> (New York City teacher arrested after his drone crashes into an empty section of seats during a match at the US Open); Ryan Kath, 'Drone Crashes, Hits 2 People During Marblehead Parade' (*CBS BOSTON*, 25 May 2015) <http://boston.cbslocal.

With increased deployment through growth in transport and delivery services industries, particularly in high-density population areas, heightened personal injury and property damage risks can be readily anticipated. Not surprisingly, given regulatory systems around the world in which burgeoning numbers of drones, many of which are unregistered or unlicensed, and, in some instances, able to be operated with limited or no training, public confidence in drones reflects wariness. A 2019 survey in the United Kingdom by PWC, for example, indicated less than a third (31%) of the public felt positive towards drone technology, with risk of accident constituting one of the top three issues of concern.[10] Further, 78 per cent wanted drone operators licensed, 77 per cent wanted insurance requirements on drone operations imposed, and 70 per cent flagged a confusion as to administrative reporting lines and oversight for drone misuse.[11]

Tension between expectations or perceptions of fast, efficient and potentially cost-saving deliveries by drone fleets and the reality of outcomes have been documented around several early delivery programmes. Drone delivery company Wing Aviation, owned by Google's parent company, Alphabet, received approval for delivery drone operations in a limited number of jurisdictions in Australia in 2018,[12] making "delivery within minutes" of coffee, sushi, soy chic candles and Oreo or salted caramel gelato a reality.[13] Community backlash[14] against noise and undue intrusion from the drones, however, precipitated a parliamentary enquiry into the technology[15] and stirred major rancour amongst neighbourhoods impacted. Although noise abatement propeller innovations and restrictions to limited numbers of day-time flights were amongst subsequent outcomes around the Australian programmes, the issues remain contentious.

Risks inherent in drone deliveries over high-density population areas were further highlighted in 2019 in Switzerland, when Swiss Post's drone delivery service was suspended in August 2019 in the wake of two crashes.[16] Swiss Post in conjunction

---

com/2015/ 05/25/drone-crashes-hits-2-people-during-marblehead-parade/> (drone crashes into building and injures two people at a Memorial Day parade in Marblehead, Massachusetts) (cited in) Hillary B Farber, 'Keep Out: The Efficacy of Trespass, Nuisance and Privacy Torts as Applied to Drones' (2017) 33(2) Georgia State University Law Review 359–410. <https://heinonlineorg.ezp01.library.qut.edu.au/HOL/Page?handle=hein.journals/gslr33&id=393&collection=jour nals&index=journals/gslr>.

10 Building Trust in Drones—public concerns remain a barrier to drone adoption, PwC, 'Building Trust in Drones' (*PWC*, 04 June 2019) <www.pwc.co.uk/trustindrones>.

11 PwC, 'Building Trust in Drones' (Report, June 2019) <www.pwc.co.uk/trustindrones>.

12 Australian government CASA, 'Industry Initiatives—Drone Delivery Systems' (*Australian Government Civil Aviation Safety Authority*) <www.casa.gov.au/drones/industry-initiatives/drone-delivery-systems>.

13 Wing, 'Canberra—Australia—Wing' (*Wing*) <https://wing.com/australia/canberra>.

14 Niki Burnside and Tahlia Roy, 'Whining Drones Bringing Burritos and Coffee are Bitterly Dividing Canberra Residents' (*ABC News*, 9 November 2018) <www.abc.net.au/news/2018-11-09/noise-from-drone-delivery-service-divides-canberra-residents/10484044>.

15 Australian government, Department of Infrastructure, Transport, Regional Development and Communication, 'Noise Regulation Review for Remotely Piloted Aircraft (RPA) and Specialised Aircraft' (*Australian Government, Department of Infrastructure, Transport, Regional Development and Communication*) <www.infrastructure.gov.au/aviation/environmental/aircraft-noise/noise_regulation_review_for_rpa_drones_and_specialised_aircraft.aspx>.

16 Léa Wertheimer, 'Experts Issue a Good Report for Swiss Post and Matternet—Drones to Take Off' (*Swiss Post*, 23 January 2020) <www.post.ch/en/about-us/news/news/2020/experts-issue-a-good-report-for-swiss-post-and-matternet-drones-to-take-off-again>; See also Brian Garrett-Glaser, 'Drone Delivery Crash in Switzerland Raises Safety Concerns as UPS Forms Subsidiary' (*Aviation Today*, 8 August 2019) <www.aviationtoday.com/2019/08/08/drone-delivery-crash-in-switzerland-raises-safety-concerns/>.

with Silicon Valley start-up Matternet pioneered a delivery programme in 2017 for healthcare products. In May, 2019, a ten-kilogram drone made an uncontrolled crash landing 50 yards away from a group of children, which, taken in conjunction with a crash landing into Lake Zurich in January of the same year resulted in the programme being grounded. In January 2020, in line with meeting recommendations set out by the Swiss Safety Investigation Board into the incident, the programme was resumed.

The rapid rise in commercial drone use by companies such as Amazon, Walmart and Wing—such as Amazon Prime Air achieving "air carrier" designation from the United States Federal Aviation Administration (FAA) in 2020 approving its fleet of drones to deliver packages—will extend both the benefits of drone delivery services and drone-related risks to increasing numbers of people.[17]

At present, there is no single data set for determining the number of incidents occurring domestically or internationally from drones involving ground risks. Moreover, national jurisdictions have different reporting rules that vary according to the mass of the drone, the purpose for which it is being flown and the extent of the injury or damage. For example, in the United States a remote pilot must report to the FAA within ten calendar days

> [A]ny operation of the small unmanned aircraft involving at least:
>
> (a) Serious injury to any person or any loss of consciousness; or
> (b) Damage to any property, other than the small unmanned aircraft, unless one of the following conditions is satisfied:
>
> (1) The cost of repair (including materials and labor) does not exceed $500; or
> (2) The fair market value of the property does not exceed $500 in the event of total loss.[18]

In addition to the report submitted to the FAA, and in accordance with criteria established by the National Transportation Safety Board (NTSB), certain drone accidents must also be reported to the NTSB where the operation of the drone results in any person suffering death or serious injury, or the drone weighed at least 300 pounds and sustained substantial damage.[19]

Drones weighing under 55 pounds and flown as hobby or recreational vehicles and otherwise falling under "model aircraft" definitions of the *FAA Modernisation and Reform Act of 2012* are not included in the FAA or NTSB reporting requirements.[20]

In Canada, drone operators are obliged to report occurrences involving drones to the Transportation Safety Board (TSB), an independent agency enabled by the *Canadian Transportation Investigation and Safety Board Act, SC 1989*. Pursuant to Transportation Safety Board Regulations (TSB Regulations) and to Guidelines issued by the TSB on 13 June 2019, the operator of a drone weighing more than 25 kilograms

17 Concepción de León, 'Drone Delivery? Amazon Moves Closer with F.A.A. Approval' *New York Times* (New York, 31 August 2020) <www.nytimes.com/2020/08/31/business/amazon-drone-delivery.html?auth=login-email&login=email>.

18 14 C.F.R § 107.9 (2018).

19 49 C.F.R § 830.5 (1988).

20 FAA Modernization and Reform Act of 2012, Pub. L. No. 112-95 § 336 (2012) (FAAMRA 2012).

that is involved in an accident must report that accident "as soon as possible by the quickest means available". The Guidelines make it clear that an accident includes a situation where a drone has come into direct contact with a person, where the person is killed or sustains serious injury, and where the drone collides with another drone or manned aircraft.[21]

One of the main considerations in assessing drone risk is loss history. With reporting requirements, such as those applicable in the United States and Canada described earlier, data in relation to drone incidents causing personal injury and damage will increase. However, with the exclusion of drones based on their mass or where they are flown for recreational purposes, the data that accumulates will be less than comprehensive. Moreover, as insurers specialising in drone insurance observe, potentially the highest risk profile pilots are the "sport or recreational" users. Simon Ritterband explains that:

> [T]hey are the ones with the lowest barrier of entry, as a pilot could simply purchase a Drone, register it, and get flying. Even if they are required to pass a theoretical competency test, which could help reiterate flight regulations, new pilots are still more likely to crash due to pilot error. Those flying for "work" purposes are more likely to operate within a well-structured process and be better trained than those that don't.[22]

It is not surprising that commentators expect that most recreational drone collisions with the ground or terrain will go unreported in the absence of any obligation to report such incidents.[23]

The lack of data at this stage in relation to accidents involving a drone means that assessing the risk sometimes must rely on evidence that is based on laboratory work or theoretical data. The paucity of real-world evidence has raised questions on how an acceptable level of safety for drone operations can best be determined to underpin appropriate and proportionate safety standards.[24]

Of considerable assistance in this regard is the comprehensive report prepared by the Alliance for System Safety of UAS through Research Excellence (ASSURE in 2017.)[25]

The UAS Ground Severity Evaluation Final Report documents the UAS platform characteristics related to the severity of Unmanned Aerial Systems ground collision based upon the literature research of over 300 publications from the automotive industry, consumer battery market, toy standards and other fields.[26] The team

21 *Transportation Safety Board Regulations*, SOR/2014-37.

22 Correspondence from Managing Director, Moonrock Insurance Solutions (www.moonrockinsurance.com/), to the General Editor Dr Anthony Tarr (31 October 2020).

23 Australian Government Department of Infrastructure, Transport, Regional Development and Communications, 'Emerging Aviation Technologies, National Aviation Policy Issues Paper' (September 2020) [hereinafter "Emerging Aviation Technologies Paper"].

24 ibid.

25 The Alliance for System Safety of UAS through Research Excellence (ASSURE) comprises 24 of the world's leading research institutions and more than a hundred leading industry/government partners. It is an FAA Center of Excellence for Unmanned Aircraft Systems. The FAA's Center of Excellence for UAS Research ASSURE, "Home" (*ASSURE*) <www.assureuas.org/>.

26 David Arterburn and others, 'Final Report for the FAA UAS Center of Excellence Task A4: UAS Ground Collision Severity Evaluation' (Report, October 2016) <www.assureuas.org/projects/deliverables/

reviewed available research and techniques used to address blunt force trauma, penetration injuries and lacerations as the most significant threats to the public and crews operating Small Unmanned Aerial System (sUAS) platforms.

Their results strongly suggest that earlier assumptions were overly conservative in terms of injury potential because they did not accurately represent the collision dynamics of elastically deformable sUAS with larger contact areas in comparison to the inelastic, metallic debris that occurs following the in-flight break-up of high-speed missiles found on the national test ranges.

Internationally, research into the potential safety risks continues to occur using simulations and theoretical data.[27] Assessment of risk involves consideration both of the probability of the hazardous event and of the severity of the resulting consequences. Both elements of that exercise are complex when considering the physical collision of drones with persons or property, not least because they are dependent on characteristics that vary widely. The risk will depend upon the size, mass, construction, speed and trajectory (flight path) of both the drone and that of the person or property that it collides with or strikes. Moreover, different operating environments pose vastly different risk profiles: operating in an urban environment with other aircraft and ground-based obstacles presents a vastly different risk profile to a farmer operating a drone on a farm in a regional area or a drone operating over the high seas.

That risk landscape will surely evolve and possibly do so rapidly as the population of drones is expected to grow and the technology, design and availability will evolve. Transport safety regulators and investigators domestically and internationally are advocating for close monitoring of drone safety occurrences as well as the need for continued research to ensure a detailed evidence base to develop robust risk mitigation strategies.[28]

Trespass and nuisance

The regulation of drones has, to date, been predominantly concerned with safety. Given the risks to persons and property this is a perfectly legitimate and supportable preoccupation. However, the extensive and increasing use of drones also raises very serious privacy issues and concerns around data collection and use especially given the intrusive potential of drones equipped with cameras and surveillance capability, which are now readily available to the public.

Privacy advocates categorise their use by government agencies for domestic surveillance as "leading to a dystopian, totalitarian government watching over its

---

sUASGroundCollisionReport.php>. The study analysed 512 impacts and simulations using 16 different drones such as the DJI Phantom and the DJI Mavic Pro with payloads and total weights from 322 grams up to six kilograms.

27 For example, Reece A Clothier, Brendan P Williams, and Kelly J Hayhurst, 'Modelling the Risks Remotely Piloted Aircraft Pose to People on the Ground' (2020) 101 Safety Science 33; J A Pérez-Castán and others, 'RPAS Conflict-risk Assessment in Non-segregated Airspace' (2019) 111 Safety Science 7 <https://doi.org/10.1016/j.ssci.2018.08.018>; Eamon T Campolettano and others, 'Ranges of Injury Risk Associated with Impact from Unmanned Aircraft Systems' (2017) 45(12) Annals of Biomedical Engineering 2733 <http://doi.org/10.1007/s10439-017-1921-6>; and Civil Aviation Safety Authority and Monash University, 'Human Injury Model for Small Unmanned Aircraft Impacts' (Report, 2013) <www.casa.gov.au/files/human-injury-model-small-unmanned-aircraft-impactspdf>.

28 Emerging Aviation Technologies Paper (n 23) 25.

citizenry—undetected but omnipresent".[29] Conversely, supporters champion such surveillance as the only way to prevent terrorist and cyberattacks with President Barack Obama defending government surveillance programmes as "modest encroachments on privacy" that strike the right balance between national security and individual liberties".[30] In this regard, it is clear that drones are extremely valuable in law enforcement since they can be outfitted with tools such as facial recognition software, infrared imaging and conversation monitoring software. As Laura La Bella[31] observes, "they are especially useful in cases where it is too difficult or risky for humans to go into a particular location" and they serve as an "'extra set of eyes and ears' in difficult or dangerous situations".[32]

Of course, privacy concerns and considerations do not only arise out of government surveillance, law enforcement and other programmes. Non-governmental agencies may use drones to collect unauthorised data through, for example, aerial surveillance of a mining company's resources or of a land developer's properties.[33] To counter these malpractices, Samantha Dorsey discusses the necessity in the United States for

> a nationally unified regulatory framework that will designate and place restrictions upon data collection, explain how that data may be used, and establish an accountability log that will provide individuals with the opportunity to access their data that is being collected by a commercial UAS entity.[34]

The protection of privacy is considered one of the most contentious issues that communities around the world will need to manage as drone use increases.[35] As the Australian government recently stated in the Emerging Aviation Technologies paper:

> Managing public perceptions of privacy and trust in technology is critical to the ability to embed and harness the benefits of technology and innovation. Privacy is a complex policy area as there is no agreed definition of what is meant by privacy.
>
> The Oxford English Dictionary defines "privacy" as: "The state or condition of being alone, undisturbed or free from public attention as a matter of choice or right; seclusion; freedom from interference or intrusion."[36]

Australia is a signatory to the International Covenant on Civil and Political Rights. This recognises a right to protection from unlawful or arbitrary interference with privacy. Privacy legislation at the Commonwealth level, and in most States and Territories, supports this right in relation to protecting personal information about individuals.

29 Koerner (n 4) 1131.

30 Justin Sink, 'Obama Defends NSA Surveillance Programs as "Right Balance"' (*HILL*, 7 June 2013) <http://thehill.com/video/administration/304165-obama-defends-nsa-programsas-striking-right-balance>.

31 Laura La Bella, *Drones and Law Enforcement* (Rosen Publishing Group INC 2017) 10.

32 See discussion in Chapter 4.

33 See, for example, Sean Valentine, 'Geophysical Trespass, Privacy, and Drones in Oil and Gas Exploration' (2019) 84 Journal of Air Law and Commerce 507.

34 Samantha Dorsey, 'They are Watching You: Drones, Data and the Unregulated Commercial Market' (2018) 70 Federal Communications Law Journal 351 (as cited in Koerner (n 4) 1132).

35 Lisa M PytlikZillig and others, 'A Drone by Any Other Name' (2018) 37(1) IEEE Technology and Society Magazine 80 <https://ieeexplore.ieee.org/ document/8307142>.

36 Emerging Aviation Technologies Paper (n 23).

There is no statutory right to sue for serious invasion of privacy in Australia, though existing actions such as breach of confidence, trespass or negligence could apply to privacy breaches. Other regulations that may be seen to support the right to privacy in Australia includes Commonwealth, State and Territory legislation, which concerns trespass, nuisance and/or surveillance issues.

Accordingly, the legal responses to potential invasions of privacy associated with the use of drones may include dedicated common law causes of action for invasion of privacy, more general common law causes of action that may extend to protect privacy, dedicated statutory causes of action for breach of privacy, privacy legislation that may extend to drones and legislation that specifically applies to invasions of privacy by drones.[37]

At common law an invasion of privacy in the form of an intrusion on an individual's seclusion may base a claim for trespass to land or private nuisance, but both causes of action have limitations which make them an imperfect response to such an intrusion.[38]

Des Butler comments, for example, that a trespass is not committed if the drone is flown above the operator's own land or above public land and is used to observe an individual and their activities on adjacent land.'[39]

Moreover, Hillary B. Farber observes that:

> Torts such as trespass, nuisance, and intrusion upon seclusion are limited in significant ways when applied to drone technology. This is due in large part to a drone's versatility to operate at lower and higher elevations without compromising its ability to capture the quality of the imagery at ground level. Highly sophisticated, sensory enhancing instruments that are equipped to the drone's platform make proximity to the target of the surveillance hardly relevant. On the other hand, physical proximity is a key element in trespass and intrusion upon seclusion claims. Moreover, because of their size, drones will not typically whip up soil, scare livestock, or disturb one's use and enjoyment of land in ways that courts have traditionally found to constitute a nuisance. In this regard, a plaintiff's circumstances in the drone context may be factually distinct from traditional claims under these three torts. This may well undermine any reliance on our current tort scheme to provide relief on controversies involving drones.[40]

The common law concerning trespass and private nuisance is supplemented by data protection legislation in a number of jurisdictions and, as is discussed more fully in Chapter 10, there are varying levels of maturity in such legislation ranging from comprehensive, principles-based data protection regimes (such as Europe's GDPR[41] or the

37 See, for example, Butler (n 5).

38 ibid.; and see *Bernstein of Leigh (Baron) v Skyviews & General Ltd* [1978] QB 479, [1977] 2 All ER 902.

39 ibid.

40 Hillary B Farber, 'Keep Out: The Efficacy of Trespass, Nuisance and Privacy Torts as Applied to Drones' (2017) 33 Georgia State University Law Review 359, 380.

41 European Parliament and of the Council Regulation (EU) 2016/679 on the protection of natural persons with regard to the processing of personal data and on the free movement of such data, and repealing Directive 95/46/EC (General Data Protection Regulation) [2016] OJ L119/1.

Australian Privacy Act)[42] to the patchwork of sectoral and state laws in the United States.[43] In emerging markets, the situation may be further complicated by the lack of any specific privacy or data protection legislation and the potential application of local criminal, media or defamation laws.[44]

In federal jurisdictions, the interplay between national, state and local (Council, local authority or municipal) laws can make for a complex interaction.[45] In the United States, for example, the Supremacy Clause of the US Constitution provides that federal laws are supreme and therefore pre-empt (override) conflicting state and local regulations.[46] Where the federal government has made clear its intention to be the sole regulator of an area, pre-emption is relatively straightforward. Difficulties arise where the federal government has not expressly pre-empted an area particularly where there is crossover with areas traditionally left to the states. An interesting consideration of this issue occurred in *Boggs v Merideth,*[47] where the complainant's drone, being flown about 200 feet above ground level, was shot down with a shotgun by his neighbour, William Merideth. Local authorities first charged William Merideth, the shooter, with wanton endangerment and criminal mischief. However, a state district court judge in Kentucky later dismissed the charges, stating that Merideth had a legal right to shoot the drone down. Merideth, who now calls himself "The Drone Slayer", claims the drone was trespassing on his property and violating his right to privacy, thus giving him the right to shoot it down.[48] Boggs filed a complaint in federal district court claiming he was legally operating his drone in the navigable airspace. He also claimed the state court's ruling conflicted with the exclusive jurisdiction of the FAA over the navigable airspace, which should result in federal law pre-empting Kentucky law. Boggs asserted that this meant Merideth had no property right over the airspace where his drone was flying and therefore no right to shoot it out of the sky. The district court failed to answer whether the drone was trespassing on private property or flying in the navigable airspace when it dismissed Boggs's complaint for lack of subject-matter jurisdiction.

Lane Page[49] points out that this federal case demonstrates the current lack of clarity on airspace property rights, presents the question of what constitutes an aerial trespass and highlights how blurry the line is between federal and state jurisdiction over airspace.

42 *Privacy Act 1988* (Cth).

43 See, for example, Council on Foreign Relations, 'Reforming the US Approach to Data Protection and Privacy; A Patchwork of Existing Protections' (*Council on Foreign Relations*, 30 January 2018) <www.cfr.org/report/reforming-us-approach-data-protection#chapter-title-0-2>.

44 See, for example, GSMA, 'Data Privacy Frameworks in MENA: Emerging Approaches and Common Principles' (Report, November 2019) <www.gsma.com/mena/resources/data-privacy-frameworks-in-mena>.

45 See detailed discussion in Chapter 13.

46 U.S. CONST. art. VI, cl. 2. 118 See, for example, *Mutual Pharmacy Co. v. Bartlett*, 570 U.S. 472 (2013), 476, 479–80 (holding that federal law pre-empted state law that directly conflicted with federal prohibition on drug manufacturers independently changing product labels). See also *Singer v. City of Newton*, 284 F. Supp. 3d 125 (D. Mass. 2017), appeal dismissed, No. 17-2045 (1st. Cir. Dec. 7, 2017) where a federal district court held that FAA regulations impliedly pre-empted sections of a Massachusetts city ordinance. Discussed fully in Chapter 13.

47 Complaint for Declaratory Judgment and Damages, *Boggs v. Merideth*, No. 3:16- CV-00006-TBR, 2017 WL 1088093 (W.D. Ky., 21 March 2017), 3–4.

48 Lane Page, 'Drone Trespass and the Line Separating the National Airspace and Private Property' (2018) 86 George Washington Law Review 1152.

49 ibid.

This presents a problem, however, because the FAA has exclusive jurisdiction over the undefined "navigable airspace", meaning that federal law will likely pre-empt any state regulation that addresses drone trespass. Any sufficient regulation covering this issue will require restrictions of the airspace that the FAA will consider to be the "navigable airspace" and thus an intrusion into its jurisdiction. This conflict will result in drone trespass remaining unregulated, leaving landowners and drone operators without any clear answer as to who is allowed to be where. Page[50] proposes that the FAA addresses this issue by defining the navigable airspace so that there is a bright-line height minimum describing where the FAA's exclusive jurisdiction ends, where drones must fly above and where in the airspace states can regulate without the fear of federal pre-emption.

While there certainly is a need for clear standards specific to drone use, it must be remembered that drones are defined as "aircraft" under US law.[51] In that regard, US law states that the United States has sovereignty over the "national airspace".[52] That being said, US law also states that the national airspace includes "airspace needed to insure safety in the takeoff and landing of aircraft".[53] Taken together, these statutes provide a federal right for a drone operator to use the national airspace for take-offs and landings irrespective of what state or local law requires. Indeed, in a case brought to invalidate local laws restricting drone flight, a federal court in Boston held in *Singer v. City of Newton*[54] that local law was pre-empted because it conflicted with Congress's direction to the FAA to integrate drones into the national airspace.

At odds with the foregoing, state and local governments in the United States have continued to be active in their legislative attempts to define the scope of landowners' property interests in low-altitude airspace, thereby balancing the interests of a burgeoning industry with those who wish to keep drones at a reasonable distance. Seemingly motivated by perceived shortcomings in existing law to address drone privacy issues there are ongoing legislative initiatives directed at giving property owners express rights to exclude drones from the navigable airspace directly above their property and to ameliorate some of the deficiencies in how existing torts are currently being applied to drones.[55]

For example, in response to the use of UAS by paparazzi, California[56] updated its privacy laws to include wording that makes entering the airspace above the land of another without permission an actionable violation for invasion of privacy.[57] Related to same, worldwide publicity recently focused on a lawsuit brought by "Harry and Meghan" against paparazzi who purportedly flew a "drone" over the couple's house in Los Angeles to photograph their son, Archie.[58]

50 ibid 1173–78.
51 FAAMRA 2012, §§331(8) and (9).
52 49 U.S.C. § 40103(a).
53 ibid § 40102(a)(30).
54 *Singer v City of Newton* (n 45) See full discussion in Chapter 13.
55 Farber (n 40) 374.
56 National Conference of State Legislatures, 'State Unmanned Aircraft Systems (UAS)–2015 Legislation' (30 September 2016) <www.ncsL.org/research/transportation/state-unmanned-aircraft-systems-uas-2015-legislation.aspx> [https://perma.cc/ V4S6-NNKW].
57 California Civ. Code § 1708.8(a) (West 2019) The law prohibits using a drone to capture an image or recording of a person engaging in a private, personal or familial activity without permission.
58 Olivia Petter, 'Harry and Meghan Sue over "Drone Photos" Taken of Son Archie at Home in Lockdown' (*Independent*, 24 July 2020) <www.independent.co.uk/life-style/royal-family/meghan-harry-archie-photos-sue-drone-a9635566.html>.

In addition to California, Louisiana updated its general trespass law to specifically address drones, criminalising the operation of UAS over the property of another with the intent to conduct surveillance of the property or an individual lawfully thereon.[59] This legislation would certainly conflict with the holding in *Singer* and reflect the confusing and still unsettled legal landscape.

Nonetheless, updates have also been made to the criminal privacy offenses of video voyeurism,[60] voyeurism,[61] and peeping tom.[62] Under each, a drone must be used for the purpose of committing the relevant offence to constitute a violation.[63] In Texas, it is a criminal offence to use a drone to capture an "image" of an individual or a privately owned real property if the operator does not destroy the image as soon as he becomes aware it was captured or if the operator discloses, displays or distributes the image to any third party.[64] Civil actions are also available to enjoin this activity, and actual damages may be recovered if disclosure, display or distribution occurred with "malice". Critically, an "image" is defined as "any capturing of sound waves, thermal, infrared, ultraviolet, visible light, or other electromagnetic waves, odor, or other conditions existing on or about real property . . . or an individual located on that property".[65] Sean Valentine comments that the law makes no general exception for commercial drones operating in compliance with FAA regulations and that while this law may afford meaningful protection to property owners, it could result in significant consequences for unaware or careless operators.[66]

Having noted the foregoing, it is relevant to note that the US Supreme Court upheld the right to take photographs from aircraft flying above someone's property while within the navigable airspace.[67] This pronouncement not only raises a clear legal conflict with local laws but also raises the question of whether local laws directed at drones are even necessary. Existing laws prohibiting voyeurism and the like are almost certainly applicable irrespective of the means used to commit such an offence. As the legal landscape in the United States becomes more defined, it is hoped that the perceived need for these conflicting laws abates.

A further national approach to trespass and nuisance issues may be drawn from Spain.[68] On the basis of the content of Article 12 of the Universal Declaration of Human rights and Article 17 of the International Covenant on Civil and Political Rights,[69] as well as the European Convention on the Protection of Human Rights

59 LA. Rev. Stat. Ann. § 14:63 (2016).
60 ibid.
61 ibid § 14:283.1. 61 I.
62 ibid § 14:284. 62.
63 See Valentine (n 33).
64 See TEXAS Gov. Code Ann. §§ 423.003-423.004.
65 ibid § 423.001.
66 Valentine (n 33) 515.
67 See, *California v Ciraolo*, 478 U.S. 1014 (1986).
68 See Chapter 16 National Regulatory Structure and Responses: Spain for more detailed discussion.
69 Both articles state that no person shall be subject to arbitrary intrusion into his/her private life, family, home or correspondence, or to any attack on his/her honour or reputation. Every person is entitled to the protection of the law against such intrusion or attack, Universal Declaration of Human Rights (adopted 10 December 1948 UNGA Res 217 A(III) (UDHR), art 12; International Covenant on Civil and Political Rights (adopted 16 December 1966, entered into force 23 March 1976) 999 UNTS 171 (ICCPR), art 17.

and Fundamental Freedoms,[70] Article 18.1 of the Spanish Constitution enshrines the fundamental right to personal privacy and self-image.[71] This fundamental right may be unlawfully interfered with as a consequence of frames or photographs being taken from a drone and extends to all the technologies used for recording and capturing of images. The protection of these rights in the event of the capture and processing of personal data and images from drones are covered under the provisions of the Spanish Criminal Code and Organic Law 1/1982, of 5 May 1982, governing civil protection of the right to personal and family integrity and privacy and to self-image (LOPH).[72] In this respect, Article 7.5 LOPH considers an "unlawful interference" to be the capture, reproduction or publication by means of a photograph, film or any other processing of images of people in places or at moments in or outside of their private lives, unless those people hold public office or exercise a public profession, and the image is captured during the course of a public activity in a public place (Article 8.2). The right to personal privacy and to self-image is not an absolute right and is therefore subject to evaluation and proportionality in order to assess the lawfulness or otherwise of the interference, taking into account not only laws but also social customs and individual circumstances.

Certain types of nuisance, such as noise, have a greater capacity to generate tension between national, state and local authorities in relation to regulatory responsibility and control. Noise is one of the most significant limiting factors impacting public acceptability of drone operations[73] and public responses to various regulatory or policy documents, such as the Australian government's Emerging Aviation Technologies paper,[74] emphasise community expectations with respect to regulation of issues around noise, amenity and privacy. Moreover, local authorities, councils and municipalities are usually the first port of call for noise complaints with strong community expectations that their locally elected and appointed officials take an active and leading role in setting and enforcing the regulatory framework relating to noise control and privacy intrusions through various planning and enforcement mechanisms.[75] Accordingly, it is not surprising to find a complex overlay of national, state and local laws endeavouring to address noise issues.

For example, in Australia the federal government has sought to maintain responsibility for the regulation of drone noise to ensure that a consistent approach is applied

70 Convention for the Protection of Human Rights and Fundamental Freedoms (European Convention on Human Rights, as amended), art 8 of the Convention provides that: 1. Every person is entitled to the respect of his/her private and family life, home and correspondence. 2. Public authorities may not interfere in the exercise of this right unless such interference is provided for by Law and constitutes a measure which, in a democratic society, may be necessary for the purposes of national security, public safety, the economic health of the country or the defence of good order and the prevention of crime, the protection of health or morals or the protection of the rights and freedoms of others.

71 BOE [OJ] nº 311, of 29 December 1978.

72 BOE [OJ] nº 115, of 14 May 1982.

73 Nesta, 'Flying High: The Future of Drone Technology in UK Cities' (Report, July 2018). <www.nesta.org.uk/report/flying-high-challenge-future-of-drone-technology-in-uk-cities/>.

74 Emerging Aviation Technologies paper (n 23).

75 See Hon George Gear JP and Cr Renee McLennan, City of Melville/Town of Bassendean, WA, Submission No 50 to the Australian Government Department of Infrastructure, Transport, Regional Development and Communication, 'National Aviation Policy Issues Paper on Emerging Aviation Technologies' (6 November 2020).

across the country to foster interoperability, enforcement and compliance by industry.[76] In addition to the aviation-specific legislation, such as the *Air Navigation (Aircraft Noise) Regulations 2018,* there is federal or Commonwealth environmental legislation that covers noise impacts. The Commonwealth administers the *Environmental Protection and Biodiversity Conservation Act 1999 (EPBC Act)*, while each state or territory administers its own environmental legislation. State and territory governments have general responsibility for ground-based noise impact (under environmental protection or nuisance laws) in their jurisdictions. State and territory noise or nuisance regulations and guidelines do not generally impose a decibel limit on objects. Instead, they consider on a case-by-case basis a number of factors to determine if the noise is inappropriate for that location at a particular point in time. Depending on the sound of a drone, it may be viewed as having the same impact as the sound of a piece of mechanical machinery such as a lawnmower being operated in an urban area. The assessment of noise needs to take into account the volume, character, timing, number of people impacted and broader community expectations.[77]

A major difficulty with applying noise regulation to most drones is that there is a lack of existing standards or conventions for drone noise and no process for noise certification. Aircraft noise has generally been in predictable patterns and scale that correlate to the location of airports and flight paths. For example, noise is regulated to some extent at all UK airports. This can include noise limits and restrictions on operations. The specific restrictions will differ from airport to airport, reflecting the types of aircraft that operate there, how busy the airport is and what the flight paths are.

Although maximum noise limits are set for occupational noise exposure, there is no limit defined for environmental noise, including aviation noise. However, in order to assess the significance of aircraft noise in the United Kingdom, it is generally assumed that if the average noise level in an area from 7.00 a.m. to 11.00 p.m. is more than 57dBA L_{eq}, it will be "significantly annoying" to the community that live and work there. The EU has established a corresponding policy threshold of 55 dB L_{den}, resulting in two different measures being used to inform policy at present. This does not mean that noise above these levels will not be allowed. But it does mean that noise will be an important factor in planning decisions within that area (for example, about airport expansion), and that there may be support available for noise mitigation (such as double-glazing).[78]

Smaller drones do not have the same geographical positioning and limitations, being able to operate anywhere within the urban environment. This complicates the measurement of noise impact and exposure.[79] The impact of a noise will be further influenced by the environment in which the drone is operating and the conditions on any given day. As well as there being no easy single measurement tool or threshold that can be applied, the noise from many drones is an atypical noise and potentially

76 Emerging Aviation Technologies paper (n 23).

77 Queensland Government Department of the Premier and Cabinet, 'Queensland Drones Strategy' (June 2018).

78 Civil Aviation Authority, 'Noise—An Overview of Aviation Noise' (*Civil Aviation Authority*) <www.caa.co.uk/Consumers/Environment/Noise/Noise/#:~:text=Aircraft%20noise%20is%20not%20currently,or%20the%20Noise%20Act%201996>.

79 Emerging Aviation Technologies paper (n 23).

viewed by some people as annoying.[80] The study of noise produced by drones and ways in that a standard could be established continue to evolve.[81] Simultaneously, drone manufacturers are working to adjust the level and type of noise generated, meaning that noise research can become quickly outdated as technology evolves.

Concluding comments

Community concerns in relation to the risks posed by drones to cause damage to persons or property on the ground and to trespass and nuisance issues are very strong.

For example, various submissions in response to the Australian government's Emerging Aviation Technologies paper[82] emphasise the necessity for safe and secure operations and consideration for the community and the environment. A Melbourne community association[83] urged consideration of mechanisms such as exclusion zones over at-risk areas, such as densely populated communities and, with respect to impacts on the community and the environment, they identified noise to be the primary issue.

They observe very cogently that:

> As with fixed wing/rotor aircraft flying over public space, just one small mistake could result in crashes that threaten the health, safety and well-being of people in public and private property. Proliferation of these new technologies and their relatively inexpensive access, heighten the level of risk. Also, crashes into public infrastructure such as electricity pylons and poles, straying into flight paths of other aircraft and protected (controlled) airspaces in particular, all urban areas in uncontrolled air space, could result in extreme danger putting many lives at risk. These factors and levels of risk must be taken into account. . . .
>
> In respect to noise the key words are . . . consistent with local community considerations. . . . With increasing use and concentration of drones and the proposed use of eVTOL aircraft into and above urban settings, this will bring into focus how noise management is undertaken to address community concerns. The current approach to aircraft noise regulation and its related legislative mechanisms are not reflective of what many communities expect and therefore not fit for purpose to be extended to regulate noise emitted from drones and eVOTL.[84]

80 Garth Paine, 'Drones to Deliver Incessant Buzzing Noise, and Packages' (*government technology*, 3 May 2019) <www.govtech.com/fs/automation/Drones-to-Deliver-Incessant-Buzzing-Noise-and-Packages.html>; Andrew J Lohn, *What's the Buzz?* (ebook, RAND Corporation 2017) <https://doi.org/10.7249/RR1718>.

81 N Kloet, S Watkins, X Wang, S Prudden, R Clothier and J Palmer, 'Drone On: A Preliminary Investigation of the Acoustic Impact of Unmanned Aircraft Systems (UAS)' (24th International Congress on Sound and Vibration, London, July 2017) <http://researchbank.rmit.edu.au/view/ rmit:46120>.

82 ibid (n 23).

83 Ian Mitchell, East Melbourne Group, Submission No 7 to the Australian Government Department of Infrastructure, Transport, Regional Development and Communication, 'National Aviation Policy Issues Paper on Emerging Aviation Technologies' (23 October 2020).

84 See also Sebastian Davies-Slate, Western Australian Local Government Association, Submission No 5 to the Australian Government Department of Infrastructure, Transport, Regional Development and Communication, 'National Aviation Policy Issues Paper on Emerging Aviation Technologies' (19 October 2020).

In responding to community concerns in relation to matters such as noise, the cautionary words of the FAA should be heeded. In a submission[85] to the Emerging Aviation Technologies paper, the FAA cautions against allowing community acceptance to solely drive any noise regulations and instead suggests considering the use of the international [ICAO] environmental standard-setting approach to take into account the effectiveness and reliability of certification schemes from the viewpoint of technical feasibility, economic reasonableness and environmental benefit to be achieved. They point to the fact that in the United States, the FAA is required[86] to consider whether the standard or regulation is economically reasonable, technologically practicable and appropriate for the applicable aircraft, aircraft engine, appliance or certificate. While this approach seems reasonable, it is pertinent to note that although drones are defined as aircraft in the United States, neither the FAA nor the US Congress requires the FAA to approve the design and noise levels for drones as they are required to do for other aircraft.

In relation to privacy in general, Hillary B. Farber[87] makes the following valid observations.

> The drone's size, versatility, and maneuverability separate it from other aircraft and satellites. When the property laws changed to accommodate high altitude aircraft, such as planes and even helicopters, it was understood that the risks to privacy were minimal and the need for air travel was great. However, drones maneuver in low altitude airspace, thereby posing new and tangible threats to privacy. As people turn to the courts for relief, the thorny issues raised . . . about the applicability of existing torts to drones will have to be resolved. The shortcomings of these doctrines will likely pave the way for the passage of new drone laws, designed to settle the ambiguity about where a property owner's rights to airspace begin and end. No doubt the new rules governing small commercial drones will exponentially increase the number of drones in our skies. At the same time, state and local governments have the opportunity to define the scope of landowners' property interest in low altitude airspace, thereby balancing the interests of a burgeoning industry with those who wish to keep drones at a reasonable distance. Shortcomings in existing torts to handle drone privacy cases will direct future legislation. To be sure, laws that give property owners express rights to exclude drones from the navigable airspace directly above their property will ameliorate some of the deficiencies in how our existing torts are currently being applied to drones.[88]

In many jurisdictions there is a lack of national consistency with regard to national and state privacy and surveillance legislation and regulations,[89] and this inconsistency

85 United States Federal Aviation Administration (FAA), 'FAA Comments on the "National Aviation Policy Issues Paper on Emerging Aviation Technologies"' (Comments, 30 October 2020) <www.infrastructure.gov.au/aviation/drones/files/submission-47-faa-comments_australia_uas_policy_oct20-v2.pdf>.

86 49 U.S.C. §44715—Controlling aircraft noise and sonic boom.

87 Farber (n 40).

88 See also Thomas Carlton, 'New Heights, New Uses, and New Questions: Can Individuals Enforece their Property Rights Against the Impending Rise of Low-Flying Drones?' (2018) 59 Boston College Law Review 2135.

89 See, for example, Australian Senate Inquiry Committee, 'Regulatory Requirements that Impact on the Safe Use of Remotely Piloted Aircraft Systems, Unmanned Aerial Systems and Associated Systems' (31 July 2018); at para 1.15. paras 7.34–7.36. Along with privacy legislation such as the *Privacy Act*

coupled with the growth of local council by-laws relating to drone operations has made compliance for drone operators extremely challenging. As Professor Des Butler noted[90] that there is not a uniform approach to privacy laws as they apply to individuals. It is therefore difficult for drone operators to establish whether they are operating within the law or not. Professor Butler continued:

> In the absence of a specific common law or statutory cause of action protecting personal privacy, [there exists] a piecemeal collection of common law causes of action such as trespass, private nuisance and breach of confidence, all of which have limitations which mean that they do not provide complete protection against invasions of privacy.

It is beyond the scope, and length, of this chapter to explore in any detail the labyrinthian detail of these privacy and surveillance laws, but it is noted that concerns as to their inconsistency is not new. For example, the 2014 House of Representatives report titled "Eyes in the sky: Inquiry into drones and the regulation of air safety and privacy"[91] made a recommendation with regard to the harmonization of privacy laws, but the Australian government responded that it is "appropriate that states and territories continue to modify their own surveillance device laws, if necessary".[92] Similar sentiments are expressed in relation to the FAA and the need for regulations to apply uniformly to all drones used for commercial purposes in the United States.[93] While these regulatory initiatives are certainly understandable, it is also relevant to note that Harry and Meghan's sister-in-law, Kate, was photographed topless by a photographer located almost a kilometre away.[94] This distance is far further than a drone could be to take such a photograph yet no global movement to ban telephotos lens has materialised.

Chapter 10 considers data protection, privacy and big data with particular reference to Europe's General Data Protection Regulation (**GDPR**)[95] and similar international legislation.

1988 (Cth), surveillance devices legislation, which governs the use of optical surveillance devices and data surveillance tracking devices, has been enacted in five jurisdictions—New South Wales, Victoria, Western Australia, South Australia and the Northern Territory. Yet, these laws create further confusion about the permissible use of RPAS.

90 Professor Des Butler, Submission No 18 to the Senate Standing Committee on Rural and Regional Affairs and Transport, 'Regulatory Requirements that Impact on the Safe Use of Remotely Piloted Aircraft Systems, Unmanned Aerial Systems and Associated Systems' (2016) 31, 3.

91 House of Representatives Standing Committee on Social Policy and Legal Affairs, 'Eyes in the Sky: Inquiry into Drones and the Regulation of Air Safety and Privacy' (July 2014) 48.

92 Australian government, 'Australian Government response to the Standing Committee on Social Policy and Legal Affairs Report—Eyes in the Sky: Inquiry into Drones and the Regulation of Air Safety and Privacy' (December 2016) 9.

93 See, for example, Farber (n 40); Page (n 47).

94 Megan Levy, 'Snapped from Afar, Topless Shots Spanned 1KM' *The Sydney Morning Herald* (Sydney, 17 September 2012) <www.smh.com.au/entertainment/celebrity/snapped-from-afar-topless-shots-spanned-1km-20120917-261a1.html>.

95 General Data Protection Regulation (n 41).

10 Data protection, privacy & big data[1]

Dino Wilkinson and Masha Ooijevaar

Introduction

Drones have long been considered as "eyes in the sky"[2] with all but the most basic consumer models routinely equipped with some form of camera for still or video image capture. More advanced surveillance technologies can combine a sophisticated camera drone's high-quality audiovisual recording and storage capabilities with data analytics tools such as facial recognition software, gait analysis and other biometric assessment techniques to identify individuals for targeted observation. The size and manoeuvrability of drones enable them to monitor individuals at a distance and to follow and track targets, potentially without the knowledge of the person who is subject to surveillance.

As technologies develop and drones become "smarter", the possibilities for data collection are almost limitless. Global positioning system (**GPS**) is a technology that is often a built-in feature of drones and allows for its location (and that of any surveillance target) to be tracked and recorded. Drones can be equipped with thermal imaging cameras that detect human presence through body heat.[3] It is also possible to use a Wi-Fi antenna affixed to a drone to locate individuals via their mobile telephones.[4]

These examples create obvious tension with legal obligations of privacy and non-intrusion into the personal lives of individuals (as distinct from the personal injury and property damage risks assessed in the previous chapter). Many legal systems consider the right to privacy as a fundamental human right and surveillance programmes are often the target of public outrage,[5] political ire[6] and regulatory clampdowns.[7]

1 The authors would like to thank Ben Gibson for his contribution to the chapter.

2 See, for example, Bart Schermer, 'An Eye in the Sky: Privacy Aspects of Drones' (*Leiden Law Blog*, 20 June 2013) <https://leidenlawblog.nl/articles/an-eye-in-the-sky-privacy-aspects-of-drones>.

3 See, for example, Fintan Corrigan, '10 Thermal Vision Cameras For Drones and How Thermal Imaging Works' (*DroneZon*, 27 February 2020) <www.dronezon.com/learn-about-drones-quadcopters/9-heat-vision-cameras-for-drones-and-how-thermal-imaging-works/>.

4 See, for example, Darren Quick, 'Students Develop Drone to Locate Survivors via their Mobile Phones' (*New Atlas*, 18 July 2014) <newatlas.com/drone-mobile-phone-location-survivors/33005/>.

5 See, for example, Haroon Siddique, 'Internet Privacy as Important as Human Rights, Says UN's Navi Pillay' *The Guardian* (London, 27 December 2013) <www.theguardian.com/world/2013/dec/26/un-navi-pillay-internet-privacy>; Amnesty International, 'Global Opposition to USA Big Brother Mass Surveillance' (18 March 2015) <www.amnesty.org/en/press-releases/2015/03/global-opposition-to-usa-big-brother-mass-surveillance/>.

6 See, for example, Zak Doffman, 'New Trump Ruling Limits AI Surveillance Exports Over China Military Fears' (*Forbes*, 5 June 2020) <www.forbes.com/sites/zakdoffman/2020/01/05/new-trump-ruling-limits-ai-surveillance-exports-over-china-military-fears/#232d6e213cc8>.

Direct surveillance by way of drone technology is no less invasive—and potentially more so—than closed-circuit television or fixed security cameras. The enhanced capabilities and potential of drone-based technologies should oblige manufacturers, operators and regulators to give due consideration to the privacy implications of drone use.

The legal and moral obligations stemming from advanced technological developments are starkly highlighted in regulatory guidance issued by the Information & Privacy Commissioner for Ontario, Canada:

> These developments oblige us to revisit fundamental issues regarding our expectations of privacy. We are called upon to once again fortify our defence of privacy, including respect for activities that occur in public spaces, in order to ensure that this central tenet of freedom remains protected in a manner that is consistent with our shared values.[8]

Even non-surveillance drone activity should be considered through a lens of privacy protection despite the less obvious risks. In many cases, the context of drone use and the type of data collected can create an indirect impact on individuals with a consequent implication under privacy laws. The inadvertent capture of persons (and their activities) recorded by drones used for surveying or research purposes is one example. Even without capturing a person's photograph, the recording of their private property or possessions could provide information that can be combined with other data to build a picture of the individual in question. This may be sufficient to consider the captured information as "personal data" or "personally identifying information" (PII) for the purposes of data protection regulation.

Principles of data protection

The legal concept of privacy centres on the right to respect for an individual's private life. Data protection is the separate—but related—concept of securing information against unauthorised access.[9] While neither concept is expressly referenced in the US Constitution, the Fourth Amendment[10] enshrines a right for people to be secure from unreasonable searches and seizures of property by the government. In Europe, the Charter of Fundamental Rights[11] provides that everyone has (a) the right to respect for his or her private and family life, home and communications,[12] and (b) the right to the protection of personal data concerning him or her.[13]

7 See, for example, James Titcomb, 'US Surveillance Makes "Safe Harbour" Data Treaty With EU Invalid, European Court Adviser Says' *The Telegraph* (London, 23 September 2015) <www.telegraph.co.uk/technology/internet/11884432/EUs-data-sharing-deal-with-US-is-invalid-European-Courts-Advocate-General-says.html>.

8 Ann Cavoukian, 'Privacy and Drones: Unmanned Aerial Vehicles' (Information & Privacy Commissioner, Ontario, Canada Report, 2012) <pbd-drones.pdf(ipc.on.ca)>.

9 See, for example, Juliane Kokott and Christoph Sobotta, 'The Distinction between Privacy and Data Protection in the Jurisprudence of the CJEU and the ECtHR' (2013) 3(4) IDPL 222.

10 U.S. CONST. amend. IV.

11 Charter of Fundamental Rights of the European Union [2012] OJ C326/3.

12 ibid art. 7.

13 ibid art. 8(1).

The Charter elaborates further in the context of data protection with additional principles. These require that personal data be processed "fairly for specified purposes and on the basis of the consent of the person concerned or some other legitimate basis laid down by law."[14] Individuals have rights to also access their personal data and to have errors in such data rectified. Compliance with such rules should be subject to control by an independent authority.[15]

The foundations of data protection in the Charter are recognised and enshrined in EU law by the General Data Protection Regulation (GDPR).[16] The GDPR marked a fundamental shift in the European and global approach to data protection regulation when it replaced the Data Protection Directive[17] in 2018 by reiterating and expanding on the core principles relating to the processing of personal data.

The six core principles of the GDPR are stated as follows:

> Personal data shall be:
>
> (a) processed lawfully, fairly and in a transparent manner in relation to the data subject ("lawfulness, fairness and transparency");
> (b) collected for specified, explicit and legitimate purposes and not further processed in a manner that is incompatible with those purposes; further processing for archiving purposes in the public interest, scientific or historical research purposes or statistical purposes shall, in accordance with Article 89(1), not be considered to be incompatible with the initial purposes ("purpose limitation");
> (c) adequate, relevant and limited to what is necessary in relation to the purposes for which they are processed ("data minimisation");
> (d) accurate and, where necessary, kept up to date; every reasonable step must be taken to ensure that personal data that are inaccurate, having regard to the purposes for which they are processed, are erased or rectified without delay ("accuracy");
> (e) kept in a form which permits identification of data subjects for no longer than is necessary for the purposes for which the personal data are processed; personal data may be stored for longer periods insofar as the personal data will be processed solely for archiving purposes in the public interest, scientific or historical research purposes or statistical purposes in accordance with Article 89(1) subject to implementation of the appropriate technical and organisational measures required by this Regulation in order to safeguard the rights and freedoms of the data subject ("storage limitation");
> (f) processed in a manner that ensures appropriate security of the personal data, including protection against unauthorised or unlawful processing and against accidental loss, destruction or damage, using appropriate technical or organisational measures ("integrity and confidentiality").[18]

14 ibid art. 8(2).
15 ibid art. 8(3).
16 Council on Foreign Relations (n 3).
17 Council Directive (EC) 95/46 on the protection of individuals with regard to the processing of personal data and on the free movement of such data [1995] OJ L281/31.
18 GDPR, art. 5(1).

In addition, the controller of personal data (i.e. the person or body which, alone or jointly with others, determines the purposes and means of the processing of personal data) is required to be able to demonstrate compliance with the aforementioned principles ("accountability").

These principles form the basis of data protection legislation in many other jurisdictions outside Europe. The Australian Privacy Principles (or **APPs**) are referred to by the national data protection regulator as "the cornerstone of the privacy protection framework" in the Australian Privacy Act.[19] They set out key pillars of openness and transparency, accuracy and security that align strongly with the GDPR. In Singapore, the Personal Data Protection Act (**PDPA**) establishes requirements for lawful data processing and principles of transparency, purpose limitation and storage limitation.[20] State or national laws in Canada, South Africa, Bahrain, Qatar and other territories, as well as the Model Code for the Protection of Personal Information published in 1996 by the Canadian Standards Authorisation are all similarly principles-based.[21]

As noted earlier, these principles protect "personal data" (also called "personally identifying information" or similar), which usually encompasses both information that can identify living individuals directly and information that can be used to identify individuals in conjunction with other data available to the controller. This could cover both audio and visual recordings of individuals collected via drone surveillance and other indirect information concerning a person's private life or activities; for example, the presence or absence of a vehicle on the driveway of a residential property may give a reasonable indication of an individual's movements.

Types of drone activity

In considering the privacy and data protection implications of drone activity, it will be necessary to distinguish between different types of operation. At one end of the scale of risk in this regard would be direct surveillance of the sort often undertaken by police, military or other security authorities and aimed at the identification and monitoring of individuals. At the other end of the spectrum, recreational drone usage may involve limited or no data collection. In between these extremes, there may be incidences of incidental personal data capture that occurs through normal corporate or personal use of drones, such as site inspection, crop monitoring or photography.

At this point, it should be noted that domestic use of personal data is often exempted from data protection legislation (the GDPR states that it does not apply to the processing of personal data "by a natural person in the course of a purely personal or household activity").[22] However, unauthorised use of a drone by an individual to capture footage of another person could amount to an invasion of privacy that may lead to civil or criminal prosecution.

When assessing the risk, it is also relevant to consider other factors such as the nature, frequency and volume of information collected. An incidental image of an

19 Privacy Act 1988 (Cth) Sch 1 ('Australian Privacy Principles').

20 Personal Data Protection Act 2012 (No. 26 of 2012, Sing).

21 Canadian Standards Association, 'National Standard of Canada: Model Code for the Protection of Personal Information' (Canadian Standards Association, 1996).

22 GDPR, art. 2(2)(c).

individual in a public place may not generate any material privacy or data protection implications. However, video footage that records more detail of their activity, or repeated or persistent images that build up a pattern of information over time, may be more likely to create an issue.

Regulatory attitudes

It is generally acknowledged and understood that initial regulatory interventions on drones in most markets have historically (and understandably) focused on safety issues.[23] However, the concerns outlined earlier are forcing regulators to adopt privacy-focused obligations into general drone legislation.

The latest European regulation on rules and procedures for drone operation includes a number of explicit references to privacy issues.[24] In order to secure an operational authorisation, an unmanned aerial system (**UAS**) operator must provide a statement that it complies with applicable laws relating to privacy and data protection,[25] and national authorities are required to register operators whose activities may present a risk to privacy or protection of personal data.[26] UAS operators are obligated to register when operating within the "open" category any drone that is "equipped with a sensor able to capture personal data, unless it complies with Directive 2009/48/EC".[27]

In Dubai, a law was passed in July 2020 as part of a framework of regulatory measures to support the Dubai Sky Dome project intended to create a commercial drone network for the delivery of packages and the transport of passengers.[28] Dubai Law No. 4 of 2020 (the **Dubai Drone Law**) regulates unmanned aerial vehicles for commercial and government purposes with a primary objective of attracting investment to the emirate's aviation industry. However, notwithstanding the absence of a national data protection or privacy law in the UAE, the Dubai Drone Law requires anyone who uses a drone to take all necessary measures to avoid violating the privacy of individuals, private property or commercial assets and to maintain the confidentiality of legally protected data. It states that the use of recording, photography or remote sensing equipment to violate the freedoms and privacy of individuals or families, the photographing of facilities, buildings and restricted or prohibited areas without authorisation from concerned entities and the installation of any equipment to collect information and data illegally are all strictly prohibited by law.

At the same time, as aviation regulators and national governments are beginning to acknowledge privacy and data risks, it is clear that data protection authorities have drone activity in their sights. The Ontario privacy regulator addressed concerns around UAVs in a 2012 paper.[29] The UK Information Commissioner

23 See Julie-Anne Tarr, Maurice Thompson and Anthony Tarr, 'Regulation, Risk and Insurance of Drones: An Urgent Global Accountability Imperative' (2019) 8 JBL 559.

24 Commission Implementing Regulation (EU) 2019/947 of 24 May 2019 on the rules and procedures for the operation of unmanned aircraft [2019] OJ L152/45.

25 ibid art. 12(2)(c).

26 ibid art. 14(1).

27 ibid art. 14(5)(a).

28 See ARN News Centre, 'Dubai Issues Law to Regulate Drone Activity' *ARN News Centre* (Dubai, 4 July 2020) <www.arnnewscentre.ae/en/news/uae/dubai-issues-law-to-regulate-drone-activity/>.

29 U.S. CONST. (n 14).

(ICO),[30] Spain's Agencia Española de Protección de Datos (AEPD),[31] Europe's Article 29 Working Party,[32] the Office of the Australian Information Commissioner (OAIC)[33] and Singapore's Personal Data Protection Commission (**PDPC**)[34] are among the authorities to have issued specific guidance on privacy issues in the context of drones.

Even more pertinently, we are seeing examples of governments and regulators moving beyond guidance on the application of existing data protection laws to drone operation and incorporating specific drone-related provisions into law. California approved an update to its Civil Code in 2016 that made a person liable for physical invasion of privacy when that person:[35]

> knowingly enters onto the land or into the airspace above the land of another person without permission or otherwise commits a trespass in order to capture any type of visual image, sound recording, or other physical impression of the plaintiff engaging in a private, personal, or familial activity and the invasion occurs in a manner that is offensive to a reasonable person.

Similarly, the State of Wisconsin added a provision on "use of a drone" which states that:[36]

> Whoever uses a drone, as defined in s. 175.55 (1) (a), with the intent to photograph, record, or otherwise observe another individual in a place or location where the individual has a reasonable expectation of privacy is guilty of Class A misdemeanor. This section does not apply to a law enforcement officer authorized to use a drone pursuant to s. 175.55 (2).

Legal and regulatory risk analysis

Comprehensive data protection regimes

Notable legal regimes

A number of countries have data protection regimes which can be regarded as comprehensive and many of these regimes are founded on common principles and similar legal obligations.

30 Information Commissioner's Office, 'Your Data Matters: Drones (FAQs)' (*Information Commissioner's Office*) <https://ico.org.uk/your-data-matters/drones/>.

31 Agencia Española de Protección de Datos, 'Drones and Data Protection' (30 May 2019) <www.aepd.es/sites/default/files/2019-09/guia-drones-en.pdf>.

32 Council Opinion 01/2015 of 16 June 2015 on Privacy and Data Protection Issues relating to the Utilisation of Drones [2015] 01673/15/EN <https://ec.europa.eu/justice/article-29/documentation/opinion-recommendation/files/2015/wp231_en.pdf>.

33 Office of the Australian Information Commissioner, 'Drones' (*Office of the Australian Information Commissioner*) <www.oaic.gov.au/privacy/your-privacy-rights/surveillance-and-monitoring/drones/>.

34 Personal Data Protection Commission Singapore, *Advisory Guidelines on the Personal Data Protection Act for Selected Topics* (Singapore: Personal Data Protection Commission, 2013 revised 2018) <www.pdpc.gov.sg/-/media/Files/PDPC/PDF-Files/Legislation-and-Guidelines/FINAL-Advisory-Guidelines-on-PDPA-for-Selected-Topics-31-August-2018.pdf>.

35 Cal. Assemb. B. 856, 2015 Leg., Chapter 521 (Cal. 2016).

36 Wis Stat s942.10 (2013).

The mutual recognition frameworks that many of these laws contain precipitate the natural occurrence of a "best practice" network of jurisdictions. By way of example, in probably the most cited exemplar of a comprehensive regime, the European Commission has the power to determine, based on Article 45 of the GDPR, whether a country outside the EU offers an adequate level of data protection. If it does so, then personal data can be transferred by controllers within the EU (and Norway, Liechtenstein and Iceland) to that other country without the need to take further specific steps to safeguard the transfer (assuming the processing itself which the transfer is facilitating is lawful). It is worth noting that adequacy decisions do not apply to data exchanges carried out by law enforcement authorities which are separately governed by the "Police Directive".[37]

At the time of writing, the European Commission has so far recognised Andorra, Argentina, Canada (commercial organisations), Faroe Islands, Guernsey, Israel, Isle of Man, Japan, Jersey, New Zealand, Switzerland and Uruguay (and previously, but no longer, the United States under first the Safe Harbor and then the Privacy Shield frameworks) as providing adequate protection, and talks are ongoing with South Korea.[38]

Aside from various small nations within the geographical purview of Europe, it is notable that only Argentina, Israel, Japan, New Zealand and Uruguay have received unqualified decisions (the Canada decision being restricted to the private sector) and, even within those decisions themselves, some reservations were noted.

In addition to the European Commission adequacy cohort, one might also describe Australia and Singapore, amongst others, as having a comprehensive data protection landscape, albeit where there are differences in approach to those taken under the GDPR. Later in this chapter, we will also look at jurisdictions with newly emergent approaches (see *Emerging Markets*).

What all the established jurisdictions have in common is an approach which includes the following.[39]

- A wide definition of personal data (not just direct identifiers such as name, image, voice, etc. but other data which could be combined to identify an individual, such as IP address, mobile phone signal, etc.)
- Recognition that individuals should have some influence over how organisations use their data
- Recognition that individuals should be informed as to how their data is to be used
- Recognition that misuse of data is a personal and societal wrong
- An obligation on the person who controls the personal data to take steps to protect it from misuse
- Recognition of the importance of establishing a competent and suitably equipped privacy regulator to enforce the laws

37 Council Directive (EU) 2016/680 on the protection of natural persons with regard to the processing of personal data by competent authorities for the purposes of the prevention, investigation, detection or prosecution of criminal offences or the execution of criminal penalties and on the free movement of such data and repealing Council Framework Decision 2008/977/JHA [2016] OJ L119/89.

38 European Commission, 'Adequacy Decisions: How the EU Determines If a non-EU Country has an Adequate Level of Data Protection' <https://ec.europa.eu/info/law/law-topic/data-protection/international-dimension-data-protection/adequacy-decisions_en>.

39 We will see that emerging regimes also tend to recognise these principles; however, the legal formulation can be somewhat blunt.

Anyone operating a drone for purposes which are not purely domestic, which records data capable of identifying a person, in one of these jurisdictions is likely to have to comply with the local data protection law. Of course, it may be that the operator is not interested in surveying any persons—it has other purposes for its drone operations notwithstanding that the collection of personal data is an inevitable consequence—and has plans to delete it or obscure it altogether. However, even where one of these techniques is to be used, there will almost certainly be some element of personal data collection and processing that occurs before the technique is applied; consequently, most mature legal regimes will require the operator to be able to demonstrate that it has considered the privacy impacts of its activities appropriately and taken steps to mitigate the risks to individuals and limit the unnecessary collection of personal data.

Fundamental legal requirements in the context of drone use

(1) INFORMATION REQUIREMENTS

As noted, data protection regimes which are mature and comprehensive inevitably require the data subject to be provided with some degree of information as to how his or her personal data will be collected and used.

The requirement set out in the GDPR for controllers who collect personal data from the data subject is as follows:

> Where personal data relating to a data subject are collected from the data subject, the controller shall, at the time when personal data are obtained, provide the data subject with all of the following information:
>
> (a) the identity and the contact details of the controller and, where applicable, of the controller's representative;
> (b) the contact details of the data protection officer, where applicable;
> (c) the purposes of the processing for which the personal data are intended as well as the legal basis for the processing;
> (d) where the processing is based on point (f) of Article 6(1), the legitimate interests pursued by the controller or by a third party;
> (e) the recipients or categories of recipients of the personal data, if any;
> (f) where applicable, the fact that the controller intends to transfer personal data to a third country or international organisation and the existence or absence of an adequacy decision by the Commission, or in the case of transfers referred to in Article 46 or 47, or the second subparagraph of Article 49(1), reference to the appropriate or suitable safeguards and the means by which to obtain a copy of them or where they have been made available.[40]

When one visits a website, this obligation can be discharged via a notice on the website. When one visits a physical business premise, this can be done by physical notices and through information provided on data collection forms.

40 GDPR, art. 13(1).

In both scenarios, the data collection environment is somewhat constrained (the websites under the top-level domain visited and the physical premises visited). A characteristic of drones is the ability to collect data over large areas without the active participation, or potentially even the awareness, of the data subject(s). Even if the data subject is aware of the presence of a drone, he or she may have no clue which person or entity is operating it and what data they are collecting. While the internet has clearly been misused on occasion as a tool to collect and use data in unlawful ways or ways which may have been unknown to the data subject, it remains the case that most notable data breaches involve personal data that was collected by virtue of some sort of relationship which existed between the consumer and the provider of a service; while an individual might be surprised to hear that a business has been hacked and their data has been exposed, he or she would probably not be surprised to hear that the business held such data in the first place. While personal data may be used for unexpected or dubious purposes, and is sometimes not kept sufficiently secure, in such circumstances, it is often data which has one way or another been volunteered at some point by the data subject or created with such data as its base.[41]

By contrast, any business or authority looking to operate a drone over a public or quasi-public space may have no prior relationship with those who are surveyed and may have difficulty ensuring that the people below are sufficiently informed, particularly if access to the surveyed site is not controlled. If entrance is controlled (i.e. with a ticketing barrier or similar), then people can be given notice; however, if filming is to occur over a large area with people coming and going freely, then this is not an option, and it is hard to conceive of a reliable method of providing sufficiently clear and complete information to people in a manner which can reasonably be assumed to be effective. The commercial drone operator in such a scenario will be faced with a predicament if no relevant exemption applies (see Exemptions, discussed later).

The British Broadcasting Corporation (BBC) publishes editorial guidelines setting out its values and standards, which apply to all BBC content. These guidelines include a guidance section around the use of drones for filming. The drones guidance sums up the situation succinctly:

> The versatility of drones and their ability to operate without the constraint of walls or fences means they can easily access private spaces. The Information Commissioner's Office (**ICO**) has warned broadcasters that their use of drones "can be highly privacy intrusive" because of the potential to capture images of individuals "unnecessarily". The ICO suggests that while individuals may not be identifiable from a wide aerial shot, they might still be identifiable from the context in which they are filmed. Individuals may also be unlikely to realise that they are being recorded, even if they are aware of the presence of the drone itself.[42]

41 See, for example, Adam Forrest, 'Facebook Data Scandal: Social Network Fined $5bn Over "Inappropriate" Sharing of Users "Personal Information"' *Independent* (London, 1 July 2010) <www.independent.co.uk/news/world/americas/facebook-data-privacy-scandal-settlement-cambridge-analytica-court-a9003106.html>.

42 British Broadcasting Corporation, 'Editorial Guidelines—Guidance: Use of Drones' *British Broadcasting Corporation* (London, December 2019) <www.bbc.com/editorialguidelines/guidance/drones>.

The ICO itself has emphasised the need to carefully consider how to provide fair processing information in its code of practice on surveillance cameras and personal information.[43] The ICO covers the use of drones to some extent in this guidance and refers to drones as unmanned aerial vehicles (**UAVs**). The guidance emphasises that a UAV is typically part of a broader UAS (the UAV may collect the data but will likely transmit it or download it onto other connected devices and storage media for further processing, which collectively comprises the UAS).

When addressing the issue of information provision, the ICO says:

> The challenge of providing fair processing information is something that you must address if you decide to purchase UAS. You will need to come up with innovative ways of providing this information. For example, this could involve wearing highly visible clothing identifying yourself as the UAS operator, placing signage in the area you are operating UAS explaining its use and having a privacy notice on a website that you can direct people to, or some other form of privacy notice, so they can access further information.[44]

(2) SECURITY OF PERSONAL DATA

Data protection laws place obligations on the controller to keep personal data secure and protected against theft, unauthorised disclosure and corruption. Due to the huge range of processing purposes and techniques, the rapid development of technology and the variation in sensitivity of different data sets, most lawmakers have tended to keep away from overly prescriptive security requirements, instead preferring to require the controllers to adopt a risk-based approach.[45] One interesting law which has adopted a slightly more comprehensive approach is the South Korean Personal Information Protection Act (SKPIPA).[46] Under SKPIPA, additional security standards have been issued which are much more comprehensive than those set out in most data protection laws.[47] However, while more granular than the requirements of some laws, even these standards operate at a reasonably high level, providing a framework for compliance rather than prescribing technical details.

When assessing the security measures that are to be deployed, the drone operator needs to take a holistic approach and consider what the ICO referred to as the UAS; the entire processing system, not just the drone itself. For example, in a typical "hobbyist" drone a camera might transmit a live feed to a mobile device via Bluetooth, but there might be no facility to record data and there may be no further onward

43 Information Commissioner's Office, 'In the Picture: A Data Protection Code of Practice for Surveillance Cameras and Personal Information' (*Information Commissioner's Office Code*, 2018) <https://ico.org.uk/media/for-organisations/documents/1542/cctv-code-of-practice.pdf>.

44 ibid 31.

45 See, for example, GDPR, art. 32.

46 Personal Information Protection Act (S.Kor), *translated in* KoreanLii, <www. koreanlii.or.kr/w/images/0/0e/KoreanDPAct2011.pdf privacy.go.kr/cmm/fms/FileDown.do?atchFileId=FILE_000000000830758&fileSn=1&nttId=8186&toolVer=&toolCntKey_1=>.

47 MOPAS Notification, 'Personal Information Safeguard and Security Standard' (30 December 2014) <www.privacy.go.kr/cmm/fms/FileDown.do?atchFileId=FILE_000000000830758&fileSn=0&nttId=8186&toolVer=&toolCntKey_1=>.

transmission. Even if such a drone is being used for commercial purposes, the risk of unauthorised loss or disclosure of personal data which is captured would seem to be small. By contrast, a sophisticated UAS might involve a drone equipped with a normal imaging camera with a powerful telephoto lens; a thermal imaging camera capable of identifying individuals "through" other physical barriers; a transmission system which sends data in real time to multiple viewing devices at various locations and also to a facility where further analysis of the data is performed by automated algorithmic means; and the system also includes real-time simultaneous back-up, or periodic back-up, to cloud servers in two geographically remote data centres. Perhaps, such a system might be used as part of the perimeter security measures of a compound of some sort. In the second case, the UAS is capable of capturing more intrusive personal data; distributes the data more widely to various points, creating a greater number of potential points of failure and maintains records of the data captured. Clearly, more comprehensive security measures are required and proportionate in the second example.

Knowledge is power, but with power comes responsibility and, in general, the cost of compliance for drone operators will increase in line with the volume, sensitivity and subsequent processing of the personal data which is collected.

(3) DATA PROTECTION IMPACT ASSESSMENTS

It is incumbent, then, on drone operators to consider how to deploy the principles of privacy by default and by design to limit the capture of unnecessary personal data and how the operation of the drone can be controlled to minimise excess data capture. For example, if a drone is to be used to survey a large area of farmland for agricultural purposes, it is possible that the flightpath required may involve some activity over or near the border of the surveyed land and a third party's private property or a public property. The operator should consider if it is necessary to survey the entire area or whether the same results can be achieved by limiting the surveyed area to a sample of the land which is not adjacent to the third party or public land. If it is necessary to survey the entire area, can the camera be adjusted so that the field of vision is limited to the edge of the farmland and images from the adjacent lands are not captured? If it is necessary to fly over third party or public land at some point, can the camera be disabled during such periods?

Mature data protection regimes, such as the GDPR and the Dubai International Financial Centre's Data Protection Law, mandate such impact assessments before certain processing activities are carried out, and the use of drones to survey large numbers of people, or smaller numbers of people in an intrusive manner would typically trigger such a requirement. Operators should be able to demonstrate that privacy issues have been considered and be able to provide their rationale for the approach they have taken if challenged by a regulator or an individual.

It is also important that participants in the activity for which the drone is to be used are clear in relation to their legal status. Many data protection regimes designate a status of "controller" or similar to the party ultimately responsible for the activity in question (in GDPR parlance, the party which controls the means and purposes of the processing), whilst a service provider providing their services which involve the processing of personal data may often be a "processor", or has similar designation; that is to say, a party who follows the instructions of the controller and does not determine the means and purposes of the processing. *Scenario A*: a television production company has a very precise and exacting vision of the drone footage it wishes to capture and engages a third-party drone operator to capture footage to its specific instructions and provide the captured footage to the TV company for editing. The drone operator is told where to film, when, from what height, what angles to use, etc. The TV company is the controller and the drone operator is the processor. *Scenario B:* A British TV company wants a montage, in a planned new series, representing a typical day in the city of Paris. It asks a local contractor to capture footage it can use in its montage and provide it with a package of suggested footage. It provides no more instruction than a high-level description of the way the montage will feature in the final programme. The local contractor is free to film what it wants, when it wants, however it wants, with the (simple) mandate to "capture the spirit of modern Paris". In this scenario, the drone operator has largely unchecked freedom to interpret an artistic requirement. It can film by drone overhead, on the subway, in parks, from boats, etc. The contractor in this scenario is a controller of the data, as is the TV company once the data has been provided to it.

In scenario B, the contractor has wider reaching legal obligations and responsibilities than the contractor in scenario A. What is more, the contractor in scenario A can legitimately ask the TV company in scenario A to contractually assume many of the legal risks associated with performing the very specific activities requested. The contractor in scenario B can hardly expect the TV company to assume the risk of it doing something unlawful when it has such wide discretion to choose how to deliver the end product.

Exemptions

Certain types of drone activity may benefit from privacy law exemptions. For example, in Canada businesses must comply with the Personal Information Protection and Electronic Documents Act (PIPEDA), including with respect to personal information gathered via the use of drones. However, PIPEDA does not apply if the personal information is being collected for purposes which are:

- journalistic
- artistic
- literary
- academic, or
- for not-for-profit organizations or charities

The GDPR takes a similar approach, requiring that member states make domestic legislation to protect the ability of journalists, academics, artists and writers to express their craft.

Certain official bodies may also benefit from wide-ranging exemptions from data protection laws or from specific case exemptions. A common exemption is the exemption of competent authorities responsible for the investigation of criminal offences.

The GDPR does not apply to processing of personal data by a natural person in the course of a purely personal or household activity. If an amateur enthusiast flies a drone for nothing other than his or her own pleasure, then data protection laws are unlikely to be a concern (although of course, there may be more general legal concepts such as voyeurism or trespass which become relevant and which could apply).

Limited or patchwork national regulation

The rights of privacy and data protection in a jurisdiction such as the United States—which lacks a comprehensive federal privacy or data protection law—will derive from a blend of principles and regulation embodied from constitutional law, the law of torts, national legislation regulating specific sectors and categories of data such as healthcare and children's information and state laws.

Since 1958, the FAA has been delegated authority in the United States to prescribe regulations governing the flight and operation of aircraft, which include drones.[48] It has exclusive jurisdiction to create and enforce laws based on airspace use and safety. The mission of the FAA is "to provide the safest, most efficient aerospace system in the world".[49] Accordingly, states and municipalities in the United States are prohibited from introducing legislation on drones that could conflict with the FAA's remit. However, the FAA has explicitly stated that its remit does not extend to regulating privacy-related issues.[50]

Many US states are therefore passing separate legislation to deal with privacy and drones. Moreover, legal protection may be relied upon under case law relating to the Fourth Amendment (against the government's use of drones for surveillance and law enforcement purposes) and privacy torts (against drone activities by commercial entities or private individuals). Further recourse may be sought under privacy-related laws, through a mix of state-specific data protection legislations, such as the California Consumer Protection Act (CCPA),[51] and federal sector-specific privacy regulations, such as the Health Information Portability and Accountability Act (HIPAA).[52]

The patchwork of privacy regulation, case law and frameworks in the United States, however, creates uncertainty for individuals who are seeking effective remedies against increasingly intrusive drone activities. It also creates ambiguity for drone operators who have to comply with, at times, overlapping and contradictory laws and principles.

Fourth Amendment and reasonable expectation of privacy

The right to privacy in the United States has evolved from the Bill of Rights,[53] particularly by way of the Fourth Amendment, which protects individuals from governmental

48 See, for example, Federal Aviation Administration, 'A Brief History of the FAA' (*Federal Aviation Administration*, 4 January 2017) <www.faa.gov/about/history/brief_history/>. See also FAA Modernization and Reform Act, Pub. L. No. 112-95; and Alissa M Dolan and Richard M Tompson II, 'Integration of Drones into Domestic Airspace: Selected Legal Issues' (Congressional Research Service, 7-5700 R42940 2013) <https://fas.org/sgp/crs/natsec/R42940.pdf>.

49 See Federal Aviation Administration, 'Mission and Responsibilities' (*Federal Aviation Administration*, 21 August 2014) <www.faa.gov/airports/central/about_airports/CE_mission>.

50 The FAA has stated that privacy "issues are beyond the scope of its rulemaking". The FAA has noted that state law and other legal protections for individual privacy may provide recourse for a person whose privacy may be affected through another person's use of UAS. See Department of Transportation, FAA Notice of proposed rulemaking on 'Operation and Certification of Small Unmanned Aircraft Systems' Billing Code 4910-13-P (15 February 2015) 36 <www.faa.gov/regulations_policies/rulemaking/recently_published/media/2120-AJ60_NPRM_2-15-2015_joint_signature.pdf>.

51 2020 Cal. Stat. Consumer Privacy Protection Act, S 2430, 2020 <http://webserver.rilin.state.ri.us/BillText/BillText20/SenateText20/S2430.pdf>.

52 Health Insurance Portability and Accountability Act of 1996, Pub. L. 104–191, 110 Stat. 1936.

53 David J Garrow, 'Privacy and the American Constitution' (2001) 68(1) Social Research 55; Samuel Warren and Louis Brandeis, 'The Right to Have Privacy' (1890) 4 Harvard Law Review 193; *Grisworld v Connecticut*, 381 U.S. 479 (1965) in which Justice William Douglas held that the "right of privacy" derived from "penumbras, formed by emanations from" various provisions of the Bill of Rights.

invasions of privacy through unreasonable searches and seizures.[54] Except in limited circumstances, warrantless searches violate the Fourth Amendment, and evidence collected during the search cannot be admitted in criminal proceedings.[55]

The evolution of drones from military instruments to small commercial tools has made them a popular technology among law enforcement and government agencies, particularly for surveillance purposes.[56] The increasing use of drones by law enforcement has led to significant concerns over privacy and how the Fourth Amendment may best serve to protect individuals against unreasonable drone surveillance. Although the US Supreme Court has to date never addressed specifically the privacy concerns that arise due to the use of drones together with its analysis of the Fourth Amendment, there are a number of precedents that relate to privacy in the home, privacy in public spaces, location tracking, aerial surveillance and advanced technologies that may act as guidance on how the Supreme Court could approach future cases relating to drones and the Fourth Amendment.

Notably, the Supreme Court established the "reasonable expectation of privacy" test to assess whether governmental surveillance or searches are in violation of the Fourth Amendment. The Supreme Court held in *Katz v United States* that wiretapping without a warrant is unconstitutional and established the right to privacy on two counts: (i) that the person must exhibit "an actual (subjective) expectation of privacy"; and (ii) "that the expectation be one that society is prepared to recognise as 'reasonable'".[57] Case law that evolved from the "reasonable expectation of privacy" test suggests that constitutional protection under the Fourth Amendment will depend on a number of factors and the context in which such surveillance takes place: for example, where the individual is located at the time of the drone surveillance or intrusion (i.e. at home, in their backyard, or on a public road) and how advanced and publicly available the drone technology is.[58]

The Supreme Court has held that the "very core" of the Fourth Amendment is the right of a person to retreat into one's home.[59] Law enforcement therefore cannot enter a person's home to secretly observe or listen without a warrant.[60] Flying a drone into a home to surveil an individual's activities or conversations will likely constitute a search under the Fourth Amendment.

54 U.S. CONST. (n 14) *states:* "The right of the people to be secure in their persons, houses, papers, and effects, against unreasonable searches and seizures, shall not be violated, and no warrants shall issue, but upon probable cause, supported by oath or affirmation, and particularly describing the place to be searched, and the persons or things to be seized".

55 *Weeks v United States*, 232 US 383 (1914).

56 Gregory S. McNeal, William Goodwin and Sezen Jones, 'Warrantless Operations of Public Use Drones: Considerations for Government Agencies (2017) 44 Fordham Urban Law Journal 703.

57 *Katz v United States,* 389 U.S. 347, 360 (1967) as quoted in Taly Matiteyahu, 'Drone Regulations and Fourth Amendment Rights: The Interaction of State Drone Statutes and the Reasonable Expectation of Privacy' (2015) Columbia Journal of Law & Social Problems 266, 270. Since *Katz* the Court has consistently held that "the application of the Fourth Amendment depends on whether the person invoking its protection can claim a justifiable, a reasonable or a legitimate expectation of privacy that has been invaded by government action"; See, for example, *Smith v Maryland*, 442 U.S. 735, 740 (1979).

58 Richard M Thompson II, 'Drones in Domestic Surveillance Operations: Fourth Amendment Implications and Legislative Responses' (2013) Congressional Research Service Report for Congress R42701, 12.

59 *Silverman v United States*, 365 U.S. 505, 511 (1961).

60 ibid 512.

However, surveillance in public spaces is likely to survive "reasonable expectation of privacy" claims. In *United States v Knotts*, a case regarding the use of an electronic surveillance device, the Supreme Court held that individuals do not have a reasonable expectation of privacy against surveillance when travelling in a car on public roads.[61] Similarly, US courts have found that flyover searches are not prohibited if the areas surveilled are "open to public view".[62] In *California v Ciraolo*, the Supreme Court held that a warrantless aerial surveillance at approximately 400 feet of a fenced-in garden was not unreasonable under the Fourth Amendment as it was observable from "navigable airspace".[63] Flying drones and tracking individuals in public areas or areas open to public view are unlikely, therefore, to violate the Fourth Amendment.

However, consideration should be taken by drone operators when encroaching on an individual's property. In *United States v Causby*,[64] the Supreme Court held that while the "air space is a public highway" and the domain of the federal government,[65] a landlord is entitled to exclusive control over the "immediate reaches of the enveloping atmosphere".[66] Nonetheless, for the landowner to recover in an action for trespass against an aircraft, he or she must show "substantial interference" with the actual use of the land, even where the aircraft is flying below "federally-regulated altitudes".[67] With small drones populating the skies at below 500 feet and disturbing residents merely by their presence, different sets of considerations and factors will have to be used to determine the "gravity of the harm" done by drones hovering over someone's home and whether they could constitute an aerial trespass.[68]

Moreover, technologies used by government actors which are not available to the public are likely to require a warrant. In *Kyllo v United States*, government agents used

61 *United States v Knotts* 460 U.S 276, 281–82 (1983). It is worth noting that in *United States v Jones* 565 U.S 400 (2012), the Supreme Court ruled that the installation of a GPS tracker on the private property of the defendant (i.e. his car) together with the prolonged surveillance to investigate the defendant for alleged narcotics violations constituted a search and required a warrant. However, the protection provided in this case did not extend to the information obtained about the defendant; the defendant did not have a reasonable expectation of privacy to the weeks of data logging the defendant's movements of his car when he was driving on a public road. Instead, merely the invasion of his private property (i.e. his car) put the case in favour of the defendant.

62 *California v. Ciraolo* 476 U.S 207, 213 (1986); See also *Florida v Riley*, 488 U.S 445, 448 (1989), where the Supreme Court held that an officer's observation of the interior of a partially covered greenhouse in a residential backyard from a helicopter circling 400 feet above the house did not constitute a search under the Fourth Amendment, since the helicopter was in navigable airspace (i.e. the airspace above minimum safe altitude that is open to any member of the public). Despite having erected fences around the property, it did not preclude the public or official observation from a helicopter flying at a minimum safe altitude. Although the lower limit of navigable airspace is 500 feet for aircraft, the Supreme Court allowed the helicopter to fly at 400 feet because it noted that helicopters are not bound by that navigable airspace limit: *Florida v Riley*, 488 U.S 445, 451 (1989).

63 *California v. Ciraolo*, 476 U.S 207 (1986).

64 *United States v. Causby*, 328 U.S 256 (1946).

65 ibid. The Causby case, however, did not define where a property's airspace ends and where the navigable airspace begins. At the time, the lowest minimum safe altitude for aircraft was designated to be 300 feet; this put a plane flying 83 feet over the defendant's land outside the publicly navigable airspace.

66 ibid 264.

67 Hillary B Farber, 'Keep Out! The Efficacy of Trespass, Nuisance and Privacy Torts as Applied to Drones' (2017) 33 Georgia State University Law Review 359, 384.

68 ibid 385.

a thermal-imaging device to determine heat patterns inside the home of the defendant. Since the imaging technology was not in the "general public use" and it allowed the police officer to obtain information about the home's interior that he could not otherwise have obtained without a physical intrusion,[69] the Supreme Court held that the surveillance constituted a search covered by the Fourth Amendment. Such a condition leaves open the possibility that drone technology that is in the "general public use" (i.e. commercial drones) could be used by law enforcement without a warrant to gather information inside the home of an individual.[70]

Common law and privacy torts

Alongside the Fourth Amendment cases, the common law of torts has been developed by US courts to provide protection to individuals from non-governmental actors through privacy torts such as "intrusion upon seclusion".[71] The intrusion upon seclusion tort focuses on invasive activities that encroach upon an individual's privacy. A claim under this tort is based on the following test: (i) the intrusion has to be intentional on the individual's "solitude", "seclusion" or "private affairs"; and (2) the intrusion would be "highly offensive to a reasonable person".[72]

Similarly, to many Fourth Amendment claims, intrusion upon seclusion cases is often decided by whether the plaintiff had a "reasonable expectation of privacy" at the time when the intrusion took place. In *Wolfson v Lewis,*[73] a television crew surveilled the home of a healthcare executive for many hours while using high-powered cameras and microphones, which was considered by the court to be intrusive upon the plaintiff's "seclusion and solitude".[74] However, conducting surveillance of a person in a public area or taking images of an individual who can be viewed from a public viewpoint are unlikely to be considered as an invasion to privacy.[75] Additionally, the intrusion has to be intentional, meaning that the defendant must have actively desired to intrude on another person's home or must have known that his or her conduct would result in an intrusion.[76] A drone that accidentally encroaches on a person's home is not likely, therefore, to be actionable under this privacy tort.

Finally, the intrusion must be "highly offensive" to a person of "ordinary sensibilities". To determine whether the intrusion would be highly offensive, the courts will take several factors into consideration, such as the degree of the intrusion, the circumstances surrounding the intrusion, the conduct of the intruder and his or her motives and objectives, and "the expectations of those whose privacy is invaded".[77] A single intrusive drone incident may not be sufficient. The intrusion must be "repeated with such persistence and frequency as to amount to a course of hounding of the plaintiff

69 *Kyllo v United States*, 533 U.S 27, 31 (2001) as quoted in Thompson II (n 58), 6.
70 Matiteyahu (n 57), 275.
71 Restatement (Second) of Torts s 652B (Am. L. Inst. 1977).
72 ibid s 652B.
73 *Wolfson v Lewis* 924 F. Supp. 1413 (E.D. Pa. 1996).
74 ibid 1432.
75 Farber (n 67), 397.
76 Restatement (Second) of Torts (n 71), s 8A as quoted in Farber (67), 396–97.
77 *Miller v National Broadcasting Co.*, 232 Cal. Rptr 668, 679.

that becomes a substantial burden to his existence",[78] which may be a high threshold to meet for intrusive drone activities.

State legislations

In terms of statutory protections, states in the United States have responded to the expanded use of drones and the privacy concerns that accompany them by introducing their own drone laws or adding drone-law protections in their existing privacy-related laws.[79] Often, such drone laws or protections are based on existing standards developed by case law, such as the "reasonable expectation of privacy" principle.

Florida enacted an amendment to its Freedom from Unwarranted Surveillance Act[80] (the first "drone" law to be introduced in the US)[81] that prohibits businesses and government actors from using drones to conduct surveillance by capturing images of private property or individuals on such property, where the individual has a reasonable expectation of privacy,[82] without a valid written consent. The term "surveillance" is widely defined to include activities that allow drone operators to observe individuals with sufficient visual clarity to be able to obtain information about an individual's identity, habits, conduct, movements or whereabouts or that allows them to determine unique identifying features or the occupancy of the property.[83] Exceptions apply to surveillance conducted by utilities, state-licensed entities and businesses delivering cargo, conducting environmental monitoring or engaging in aerial mapping.

Wisconsin has had a law regulating drone activities in effect since April 2014.[84] In particular, it prohibits private citizens from using a drone "with the intent to photograph, record or otherwise observe" another individual who is in a place or location where that individual has a reasonable expectation of privacy.

California also introduced an amendment to its existing invasion of privacy statute in the California Civil Code to ban the use of drones "in a manner that is offensive to a reasonable person".[85] Drone activities that capture the intimate details of an

78 Restatement (Second) of Torts (n 71), s 652B.

79 Since 2013, 24 states (Alaska, Arkansas, California, Florida, Idaho, Illinois, Indiana, Iowa, Kansas, Maine, Mississippi, Montana, Nevada, North Carolina, North Dakota, Oregon, Pennsylvania, Tennessee, Texas, Utah, Vermont, Virginia, West Virginia, Wisconsin) have passed legislation that falls within the broad category of privacy. Such legislation includes warrant requirements for UAS use by law enforcement agencies and protection from privacy violations committed by non-government drone operators; see 911 Security, 'U.S. Drone Laws: Overview of Drone Rules and Regulations in USA By State (2019) 911 Security Report 3 <www.utsystem.edu/sites/default/files/offices/police/policies/USDroneLaws.pdf>.

80 Freedom from Unwanted Surveillance Act, Fla. Stat. s 934.50 (2015).

81 Gregory McNeal, 'Drones and Aerial Surveillance: Considerations for Legislatures' (*Brookings*, November 2014) <www.brookings.edu/research/drones-and-aerial-surveillance-considerations-for-legislatures/>.

82 Under the statute there is a presumption that a person has a "reasonable expectation of privacy on his or her privately owned real property if he or she is not observable by persons located at ground level in a place where they have a legal right to be, regardless of whether he or she is observable from the air with the use of a drone": Freedom from Unwanted Surveillance Act (n 84), s 934.50, 3(b).

83 ibid. s 934.50 1(e).

84 WIS. STAT. s 114 (2013).

85 CAL. CIV. CODE s 1708.8 California Civil Code (West 2015–2016).

individual's personal life, his or her interaction with family or any activity that occurs in their homes would be in violation of this statute.[86]

State-level privacy frameworks

State data protection laws have further added to the patchwork of privacy regulation in the United States. With the rise in cybercrime and collection of large amounts of data, states are rushing to enact their own data privacy legislations.[87] The State of California recently passed the California Consumer Privacy Act (CCPA)[88] which came into effect on 1 January 2020 in order to extend consumer privacy protections to the internet.[89]

Drone operators that capture "personal information" (or PI) of California residents will have to ensure they comply with the CCPA. The CCPA defines "personal information" very broadly to include biometric information, such as faces captured by surveillance cameras or other means of video recording used by drones.[90] However, PI specifically excludes publicly available information and de-identified information.[91] It is important to note that publicly available information does not mean information collected by a business about a consumer in a public place "without the consumer's knowledge". This means that photos, videos and audio and other data captured by drone operators without the individuals' knowledge are likely to fall under the definition of PI.

The CCPA grants consumers a number of rights with regard to their PI held by businesses, including the right to opt out of the sale of PI, a right to know what IP has been collected about them and the right to non-discrimination for having exercised any of these rights. Drone operators, therefore, will face challenges on how to make consumers aware of their rights at the time of collection of their PI and how to create business processes to ensure compliance with consumer rights requests. Businesses that collect "de-identified information" are not obliged to comply with consumer requests to provide or delete their information or to re-identify individual data to verify a consumer

86 Additionally, where surveillance has been conducted for financial gain, courts may award significant damages, including punitive damages and civil fines: ibid. s1708.8 (a), (b) and (l).

87 There are currently around 100 bills addressing privacy, cybersecurity and data breaches that are pending across the 50 states. See LegiScan, 'National Legislative Search' (*LegiScan*, 18 January 2021) <https://legiscan.com/>.

88 CAL. CIV. CODE s 1798.100-1798.199 California Civil Code (West 2018).

89 The CCPA has influenced at least nine similar regulations in Maryland (see Personal Information Protection Act (PIPA), Md. Code Ann. Comm. Law 14-3504), Nevada (see S.B. 220, 2019, 80th Sess (Nev, 2019)), Massachusetts (see S. 120, 2019–2020, 191st Sess. (Mass. 2019–2020) which has been put on hold by the Joint Committee on Consumer Protection and Professional Licensure in February 2020), Rhode Island (see S. 2430, Gen. Assemb., Reg. Sess. (R.I. 2020)) and New York (see S.B 5642, Gen. Assemb., Reg. Sess. (N.Y. 2019–2020)). Further data protection statutes are likely to meet the rising demand for robust privacy protections in the United States.

90 CAL. CIV. CODE s 1798.140(o)(1) California Civil Code (West 2018) defines "Personal Information" as: "information that identifies, relates to, describes, is reasonably capable of being associated with, or could reasonably be linked, directly or indirectly, with a particular consumer or household".

91 ibid. s1798.140(o)(2). "De-identified information" includes any information that "cannot reasonably identify, relate to, describe, be capable of being associated with, or be linked, directly or indirectly, to a particular consumer".

request.[92] Drone operators, therefore, should consider taking steps to de-identify the information they collect in order to fall outside the purview of the CCPA, for example, by blurring the images that they collect.

It is worth noting that the patchwork of state-level regulations that exist in the United States often overlap and contain contradictory provisions. For example, while all 50 US states have adopted data breach notification laws, many appear to contain differences in definitions for "personal information" (and, therefore, what information is protected by the statute) and what constitutes a data breach. Privacy advocates and legislators have been calling for a federal privacy law to resolve such overlapping and contradictory provisions.

Impact of sector-level regulation

In contrast to the European Union, there is no single, comprehensive federal law in the United States that regulates the collection and use of personal data. Instead, the US federal government has addressed privacy by regulating only specific sectors and categories of information such as health information through HIPAA,[93] financial information through the Gramm-Leach-Bliley Act,[94] and information relating to children through the Children's Online Privacy Protection Act (COPPA).[95]

HIPAA, in particular, may be cause for concern for drone operators that collect and process "protected health information" (PHI). HIPAA protects the privacy and security of PHI transmitted and maintained in any form or medium. Under the HIPAA Privacy Rule, patient consent for the use and disclosure of PHI is required unless there is a serious threat to health and safety of the patient. PHI can include a patient's social security number, individual names as well as biometric identifiers, including finger and voice prints, and full-face photographic images.[96]

Drones are increasingly used in the field of healthcare, particularly for emergency medical services (EMS). Drones may be used to survey potentially unsafe scenes before human resources are deployed, or drone cameras may assist in documenting a scene

92 However, certain requirements still remain for de-identified information: businesses that use de-identified information must still (i) implement technical safeguards that prevents re-identification; (ii) implement business processes that specifically prohibit re-identification; (iii) implement business processes that prevent the inadvertent release of de-identified information and (iv) make no attempt to re-identify the information. It is arguable whether with robust facial recognition databases and cyber tools being widely available, whether de-identified information can truly remain de-identified: ibid s1798.140(7)(h) (definition of 'Deidentified').

93 Health Insurance Portability and Accountability Act of 1996, Pub. L. No. 104–191 (1996).

94 Financial Modernization Act of 1999, Pub. L. No. 106–102 (1999).

95 Children's Online Privacy Protection Act, 15 U.S.C. ss 6501–6506 (1998).

96 Additionally, business associates of entities that are covered under HIPAA (i.e. covered entities) will be held directly liable for compliance with certain requirements of the HIPAA Rules, including failure to comply with the requirements of the HIPAA Security Rule, making impermissible uses and disclosures of PHI and failure to provide breach notification to a covered entity or another business associate. Partners and associates of drone operators who collect PHI will, therefore, need to take account of their responsibilities under HIPAA: Health Information Technology for Economic and Clinical Health Act of 2009, Pub. L. 111-5, 123 Stat.226. Please see further guidance at Office for Civil Rights, 'Direct Liability of Business Associates' (*Office for Civil Rights*, 31 January 2020) <www.hhs.gov/hipaa/for-professionals/privacy/guidance/business-associates/factsheet/index.html#footnote8_c0m70ao>.

such as a traffic accident or a specific patient encounter, thereby capturing PHI (for example, a video of a patient or the audio revealing the patient's name). HIPAA would then apply to that PHI, despite it being captured by a drone.[97] To avoid significant liabilities under HIPAA, drone operators would need to ensure that any PHI is strictly encrypted, secured and disclosed only to healthcare institutions that are authorised to receive such data. Drone operators who accidentally or innocently capture images of accidents or where PHI is displayed should consider deleting such information or sufficiently degrading the images by blurring facial images and identifiers of PHI before disclosing such information.

Moreover, drone operators who surveil or capture information related to children may be captured by COPPA.[98] The purpose of COPPA is to catch sites and services that use tracking tools to follow children (i.e. across websites for behavioural advertising purposes). Drone operators who track or capture activities of children or collect their personal information would need to ensure they take extreme care when planning flights over areas that include young children and when capturing their information, which can include photos, videos, audio files that contain the child's image or voice, as well as their geolocation information.

Emerging markets

In territories that lack a comprehensive data protection or privacy regime, the business of drone usage can involve additional complexities that can present genuine risks to the unwary. Such territories quite often prioritise national security over individual rights, whether driven by cold-headed pragmatism (being in a tough neighbourhood) or ideological approaches. Whatever the reason, in such a territory, the risks which the drone operator may need to pay particular attention to are risks which may be more likely to manifest in serious criminal consequences rather than a regulatory fine or administrative sanction.[99]

Of course, security and public safety drone regulations are not the preserve of countries lacking a comprehensive data protection regime. Virtually, all territories will have laws which might criminalise particularly bothersome or dangerous acts, such as flying a drone over an airport, and many countries which do possess a comprehensive data protection law regime will also have licensing and permission-based frameworks for the operation of drones.[100] The drone performs two main activities: it flies and it

97 Doug Wolfberg, 'EMS Lawline: Legal Questions Arise in EMS Drone Use' (2019) Journal of Emergency Medical Services <www.jems.com/2019/12/13/ems-lawline-legal-questions-arise-in-ems-drone-use/>.

98 Operators of websites or online services must give notice to parents and get their verifiable consent before collecting, using or disclosing personal information from children when either: (a) the website or online service is directed to children who are younger than 13 years of age (e.g. interactive drone games for children), or (b) when operators of websites or online services have actual knowledge that they are collecting personal information from children younger than 13: Children's Online Privacy Protection Act (n 98) s6501(9) (definition of 'verifiable parental consent').

99 Whilst inadvertently committing a crime is a notable risk when operating in countries without a formalised legal regime which addresses data protection as a civil issue, the inquisitive lensman would do well to note the potential for trouble even in data protection law hotspots, such as Europe: Derek Gatopoulos, 'Greek Court Convicts UK Plane-Spotters' *Independent* (London, 17 September 2011) <www.independent.co.uk/news/world/europe/greek-court-convicts-uk-plane-spotters-5362102.html>.

100 See, for example, Civil Aviation Authority, 'Drone and Model Aircraft Registration' (*Civil Aviation Authority*, 5 November 2019) <www.caa.co.uk/Consumers/Unmanned-aircraft/Our-role/Drone-and-model-aircraft-registration/> which requires operators of drones (or indeed any unmanned aircraft) weighing between 250 grams and 20 kilograms to be registered.

collects information. Whilst both activities are regulated in most territories, regulation of the second would typically only be of a criminal nature in many countries where the information collected is subject to special classification on the grounds of national security or where the collection of the information is nefarious by nature. Conversely, in other territories, the security and criminal laws may be broad enough to apply to any information gathering, without specific requirement for any criminal intent.

Where laws are drafted in a very broad way—which is often the case in emerging legal jurisdictions and developing markets—the prosecuting authorities naturally have a wide degree of discretion to come down hard on acts which might be perceived as contrary to public or national interest, or injurious to personal privacy, in certain circumstances but entirely frivolous and innocent in others. The camera has a huge range of uses: documenter of children's parties; travel guide; gatherer of intelligence; exposer of abuses. Context is everything but is not just in the eye of the beholder, it is also in the eye of the subject (and the legislator).

As well as being drafted broadly in and of themselves, legal provisions pertaining to privacy may be broadly distributed across various statutes in a territory without a consolidated privacy law.

One country where photography has played an important role in its growing international recognition is the United Arab Emirates. The Emirate of Dubai hosts the world's tallest building, the largest man-made island, the largest shopping mall, etc., and pictures of Dubai adorn many a popular Instagram account. Yet, outside certain special economic zones, the UAE does not have a codified data protection law and using a drone to film in public places without an official authorisation would not be a well-advised move. In addition to the usual civil aviation regulations,[101] there are several legal provisions relevant to the capturing of images and videos using electronic equipment. The most apposite example is Article 21 of the Law on Combatting Cybercrimes:[102]

> Punishment of Assaulting the Privacy of a Person in Cases other than those Permitted in Law by using an Information Network, Electronic Information System or any of the Information Technology Tool
>
> Any person who used an Information Network, Electronic Information System or any of the Information Technology Tools in assaulting the privacy of a person in cases other than those permitted in Law shall be punished by imprisonment for a period not less than six months and a fine not less than AED 150,000 and not more than AED 500,000 or by any of these punishments by any of the following methods:
>
> 1 Overhearing, interception, recording, transferring, transmitting or disclosure of conversations, communications or audio or visual materials.
> 2 Capturing pictures of third party or preparing electronic pictures or transferring, exposing, copying or keeping those pictures.

101 See *Civil Aviation Law* (United Arab Emirates) as amended by Federal Act No. 20 of 1991, art. 69–70, to include drones within its purview. In particular, note that operation of an aircraft without the appropriate licence can attract up to one year in prison, and operation of an aircraft in a prohibited zone can attract up to three years in prison.

102 *Federal Decree Law No. 5 of 2012 on Combatting Cybercrimes* (United Arab Emirates), art. 21.

> 3 Publishing electronic news or pictures or photographs, scenes, comments, statements or information even if they were correct and real.
>
> Any person who used an Electronic Information System or any of the Information Technology Tool to perform any amendment or processing on a recording, picture or scene for the purpose of defamation or insulting another person or assaulting or violating his privacy shall be punished by imprisonment for a period not less than one year and a fine not less than AED 250,000 and not exceeding AED 500,000 or by any of these punishments.

This type of provision has an equivalent in the cybercrime legislation of many of the Arabian Gulf countries. In practice, the effect of this provision is that if you do not have a legal mandate for doing so, then you risk imprisonment for capturing, publishing or even possessing images or recordings of people obtained without their prior permission (whether captured by drone, smartphone or another digital device). Obtaining advance permission from swathes of the general public will not be easy, so, in effect, any large-scale filming will always require clear official authorisation to mitigate risk, and individual subjects should be asked to provide advance consent if at all possible.

This principle similarly flows through other parts of the country's legislation: media laws require licences or government approvals for filming and photography; copyright or criminal laws can be used to grant quasi-privacy rights (the UAE Copyright Law provides that a photograph featuring any person may not be kept, exhibited, published or distributed without the consent of the person appearing in the photograph);[103] and publishing laws contain sanctions for dishonouring a person's reputation or family name.

As noted, these laws may be broadly drafted and courts can have considerable freedom to interpret the legislation to protect national interests and public policy. In the case of photography or filming, the subsequent use of images that have already been captured (for example, by posting on social media or incorporating into broadcasts) can also constitute an offence, in addition to the act of capturing itself.

It may be considered that such laws are deliberately drafted in a way that leaves them open to wide interpretation. This may be a means of giving the authorities freedom to respond to perceived threats or simply to allow emerging economies to evolve quickly by way of policy decisions without the need to formally regulate at every step. In the Islamic countries of the Middle East and Africa, there is also strong recognition of the general Shari'ah principle of respect for private life, which is afforded high importance in the Islamic culture.

Naturally, numerous territories which do not currently have a comprehensive data protection regime may be looking to develop one. Among the emerging markets of the Middle East, national data protection laws have been passed in Bahrain, Egypt, Lebanon and Qatar during the four-year period from 2016 to 2020 and it is widely anticipated that more countries in the region will follow suit. As privacy law momentum grows in a region, it is hard for countries to adopt an outlier status whilst holding themselves up as sophisticated technology hubs and retaining mainstream international investment appetite.

103 See *Federal Law No. 7 of 2002 on Copyright and Related Rights* (United Arab Emirates), art. 43.

We expect similar trends in Africa. To take another example of a relatively small country with an ever-growing economic profile, Rwanda enacted protection laws in 2020.[104] It is anecdotal, perhaps, but to support the point made in the previous paragraph—that governments recognise the importance of a sensible data governance framework as a tool to attract international investment, particularly in technology—it is worth noting that the responsible ministry is the Ministry of ICT & Innovation.[105] Unsurprisingly, the law appears to have been heavily influenced by the GDPR.

Measured and appropriate data protection laws are important if drone use is to be sensibly and even-handedly regulated. The existing panoply of civil aviation laws tend to focus on the "flight" aspect of drone activity, rather than the information gathering aspect. Broadly drafted security or privacy laws intended to clamp down on criminal acts but with the potential to be used in a way which criminalises all but the most focused and consent-driven information gathering may be overly restrictive to drone operation. In India, the Ministry of Civil Aviation, has run a public consultation on draft Unmanned Aircraft System Rules, 2020. The draft rules have faced criticism for their limited attempts to deal with privacy issues and the absence of a more comprehensive data protection framework in India has left certain groups concerned.[106] In addition, the draft rules offer wide exemptions to public authorities, effectively enabling them to operate drones for surveillance purposes without needing to justify the need or obtain further authorisation. This wide-ranging exemption for public authorities is characteristic of the approach in many emerging economies, where government bodies are routinely exempted from compliance with regulatory controls that commercial operators may need to adhere to.

Risk mitigation

Adopting a risk-based approach

Drones have ever-increasing capabilities to collect large amounts of personal information; through video-cameras that easily record, store and upload images, to detectors and sensors that can interfere with a person's private life and property. Commercial and recreational drone operators should be aware of local, state, federal and international laws relating to privacy and data protection that may directly or indirectly impact their drone activities. Drones that violate the privacy of individuals may expose their owners and their employees to civil and criminal liabilities, including hefty fines and adverse court awards or high settlements.

Drone operators should consider risk-based and risk-management strategies when setting up and operating their drones. In particular, they should conduct an analysis

104 Office of the Prime Minister of the Republic of Rwanda, 'Statement on Cabinet Decisions of 27th October 2020' (*Office of the Prime Minister*, 27 October 2020) <www.primature.gov.rw/index.php?id=131&tx_news_pi1%5Bnews%5D=933&tx_news_pi1%5Bcontroller%5D=News&tx_news_pi1%5Baction%5D=detail&cHash=7a012c144e6b2eb6d384a0bf1f153c2>.

105 See Ministry of ICT & Innovation, 'MINICT' (*Republic of Rwanda*, 2021) <www.minict.gov.rw>.

106 See, for example, Internet Democracy Project, 'Comments on the draft Unmanned Aircraft System Rules, 2020' (*Internet Democracy Project*, 17 December 2020) <www.medianama.com/wp-content/uploads/Internet-Democracy-Projects-submission-on-the-draft-Unmanned-Aircraft-System-Rules-2020.pdf>.

of potential privacy risks before deploying unmanned aircraft systems:[107] a balance should be struck between the threats to privacy of individuals who may be affected by the drone and the benefits and interests derived by the drone operator. Interference with privacy and data protection rights can be minimised at the outset when planning: (i) the flight path intended; (ii) the drone and equipment used; and (iii) the management of collected data.[108]

Privacy or data protection impact assessments (PIAs or DPIAs) are useful tools to allow a drone operator to examine critically its activities against any applicable data protection principles and legal requirements. It helps the drone operator to identify the key risks and to assess their impacts on individuals' privacy and data protection rights and to guide the operators to plan for appropriate solutions and safeguards that eliminate, mitigate or transfer the relevant risks.[109] DPIAs in particular encourage organisations or individual drone operators to:[110]

(i) map their operations and the personal data flows that are collected and processed;
(ii) identify the data protection risks and the likelihood and severity of the risks to understand their potential impacts on individuals, the drone operator and its partners;
(iii) identify solutions to respond to the risks identified such as technical safeguards (i.e. security measures or technical means to minimise data collected or to protect from unauthorised access) and procedural safeguards (i.e. internal guidance for handling data, data breach responses, and structures to ensure employees comply with internal procedures) and;
(iv) prepare a finalised list of all identified risks and safeguards to remind drone operators and relevant actors of the safeguards they need to implement to support a risk-based approach to drone missions, as well as being a "privacy reference sheet for pilots and staff involved in the mission".[111]

Similarly to how an aircraft may plan and approach a flight, drone operators should carefully pre-plan their flights at the outset. Pre-flight planning should take into consideration any privacy implications that could arise: drone operators should map out the location where the drone will be flown; plan how to fly over or near them; identify

107 In certain countries and territories this is an obligation and not merely a requirement. A Data Protection Impact Assessment (DPIA) is a risk management procedure that is required whenever personal data is processed and when such processing is "likely to result in a high risk to the rights and freedoms of natural persons": GDPR, art. 35.

108 DroneRules.EU PRO, 'Privacy Code of Conduct: A Practical Guide to Privacy and Data Protection Requirements for Drone Operators and Pilots' (*European Unions' COSME Programme*, 2014–2020) 11 <https://dronerules.eu/assets/files/PCC_DR_final-for-printing_9-November-2018.pdf>.

109 DroneRules.EU PRO, 'Data Protection Impact Assessment Template: A DroneRules.Eu PRO Resource for Drone Operators and Pilots' (*DroneRules.EU*, 19 January 2020) 3 <https://dronerules.eu/assets/files/DRPRO_Data_Protection_Impact_Assessment_EN.pdf>; See also DroneRules.EU PRO, 'Professional Users Privacy Impact Assessment (PIA) Checklist (*DroneRules.EU*, 19 January 2020) <https://dronerules.eu/en/professional/resources/professional-users-pia-checklist>.

110 DroneRules.EU PRO, 'Data Protection Impact Assessment Template: A DroneRules.Eu PRO Resource for Drone Operators and Pilots' (*DroneRules.EU*, 19 January 2020) 10, 14, 30 and 37.

111 DroneRules.EU PRO, 'Professional Users Privacy Impact Assessment (PIA) Checklist (*DroneRules.EU*,19January2020)<https://dronerules.eu/en/professional/resources/professional-users-pia-checklist>, 37.

the number and type of individuals that may be affected (i.e. a few individuals versus a big crowd); and the type of information that will be collected and processed by the drone. If operating in public spaces, drone operators may need to be vigilant not to target, follow or continuously capture people without their knowledge or consent.[112] Drone operators should minimise their flight paths that may go over or near private spaces such as homes, terraces or gardens.[113] By planning flight paths and angles at which data is captured by drone sensors, drone operators can minimise the risk of capturing people within their private locations, which could trigger privacy, trespass and nuisance claims.

Privacy measures should be incorporated even before pre-flight and operation of the drone. Organisations or individuals who develop or purchase drones should assess whether privacy has been fully factored into the design and use of the drone. The GDPR standard of data protection by design and default[114] aims to ensure that data protection and privacy considerations are entrenched in the design and development of new technologies, processes and flight plans from the very beginning and they ensure that as little personal data is collected and processed by default.[115] By incorporating privacy measures into drone manufacturing, including in the design (i.e. colour, size and sound of drones), the hardware and software, drone operators can better plan privacy-compliant drone operations.[116] Examples of drone features that may help to achieve privacy by design and default include:[117]

- making drones noticeable and implementing design elements which can signal to people on the ground that the drone's sensors are currently active and capturing data;
- providing the drone with geofencing (i.e. a virtual perimeter programmed with GPS data that prevents drones from deviating into restricted air space)[118] and other limitation sensing technology;
- incorporating software into the drone or functionalities in the software to control the drone, allowing users to activate or deactivate drone sensors when required and;
- securing drone systems through, for example, encryption software to protect the drone and access to its data.

Once the privacy risks have been identified, operators can put in place measures and safeguards to minimise such risks. Anonymisation[119] is a key mechanism to ensure that the information collected by a drone does not include personal information which may trigger the application of certain data protection and privacy laws. Personal data

112 Privacy Code of Conduct (n 108), 12.
113 ibid.
114 Article 25, GDPR.
115 DroneRules.Eu PRO, 'Privacy-By-Design Guide: A DroneRules.EU PRO Resource for Drone Manufacturers' 2. <https://dronerules.eu/assets/files/DRPRO_Privacy_by_Design_Guide_EN.pdf>.
116 ibid 3.
117 ibid 4.
118 Drew Dixon, 'Geofencing Stops Drones in Their Tracks' *The Florida Times-Union* (Jacksonville, 1 August 2017). <www.govtech.com/public-safety/Geofencing-Stops-Drones-in-Their-Tracks.html>.
119 Anonymisation is the process of either encrypting or removing personally identifiable information from data sets so that individuals whom the data describes remain permanently anonymous. See, for example, Recital 26 of the GDPR.

(or personal identifiable information) relates to data that allows the direct or indirect identification of individuals. Blurred images, therefore, or glimpses of people from a distance are not likely to be considered personal data. However, images of people's faces, recognisable clothes, haircuts, as well as vehicle licence plates will constitute personal data.[120] Even indistinct images may qualify as personal data if they can be combined with additional information; for example, if the name of a person tracked by a drone is known, blurred images of that person may still allow the successful surveillance of his or her movements. Additional software features can be implemented that can minimise the collection of data by, for example, turning off data collection when the drone strays, automatically erasing all data on the drone after it has been downloaded following a flight, or automatically anonymising personal data captured by detecting human shapes and blurring, hiding or blanking them.[121]

If the drone operation specifically requires the collection and processing of personal data, then drone operators should consider categorising the data collected. Any collection of personal data that is required for a specific, legitimate purpose should be clearly identified prior to conducting the drone operation. Data can also be divided into general personal data and sensitive personal data; which may include data consisting of racial or ethnic origin, religious beliefs, genetic data, biometric data, data concerning health or a natural person's sex life or sexual orientation.[122] Any incidental, collateral or unintentional data that is collected at the same time should be separated and either immediately deleted or anonymised.

Where countries lack specific privacy laws that regulate how drone operators should effectively manage privacy risks, a comparable approach can be made with policies and procedures available for camera surveillance systems such as CCTV. For example, the UK Information Commissioner Office's guidance on CCTV recommends incorporating privacy mechanisms relating to data retention, disclosures and governance when setting up and operating a surveillance system,[123] which can be applied to drone surveillance as well. However, such policies and guidance should be carefully tailored to drones. Since drones are small and stealthy, on many occasions, individuals may not realise that a drone has a camera or sensors attached and that they are being surveilled or recorded. Drone operators therefore need to find suitable methods to ensure transparency by providing relevant information to individuals regarding the processing of their personal data.

The case for specific regulation

While a number of countries have implemented separate privacy laws and drone regulations, legislators may wish to consider adopting privacy and data protection regulations specifically for drones. A regulation that identifies explicit privacy responsibilities when using drones would provide consistency and certainty for drone operators, insurance companies, courts and individuals.

120 Data Protection Impact Assessment Template (n 113) 7.

121 Privacy-By-Design Guide (n 115) 4.

122 See the definition of "special categories of personal data", Article 9 GDPR.

123 ICO, 'In the Picture: Data Protection Code of Practice for Surveillance Cameras and Personal Information' <https://ico.org.uk/media/1542/cctv-code-of-practice.pdf>.

Such laws would set forth specific privacy principles and requirements tailored to drone usage and mirror existing gold standards of data protection, such as the GDPR. For example, such laws should prescribe the adoption of data retention procedures and procedural protections for accessing data. Many critics of drones have raised concerns that the collection of aerial imagery and videos will enable pervasive surveillance that allows drone operators (whether a governmental agency or a private individual) to know what individuals are doing at different points in time. Such footage may be retained indefinitely, revealing private details of a person's life. Legislators, therefore, should adopt policies and procedures to address the retention of information, which focus "on the information that is collected, how it is stored, and how it is accessed, rather than the particular technology used to collect the information".[124]

Additionally, legislators should implement transparency and accountability measures requiring drone operators to publish on a regular basis "usage logs" which document the activities conducted by the drones and the information collected during such activities.[125] Such usage logs would detail who operated the system, when it was operated, where it was operated (including GPS coordinates) and what the purposes are for the operation,[126] as well as other details in line with existing data protection principles (for example, the accountability principle of the GDPR). Drone operators could even be obligated to implement specific software and systems to allow for easy access to flight logs that contain information, allowing regulators to monitor how such drones are being used and enable them to hold operators accountable.

Privacy laws regulating drones could also allow legislators to clarify what they mean by specific terminology and to specify what places should be entitled to specific privacy protections.[127] At the moment, conflicting laws and frameworks have caused confusion in certain countries as to the types of activities that are prohibited and the areas that are protected.[128] Legislators could choose to prohibit or limit certain types of surveillance that may impose serious risks to individual privacy. They could also clarify terms such as "surveillance", "reasonable expectations", "private property" and "public place" to avoid inconsistent interpretations by individuals, lawmakers and courts. Legislators may even wish to adopt entirely new terminology that can be easily understood by different parties and would avoid misperceptions.

Key privacy responsibilities for drone operators

Drone operators should be aware of their responsibilities, whether under specific drone regulation, federal or state privacy laws or other applicable criminal or civil laws that may regulate the way drones can be used when collecting data and adopt appropriate procedures to ensure compliance. A number of regulators and organisations have sought to introduce best practices for drone operations in line with applicable data protection laws and international standards.

124 Gregory McNeal, 'Drones and Aerial Surveillance: Considerations for Legislatures' The Project on Civilian Robotics Series (*Brookings*, November 2014) <www.brookings.edu/research/drones-and-aerial-surveillance-considerations-for-legislatures/>.

125 ibid.

126 ibid.

127 ibid.

128 See, for example, the section in this chapter on the United States.

Barack Obama issued a US Presidential Memorandum in February 2015 instructing the National Telecommunications and Information Administration (**NTIA**) to develop best practices for privacy, accountability and transparency issues regarding the use of unmanned aircraft systems (**UAS**).[129] In particular, it recognises that the "very characteristics that make UAS so promising for commercial and non-commercial uses, including their small size, manoeuvrability and capacity to carry various kinds of recording or sensory devices, can raise privacy concerns".[130] The "voluntary best practices" recommended by the NTIA include:

- making a "reasonable effort" to provide information to individuals of the "general timeframe and area" when a drone may collect their "covered data";[131]
- showing care when operating drones or collecting and storing "covered data" by avoiding using drones to intentionally collect such data when the operator knows that the individual has a "reasonable expectation of privacy"[132] and not use drones to carry out "persistent and continuous collection" of the data unless there is a compelling need to do so;[133]
- limiting the use and sharing of "covered data" without consent when it relates to employment eligibility, promotion, retention, credit eligibility or healthcare treatment eligibility;[134]
- securing "covered data" by implementing a programme that contains "reasonable administrative, technical and physical safeguards appropriate to the operator's size and complexity, the nature and scope of its activities and the sensitivity of the covered data";[135]
- monitoring and complying with evolving federal, state and local UAS laws.[136]

Drone operators should also consider the eight guiding principles of the European Commission,[137] either as guidance or to support compliance with the GDPR when they collect personal information. It is important that drone operators incorporate sufficient mechanisms and procedures for their drone activities to minimise risks to privacy.[138] The European Commission principles are the following.[139]

1 Inform: inform individuals whenever any information about a person is captured or recorded, especially clear images of their face.

129 NTIA, 'Voluntary Best Practices for UAS Privacy, Transparency and Accountability' (18 May 2016) <www.ntia.doc.gov/files/ntia/publications/uas_privacy_best_practices_6-21-16.pdf>.
130 ibid 2.
131 ibid. s 1(a), 5.
132 ibid. s 2(a), 5.
133 ibid. s 2(b), 6.
134 ibid. s 3(a), 6.
135 ibid. s 4(a), 6.
136 ibid. s 5, 7.
137 See DroneRules.EU PRO, the European Commission's reference resource in Europe for Remotely Piloted Aircraft Systems.
138 DroneRules.EU PRO, 'Privacy Handbook for Recreational Users' 8 <https://dronerules.eu/assets/handbooks/PrivacyHandbook_EN.pdf>.
139 DroneRules.EU PRO, 'Data Protection Guiding Principles under the GDPR' <https://dronerules.eu/assets/covers/DroneRules_factsheet_0vf.pdf>.

2 Listen: get acquainted with the data protection rights of individuals.
3 Minimise: capture the least amount of data about people in the area of the drone operation and anonymising where possible.
4 Respect: ensure that people can exercise their rights.
5 Limit: limit storage and use of personal data to the purpose for which the data is collected and for the minimum period required.
6 Protect: provide adequate security for processing and disclosing personal data.
7 Assess: conduct DPIAs and follow privacy-by-design principles.
8 Demonstrate: make a privacy notice (and DPIA) publicly available to demonstrate lawful or best practice compliance with data protection principles.

Importantly, best practices and applicable laws require drone operators to act visibly and transparently.[140] The GDPR requires data controllers (in this case, drone operators that determine the purpose and means of processing personal data collected by the drones) to provide individuals at the time of data collection (or as soon as possible after collection) with sufficient information about their data processing activities. In particular, people should be aware if there is a drone operating near them that is processing their personal information. People "have a right to be informed about the processing of their personal data and, out of respect for their privacy, people should be informed of any potential interference with their privacy by drone operations".[141] Drone operators should inform individuals who are in close proximity of the drone about the nature of the drone operation, relevant details about how personal data that is captured shall be treated, their rights and how they can exercise them and the contact information of the drone operator.

It may be difficult for drone operators to provide such information to individuals at the time of data collection. They, therefore, need to identify a variety of communication channels to inform individuals about their drone operations and refer them to their privacy notices which details how personal data is processed. Available communication channels could include:[142]

- posters or billboards close to the flight location;
- adverts in media, such as local newspapers or targeted online media campaigns;
- flyers and leaflets or
- up-to-date information on the drone operator's website and social media.

Additionally, drone operators could choose drone equipment that enhances the visibility of the drone, for example, by continuously transmitting the registration number of the drone operator or by adding unique serial numbers or electronic identifications on the drone.[143]

A number of existing data protection legislations prescribe a set of rights which individuals have with regard to their personal data. The GDPR provides individuals

140 Privacy Code of Conduct (n 108) 15.
141 ibid.
142 ibid 17.
143 ibid 16.

with rights that include: the right of access to their personal data; the right to erase or restrict the processing of their personal data and the right to object to certain processing of their personal data, including automated decision-making and direct marketing. Where drone operators act as data controllers, they will be responsible for ensuring that the rights of individuals are respected.[144] To ensure that drone operators comply with individual rights, they should put in place internal policies and procedures to enable the efficient and timely exercise of rights by individuals.

Finally, drone operators must ensure that the data they collect via drones are treated diligently and securely at all times. A number of countries have implemented data breach notification requirements which requires data controllers under certain circumstances to report data breaches to regulatory authorities and individuals. With the inexorable rise of cybercrime, robust technical and organisational security measures should be implemented to ensure that personal data captured during drone operations are protected. This protection should apply to the full life cycle of personal data: from its collection, processing and storage, to its anonymisation or destruction.[145] Where sensitive data or personal data, which if lost or stolen may cause gross harm to individuals, is collected, stronger security measures should be implemented. Failure to secure personal information and to swiftly and efficiently deal with data breaches could result in heavy penalties under applicable cybercrime laws and cause significant reputational damage.

144 ibid 21.
145 ibid 24.

11 Cyber risks

Reece Corbett-Wilkins and Alastair Long[1]

Introduction

In most jurisdictions, the law does not comprehensively address cybersecurity issues specific to the operation of drone technology. Around the world, governments and regulators have typically absorbed the various registration, safety and air-flight navigation issues posed by drone use into aviation laws. However, these laws generally fail to address the cyber risks relevant to drone technology. They are often silent or vague on cyber-risk issues or leave it to privacy regulators to manage the risk through the lens of data privacy protection.

As examined in the previous chapter,[2] it is true that privacy protection is a relevant consideration. However, data privacy risk and protecting personal data from unauthorised access/disclosure/loss or misuse is only one aspect of the broader cyber risks associated with drone usage. Further, privacy laws are mostly principle based and technology neutral, and do not comprehensively impose information security or systems integrity best practice requirements and standards specific to drone technologies. They also tend to be limited in scope, applying only to commercial operators and not individuals collecting data (drone footage or audio) for personal or non-commercial use. In other words, the privacy laws typically will not apply to recreational drone operators, leaving a gap in regulatory oversight of a large proportion of users.

Privacy laws also apply practically to activities relating specifically to data handling, that is, collecting, holding or disclosing data. Commonly, these laws will govern the activities of the drone operator or the customer who engaged the drone operator, and not the drone manufacturer. The latter would instead be primarily responsible for building security controls into the device or associated applications to guard against cyber attacks (and instead of privacy laws, consumer protection laws may well apply).

The aforementioned regulatory oversight gaps need to be addressed if confidence in burgeoning drone technology is to be maintained.

Moreover, as discussed earlier,[3] it is important to recognise that privacy risk extends beyond the personal data collected by the drone itself, such as audio/image/video footage and surveillance /tracking data. Rather, drones should be viewed as part of

1 The authors would also like to thank Clyde & Co colleagues Joowon Park (Hong Kong), Justin Yuen (Hong Kong), Alison Godbier (Australia), Ruth Yeend (Australia), Caitlyn Bellis (Australia), James Wong (Australia) and Ashley Wong (Australia) for their contributions to the chapter.

2 See discussion in Chapter 10.

3 See discussion in Chapter 10.

a broader unmanned aerial system (UAS) which includes the drone and other connected devices, including any subsequent data processing activities undertaken on associated computer systems by the drone operator.

This concept has important implications for information security and cyber risk as it acknowledges the fuller picture of drone usage and the interconnectivity between multiple systems in drone use, and the flow of data from one system to the next; that is, it is not just the security of the drone itself that must be regulated but also the data collected, transmitted and stored by associated computer systems.

This chapter is divided into three parts.

The first section (Part A) will look at a number of vulnerabilities relevant to drones that have the potential to be exploited, through the use of case studies. It will be highlighted that like most technologies, drones are inherently vulnerable to cyber attacks due to their dependency on communications signals and connectivity to operate.

The second section (Part B) will examine key jurisdictions to explore how various legislative regimes have chosen to tackle the cyber risks posed by drones. It will highlight that aviation laws are relatively silent when it comes to information security; and drone-related cyber risk remains unaddressed in broader computer offence laws. This leaves a gap whereby data privacy laws (and to some extent consumer protection laws) are the main method of governing drone information and cybersecurity risks (which we address in Part C).

The third section (Part C) will use Australia as a case study to examine how data privacy, consumer protection and Internet of Things (IoT) frameworks can be used as a roadmap to navigate cybersecurity risk and implement best practice requirements.

Part A: drone-related cybersecurity vulnerabilities

As the market for drones expands to a range of use cases across a plethora of sectors, it is vital that manufacturers, operators, consumers and policymakers are able to identify and understand the technological risks that can make drones vulnerable to cyber threats. This will allow steps to be taken to minimise cyber risk to maintain market confidence in the use of drone technology.

In short, drones are particularly vulnerable to cyber threats as a result of their dependency on external wireless input channels, such as GPS, radiofrequency, radar, infrared and Wi-Fi sensors to operate effectively. Drones use information signals between a ground control station and the drone's communications links, navigation sensors and onboard flight controller. It is these components and the interoperability between communications components that can leave them open to interference.

Drones are internet-connected "IoT" devices, meaning that they are inherently vulnerable to interception by unauthorised third parties if security controls are bypassed to connect to the device or broader UAS network. Like any internet-connected computer device or interconnected computer system, the main security challenges are protecting the transmission of information between authorised devices and preventing unauthorised users from accessing systems.

The bedrock model for upholding information security focusses on three basic concepts: confidentiality, integrity and availability. Confidentiality refers to information being protected from those who are not authorised to access it. Integrity refers to information remaining accurate and the ability to prevent information from being interfered with or manipulated. Availability refers to information remaining intact and free to access in a timely fashion, or systems remaining online and free from interception.[4] These concepts are relevant to approaching drone cybersecurity risk and will be drawn upon in the following.

Practically speaking, exploiting drone vulnerabilities may empower a malicious actor to:

- take control over the flight path (i.e. hijack navigation);
- crash/land the drone at will (i.e. hijack control); and/or
- gain access to file system/access to media files (i.e. access data).

The following case studies will highlight these consequences.

GPS spoofing and jamming

GPS spoofing and jamming is a way to intercept and prevent a drone from receiving legitimate GPS signals to hijack or bypass the legitimate operation of the drone.

In a GPS jamming attack, signals are directed to a drone to interfere with the legitimate GPS signals received by the drone, causing the GPS receiver to malfunction.[5] In a GPS spoofing attack, fake GPS signals are transmitted, which cause the drone to alter its position and steer off course.[6]

For example, in 2014, a team of researchers from the University of Texas successfully hacked a Hornet Mini-rotorcraft UAV in a GPS spoofing attack.[7] First, they used a custom-made GPS spoofing device located about 500 m from the UAV to transmit weak counterfeit GPS signals towards the hovering UAV. Then, they rapidly increased the fake signal power which brought the drone under their control. This was done by simply inducing a false signal to make it appear that the drone had flown upwards which led the flight controller to mistakenly command it to dive, resulting in a crash.

This experiment demonstrated how it is possible to produce fake GPS signals that are almost indistinguishable from legitimate ones. It also drew attention to how critical GPS function is for successful drone use, control and safety.

In 2011, this risk was further highlighted when an Iranian cyber warfare unit successfully used GPS jamming and spoofing to trick a US military drone into landing in Iran that was allegedly violating its airspace.[8] Although the exact techniques used in the attack are unknown, it is believed that communications to the drone were jammed, and then spoofed GPS signals were sent, tricking the drone into thinking it was landing at its home base.[9]

4 Corey Schou and Steven Hernandez, *Information Assurance Handbook: Effective Computer Security and Risk Management Strategies* (McGraw-Hill Education September 2014) 27.

5 Elsa Dahlman and Karin Lagrelius, 'A Game of Drones: Cyber Security in UAVs' (DPhil thesis, KTH Royal Institute of Technology June 2019) 9.

6 ibid 9.

7 Jean-Paul Yaacoub and others, 'Security Analysis of Drones Systems: Attacks, Limitations, and Recommendations' (2020) 11 Internet of Things 25.

8 Riham Altawy and Amr M Youssef, 'Security, Privacy, and Safety Aspects of Civilian Drones: A Survey' (2016) 1(2) ACM Transactions on Cyber-Physical Systems 2.

9 ibid 2.

GPS jamming and spoofing threaten to undermine the integrity of drones. It is vital that information is not manipulated in its transmission from sender to receiver, which is an underpinning tenet of information technology security.

Denial-of-service

In a denial-of-service (DoS) attack, the threat actor prevents the legitimate user from controlling the drone through flooding the drone's components with malicious communications. The computing power or memory is drained, causing the component(s) to become overloaded and malfunction.[10] To give a very practical example, a DoS attack is like a crowd of people gathered at the entrance to a shop.[11] This makes it difficult for legitimate customers to enter and disrupts trade. Much like a crowd prevents foot traffic, a DoS attack prevents legitimate network traffic from reaching the device for communications purposes. In the drone context, a DoS attack could involve flooding the drone's network with navigation requests continuously at a fast pace, which prevents an operator communicating with the drone.[12]

In 2018, security researchers performed a DoS attack on a Parrot AR Drone by attacking its communication system.[13] In the attack, the researchers disconnected the initial user by sending a de-authentication command, and then continuously sent the same command, exhausting the UAV's memory.[14] This prevented the user from reconnecting to the device.

The experiment was undertaken with the intention to crash the drone (which was successful) and highlighted the ease with which such attacks can be carried out. Drones must be guarded against DoS attacks so that all elements of their system can be guaranteed to perform their required functions without disruption.[15] It is this availability which ensures that information systems can be accessed in a timely and reliable fashion.

Man-in-the-middle

Drones are vulnerable to "man-in-the-middle" (MitM) attacks, where the threat actor gets "in the middle" of two systems to access information, usually on a clandestine basis without the knowledge of users. A classic example is where a threat actor sees a transaction being made and intercepts it to change the destination account number to commit financial fraud.[16]

In the case of drones, a MitM attack is a violation of authentication to control the communication between the device (UAV) and the user (remote control),[17] and allows

10 Mehdi Karimibiuki, 'Addressing Security in Drone Systems through Authorization and Fake Object Detection' (Thesis, University of British Columbia April 2020) 2.

11 IT Perfection Network Security, 'DoS and DDoS Attacks' <www.itperfection.com/network-security/dos-and-ddos-attacks-denial-of-service-attack-ping-cybersecurity-network-cyber/>.

12 Dahlman and Lagrelius (n 5) 9.

13 ibid 16.

14 ibid 17.

15 Altawy and Youssef (n 8) 15.

16 Dan Swinhoe, 'What is a Man-in-the-Middle Attack? How MitM Attacks Work and How to Prevent Them' (*CSO Australia*, 13 February 2019)<www.csoonline.com/article/3340117/what-is-a-man-in-the-middle-attack-how-mitm-attacks-work-and-how-to-prevent-them.html>.

17 Dahlman and Lagrelius (n 5) 16.

an unauthorised party to access data collected by the drone. Drones are particularly vulnerable to these types of attack as they continuously broadcast their location and flight information, making them easy target.[18]

In 2016, security researchers performed a MitM attack on a drone by targeting its radio link.[19] The researchers were able to ascertain the connection parameters for the drone (which were set to default) and then remotely changed the relevant parameters to communicate with the flight computer, and control the communication between the vehicle and the remote control.[20]

This attack exposed flaws in the radio communication system and highlighted how the continued use of default manufacturer authentication settings can be exploited to spoof legitimate users' connections to drone devices. This creates opportunity for a MitM attack.

MitM attacks threaten the confidentiality of drone systems through unauthorised disclosure of information.[21] If drones are to play an increased operational role across many sectors as well as personal use, it is necessary that the information is protected and confidentiality is maintained.

Malware infection

Both the flight controller (within the drone) and ground control unit (i.e. remote control/operations systems) are vulnerable to malware infections (i.e. viruses/trojans).[22] These are typically injected through users inadvertently installing malicious software updates, or through threat actors gaining access to systems and installing malware on end point devices.

One example of malware is "Maldrone" (a malicious computer virus) which once installed, enables the threat actor to take control of the drone.[23] It is concerning that the source code of Maldrone is open to the public and can be uploaded remotely, so could be easily used to infect drones.[24] Malware infections compromise the confidentiality of information through unauthorised disclosure, which also violates the integrity of system as a whole.[25]

In 2011, malware was discovered in the ground control unit in the Creech Air Force base in the United States.[26] The malware was a keylogging virus which created a backdoor into the computers to allow remote access. The keylogger tracked keyboard strokes made by UAV operators to manage the drone fleet over Iraq and Afghanistan.[27] Although there were no reported consequences of the incident, it demonstrates

18 Karimibiuki (n 10) 2.
19 Dahlman and Lagrelius (n 5) 16.
20 ibid.
21 Altawy and Youssef (n 8) 15.
22 ibid 10.
23 Charlie Osborne, 'Maldrone: Malware Which Hijacks Your Personal Drone' (*Zero Day*, 27 January 2015) <www.zdnet.com/article/maldrone-malware-which-hijacks-your-personal-drones/>.
24 Katharina Ley Best and others, *How to Analyze the Cyber Threat from Drones* (Rand Corporation 2020) 46.
25 Karimibiuki (n 10) 2.
26 Altawy and Youssef (n 8) 10.
27 ibid 10.

the potential severity that malware attacks can have, including the loss of sensitive data or the loss of control of UAVs.

Wi-Fi jamming

Similar to GPS jamming (mentioned earlier), drones are vulnerable to hijacking through Wi-Fi jamming, which targets the communication between the ground control device (phone, tablet, etc.) and the Wi-Fi wireless access point in the drone.[28] This process typically involves sending a de-authentication process, which allows the threat actor to connect to the drone through their own Wi-Fi network, thereby gaining control over the drone.

For example, security researcher Samy Kamkar has developed a drone called "SkyJack" that is capable of Wi-Fi-Jamming in order to hack other drones within wireless distance.[29] "SkyJack" can autonomously scan, hack and wirelessly take full control over any other drones thereby creating a "zombie drone".

SkyJack scans for wireless addresses that match the address of the drone and then sends authentication requests using a software called "aircraft". Aircraft has the ability to crack and de-authenticate the Wi-Fi network. Signals from the operator are then disconnected by the SkyJack signal and it pretends to be the operator, taking control of the drone.[30]

This demonstrates the vulnerabilities that exist through Wi-Fi network connectivity. Through Wi-Fi Jamming, the threat actors are able to disrupt communications and the reception of messages, which diminishes the integrity and ultimately security of drone systems.

Wi-Fi aircrack

Drones can be subject to an "Aircrack-ng" attack, which de-authenticates the user and gives control over the device to the threat actor.

"Aircrack-ng" is software that can be used to detect nearby wireless networks and drone systems, which then deactivates the drone's controller and connects it to the attacker.[31] This results in the threat actor having full control over the drone which ultimately undermines the integrity of the system.

In 2016, security researchers performed a cyber attack against a Parrot AR Drone. They took advantage of weaknesses in the Wi-Fi-based communication system to gain access to the device.[32] After taking control of the drone, they manipulated it using a Robot Operating System (ROS), an open-source platform which can be used as an operating system for simple devices.[33] As a result, they gained full control of the UAV.

This example highlights that open-source tools are freely available for exploiting Wi-Fi-enabled technology.

28 Yaacoub (n 7) 19.
29 Manimaran Mohan, 'Cybersecurity in Drones' (Capstone Project, *Utica College*, May 2016) 28.
30 ibid 28.
31 Dahlman and Lagrelius (n 5) 14.
32 ibid 14.
33 ibid.

Replay

Replay is similar to a denial-of-service attack, which intercepts the data that is transmitted between the drone and the ground control system then either delays it or re-transmits it at a later time.[34] This may then become part of a later spoofing attack used to gain control of the drone.

Buffer overflow

Buffer overflow is also similar to a DoS attack, which intercepts the transmission of data between the drone and ground control system and floods it with illegitimate requests.[35] As a result, the connection between the drone and operator is disrupted and the threat actor gains control.

For example, security researchers performed a buffer-overflow attack on a Parrot Bebop drone.[36] They sent a request from their laptop to the UAV asking to be the controller. The request was sent as a JSON record (a certain type of file format), but in the wrong format and containing too many characters in one field. A buffer overflow occurred when the drone's CPU and memory usage dropped to approximately 10%, preventing the operator from accessing the device. It then stopped mid-air and crashed.

This attack demonstrates drones' vulnerability to basic denial-of-service buffer-overflow attacks—exploitation of which can result in catastrophic and immediate disabling of the drone's rotors midflight.[37]

Remote injection

Drones are also able to be used to communicate with other IoT devices.

A 2016 report was published by university researchers in Israel and Canada who used a DJI drone to inject a worm to take control of smart light bulbs in an office building in Israel.[38] The security researchers used the drone to hover close to the light bulbs to issue a factory reset command. The drone's software then updated the devices firmware, took control of the light bulbs, and made them blink "SOS" in Morse code.

This demonstrates how drones can be used as a communication medium to spread infectious malware from one IoT device to those around it, which undermines the integrity and legitimate use of the drone. In the future, hackers may be able to use drones to cause rapid citywide disruptions which are difficult to prevent and investigate.[39]

While the risk of this may be remote, this question will become more relevant as our cities adopt widespread IoT sensors and devices in the future.

Manipulating captured footage

Drones rely on the video captured by their cameras for navigation and collision avoidance. A threat actor who has knowledge of the system parameters and is able to gain

34 Yaacoub (n 7) 25.
35 ibid.
36 Dahlman and Lagrelius (n 5) 20.
37 Michael Hooper and others, 'Securing Commercial WiFi-based UAVs from Common Security Attacks' (IEEE Military Communications Conference, Baltimore, 1–3 November 2016) 1.
38 Best (n 24) 23.
39 ibid 23.

access to the flight controller can intercept the data transmission and replace the genuine footage with a fabricated one.[40]

This manipulation process often starts when the flight controller requests the captured video from the operating system of the flight controller computer by issuing a system call. A threat actor that can gain access to the flight controller can intercept the system calls issued and replace the genuine footage with the fabricated one.[41]

Again, while this risk may be remote it highlights the type of activity that may occur should a threat actor have the resources or be sufficiently motivated.

Unauthorised disclosure of communication

A central vulnerability of drones is the exchange of information between the drone and ground control system, including the telemetry feeds and signals.[42]

For example, a cyber attack was carried out on the United States Reapers and Predators drone fleet operating in Iraq.[43] During this attack, the captured live video feeds sent by the UAVs to the ground control system was intercepted by Iraqi militants. They were able to do this using an off-the-shelf product called "*SkyGrabber*". The attack was possible because encryption of the video feeds was disabled.

This demonstrates the need to have systems in place to protect against the unauthorised disclosure of communication should a drone be intercepted which threatens the confidentiality of the system.[44]

Reverse engineering

Reverse engineering is not a vulnerability exploit but is a practical technique that can be used to design and facilitate cyber attacks on drones.[45] This occurs through reverse engineering the technology, which involves reviewing software code or system design and configuration to decipher how the drone works with the intention of configuring an attack or stealing intellectual property.

In 2011, the US drone RQ-170 Sentinel was allegedly captured by Iranian hackers. It has been suggested that they used the drone to reverse engineer its technology for their own advantage.[46]

While the United States authorities maintain that Iran will find it difficult to exploit any data and technology, it still serves to highlight the potential risks should drones be captured, particularly in a military context.[47]

40 Altawy and Youssef (n 8) 10.
41 ibid.
42 ibid 11.
43 ibid.
44 ibid.
45 Dahlman and Lagrelius (n 5) 9.
46 Kim Hartmann and Keir Giles, 'UAV Exploitation: A New Domain for Cyber Power' (International Conference on Cyber Conflict, 3 June 2016).
47 AirForce Technology, 'RQ-170 Sentinel Unmanned Aerial Vehicle' (*Projects*, 19 January 2021) <www.airforce-technology.com/projects/rq-170-sentinel/>.

Summary of examples

As highlighted earlier, there are a number of ways in which drone technology and data can be interfered with or intercepted. While the overall risk of exploitation may be relatively low, it is nevertheless important that manufacturers and users of drones are aware of these risks and take appropriate measures to guard against known and foreseeable risk. We will address measures which should be considered in Part C.

We now summarise the aviation and cybersecurity approach to regulating drone technology.

Part B: aviation/cybersecurity regulatory approach to drones

The current aviation regulations applicable to drone operations view drones primarily as a form of "aircraft" and consequently focus on the risks around the vehicles causing physical injury or accidents. Cyber risk is often buried in the regulatory text or as an afterthought.

This part examines the legislative regimes of different nations to see how various jurisdictions have chosen to tackle the risk posed by drones to information security.

International Civil Aviation Organisation

The United Nations body in charge of international civil aviation—International Civil Aviation Organisation (ICAO)—has issued guidance material entitled "*Unmanned Aircraft Systems Traffic Management (UTM)—A Common Framework with Core Principles for Global Harmonisation*".[48] The ICAO guidance cites cybersecurity as a parameter with which to measure the overall effectiveness, safety and efficiency of a UTM system involving airborne and ground-based functions.[49]

This guidance material encourages aviation authorities to harmonise UTM systems globally and to report cybersecurity issues. It encourages civil aviation authorities and regional safety oversight organisations to take into consideration "*cybersecurity risks and vulnerabilities*" and to establish a robust security framework. Cybersecurity is cited as part of a gap in data standards to support UTM safety-related services[50] and for drone identification purposes.[51]

An important statement from ICAO about cybersecurity is as follows:

> There are significant cybersecurity risks and vulnerabilities that must be taken into consideration. A robust security framework must be established to address potentially malicious attacks to communication systems, including C2 Link disruptions, Global Navigation Satellite System (GNSS) jamming or spoofing attacks, and the manipulation of information exchanged between UAS and

48 International Civil Aviation Organization, 'Unmanned Aircraft Systems Traffic Management (UTM)—A Common Framework with Core Principles for Global Harmonization' (Framework, 2018); International Civil Aviation Organization, 'Unmanned Aircraft Systems Traffic Management (UTM)—A Common Framework with Core Principles for Global Harmonization' (Framework, 2019).

49 ibid (2019) 7.

50 ibid 12.

51 ibid 17.

> between UAS and UTM systems, which may result in erroneous advisories, unwanted changes in flight paths and increased risk of collision.[52]

While the guidance clearly picks up on cybersecurity risks as an issue to be addressed, the material is very high level in nature. It does not expressly address implications related to cybersecurity breaches or system failures leading to physical impact or collision of drones whilst in flight.

At the time of writing, ICAO had launched a Request for Information to the international aviation community for part 4 of its DRONE ENABLE consultation in the development of an integrated UTM. It does not however expressly seek information and view on cyber threats to drone operations.[53]

It remains to be seen what further advisory content the ICAO issues in its global supervisory role, to address cyber risk.

Hong Kong

The Air Navigation (Hong Kong) Order 1995 (Cap. 448C) applies in full to the use of drones as aircraft in the Hong Kong Special Administrative Region. In particular, Article 48 of the Order stipulates that no person shall "recklessly or negligently cause or permit an aircraft to endanger any person or property", with offenders being liable to prosecution and upon conviction to a fine and up to two years' imprisonment.

A public consultation by the Civil Aviation Department in July 2018 was launched with an aim to introduce an updated legal and regulatory framework on the use of drones. However, at present no new framework has yet been introduced.

More importantly, cybersecurity and cyber risk does not feature in local aviation laws. References are invariably made to the Hong Kong Privacy Commissioner for Personal Data (PCPD) and the Personal Data (Privacy) Ordinance (Cap 486) (PDPO) for any data or privacy issues. The PCPD has issued guidance on the use of drones in the context of surveillance.[54]

Cyber-security issues are not specifically addressed, but on page 5 of the Guidance there is some high-level consideration to cyber risk with the PCPD stating that:

> If images are transmitted through wireless means, encryption should be considered to avoid the adverse consequences of interception by unrelated parties. If the drone has a recording function, access control should be considered to prevent the recording from falling into the wrong hands in the event the drones are accidentally lost.

More broadly, the Hong Kong Air Traffic Engineering Services Division (AESD) has worked with ICAO and the Airport Authority Hong Kong (AAHK) since 2018 to

52 ibid 19.

53 International Civil Aviation Organization, 'International Civil Aviation Organization Unmanned Aircraft System Traffic Management (UTM) Request for Information' (Request for Information, 2020).

54 Privacy Commissioner for Personal Data Hong Kong, 'Guidance on CCTV Surveillance and Use of Drones' (Guidance Note, March 2017).

share information and to raise awareness on cyber threats and safety risks, policy, procedures and technology.[55]

However, this is regulated airspace where drones are forbidden to operate. Nevertheless, the same principles of cyber-risk mitigation can equally apply to uncontrolled (Class G) airspace.

The People's Republic of China (PRC)

In mainland China, the laws governing the use of drones focus on aviation safety. The Civil Aviation Administration of China (CAAC) is the main responsible regulator. Since 2017, CAAC required all drone users with a device over 250 g to register on their system before their drones are allowed to take off. Personal information, such as names, addresses, contact methods and product serial codes would be collected by the CAAC. Users are also required to explain the reasons for using the drones.

The authority also developed a risk-based airworthiness certification mechanism in 2019, as the drone industry is moving towards the development of drones to carry heavy cargo or passengers. Drones are categorised based on their respective operational risks (i.e. risk of collision, both on ground or mid-air) and there are different certification requirements for each category. CAAC requested all manufacturers to follow and apply for airworthiness certification for their products.

In terms of drones' operations, the authority has barred drone usage in "densely populated" areas, such as cities and villages, roads and major attractions. Various safety regulations have been implemented to set up no-fly zones in particular cities, areas and attractions, which poses a great hindrance for drone usage in mainland China. It also restricts any drone usage that has an impact on public order. There have been cases in which tourists have been fined for filming with drones and individuals sentenced for violating public order and aviation safety.

Nevertheless, recent updates in laws governing the use of drones see a shift towards cybersecurity issues. From May 2020, drones that weigh below 7 kg are required to submit real-time operation data to CAAC via the Unmanned Aircraft System Traffic Management Information Service System (UTMISS). Information, such as the owner's identity, coordinates, altitudes and speed will be collected for each operation.

CAAC aims to regulate drone activities through this platform, while it also allows other government divisions in mainland China to apply for the data which is being collected. Failure to provide such data would lead to penalty by the authority and if any of the drone activities contravene any national security legislation, the relevant authorities may impose penalties on those users pursuant to the applicable laws.

In addition, Chinese lawmakers are currently reviewing national data security legislation. The new law covers any data collection by electronic means, and therefore it is our view that footage captured by drones would fall under the ambit of this proposed legislation. It is expected that further regulations on drone usage would be published to regulate any contravention of the interests of public and the country through flying a drone to ensure any drone operations satisfy the requirements in the regime.

55 Civil Aviation Safety Authority, 'Annual Report 2018–2019' (*Australian Government*, 2019).

United States

In the United States, the biggest recent development in laws governing drone usage is the implementation of the *FAA Reauthorization Act of 2018*.[56] The law has subdivided the previous categorisations of unmanned aircraft systems and now governs the use of recreational drones in the United States. It sets out new conditions and requirements for recreational drone users and repealed the predecessor Special Rule for Model Aircraft framework. However, as always, the focus is on physical safety rather than cyber and information security risks.

Previously, drones weighing under 55 lb (~25 kg) were classified as model aircraft and registration with the FAA was not required, meaning that recreational drones could be launched from most locations by users that were not required to have any special knowledge in such operations. The recent framework has restricted this by setting out limitations with which drone users are required to comply, failing which they must obtain special certification or operating authority from FAA.[57]

The drone must be registered with FAA. It must be flown strictly for recreational purposes only and operated within the safety guidelines issued by FAA and the respective community-based organisations where the drones are flown. Broadly speaking, recreational drones can only be flown at or below 400 feet above ground in uncontrolled airspace; for controlled airspace, prior authorisation from the relevant air traffic administrator is required.

Other requirements in the law include non-interference with other manned aircraft and rescue operations; flight carried out within the visual line of sight; and no night-time flying without full knowledge of the drone's location throughout the flight. If any user operates his or her drone in a careless or reckless manner so as to endanger the life or property of another, that user could be liable for criminal and/or civil penalties.

It also requires the drone operator to pass an aeronautical knowledge and safety test, maintain the document proof and make such document available upon request. The test aims to equip drone operators with an understanding of aeronautical safety knowledge, knowledge of FAA regulations and requirements on drone operations within the US national airspace system. The FAA is still developing the framework and inviting industry stakeholders' feedback for such testing framework.

The FAA is also developing the Low Altitude Authorization and Notification Capability (LAANC). It automates the application and approval process for airspace authorisations. This is to allow recreational drone users to obtain automated authorisation to fly at or below 400 feet at controlled airspace. It will also provide information as to where can the drones be flown to drone users, and drone operating information (i.e. altitude and location of the drones) to air traffic officials.

Cyber-security issues are expected to have some prominence in the LAANC advisory. Indeed, from a cybersecurity perspective, new developments are anticipated. Under section 509 of the law, the FAA is required to review its cybersecurity plan within a year from its enactment.[58] There was also a separate audit report on FAA's cybersecurity

56 Generally see discussion in Chapter 15, National Regulatory Structure and Responses: USA.

57 Federal Aviation Administration, 'Fact Sheet—Small Unmanned Aircraft Systems (UAS) Regulations (Part 107)' (*Federal Aviation Administration*, 6 October 2020) <www.faa.gov/news/fact_sheets/news_story.cfm?newsId=22615>.

58 CAA Reauthorization Act of 2018, Pub. L. No. 115-254, s 509, 132 Stat 3186 (2018).

plan,[59] in which it recommended FAA to develop cybersecurity risk management plans, and to enhance aircraft systems' cybersecurity. Finally, in FAA's strategic plan (2019–2022), reference is made to ensure the aviation system is resilient enough to withstand security events (including cybersecurity), which could otherwise disrupt the NAS.

It remains to be seen what further cybersecurity measures are implemented in respect of cybersecurity from the FAA.

Canada

Part IX (Remotely Piloted Aircraft Systems) of the Canadian Aviation Regulations sets out a general prohibition on reckless and negligent flying, a requirement to register ownership, visual line of sight flying, avoiding emergency security perimeters (unless operating to save human life, police operations, firefighting or some other public authority service), controlled and restricted airspace, payload and flight operations.

It does not refer to cybersecurity, geo-fencing or secure communications as between the operator and the drone under aviation regulations.

South Korea

Regulation and governance of drone use in South Korea is undertaken by the Korea Office of Civil Aviation (KOCA) as part of the Ministry of Land, Infrastructure and Transport (MOLIT). The latest drone law came into effect on 1 May 2020 to provide a framework for the use of drones and to facilitate the drone industry. However, this does not include anti-drone activities, such as the GPS jamming.

According to a policy briefing in 2020 (available in Korean only), MOLIT is planning to develop anti-drone technologies, such as radar and drone jammer to stop illegal drone use and to protect key infrastructures from drone attacks.

Furthermore, the Korean government is planning to introduce regulations such as requiring drone users to attach GPS trackers on their drones when flying drones near key government infrastructure or airports.

Singapore

The Air Navigation (101—Unmanned Aircraft Operations) Regulations 2019 do not expressly refer to cybersecurity, privacy or data protection within the rules for governing the use of drones in Singapore.[60] However, Singapore does have an explicit cybersecurity law and other ancillary legislation that deals separately with cyber threats and would apply in the context of drone use.

United Kingdom and the European Union (EU)

Aviation rules and regulations surrounding UAVs are rapidly evolving within the EU. Under the Brexit treaty, the UK has agreed to be bound by the latest regulations with respect to drones. Regulation (EU) 2018/1139 of 4 July 2018 has updated common

59 FAA Report No AV2019021 (March 2019).
60 Air Navigation (101—Unmanned Aircraft Operations) Regulations 2019 (Cap 6, 2019 Rev Ed).

aviation rules within the EU and expressly refers to the governance of unmanned aircraft in the context of wider civil aircraft.[61]

More importantly, Article 4.1(d) of Regulation (EU) 2018/1139 requires the Commission, EASA and Member States to: "take into account interdependencies between the different domains of aviation safety, and between aviation safety, cybersecurity and other technical domains of aviation regulation". This is one of several references in which cybersecurity and risk is expressly acknowledged as an integral part of the EU's aviation safety strategy.

In October 2019, European Parliamentary Research Service paper entitled "Civil and military drones: Navigating a disruptive and dynamic technological ecosystem",[62] information security and cyber risks were identified among a number of key remaining challenges, namely the risks associated with remote hijacking of a drone's command and control system for nefarious purposes.

New EU legislation dedicated to UAVs (the EU UAS Implementing Regulation) came into effect from 31 December 2020, and in Article 19.4 of Regulation (EU) 2019/947 of 24 May 2019 the requirement to take into account cybersecurity within a wider safety matters and procedures for the efficient exchange of safety information between Member States is repeated.[63]

Australia

Australia was the first jurisdiction to enact regulations specific to unmanned aircraft.[64]

Part 101 of the Australian Civil Aviation Safety Regulations 1998 (Cth)[65] is the primary legislative source for the use of unmanned aircraft and rockets. It gives the Civil Aviation Safety Authority (**CASA**) the power to supervise and govern certain drone operations.

It is the body responsible for:

- the registration of Australian drones;
- the issuing of certification for commercial drones;
- the accreditation of certain types of drones (e.g. operators of drones exceeding 250 g in weight will required from 2021 to show they understand drone safety rules); and
- the investigation of unsafe drone operations.

CASA has published various bespoke rules and regulations with respect to safe flight for civil drone operators in Australia. In addition, CASA also aims to educate the populace about drone regulation through guidelines on its website and a safety app called "Airmap", which shows the areas a drone can or cannot be flown.

61 Regulation (EU) 2018/1139 [2018] OJ L212/1.

62 Tania Latici, 'Civil and Military Drones: Navigating a Disruptive and Dynamic Technological Ecosystem' (European Parliamentary Research Service, 2019)<www.europarl.europa.eu/RegData/etudes/BRIE/2019/642230/EPRS_BRI(2019)642230_EN.pdf>.

63 Commission Implementing Regulation (EU) 2019/947 of 24 May 2019 on the rules and procedures for the operation of unmanned aircraft [2019] OJ L152/45.

64 Australian Association for Unmanned Systems and Liberty Victoria, 'The Use of Drones in Australia: An Agenda for Reform' (Report, 2015) <https://libertyvictoria.org.au/sites/default/files/relocated/reports/LV_AAUS_Use_of_drones_in_Australia_agenda_for_reform_27042015.pdf> 11.

65 *Civil Aviation Safety Regulations 1998* (Cth) pt 101.

However, despite the wealth of aviation legislative and regulatory instruments, cyber risk, incidents and security are not mentioned in any prominent detail. Further, CASA's investigatory powers only extend to aviation safety breaches. CASA does not investigate or enforce cyber incidents or privacy-related concerns, directing such queries instead to the Office of the Australian Information Commissioner (OAIC).[66]

However, this space is under review. In October 2020, the Department of Infrastructure, Transport, Regional Development and Communications (DITRDC) released the "Emerging Aviation Technologies—National Aviation Policy Issues Paper" as a first step towards the development of a national policy for the management of drones and other emerging aviation technologies.[67] The paper seeks contributions from the community about issues relating to cybersecurity (including the use of counter-drone technology) to develop a drone security framework to manage the physical, cyber and socioeconomic risks associated with drones.

It remains to be seen what further developments come out of any national framework.

New Zealand

The Civil Aviation Authority (**CAA**) is the primary governing body for drone regulation in New Zealand.

Similar to CASA, the CAA provides guidelines around the operation and certification of drones. In addition, it also serves as the investigatory body for drone safety complaints. If a drone operator is found to have violated the rules, the CAA can issue a written warning, a fine, or even prosecute the person in breach. The New Zealand app for drones is "Airshare".[68]

Drone usage in New Zealand is primarily governed by the New Zealand Civil Aviation Rules. The most relevant parts are Part 101,[69] which contains the rules for operating drones, and Part 102, which allows for the certification of drones so they can operate outside the rules established in Part 101. Akin to the Australian drone regulatory framework, non-legislative but advisory circulars have been developed in New Zealand in respect of Parts 101 and 102. Similar to Australia, New Zealand's drone rules focus on flight safety.

There currently appear to be no specific references in its aviation legislation.

General cybersecurity laws and drones

Based on our assessment of current aviation-specific regulatory frameworks in various jurisdictions, there is room for bolstering legislation to manage, govern, protect, mitigate or punish cyber attacks conducted on or in using drones.

To complete the picture, in this section we will consider general cybersecurity laws in the same jurisdictions mentioned earlier to assess what other laws may apply to drone use to prohibit cyber attacks.

66 Civil Aviation Safety Authority, 'Notify and Report' (Report)<www.casa.gov.au/about-us/contact-us/notify-and-report>.

67 Department of Infrastructure, Transport, Regional Development and Communications, 'Emerging Aviation Technologies: National Aviation Policy Issues Paper' (Issues Paper, Commonwealth of Australia, September 2020) <www.infrastructure.gov.au/aviation/drones/index.aspx>.

68 Air Share, 'AirShare is the UAV and Drone Hub for New Zealand' (*AirShare*, 2020) <www.airshare.co.nz>.

69 *Civil Aviation Rules* (NZ) pt 101.

Like aviation laws, the general laws do not neatly apply to govern or regulate drone-related cybersecurity issues, nor establish positive obligations on manufacturers and users in respect of maintaining cybersecurity best practice and preventing attacks (rather, they outlaw committing attacks).

Hong Kong

Hong Kong does not currently have dedicated cybersecurity laws.

However, illicit interception of UAV communications containing personal data would, for example, trigger potential liability under the Personal Data (Privacy) Ordinance (Cap 486). In this regard, personal data that is lost or stolen (whether it takes the form of photos, video footage or any other information that identifies an individual), by a remote threat actor on the ground or through another device will most likely trigger data privacy laws as opposed to any violation of aviation laws.

Other legislation may be applicable to drones as computer technology. For example, unauthorised access to a computer is an offence under s27A of the Telecommunications Ordinance (Cap 106). Further, the misuse of a computer program or data and access to a computer with criminal or dishonest intent are offences contrary to s60 and s161 of the Crimes Ordinance (Cap 200), respectively.

The People's Republic of China (PRC)

In contrast to the patchwork of telecommunications and computer laws in Hong Kong, the PRC does have a dedicated cybersecurity law regime. The relevant legislation is the Cybersecurity Law of the People's Republic of China.

Of particular relevance are Articles 27, 44 and 48. Article 27 forbids individuals or entities from conducting any activity endangering cybersecurity. Article 44 likewise forbids stealing or otherwise illegally obtaining personal information.

Article 48 states information and application sent to third parties should be free from malware. While none of these articles explicitly mentions drones, due to how broad these provisions are drafted, it is likely drone hackers and drone operators will be caught under these provisions.

Article 63 states that breach of Article 27 can lead to short-term imprisonment or fines. Articles 64 and 60 likewise impose fines on offenders for breaches of Articles 44 and 48, respectively.

While these laws do not specifically reference drone technology, their broad scope may have application to drone manufacturers and users.

United States

Cybersecurity law in the United States is underpinned by the Federal Computer Fraud and Abuse Act 18 U.S.C. 1030 (**CFAA**). The CFAA's focus is on the hacking of, and unauthorised access to, computers to obtain national security information, interstate or foreign commerce information, non-public government computers, reckless and intentional damage to computers, password trafficking and access to defraud, extort and cyber-extortion. Ancillary legislation includes the Electronic Communications Protection Act (ECPA) 18 U.S.C. to protect communications in transit or in storage.

The ECPA includes within its remit the Stored Communications Act (18 U.S.C. 2702) which makes it a criminal offence to access an electronic communications service without authority and the Wiretap Act (18 U.S.C. 2511) that prohibits intentionally intercepting electronic communication, with certain exceptions for law enforcement etc. There are also individual state laws that prohibit and sanction unauthorised access to computer systems, for example, New York's Penal Law 156.05, 156.20.

The CFAA covers a range of offences, including denial-of-service, phishing, identity theft, malware use and the possession of hardware, software or other tools to commit cybercrime. In theory, therefore, that would include the use of a drone as a tool for advancing a criminal enterprise that might involve data theft or compromising IT systems and infrastructure. Critical infrastructure is protected by the US Cybersecurity and Infrastructure Security Agency (CISA) as part of the Department for Homeland Security.

CISA will coordinate with other government agencies to protect operators of transport which in this instance would include aviation authorities who oversee airports, airspace and air traffic management. Finally, incident reporting is encouraged. Under the Cybersecurity Information Sharing Act 2015, sharing about threats, and measures taken to mitigate against such threats, is facilitated and it does not prejudice other rights such as maintaining legal privilege.

There are sector specific laws that deal with cybersecurity but these predominantly relate to financial services, telecommunications and healthcare, and are not expressly relevant to drones or related computer technology.

Canada

The Canadian Criminal Code, RSC 1985 c C-46 prohibits a number of different cyber-related acts, including hacking, computer misuse to commit fraud or steal money or other property, DoS attacks, phishing, infecting IT systems with malware, possession or use of hardware, software or other devices to hack into or cause mischief to other systems, identity theft and terrorist activities if such activities involve acts done with the intention to cause serious interference or disrupt essential services, facilities and systems in both the public and private domains. As such, the Criminal Code is expansive and would likely be the first point of call for authorities dealing with cybercrime through the operation or use of drone technology.

There are also more specific pieces of legislation dealing with electronic communications and computer use. Canada's Anti-Spam Legislation[70] prohibits both unauthorised changes to the destination of electronic communications and the unauthorised installation of computer programs on someone else's computer system in the course of commercial activities, as well as aiding abetting either of those two activities.

Finally, the Communications Security Establishment (CSE) is Canada's cybersecurity watchdog. CSE advises the Canadian government on the protection of computer networks and safeguarding critical electronic information and has created IT

70 An Act to promote the efficiency and adaptability of the Canadian economy by regulating certain activities that discourage reliance on electronic means of carrying out commercial activities, and to amend the Canadian Radio-television and Telecommunications Commission Act, the Competition Act, the Personal Information Protection and Electronic Documents Act and the Telecommunications Act SC 2010, c23.

standards, practices and directives at a federal level throughout Canada. As with the United States and other jurisdictions, the main regulatory and legislative focus is on financial services and healthcare.

South Korea

The relevant act in governing cybersecurity is the Act on Promotion of Information and Communications Network Utilisation and Information Protection.

The sections of note here are Articles 48 and 49. Article 48 prohibits a person from performing intrusive acts on information and communication networks. This article can be interpreted to prohibit hackers from hacking into the Wi-Fi or Bluetooth networks connecting the drone to the ground station. Article 49 then relates to the protection of secrets. It disallows unauthorised infringement, disclosure, misappropriation or "mutilation" of others' information processed, stored or transmitted through an information and communications network. Article 49 is straightforward in its application to drones—it disallows a person from accessing the content stored within drones without due authorisation.

Violation of the Act can lead to a five-year prison sentence or a very significant fine in South Korea.

Singapore

There are two primary pieces of legislation relevant to cybersecurity in Singapore.

The first is the Cybersecurity Act 2018. This Act does not cover the majority of drone users given it only imposes cybersecurity obligations on owners of critical information infrastructure (e.g. energy providers).

The second Act is the Computer Misuse Act (CMA). This act is applicable to drones as a form of computer technology. The CMA is applicable to persons both inside and outside Singapore.

The most relevant provisions in the CMA are sections 3, 4, 6 and 7. Section 3 forbids individuals from accessing computer materials without authorisation. Section 4 bars individuals from accessing computer programs or data with the intention of committing a crime. Section 6 disallows individuals from using or intercepting computers (e.g. services relating to data processing and storage of data) without authorisation. Finally, section 7 forbids persons from interfering or interrupting lawful access and/or use of computers.

A breach of any of these four sections can result in significant fines or imprisonment.

United Kingdom

The regulations applicable to cybersecurity in the UK are the Network and Information Systems Regulations 2018/506 and the *Computer Misuse Act 1990*.

The former set of regulations brings into effect the EU Network and Information Systems Directive passed in the EU (see the following subsection for more information).

Section 1 forbids unauthorised access to computer materials. Section 2 forbids unauthorised access to computers if the person intends to facilitate or commit crimes. Section 3 forbids unauthorised attempts to impair the operation of a computer/drone. Section 3A also forbids the facilitation of acts outlawed in sections 1 and 3.

The European Union (EU)

In June 2015, the Article 29 Data Protection Working Party (the EU's data privacy watchdog pre-GDPR) published an opinion on privacy and data protection issue relating to the utilisation of drones. It details requirements to consider risk of electronic and cyber attacks on drones in the context of ensuring that controllers implement appropriate technical and organisational measures to protect personal data under Article 17 of the then EU Data Protection Directive.[71]

More broadly, there are three pieces of regulation relevant to cybersecurity that indirectly impact on drone use within the European jurisdiction.

The first is the EU Network and Information Systems Directive, EU Regulation 2016/1148. This directive strives to ensure that: (i) EU's member states have in place resilient and effective national cybersecurity regimes which cooperate with each other and (ii) operators of essential services and certain digital service providers within member states have appropriate and proportionate cybersecurity measures in place.

The second relevant directive is Directive 2013/40/EU. This directive deals with attacks against information systems by establishing minimum rules, including sanctions. The relevant provisions are Articles 3–7. Article 3 prohibits illegal access, Article 4 prohibits undue system interference, Article 5 prohibits data interference, Article 6 prohibits undue interception and Article 7 is in relation to tools used to commit the offences in Articles 3–6.

The third relevant directive is Regulation EU 2018/1139—section VII ("Unmanned Aircraft"). There are three parts to section VII:

1 centralising regulatory assets—this allows the Union (European Commission, EASA) to intervene when the individual effects of a state isn't enough;
2 competences—this allows member states to lay down specific national rules on drones, grant specific exemption for some European requirements, and amends implementing or delegated acts of the Commission; and
3 sectorial laws—for example, public security legislation, telecommunication laws, criminal law that can be applied to the operation of drones.

Australia

As mentioned previously, CASA has explicitly confirmed they focus mainly on the physical safety drones rather than cybersecurity risks.

However, in terms of broader legislation, criminal laws in Australia and at the State and Territory level operate to proscribe certain criminal conduct in relation to computer offences, similar to that addressed in other jurisdictions previously and New Zealand in the following.

Additionally, drone operators may be caught by the following Act and recently proposed legislation in respect of their data and cyber security obligations:

- *Telecommunications and Other Legislation Amendment (Assistance and Access) Act 2018* (Cth) likely broad enough to be used by Australian law enforcement agencies as a basis for requesting access to encrypted data stored within a UAS; and

71 Opinion 01/2015 on Privacy and Data Protection Issues Relating to the Utilisation of Drones [2015] OJ WP231.

- *Security Legislation Amendment (Critical Infrastructure) Bill 2020* (Cth) UAS with nexus to a 'critical infrastructure sector' may be subject to additional cybersecurity obligations.

New Zealand

Similar to the Regulations in Australia, the New Zealand Civil Aviation Rules does not regulate issues pertaining to cybersecurity. Rather, it is the *Crimes Act 1961*—New Zealand's central piece of criminal legislation—that deals with computer crimes (and, by extension, crimes relating to drones).

For example, section 249 of the Act criminalises unlawfully accessing and performing wrongful acts upon a computer. Meanwhile, section 250 criminalises the damaging of a computer/drone system, in the sense of interfering with its data or its ability to function.

Summary of laws

As we have demonstrated in this Part B, aviation laws focus primarily on wrongdoing as an operator of an aircraft which endangers the travelling public. Cybersecurity laws focus on penalising the wrongdoer committing a computer-related offence rather than establishing positive duties on drone manufacturers or users to ensure cybersecurity best practice is implemented. Although this is slowly changing, a user or operator of drones would still have to pivot between two separate bodies of law in order to see the wider picture.

Part C: how to navigate drone-related cybersecurity risk

In this part, we will consider how drones should be treated as internet-connected computer devices as much as they are considered to be aircraft.

The world has never been more interconnected, and we are increasingly reliant on internet-connected devices to provide convenience to our lives (i.e. the IoT).

It is estimated that by 2030, there will be more than 21 billion IoT devices connected to the internet around the world, with some estimates placing the figure at over 64 billion devices.[72] IoT devices connect in a shared network through a common communication link, the internet. They are made up of various sensor, actuator and controller components which produce live-stream data, allowing them to make decisions and take actions autonomously based on that shared data.[73]

However, as opportunities in the digital world have increased, so have cyber threats.[74] Many IoT devices are developed with functionality as the top priority, meaning security often becomes a secondary consideration.[75] A central security challenge

72 Australian Department of Home Affairs, 'Code of Practice: Securing the Internet of Things for Consumers' (*Australian Government*, 2020) <www.homeaffairs.gov.au/reports-and-pubs/files/code-of-practice.pdf> 1.

73 Karimibiuki (n 10).

74 Australian Department of Home Affairs, 'Australia's Cyber Security Strategy 2020' (*Australian Government*, 2020) <www.homeaffairs.gov.au/cyber-security-subsite/files/cyber-security-strategy-2020.pdf> 4.

75 ibid 1.

to the growing IoT environment is protecting shared information between authorised devices and users, while identifying legitimate objects in the network from illegitimate ones.[76] As cyber threats continue to increase in scale and sophistication, it is vital that the IoT has cybersecurity provisions that defend against potential threats.

The current aviation regulations applicable to drone operations view drones primarily as a form of "aircraft". However, drones can also be seen as complex autonomous IoT systems.[77] They are dynamic mobile IoT systems that move around and broadcast their sensitive information, including mission planning data without authorisation checks.[78]

Using Australia as an example, we now review a number of legal frameworks which are re-shaping the IoT and cybersecurity policy landscape.

IoT code of practice

On 3 September 2020, the Australian Government released the "*Voluntary Code of Practice: Securing the Internet of Things*", representing one of the first key steps in improving the security of IoT devices in Australia.[79] It sets out voluntary measures that the Australian Government recommends be adopted as the minimum standard for IoT devices.

The purpose of the Code is to raise awareness of the security safeguards of the IoT landscape and to build consumer confidence in IoT technology.[80] By increasing the cybersecurity of IoT devices, it is hoped that this will deter the threats posed to IoT devices in Australia.[81]

The Code of Practice was developed after engagement with industry professionals and the public by the Department of Home Affairs, in partnership with the Australian Signals Directorate's Australia Cyber Security Centre (ACSC). The ACSC is responsible for leading the government's efforts to improve cybersecurity. They work with businesses and experts in Australia to develop solutions to cybersecurity threats and provide advice to people about how to protect themselves online.[82]

The Code sets out 13 voluntary principles to provide industry with a best practice guide on how to design IoT devices with cybersecurity features in mind:

- Principle 1: No duplicated default or weak passwords.
- Principle 2: Implement a vulnerability disclosure policy.
- Principle 3: Keep software securely updated.
- Principle 4: Securely store credentials.
- Principle 5: Ensure that personal data is protected.
- Principle 6: Minimise exposed attack surfaces.
- Principle 7: Ensure communication security.
- Principle 8: Ensure software integrity.
- Principle 9: Make systems resilient to outages.

76 Karimibiuki (n 10) 2.
77 ibid 3.
78 ibid 5.
79 Australian Department of Home Affairs (n 72) 1.
80 ibid.
81 ibid.
82 Australian Signals Directorate, 'About the ACSC' (*Australian Government*, October 2020) <www.cyber.gov.au/acsc>.

- Principle 10: Monitor system telemetry data.
- Principle 11: Make it easy for consumers to delete personal data.
- Principle 12: Make installation and maintenance of devices easy.
- Principle 13: Validate input data.

The Code recommends prioritising the first three principles (taking action on default passwords, vulnerability disclosure and security updates) as these will bring the largest security benefits in the short term.[83]

The full 13 principles will be outlined in the checklist at the end of the chapter. Compliance with the principles is optional but encouraged and any entity that chooses to comply can do so in accordance with all or only some of the principles.[84] Organisations that can demonstrate compliance with the code will be able to argue that they have taken reasonable steps to comply with best practice requirements.

IOTAA Provider and User Security Awareness Guides

In line with the Australian Government's goal of increasing public confidence in IoT technology, IoT Alliance Australia (IOTAA) has recently released two separate guides; one for providers and one for users of IoT technology to increase security, safety, and privacy practices within all IoT products and services. The guides provide accessible tips and techniques, and the annexure of the guides provide a particularly useful and digestible list of possible vulnerabilities in IoT products.

Amongst other things, the provider security awareness guide recommends that providers:

- define the end-of-life term and policy and provide to the user at time of purchase;
- design and implement products to avoid duplicated default or weak passwords, no default administration credentials or passwords;
- plan for secure and automated software updates without disrupting functionality;
- design and deliver the functionality of secure storage of credentials, certificates, keys and secrets. Avoid hard coding these, (i.e. administration access credentials);
- implement authentication and access privileges that can be easily set up by users;
- provide privileges for the user to disable unused features and ports on IoT products;
- ensure capabilities are in place for data encryption from the source to the destination;
- validate consistency and authenticity of data as it is delivered;
- empower the user with audit privileges, (i.e. system, network and user logs);
- provide the user with guidelines or steps to understand, report or resolve issues for any unprecedented incidents starting from situational awareness, problem confirmation, severity of the issue, and to isolate/rectify and eradicate the problem; and
- ensure IoT products are designed to fail safe and secure, not fail open.[85]

Amongst other things, the user security awareness guide recommends that users:

- protect networks, wireless networks and IoT devices with strong passphrases;
- never use the same passphrase across networks or devices;

83 Australian Department of Home Affairs (n 72).

84 ibid.

85 IoT Alliance Australia, 'Ensuring your IoT is secure: A provider's guide' (*Australia Government 2020)* <https://iot.org.au/wp/wp-content/uploads/2021/02/IoTAA-IoT-Providers-Security-Awareness-Guide-Ebook.pdf>.

- seek providers who offer multifactor authentication on products and enable it;
- always change the default administrator usernames and passphrases on new network equipment and IoT devices and accounts;
- with all new network and connected device products, install firmware updates (available from vendor websites) and
- read IoT user guide and take advantage of resources from organisations like the Office of the eSafety Commissioner (https://esafety.gov.au) and the IoT Security Foundation (https://www.iotsecurityfoundation.org).[86]

ACSC consumer guidelines

Alongside the Code of Practice, the ACSC released an IoT guide for consumers and small and medium-sized businesses on how to protect themselves against cyber threats when buying, using, and disposing of IoT devices. This is important as many IoT devices found in Australian homes and businesses were not created with security as a priority.[87]

As a result, many devices are vulnerable to compromise, leading to incidents where threat actors have gained access to devices and personal data for malicious purposes.[88] The advice relates to before purchasing, setting up, maintaining and disposing of an IoT device. This guide is relevant for drone users, who are largely hobbyists using them for recreational purposes.[89]

It is vital that the everyday consumer is educated about how to take steps to protect their IoT devices.

ACSC manufacturer guidelines

The ACSC have also released a guide to help manufacturers implement the IoT Code of Practice. This is vital as threat actors regularly target information held by company contractors, both classified and unclassified, in an attempt to gain an economic or strategic advantage.[90]

The ACSC has produced this guide to help manufacturers implement the 13 principles outlined in the Voluntary Code of Practice. They do this by stating good and bad examples of implementation of the Code. These will be outlined in the checklist at the end of the chapter.

Australia's Cyber Security Strategy 2020

Another key source driving Australia's evolving IoT and cybersecurity landscape is Australia's 2020 Cyber Security Strategy, of which the IoT Code of Practice was a

86 IoT Alliance Australia, 'Ensuring your IoT is secure: A user's guide' (*Australian Government 2020*) <https://iot.org.au/wp/wp-content/uploads/2021/02/IoTAA-IoT-Users-Security-Awareness-Guide.pdf>

87 Australian Signals Directorate, 'Internet of Things Devices' (Web Page) <www.cyber.gov.au/acsc/view-all-content/advice/internet-things-devices>.

88 ibid.

89 Altawy and Youssef (n 8) 2.

90 Australian Signals Directorate, 'IoT Code of Practice: Guidance for Manufacturers' (*Australian Government*, 19 January 2021) <www.cyber.gov.au/acsc/view-all-content/publications/iot-code-practice-guidance-manufacturers>.

key deliverable. The strategy outlines that malicious cyber activity is one of the most significant threats impacting Australians.[91]

The vision of the strategy is to create "*a more secure online world for Australians*" which is promised to be delivered through complementary action by government, businesses and the community.[92]

Therefore, the 2020 Strategy and Code indicate how the government will approach cybersecurity obligations of the drone industry in the future, including through regulatory reform.[93] This is particularly relevant as the IoT expands in Australia and drone devices develop new capabilities.

"Five Eyes" statement of intent

In 2019, Australia co-signed a statement of intent with the other Five Eyes nations (Canada, New Zealand, the United Kingdom and the United States) regarding IoT devices.

The document is an acknowledgement that the IoT is growing rapidly yet many devices lack basic security features and that the vulnerabilities of compromised devices have serious consequences.[94] It also acknowledges that more needs to be done to protect people from the risks posed by IoT devices and that it is a global issue.

Through signing the Statement of Intent, the Five Eyes nations agree to provide better protection to users through raising awareness of security safeguards associated with IoT devices and agree to encourage international alignment on IoT security.[95]

Australia's Code of Practice aligns with and is built upon this statement.[96] It is a useful reference point for understanding the key underpinnings of Australia's overall strategy for improvement of IoT security into the future.

Essential Eight mitigation strategies

In addition to the aforementioned codes specifically relevant to IoT devices, the "Essential Eight" are a baseline information security mitigation roadmap prepared by the ACSC.[97] These strategies can assist drone operators in preventing malware delivery and execution, can limit the extent of cybersecurity incidents and help in data recovery and system availability.

In complying with best practice information security requirements, drone operators (particularly commercial operators) should adhere to these principles to reduce the threats to their wider UAS computer environment (i.e. computer system on which data is stored and processed) and ensure compliance with information security best practice.

91 Australian Department of Home Affairs (n 74) 10.

92 ibid 8.

93 ibid.

94 Government of the United Kingdom, 'Statement of Intent Regarding the Security of the Internet of Things' (Government Guidance, 2019) <www.gov.uk/government/publications/five-country-ministerial-communique/statement-of-intent-regarding-the-security-of-the-internet-of-things>.

95 ibid.

96 Aimee Chanthadavong, 'Australian Government Releases Voluntary IoT Cybersecurity Code of Practice' (*ZDNet*, 3 September 2020) <www.zdnet.com/article/australian-government-releases-voluntary-iot-cybersecurity-code-of-practice/>.

97 Australian Signals Directorate, 'Essential Eight Explained' (*Australian Government*, June 2020) <www.cyber.gov.au/acsc/view-all-content/publications/essential-eight-explained>.

The "Essential Eight" principles are set out in the following:

1 **Application control** to prevent execution of unapproved/malicious programs, including .exe, DLL, scripts (e.g. Windows Script Host, PowerShell and HTA) and installers.
2 **Configure Microsoft Office** macro settings to block macros from the internet, and only allow vetted macros either in "trusted locations" with limited write access or digitally signed with a trusted certificate.
3 **Patch applications,** for example, Flash, web browsers, Microsoft Office, Java and PDF viewers. Patch/mitigate computers with "extreme risk" vulnerabilities within 48 hours. Use the latest version of applications.
4 **User application hardening.** Configure web browsers to block Flash (ideally uninstall it), ads and Java on the internet. Disable unneeded features in Microsoft Office (e.g. OLE), web browsers and PDF viewers.
5 **Restrict administrative privileges** to operating systems and applications based on user duties. Regularly revalidate the need for privileges. Don't use privileged accounts for reading email and web browsing.
6 **Multi-factor authentication** for VPNs, RDP, SSH and other remote access, and for all users when they perform a privileged action or access an important (sensitive/high availability) data repository.
7 **Patch operating systems.** Patch/mitigate computers (including network devices) with "extreme risk" vulnerabilities within 48 hours. Use the latest operating system version. Don't use unsupported versions.
8 **Daily backups** of important new/changed data, software and configuration settings, stored disconnected, retained for at least 3 months. Test restoration initially annually and when IT infrastructure changes.

Against the background of the evolving information security frameworks, we now review the role of privacy laws in enforcing cybersecurity requirements for the drone industry.

Drones and privacy/Security laws

The Office of the Australian Information Commissioner (OAIC) is the primarily relevant data protection regulator in Australia. The OAIC is responsible for enforcing the Privacy Act 1988 (Cth) which is the key statute governing the handling of personal information. Corresponding state and territory laws may also apply in limited circumstances but are not considered in the following.

Any organisation with an annual turnover exceeding AUD $3 million will be subject to the *Privacy Act*. Such organisations are known as "APP entities" and are subject to the Australian Privacy Principles (APP), an integral part of the Privacy Act which sets out the various obligations including those relating to information security.

Currently, private individuals and entities with an annual turnover below AUD $3 million are generally not caught by the *Privacy Act*, unless certain exceptions apply. This presents a legislative gap, as recreational drone users and smaller businesses utilising drones are not subject to the remit of the OAIC and therefore cannot be held accountable for their failure to safeguard personal information.[98]

98 Office of the Australian Information Commissioner, 'Drones' (*Australian Government,* 2020) <www.oaic.gov.au/privacy/your-privacy-rights/surveillance-and-monitoring/drones/>.

Currently the scope of the Privacy Act is the subject of review, with law reform currently being considered by the Attorney General's Department.[99] Should the changes proposed by the OAIC be accepted, the scope of the Act will be significantly expanded to apply to small businesses that turn over less than AUD $3 million. Practically speaking, this will apply to approximately 2 million small business in Australia. As a result of these changes, it is essential that smaller / start up drone operators and their clients be alive to possible changes in their privacy obligations.

As it currently stands, for organisations whose turnover is more than $3 million annually, the collection and storage of information by or through drones falls under the jurisdiction of the *Privacy Act* if the information can be classified as "personal information". Information qualifies as "personal information" if it is "information or an opinion about an identified individual, or an individual who is reasonably identifiable" (see Chapter 9).[100]

Examples of personal information relevant in the context of drones include photos, sound recordings or videos that could reasonably identify an individual—for instance, footage that indicates where a person works, a recording of a person's voice (as long as the recording is sufficient in length and clarity to identify the person).

APP principles

There are a total of 13 APPs which apply to all stages of the information lifecycle—that is, the collection, use and disclosure, and destruction of personal information. The APPs are principles-based law and technology neutral which means they can be adapted to technological changes, including drones.[101]

In relation to cybersecurity and data security, the relevant obligations are addressed in APP 11.1, which governs the protection of personal information.

APP 11.1—security of personal information

APP 11.1 is the key provision in ensuring that APP entities take reasonable steps to protect against cybersecurity incidents.

An APP entity operating drones is obliged under APP 11.1 to take *reasonable steps* to protect personal information it holds (stored within the drone's system or related data processing computer systems) from misuse, interference and loss, as well as from unauthorised access, modification or disclosure.

Whether steps are reasonable in the circumstances turns on a number of factors, including: the nature of the entity; the amount and sensitivity of the personal information held; the possible adverse consequences for an individual in the case of a breach; the practical implications of implementing the security measure, including the time and cost involved; and whether a security measure is itself privacy invasive.

99 Australian Government, 'Review of the Privacy Act 1988' (*Attorney-General's Department*) <www.ag.gov.au/integrity/consultations/review-privacy-act-1988>.

100 *Privacy Act 1988* (Cth) s 6.

101 Office of the Australian Information Commissioner, 'Australian Privacy Principles' (*Australian Government*, 19 January 2021) <www.oaic.gov.au/privacy/australian-privacy-principles/>.

What steps should drone operators take to safeguard personal information?

To assist organisations in complying with APP 11.1, the OAIC has published guidelines relevant to whether reasonable steps have been taken to protect personal information.[102] The OAIC specifically references that APP entities should focus on the following areas:

- governance, culture and training:
  - fostering a privacy and security aware culture;
  - establishing oversight, accountability and decision-making responsibility; and
  - implementing personnel security and training;
- developing internal practices, procedures and systems;
- implementing strong information and community technology (ICT) security:
  - software security;
  - encryption;
  - network security;
  - whitelisting and blacklisting;
  - vulnerability testing;
  - backing up data; and
  - email security.
- implementing access security:
  - trusted insider risk;
  - identity management and authentication;
  - access to non-public content on web servers;
  - passwords and passphrases;
  - collaboration with third parties when handling data;
  - audit logs, audit trails and monitoring access; and
  - individuals accessing and correcting their own personal information;
- third-party providers (including cloud service providers);
- data breach preparedness;
- physical security;
- destruction or de-identification of personal information when no longer required; and
- obtaining certification/complying with industry standards.

By being able to actively demonstrate compliance with the aforementioned requirements, drone operators will be able to show that they have taken reasonable steps to comply with information security requirements.

102 Office of the Australian Information Commissioner, 'Guide to Securing Personal Information' (*Australian Government*, 5 June 2018) <www.oaic.gov.au/privacy/guidance-and-advice/guide-to-securing-personal-information/>.

Organisations that contract with drone operators should also ensure that any agreement with the operator addresses data handling requirements, as both the drone operators and the contracting party will be responsible for ensuring data is protected.

Drones and consumer laws

A final point to note is how drones fit into the Australian consumer protection legislative regime. The following case study demonstrates how Australian Consumer Law (ACL) is being re-examined in light of advances in technologies and expansion of the IoT.

The Australian Competition and Consumer Commission (ACCC) is the government agency responsible for ensuring that individuals and businesses comply with Australian competition, fair trading and consumer protection laws.[103] Its aim is to protect people from scams, unsafe products and unfair treatment from businesses.[104]

In June 2020, the ACCC entered into an undertaking with Lime Network Pty Ltd (Lime), who provides rental dockless bicycle and e-scooters to metropolitan areas and universities around the world.

By way of background, when people rode downhill at speed or hit an obstacle, the Gen 2 e-scooters would apply excessive brake force causing the scooter to stop suddenly. On a number of occasions, many people suffered serious injuries, including broken bones, damaged teeth, cuts and abrasions.

It was found that on at least 50 occasions, Lime had become aware of this problem and that it had caused or was likely to cause serious injury to customers.[105] They failed to report this to the Commonwealth Minister as per the obligation under section 131 of the ACL.[106] Furthermore, on three occasions in early 2019, Lime applied remote firmware updates to its Gen 2 e-scooters to address the safety issues. Again, they failed to appropriately notify the Commonwealth Minister of the firmware updates.[107]

Importantly, with regard to the serious injury, the ACCC considered that Lime misrepresented its product safety and failed to comply with mandatory injury-reporting obligations under the ACL.[108] With regard to the firmware updates, the ACCC considered each firmware update to constitute a voluntary recall under the meaning of section 128 of the ACL. Therefore, Lime failed to provide notice to the Commonwealth Minister which was a breach of its obligations under the ACL.[109] The undertaking addresses the ACCC's concerns about misrepresentations regarding the safety of Lime's e-scooters and about their product safety reporting obligations under the ACL.

103 Australian Competition & Consumer Commission, 'About Us' (Australian Competition & Consumer Commission, 19 January 2021) <www.accc.gov.au/>.

104 ibid.

105 Lime Network Pty Ltd, 'Undertaking to the Australian Competition and Consumer Commission Given for the Purposes of Section 87B' (*Australian Competition & Consumer Commission*, 16 June 2020) <www.accc.gov.au/system/files/public-registers/undertaking/EO%20-%20s87B%20 undertaking%20-%20Lime%20Network%20Pty%20Ltd%20-%20signed%20by%20Chair%20 16%20June%202020.pdf> 2.

106 ibid.

107 ibid.

108 ibid 2.

109 ibid.

Specifically, the undertaking from Lime includes commitments to:

- publish a statement about the undertaking on its website and in an email to users of the Lime App;
- supply only Gen 3 or later model e-scooters if Lime recommences operations in Australia (once COVID-19 restrictions have been lifted);
- take timely actions to address any safety issues or defects affecting its e-scooters, including by directly and prominently notifying users of any safety hazards as soon as it becomes aware; and
- implement a comprehensive Consumer Compliance Programme containing improved injury-reporting systems and stringent product safety procedures.

This case brings to light key requirements that device manufacturers, IoT service providers and mobile application developers need to be following, for example, rectifying a product's safety defect or hazard, including issuing firmware updates, and recognising that such action will likely be considered a voluntary recall under the ACL.

As the IoT grows and more products (including drone technology) become connected, this issue will come into sharper focus.

National Drone Detection Network

The May 2021 Budget includes the 'Digital Economy Strategy' in which the Australian Government has committed $32.6 million over two years to establish an '*Emerging Aviation Technology Partnerships*' program. This reflects the need to support emerging aviation technologies, including drones and the drone industry.[110]

The investment includes a new framework called the '*National Drone Detection Network*', which is expected to be "*a coordinated system of scalable and modular infrastructure to detect drone activity around airports, flightpaths and other sensitive areas and provide relevant data to a wide range of users*". The government states that this network will be essential to address security risks related to drones, and will also assist with administering regulations relating to safety, privacy, noise, spectrum and environmental impacts.[111]

At the same time the Digital Economy Strategy was announced, the Australian Government released a policy statement addressing "*National Emerging Aviation Technologies*", in which it specifically addresses its strategy to approaching cyber and physical security, as well as the National Drone Detection Network. The report details a number of proposals which if introduced will contribute to the raising awareness of cyber security risks as well as obligations on the industry to increase the security of technology to be consider 'cyberworthy'.[112]

110 Australian Government, 'Australia's Digital Economy Strategy' (*Department of Prime Minister and Cabinet*) <https://digitaleconomy.pmc.gov.au/>.

111 'Australia's Digital Economy Strategy – Emerging Aviation Technologies' (*Department of Prime Minister and Cabinet*) <https://digitaleconomy.pmc.gov.au/fact-sheets/emerging-aviation-technologies>.

112 Australian Government, 'National Emerging Aviation Technologies' (*Department of Infrastructure, Transport, Regional Development and Communications*) <www.infrastructure.gov.au/aviation/technology/files/national-emerging-aviation-technologiespolicy-statement.pdf>.

In our view, this is a promising development and reflects the growing awareness of the need for a national regulation of drone technologies from a cyber security perspective.

Thoughts for the future

As technologies evolve so do cybersecurity threats. In the context of UAVs, while the probability of such threats being exploited may generally be low, their impact can be high with dangerous and devastating effects.[113]

It is important that all parties in the drone industry are educated about the cyber risks so that steps can be taken to uphold information security through the entire supply chain. However, raising awareness can only go so far.

Ultimately, there needs to be uniformity across the world on which regulatory authority is responsible for ensuring cybersecurity—and whether such laws should sit within the aviation, cybersecurity, privacy and data protection or consumer protection legal domain. Further, global standards should be set to clearly outline best practice requirements noting that technology will continue to evolve and outpace the change of law, and measures by which these can be enforced in light of this.

As stated by Tim Berners-Lee in 2009, the inventor of the World Wide Web: "*The Web as I envisaged it, we have not seen it yet. The future is still so much bigger than the past*".[114] The future of technology is full of promise. However, it must not be forgotten that this will inevitably come with risks which need to be addressed by all stakeholders to ensure that industry confidence remains.

Internet of things information security checklist

In light of the earlier discussion regarding information security and drones, specifically obligations relating to personal information and data, we recommend that individuals and businesses adhere to the following checklist, based on the IoT Code of Practice, to ensure cybersecurity is upheld.[115]

113 Yaacoub (n 7) 1.

114 Daniel Silva, 'Internet Has Only Just Begun, Say Founders' (Phys Org, 22 April 2009) <https://phys.org/news/2009-04-internet-begun-founders.html>.

115 See Australian Department of Home Affairs (n 72); and <www.cyber.gov.au/acsc/view-all-content/guidance/setting-iot-device>; and <www.cyber.gov.au/acsc/view-all-content/publications/iot-code-practice-guidance-manufacturers>; Australian Signals Directorate, 'Setting Up an IoT Device' (*Australian Government*, 2020) <www.cyber.gov.au/acsc/view-all-content/guidance/setting-iot-device>; and Australian Signals Directorate (n 88).

Principle	*Description*	*Manufacturers Do's*	*Manufacturers Don'ts*	*Consumers Do's*	*Consumer Don'ts*
1. No duplicated default or weak passwords	Passwords should be unique, unpredictable, complex and unfeasible to guess.	• Do change passwords from the default to something of at least the minimum length and complexity as articulated in the Australian Government Information Security Manual. • Do require WebAuthn or multi-factor authentication. • Do require users to authenticate Wi-Fi Access points.	• Do not publish default passwords. • Do not make passwords unable to be changed. • Do not have devices disclose account passwords without authentication.	• Do change your password, especially if the device is shipped with a weak default password. • Do use a strong password or passphrase. • Do purchase a device that uses multi-factor authentication.	• Do not use a weak password. • Do not purchase a device that has a password you are unable to change.
2. Implement a vulnerability disclosure policy	Provide a public point of contact as part of a vulnerability disclosure policy in order for security researchers and others to report issues.	• Do make a clear and detailed disclosure policy readily available. • Do provide a specific point of contact for reporting vulnerabilities. • Do develop and distribute updates in a timely manner once vulnerabilities are identified. • Do create a bug bounty program to encourage reporting of vulnerabilities. • Do have a service legal agreement which outlines expectations and strategies to remediate or defend device.	• Do not ignore vulnerabilities. • Do not have a policy that contradicts elements of the Australian Privacy Principles.	• Do check whether the manufacturer provides regular updates to fix vulnerabilities as they are discovered. Do purchase a device made by a well-known reputable company and sold by a well-known reputable store.	• Do not purchase a device that does not have a disclosure policy.

(*Continued*)

(Continued)

Principle	*Description*	*Manufacturers Do's*	*Manufacturers Don'ts*	*Consumers Do's*	*Consumer Don'ts*
3. Keep software securely updated	Software (including firmware) on IoT devices, including third-party and open-source software, as well as associated web services, should be securely updateable. Updates should be timely and not impact the device's functionality. Updates should also not change user-configured preferences, security or privacy settings without prior approval from the user.	• Do provide automatic updates and make users aware via reliable communication. • Do digitally sign updates. • Do always provide updates over secure network protocols • Do ensure updates are easy for the user to find and apply. • Do make a change log available to users detailing the purpose of each update. • Do make end-of-life policy available to users. • Do ensure the device checks for updates daily and highlights the availability of updates to the user. • Do ensure the device validates updates through cryptographically secure mechanisms prior to installation.	• Do not introduce new features before remediating weaknesses and vulnerabilities • Do not require users to pay a subscription fee for updates • Do not make updates that reduce the device's functionality.	• Do apply regular updates. • Do consider upgrading to a newer device when updates are no longer available for your device. • Do ensure the Wi-Fi network is set up securely with a secure password.	• Do not purchase a device that requires a subscription fee for updates. • Do not purchase a device that no longer provides updates.

Principle	*Description*	*Manufacturers Do's*	*Manufacturers Don'ts*	*Consumers Do's*	*Consumer Don'ts*
4. Securely store credentials	Any credentials should be stored securely within devices and on services. Hard-coded credentials (e.g. usernames and passwords) should not be embedded in device software or hardware since they can be discovered via reverse engineering.	• Do ensure passwords stored on the device are encrypted using algorithms, as articulated in the Australian Government Information Security Manual. • Do ensure all passwords and sensitive data exchanged during device set-up are done so using cryptographically secure mechanisms.	• Do not have hardcoded credentials contained within the firmware which are common multiple devices. • Do not store passwords in configuration or firmware. • Do not share or extract passwords for Wi-Fi networks without encryption. • Do not reuse Private Key material between multiple devices.	• Do ensure the device is made by a well-known reputable company and sold by a well-known reputable store.	• Do not purchase a device that does not store passwords through encryption.
5. Ensure that personal data is protected	Where devices and/or services process personal data, they must do so in accordance with data protection law, e.g. the Privacy Act 1988 and Australian Privacy Principles. Personal data should only be collected if necessary for the operation of the device, and privacy settings on a device should be set to privacy protective by default.	• Do have a privacy policy that clearly describes personal data collected, including how it will be stored and used. • Do ensure only personal data needed to operate the device is collected. • Do ensure encryption, as articulated in the Australian Government Information Security Manual is used for data in transit and at rest.	• Do not transmit personal data in clear text. • Do not encourage users to connect with third-party online platforms for data sharing without being informed of the risks.	• Do check what data the device will collect and who the data will be shared with.	• Do not purchase a device that is not compliant with the Australian Privacy Principles. • Do not connect with third-party online platforms to share data without being informed of the risks.

(*Continued*)

(Continued)

Principle	*Description*	*Manufacturers Do's*	*Manufacturers Don'ts*	*Consumers Do's*	*Consumer Don'ts*
		• Do ensure all personal data transmitted between the device and the mobile application is encrypted. • Do ensure metadata and content associated with sensitive personal data is encrypted. • Do comply with relevant regulatory and statutory requirements (e.g. Australian Privacy Principles and Australian Consumer Law).			
6. Minimise exposed attack surfaces	Devices and services should operate on the "principle of least privilege".	• Do ensure during set-up, the device only opens required physical interfaces or network port. • Do ensure after the set-up process is complete, physical interfaces or network ports that were only required for device set-up are closed. • Do ensure physical interfaces or network ports required for configured functionality are only exposed when the user has securely configured that functionality.	• Do not have multiple unused network ports that are open and listening for connections. • Do not keep Bluetooth pairing active once the device has been set up. • Do not have unencrypted protocols (e.g. Telnet) for the exchange of usernames and passwords. • Do not have unused physical interfaces (e.g. USB ports) available.	• Do check the device only does what you want it to do. • Do check if the device needs to be connected to the internet.	• Do not leave Bluetooth pairing active once the device has been set up. • Do not leave unnecessary features (such as cameras or microphones) active when not in use.

Principle	*Description*	*Manufacturers Do's*	*Manufacturers Don'ts*	*Consumers Do's*	*Consumer Don'ts*
		• Do disable manufacturing and debug interfaces (e.g. JTAG and UART) on production hardware. • Do make the web management interface only accessible to the local network unless the device needs to be managed remotely via the internet. • Do implement secure software development process that includes penetration testing. • Do ensure backups of configuration data are only available after authentication.			
7. Ensure communication security	Data requiring confidentiality or integrity protection, or associated with remote management and control, should be encrypted in transit, appropriate to the properties of the technology and usage. All credentials and certificates should be managed securely.	• Do ensure data, especially sensitive data, in transit to and from the device is encrypted, as articulated in the Australian Government Information Security Manual. • Do use Encryption for communication during device set-up. • Do provide logs detailing remote access to the device to the user. • Do encrypt all remote access to the device.	• Do not use encoding, rather than encryption to protect sensitive data. • Do not send Wi-Fi SSID and password in plain text between the application and the device during set-up. • Do not transfer user's activity unencrypted across a network.	• Do check your Wi-Fi network is set up securely, and does it have a secure password. • Do check the device is made by a well-known reputable company and sold by a well-known reputable store.	• Do not purchase a device that does not use encryption. • Do not connect with unknown or unsecured devices or networks.

(*Continued*)

(Continued)

Principle	*Description*	*Manufacturers Do's*	*Manufacturers Don'ts*	*Consumers Do's*	*Consumer Don'ts*
8. Ensure software integrity	Software (including firmware) on IoT devices should be verified using secure boot mechanisms. If an unauthorised change is detected, the device should alert the consumer/administrator to an issue and should not connect to wider networks than those necessary to perform the alerting function	• Do ensure the device requires updates to be digitally signed by the manufacturer. • Do have a boot mechanism that checks for errors and notifies the user of any failed updates. • Do only allow plug-ins or extensions to communicate with online resources using secure mechanisms which confirm the integrity of remote resources. • Do provide change logs to identify changes to the device.	• Do not allow the device to use anything other than signed plug-ins or extensions.	• Do check the device is made by a well-known reputable company and sold by a well-known reputable store. • Do enable automatic software updates.	• Do not ignore updates. • Do not purchase a device that no longer offers software updates.
9. Make systems resilient to outages	Resilience should be built into IoT devices and services where required by their usage or by other relying systems, taking into account the possibility of outages of data networks and power.	• Do notify the user immediately about the device going offline when network connectivity is lost. • Do ensure the device reconnects to the network automatically and notifies the user once the device reconnects. • Do provide battery backups for relevant devices. • Do secure alternative communication mechanisms (e.g. Bluetooth and Wi-Fi) are provided in the event of network loss. • Do ensure the device maintains essential functionality if network connectivity is unavailable.	• Do not require user interaction following unexpected loss of power to turn the device back on and reconnect to the network.	• Do set up the device in a secure location. • Do ensure your device has alternative communication mechanisms.	• Do not set up the device in an unsecure location. • Do not purchase a device that does not have battery backups.

Principle	*Description*	*Manufacturers Do's*	*Manufacturers Don'ts*	*Consumers Do's*	*Consumer Don'ts*
10. Monitor system telemetry data	If telemetry data is collected from IoT devices and services, such as usage and measurement data, it should be monitored for security anomalies.	• Do inform the user whether or not telemetry data is collected.	• Do not collect telemetry data for purposes other than to improve device functionality, integrity, security and monitor for security anomalies.	• Do watch for a significant increase in your monthly internet usage or bill. Significant increases in internet usage or billing charges can indicate that your device has been compromised.	• Do not purchase a device that collects telemetry data for purposes other than to improve device functionality, integrity, security and monitor for security anomalies.
11. Make it easy for consumers to delete personal data	Devices and services should be configured such that personal data can easily be removed when there is a transfer of ownership, when the consumer wishes to delete it and/or when the consumer wishes to dispose of the device.	• Do put the processes for deleting personal data on the manufacturer's website. • Do have a user-friendly factory reset process that is clearly outlined in the device manual, is easy to complete and includes the removal of user-provided data and configuration. • Do allow the user to delete single pieces of data while maintaining other data. • Do ensure all personal data is securely deleted upon removal of an account. • Do ensure all configuration data is securely deleted at the request of the user.	• Do not require the user to incur extra cost to delete their personal data from both their device and the associated online accounts. • Do not have the only way to delete personal data through "ageing". • Do not maintain user's data on their device even after the user intentionally attempts to delete it. • Do not require users to contact the manufacturer in order to delete personal data.	• Do erase all data and personal information, perform a factory reset of the device, disassociate the device from mobile phones and other devices and remove any removable media (e.g. USB flash drives, memory cards, etc.) attached to the device when disposing of it.	• Do not purchase a device that makes it difficult to delete personal data. • Do not retain unnecessary personal data on your device.

(Continued)

(Continued)

Principle	*Description*	*Manufacturers Do's*	*Manufacturers Don'ts*	*Consumers Do's*	*Consumer Don'ts*
12. Make installation and maintenance of devices easy	Installation and maintenance of IoT devices should employ minimal steps and follow Australian Government best practice on security and usability.	• Do provide tips for the user on how to set up the device securely. • Do explain how to use the device through a short video or interactive demo. • Do ensure installation and secure configuration of the device is easy. • Do provide device documentation that clearly describes how to install and configure the device. • Do ensure the application or online interface provides a step-by-step set-up process. • Do ensure device documentation clearly matches the actual user experience with the device. • Do automatically apply updates. • Do ensure the device immediately notifies the user when the batteries are running low where continuous battery operation is expected.	• Do not allow installation to cause issues that require a factory reset to remedy them. • Do not require substantial user training for maintenance of the device.	• Do reboot your device regularly. • Do apply regular updates.	• Do not leave your device turned on when it is not in use. • Do not ignore updates (of device software and applications). • Do not purchase a device that you do not understand or cannot learn how to maintain.

Principle	*Description*	*Manufacturers Do's*	*Manufacturers Don'ts*	*Consumers Do's*	*Consumer Don'ts*
13. Validate input data	Data received via user interfaces, application programming interfaces (APIs) and network interfaces should be validated. Ensure data input is authorised and conforms to expectations.	• Do follow best practice advice in order to reduce the attack surface of strings designed to encode or carry content beyond expected user input. • Do ensure the device defends itself against exploitation techniques such as SQL injection. • Do perform both client-side validation and server-side validation.	• Do not accept non-authorised and invalid input. • Do not allow a user to input data unless authentication is provided. • Do not let the device crashes due to unexpected input.	• Do check the device is made by a well-known reputable company and sold by a well-known reputable store. • Do check what data the device collects and who will the data be shared with. • Do check the legitimacy of applications and networks before downloading or connecting.	• Do not connect to unsecured networks. • Do not download applications that are untrustworthy.

12 Product liability

Christopher Carlsen and Julie-Anne Tarr

Introduction

Preceding chapters make it clear that any regulatory framework must address the complex web of airspace integration, safety, security, noise, environment, privacy, safe and efficient electric take-off and landing vehicles, infrastructure, technology trials and central coordination. Such issues and are integral to the development of a comprehensive regulatory structure that will enable countries to benefit from the considerable opportunities provided by drones.

Regulators have been very conscious of the need to tread a path that does not stifle innovation by introducing measures which excessively load liability on manufacturers, when the users of the automated technology, or their insurers, may be better positioned to bear the risk.[1] As the European Commission[2] recently observed:

> An enabling environment for such game-changing mobility technologies[3] is key, so that the EU can become a prime deployment destination for innovators. Start-ups and technology developers need an agile regulatory framework to pilot and deploy their products. The Commission will work towards facilitating testing and trials, and towards making the regulatory environment fit for innovation, so as to support the deployment of solutions on the market.[4]

1 Alison Newstead, 'Drones and Robots: Liability for Designers, Manufacturers and Insurers' (March 2014)<www.inhouselawyer.co.uk/legal-briefing/drones-and-robots-liability-for-designers-manufacturers-and-insurers/>. See, also, Kyle Bowyer, 'The Robotics Age: Regulatory and Compliance Implications for Businesses and Financial Institutions' (*The European Financial Review*, 21 April 2018)<www.europeanfinancialreview.com/ the-robotics-age-regulatory-and-compliance-implications-for-businesses-and-financial-institutions/>. "Regulation needs to strike a balance between controlling risk and stifling growth. Interestingly, the call for regulation often comes from innovators and thinkers such as Elon Musk and Bill Gates and it is becoming increasingly evident that existing laws regulating product liability, consumer rights, property law, intellectual property and tort law, to name but a few, may not be adequate to manage and control the risks associated with rapidly advancing AI (including technologies such as drones)."

2 Commission, 'Communication from the Commission to the European Parliament, the Council, the European Economic and Social Committee and the Committee of the Regions Sustainable and Smart Mobility Strategy—Putting European Transport on Track for the Future' COM (2020) 789 final.

3 Including use of drones (unmanned aircraft) for commercial applications.

4 Commission (n 2), 15 [64].

Such strongly articulated frames of reference when combined with the reality of rapidly evolving technology and the emergence almost daily of new, innovative drone uses understandably challenges national authorities capacities to keep pace across the full regulatory framework. It is therefore not surprising that regulatory focus globally has been upon imposing strict operating limitations on drone activities impacting other aircraft or safety of those on the ground through restriction of drone use in populated areas and proximate to airfields.

Nevertheless, increasing attention is being paid to the implementation of design specifications and productions standards, and to the imposition of obligations upon manufacturers and those responsible for the design and production of drones by regulators and international organisations, such as the International Civil Aviation Organisation (ICAO) and the International Organisation for Standards (ISO). More generally, debate is emerging in relation to product liability with respect to the manufacture of drones and other autonomous vehicles. For example, it is interesting to note that certain leading car manufacturers have expressed strong support for the legal position that all manufacturers who sell fully driverless cars must accept liability for cars involved in accidents that were in full autonomous mode at the time of the accident.[5]

Developing a consistent regulatory and operational framework for drones must of necessity consider product liability issues which, in turn, closely connect to development of drone-specific airworthiness standards, including mandated "fail-safe" functions. The Australian Senate Inquiry Committee[6] in 2018 recognised that to allow drones to fully integrate into shared airspace, they must be subject to standards of airworthiness. The committee recommended that airworthiness standards should extend to drones that arrive in the country through foreign imports, similar to model rockets and laser pointers. It further recommended that drones should include a number of fail-safe redundancies, such as return-to-home functionality and forced flight termination.

The ever-increasing use of drones is certain to be accompanied by an increase in misuse and mishaps, leading to an inevitable rise in litigation involving bodily injury, death and property damage caused by drone accidents. Such litigation may require

5 See, for example, Parliament of Australia, 'Inquiry into Social Issues Relating to Land-based Automated Vehicles in Australia' (August 2017) <www.aph.gov.au/Parliamentary_Business/Committees/House/Industry_Innovation_Science_and_Resources/Driverless_vehicles/Report/section?id=committees%2Freportrep%2F024056%2F24939> and specifically Volvo Car Australia, 'Submission No 11 to the Standing Committee on Industry, Innovation, Science and Resources, Inquiry into Social Issues Relating to Land-based Driverless Vehicles in Australia' (6 February 2017) 7; See also Parker O'very, '3 Ways Self-driving Cars Will Affect the Insurance Industry' (*VentureBeat*, 26 January 2018) <https://venturebeat.com/2018/01/26/3-ways-self-driving-cars-will-affect-the-insurance-industry/> where it is stated that "Google, Volvo, and Mercedes-Benz already accept liability in cases where a vehicle's self-driving system is at fault for a crash. Tesla is taking things a step further byextending an insurance program to purchasers of Tesla vehicles".

6 Rural and Regional Affairs and Transport Committee, Parliament of Australia, 'Report on the Regulatory Requirements that Impact on the Safe Use of Remotely Piloted Aircraft Systems, Unmanned Aerial Systems and Associated Systems' (Report, 31 July 2018), [8.27]—[8.38] <www.aph.gov.au/Parliamentary_Business/Committees/Senate/Rural_and_Regional_Affairs_and_Transport/Drones/Report>; (Australian Senate Inquiry Committee).

resolution of complex issues involving allocation of liability for the damage inflicted by drones between and among the owners, designers, manufacturers and distributors.

Unless and until uniform civil liability laws are enacted, the allocation of liability for drone-caused injuries will continue to be governed by existing principles of tort law and national legislation directed generally, for example, at defective products.[7]

This chapter examines the existing and well-developed body of products liability law as this provides an effective analytical framework to address such claims against manufacturers and others in the chain of distribution of drones. Particular reference is made to the law in the United States as space constraints preclude a general treatise on product liability law. The chapter concludes with a brief consideration of global initiatives that have commenced to implement design specifications and production standards, and to impose compliance obligations upon manufacturers and those responsible for the design and production of drones.

The theories of liability under products liability law

For centuries, tort law has required product manufacturers and distributors to ensure that their products perform in a reasonably safe manner. Products liability law provides the basis for seeking remedies when a defective product causes harm to persons or property.

Drones are equipped with novel and complex technologies and are being used in an ever-expanding variety of new applications. Although some commentators have questioned whether new legal theories and doctrines will be required to address issues of liability arising from drone-induced injuries, there already exists a highly developed and comprehensive framework of products liability law capable of addressing the claims that will arise out of drone mishaps. This system of products liability law has proven itself to be remarkably adaptive to new technologies and products, and to resolving the initially novel questions posed, for more than half a century. The same will hold true for drones. As the California Supreme Court observed more than 40 years ago:

> The technological revolution has created a society that contains dangers to the individual never before contemplated. The individual must face the threat to life and limb not only from the car on the street or highway but from a massive array of hazardous mechanisms and products. The radical change from a comparatively safe, largely agricultural, society to this industrial unsafe one has been reflected in the decisions that formerly tied liability to the fault of a tortfeasor but now are more concerned with the safety of the individual who suffers the loss. As Dean Keeton has written, "The change in the substantive law as regards the liability of makers of products and other sellers in the marketing chain has been from fault to defect. The plaintiff is no longer required to impugn the maker, but he is required to impugn the product".[8]

Products liability law has two primary purposes: (1) to incentivise product manufacturers to make their products safer and (2) to compensate victims harmed by those products.[9] It has long been established that imposing strict liability on manufacturers is designed

7 In the EU, a directive concerning liability for defective products exists: Council Directive (EEC) 85/374 on the approximation of the laws, regulations, and administrative provisions of the Member States concerning liability for defective products [1985] OJ L210/29.

8 *Barker v. Lull Engineering Co., Inc.*, 20 Cal.3d 413, 434–35 (1978) (citation and quotation omitted).

9 *See* George L. Priest, 'Modern Tort Law and its Reform' (1987) 22 Valparaiso University Law Review 1, 8.

to "insure that the costs of injuries resulting from defective products are borne by the manufacturers that put such products on the market rather than by the injured persons who are powerless to protect themselves".[10] The liability risks to the manufacturer can be insured and those costs can be distributed among the public as a cost of doing business.[11] An injured plaintiff need only prove that he was using the product in the manner intended and was injured "as a result of a defect in design and manufacture of which the plaintiff was not aware that made the product unsafe for its intended use".[12]

Under the broad umbrellas of tort law and contract law, there exist multiple theories of liability that can be asserted in a products liability claim. These include negligence, manufacturing defects, design defects, failure to warn and breach of warranty.[13]

A product claim based on negligence focusses on the *behaviour* of the developer, manufacturer or distributor. The key question in an ordinary negligence action will be whether the defendant acted reasonably under the circumstances. In a strict products liability case, the focus is on the *product* itself. In other words, in a strict liability claim, the defendant is liable if the product itself is defective. Strict products liability for design defect thus differs from a cause of action for a negligently designed product in that the injured party is not required to prove that the manufacturer acted unreasonably in designing the product. The focus shifts from the conduct of the manufacturer to whether the product, as designed, was not reasonably safe.[14] A manufacturer is held liable regardless of its lack of actual knowledge of the condition of the product because it is in the superior position to discover any design defects and alter the design before making the product available to the public. Liability attaches when the product, as designed, presents an unreasonable risk of harm to the user.[15] It is unnecessary in a strict liability action to show that the manufacturer has been negligent in any way, "[i]n fact, [it] can be found liable even though [i]t was utterly non-negligent".[16]

The doctrine of strict liability originally was articulated in a 1963 court decision issued by the California Supreme Court.[17] In 1965, the doctrine was incorporated by the American Law Institute[18] in the Restatement (Second) of Torts,[19] and in the

10 *Greenman v. Yuba Power Products*, Inc., 59 Cal.2d 57, 63 (1963).

11 ibid 64.

12 ibid.

13 See *Voss v Black & Decker Manufacturing Co.*, 59 N.Y.2d 102, 106 (1983) where it was stated "A plaintiff injured by an allegedly defective product may seek recovery against the manufacturer on the basis of any one or more of four theories of liability. Depending on the factual context in which the claim arises, the injured plaintiff, and those asserting derivative claims, may state a cause of action in contract, express or implied, on the ground of negligence, or . . . on the theory of strict products liability."

14 ibid 107.

15 ibid 107–8.

16 *Moorman v. Am. Safety Equip.*, 594 So.2d 795, 800 (Fla. Dist. Ct. App. 1992).

17 *Greenman* (n 10) 57.

18 The American Law Institute is a research and advocacy group founded in 1923 comprised of leading judges, lawyers and legal scholars to promote the clarification and simplification of United States common law. It publishes "Restatements" of the law which essentially are codifications of case law that are meant to reflect the consensus of the American legal community as to what the law is and, in some cases, what it should become. The Restatements are not binding on courts, but are considered highly persuasive authority because they are formulated over a number of years with extensive input from law professors, practicing attorneys, and judges: American Law Institute, 'About ALI' (*American Law Institute*, 20 January 2021) <www.ali.org/about-ali/>.

19 Restatement (Second) of Torts §402A (Am. L. Inst. 1965).

following decades it was adopted by virtually all state courts in the United States.[20] Under the Second Restatement, and the substantial body of products liability case law applying its principles,[21] a manufacturer can be liable for the sale of a product containing an "unreasonably dangerous" defect even if it has "exercised all possible care in the preparation and sale" of the product.[22]

In 1998 the American Law Institute published the "Restatement (Third) of Torts: Products Liability".[23] The Third Restatement specifically addresses manufacturing defects, design defects, and failure to warn but, notably, ties liability for design defects and failure to warn to "foreseeable risks". Under the Restatement (Third) of Torts, a product contains a design defect when the foreseeable risks of harm posed by the product could have been reduced or avoided by the adoption of a reasonable alternative design by the manufacturer.[24] Under this framework, the failure of a manufacturer to identify and mitigate a dangerous "foreseeable" risk is closer to negligence than to strict liability.[25]

In cases of physical harm, the manufacturer as well as all entities in the chain of distribution are subject to liability for damage injuries caused by the defective product, and that potential liability extends to both consumers and third parties injured by the product.[26] Although any entity in the distribution chain potentially is liable, the retailer typically will seek to shift the liability by impleading the product manufacturer.

Negligence

A product liability action asserting a claim based on negligence, such as negligent design, is based on fundamental concepts of common law negligence.[27] As in any negligence action, a plaintiff must establish: (1) a legal duty on the part of the defendant towards the plaintiff under the circumstances; (2) a breach of that duty by the defendant; (3) the defendant's breach of the duty was both the actual and proximate cause of the plaintiff's injuries; and (4) the plaintiff suffered damages as a result of the breach.[28] A plaintiff alleging negligent design also must show that the product was unreasonably dangerous.[29] The design must take into account currently available

20 John Villasenor, 'Products Liability and Driverless Cars: Issues and Guiding Principles for Legislation' (*Brookings Institution*, 24 April 2014) 7.

21 Most states apply the principles of products liability law set forth in the Restatement as part of their common law. See, e.g., *George v. Celotex Corporation*, 914 F.2d 26, 28 n. 1 (2d Cir. 1990) where it was stated that "New York's doctrine of strict products liability generally follows the guidelines set forth in [Restatement (Second) of Torts, Products Liability] §402. (quotation and citation omitted). However, some states have enacted statutes codifying the law. For example, Georgia's product liability statute is codified in O.C.G.A. §51-1-11.

22 Villasenor (n 20) 7.

23 Restatement (Third) of Torts: Products Liability (Am Law. Inst, 1998).

24 ibid § 2 (1998).

25 Villasenor (n 20) 7.

26 See Restatement (Third) of Torts (n 24) § 1 (1998): "One engaged in the business of selling or otherwise distributing products who sells or distributes a defective product is subject to liability for harm to persons or property caused by the defect".

27 See *Jablonski v. Ford Motor Co.*, 353 Ill. Dec. 327, 955 N.E.2d 1138 (Ill. 2011).

28 See *Pinchinat v. Graco Children's Products*, Inc., 390 F. Supp. 2d 1141, 1149 (M.D. Fla. 2005).

29 See *Marzullo v. Crosman Corp.*, 289 F.Supp. 2d 1337, 1342 (M.D. Fla. 2003).

technologies, and failing to use an available and appropriate technology in the product can constitute a breach of duty.[30]

A manufacturer has a non-delegable duty to design a reasonably safe product.[31] Thus, the key question in a negligent design case is whether the manufacturer exercised reasonable care in designing the product.[32] "In determining whether the manufacturer's conduct was reasonable, the question is whether in the exercise of ordinary care the manufacturer should have foreseen that the design would be hazardous to someone".[33] To establish that the harm was foreseeable, the plaintiff must show that the manufacturer knew or should have known of the risk posed by the product design at the time of manufacture of the product.[34]

Design defects

A design defect claim asserts that the product is inherently dangerous based on its design alone, and not based upon an error that may have occurred during the manufacture of the product. A design defect exists when:

> foreseeable risks of harm posed by a product could have been reduced or avoided by the adoption of a reasonable alternative design by the seller or other distributor, or a predecessor in the commercial chain of distribution, and the omission of the alternative design renders the product not reasonably safe.[35]

The key question in a lawsuit against a drone manufacturer in most states will be whether there was a "reasonable alternative design" that, if it had been adopted, would have avoided the accident.

A number of factors may be considered when evaluating whether an alternative design is reasonable, and if the omission of that design rendered the product not reasonably safe. These factors, which are considered on a case-by-case basis, include the magnitude and probability of the foreseeable risks of harm, the instructions and warnings accompanying the product, and the nature and strength of consumer expectations regarding the product and the relative advantages of the alternative design, including its production costs, and its effect on product longevity, maintenance and repair.[36]

A product may be found defective in design under either of two alternative tests. Under the consumer-expectation theory, "a product is defectively designed if the plaintiff is able to demonstrate that the product did not perform as safely as an ordinary consumer would expect when used in the intended or reasonably foreseeable manner".[37] In other words, this test looks to see if the product reasonably conforms to the expectations of the consumer. This determination is made based on whether the

30 See, for example, *T.J. Hooper v. N. Barge Corp.*, 60 F.2d 737 (2d Cir. 1932).

31 See *Calles v. Scripto-Takai Corp*., 224 Ill.2d 247, 270, 309 Ill. Dec. 383, 864 N.E.2d 249 (2007).

32 ibid.

33 ibid 271 (quotation omitted).

34 ibid.

35 Restatement (Third) of Torts (n 23) § 2(b)(1998).

36 See ibid cmt. f.

37 *Force v. Ford Motor Company*, 879 So.2d 103, 106 (Fla. 5th DCA 2004) citing *Fremainst v. Ford Motor Company*, 258 F.Supp.2d 24, 29 (D.P.R. 2003).

"the danger posed by the design is greater than an ordinary consumer would expect when using the product in an intended or reasonably foreseeable manner".[38] In a purely design defect analysis, the consumer expectation test does not merely look at foreseeability; it looks at an unreasonably dangerous standard.[39]

The more complex the product, the harder it is to define reasonable consumer expectations, because the average consumer likely has no realistic way to understand how the product functions. This test is even more challenging to use when dealing with new technology, where the product has not been used widely and cannot be compared to other models, and so it is nearly impossible to identify reasonable consumer expectations.[40] The difficulty in defining consumer expectations with respect to new and complex products and technology has caused many jurisdictions to abandon the consumer expectation test in favour of the risk-utility test.[41]

The risk-utility test is the predominant test for determining design defects in products liability cases.[42] The Restatement (Third) of Torts endorses the risk-utility test as the sole test for design defects, and provides as follows:

> A product . . . is defective in design when the foreseeable risk of harm posed by the product could have been reduced or avoided by adoption of a reasonable alternative design by the seller . . . and the omission of the alternative design renders the product not reasonably safe.[43]

This test seeks to determine whether a product is unreasonably dangerous under the totality of the circumstances by viewing the safety benefits of a proposed design compared to alternative models for the same product.[44]

The risk-utility test does not require a manufacturer to use the safest design possible.[45] Rather, under this test, "[a] product is defective in design if the safety benefits from altering the design as proposed by the plaintiff would have exceeded the costs of such an alteration".[46] In order to prevail under this test, a plaintiff must present a reasonable alternative design that would have prevented the accident.[47] In applying the risk-utility test, courts look at a number of factors, including:

38 Terrence F Kelly and Bruce L Ottley, *Understanding Products Liability Law* (LexisNexis 2006).

39 Jeffrey R Zohn, 'When Robots Attack: How Should the Law Handle Self-Driving Cars that Cause Damage' (2015) 2 University of Illinois Journal of Law, Technology & Policy 475.

40 ibid 476.

41 ibid. See also David G. Owen, 'Design Defects' (2008) 73 Missouri Law Review 291, 301 where it was said that "[M]ost modern courts have abandoned consumer expectations as the predominant test for design defectiveness".

42 See *Branham v. Ford Motor Company*, 701 S.E.2d 5, 14–15 (S.C. 2010): "Some form of a risk-utility test is employed by an overwhelming majority of jurisdictions in the country."

43 Restatement (Third) of Torts (n 23) § 2(b) (1998).

44 See Zohn (n 39) 477.

45 See Restatement (Third) of Torts (n 23) cmt a: "Society does not benefit from products that are excessively safe . . . any more than it benefits from products that are too risky. Society benefits most when the right, or optimal, amount of product safety is achieved".

46 David G. Owen, 'Toward a Proper Test for Design Defectiveness: "Micro-Balancing" Costs and Benefits' (1997)75 TexasLawReview1661, 1689.

47 See, e.g., *Voss* (n 13) 109.

> (1) The utility of the product to the public as a whole and to the individual user; (2) the likelihood that it will cause injury; (3) the availability of a safer design; (4) the potential for designing and manufacturing the product so that it is safer but remains functional and reasonably priced; (5) the ability of the plaintiff to avoid injury by careful use of the product; (6) the degree of awareness of the potential danger of the product; (7) the manufacturer's ability to spread any cost related to improving the safety of the design.[48]

Given the central and increasing role that software plays in the operation of drones, an issue that likely will arise in future drone product liability litigation is whether malfunctioning software constitutes a product or a service. A "product" is defined under the Restatement (Third) as a "tangible personal property distributed commercially for use or consumption".[49] The Restatement does not consider services to be products.[50] However, software likely will be viewed as a product, particularly if it is sold as a general purpose package or is designed to control the drone.[51] This is so because no matter what form the product design takes, the manufacturer is required to ensure that the design causes the product to perform in a reasonably safe manner.[52]

Another issue likely to arise in drone design defect cases is the manufacturer's liability for "hacking". Like autonomous vehicles and other products that make up the "Internet of Things", drones equipped with automated operating technologies are subject to being accessed by unauthorised third parties. For example, researchers have demonstrated that it is possible to take over the brakes, engines and other components of automobiles remotely. This forced the auto industry to enact measures to seek to prevent such cyber attacks.[53] Because hacking has become commonplace, and therefore clearly is foreseeable, drone manufacturers are required to design their products to protect against this foreseeable harm. A drone operating system that is not reasonably designed to withstand cyber attacks would be defective under the risk-utility test, subjecting the manufacturer to liability for resultant crashes.[54] This duty is no different from the one many businesses face today to prevent hackers from gaining access to confidential consumer information like credit card numbers.[55]

The malfunction doctrine

Under the malfunction doctrine, a variation of the manufacturing defect doctrine, a plaintiff can show a manufacturing defect without specifically proving how the

48 ibid.
49 Restatement (Third) of Torts (n 23) § 19(a) (1998).
50 ibid 19(b).
51 See ibid rptr. n. to cmt. d 278.
52 See Restatement (Third) of Torts (n 23) § 2(b) (1998) defining the duty to design without any limitation regarding the form of the design.
53 See Tom Simonite, 'Your Future Self-Driving Car Will be Way More Hackable' (*MIT Technology Review*, 26 January 2016).
54 ibid 1662.
55 See Mark Geistfeld, 'A Roadmap for Autonomous Vehicles: State Tort Liability, Automobile Insurance, and Federal Safety Regulation' (2017) 105 California Law Review 1611, 1661.

product was defective.[56] Under this theory of liability, the injured party must prove that: (1) the product malfunctioned; (2) the malfunction occurred during proper use; and (3) the product had not been altered or misused in a manner that probably caused the malfunction.[57] The major benefit to the injured party of the malfunction doctrine is that the product malfunction can be proven with circumstantial evidence.[58]

A malfunction is defined by reference to the product's expected performance.[59] Under the Restatement (Third), the relevant expectation involves the product's failure to "perform its manifestly intended function".[60] For example, in respect of the design of an operating system of a drone intended for commercial package delivery, that function would be to safely deliver the package to the correct destination, and then return to its base.[61] Based on this coding objective for a drone's operating system, any crash arguably would involve a failure of the drone's manifestly intended function, constituting a product malfunction and subjecting the manufacturer to strict liability.[62] The malfunction doctrine also would be applicable in the case of a hacked drone. The manufacturer obviously would not intend for the drone to be controlled by an unknown third party, and the ordinary consumer presumably would expect that the operating system, not a hacker, would determine the drone's operating behaviour.

Manufacturing defects

A manufacturing defect occurs "when the product departs from its intended design even though all possible care was exercised in the preparation and marketing of the product".[63] As a result of this departure, the product fails to perform as safely as the intended design would have performed.[64] A manufacturing defect claim is based on the expectation that "a mass-produced product will not differ from its siblings in a manner that makes it more dangerous than the others".[65] Liability is imposed whether or not the manufacturer's quality control efforts satisfy standards of reasonableness.[66] This is strict liability in its truest sense.[67] "In general, a manufacturing or production defect is readily identifiable because a defective product is one that differs from the manufacturer's intended result from other ostensibly identical units of the same product line".[68] Defects of this type occur for different reasons. Materials or component parts of the product can be contaminated or otherwise manufactured in a flawed

56 See Restatement (Third) of Torts (n 23) § 2(a) cmt. a (1998) describing the method as "a function similar to the concept of res ipsa loquitor, allowing deserving plaintiffs to succeed notwithstanding what would otherwise be difficult or insuperable problems with proof".
57 David G. Owen, 'Manufacturing Defects' (2002) 53 South Carolina Law Review 851, 873; See also *White v. Mazda Motor of Am., Inc.*, 99 A.3d 1079, 1090 (Conn. 2014).
58 Restatement (Third) of Torts (n 23) § 3 cmt. c (1998): "The inference of defect may be drawn . . . without proof of the specific defect".
59 See Geistfeld (n 55) 1637.
60 Restatement (Third) of Torts (n 23) § 3 cmt b.
61 See Geistfeld (n 55) 1637.
62 ibid.
63 See Restatement (Third) of Torts (n 23) § 2(a) (Am. Law. Inst. 1998) defining "manufacturing defect".
64 *Force* (n 37)106.
65 *Casey v Toyota Motor Eng'g & Mfg. N. Am., Inc.*, 770 F.3d 322, 329 (5th Cir. 2014) (citation omitted).
66 Restatement (Third) of Torts (n 23) § 2 at cmt. a. (1998).
67 ibid.
68 Barker (n 8) 429.

manner due to an error in the production process; the product can be improperly assembled or constructed; or the product can be improperly packaged. Because these defects depart from design specifications, they exist only in aberrant products that would not satisfy quality-control standards.[69]

A manufacturing defect theory of liability would not exist in cases involving defects in the software used to control the drone. Although, for example, the operating system might have a programming bug caused by a typo, that coding is still part of the operating system, making it part of the drone's design. All drones with this operating system would contain that coding error, unlike manufacturing defects that affect only particular products within the entire product line.[70]

Liability for manufacturing defects is not limited to the product manufacturer, but also may be extended to distributors and sellers of the defective products as well:

> An often-cited rationale for holding wholesalers and retailers strictly liable for harm caused by manufacturing defects is that, as between them and innocent victims who suffer harm because of defective products, the product sellers as business entities are in a better position than are individual users and consumers to insure against such losses. In most instances, wholesalers and retailers will be able to pass liability costs up the chain of product distribution to the manufacturer. When joining the manufacturer in the tort action presents the plaintiff with procedural difficulties, local retailers can pay damages to the victims and then seek indemnity from manufacturers. Finally, holding retailers and wholesalers strictly liable creates incentives for them to deal only with reputable, financially responsible manufacturers and distributors, thereby helping to protect the interests of users and consumers.[71]

Warning and labelling defects

In warning or labelling defect claims, the injured party asserts that the product had some sort of inherent danger that the product manufacturer (or distributor or seller) had a legal duty to warn about but failed to do so. With respect to warning defects, that Restatement (Third) provides as follows:

> A product . . . is defective because of inadequate instructions or warnings when the foreseeable risk of harm posed by the product could have been reduced or avoided by the provision of reasonable instructions or warnings by the [manufacturer] . . . and the omission of the instructions or warnings renders the product not reasonably safe.[72]

The standard focusses on whether the warnings provided were adequate.[73] Manufacturers are not required to warn of every possible risk, but only those risks that

69 See Geistfeld (n 55) 1611.

70 ibid 1633.

71 Restatement (Third) of Torts (n 23) § 2 (1998).

72 ibid 2(c).

73 See, for example, *Pavlides v. Galveston Yacht Basis*, 727 F.2d 330, 338–39 (5th Cir. 1984): "The question of whether or not a given warning is legally sufficient depends upon the language used and the

are discoverable in light of the generally recognised and prevailing best knowledge available.[74]

Generally, the duty to warn will be found in situations where: (1) the product supplied is dangerous; (2) the danger is or should be known by the manufacturer; (3) the danger is present when the product is used in the usual and expected manner; and (4) the danger is not obvious or well known to the user.[75] Even when a warning is given, it may be found to be defective because of the use of inadequate wording, the location of the warning, or other circumstances concerning the manner in which the warning is conveyed. Even absent a manufacturing or design defect, a manufacturer still might be found liable for failing to provide an adequate warning for a product.[76] And, an adequate warning does not absolve the manufacturer of liability for other defect claims.[77]

As a general matter, tort law requires manufacturers to adopt fault-tolerant product designs. Accordingly, the concepts of design defect and warnings must be considered concurrently. As the Restatement (Third) of Torts explains, "instructions and warnings may be ineffective because users of the product may not be adequately reached, may be likely to be inattentive, or may be insufficiently motivated to follow the instructions or heed the warnings".[78] A manufacturer may be obligated to design away dangers when it is reasonable to do so because, given the nature of the user or the product use, it is foreseeable that warnings or obvious dangers will either not be seen or will be disregarded.[79] In other words:

> [b]alanced against the somewhat limited effectiveness of warnings is the designer's ability to anticipate and protect against possible injuries. If a slight change in design would prevent serious, perhaps fatal, injury, the designer may not avoid liability by simply warning of the possible injury. We think that in such a case the burden to prevent needless injury is best placed on the designer or manufacturer rather than on the individual user of a product.[80]

Contract based liability

Product liability claims also can be based on principles of contract law as a result of the warranties created as part of the process of marketing and selling drones. Warranties are assurances, either explicit or implicit, that the goods being sold are of sufficient quality. If that turns out not to be true, and an injury to a purchaser of the product occurs as a result, the basis exists for a products liability claim based on breach of warranty.

---

impression that such language is calculated to make upon the mind of the average user of that product." (citations omitted).

74 See *Brown v. Glade & Grove Supply*, 647 S.2d 1033 (Fla. 4th DCA 1994).

75 *Billiar v. Minnesota Mining & Manufacturing Co.*, 623 F.2d 240, 243 (2d Cir. 1980).

76 See *Battersby v. Boyer*, 241 Ga. App. 115, 117, 526 S.E.2d 159, 162 (1999): "[A] duty to warn can arise even if a product is not defective".

77 See *Uloth v. City Tank Corp.*, 376 Mass. 874, 879–80, 384 N.E.2d 1188, 1192 (1978): "Whether or not adequate warnings are given is a factor to be considered on the issue of negligence, but warnings cannot absolve the manufacturer or designer of all responsibility for the safety of the product".

78 Restatement (Third) of Torts (n 23) § 2 cmt. 1 (1998).

79 ibid § 2.

80 *Uloth* (n 77) 880.

Product warranties are addressed in the Uniform Commercial Code ("UCC"), which was created to help provide uniformity of law with respect to commercial transactions. The UCC has been adopted by every state in the United States, although sometimes with minor variations.[81] With respect to products liability, the most relevant portions of the UCC are those addressing express and implied warranties. An express warranty is created though promises made by the seller of the goods, and can be created in three ways: (1) any affirmation of fact or promise made by the seller to the buyer which relates to the goods; (2) any description of the goods which is made part of the basis of the bargain creates an express warranty that the goods shall conform to that description; and (3) any sample or model that is made part of the basis of the bargain creates an express warranty that the whole of the goods shall conform to the sample or model.[82] In the context of drones, express warranties can be created through explicit promises made by the seller, or through advertising.

Warranties also can be implied. Unless there is an explicit exclusion in the parties' contract, goods are sold subject to an implied warranty of merchantability[83] and, where appropriate, an implied warranty of fitness for a particular purpose.[84] To be "merchantable", the goods must be: (1) fit for the ordinary purpose for which they are used; (2) capable of passing without objection in the trade under the contract description; and (3) of fair and average quality for such goods.[85] An implied warranty of fitness for a particular purpose exists where the seller, at the time of contracting, has reason to know any particular purpose for which the goods are required and that the buyer is relying on the seller's skill or judgment to select or furnish suitable goods.[86]

Defences to product liability claims

There are a number of defences available to manufacturers and other entities in the chain of distribution in product liability cases. Four defences generally apply to products liability claims: comparative negligence, misuse, state of the art and assumption of risk. Under the comparative negligence defence, the manufacturer asserts that it should not be fully liable, or liable at all, because the injured party's own negligence caused or contributed to the accident and his injuries.[87] Misuse of the product is another defence that may be raised in a drone case. A manufacturer does not have a duty to protect against all misuses of its product, but it does have "a duty to prevent an injury caused by the foreseeable misuse of its product".[88]

The state-of-the-art defence can be a powerful defence to design defect and warning defect claims.[89] For design defects, the state-of-the-art defence "involves the feasibility of adopting curative design measures to reduce or eliminate a risk of which the

81 See, for example, New York Uniform Commercial Code § 1-101 and those that follow.
82 ibid § 2-313 (1)(a), (b) and (c).
83 ibid § 2-314.
84 ibid § 2-315.
85 ibid § 2-314.
86 ibid § 2-315.
87 See *Cedeno v. Broan-Nutone*, LLC, 2019 WL 4751913 *7 (E.D.N.Y.,30September2019).
88 *Jurado v. Western Gear Works*, 619 A.2d 1312, 1318 (N.J. 1993).
89 See, for example, *Geressy v. Digital Equipment Corp.*, 980 F.Supp. 640, 649 (E.D.N.Y. 1997) (elaborating upon a manufacturer's duty to warn based upon its knowledge of foreseeable risk).

manufacturer is aware".[90] Although the manufacturer may be aware of a danger, current technological and scientific limits may make the risk unavoidable or protecting against the risk financially unfeasible to research.[91]

The assumption of risk defence provides that a product user who knowingly accepts the risks of a potentially hazardous product assumes some or all of the responsibility for any harm that may result from the use of the product.[92] The defence asserts that a "user has fully consented to incur a risk which he or she fully comprehends".[93] The defence has two elements: (1) the plaintiff must know and understand the risk and (2) the plaintiff's choice to encounter it must be free and voluntary.[94] The knowledge and understanding element requires a subjective look into the plaintiff's state of mind to show that the plaintiff knew the risks; thus this defence does not take an objective look at what a reasonable plaintiff would know.[95] For this defence to apply to drones, the manufacturer would have to fully disclose the potential risks associated with the drone, including any likely failure modes and some approximate sense of their probability.[96] The free and voluntary element requires that the "plaintiff ma[de] a true and meaningful choice to engage a particular risk, presumably to advance an interest (even mere convenience) that the plaintiff considers more valuable than avoidance of the risk".[97]

Courts also have considered what is called the "sophisticated user defence", which can exempt manufacturers from their typical obligation to provide product users with warnings about the product's potential hazards.[98] Under the sophisticated user defence, such users need not be warned about dangers of which they are already aware or should be aware. Because these sophisticated users regularly use and are charged with knowing the particular product's dangers, the failure to warn about those dangers is not deemed to be the legal cause of any harm.[99] The sophisticated user's knowledge of the dangers is deemed to be the equivalent of prior notice.[100] This defence applies equally to strict liability and negligent failure to warn cases.[101]

Regulatory, design and compliance initiative

As mentioned previously, there is increasing attention being paid by regulators and international organisations, such as the International Civil Aviation Organisation (ICAO) and the International Organisation for Standardisation (ISO), to the implementation of design specifications and production standards, and to the imposition of obligations upon manufacturers and those responsible for the design and production

90 Gary C. Robb, 'A Practical Approach to Use of State of the Art Evidence in Strict Products Liability Cases' (1982) 77 Northwestern University Law Review 1, 22–25.

91 ibid.

92 Eric C. Feldman and Alison Stein, 'Assuming the Risk: Tort Law, Policy, and Politics on the Slippery Slopes' (2010) 59 DePaul Law Review 259.

93 David G Owen, 'Products Liability: User Misconduct Defenses' (2000) 52 South Carolina Law Review 1, 24 citing *Rahmig v. Mosley Mach. Co.*, 412 N.W.2d 56, 74 (Neb. 1987).

94 ibid 25.

95 ibid 29.

96 Feldman and Stein (n 92) 263.

97 Owen (n 93) 31.

98 See, for example, *Johnson v. Am. Standard, Inc.*, 43 Cal. 4th 56, 65–66 (2008).

99 David G Owen, *Products Liability Law* (Thomson/West 2005) § 9.5, 599.

100 *Billiar* (n 75) 243.

101 See, for example, *Humble Sand & Gravel*, Inc. v. Gomez, 146 S.W.3d 170, 183 (Tex 2004).

of drones. These initiatives potentially have significant impacts upon product liability claims and determinations in the future. Some of these initiatives are briefly mentioned in the following.

International Civil Aviation Organisation (ICAO)[102]

ICAO is a specialised agency of the United Nations funded and directed by 193 national governments to support their diplomacy and cooperation in air transport as signatory states to the Chicago Convention (1944).[103] ICAO is not an international aviation regulator and as such ICAO standards never supersede the primacy of national regulatory requirements. It is always the local, national regulations which are enforced in, and by, sovereign states, and which must be legally adhered to by air operators making use of applicable airspace and airports.

However, ICAO, with its Member States, has developed a draft regulatory framework for UAS[104] based upon a review of existing regulations in Member States in a bid to share best practices that can be implemented by countries seeking to improve, or introduce, UAS regulation. This has resulted in ICAO Model UAS Regulations Parts 101, 102 and 149 which are discussed in detail in Chapter 14. However, at this juncture it should be mentioned that for higher risk operations[105] requirements in respect of the UAS are imposed both upon the operator when the national authority is considering its application for authorisation, and upon the manufacturer, which will be obliged to provide documentation and details to both the authority and operator. Moreover, the UAS is required to be designed, produced or modified such that it does not contain any safety defects identified by the authority, display a label indicating eligibility to conduct operations in the specific category (in English, legible and permanently affixed to the UA), and have detailed current remote pilot operating instructions for the operation of the UAS. The UAS may only be operated after the person who designed, produced or modified the UAS has received notification that the regulator has accepted the Declaration of Compliance or received an approval from an approved aviation organisation; and it must have a current aircraft registration.[106]

Separately, the manufacturer must make a declaration to the national authority specifying the manufacturer of the UAS, the model of the system, the maximum take-off weight of the UA, the operations that the UA is intended to undertake and the category of UA; as well as specifying that the system meets the means of compliance

102 See discussion in Chapter 14.

103 The Convention on International Civil Aviation, drafted in 1944 by 54 nations, was established to promote cooperation and "create and preserve friendship and understanding among the nations and peoples of the world." Known more commonly today as the 'Chicago Convention', this landmark agreement established the core principles permitting international transport by air, and led to the creation of the specialised agency which has overseen it ever since—the International Civil Aviation Organization (ICAO): ICAO, 'The History of ICAO and the Chicago Convention' (*ICAO*, January 2021) <www.icao.int/about-icao/History/Pages/default.aspx>.

104 ICAO, 'ICAO Model UAS Regulations: Introduction to ICAO Model UAS Regulations and Advisory Circulars' (*ICAO*, 20 January 2021) <www.icao.int/safety/UA/Pages/ICAO-Model-UAS-Regulations.aspx>. (Model UAS Regulations).

105 ibid (definition of 'higher risk operations') pt 102 also discussed in Chapter 14.

106 ibid 102.19.

applicable to the operations for which the declaration was made.[107] The means of compliance shall consist of data (tests, analysis, industry consensus standards) and the results or justification used to demonstrate the UAS meets the predetermined level of safety the authority has established as acceptable.[108]

In addition, the manufacturer is required to provide specified documentation to owners,[109] the purpose being to allow the owners to operate UAS safely. These include a maintenance programme that includes instructions for the servicing and maintenance of the system, and an inspection programme to maintain system readiness, any mandatory actions the manufacturer issues in respect of the system; and a comprehensive UAS operating manual.

European Union[110]

Commission Implementing Regulation (EU) 2019/947 of 24 May 2019 and Commission Delegated Regulation (EU) 2019/945 of 12 March 2019 on Unmanned Aircraft Systems lay new cornerstones for European UAS regulation commencing 31 December 2020.

The EU Regulations[111] are interesting in that they seek to address not just safety issues, but wider concerns around privacy, security and data protection. They also go further by considering product safety and design requirements. The Regulations were enacted to replace most of the existing domestic or national provisions on drone operations in EU member states, to in effect create a homogenisation of drone-related legislation across the EU reducing the variety of operational requirements, obligations and restrictions between member states. They also encourage drone operators to freely circulate within the EU without further registration or paperwork required.

In a similar vein to the ICAO Model Regulations, the EU Regulations seek to target the heaviest regulatory burden at the areas of highest perceived risk while maintaining a relatively light touch approach to those operations considered lower risk. It does this by the separation of operations into three categories: Open, Specific and Certified.

The Open category is characterised by a set of operational restrictions depending on the subcategories of operation (A1, A2 or A3) with the most important operational restriction being that all the subcategories of operation must be operated in visual line of sight. This category captures low-risk operations. Product safety and design requirements being implemented by the European Aviation Safety Agency (EASA) require the placing of CE Marking on products made available on the European Union market, confirming that the product has been assessed by the manufacturer and that it is in conformity with EU health, safety and environmental protection requirements.[112] All EU UAS will have assigned a CE marking with a number between 0 and 4, that

107 ibid 102.307.
108 ibid 102.305.
109 ibid 102.311.
110 Generally, see discussion in Chapters 14, 16 and 17.
111 Commission Implementing Regulation (EU) 2019/947 of 24 May 2019 on the rules and procedures for the operation of unmanned aircraft [2019] OJ L152/45; and Commission Delegated Regulation (EU) 2019/945 of 12 March 2019 on unmanned aircraft systems and on third-country operators of unmanned aircraft systems [2019] OJ L152/1.
112 See Your Europe, 'CE Marking' (*Your Europe*,4 November 2020) <https://europa.eu/youreurope/business/product-requirements/labels-markings/ce-marking/index_en.htm>.

will specify the class of the UAS (C0, C1, C2, C3 and C4) and be accompanied by consumer information on how to fly a UA safely with "do's and don'ts" related to each class. The classification system will allow operators to easily identify the type of UAS they are permitted to operate. The classification system came into force on 31 December 2020, but operators will still be permitted to operate unclassified UAS until 1 January 2023.

The Specific category of operation—covering medium risk operations—is based on a risk assessment performed by the Operator according to Article 11 of the Implementing Regulation and on an operational authorisation provided by the Competent Authority based on that risk assessment. The European Aviation Safety Agency (EASA) on 17 December 2020 published the accepted rules and methodology for this risk assessment in a document entitled Special Condition Light Unmanned Aircraft Systems—Medium Risk (hereafter referred to as the "Special Condition").[113]

The Certified category covers high-risk operations requiring a certification process consisting of: (i) the certification of the UAS, (ii) a licenced remote pilot and (iii) an operator approved by the competent authority.[114] At the time of writing, rule-making on the certified category of operation is ongoing.[115]

The Special Condition described previously is of particular relevance in this chapter as it prescribes detailed airworthiness standards covering structures, design and construction, lift/thrust/power system installation, and systems and installation.[116] The obligations are very extensive and are broadly applicable to unmanned aircraft under 600 kg, with most drones currently under certification in EASA anticipated to adopt this certification basis.[117] Two examples of requirements imposed are as follows:

> Light-UAS.2250 Design and construction principles (a) The design of each part or assembly must be suitable for the expected operating conditions of the UA. (b) Design data must adequately define the part or assembly configuration, its design features, and any materials and processes used. (c) The suitability of each design detail and part having an important bearing on safety in operations must be determined.
>
> Light-UAS.2305 Landing gear systems (a) The landing gear system, if installed, must be designed to: (1) provide stable support and control to the UA during surface operation; and (2) account for probable system failures and the operation environment. (b) The UA must be designed to absorb the kinetic energy of the

113 This document in EASA's terminology describes the Acceptable Means of Compliance (ACM) and Guidance Material (GM) for the specific category: See European Union Aviation Safety Agency, 'Special Condition for Light Unmanned Aircraft Systems—Medium Risk' (*European Union Aviation Safety Agency*, 17 December 2020) <www.easa.europa.eu/sites/default/files/dfu/special_condition_sc_light-uas_medium_risk_01.pdf>.

114 Commission Implementing Regulation (EU) 2019/947 of 24 May 2019 on the rules and procedures for the operation of unmanned aircraft [2019] OJ L152/45 Article 3.

115 European Union Aviation Safety Agency (n 113).

116 ibid subparts C, D, E and F.

117 European Union Aviation Safety Agency, 'EASA Publishes Proposed Standards for Certification of Light Drones' (*European Union Aviation Safety Agency*, 20 July 2020) <www.easa.europa.eu/newsroom-and-events/press-releases/easa-publishes-proposed-standards-certification-light-drones>.

landing performance. (c) Adverse landing conditions must not cause damage to the essential systems of the UA, which could lead to a hazardous or catastrophic event if not detected.[118]

It is beyond the scope of this chapter to itemise and consider all the requirements specified in the Special Condition, but they cover the full spectrum of airworthiness standards and even extend to addressing the risk of unauthorised access or takeover of a drone's controls.[119] This level of detail clearly has significant implications for product liability claims and determinations impacting upon matters, such as reasonable care, reasonable design and state-of-the-art defences.

United States

The Federal Aviation Administration (FAA) has, pursuant to section 345 of *Federal Aviation Authority Reauthorization Act* of 2018, established a process for accepting risk-based consensus safety standards related to the design, production and modification of small unmanned aircraft systems (sUAS). This legislation also authorises the FAA to certify a manufacturer of sUAS, or an employee of such manufacturer, that has demonstrated compliance with the consensus safety standards and met any other qualifying criteria, as determined by the FAA.

A manufacturer is, under the legislation, able to self-certify a sUAS system make or model that complies with these consensus safety standards.

Before accepting consensus safety standards, the FAA is obligated to consider a variety of matters and circumstances,[120] including the following:

- Technologies or standards related to geographic limitations, altitude limitations, and sense and avoid capabilities.
- The varying levels of risk posed by different sUAS and their operation and tailoring performance-based requirements to appropriately mitigate risk.
- Predetermined action to maintain safety in the event that a communications link between a sUAS and its operator is lost or compromised.
- Detectability and identifiability to pilots, the FAA and air traffic controllers, as appropriate.
- Means to prevent tampering with or modification of any system, limitation, or other safety mechanism or standard, including a means to identify any tampering or modification that has been made.
- Consensus identification standards under section 2202 of the FAA Extension, Safety and Security Act of 2016.[121]
- Any technology or standard related to sUAS that promotes aviation safety.

118 Both examples taken from European Union Aviation Safety Agency (n 113) Subpart D—Design and Construction.

119 European Union Aviation Safety Agency (n 113) Subpart F Systems and Equipment notes that improper functioning of equipment and systems may be caused by intentional unauthorised electronic interaction (IUEI). The applicant is therefore advised to consider cybersecurity threats as possible sources of 'improper functioning' of equipment and systems.

120 Federal Aviation Authority Reauthorization Act of 2018, s 345(b).

121 Public Law 114–190; 130 Stat. 615.

The FAA is directed to have regard to cost-benefit and risk analyses of consensus safety standards that may be accepted pursuant to the Federal Aviation Authority Reauthorization Act of 2018 for newly designed sUAS.[122] As Kenji Sugahara observes:

> This is important as it should help keep costs down. What is good enough? As an analogy- do we need Fort Knox cybersecurity or just a firewall for something like a 300 gram FPV racer?[123]

The FAA is also directed to look at the applicability of the consensus safety standards to any category of unmanned aircraft systems that should be exempt from the consensus safety standards based on risk factors, and to the applicability of consensus safety standards to sUAS that are not manufactured commercially.[124] The FAA is expressly authorised to exempt from these standards sUAS that are not capable of navigating beyond the visual line of sight of the operator through advanced flight systems and technology, if the FAA determines that such an exemption does not pose a risk to the safety of the national airspace system.

In determining whether to accept risk-based consensus safety standards related to the design, production and modification of any sUAS, the FAA may require a manufacturer of sUAS to provide the aircraft system's operating instructions, the aircraft system's recommended maintenance and inspection procedures, a sample aircraft to be inspected, and the manufacturer's statement of compliance. A manufacturer's statement of compliance[125] shall identify the aircraft make, model, range of serial numbers, and any applicable consensus safety standards used and accepted by the FAA. It shall then state that:

- The aircraft make and model meets the provisions of the consensus safety standards.
- The aircraft make and model conforms to the manufacturer's design data and is manufactured in a way that ensures consistency across units in the production process in order to meet the applicable consensus safety standards.
- The manufacturer will make available to the FAA, operators or customers the aircraft's operating instructions, which conform to the consensus safety standards; and the aircraft's recommended maintenance and inspection procedures, which conform to the consensus safety standards.
- The manufacturer will monitor safety-of-flight issues and take action to ensure it meets the consensus safety standards and report these issues and subsequent actions to the FAA.
- At the request of the Administrator, the manufacturer will provide reasonable access for the FAA to its facilities for the purposes of overseeing compliance.
- The manufacturer, in accordance with the consensus safety standards accepted, has ground and flight-tested random samples of the aircraft; found the sample aircraft performance acceptable; and determined that the make and model of aircraft is suitable for safe operation.

122 Federal Aviation Authority Reauthorization Act of 2018, s 345(b) (8).
123 Kenji Sugahara, 'Analysis of the FAA Reauthorization Act' (13 December 13 2018)<www.ariascend.com/analysis-of-the-2018-faa-reauthorization-act/>.
124 Federal Aviation Authority Reauthorization Act of 2018, s 345(b) (9); (11).
125 ibid, s 345(h).

The focus of the FAA, to date, in relation to the implementation of the FAA Reauthorization Act of 2018, has been upon remote identification as being fundamental to both safety and security of UAS operations. As the Deputy Administrator of the FAA states:

> Remote identification will be necessary for routine beyond visual line-of-sight operations, operations over people, package deliveries, operations in congested areas, and the continued safe operation of all aircraft in shared airspace. It will also be foundational for the advancement of automated passenger or cargo-carrying air transportation, which is often referred to as Urban Air Mobility. With remote identification, the FAA and our national security and public safety partners will be better able to identify a UAS and its operator, assess if a UAS is being operated in a clueless, careless, or criminal manner, and take appropriate action if necessary. Remote identification is the FAA's highest priority UAS-related rulemaking effort.[126]

This focus has culminated in the submission by the FAA of a Final Rule "Remote Identification of Unmanned Aircraft" to the Federal Register for publication.[127] This Rule establishes requirements for the remote identification of unmanned aircraft operated in the airspace of the United States and with very limited exceptions all unmanned aircraft operating in the airspace of the United States are subject to the operating requirements of this rule, irrespective of whether they are operating for recreational or commercial purposes. Standard remote identification unmanned aircraft and remote identification broadcast modules must be designed and produced to meet the requirements of this rule. A person designing or producing a standard remote identification unmanned aircraft or broadcast module for operation in the United States must show that the unmanned aircraft or broadcast module meets the requirements of an FAA-accepted means of compliance.[128]

The FAA acknowledges that UAS may have components produced by different manufacturers (e.g. an unmanned aircraft could be manufactured by one manufacturer and the control station could be manufactured by another). In addition, unmanned aircraft that operate beyond the radio line of sight may use third-party communication links. As finalised, the remote identification requirements in this final rule apply to the operation and the design and production of unmanned aircraft. Unmanned aircraft producers are responsible for ensuring that the unmanned aircraft comply with the design and production requirements of this rule even when the unmanned aircraft uses control station equipment (such as a smart phone) or communication links manufactured by a different person. The unmanned aircraft producer must address

126 Statement of Daniel K. Elwell, Deputy Administrator, Federal Aviation Administration, before the Transportation and Infrastructure Subcommittee on Aviation, United States House of Representatives, 'Implementation of the FAA Reauthorization Act 2018' (26 September 2019) <www.transportation.gov/testimony/implementation-faa-reauthorization-act-2018>.

127 Department of Transportation, 'Federal Aviation Administration, 14 CFR Parts 1, 11, 47, 48, 89, 91, and 107 [Docket No.: FAA-2019-1100; Amdt. Nos. 1-75, 11-63, 47-31, 48-3, 89-1, 91-361, and 107-7], RIN 2120–AL31, Remote Identification of Unmanned Aircraft'<www.faa.gov/news/media/attachments/RemoteID_Final_Rule.pdf>.

128 ibid 13.

how any dependencies on control station functionality are incorporated as part of the remote identification design and production requirements.[129]

International Organisation for Standardisation (ISO)

ISO is a global federation of national standards bodies (ISO member bodies) and the work of preparing International Standards is normally carried out through ISO technical committees.[130]

The world's first ISO approved Drone Safety Standard—ISO 21384-3, *Unmanned aircraft systems—Part 3: Operational procedures*, was launched in December 2019. This international standard applies to all commercial UAS operations regardless of size, categorisation, application or location and endeavours to represent international best practice for the safe operation of all types of use and missions.

As Gigi Onag explains:

> The new standards promote an "etiquette" for drone use that reinforces compliance towards no-fly zones, local regulation, flight log protocols, maintenance, training and flight planning documentation.[131]
>
> Social responsibility is also at the heart of the standards, which strengthens the responsible use of a technology that aims to improve and not disrupt everyday life.
>
> The new standards also seek to address public concerns surrounding privacy and data protection, demanding that operators must have appropriate systems to handle data alongside communications and control planning when flying.
>
> The hardware and software of all related operating equipment must also be kept up to date. Significantly, the fail-safe of human intervention is required for all drone flights, including autonomous operations, ensuring that drone operators are held accountable.

It is the first in a series of emerging standards for air drones, with others due to address General Specifications, Product Manufacture and Maintenance, Unmanned Traffic Management (UTM) and Testing Procedures.[132]

Standardisation in the field of unmanned aircraft systems (UAS), including, but not limited to, classification, design, manufacture, operation (including maintenance) and safety management of UAS operations will, like the ICAO Model Regulations and

129 ibid XIV Remote Identification Design and Production.

130 It is an independent, non-governmental international organisation with a membership of 165 national standards bodies. See International Organization for Standardization, 'About Us' (*ISO*, 20 January 2021) <www.iso.org/about-us.html>.

131 Futureiot, 'ISO Approved International Standards for Drones' (*Futureiot*, 6 December 2019) <https://futureiot.tech/iso-approved-international-standards-for-drones/>.

132 These include ISO21384-4, 'Unmanned Aircraft Systems—Part 4: Vocabulary' (*ISO*, May 2020) <www.iso.org/standard/76785.html>; ISO23665, 'Unmanned Aircraft Systems—Training for Personnel Involved in UAS Operations' (*ISO*, January 2021) <www.iso.org/standard/76592.html>; Clare Naden, 'Drone Market Set to Take Off with New ISO Standard' (*ISO*, 5 December 2019) <www.iso.org/news/ref2461.html>; Professional Security, 'ISO-approved Drone Standards' (*Professional Security Magazine Online*, 6 December 2019) <www.professionalsecurity.co.uk/news/transport/iso-approved-drone-standards/>.

European Union Regulations discussed earlier, have major implications for product liability litigation.

Concluding comments

The drone industry is in its infancy and, given the tremendous economic efficiencies offered by this new technology, the commercial use of drones is certain to expand significantly in the coming years. An unfortunate, but unavoidable, result of the increased use of drones will be an increase in mishaps, resulting in increased litigation involving personal injury, death and property damage caused by drone accidents. Although drones incorporate new and complex technologies, the existing framework of tort law, and specifically products liability law, is available and capable of addressing the allocation of liability between and among the manufacturers and other entities in the chain of distribution. For those entities, an understanding of their potential liability exposure under that framework, and the steps needed to avoid such exposure, is key to the future success of the drone industry.

The increasing attention being paid by regulators and international organisations to the implementation of design specifications and production standards, and to the imposition of obligations upon manufacturers and those responsible for the design and production of drones, already has, and will continue to have, product liability repercussions for the many different parties in the supply chain where drones may be used. Manufacturers will need to ensure that they comply with design specifications and that sufficiently rigorous quality control checks are in place to ensure that the products manufactured meet the requisite design and safety standards.[133]

133 Alison Newstead, 'Drones and Robots: Liability for Designers, Manufacturers and Insurers' (*Inhouse Lawyer*, March 2014) <www.inhouselawyer.co.uk/legal-briefing/drones-and-robots-liability-for-designers-manufacturers-and-insurers/>.

Part D
Regulation

13 Regulatory overview

Chris Morrison, Alan Kells, Jeffrey Ellis, Maurice Thompson and James M. Cooper

Introduction

This chapter provides an overview of the evolving regulatory environment in which Unmanned Aircraft (UA) and Unmanned Aircraft Systems (UAS),[1] or Remotely Piloted Aircraft (RPA) and Remotely Piloted Aircraft Systems (RPAS),[2] operate. As stated in Chapter 1, unless the context demands more "jurisdiction specific" language, unmanned aircraft and remotely piloted aircraft will be referred to as "drones". The regulatory chapters do require more specific language. This and the following chapters look at guidance provided by international and transnational organisations, how individual countries are approaching the topic, and at some of the key issues attracting the attention of regulators and of the broader community.

We live in a time of extraordinary and rapid change. The 21st century is still quite young but has already spawned technology that would have been deemed fantastical only a few short years ago. Driverless cars, 3D printers, fibre optics, social media and Bluetooth are only some of the new technology applications that are already transforming the way we live. But with each wondrous new use, there is almost always a troubling potential for misuse. Health hazards, cyber hacking, invasions of privacy and the danger of physical harm arising from product malfunction are all causes for concern and some type of regulation.

Calls for regulation, however, are not limited only to those seeking to deter and police the potential for misuse. Regulators are also lobbied by those who want to remove or alter existing laws and regulations so as to encourage the growth and beneficial uses of new technologies. Irrespective of what the regulator is requested to do, the regulator must first understand the good and bad of what the new technology is capable of before it can act. The regulator must also determine whether existing laws are suitable to accomplish these goals. If new laws are needed, the regulator also has

1 The term Unmanned Aircraft (UA) is used to describe the aircraft itself, whereas the term Unmanned Aircraft System (UAS) is generally used to describe the entire operating equipment including the aircraft, the control station from where the aircraft is operated and the wireless data link. See, for example, Federal Aviation Administration, 'Unmanned Aircraft Systems' (*United States Department of Transport*, 5 January 2021) <www.faa.gov/uas/>.

2 The International Civil Aviation Organization (ICAO) employs the acronym RPAS (standing for Remotely Piloted Aircraft System) or RPA (Remotely Piloted Aircraft). The term RPAS appears to be the preferred terminology used by international aviation related agencies like ICAO, Eurocontrol, the European Aviation Safety Agency (EASA), the Civil Aviation Safety Authority (CASA—Australia) and the Civil Aviation Authority (CAA—New Zealand.

to attempt to craft these laws without undermining the existing regulatory structure and then determine how to police the new laws which are enacted.

Understanding how the regulatory process functions is of fundamental importance when trying to predict what a regulatory structure will look like for any emerging technology. It is particularly important when considering what the regulatory structure for drones will be in the coming years. That is because the regulatory framework for this developing technology is still very much a work in progress and is far less developed than the technology which it seeks to regulate.[3] This is not surprising when one considers the regulatory process for new technology. The law traditionally develops at a measured pace while technology and innovation are frequently borne of inspiration and as fast as possible realisation. Although both require hard work to reach fruition, the persons driving new technology development are focussed on bringing that technology into use as quickly as possible. The motivations for doing so are both economic and practical. New technology development is costly, and those costs need to be recouped before the profits that motivated an initial investment can be achieved. On a practical level, new technology also has to be widely used before its full potential can be realised and the unforeseen problems that inevitably surface can be corrected. The law develops far differently.

The law develops first by analysing whether there is a need for a new law. Usually, this begins with a person or group raising concerns about potential problems that may arise if a new law is not passed. This in turn requires an analysis as to whether existing laws are sufficient to deal with these potential problems. If the answer is no or even maybe, then the next step is to analyse more fully the potential problem to determine how significant it may be. If deemed significant, the regulators must analyse and debate potential laws that might be enacted to address the problems that have been identified.

The foregoing usually takes place in a partisan political environment with various special interest groups weighing in on perceived benefits and harms to their interests if a particular law is passed. This is often a convoluted and protracted process[4] with the first step in this process being a legislative or regulatory acknowledgement of societal concerns. The next step is to consider whether existing law and related regulatory structures are adequate to address these concerns. If not, then various modifications to existing laws and structures must be considered and the consequences of their implementation carefully analysed. Needless to say, the more concerns voiced by various stakeholders in this regulatory agenda, the more complex and time consuming the process becomes. Given the rapid development of drone technology, the constantly widening areas for its use and the myriad safety, security and privacy concerns that arise, it is easy to see why the development of the law and regulatory structure in this area is complex and still a work in progress. Comfort perhaps can be derived from an observation of the Supreme Court of Oregon in 1960:

3 See discussion at Chapter 19 Technological Challenges Inherent in Safety Regulation.

4 Since the length of this chapter does not permit a detailed discussion of how this process plays out and all the various interests that come into play, a diagram prepared by the Legislature of the State of Oregon provides a "simple view" of what usually takes place: See Oregon State Legislature, 'How an Idea Becomes Law: A Simple View of the Oregon Legislative Process' (*Oregon State Legislature*, 19 January 2021).

> If the mind of man can invent and operate a flying machine, it ought to be able to devise a rule of law which is adequate to deal with the problems flowing from such inventiveness.[5]

Regulator or regulators

Up to this point in time, most aviation laws and regulation centred around the delivery of aviation services by aviation companies to users of discreet aviation services (e.g. passenger and cargo transit by aviation carriers to consumers of those same aviation services). In the age of drones, however, companies with historically no aviation experience are pivoting their offerings to take advantage of drones' technology and are entering into and impacting the aviation sector. Whether they appreciate it yet or not, this will have a profound impact on the response needed by governments and their regulators and a knock-on impact for insurers.

Since the advent of aviation, regulators have largely needed to regulate only the pilot, the aircraft and the airport for the purpose of carrying persons and/or cargo. Requirements for safety and standards were essentially uniform. Whether it was a passenger airliner or a cargo plane, once in the air, barring exceptional circumstances of a mid-air collision, weather events, machinery malfunction, human error or mischief, the aircraft would be loaded and would take off from point "A" and would land and be unloaded at point "B". Subject to matters concerning sovereignty of the airspace, the journey of the aircraft through the skies was quite uneventful. Indeed, on long-haul flights, it gave rise to the development of the auto-pilot function on many aircraft.

To make a point, however, consider the absurd implications if those same aircraft had to fly from point "A" to point "B" at an altitude of less than 400 feet. All of a sudden, the land environment and the pilot and the aircraft's ability to respond to it would become critical factors. The flight path of the aircraft would then need to take account of cities and towns, large infrastructure, mountainous regions, etc. If flights were anticipated through or in the vicinity of such environments, regulators would then have the added task of seeking to regulate higher degrees of pilot competency. For example, the risk associated with an aircraft flying over an uninhabited desert or agricultural land might require one level of pilot competency, whereas the risks associated with an aircraft flying over or through a city would understandably require a much higher degree of pilot competency. Similarly, the aircraft would require a completely different level of responsiveness.

Modern aircraft, like many ocean-going vessels, have grown steadily in size for economies of scale. Neither is required to have the ability to make drastic deviations in direction or speed. The linear momentum of an A380 aircraft in flight travelling at 1,185 km/hour, or a fully laden 400-m-long Ultra Large Crude Carrier (ULCC) vessel with a 550,000-deadweight tonnage is astonishingly large. To illustrate, for a ULCC bulk carrier vessel to come to a stop after forward propulsion at a cruising speed of 16 knots (30 km/hour) has ceased, might take 20–25 minutes over a distance of possibly 25 km. Or consider that if an A380 aircraft travelling at 1,185 km/hour detects an obstacle hovering stationary in its direct flight path 1 km in the distance, the aircraft

5 *Atkinson v. Bernard,* Inc 223 Or. 624, 232 (1960).

would meet that obstacle a mere 3 seconds later. Stopping both craft safely typically requires meticulous planning, time, a considerable distance of unencumbered flight path or water and methodical execution.

These limitations in maneuverability are tempered by the helpful reality that the aircraft may be travelling some 13 km above the ground, and ocean-going vessels may effectively be alone on the high seas for days or weeks. As a consequence, aviation regulators have not needed to consider the land environment relative to flight in the detail now required to appropriately consider the safe deployment and regulation of drones, especially in high density environments. Drones will be navigating populated areas in close proximity to people, buildings, infrastructure and the like and carrying out tasks that one never previously even contemplated in respect of regulated classic aircraft. In addition, by the time the first edition of this book is available for sale or only shortly thereafter, drones may also be carrying people. With the exponential use of drones, there will be a need for regulators to completely overhaul their attitude to risk. As well as needing to reconsider relative pilot competencies and drone responsiveness, regulators will need to have access to a comprehensive understanding of the risks arising from flying over, under and through, different environments.

This need for change has caught most governments and regulators completely off-guard. Many will be reluctant to even concede that the age of drones is breaking the classic stereotype of aviation and bridging into other sectors. From a maritime perspective, for instance, it would be surprising if a classic aviation regulator were familiar with the risks associated with: (i) offshore oil rigs, (ii) ocean going vessels, (iii) port operations, (iv) confined tanks, (v) climate environments that can form inside cargo holds and storage tanks and facilities loaded with various commodities, (vi) deep sea mining at 3 km below the ocean's surface or (vii) maritime law.[6] While that has been acceptable to date for classic aviation, it is these and other risks that these same aviation regulators will now need to grapple with if they are to comprehensively consider navigating the way forward with drones if drones are to fulfil their potential in sectors like maritime; that is, if drones are to be subsumed under the regulatory oversight of aviation regulators at all. With drones now being so heavily used in the maritime, offshore oil and gas, natural resources, mining and transport sectors, among many others, it could be argued that drones should be regulated separately to classic aviation. Given we are only now starting to address many of the challenges presented by the drones age, such a wholesale change in perspective would be possible at this time. At the least, consideration could be given to some dual regulatory oversight, of which there are a number of good examples internationally.[7]

If drones are to remain within the bailiwick of classic aviation regulators, consider the changes required. In addition to having to upskill and change their mindsets as noted earlier, one also needs to factor in the reality that the number of these new

6 See discussion in Chapter 5 Maritime Uses of Drones.

7 For example, offshore oil & gas rigs in Australia are regulated by two authorities: the National Offshore Petroleum Safety and Environmental Management Authority (NOPSEMA) and the Australian Maritime Safety Authority (AMSA), with the jurisdiction between the two grey to say the least, but competently dealt with via an MOU between the two authorities to cooperate in their dealings with such 'maritime' and 'offshore' assets and services. A similar obvious example is the USA's Federal Aviation Authority (FAA) which entered into an MOU with the Occupational Safety and Health Administration (OSHA) to jointly regulate in respect of airport ramp safety issues.

"aircraft" requiring regulation is increasing daily. The number of drones deployed and operating globally has already outstripped the expectations and resourcing capabilities of the most advanced aviation regulatory entities and their numbers will continue to increase exponentially.

To put this in perspective, the active global commercial aircraft fleet currently stands at 25,368 aircraft, with the next 10 years expected to see 3.4% net annual growth, increasing the number to 35,501.[8] In comparison, in one country alone, the United States, in early 2018, the United States' FAA's drone registry passed a million listings,[9] increasing to 1.66 million in 2020.[10] Obtaining accurate numbers of drones globally at present is a challenge because many countries still do not have compulsory registration of drones and/or means of policing registration, but it is abundantly clear that the number of drones dwarfs the number of commercial aircraft in operation.

This provides an appreciation of the monumental task facing governments and regulators globally. Just as they seek to plan or take steps to upskill their personnel and drastically increase the numbers in their departments, the technological advancements in drone technology, their usage across multiple sectors and their numbers continue to outstrip any such efforts. In effect, governments and their regulators have been overtaken and are now playing a game of catch-up they will not win unless serious adjustments and investments are made. This raises the question as to whether governments and regulators should continue to build out from the classic aviation regulatory bodies that exist and into whose jurisdiction drones have almost been assumed to fit, or whether it would be best to create completely new departments, cross-pollinated with not just aviation talent, but talent from various sectors recognised to be heavy users or potential users of drones technology, in other words, create purpose-built authorities.

Constitutional issues

One important aspect of regulation is the interplay between national and state laws in federal jurisdictions. For the sake of consistency and certainty, aviation law is generally within the sole remit of a country's national government. For reasons explained in the following,[11] there are strong arguments that in relation to commercial aviation using recognised aerodromes it is (for the most part) clear cut where the boundaries of national and local legislation are drawn.[12] The battle for control between national and local government is nothing new, and while on the one hand it may seem sensible for control of drones, like aviation, to remain with the national government, unlike aviation, drones do not solely operate along agreed flight paths, from specified aero-

8 See Oliver Wyman, 'Global Aircraft Demand Forecast' (*Oliver Wyman*, 19 January 2021) <www.oliverwyman.com/our-expertise/insights/2017/jun/paris-air-show/global-commercial-aircraft-fleet-to-grow-to-more-than-35000.html>.

9 US Department of Transportation, 'FAA Drone Registry Tops One Million' (*US Department of Transportation*, 10 January 2018) <www.transportation.gov/briefing-room/faa-drone-registry-tops-one-million>.

10 Federal Aviation Administration, 'Press Release—U.S. Transportation Secretary Elaine L. Chao Announces $7.5 Million in 19 Unmanned Aircraft System Research Grants to Universities' (*United States Department of Transport*, 21 August 2020) <www.faa.gov/news/press_releases/news_story.cfm?newsId=25199&omniRss=press_releasesAoc&cid=102_P_R>.

11 See, for example, the judgment of the High Court of Australia in *Airlines of New South Wales Pty Ltd v New South Wales [No 2]* (1965) 113 CLR 54.

12 ibid.

dromes, and are operated by remote pilots with varying degrees of skill and experience. As such, there is an argument that local authorities will be far more familiar with the risks of operating drones in local areas and therefore better able to regulate this.

Resolutions in relation to the interplay between federal, state and local laws from two jurisdictions—Australia and the United States—are considered in the following.

Australia—commingling theory[13]

Constitutional limitations restrict the scope to which the federal government can legislate in respect to civil aviation operations and, as a consequence, cooperation with the states[14] was, and still is, necessary to provide uniform aviation laws throughout Australia. While it is beyond the scope of this chapter to provide a full discourse on this topic, the distinction in the Australian Constitution between intrastate and interstate commerce, confining the power of the Commonwealth to the latter, significantly impacts the power of the Commonwealth to legislate in respect of intrastate trade and commerce.

In *Airlines of NSW v New South Wales (No 1) (Airlines of NSW Case (No 1)*,[15] the High Court of Australia (i.e. Australia's highest court) conceded that in relation to the regulation of aviation there was considerable scope for the Commonwealth to move into much of the field then occupied by the states under the State Acts; however, the Court held that the states still had extensive powers in relation to civil aviation.

The Commonwealth government, in the aftermath of the judgment handed down in the *Airlines of NSW Case (No 1)*, amended its *Air Navigation Regulations 1947* so as to apply to all classes of air navigation—international, interstate and intrastate. It also established a Commonwealth licencing system for intrastate air transport services. The validity of these far-reaching provisions was once again tested by the High Court in *Airlines of New South Wales Pty Ltd v New South Wales (No 2)*.[16] It was in this landmark aviation case that the High Court of Australia endorsed a "commingling theory", recognising that aircraft with different points of departure (or more accurately departures from different states) were flying in common airspace—or commingling with other aircraft, with obvious regulatory and safety implications.

Barwick CJ recognised that significant changes had taken place in Australia's aviation industry:

> The speeds at which aircraft move in the air, the narrow, and narrowing, margins of time in which consequences of error or malfunction may be avoided or reduced, the increasing density of air traffic, the interdependence of safety of one aircraft upon the performance of other aircraft, the hazards of weather and the

13 Generally, see Julie-Anne Tarr and others, 'Drones in Australia—Rapidly Evolving Regulatory and Insurance Challenges' (2019) 30 ILJ 135, 141–43; RIC Bartsch, 'Unmanned and Uncontrolled: The Commingling Theory and the Legality of Unmanned Aircraft System Operations' (2015) 4 Journal of Aeronautics & Aerospace Engineering 1.

14 See, for example, the adoption of the Commonwealth *Air Navigation Regulations 1937 (Cth)* as State Law by enactment of *Air Navigation Act 1938 (NSW); Air Navigation Act 1937 (Qld); Air Navigation Act 1937 (SA); Air Navigation Act 1937 (Tas); Air Navigation Act 1937 (Vic); and Air Navigation Act 1937 (WA)*.

15 (1964) 113 CLR 1.

16 (1965) 113 CLR 54.

variable performance of aircraft, leading to diversion and re-routing of aircraft in flight, the need for use of common facilities . . . all combine to demonstrate that all air operations irrespective of destination or of their particular nature must be subject to the same control if the air is to be safe.

Accordingly, the High Court upheld a federal power to licence all air navigation on the basis of safety, regularity and efficiency of the operations, including purely intrastate operations. One of the reasons relied on was that the safety of interstate and overseas air navigation could be assured only by the Commonwealth regulating the safety aspects of all air navigation in Australia. Professor Leslie Zines explained the significance of this judgment in respect to the regulation of aviation in Australia:

> A law therefore operating on purely intrastate carriage of goods and passengers by air was held to be a law with respect to trade and commerce with other countries and among the states. No doubt, if the Founding Fathers had been asked whether they could conceive of a situation where the power they had given the Commonwealth could be used to control an entire area of domestic trade and commerce within a state, they would have said "No". But that is because they were unaware of the hazards, speeds and complexity of modern forms of travel. It is probable that the framers certainly intended that the Commonwealth should be empowered to protect interstate and overseas trade. What has changed since then are simply the facts of the world not the nature or object of the power.[17]

The High Court held in order to ensure the safety, regularity and efficiency of interstate and overseas air travel it was necessary for the Commonwealth to exercise a wide measure of control over intrastate navigation, with the real question being how far that control could lawfully go.[18] Accordingly, it is clearly established in *Airlines of New South Wales (No 2)* that the Commonwealth has unlimited (de facto) power in Australian domestic aviation on any safety, operational or technical aspects of air navigation.

Of critical importance in this context is the extent to which the power of the Commonwealth may extend in respect to the regulation of drones that are incapable of flying into navigable airspace, either due to their inherent performance capabilities or through an internal system—electronic fences or G-gates[19]—in the case of certain drones. These drones would not be capable of "commingling" with other aircraft operating in navigable airspace. If it can be shown that the Commonwealth's, or its regulator in this context CASA's, authority is limited to regulating only in "navigable airspace" then the class of drones that are "not capable of" operating in navigable airspace will not be within CASA's authority to control and hence any purported

17 Leslie Zines, 'What the Courts have Done to Australian Federalism' (*Parliament of Australia*, November 1991) <www.aph.gov.au/About_Parliament/Senate/Powers_practice_n_procedures/~/~/link.aspx?_id=3DC6260FAE2F4BB79164DCA97B2AF5A9>.

18 *Airlines of New South Wales Pty Ltd v New South Wales (No 2)* (1965) 113 CLR 54, 128.

19 Geo-fencing is a feature in a software program that uses the global positioning system (GPS) or radio frequency identification (RFID) to define geographical boundaries. See, for example, Sarah K White, 'What is Geofencing? Putting Location to Work' (*CIO Australia*, 2 November 2017) <www.cio.com/article/2383123/mobile/5-things-you-need-to-know-about-geofencing.html>; Techopedia, 'Geofencing' (*techopedia*, 23 February 2012) <www.techopedia.com/definition/14937/geofencing>.

authority to do so will be *ultra vires* and therefore void. In other words, already the established classic "aviation" concepts of "navigable airspace" and "commingling" are challenged in the context of drones.

For example, a question arises as to whether the Commonwealth (under civil aviation law) has jurisdiction to regulate any aircraft (i.e. manned or unmanned) when operated within confined spaces. Does CASA have jurisdiction to regulate helicopter activities when operated inside, by way of example, Etihad Stadium in Melbourne, when the roof is closed? In consideration of the constitutional limitations briefly discussed in this section, and in applying the commingling theory, the answer may not be straightforward.

Finally, the scope of Commonwealth "aviation" powers, with respect to purely intrastate services, does not extend to commercial aspects of aviation. Nor, from the recent decision of the High Court in *Work Health Authority v Outback Ballooning Pty Ltd*,[20] does the body of Commonwealth civil aviation laws[21] exclude the application of state and territory occupational health and safety laws. The *Outback Ballooning Pty Ltd* case, while not specifically about drones, demonstrates the overlapping regulatory burdens of local and national requirements that may be placed on operators. The respondent ballooning business provided hot air balloon rides to passengers. Tragically, a passenger while boarding sustained fatal injuries. Action was taken against the company by the health and safety regulator under local (rather than national) legislation. Following differing decisions in the courts below as to whether local workplace health and safety legislation could apply, or if the regulatory landscape was solely occupied by national aviation law, in the circumstances where boarding had commenced, the case came before the High Court.

The majority in the High Court (Kiefel CJ, Bell, Keane, Nettle and Gordon JJ) found that the local legislation was not inconsistent with Commonwealth civil aviation law and that it applied to operations associated with aircraft, including the embarkation of passengers. The effect of this decision is that operators are now subject to both Commonwealth laws in relation to aviation safety and to state and territory laws—including occupational health and safety laws. The risk of subjecting operators to a multitude of non-uniform laws was addressed by Edelman J in dissent:

> it would be surprising, confusing, and potentially dangerous if the Civil Aviation Law were to have the effect that the rules of the air on a flight from Darwin to Melbourne, via Sydney, could be regulated not merely by the comprehensive and uniform rules policed by the Commonwealth Civil Aviation Authority ("CASA"), but also, depending upon the airspace, by separate and different rules policed by the Work Health Authority and its inspectors in the Northern Territory, or regulators in New South Wales and Victoria.[22]

The potentially overlapping requirements of different aspects of local and national legislation provide added complexity to the regulatory oversight of operators, particularly

20 [2019]HCA 2.
21 Including the *Civil Aviation Act 1988(Cth)*.
22 [2019] HCA 2, 34 [93].

those that may cross state boundaries in the course of their operations.[23] How will an incident that results in alleged breaches of both the local and national regulations be dealt with in practice? Which regulator takes action? Who takes the lead? Surely a single regulator dealing with this ever-evolving area is the way forward? In light of the discourse in this text, however, the question remains as to whether that single regulator evolves from the current "classic" aviation regulator or whether now would be the appropriate time to consider an autonomous regulator.

USA—Singer[24]*—national versus local regulation*

In 2017, the case of *Singer v City of Newton* came before the District Court of Massachusetts. The case was brought by Dr Michael Singer, a resident of Newton. The City had introduced a local Ordinance[25] regulating UAS operations with the purpose of "*protecting the privacy of residents . . . [and] . . . to prevent nuisances and other disturbances of the enjoyment of both public and private space*". In order to do so the Ordinance imposed registration requirements; a ban on operating below 400 feet over private property without the express permission of the owner; prevented BVLOS operation; prevented interference with other aircraft; a ban on operating over City property without prior permission; and prevented surveillance or invading any place where a person has a reasonable expectation of privacy.

These requirements would be applied locally in addition to national and FAA requirements. The net effect of them, it was argued, would be to make UA use in the City virtually impossible. Singer challenged four provisions of the Ordinance arguing the Ordinance was preempted (or the area occupied) by national federal law. The Supremacy Clause of the US Constitution provides that federal laws are supreme and therefore preempt (override) conflicting local regulations. Where the federal government has made clear its intention to be the sole regulator of an area, preemption is relatively straightforward. Difficulties arise where the federal government has not expressly preempted an area particularly where there is crossover with areas traditionally left to the states, which was the case in point here, where aviation (a federal area of regulation) interacts with privacy (traditionally an area for states). The courts will then have to consider whether preemption can be inferred from the way the federal government has regulated—is regulation so pervasive that it demonstrates intent to occupy the field (field preemption)? Or is compliance with both state and federal regulations impossible (conflict preemption)?

The court found that field preemption did not apply. Despite aviation traditionally being an area occupied by federal law, the court noted a fact sheet published by the FAA envisaging states regulating UA use, around issues such as privacy, zoning and law enforcement operations, defeating the field preemption argument. As a result,

23 Ben Martin and Jayne Heatley, 'Judicial Decisions Requiring Urgent Legislative Attention' (Norton White Briefing Paper, 2019)<www.aph.gov.au/DocumentStore.ashx?id=cbc1a90a-7031-48fc-adba-31d54d50078a> comment that the decision in *Work Health Authority v Outback Ballooning Pty Ltd* [2019] HCA 2, is "likely to add to costs for air operators who will be required to comply with up to 9 sets of safety laws (that may not be consistent) and deal with safety regulators in each State and Territory in addition to CASA."

24 284 F. Supp. 3d 125 (2017).

25 Newton Ordinances § 20-64 (26 March 2020).

the issue became whether the aspects challenged were conflict preempted. The court found they were and struck them down for the following reasons:

Registration—the court noted the existence of the FAA registration scheme clearly demonstrated its intent to be the exclusive registration scheme for UAS. This clearly conflicted with the Ordinance's requirement to register "*all drones without limit as to the . . . altitude they operate, in clear derogation of the FAA's intended authority*".

400 feet over private property—it was found that this provision, in tandem with the public property ban, essentially created a UA ban within city limits, noting "*Nowhere in the city may an individual operate a drone without first having permission from the owner of the land below, be that Newton or a private landowner*". The FAA requires UA to be operated below 400 feet (without a waiver), the City restriction essentially eliminated UA use in the City without prior permission, thwarting the intention of the government and FAA to integrate UA into national airspace.

BVLOS—this requirement went beyond the FAA's (option for an observer), and (given the altitude requirements) impacted upon navigable airspace, which is an area of federal regulation.[26]

Public property ban—the court noted the ban "*does not limit its reach to any altitude. This alone is a ground for preemption of the subsection because it certainly reaches into navigable airspace*" which is an area occupied solely by federal law.

It should be noted the court struck down the four provisions only. It did not strike down the whole Ordinance, nor did the court find that field preemption applied, thus allowing local regulation in areas of UAS regulation not regulated by the national government. Had Newton drafted its Ordinance with more care, the provisions may not have been struck down, so local governments may go above and beyond FAA requirements if this can be justified by local circumstances. For example, the registration provision was struck down for requiring all UA be registered, necessitating dual registration where FAA requirements apply. Had the City looked to register those UA not required to be registered by the FAA (up to 250 g) this may have been successful.[27]

One interpretation of this decision which appears to go to the heart of the matter is that the court felt:

> *operational safety and licensing matters ought to be targets of exclusive federal regulation. The States, for their part, should get to regulate drone purpose and function—what drones can be used for and what types of things they can do.*[28]

26 While held to be a matter of conflict preemption, the court's reasoning infers field preemption where aircraft safety is concerned.

27 FAA approval is required for any local registration scheme.

28 See Harvard Law Review, 'Singer v City of Newton Massachusetts District Court Finds Portion of Local Drone Ordinance Preempted by FAA Regulation' (2018) 131 Harvard Law Review 2057.

Transnational and national regulatory structures and responses

At present, the regulatory landscape is at best piecemeal. National authorities have begun to develop regulations, but with the technology developing at such a rapid rate, alongside new and innovative uses for drones being found almost daily, it is understandably difficult for national authorities to keep pace. As Dr Jonathan Aleck, Head of Legal Affairs at the Australian Civil Aviation Safety Authority noted at the IBA (International Bar Association) annual conference held in Sydney in October 2017, "the moment you put your finger on the technology, it has changed and advanced . . . Every jurisdiction has a roadmap and a plan. Everyone is looking at this and struggling".[29]

Currently, only around half of the 193 contracting states to the International Civil Aviation Organization ("ICAO"), a specialised agency of the United Nations, have civil drone regulations in force. States that have promulgated domestic regulations have generally done so by imposing strict operating limitations on all drone activities with limitations targeted at the safety of those on the ground and other aircraft through the restriction of the use of drones in populated areas and in the proximity of airfields.

ICAO has prepared a draft regulatory framework for UAS[30] based upon a review of existing regulations in Member States in a bid to share best practices that can be implemented by countries seeking to improve, or introduce, UAS regulations. These Model UAS Regulations and companion Advisory Circulars offer a template for the 193 Member States to implement, or to supplement their existing UAS regulations. There is little doubt that agreed international regulatory requirements and standards for drones akin to that for manned aviation would bring enormous benefits both in terms of safety and efficiency in manufacturing and design standards. Accordingly, the next chapter in this book, Chapter 14, will look at the work being undertaken by Transnational Organisations to achieve regulatory consistency, effectiveness and efficiency. For example, this chapter will review the ICAO draft regulatory framework, initiatives of the European Commission,[31] the European Union Aviation Safety Agency (EASA), Pacific Aviation Safety Office (PASO) and other bodies such as the Joint Authorities for Rulemaking on Unmanned Systems (JARUS).[32]

In the four chapters that immediately follow, the regulatory regimes for drone operations in the United States, Spain, the United Kingdom and Australia are outlined. These chapters serve to highlight the similarities and differences between domestic regulations. The first country to implement regulations in this field was Australia

29 As reported by Tom Madge-Wyld, 'Australian Safety Regulator Says Drones "Cannot Be Managed"' (*Getting the Deal Through*, 12 October 2017)<https://gettingthedealthrough.com/article/5798/australian-safety-regulator-says-drones-cannot-managed>.

30 ICAO, 'Introduction to ICAO Model UAS Regulations and Advisory Circulars' (*ICAO Safety*, 19 January 2021) <www.icao.int/safety/UA/Pages/ICAO-Model-UAS-Regulations.aspx>.

31 See, for example, Commission, 'Communication from the Commission to the European Parliament, The Council, The European Economic and Social Committee and the Committee of the Regions: Sustainable and Smart Mobility Strategy—Putting European transport on Track for the Future Brussels' COM (2020) 789 final <https://ec.europa.eu/transport/sites/transport/files/legislation/com20200789.pdf>.

32 JARUS is a group of experts from National Aviation Authorities and regional aviation safety organisations that works on recommending a single set of technical, safety and operational requirements for the certification and safe integration of UAS into airspace and at aerodromes.

in 2002 with the introduction of the Civil Aviation Safety Regulation Part 101. The chapter describing the aviation regulatory system in the United States provides a good example of how the manned aviation regulatory system developed and subsequently began to incorporate UAVs beneath its regulatory umbrella. Spain affords a good example of an EU Member State approving its own domestic or national regulations governing the use of drones, but subject to overarching EU Community Regulations.

Registration and licencing

The registration of drones, and the licencing of those who operate or own them, are seen as key considerations in any comprehensive and robust regulatory framework governing drone operations. The trend globally in recent years has been for states to enact more stringent rules around registration and licencing. That development is inexorably linked to the continued proliferation of drone use in that time and the resultant increased risk of collisions and other hazardous events.

The key driver underlying the need for registration is to ensure the operator and/or owner of the drone can easily be identified. It is the same reasoning behind why other traditional modes of transport (motor vehicles, vessels, manned aircraft, among others) have well-established registration systems in place. Ease of identification has many benefits. It assists incident investigation. It allows enforcement agencies to monitor and penalise unlawful activity, both in terms of actions by or against the drone in question. It promotes systems where airworthiness or mechanical issues can be monitored and checked for compliance. Most importantly, it creates accountability for those responsible for the drone's activity, thereby promoting the safe and responsible use of drones and, in turn, minimising the risk of unlawful activity.

Licencing and certification requirements in relation to drone pilots and operators are also centred on issues of safety. Minimum standardised training and education obligations ensure that those individuals ultimately in control of the drones in our skies have a clear understanding of the authorised operating conditions, the limits on where and in what circumstances a drone can be flown, and the potential dangers associated with unlawful activity. Those precautions ultimately reduce the risk to public safety.

Despite the obvious importance of registration and licencing as part of an overall drone regulation framework, a consistent approach on a national level is yet to have been reached. In the Regulation chapters that follow, consideration is given to how various countries in different regions are currently addressing these issues and, where relevant, the likely future developments. There is also commentary on the discussions that are occurring at a multilateral level through organisations such as ICAO, with a view to promoting a common global framework.

Technology-based solutions

The final chapter dealing with regulation in Part D of this book, Chapter 19, looks at Technological Advances. As an Australian Senate Inquiry Committee noted,[33] the inte-

33 Senate Rural and Regional Affairs and Transport References Committee, Parliament of Australia, 'Regulatory Requirements that Impact on the Safe Use of Remotely Piloted Aircraft Systems, Unmanned Aerial Systems and Associated Systems' (Report, 31 July 2018); 89 [6.50] <www.aph.gov.

gration of RPAS into Australian airspace requires a balance between effective enforcement measures, such as sufficient penalties, registration and restricted flight zones, with that of technology-based solutions.

An example of this is Amazon's suggested solution:

> airspace could be segregated to ensure safe and efficient drone use. In this model, the area between 200 and 400 feet is reserved as a "drone highway" where drones operate autonomously and are equipped with "sense and avoid" technologies that allow them to dodge other vehicles and potential hazards like birds and tall buildings. If properly introduced, drones could be used for last mile freight delivery as well as the surveillance and rapid deployment of emergency personnel, maintenance crews or equipment.[34]

In relation to technology-based solutions there are an array of technologies currently being developed to enhance the safety mechanisms built into RPAS, including geo-fencing, collision avoidance, and other transponder-based systems such as Automatic Dependent Surveillance Broadcast (ADS-B).

Geo-fencing is technology that creates a virtual boundary to keep drones from entering restricted airspace and a large proportion of commercially available drones already include geo-fencing capabilities (software and data contained in the drone that can restrict it from flying in certain areas, such as airports).

Electronic conspicuity is another initiative which will allow the automatic identification of all airspace users, including drones. Aircraft equipped with electronic conspicuity equipment can actively signal their presence to other airspace users. Such devices also receive signals which can alert the pilot to other aircraft in the vicinity thus enabling the pilot to see that aircraft and to take action to avoid it. For example, ADS-B technology is an electronic system that allows an aircraft to automatically broadcast its precise location via a digital link. These and other technology-based solutions are discussed in Chapter 19.

---

au/Parliamentary_Business/Committees/Senate/Rural_and_Regional_Affairs_and_Transport/Drones/Report>.

34 See New South Wales Government, 'Transport for NSW: Future Transport Strategy 2056' (*New South Wales Government*, March 2018)66<https://future.transport.nsw.gov.au/sites/default/files/media/documents/2018/Future_Transport_2056_Strategy.pdf>.

14 Transnational organisations

Chris Morrison, Alan Kells, Julie-Anne Tarr and Anthony A. Tarr

Introduction

The European Commission[1] in a communication dated 9 December 2020 emphasised the necessity to put European transport on track for the future, the importance of a coordinated European approach to connectivity and transport activity to overcome crises such as the COVID-19 pandemic, and to strengthen the European Union's strategic autonomy and resilience.[2] In pursuit of these objectives the Commission recognises that "proactively shaping our future mobility by developing and validating new technologies and services is key to staying ahead of the curve"[3]. It commits to put in place favourable conditions for the development of new technologies and services, and all necessary legislative tools for their validation. Of particular significance to this book is the Commission's declaration that:[4]

> The Commission fully supports the deployment of drones and unmanned aircraft, and will further develop the relevant rules, including on the U-space,[5] to make it fit for enhancing safe and sustainable mobility. The Commission will also adopt a "Drone Strategy 2.0" setting out possible ways to guide the further development of this technology and its regulatory and commercial environment.

1 European Commission, 'Communication from the Commission to the European Parliament, The Council, The European Economic and Social Committee and the Committee of the Regions: Sustainable and Smart Mobility Strategy—Putting European Transport on Track for the Future Brussels' COM (2020) 789 final <https://ec.europa.eu/transport/sites/transport/files/legislation/com20200789.pdf>.

2 ibid paras 1–5.

3 ibid para 64.

4 ibid para 66.

5 U-space is a set of new services and specific procedures designed to support safe, efficient and secure access to airspace for large numbers of drones. These services rely on a high level of digitalization and automation of functions, whether they are onboard the drone itself, or are part of the ground-based environment. U-space provides an enabling framework to support routine drone operations, as well as a clear and effective interface to manned aviation, ATM/ANS service providers and authorities. U-space is therefore not to be considered as a defined volume of airspace, which is segregated and designated for the sole use of drones. U-space is capable of ensuring the smooth operation of drones in all operating environments, and in all types of airspace (in particular but not limited to very low level airspace). It addresses the needs to support all types of missions, and may concern all drone users and categories of drones. See 'U-Space Blueprint' (9 June 2017)<www.sesarju.eu/u-space-blueprint>.

The Commission acknowledged the emergence and wider use of drones (unmanned aircraft) for commercial applications, autonomous vehicles, hyperloop, hydrogen aircraft, electric personal air vehicles, electric waterborne transport and clean urban logistics in the near future and declared that:

> An enabling environment for such game-changing mobility technologies is key, so that the EU can become a prime deployment destination for innovators. Start-ups and technology developers need an agile regulatory framework to pilot and deploy their products. The Commission will work towards facilitating testing and trials, and towards making the regulatory environment fit for innovation, so as to support the deployment of solutions on the market. The Commission will drive the research and deployment of innovative and sustainable technologies in transport. Investment in disruptive solutions will pave the way for important breakthroughs and environmental gains in the years and decades to come.[6]

This is a very encouraging communication as coordinated action has the potential to drive international standards for drones akin to that for manned aviation and bring enormous benefits in terms of safety, efficiency of operations, uniform and technological innovations.

For the most part, as previously discussed, regulatory emphasis has understandably focussed on operational safety. Less attention and rigour has been applied to design standards which will also serve to improve safety. As has been stated previously, the speed with which the technology is developing presents difficulties for regulators in nailing down specified design standards. By the time these have been looked at, the technology has developed again. Moreover, one of the main reasons design standards languish is because regulators do not yet know what such standards look like. In order to achieve a suitable set of design standards, regulators will have to work closely with industry. This process of the regulator issuing a design standard or specification and then industry demonstrating a better way of doing things, resulting in an adjustment in the regulators' approach, is not new.

A very good example of this occurred in 1930 in the UK when the Air Ministry (AM) issued AM Specification F7/30 for a new and modern fighter which had to be capable of speeds of 250 miles/hour and had to be able to carry 4 machine guns. Of the seven designs tendered, only one aircraft was accepted as being suitable, the Gloster Gladiator biplane. A number of the other designs came close, but all had some deficiencies. One of the other designers embarked on a series of "cleaned-up" designs in an attempt to show the Air Ministry that he could meet the specification. In July 1934, he submitted a new aircraft design to the Air Ministry, which had a retractable undercarriage and a smaller wingspan, but again, it was rejected. The intrepid designer continued to persevere, and in December 1934, he presented yet another design. This time the Air Ministry accepted the design as being superior and issued contract AM 361140/34 and provided £10,000 for the construction of his improved F7/30 design. Then on 3 January 1935, the Air Ministry formalised the contract and issued a whole new specification, F10/35, which was written around that specific aircraft. The young aircraft designer was RJ Mitchell and the aircraft of course was the

6 European Commission (n 1) paras 64–65.

Spitfire. So, if aircraft designers keep putting their experimental UAS to the regulators, eventually there might be a "light-bulb" moment and everybody will know what a type certificated UAS looks like.

The ensuing paragraphs look at the work being undertaken by Transnational Organisations to achieve regulatory consistency, effectiveness and efficiency. The chapter also outlines work being done on recommending a single set of technical, safety and operational requirements for the certification and safe integration of drones into airspace and at aerodromes. For example, this chapter will review the ICAO draft regulatory framework and work of the European Union Aviation Safety Agency ("EASA") in some detail. Mention is also made of other transnational initiatives such as the Pacific Aviation Safety Office (PASO) and the Joint Authorities for Rulemaking on Unmanned Systems ("JARUS").[7]

International Civil Aviation Organisation (ICAO)

ICAO is a specialised agency of the United Nations funded and directed by 193 national governments to support their diplomacy and cooperation in air transport as signatory states to the Chicago Convention (1944).[8] ICAO is not an international aviation regulator and as such ICAO standards never supersede the primacy of national regulatory requirements. It is always the local, national regulations which are enforced in, and by, sovereign states, and which must be legally adhered to by air operators making use of applicable airspace and airports.

However, ICAO, with its Member States, has developed a draft regulatory framework for UAS[9] based upon a review of existing regulations in Member States in a bid to share best practices that can be implemented by countries seeking to improve, or introduce, UAS regulation. This has resulted in ICAO Model UAS Regulations Parts 101, 102 and 149. These Model Regulations are supported by Advisory Circulars (AC) which provide guidance to support the implementation of the Model Regulations.

The Model Regulations are targeted at the certification and safe operation of UAS. If adopted, they should help provide more certainty around operational and organisational requirements, making selection of UAS more straightforward for operators, while at the same time improving safety for the wider community. Given those countries that have already implemented legislation have understandably focussed on the safe operation of UAS, it is appropriate the draft ICAO regulations do likewise.

By limiting the scope to certification and safe operations, the Model Regulations allow for additional input from nations to further develop their regulations for specific

7 JARUS is a group of experts from National Aviation Authorities and regional aviation safety organisations that works on recommending a single set of technical, safety and operational requirements for the certification and safe integration of UAS into airspace and at aerodromes.

8 The Convention on International Civil Aviation, drafted in 1944 by 54 nations, was established to promote cooperation and "create and preserve friendship and understanding among the nations and peoples of the world." Known more commonly today as the Chicago Convention, this landmark agreement established the core principles permitting international transport by air, and led to the creation of the specialised agency which has overseen it ever since—the International Civil Aviation Organisation (ICAO) <www.icao.int/about-icao/History/Pages/default.aspx>.

9 ICAO, 'ICAO Model UAS Regulations: Introduction to ICAO Model UAS Regulations and Advisory Circulars' (*ICAO*, 20 January 2021) <www.icao.int/safety/UA/Pages/ICAO-Model-UAS-Regulations.aspx> [hereinafter "ICAO Model UAS Regulations and AC's"].

issues in each individual jurisdiction. For instance, by not attempting to address considerations such as privacy (a growing issue globally), insurance or economic authority, the Model Regulations leave it to the national jurisdictions to address these issues according to national requirements.

The Model Regulations do not define the purpose of the operation, namely whether it is for commercial or recreational use, on the assumption that the aviation-related risk posed by UA differs very little between a UA that is used for recreational, commercial or professional purposes.[10]

Further to commentary in Chapter 13 (Regulatory Overview) and Chapter 5 (Maritime Uses of Drones), the authors would challenge the accuracy of this assumption and suggest that it does not do justice to an effective additional layer of perspective required; that is, there is a significant aviation-related risk differential that needs to be addressed within the individual layers of recreational, commercial or professional operations, which in turn poses a direct challenge to the appropriateness of placing all operational purposes in the same basket.

In any event, the Model Regulations in their present form are separated into three parts in which consideration has been given to the layering of the aviation-related risks. Part 101 is aimed at lower risk operations, UA 25 kg or less which can be operated within restricted parameters. Part 102 is directed towards those UA which are not covered within Part 101, UA weighing more than 25 kg or those operations considered as more high risk such as night-time flights or in proximity to people and structures. Part 149 sets out draft regulations for the certification and operation of Approved Aviation Organisations, which it is envisaged will undertake tasks such as issuing competency certificates to operators, approving UAS for use and authorising UAS operations. A third category of UAS operations is under development by ICAO. This third category will cover international Instrument Flight Rules operations.

Part 101

Part 101 is aimed at those lower risk operations to ensure safety whilst at the same time reducing the regulatory and administrative burdens on operators. It applies to those UA weighing between 15 and 25 kg. Where the operation cannot comply with Part 101, whether because the UA is heavier than 25 kg or it is to be used in what are viewed as more high-risk operations, such as at night, in the proximity of people or structures or beyond visual line of sight, then the operator must comply with the more stringent requirements under Part 102. It is anticipated that most current commercial operations will be capable of compliance with this Part.

The operations deemed lower risk for the purposes of Part 101 are daylight operations within the visual line of sight of the operator (or observer in direct communication with the operator), which take place in a location away from people, structures and other air traffic. The key requirements are that the UAS is registered with the authority and inspected/approved by a reputable organisation. Given the lower risk nature of these operations, there is no requirement for the operator to obtain a remote

10 ibid AC 101-1 p 6.

pilot's licence[11] or for the specific operation to be authorised by the authority. We will consider some of these key factors in more detail in the following.

The key features for operating under the lower regulatory burdens of this Part includes registration, operating conditions, operator obligations and the UAS itself.

Registration

The requirement to register the UAS and hold a valid certificate of registration:

> *allows identification of the aircraft and owner and provides the [authority] with data regarding the industry. Registration is also a way to record experience with a particular model of UA should the operator elect to expand operations into [Part 102].*[12]

Mandatory registration would provide considerable benefits. As the use of UA becomes more prevalent, so too does the potential for accidents. If someone suffering damage/injury as a result of UA operation is unable to identify the operator, they will have difficulty securing recompense. It further enables information to be obtained and studied around UA use in particular areas and about the operational performance of specific models in various operational conditions. As noted by the ICAO in the Advisory Circular it further serves to provide the authority with details on the operational background of an operator, such as any accident or incidents (required to be reported under Part 101 where injury or property damage is sustained[13]; however, we would expect most states to go further, requiring near misses and operational failures to also be reported), should that operator apply for authorisation to undertake higher risk operations (under Part 102).

Given the primary concern with the new technology will be safety, registration and contact information will also allow for the inspection of a UAS by the relevant authority to ensure compliance.[14]

Operating conditions

The Model Regulations set out *standard unmanned aircraft operating conditions*[15] (which can alter in certain circumstances) allowing UAS to be operated under the reduced administrative and regulatory burdens of Part 101. These include:

- UA to be operated in the visual line of sight of the operator (or UA observer in direct communication with the operator).
    - This is not a specified distance but involves taking account of views of the surrounding airspace and weather conditions which could affect this.
    - The UA is to remain visible within the normal range of sight of the operator (with glasses/contact lenses if used) but the introduction of additional

11 ibid 101.41(a).
12 ibid AC 101-1 p 8.
13 ibid 101.009.
14 ibid 101.007(3).
15 ibid 101.7.

electrical/mechanical aids or similar equipment such as binoculars or a telescope to improve vision is not permitted.
- If used, the observer must maintain visual line of sight of the UA and surrounding airspace and be in *direct communication* with the operator. The purpose of this is to allow the operator to take immediate corrective action; therefore it would be sensible to have backup means of communication in the event the primary means fails.

- At or below 400 feet.
  - If above this height approval is needed under Part 102.
- During daylight.
  - Only in Visual Meteorological Conditions therefore pre-flight weather checks are key.
- Not within airspace 30 m (horizontally) of a person not associated with the operation or who has not given consent (unless in airspace of approved aviation organisation and approved by that organisation).
  - Exceptions include persons inside a structure/vehicle which can provide a degree of protection.[16]
  - If the person has consented, the distance is reduced to within 15 m horizontally.[17]
  - It is important to note that consent is only one aspect of risk mitigation[18] and that the ICAO is clear consent does not obviate issues around local legislation relating to privacy and nuisance.[19]
- Not over restricted/prohibited areas.
  - The Part makes provision to restrict use around airports and populated areas, but also allows for national governments to impose further restricted areas—for example, military bases, utility infrastructure, roads or to set policies for parks and similar public spaces such as the ordinance in *Singer*[20] (discussed in chapter 13) which concerned a prohibition of UA use over public land amongst other locations. In that case the legislation was struck down; however, more limited restrictions, such as over a specific park, could well be upheld.
- Not over an emergency services operation.[21]
- Operator is only operating that single UA.[22]
- Give way to aircraft.[23]

16 ibid 101.35 (b).
17 ibid 101.35 (d).
18 ibid AC 101-1 11.
19 ibid.
20 *Singer v. City of Newton*, 284 F. Supp. 3d 125, 128 (D. Mass. 2017).
21 ICAO Model UAS Regulations and AC's (n 9) 101.7(c).
22 ibid 101.7(d).
23 ibid 101.33.

- Not within 4 km of a controlled aerodrome.[24]
  - The exceptions to this include the operator to be the holder, or under the supervision, of a qualified pilot (remote or manned), or approved by an approved organisation and to have knowledge of airspace.[25] Given that the risks to aviation are highest in these locations the ICAO suggests the operator or supervisor should have: "*The ability to read and understand an aeronautical chart identifying restricted, military operating and danger areas, as well as controlled airspace would be an acceptable means of demonstrating an awareness of airspace designations and restrictions required*"[26] which may come from an approved organisation, flight school or qualified pilot.

Operator obligations

While there is no requirement for the operator to obtain a certification of competency, there is a requirement on the operator to understand the airspace they are operating in which will include checking for restrictions pre-flight and being aware of them. If operating a UA within 4 km of an aerodrome knowledge of the use of aeronautical charts and airspace is required.[27]

There is an overriding obligation on the operator to take all practicable steps to minimise hazards.[28] A corollary can be drawn with workplace health and safety legislation which places similar requirements on employers and those responsible for workplace operations to take *reasonably practicable* measures to protect from risks arising from the work. In certain jurisdictions, notably the UK, such legislation carries a reverse burden of proof, providing that following a workplace incident, the onus is on the person or organisation with the duty to demonstrate that such steps were in fact taken. This makes taking enforcement action against the duty holder more straightforward than might otherwise be the case. Should this be incorporated into domestic legislation, it will mean operators could face an uphill struggle to defend themselves following an incident unless the very highest standards have been observed.

The Model Regulations set out prohibitions on use in a careless or reckless manner as well as while operating another vehicle[29] or when under the influence of alcohol or drugs.[30] It is expected states will implement criminal penalties for breaches of these types as is currently the case with other forms of machinery.

UAS

The Part applies only to UA weighing 15–25 kg. Any UA over this weight requires approval under the more stringent requirements of Part 102.[31] The Model Regulations envisage the use of approved bodies or individuals for issuing operator's quali-

24 ibid 101.7(b)(4).
25 ibid AC 101-1 p 5.
26 ibid AC 101-1 p 9.
27 ibid 101.41.
28 ibid 101.17(a).
29 ibid 101.43.
30 ibid 101.45.
31 ibid 101.37(a).

fications (for Part 102 type operations), as well as authorising and approving UAS for use. These bodies will have to apply for, and be granted approval by, the relevant authority.

The UAS (and any modification) has to be either constructed by/under the authority of, or be inspected and approved by, an *Approved Person* or *Approved Organisation*[32] or have a *Declaration of Compliance* issued by the manufacturer and accepted by the national authority.[33] A key point for end users is the requirement for any modification to be approved; therefore, buying an approved version off the shelf and fitting tools, cameras or other devices is likely to lead to further approval being required. Despite this requirement, the regulatory burden remains low. Provided the declaration or approval is in place (which with a relevant declaration it will be when bought off the shelf), these UA "*do not require authorisation. . . to operate*".[34]

In respect of UA weighing under 15 kg the approval or declaration is not required. The reason for the distinction at 15 kg is that this provides "*additional division . . .* [providing] *. . .additional flexibility to delineate between UA that warrant additional scrutiny without requiring additional remote pilot qualifications*".[35]

Despite the lack of recognised standards, regulations which would be expected to cover these operations as well as other safety legislation, will likely require the operator to consider the UA's suitability for its intended use, maintenance and operation in accordance with the manufacturer's instructions, pre-flight checks and risk mitigation.

The ability to operate under this Part is helpfully summarised in the AC with the key elements[36] set out as follows:

(1) operate a UA that weighs [25 kg or less] and always ensure that it is safe to operate;
(2) assure that UA weighing more than [15 kg] and [25 kg or less] has been approved under the authority of an AAO, or a Declaration of Compliance is on record with the CAA;
(3) take all steps practicable to minimise hazards to persons, property and other aircraft (i.e. don't do anything hazardous);
(4) fly only in daylight;
(5) give way to all manned aircraft;
(6) be able to see the UA with your own eyes (e.g. not through binoculars, a monitor, or smartphone), which also applies to a UA observer;
(7) maintain flight at or below [120 m (400 ft)] above ground level (AGL) (unless certain conditions are met);
(8) have knowledge of airspace restrictions that apply in the area of operation;
(9) fly no closer than [4 km] from any aerodrome (unless certain conditions are met)';
(10) obtain an air traffic control (ATC) clearance issued by the local ATC unit, if planning to fly in controlled airspace;

32 ibid 101.37(b)(1).
33 ibid 101.37(b)(3) and 102.301.
34 ibid AC 101-1 p 6.
35 ibid AC 101-1 p 5.
36 ibid AC 101-1 p 6–7.

(11) *remain clear of special-use airspace unless permission is given by the administering authority of the area (e.g. restricted or military operating areas);*
(12) *obtain consent from anyone you plan to fly above; and*
(13) *obtain consent from the property owner or person in charge of the area you plan to fly above.*

Part 102

This Part of the Model Regulations is designed for higher risk operations, which are those not capable of operating under the standard conditions of Part 101, whether through size of the UA (+25 kg including any payload carried)[37] or because of the nature of the operating environment; for example, at night, beyond visual line of sight, etc. The aim is to be:

> *flexible in that very few activities are prohibited. Instead . . . authorisation . . . will be granted on a case-by-case basis once the [authority] is satisfied that the operator has identified the hazards associated with the intended operation(s) and the associated consequences and has a plan in place to mitigate those risks.*[38]

The key therefore is the assessment by the national authority and the risk mitigation measures that can be put in place which will convince the national authority the proposed operations can take place safely. Not surprisingly, the safety aspect remains the key issue.

In order to operate under the perceived greater risk conditions of Part 102, key features include the competency of the operator, risk mitigation measures and the safety of the UA itself. These factors will allow the national authority to assess the request for permission and authorise as appropriate.

Operator competency

For operations that fall outside of the Part 101 arrangements, it is envisaged the operator will obtain a remote pilot's licence[39] ("RPL") which will require both general aviation knowledge and knowledge of the UAS being operated. There are a number of ways it is proposed individuals can demonstrate these requirements. A RPL applicant must be at least 16 years of age. The two-step process will involve:

- Step 1—general aviation knowledge (one of):
    - aeronautical knowledge examination; or
    - aviation theory examination; or
    - remote pilot theory examination; or
    - an acceptable foreign equivalent.

37 ibid AC102-1 p 10.
38 ibid AC 101-1 p 5.
39 ibid 102.1.

For these purposes it is envisaged any of the following currently held will be sufficient: a flight crew licence or military equivalent; a foreign RPL that meets the country's RPL requirements; or an air traffic control licence or military equivalent.

- Step 2—knowledge of UA operating (one of):
  - RP training course in category of UA operator will use; or
  - manufacturer's training course for category of UA; or
  - regulator's flight test; and
  - have demonstrated the competencies required for the safe operation of the applicable type of UAS and associated control station, under standard operating conditions.

In order to allow the authority to assess competency adequately, the application for a RPL is to be made in writing (or other specified means) confirming and evidencing qualifications, examinations and training courses completed as well as aeronautical and UAS experience.[40] Given the potential varied operations and skill levels, the Model Regulations envisage the possibility of conditions being placed upon RPL,[41] limiting the types of UAS, areas and conditions of operation.

Unless otherwise indicated, it is proposed standard conditions will be applicable to all RPL, such as not to operate above 400 feet or within 4 km of the movement area of an aerodrome without additional qualifications such as a flight crew or air traffic control licence or military equivalent.[42] In addition, it is a condition of a RPL that a UA shall not operate outside of visual line of sight without additional qualifications and approvals,[43] and the licence holder shall not operate more than one UA at a time without approval.[44]

As would be expected, licences can be cancelled or suspended.[45] The authority must give notice and consider any representations by the licence holder.[46] The Model Regulations posit the following reasons the licence may be revoked (which may of course be further built upon by national authorities):

- operating a UA in contravention of regulations or a licence condition;
- operating a UA negligently or carelessly; or
- recklessly endangering life or property.

Further, for organisations operating outside of Part 101, it is proposed an Unmanned Aircraft System Operator Certification will be required.[47] This will include an organisational role of Chief Remote Pilot[48] to ensure a dedicated individual responsible for safe operations. This person's responsibilities will include ensuring the operator

40 ibid 102.3.
41 ibid 102.5.
42 ibid 102.5(b).
43 ibid 102.5(c).
44 ibid 102.5(d).
45 ibid 102.9.
46 ibid 102.11.
47 ibid 102.13(a)(1).
48 ibid 102.17.

remains compliant with aviation regulations, record keeping, monitoring operational standards and the proficiency of individual and operators and maintaining a complete and up-to-date reference library of operational documents required by the authority for the types of operations conducted by the operator. The identification of an individual to undertake this role envisages a considerable degree of responsibility and potential liability upon the Chief Remote Pilot.

Risk mitigation

By way of example, we will look at some of the specific category operations[49] which a RPL and authorisation will be required for.

Night operations—the availability of aircraft lighting/aids to ensure the UA is visible to other UA operations or manned aircraft; thought must be given to how visual contact with the aircraft will be maintained; the areas of proposed operations; the risks to persons or property on the ground; and how notification of UA flights will be made to emergency services in the area.[50]

Crowds/congested areas—the application will be expected to confirm the identification of the hazards and risks, including those that might be exacerbated by people being present; the configuration of the aircraft (fixed wing versus multi rotor, etc.); reliability of the UA (to include manufacturer's declaration); reliability of the control system; mitigations in place in the event of any system failure; system redundancy (such as an acceptable automatic recovery parachute); and, if practicable, the steps the operator proposes to obtain the consent of or to give notice to people affected by the operation.[51]

Proximity of buildings or structures—if people are present or in close proximity, this may also be hazardous. If the UA is used close to buildings, additional concerns will need to be addressed, such as procedures for dealing with the impact into a structure or object; and crowd/access control to ensure a safety perimeter in the event the aircraft falls to the ground.[52]

Beyond visual line of sight—it is expected VLS will be standard for the foreseeable future. For BVLOS operations, *a strong safety case*[53] in the application will be required.

Other scenarios include (but are not limited to) above 400 feet and within 4 km of an aerodrome. Carrying dangerous or hazardous items[54] is supported by its own AC.[55]

UAS safety

In addition to the requirements placed on the operator, more stringent requirements are also to be placed on the UAS itself for these higher risk operations. Requirements

49 ibid 102.19.
50 ibid AC 102-1 p 10.
51 ibid 101.35.
52 ibid AC 102-1 p 11.
53 ibid.
54 ibid AC 102-37 p 4, 'Articles or substances that are capable of posing a hazard to health, safety, property or the environment'.
55 ICAO Model UAS Regulations and AC's (n 9) AC 102-37.

in respect of the UAS are imposed both upon the operator when the authority is considering its application for authorisation, and upon the manufacturer, which will be obliged to provide documentation and details to both the authority and operator. The requirement for manufacturers to publish safety data appears to be growing and we can expect further obligations to be placed upon them by regulators as the availability and use of UAS continues to grow.

The key requirement is for the UAS to be registered with the authority, enabling data collection by the authority on UAS use and operations, as well as feedback on specific designs and models, and for the operator to be identified in the event of an incident. This can be further strengthened by a condition of an authorisation requiring identification markings.[56]

The UAS is required to be:

- Designed, produced or modified such that it does not contain any safety defects identified by the authority.
- Display a label indicating eligibility to conduct operations in the specific category (in English, legible and permanently affixed to the UA).
- Have current remote pilot operating instructions for the operation of the UAS. There is an obligation on the person who designed, produced or modified the UAS to make available the instructions upon sale, transfer or use of the UA by someone else. Such instructions shall address, as a minimum:
    - A system description that includes the required UAS components, any system limitations, and the declared category or categories of operation.
    - Permitted modifications that will not change the ability of the UAS to meet the requirements for the category or categories of operation it is eligible for.
    - Instructions that explain how to verify and change the mode or configuration of the UA, if they are variable.
- Operated only after the person who designed, produced, or modified the UAS has received notification that the authority has accepted the Declaration of Compliance or received an approval from an approved aviation organisation.
- Have a current aircraft registration.[57]

Separately, the manufacturer must make a declaration to the national authority specifying the manufacturer of the UAS, the model of the system, the maximum take-off weight of the UA, the operations that the UA is intended to undertake and the category of UA; as well as specifying that the system meets the means of compliance applicable to the operations for which the declaration was made.[58] The means of compliance shall consist of data (tests, analysis, industry consensus standards) and the results or justification used to demonstrate the UAS meets the predetermined level of safety the authority has established as acceptable.[59]

56 ibid 102.25.
57 ibid 102.19.
58 ibid 102.307.
59 ibid 102.305.

There is also an obligation to report to the authority if the UAS is found to no longer be compliant.[60]

In addition, the manufacturer is required to provide specified documentation to owners.[61] The purpose is to allow the owners to operate UAS safely. These include:

- A maintenance programme that includes instructions for the servicing and maintenance of the system, and an inspection programme to maintain system readiness.
- Any mandatory actions the manufacturer issues in respect of the system.
- A UAS operating manual that includes details of safe operating conditions, the impact of foreseeable weather conditions, safety features and warnings which will be provided in the event of unsafe system operating conditions.

Authorisation

The application by the operator to the authority is required to be made in writing with details of[62]:

- The person with primary responsibility for operations (placing scope for individual criminal or civil liability on this person).
    - The AC suggests providing an organisation chart to clearly set out responsibilities.[63]
    - It is suggested the person will require:

      knowledge of the aviation regulatory environment and experience in the transport industry, it is anticipated that the primary person(s) may undergo evaluations such as a criminal background check, driving records review, compliance with transport safety regulatory requirements, conviction record for transport safety offences, pilot records history or other pertinent aviation records reports.[64]

    - Those who will/likely have control of the privileges of the certificate—that is, those controlling flights, maintenance or training.
- Locations of use.
- An operational risk assessment considering the known and likely hazards to people, property and aircraft and details the mitigation/control measures.
    - Understandably the safety management system requirement is key. This will include a written safety policy, risk management processes, internal reporting, investigation and learning from incidents and accidents, measuring attainment against set goals and internal audits and reviews. Further requirements include the training of staff and documented processes.[65]

60 ibid 102.309.
61 ibid 102.311.
62 ibid 102.23.
63 ibid AC 102-1 p 15.
64 ibid.
65 ibid 102.49.

- Reporting process for accidents, incidents and near misses.
  - Not just injury or property damage but fly away and loss of control, mechanical failures and incursion into unauthorised airspace are envisaged.[66]
- Licencing and training requirements for operators.
- Details of UAS to be used, including identifiers (colour schemes etc.).
- Control system.
  - The C2 or Command and Control link.
  - Currently, there are no design standards or configuration requirements that apply to UAS control systems. Work is progressing internationally by RTCA, to develop standards in this area, but this is yet to be completed.
- Maintenance, etc.
  - Pre- and post-flight inspections, regular inspections, retirement life, responsibility, compliance with manufacturer's service requirements, damage tolerance criteria (i.e. when components such as a propeller must be changed).[67]

The suggestion is that the authority will take a holistic approach, looking:

> *at the people involved in the operation, the aircraft, and the scope of the operation. The [authority] must be satisfied that the operation is safe, and that the operator is able to mitigate and control the safety risks before issuing the authorisation.*[68]

It is proposed an authorisation will last for three years or shorter if determined to be appropriate by the authority.[69] The certificate holder has responsibility to make all those operating on its behalf aware of the general operating requirements and its conditions and limitations.[70] Records must be kept of operators and crew members, flights, maintenance operations, that pass over on sale/transfer and such records are retained for inspection by the authority.[71]

The authorisation can be suspended[72] or revoked[73] for the same reasons as under Part 101—a breach of regulations or condition of the certificate; a person engaged/employed has operated a UA negligently or carelessly; or a person engaged/employed by the operator has recklessly endangered human life or property by operating a UA.

There is a requirement on those employed to assist by complying with specified practices and procedures[74] akin to legislation to follow employer's instructions in workplace safety legislation.[75]

66 ibid AC 102-1 p 16.
67 ibid AC 102-1 p 20.
68 ibid AC 102-1 p 14.
69 ibid 102.31.
70 ibid 102.33(b).
71 ibid 102.39.
72 ibid 102.41.
73 ibid 102.43.
74 ibid 102.45.
75 For example, see the Health and Safety at Work etc. Act 1974 (UK), s 7.

Overall, the key requirement for authorisation is whether the operator performs the envisaged operation safely. We expect authorities to be initially reluctant to go too far outside the scope of the standard operating conditions envisaged in Part 101 without a good safety case. As use becomes more prevalent, design and safety features become standardised, and authorities become more used to seeing UA operated safely without incident, authorisation is likely to be more relaxed; however, those trailblazers may find authorities initially reluctant to authorise operations beyond the norm.

Part 149

There is currently no supporting AC for this Part. It deals with the certification and operation of Approved Aviation Organisations ("AAO"). As mentioned briefly earlier, an AAO will be approved by the national authority of a country to undertake tasks such as issuing competency certificates to operators, authorising instructors, inspecting and approving the construction of UAS as well as any other task approved by the relevant national authority.[76]

In order to be deemed competent to be an AAO, the organisation must make an application in writing demonstrating it is a competent organisation to exercise these privileges. This will include a check on personnel,[77] resources and facilities,[78] documentation (to include equipment manuals, technical standards and legislation),[79] processes for assessing the competency of operators[80] and an internal safety management system.[81] As would perhaps be expected, there is significantly more detail around the safety management system requirements than other factors. That system includes relevant policies and procedures, quality monitoring, processes for corrective and preemptive actions to address any issues, an internal audit requirement and a management review.

European Union and the European Aviation Safety Agency (EASA)

The European Commission lay new foundations for European UAS regulation commencing 31 December 2020 by promulgating two delegated regulations on the systems of unmanned aircraft, drones or UAS and on their rules and procedures for use. These are the Delegated Regulation (EU) 2019/945 of the Commission of 12 March 2019 and Implementing Regulation (EU) 2019/947 of the Commission of 24 May 2019.

These EU Regulations are interesting in that they seek to address not just safety issues, but wider concerns around privacy, security and data protection.[82] They also go further by considering product safety and design requirements.[83]

76 ICAO Model UAS Regulations and AC's (n 9) 149.9.
77 ibid 149.21.
78 ibid 149.23.
79 ibid 149.25.
80 ibid 149.29.
81 ibid 149.33.
82 See Council Regulation (EU) 2016/679 of 27 April 2016 on the protection of natural persons with regard to the processing of personal data and on the free movement of such data, and repealing Directive 95/46/EC (General Data Protection Regulation) OJ L119/1 (GDPR) and detailed discussion in Chapter 10.
83 See below re Design.

The Regulations were enacted to replace most of the existing domestic or national provisions on drone operations in EU member states, to in effect create a homogenisation of drone-related legislation across the EU reducing the variety of operational requirements, obligations and restrictions between Member States. They also encourage drone operators to freely circulate within the EU without further registration or paperwork required.

The key agency of the EU in this context is EASA which was established by the EU in 2002 with the aim of ensuring safety and environmental protection within the European Union. Its goals in relation to UAS include *managing the safe introduction of UAS into the airspace*[84] as well as the admirable goal of simplifying the regulatory sphere by adopting a single regulatory and certification process among Member States.[85] Such a clear transnational policy will be of assistance in aiding the development of both safety and technology as well as simplifying the process for operators across the EU.

Despite the harmonisation of rules, Member States will be free to define "zones" within their respective airspace to restrict drone operations. Hence, the flight zones will still be designated and regulated by respective national legislation. Any registrations or authorisations required under the harmonised rules will also be implemented at the national level.

The system of regulation is based upon the registration of operators enabling identification in the event of an incident and for data to be collected to track UAS use and aid in the development of standards and regulations. The operator will need to be registered with the national civil aviation authority of the country of operation as well as displaying a sticker on the UA showing this and uploading it to the UA's remote identification system.[86]

In a similar vein to the ICAO Model Regulations, the EU Regulations seek to target the heaviest regulatory burden at the areas of highest perceived risk while maintaining a relatively light touch approach to those operations considered lower risk. It does this by the separation of operations into three categories:

- i Open—low-risk operations not requiring authorisation or declaration before flight.
- ii Specific—medium-risk operation requiring authorisation by the competent authority pre-flight, taking into account the mitigation measures identified in an operational risk assessment; or a pre-flight declaration for certain standard scenarios[87]; or when the operator holds a light UAS operator certificate with the appropriate privileges; or under the auspices of a model aircraft club/association.
- iii Certified—high-risk operation requiring a certification process consisting of: (i) the certification of the UAS, (ii) a licenced remote pilot and (iii) an operator approved by the national competent authority.[88]

Based on market needs, priority has been given to the development of Acceptable Means of Compliance (AMC) and the Guide Material (GM) for operations in the "Open" and

84 EASA, 'The European Plan for Aviation Safety (EPAS) 2020–2024' (13 November 2019) 14.1.

85 The UK will be treated as a Member State until 31 December 2020 under the terms of its withdrawal agreement. Following this it will be treated as a Third Country, subject to any subsequent agreement.

86 Article 14 EU Regulation 2019/947.

87 Annex EU Regulation 2019/947.

88 Article 3 EU Regulation 2019/947.

"Specific" categories and on 17 December 2020 EASA published Special Condition Light Unmanned Aircraft Systems—Medium Risk.[89] This Special Condition prescribes detailed airworthiness standards covering structures, design and construction, lift/thrust/power system installation, and systems and installation.[90] The obligations are very extensive and are broadly applicable to unmanned aircraft under 600 kg, with most drones currently under certification in EASA anticipated to adopt this certification basis.[91]

The framework for operations in the "Certified" category is currently under development.

Open

The Open or lower risk operations requiring operator registration but no further authorisation or declaration pre-flight can be undertaken in the following circumstances:

- The UA bears one of the CE class marks 0–4[92]; or is privately built and with a weight less than 25 kg; or is purchased before 1 January 2023, with no CE class marking.[93]
- It will not be operated directly over people unless it bears a CE class mark or is lighter than 250 g.
- Visual line of sight will be maintained by the operator or UA observer.
- It is flown at a maximum altitude of 120 m.
- It will not carry dangerous goods or drop any material.[94]

The Open category is broken down further into separate categories of permission (A1–A3) subject to the UAS and the intended area of operation, with specific focus on the weight of the UA and the proximity of people and buildings. Heavier UA are required to keep a greater distance from populated areas and will require additional training for the operator based on the potential consequences of a failure. A UA weighing less than 250 g requires no additional training and can fly over people (category A1) whereas a UA between 4 and 25 kg (category A3) requires the completion of an online training course.

A1

- Includes privately built UA of less than 250 g,[95] Class C0 (up to 250 g) and C1 (up to 900 g)[96] and other commercially built UA weighing less than 250 g that were placed on the market prior to 1 July 2022.[97]

89 This document in EASA's terminology describes the Acceptable Means of Compliance (ACM) and Guidance Material (GM) for the specific category. See <www.easa.europa.eu/sites/default/files/dfu/special_condition_sc_light-uas_medium_risk_01.pdf>.

90 ibid, Subparts C, D, E and F.

91 'EASA Publishes Proposed Standards for Certification of Light Drones' (20 July 2020) <www.easa.europa.eu/newsroom-and-events/press-releases/easa-publishes-proposed-standards-certification-light-drones>.

92 See Design below for further.

93 UA without CE marking may operate until 1 January 2021 according to the requirements in Article 22 EU Regulation 2019/947.

94 Article 4 EU Regulation 2019/947.

95 With a maximum operating speed of less than 19m/s, see UAS.OPEN.020 (5)(a) (Annex).

96 See Design section in Chapter 14.

97 EU Regulation 2019/947, Annex Part A, UAS.OPEN.020 (5)(b) & Regulation (20)(a).

- Permits UA weighing less than 250 g to overfly uninvolved people (but not crowds),[98] but requires heavier UA permitted to operate under this classification (250–900 g) to remain 50 m from people.
- The competency requirements[99] include familiarisation with the manufacturer's manual for UA weighing up to 250 g. For those heavier UA (C1), an online training course is required followed by a multiple-choice examination, including questions on the following topics—air safety, airspace restrictions, aviation regulation, human performance limitations, operational procedures, UAS general knowledge, privacy and data protection, insurance and security.

A2

- Covers class C2 UA (weighing less than 4 kg).[100]
- Requires the UA to remain at least 30 m from uninvolved persons, which can be reduced to 5 m where the UA operates an active low-speed mode after the remote pilot has evaluated the safety of doing so by considering weather conditions, performance of the UA and the segregation of the overflown area.[101]
- Given the heavier UA involved and the potential for flying in close proximity to people, unsurprisingly, there are additional competency requirements when compared to the A1 category. The requirements are:
  - Familiarisation with the manufacturer's manual.
  - Remote pilot certification—obtained following an online training course and examination (as per the A1 C1 requirements mentioned earlier), self-practical training, and further examination aimed at assessing the remote pilot's knowledge of the technical and operational mitigations for ground risks.[102]

A3

- UA operating under this subcategory include C2 (up to 4 kg), C3 (up to 25 kg and dimensions of up to 3 m) and C4[103] (up to 25 kg), privately built UAS weighing less than 25 kg[104] and other commercially built UA weighing less than 25 kg which were placed on the market prior to 1 July 2022.[105]
- Operations are to be conducted in an area the remote pilot reasonably expects to be one where no uninvolved person will be endangered within the flight range.[106] In addition, operations must also be at least 150 m (horizontal) from residential, commercial or recreational areas.[107]
- In light of the greater distance from people and structures, the competency requirements are reduced from A2. This subcategory requires the online training course

98 ibid UAS.OPEN.020 (2).
99 ibid UAS.OPEN.020 (4).
100 and operated with active and updated direct remote identification and geo-awareness system—EU Regulation 2019/947, Annex Part A, UAS.OPEN.030 (3).
101 EU Regulation 2019/947, Annex Part A, UAS.OPEN.030 (1).
102 ibidUAS.OPEN.030 (2).
103 ibidUAS.OPEN.040 (4)(c)-(e).
104 ibidUAS.OPEN.040 (4)(a).
105 ibidUAS.OPEN.040 (4)(b).
106 ibidUAS.OPEN.040 (1).
107 ibidUAS.OPEN.040 (3).

(as per A1, C1 and A2) and the self-practical training required by A2, but not the subsequent examination.

While the A2 category involves freedom to operate in closer proximity to people, it is perhaps the A3 category that causes the greatest difficulties for the remote pilot. It is the responsibility of the remote pilot to operate in an area they reasonably expect to be away from people. This could cause difficulties for pilots operating in more remote locations and across wider geographical areas. While they may not expect people to be present, is that expectation "*reasonable*" in the circumstances? If a pilot operates a UAS in a rural location in the vicinity of a seldom-used public right of way, is the pilot's expectation that people will not be present reasonable or should operations be moved to another category? The requirement to stay 150 m from residential, commercial and recreational areas, could present a similar problem. The former two are likely to be more easily monitored, but the latter may cause issues. It is now a criminal offence for a remote pilot to breach these (and other) obligations of the Regulations if the pilot does not "*reasonably hold[s] the view*"[108] that they are met. For this reason it would be sensible for remote pilots operating under this category to record the reasons for their expectations pre-flight, in the event they are challenged on this point at a later date.

If the operation does not fulfil the aforementioned criteria, it must be operated in the Specific or Certified category[109] requiring authorisations and the input of a national competent authority.

Specific

An approval from, or declaration to, the national competent authority will be required to operate in the Specific category. The four routes to operating under the category are:

1. The preparation and submission of a risk assessment[110]; or
2. Hold a Light UAS Operator Certificate ("LUC") enabling an operator to authorise its own operations[111]; or
3. Hold a model aircraft club authorisation from the CAA[112]; or
4. Submit a declaration to the national competent authority that the flight falls within a *standard scenario*.[113]

Standard scenarios

Should the operator be capable of operating within specified *standard scenarios* then an authorisation is not required, simply a declaration that the requirements of the specific scenario have been met.

108 Air Navigation Order 2016, Article265.
109 Articles 4 and 20 of EU Regulation 2019/947; Annex part A and Article 5(1) of EU Regulation 2019/947, Part1 to 5 Annex of EU regulation 2019/945.
110 EU Regulation 2019/947 Articles 5(1) & (2) and 12.
111 ibid Article 5(6)(a) .
112 ibid Article 5(6)(b) .
113 ibid Article 5(5).

The *standard scenarios* are yet to be implemented; however, it is proposed that these will be added to Appendix 1 of the Regulations in due course.[114] There are two proposed standard scenarios: (i) STS-01—VLOS operations at a maximum altitude of 120 m and ground speed of less than 5 m/s with a UA up to 25 kg in areas that can include urban environments (an extension of Open subcategory A2 to heavier UA) and (ii) STS-02—BVLOS operations with an observer with the same additional requirements as STS-01.[115]

The declaration is made to the competent authority by the operator providing administrative information about the operator, a statement that the requirements of the standard scenario are complied with, a commitment to comply with relevant mitigation measures and that appropriate insurance cover will be in place where required.[116] In addition to confirming compliance with the relevant standard scenario, the declaration should also contain confirmation as to which of the following are applicable:

- UAS with:
  - Dimensions up to 3 m in VLOS over controlled ground area except over assemblies of people.
  - Dimensions up to 1 m in VLOS except over assemblies of people.
  - Dimensions up to 1 m in BVLOS over sparsely populated areas.
  - Dimensions up to 3 m in BVLOS over controlled ground area.
- Operations below 120 m, and:
  - In uncontrolled airspace (class F or G); or
  - In controlled airspace after coordination and individual flight authorisation in accordance with published procedures for the area of operation.

The competent authority will verify the declaration is correct and provide the operator with confirmation "*without undue delay*".[117] Once this confirmation is received from the competent authority, the operator can commence operations.[118] There remains an obligation on the operator to notify the competent authority of any changes in the declaration submitted.[119]

Operators will undoubtedly want to see if their operations can be brought within a *standard scenario* as this negates the need to apply for, and obtain, an authorisation from the national competent authority. It will be important that care is taken by operators so that it can properly be demonstrated the operation falls within one of the scenarios. If it cannot, to avoid repeated applications to the national competent authority it may be appropriate to consider obtaining a LUC.

114 The standard scenarios will be incorporated into Appendix 1 of EU Regulation 2019/947.

115 EASA, 'Standard Scenarios for UAS Operations in the "Specific Category" (Opinion No 05/2019)<www.easa.europa.eu/sites/default/files/dfu/Opinion%20No%2005-2019.pdf>.

116 'Responsibilities of the UAS operator', UAS SPEC.050 (Annex).

117 EU Regulation 2019/947, para 3 & Art. 12(5).

118 EU Regulation 2019/947, Annex UAS.SPEC.050 para 4.

119 ibid para 5.

Authorisation

In order to obtain authorisation from the competent national authority, the operator needs to demonstrate to the authority that its operation(s) can be conducted safely taking account of the UAS, operation and competencies of those involved. In order to do so the operator is required to submit a risk assessment for evaluation.

That assessment should describe the proposed operation(s) and adequate safety objectives, identifying the risks both on the ground and in the air along with a range of possible mitigation measures, selecting those measures which allow "*that the operation can be conducted safely*" in light of the risks inherent in the operation, the UAS itself, and risks to persons and property.[120]

The description of the operation is required to include detail of the activities involved, the operating environment and geographical area with particular focus on populations, terrain and the airspace; information on the personnel's experience; and the UAS' performance in the circumstances of the proposed operation.

The risks which must be considered both on the ground and in the air include:[121] whether the operation is VLOS or BVLOS; the population density of the area; whether people will be overflown; the dimensions of the UA; the volume of airspace including that necessary for contingency procedures; the class of airspace; the impact on other air traffic and air traffic management in particular the altitude, whether the airspace is controlled or uncontrolled; whether the operation is in/near an aerodrome; whether the airspace is over an urban or rural environment; and the separation from other traffic.

Key mitigation measures will include[122]: containment measures for people on the ground; operational limitations such as restricting the geographical area of operation, the duration or scheduled time of the operation; strategic mitigation by common flight rules or common airspace structure and services; capability to cope with possible adverse operating conditions; operational and maintenance procedures; individual competency; the risk of human error; and the UAS design features and performance, specifically fail-safe features and those designed to minimise the impact of a collision. As the risk assessment will include relevant training for operators and remote pilots, once authorisation is given, that training becomes the required training for the operation.

In addition, the operator is obliged to provide additional information[123] which will include the name of an accountable person at the operator. This person will not only have to be suitable, experienced and trained, but also have to be aware that in the event of any issues, they can expect to be the authority's first port of call.

Upon receipt of the application, it will be assessed by the authority. Authorisation will be granted where it is satisfied the risks are sufficiently addressed by the operational safety objectives and mitigation measures in place, and where the operator has provided a statement confirming that the intended operation complies with applicable rules, in particular, with regard to privacy, data protection, liability, insurance,

120 EU Regulation 2019/947 Article 11(1)(e).
121 ibid Article 11(4).
122 ibid Article 11(5).
123 EU Regulation 2019/947, Annex Part A, UAS.OPEN.030.

security and environmental protection.[124] The authorisation will set out the specific operational limitations, which can include competency requirements and the technical features of the UAS[125] as well as whether it relates to a single, or number of operations, specifying the time and locations along with a list of the mitigation measures.[126] Should the operation be considered not sufficiently safe, the authority will notify the operator providing reasons.[127]

In the event of any "*significant changes to the operation or to the mitigation measures listed in the operational authorisation*", the Operator is obliged to notify the authority and submit an application for an updated authorisation.[128]

Light UAS operator certificate

The benefit of a LUC is that it enables the operator to authorise its own operations without recourse to applying for an authorisation. As one would expect, the process for being certified as a LUC is to be thorough with considerable focus on the competency of those involved and the risk mitigation and management measures in place. An individual or organisation (although it is expected the majority of applications will be from organisations) can apply to be recognised as a LUC.[129]

The application is made to the authority. It shall contain a description of the management system, details of individuals responsible for operations and for authorising operations, and a statement that the applicant has verified the documentation submitted as complying with the requirements for granting a LUC.[130]

If granted the operator is under an obligation to comply with the scope of the LUC, including any limitations, carry out risk assessments where required, and keep records for at least three years[131] of the risk assessment, mitigations taken and competencies of the people involved.[132] Further obligations include the need to establish, implement and maintain a safety management system[133] and provide a manual of the organisation's procedures and activities.[134] These last two points are key. For an operator to convince the competent authority it should be allowed to authorise its own operations, it has to demonstrate it has the skills, knowledge and experience supported by suitably robust procedures, to do so safely. A key theme of this book has been that when it comes to regulation, safety is paramount, perhaps no more so than in these circumstances where a regulator ceases to have as much control as it otherwise may.

The safety management system needs to be proportionate to the size of the operator and the nature and complexity of its operations.[135] The greater the risks involved, the

124 EU Regulation 2019/947 Article 12(2).
125 ibid Article 12(4).
126 ibid Article 5(4)(a).
127 ibid Article 12(3).
128 EU Regulation 2019/947, Annex Part A, UAS.SPEC.035.
129 ibid para 1, UAS. LUC.010.
130 ibid para 2, UAS. LUC.010.
131 Protected from damage alteration and theft.
132 EU Regulation 2019/947 Annex Part A para 1, UAS.LUC.020.
133 ibid para 1, UAS.LUC.030.
134 ibid para 1, UAS.LUC.040.
135 ibid.

more robust and thorough safety system the authority will expect to see. Some of the key requirements of the system are:

- The nomination of:

  an accountable manager with authority for ensuring that within the organisation all activities are performed in accordance with the applicable standards and that the organisation is continuously in compliance with the requirements of the management system and the procedures identified in the LUC manual.[136]

  Clearly this person will need to be sufficiently senior to ensure compliance throughout the organisation and will be the first point of call if anything goes wrong. This appears a particularly onerous requirement for that individual if we consider the wording—"*ensuring . . . the organisation is continuously in compliance with the requirements of the management system*"—anyone with experience of auditing policy compliance will no doubt agree that ensuring continuous compliance is an admirable goal all responsible organisations seek to achieve but is extremely difficult to meet in practice;
- Establish and maintain a safety policy and objectives and appoint key personnel to execute that policy;[137]
- Establish and maintain a safety management process to identify hazards associated with the operations, to evaluate and manage risks and to verify the effectiveness of actions;[138]
- Document the key processes of the safety management system which will include safety reporting and internal investigations,[139] compliance monitoring and the use of subcontractors and partners;[140] and
- An independent function to monitor and provide feedback on compliance with its obligations to allow corrective actions to be taken.[141]

As mentioned in relation to previous provisions, it will be important for operators to document compliance with these requirements.

Model aircraft clubs

The final route for Specific category authorisation relates to operations that are not within the Open category but are conducted within the framework of duly authorised model aircraft clubs and associations.[142]

The authority is able to authorise such clubs to operate upon application.[143] That application will require the club to have in place established procedures, along with an

136 EU Regulation 2019/947 Annex Part A para 2(a), UAS.LUC.030.
137 ibid paras 2(c) and (d).
138 (n 136) 2(e).
139 An organisation may wish to consider whether its internal investigation should be undertaken in conjunction with legal representatives under Legal Professional Privilege.
140 EU Regulation 2019/947 Annex Part A para 2(g), UAS.LUC.040.
141 ibid para 2(h).
142 EU Regulation 2019/947 Article 5(6)(d).
143 ibid Article 16(1).

organisational structure and management system to ensure operations are undertaken safely by ensuring:

- Remote pilots are aware of the conditions and limitations of the club's authorisation.
- Remote pilots are assisted to achieve the minimum competency to operate safely within the club's authorisation.
- The club takes action when informed a remote pilot does not comply with the limits of the authorisation.
- The club provides documentation necessary for oversight and monitoring to the CAA upon request.[144]

Certified

The Certified category is aimed at the highest risk operations. Fundamentally it concerns large drones operating in controlled airspaces, which by the very nature of the operation, presents enhanced risks to people and property. To address the enhanced risks, certification of the UAS and the operator and a licenced remote pilot will be required. The key differences are that each individual UAS must be registered in this category as opposed to simply the operator (who in turn is responsible for labelling and uploading its registration information to the UA(s)) and the requirement for a licenced remote pilot (however, equivalent training requirements *may* be imposed by way of the authorisation/LUC, as advised by the risk assessment in the Specific category).

For UAS operations to be classified in the Certified category, one of two scenarios must apply:

> For the Certified category to apply, one of two scenarios has to apply:
>
> 1 UAS Certification and Operating Conditions[145]
>
> a One of the following conditions[146] applies:
>
> i Dimension of 3 m or more and designed to be operated over assemblies of people; or
> ii Designed for transporting people; or
> iii Designed for transporting dangerous goods and requires a high level of robustness to mitigate the risks for third parties in the case of accident;
>
> b And one (or more) of the following operating conditions applies:
>
> i Over assemblies of people; or
> ii Involves the transport of people; or
> iii Involves the carriage of dangerous goods, which may result in high risk for third parties in the case of accident.
>
> 2 Opinion of the national competent authority[147]

144 ibid Article 16(2)(b)(i)-(iv).
145 ibid Article 6(1).
146 ibid Article 40(1).
147 ibid Article 6(2).

If, based upon the risk assessment (for a Specified category application), the national competent authority is of the view that the risks presented by the proposed operation cannot be adequately mitigated without the enhanced checks brought by certification of the UAS and the operator, and without the licencing of the remote pilot.

Training

Similar to operations, the training requirements are dependent on the perceived risk inherent in the UAS and operation. All operators are required to be 16 years of age.[148] Training requirements are dictated by the level of operation. For instance, training is not required for very light UA (up to 250 g). For CE marked UA of this weight, there is a requirement to be familiar with the manufacturer's instructions only. For all heavier UA some form of training is required. For lower weight (up to 900 g) (A1) or heavier drones (9–25 kg) which will not be operated near urban areas (A3) familiarisation with the user manual, an online training course and an online test of 40 multiple-choice questions is required.[149]

In addition to what has been mentioned earlier, for the highest risk operation in the Open category (A2), that is operating a UA (900 g–4 kg) in an urban environment, at least 30 m horizontal distance from people (or 5 m away if a low-speed function is available and activated), self-practical training must be completed by the operator to familiarise themselves with the UAS and an examination provided by the national aviation authority (or recognised body) consisting of 30 multiple-choice questions, including knowledge on mitigation of ground risks, meteorology and flight performance.[150]

If the operation falls under the "Specific" category the training depends on the proposed operation. If the proposed operation falls outside a standard scenario (e.g. during the hours of darkness, proximate to an aerodrome) a risk assessment will need to be prepared and submitted to the national authority. The mitigation measures will include relevant training for operators. Once approved by the national authority that training becomes the required training for the operation. If the operation falls in a standard scenario the remote pilot will be required to hold a certificate of remote pilot theoretical knowledge for operation under the standard scenarios and hold an accreditation of completion of practical skill training (by completion of an online training course).[151]

Operations in the Certified category will require a licenced remote pilot.[152]

Finally, it is worth noting that the Regulations place certain responsibilities upon both operators and remote pilots in the Open and Specific categories.[153] For operators this will include implementing safe procedures and designating a competent remote pilot. For remote pilots this will entail ensuring competency, undertaking pre-flight checks and complying with operational limitations and procedures.

148 The individual state may reduce that age, but that authorisation will only be valid in that state.

149 EU Regulation 2019/947, Annex Part A, UAS.OPEN.020.

150 ibid UAS.OPEN.030.

151 ibid UAS.SPEC.050 (d) and UAS.SPEC.060 (b).

152 EU Regulation 2019/947 Article 3(c).

153 See, EU Regulation 2019/947, Annex Part A, UAS.OPEN.050, UAS.OPEN.060, UAS.SPEC.030 and UAS.SPEC.040.

The EU Regulations also require any operator using a UA above 20 kg to have insurance in place.[154] States are able to require insurance for lighter UA.

Timeframe for implementation

As a result of the COVID-19 pandemic, the implementation of the Regulations was pushed back from 1 July 2020 to 31 December 2020. On that date the following aspects come into force:

- Registration of UAS operators and certified UAS (which will be recognised EU wide) becomes mandatory; however, there is no need to register if the UA weighs less than 250 g and has no camera or other sensor able to detect personal data.[155]
- The "UAS operator registration number" received following registration is required to be displayed with a sticker and uploaded to the remote identification system on all UA operated.
- Operations in the Specific category may be conducted after the authorisation has been given by the relevant national authority.
- Limited Open category operations can commence.

Other key dates are as follows:

1 July 2021—National authorisations, certificates, declarations are to be fully converted to the new EU system. Member States need to complete the definition of geographical zones where drones are forbidden or where special authorisation is needed.

1 January 2022—National authorisations, certificates, declarations are fully converted to the new EU system.

EASA Member States must make available information on geographical zones for geo-awareness in a digital format harmonised between EU countries.

1 January 2023—All operations in the Open category and all UAS operations are conducted according to the EU Regulations.

Design

As mentioned earlier, EASA is also implementing product safety and design requirements within the European Union requiring smaller UA to be CE marked. CE marking being the administrative marking that indicates that a product has been assessed by the manufacturer and that it is in conformity with EU health, safety and environmental protection requirements.[156] All EU UAS will have assigned a CE marking with a number between 0 and 4, which will specify the class of the UAS (C0, C1, C2, C3 and

154 EU Regulation 2019/947 Article 14 (2) (d). Discussed in detail in Chapter 22.

155 ibid Article14(5)—Unless capable of being considered a "toy" for the purposes of Article 2 of Directive 2009/48/EC of the European Parliament and of the Council)19 June 2009) on the safety of toys.

156 See, Your Europe, 'CE Marking' (4 November 2020) <https://europa.eu/youreurope/business/product-requirements/labels-markings/ce-marking/index_en.htm>.

C4) and be accompanied by consumer information on how to fly a UA safely with "do's and don'ts" related to each class. The classification system will allow operators to easily identify the type of UAS they are permitted to operate. The classification system comes into force on 31 December 2020, but operators will still be permitted to operate unclassified UAS until 1 January 2023.

The classifications contain a number of similar provisions,[157] such as use of a label identifying the class on the UA, to be safely controllable under all anticipated operating conditions, be designed and constructed to minimise injury during operation, be accompanied with a user manual providing details of the UAS characteristics, operational limitations, its behaviour in the event of a lost data link and an EASA information notice with the applicable limitations and obligations under EU law.

Key features (non- exhaustive) of each class (in addition to the ones discussed earlier) are set out in the following.

Class 0

- Have a maximum take-off mass ("MTOM") of less than 250 g, including payload.
- Have a maximum speed in level flight of 19 m/s.
- Have a maximum attainable height above the take-off point limited to 120 m.
- Be powered by electricity and have a nominal voltage not exceeding 24 V DC or equivalent AC voltage.

Class 1

- Have an MTOM of less than 900 g, including payload.[158]
- Have a maximum speed in level flight of 19 m/s.
- Have a maximum attainable height above the take-off point limited to 120 m or be equipped with a system that can restrict it to this limit.
- Be of sufficient strength to withstand any stress during use without any breakage or deformation that might interfere with its safe flight.
- In the case of a loss of data link, have a reliable and predictable method for the UA to recover the data link or terminate the flight in a way that reduces the effect on third parties in the air or on the ground.
- Be powered by electricity and have a nominal voltage not exceeding 24 V DC or the equivalent AC voltage.
- Have a unique physical serial number compliant with standard ANSI/CTA-2063 Small Unmanned Aerial Systems Serial Numbers.
- Have a direct remote identification that cannot be altered and (a) allows the upload of the UAS operator registration number; (b) ensures, real time data transmission during flight, including the operator registration number; serial number of the UA; and position and height of the UA.

157 Contained within EU regulation 2019/947, Annex.

158 Or "Be made of materials and have performance and physical characteristics such as to ensure that in the event of an impact at terminal velocity with a human head, the energy transmitted to the human head is less than 80 J," EU regulation 2019/947, Annex, Part 2 (1).

- Be equipped with a geo-awareness system that can be updated with flight limitations, warns the remote pilot of a potential breach.
- Provide the remote pilot with clear warning when the battery of the UA or its control station reaches a low level so that the remote pilot has sufficient time to safely land the UA.
- Be equipped with lights for the purpose of control and conspicuity.

Class 2

- Have an MTOM of less than 4 kg, including payload.
- Similar features to Class 1 in relation to maximum attainable height (120 m), strength and data link recoverability.
- Be equipped with a data link protected against unauthorised access to the command-and-control functions.
- Be equipped with a selectable low-speed mode (3 m/s).[159]
- Be powered by electricity and have a nominal voltage not exceeding 48 V DC or the equivalent AC voltage.
- Have a unique physical serial number compliant with standard ANSI/CTA-2063 Small Unmanned Aerial Systems Serial Numbers.
- Have a direct remote identification system, geo-awareness system, battery warning and lights as per Class 1.

Class 3

- Have an MTOM of less than 25 kg, including payload.
- Have a maximum characteristic dimension of less than 3 m.
- 120 m maximum attainable height or capable of being limited as discussed earlier.
- Data link recovery/flight termination system.
- Be powered by electricity and have a nominal voltage not exceeding 48 V DC or the equivalent AC voltage.
- Have a unique physical serial number compliant with standard ANSI/CTA-2063 Small Unmanned Aerial Systems Serial Numbers.
- Have a direct remote identification system, geo-awareness system, battery warning and lights as per Classes 1 and 2.
- Unless tethered, be equipped with a data link protected against unauthorised access to the command-and-control functions.
- Battery warning and lighting requirements as per Classes 1 and 2.

Class 4

- Have an MTOM of less than 25 kg, including payload.
- Be incapable of automatic control modes except for flight stabilisation assistance with no direct effect on the trajectory and lost link assistance provided that a pre-determined fixed position of the flight controls in case the lost link is available.

159 Unless it is a fixed-wing UA.

Cybersecurity

EASA has also been active in addressing the risk of unauthorised access or takeover of a drone's controls. The EU is moving to address this by requiring data links to be secure in its classification system. UA are increasingly a target for cyber attackers. The software and data used to operate the UA can be unencrypted. EASA signed a Memorandum of Cooperation with the Computer Emergency Response Team (CERTEU) of the EU Institutions on 10 February 2017 and these bodies have established a European Centre for Cyber Security in Aviation (ECCSA). The ECCSA's mission is to provide information and assistance to European aviation manufacturers, airlines, maintenance organisations and others in order to protect critical elements of the system, such as aircraft, navigation and surveillance systems. The ECCSA will cover the full spectrum of aviation. In addition to the information-sharing initiatives intended to be implemented through the ECCSA, the strategy to address cybersecurity risks should be focussed on research and studies, event investigation and response, knowledge and competence building, international cooperation and harmonisation and regulatory activities and development of industry standards. This will include implementing a regulatory framework for cybersecurity covering all aviation domains (RMT.0720); and new cybersecurity provisions in the certification specifications (RMT.0648).[160]

Pacific Aviation Safety Office (PASO)

The Pacific Aviation Safety Office (PASO)[161] was established in 2004 through the Pacific Islands Civil Aviation Safety and Security Treaty (PICASST) with support from an Asian Development Bank (ADB) regional loan. Its primary function is to provide regulatory aviation safety and security services across the Pacific Region.

An international organisation, PASO is a member of the Council of Regional Organisations in the Pacific (CROP) and consists of the following Member States: the Cook Islands, Kiribati, Nauru, Niue, Papua New Guinea, Samoa, Solomon Islands, Tonga, Tuvalu and Vanuatu. Associate Member States of PASO are Australia, Fiji and New Zealand.

PASO is currently implementing the Pacific Aviation Safety Office Reform Project (PASO Reform Project), supported by financing from the World Bank. The PASO Reform Project has the development objective of ensuring effective regional delivery of aviation safety and security oversight in Pacific Island countries, by strengthening PASO's technical and coordination capacity. Drones are an integral part of this Project as PASO and its Member States want to take a proactive approach to RPAS management and regulation.

Drones are increasingly present in the Pacific with the falling cost of the technology making them more accessible to local businesses and individuals. In addition, tourists to the Pacific are increasingly using drones during their visits. Post COVID-19 there is an expectation that the number of tourism arrivals will grow significantly, with the safety and security risks associated with RPAS technology expected to grow

160 EASA, 'The European Plan for Aviation Safety (EPAS) 2020–2024' (13 November 2019). Generally, see Chapter 11 Cyber risks.

161 <www.forumsec.org/pacific-aviation-safety-office-paso/>.

concurrently. There is also a strong imperative to finesse a regulatory and operating framework for deployment of drones to support emergency and recovery services and to ensure that the general public and other key stakeholders have improved awareness of drone regulation in the Pacific, and of drone use during response to disasters.

While some Pacific Island countries have been able to keep abreast of international and domestic RPAS developments, including deploying varying levels of regulatory frameworks, in most PASO member states, Civil Aviation Authorities (CAAs) face staff shortages and limited resources. As a result, they do not have robust approaches for the safe management of RPAS and enforcement of relevant legislation.[162]

Under financing from the World Bank agreed in July 2018, PASO has commenced a programme of activities with a view towards the development of a consistent regulatory framework for RPAS (including legislation, policies and procedures) that is compliant with ICAO Standards and Recommended Practices and is in place in PASO member states. Unfortunately, COVID-19 has stalled progress at this time, but it is hoped that PASO will succeed in its ambitions to achieve a regulatory environment congruent with safe and efficient deployment of drones in the Pacific region.

Concluding comments

The work being undertaken by Transnational Organisations to achieve regulatory consistency, effectiveness and efficiency is vital. The same is true for initiatives designed to promote and establish a single set of technical, safety and operational requirements for the certification and safe integration of drones into airspace and at aerodromes.

The ICAO and EASA approaches towards permissible operations have followed a safety-first approach. The standard operating conditions developed impose reduced regulatory burdens on lower risk operations—those away from people, structures and aerodromes, during daylight hours and within visual line of sight (of the operator or observer). Those higher risk operations outside of the standard operating conditions, whether due to the size of the drone involved or the proposed conditions, will involve greater regulatory burdens, including the submission of a safety case, risk assessments and further remote pilot qualifications. Commercial operators will need, in those jurisdictions where the ICAO model regulations are enacted, or the EU Regulation equivalents apply, to carefully consider whether their operations can be brought within the reduced burdens imposed by standard operating conditions, or if it is in the organisation's interests to meet stricter regulatory requirements.

The next step both for the development of the technology and to promote certainty for operators has to be around the regulation of design or at least design parameters. This will enable the technology to become safer if agreed standard safety features and responses to system failures can be incorporated into designs that manufacturers know will be acceptable to regulators. As well as safety, agreed security features reducing the risk of cyber attack can only enhance safety. Setting clear parameters will assist designers and manufacturers. Once businesses have clearly set design parameters to work with (e.g. specific safety features a regulator will expect to see included such as

162 See, The World Bank, 'Combined Project Information Documents/Integrated Safeguards Datasheet (PID/ISDA)' (Report No: PIDISDSA24046, Appraisal Stage, 30 March 2018) <http://documents1.worldbank.org/curated/pt/758341522738820811/pdf/Project-Information-Document-Integrated-Safeguards-Data-Sheet-Pacific-Aviation-Safety-Office-Reform-Project-Additional-Financing-II-P164468.pdf>.

a return to home function), public trust in the technology can only improve. Manufacturers avoid the risk of developing a product which will be rejected by a regulator and end users have certainty that the drone being purchased can conduct envisaged operations. Agreed standards will only serve to enhance safety and ensure a clear and consistent approach to regulation and enforcement.

The European Commission[163] observes that "proactively shaping our future mobility by developing and validating new technologies and services is key to staying ahead of the curve".[164] Chapter 20 will consider technologies such as geofencing and electronic conspicuity in more detail but the inclusion of these or similar technologies in design standards could go a significant way to addressing safety concerns if the technology can be incorporated in designs as standard. A number of these technologies are still being developed, but the implementation of geofencing—used to contain drones within, or exclude them from, a particular area, would serve to reduce issues around drones endangering aircraft or large events. Other possible design features may include electronic conspicuity—which allows the automatic identification of all airspace users, including ADS-B technology, a system that enables an aircraft to automatically broadcast its precise location and airborne collision avoidance systems.

163 European Commission, 'Communication from the Commission to the European Parliament, The Council, The European Economic and Social Committee and the Committee of the Regions: Sustainable and Smart Mobility Strategy—Putting European Transport on Track for the Future Brussels' COM (2020) 789 final <https://ec.europa.eu/transport/sites/transport/files/legislation/com20200789.pdf>.

164 ibid para 64.

15 National regulatory structure and responses

USA

Jeffrey Ellis

Introduction

This chapter and the three following will now consider how specific countries have approached the topic of drone regulation. Every country has its legal idiosyncrasies that will impact upon how regulations can, and will, be implemented and adopted. This may involve the segregation of regulatory spheres between different regulatory bodies, as can be seen in the member states of the European Union, or the inherent tension between national and local legislation in Federal jurisdictions like Australia and the United States (US).[1]

This chapter provides an overview of how the law regarding UAVs has developed primarily in the United States where drone use is rapidly accelerating, and considerable time and effort has been spent integrating drone regulation into a well-developed legal framework.[2] The regulatory structure in the US provides a good indicator as to where future drone regulation is likely headed in the US and is a good potential marker for other jurisdictions currently less advanced in their consideration of drones issues. Reviewing this regulatory structure also provides valuable information about how effective existing regulatory approaches actually are and provides a good foundation for navigating the uncertain regulatory outlook in the coming decade.

Aviation regulation in the United States

It was only a matter of a few years after the very first flight that the United States Congress recognised the need for national regulation of aviation. The legislative history of the very first Federal aviation statutes are particularly instructive as to why it was determined that aviation safety and flight operations had to be regulated uniformly by the Federal government and not subject to the potentially different and/or conflicting regulation of the various States and Territories.

At the Congressional hearings prior to passage of the original 1926 *Air Commerce Act* one of the witnesses who testified was William MacCracken. Mr MacCracken was Chairman of the American Bar Association Committee on the Law of Aeronautics which had been appointed by Congress to assist it in drafting federal legislation

1 See, for example, the discussion of Constitutional issues in Chapter 13.

2 References in this chapter to a 'drone' will typically refer to UAS where appropriate in the context. References to small unmanned aircraft (SUA) later in this chapter are similarly referenced as a 'drone'.

and "solving the legal problems that have been presented".[3] In explaining the legislation's legal framework, Mr MacCracken stated:

> There were two things that were of controlling importance. One was that there should be exclusive regulatory power in the Commissioner to the end that there might be uniformity throughout the States.[4]

He then testified about the *exclusivity* of Federal regulations when questioned by members of the Congressional committee.

MR BURTNESS: Mr MacCracken, the men responsible for the drafting of this bill, they, *do they feel that there would be objections to concurrent jurisdiction on the part of the State Government?*

MR MACCRACKEN: *Absolutely. There is no question about that.*

MR BURTNESS: Just briefly, what would be the main objection to the States exercising "concurrent jurisdiction", insofar as the intrastate traffic is concerned?

MR MACCRACKEN: One difficulty is determining your exact location over a State when you are in the air. In other words, there is no way of indicating when you cross the boundary line. In travelling on the earth's surface along the railroads or highway, the boundary line can be marked, but there is no way of outlining a State boundary line so it can be seen at all times in the air. Furthermore, as air traffic, air navigation, becomes more popular and more generally used it would be chaotic if you had six different sets of regulations to observe or to take cognizance of in flying from New York to Washington, which is a matter of a few hours' journey, at the most, in the air.[5]

The foregoing clearly demonstrates what seems almost beyond debate. The nature of aviation is such that it must be regulated uniformly on the Federal level and not subject to differing and potentially contradictory regulations that might be enacted on the State or local municipal level. This principal of uniform federal regulation is embedded in both the legislative and judicial underpinnings of how aviation is regulated in the United States.

Justice William Douglas of the United States Supreme Court explained the fundamental principle of all US aviation regulation almost 75 years ago. The issue before him arose as the result of a dispute between a farmer and the US government regarding take-offs and landings of military aircraft at a nearby airport that were alleged to be causing great damage to the farmer's chickens. In resolving this dispute, Justice Douglas explained the legal doctrine that remains fundamental to the regulation of both manned and unmanned aviation:

> It is ancient doctrine that at common law ownership of the land extended to the periphery of the universe—*Cujus est solum ejus est usque ad coelum*. But that doctrine has no place in the modern world. The air is a public highway, as

3 See 68th Cong., 2nd Sess., H.R. 10522, p 54–55; also referred to at p 30 of the 'History of the Legislation' section of the Legislative History for the Air Commerce Act of 1926. (HR).

4 ibid H.R. 10522 p 55.

5 ibid H.R. 10522 p 63, 64.

> Congress has declared. Were that not true, every transcontinental flight would subject the operator to countless trespass suits. Common sense revolts at the idea. To recognize such private claims to the airspace would clog these highways, seriously interfere with their control and development in the public interest, and transfer into private ownership that to which the only public has a just claim.[6]

This judicial recognition that private property rights do not take precedence over the establishment and right to use the air as a public highway reflects a continuing and important regulatory trend even though it continues to be a point of contention. This is because property interests on the ground do not want their commercial activities and privacy rights interfered with by objects flying above.

As will be illustrated in the following, the desire of property interests to be free from interference from above continues to be an important factor in the development of a UAV regulatory structure. To date, however, this interest has not hindered the development of a regulatory framework that promotes the development of aviation. Indeed, as the aforementioned US Supreme Court decision also noted, it took only a few years after the Wright Brothers first flight for the Congress of the United States to declare in both the *Air Commerce Act* of 1926[7] and the *Civil Aeronautics Act* of 1938[8] that the United States has "complete and exclusive national sovereignty in the air space over this country".[9] This provision was also subsequently made part of the 1958 *Federal Aviation Act* and continues in effect to this day.[10]

The legislative and judicial recognition that aviation development requires centralised (as opposed to local) regulation and the recognition that the air is a public highway (as opposed to being privately owned) are cornerstones of the regulatory structure for aviation and continue to be important factors in the ongoing debate for how UAS should be regulated.

As manned aviation continued to mature, the US Supreme Court and the US Congress continued to build upon the need for centralised control and the public interest in having access to the navigable airspace as taking precedence over private and local interests looking to restrict the same. In that regard, the US Supreme Court voided a municipal airport curfew that was intended to limit aircraft noise around an airport during evening hours.[11]

The Supreme Court first noted that the airspace within which these flights were operated had been recognised by Congress to be under federal, not state or local control.[12] The Supreme Court then noted that the Administrator of the Federal Aviation Administration (FAA) had broad authority to regulate the use of the navigable airspace "in order to insure the safety of aircraft and the efficient utilization of such airspace . . . and for the protection of persons and property on the ground".[13] It then

6 *United States v. Causby*, 328 U.S. 256, 260, 261 (1946).
7 44 Stat. 568, 49 U.S.C. § 171.
8 52 Stat. 973, 49 U.S.C. § 401.
9 49 U.S.C. § 176(a), *United States* (n 6) 260.
10 49 U.S.C. 40103(a).
11 *City of Burbank v. Lockheed Air Terminal, Inc.*, 411 U.S. 624 (1973).
12 411 U.S., 626, 627.
13 ibid.

continued by noting that "controlling the flight of aircraft" was clearly under Federal control and that noise related issues clearly fell under this umbrella.[14] The Supreme Court then summarised its holding as follows:

> the Administrator has imposed a variety of regulations relating to takeoff and landing procedures and runway preferences. The *Federal Aviation Act* requires a delicate balance between safety and efficiency,[15] and the protection of persons on the ground.[16] Any regulations adopted by the Administrator to control noise pollution must be consistent with the "highest degree of safety".[17] The interdependence of these factors requires a uniform and exclusive system of federal regulation if the congressional objectives underlying the Federal Aviation Act are to be fulfilled.[18]

Despite the repeated attempts by local interests to restrict flight operations, the regulatory system in the United States recognises that the nature of aviation is such that it has to be regulated in a uniform, centralised manner and not subject to the differing regulatory schemes that might be enacted if the individual States or municipalities were authorised to do so. It is in this context that the regulatory structure for UAS began to take shape.

The origin of UAV regulation

The origin of a specific regulatory regime regarding UAV can be traced back to the first attempts to regulate the use of model aircraft. Model aircraft are, as the name suggests, small-scale models of larger aircraft. Such models and persons flying same have been in existence since the early 1900s.[19]

The technology used in developing model aircraft tracked along a similar course as that being utilised by the aircraft that the models tried to emulate. Thus, by the 1930s, small, gas-powered model airplane engines were being manufactured and used on model aircraft. As happened with manned aviation, local interests sought to regulate this new technology and in 1937, Connecticut and Massachusetts banned the flying of gas models. Massachusetts stipulated "that no gas model may be flown unless licensed, nor may it be flown by anyone unless that person is a licensed pilot".[20]

In response to those who were pushing back against model aircraft flight, safety rules were proposed, and it was noted that there had not been any accidents between full-scale and gas model aircraft. The US Department of Commerce not only rejected an attempt to impose a national ban on gas models but instead issued a statement of endorsement, setting out aeromodelling's value to youth.[21]

14 411 U.S., 635.
15 49 U.S.C. § 1348(a).
16 49 U.S.C. § 1348(c).
17 49 U.S.C. § 1431(d)(3).
18 411 U.S.,638, 639.
19 Academy of Model Aeronautics, 'The History of the AMA' <www.modelaircraft.org/sites/default/files/gov/docs/AMA75-ONLINESUPPLEMENT.pdf>.
20 ibid, citing to Model Airplane News magazine, October 1937.
21 ibid.

The technology for model aircraft continued to improve and began to incorporate radio-controlled guidance systems.[22] The Academy of Model Aeronautics focussed their efforts on working with the Federal government and in 1947, the Federal Communications Commission (FCC) agreed to open a single channel on the citizens band (27.255 MHz) for radio-controlled (RC) flying and by the 1980s, the Academy had over 100,000 members.[23]

With the growth of model aircraft flying, the FAA saw the need to issue an advisory circular in 1981 which established an informal agreement between the FAA and the radio-controlled (RC) aircraft community.[24] The advisory circular "encourages voluntary compliance with, safety standards for model aircraft operators" and notes that "model aircraft can at times pose a hazard to full-scale aircraft in flight and to persons and property on the surface".[25]

The voluntary operating standards proposed by the FAA for model aircraft in 1981 echoed what it subsequently mandated for UAS operators more than three decades later. In that regard, the 1981 standards for model aircraft included the following:

a *Select an operating site that is of sufficient distance from populated areas. The selected site should be away from noise sensitive areas, such as parks, schools, hospitals and churches.*

b *Do not operate model aircraft in the presence of spectators until the aircraft is successfully flight tested and proven airworthy.*

c *Do not fly model aircraft higher than 400 feet above the surface. When flying aircraft within 3 miles of an airport, notify the airport operator, or when an air traffic facility is located at the airport, notify the control tower, or flight service station.*

d *Give right of way to, and avoid flying in the proximity of, full-scale aircraft. Use observers to help if possible.*[26]

The foregoing informal and voluntary standards for model aircraft regulation continued in force for more than three decades as those users literally and figuratively flew under the radar and attracted little attention from either the FAA or local municipal regulators. That began to change as decades later, drones burst upon the scene and it became quite apparent to Federal, State and municipal regulators that a specific definition of "model aircraft" was needed along with some means of policing flight that posed a danger to individuals and other aircraft.

The inception of UAV and UAS regulation

The FAA's first policy statement regarding the uses of drones was issued in September 2005.[27] The policy articulated therein was developed in conjunction with the FAA's

22 ibid.
23 ibid.
24 FAA Advisory Circular, 'Model Aircraft Operating Standards' 91-57 (9 June 1981) <www.faa.gov/documentLibrary/media/Advisory_Circular/91-57.pdf>.
25 ibid.
26 ibid.
27 Federal Aviation Admin, AFS-400 UAS policy 05-01, unmanned aircraft systems operations in the US National Airspace system—interim operational approval guidance (2005).

1998 Safety Risk Management policy which required that risks be assessed based on the "*severity of the hazard and likelihood of occurrence*".[28] In accordance with that directive, the FAA considered the risk posed by the increasing number of drones that were then being used in the US.

The FAA's 2005 guidance first noted that "*Unmanned aircraft (UA) operations have increased dramatically during the past several years in both the public and private sectors*".[29] It was then stated that as a result, it had become "*necessary to develop guidance*" for Federal Aviation Administration organisations to use to determine whether UAS should be "*allowed to conduct flight operations in the U. S. National Airspace System (NAS)*".[30] The FAA then stated that it would authorise such use if it could be demonstrated by the applicant that a "*collision with another aircraft, parachutist or other civil airspace user is extremely improbable*".[31]

In conjunction with the foregoing statements, the FAA's 2005 guidance also provided a definition of unmanned aircraft operations. That definition was stated as follows:

> *Unmanned Aircraft—a device that is used or intended to be used for flight in the air that has no onboard pilot. This includes all classes of airplanes, helicopters, airships, and translational lift aircraft that have no onboard pilot. A UA is an aircraft as defined in 14 CFR 1.*[32]

It is significant to note that the foregoing definition is not only extremely broad but also that it makes no attempt to differentiate "unmanned aircraft" from "model aircraft". Indeed, the FAA's non-mandatory 1981 guidelines regarding use of the latter also do not contain a definition of model aircraft. This is likely because model aircraft were considered akin to a hobby activity and prior to 2005, drone technology had been developed for military use drones. Nonetheless, it seems pretty clear that model aircraft would also fall within the definition of "unmanned aircraft" set forth in this 2005 guidance since model aircraft are "devices" "used for flight" that have "no onboard pilot".

Irrespective of why the FAA did not distinguish "unmanned aircraft" from "model aircraft" in 2005, its broad definition of the former as falling within the definition of "aircraft" provided the regulatory predicate for the FAA to exercise its authority. This is because as noted previously, the Supreme Court had specifically held that "controlling the flight of aircraft" was clearly under the FAA's control.[33] Similarly, the Supreme Court had also held that the FAA also had broad authority to regulate the use of the navigable airspace.[34]

Thus, the FAA's initial guidance for "unmanned aircraft" is entirely consistent with the existing regulatory structure establishing the FAA's authority over both "aircraft" and the use of the "navigable airspace". Nonetheless, by making no mention of any

28 FAA Order 8040.4, 'Safety Risk Management' (26 June 1998) <www.faa.gov/documentLibrary/media/directives/ND/ND8040-4.pdf>; *cancelled by* FAA Order 8040.4A, 'Safety Risk Management Policy' (30 April 2012) <www.faa.gov/documentLibrary/media/Order/8040.4A%20.pdf>.

29 AFS-400 UAS Policy 05-01.

30 ibid.

31 ibid.

32 ibid.

33 *City of Burbank* (n 11) 635.

34 ibid 626, 627.

distinction with "model aircraft", the FAA apparently saw no need to address the non-mandatory 1981 model aircraft guidelines which allowed operations of same below 400 feet.[35] As UAS technology developed rapidly, this issue could not be ignored much longer.

In 2007, the FAA issued another Policy Statement clarifying its earlier guidance regarding operation of unmanned aircraft in the National Air Space.[36] That statement specifically addresses the regulatory distinction between "unmanned aircraft" and "model aircraft". In the relevant part it states:

> The FAA recognizes that people and companies other than modelers might be flying UAS with the mistaken understanding that they are legally operating under the authority of AC 91-57. AC 91-57 only applies to modelers, and thus specifically excludes its use by persons or companies for business purposes.[37]

This policy statement provides no concrete rationale for this distinction but does note that the FAA will undertake:

> a safety review that will examine the feasibility of creating a different category of unmanned "vehicles" that may be defined by the operator's visual line of sight and are also small and slow enough to adequately mitigate hazards to other aircraft and persons on the ground. The end product of this analysis may be a new flight authorization instrument similar to AC 91-57 but focused on operations which do not qualify as sport and recreation, but also may not require a certificate of airworthiness. They will, however, require compliance with applicable FAA regulations and guidance developed for this category.[38]

So two years after the FAA's initial guidance, it acknowledges its different treatment of "model aircraft" and "unmanned aircraft" without explaining any concrete rationale for doing so. That issue aside, this guidance foreshadows future FAA regulation of unmanned aircraft by noting that it may create a "new category of unmanned vehicles" that may be tied to operations being conducted in the visual line of sight of the operator as well as by the size of the vehicle.

It is also significant to note that the FAA's initial guidance states that it may not require a certificate of airworthiness for this new category of aircraft. This is particularly striking because the regulatory predicate that the FAA was using was based on defining "unmanned aircraft" as falling within the existing definition of aircraft. The existing regulatory scheme for aircraft, however, specifically required aircraft to possess a certificate of airworthiness; that is, the aircraft conformed to FAA design and manufacturing criteria for safe operation.[39] Thus, the FAA's regulatory predicate

35 Model Aircraft Operating Standards.

36 Unmanned Aircraft Operations in the National Airspace Systems, 72 Fed. Reg. 29, 6689 (13 February 2007) <www.tc.faa.gov/its/worldpac/techrpt/ar097.pdf>; <www.govinfo.gov/content/pkg/FR-2007-02-13/html/E7-2402.htm>.

37 ibid.

38 ibid.

39 14 C.F.R. § 91.203(a)(1).

for UAS was not only inherently inconsistent but also acknowledged the necessity for both a new definition and a different regulatory scheme.

Not surprisingly and shortly after the issuance of the foregoing "clarification", the FAA commissioned Embry Riddle Aeronautical University to research and analyse the regulatory issues related to "unmanned aircraft".[40] That research found that when the definition of "aircraft" was first issued, the authors of those regulations likely did not consider "radio-controlled model aircraft".[41] It further noted that some model aircraft are "larger and, in some cases, much faster than many commercial UAs, yet they remain an unregulated UA".[42] Even more significantly, it was also observed that these guidance documents were not "a regulation".[43] The research study recommended that additional analysis and regulatory action needed to be undertaken.[44]

Not surprisingly, while the FAA struggled to develop an appropriate regulatory framework, UAS technology continued to develop rapidly. Small, easy to operate quadcopters were developed and coupled with smartphone microchip technology. These developments gave birth to flying cameras that were relatively affordable for many private citizens and fairly easy to operate.[45] The affordability of same, the wondrous vistas they opened, and the myriad new uses being explored dramatically increased the number of drones and users.[46] It also brought about the FAA's first enforcement action and judicial review of same.

Regulatory structure begins to take shape

The FAA's first enforcement action was instituted against the operator of a small drone being used to photograph and film on a college campus.[47] The FAA sought a $10,000 fine and alleged that the October 17, 2011 flight was for commercial purposes, that the drone was defined as an "aircraft" and was operated in violation of a regulation prohibiting "careless and reckless" operation.[48]

The operator moved to dismiss the FAA's complaint and argued that the drone or device being operated should be considered a "model aircraft" and per the FAA's 1981 guidance material, not included within the regulatory definition of aircraft and therefore, not subject to FAA enforcement.[49] The FAA countered by arguing that model aircraft are aircraft, subject to regulatory enforcement and that its 1981 non-mandatory guidance materials did not exempt operators of model aircraft from regulatory enforcement for careless or reckless operation.[50]

40 FAA, 'Unmanned Aircraft System Regulation Review' (September 2009) DOT/FAA/AR-09/7 <www.tc.faa.gov/its/worldpac/techrpt/ar097.pdf>.

41 ibid 6.

42 ibid.

43 ibid 14.

44 ibid 17, 18.

45 The Economist, 'Taking Flight' (*The Economist Technology Quarterly*, 8 June 2017) <www.economist.com/technology-quarterly/2017-06-08/civilian-drones>.

46 ibid.

47 See, *Michael P Huerta, Administrator, Federal Aviation Administration v Raphael Pirker*WL 8095629 (2014) 7.

48 ibid.

49 ibid 7–8.

50 ibid.

The administrative judge hearing this issue first noted that the FAA had historically treated model aircraft differently than other aircraft subject to the FAA's regulatory jurisdiction. In that regard, the judge noted that unlike other types of aircraft, model aircraft were not required to have certificates of airworthiness and that the FAA had offered no explanation as to whether they would now deem paper airplanes as subject to its regulatory jurisdiction.[51]

The judge also noted that subsequent to the date of the 2011 alleged violation, the US Congress had passed legislation requiring the FAA "to develop a plan for integration of civil UAS into the NAS, specifying that the plan contain recommendations for rulemaking to define acceptable standards for operation and certification of civil UAS".[52] The administrative judge held that the foregoing reflected a Congressional understanding that the FAA's regulatory structure did not include UAS. Based on the foregoing, the judge granted the motion and dismissed the FAA's enforcement action.[53]

The FAA appealed the administrative judge's decision and on appeal, that decision was reversed and the matter remanded for prosecution.[54] The primary legal reasons for reversal were noted to be that the FAA's broad definition of aircraft clearly included the drone at issue and that the FAA's guidance regarding model aircraft neither defined what constituted same nor precluded enforcement for regulatory violations.[55]

While the foregoing explanation as to the legal issues involved in this prosecution are clearly relevant to the decision to reverse the judge's dismissal, the alleged recklessness of the operator's actions also likely contributed to this result. In that regard, the decision reversing the judge's dismissal notes the following about the alleged manner in which the drone was operated:

> *directly towards an individual standing on a . . . sidewalk causing the individual to take immediate evasive maneuvers so as to avoid being struck by [the] aircraft; through a . . . tunnel containing moving vehicles; under a crane; below tree top level over a tree lined walkway; under an elevated pedestrian walkway; and within approximately 100 feet of an active heliport.*[56]

It is not unreasonable to assume that these allegations of careless and reckless operation played a role in how the appeal was decided. That is not stated, however. Instead, the decision focusses on factors which purport to support interpreting the existing regulatory scheme as applying to drones,[57] while omitting discussion of factors cited by the administrative judge for reaching the opposite conclusion. In this regard, the appeals board also omits any discussion of the law judge's finding that Congress' subsequent passage of legislation directing the FAA to establish a regulatory structure for UAS indicated that the pre-existing one did not apply.

51 ibid.
52 ibid 10–11.
53 ibid.
54 ibid 1.
55 ibid 2–5.
56 ibid 1.
57 ibid 2–5.

It is likely that all parties were quite aware of the thorny legal issues that were presented and the uncertainty if any further appeals were pursued. Thus, it is not surprising that on remand, the FAA settled the matter for a small fraction of the $10,000 fine it sought in the complaint.[58]

The foregoing decisions and the settlement on remand seem more appropriate to be considered reflective of a still-uncertain regulatory scheme than specific guidance to be applied prospectively. Indeed, as the law judge noted, subsequent to the flight at issue, Congress had enacted the FAA *Modernization and Reform Act* of 2012 ("2012 FMRA").[59] That statute confirmed the FAA's prior guidance defining "unmanned aircraft" as "aircraft",[60] directed the FAA to "develop a comprehensive plan to safely accelerate the integration of civil unmanned aircraft systems into the national airspace system"[61] and precluded regulation of model aircraft weighing less than 55 lb if flown recreationally.[62] With respect to the latter, Congress defined model aircraft as:

(1) capable of sustained flight in the atmosphere;
(2) flown within visual line of sight of the person operating the aircraft; and
(3) flown for hobby or recreational purposes.[63]

The foregoing statute is important for several reasons. First, it formalises in a legislative directive that devices that fly should be regulated by the entity that regulates flight and the national airspace, that is, the FAA. Second, it recognises that the use of unmanned aircraft should be integrated into the national airspace. Third, it also recognises that small model aircraft used for recreational purposes need not be subsumed into a regulatory system that was set up to manage and regulate entirely different types of flight.

It is also relevant to observe that it took seven years after the FAA's first guidance on UAS and 31 years after the FAA issued guidance on model aircraft for Congress to pass legislation formally directing the FAA integrate UAS into the national airspace and exempting model aircraft from formal FAA regulation. This legislation clearly favours entities wanting more access to the national airspace and less restrictions on use. Not surprisingly, those who were concerned more about the potential risks raised by this technology also pushed their concerns and several years later, Congress passed the *FAA Extension, Safety, and Security Act* of 2016.[64] That statute aimed to expedite approval for UAS deployment in emergencies but also prohibited UAS from interfering with emergency response activities and precluded unauthorised UAS operation around airports and critical infrastructure.[65]

58 The defendant operator stated that the matter resolved for a payment of $1,100. See, 'Team BlackSheep Drone Pilot Raphael Pirker Settles FAA Case' (22 January 2015)<www.team-blacksheep.com/docs/pirker-faa-settlement.pdf>.
59 PL 112-95, codified at 49 USC §40101, note.
60 See §§331(8) and (9) of 2012 FMRA.
61 See 2012 FMRA section 332, 'Integration of Civil Unmanned Aircraft Systems into National Airspace System'.
62 See 2012 FMRA, s336, 'Special Rule for Model Aircraft'.
63 ibid.
64 Pub.L. 114-190, codified at 49 USCA § 40101, note.
65 ibid Subtitle B—UAS Safety.

Concurrent with the foregoing legislation and consistent with the manner in which local governments had historically sought to independently regulate manned flight, local municipalities were becoming increasingly concerned with privacy and security related issues arising from the increasing number of small drones that were being flown in their areas. Since nothing in either the FAA guidance or Congressional legislation indicated any intent to alter the pre-existing and uniformly federal regulation of flight and the navigable airspace, the FAA decided that it was necessary to issue guidance to State and local jurisdictions regarding their limited role in the overall regulatory structure.[66]

The FAA specifically advised State and local jurisdictions that they lack authority to regulate airspace and flight operations. In so doing, the FAA stated:

> "[s]ubstantial air safety issues are raised when state and local governments attempt to regulate the operation or flight of aircraft",
>
> "[a] navigable airspace free from inconsistent state and local restrictions is essential to the maintenance of a safe and sound air transportation system".

This guidance is entirely consistent with the prior Supreme Court holdings previously cited herein and also consistent with Congress' directive to the FAA to "integrate" UAS into the pre-existing navigable airspace.[67] While the foregoing guidance and directive clearly are intended to preserve the existing regulatory framework governing flight, the FAA also provided guidance to State and local governments that certain types of regulations were permitted and outside the scheme of federal control. These included requirements for police to obtain a warrant prior to using a UAS for surveillance, specifying that UAS may not be used for voyeurism and prohibitions on using UAS for hunting or fishing, or to interfere with or harass an individual who is hunting or fishing as well as prohibitions on attaching firearms or similar weapons to UAS.[68] These types of regulatory initiatives did not involve controlling actual flight and therefore would not interfere with the FAA's exclusive authority in this area.

FAA regulatory initiatives begin to be implemented, and challenged

In accordance with its Congressional mandate to integrate drones into the national airspace, the FAA issued an Advisory Circular in June, 2016 regarding UAS classification, pilot certification and operational limitations.[69] This regulatory initiative was coupled with the FAA promulgating a new chapter of regulations dealing with small UAS that were specifically intended to "*allow the operation of small unmanned aircraft systems in the National Airspace System*".[70]

The FAA explained that its regulations were promulgated as interim rules that would allow "societally beneficial applications of small UAS" that posed the "least amount

66 FAA, 'State and Local Regulation of Unmanned Aircraft Systems (UAS) Fact Sheet' (17 December 2015) <www.faa.gov/uas/resources/policy_library/media/UAS_Fact_Sheet_Final.pdf> (hereinafter "FactSheet").

67 2012 FMRA section 332.

68 Fact Sheet (n 66).

69 AC No: 107-2, Small Unmanned Aircraft Systems (21 June 2016).

70 14 CFR Part 107; see also 81 FR 42063 (26 June 2016).

of public risk and no threat to national security".[71] In that regard, the FAA listed the following small UAS operations that could be conducted under the framework in this rule: Crop monitoring/inspection; Research and development; Educational/academic uses; Power-line/pipeline inspection in hilly or mountainous terrain; Antenna inspections; Aiding certain rescue operations; Bridge inspections; Aerial photography; and Wildlife nesting area evaluations.[72]

The FAA rule also set forth numerous operational requirements and limitations as well as clarifying that model aircraft are generally exempt from regulation but subject to FAA enforcement action if they endanger the safety of others. The specific issues addressed in this rule-making include the following:

Operational limitations

- Unmanned aircraft must weigh less than 55 lb (25 kg).
- Visual line of sight (VLOS) only; the unmanned aircraft must remain within VLOS of the remote pilot in command and the person manipulating the flight controls of the small UAS. Alternatively, the unmanned aircraft must remain within VLOS of the visual observer.
- At all times the small unmanned aircraft must remain close enough to the remote pilot in command and the person manipulating the flight controls of the small UAS for those people to be capable of seeing the aircraft with vision unaided by any device other than corrective lenses.
- Small unmanned aircraft may not operate over any persons not directly participating in the operation, not under a covered structure, and not inside a covered stationary vehicle.
- Daylight-only operations, or civil twilight (30 minutes before official sunrise to 30 minutes after official sunset, local time) with appropriate anti-collision lighting.
- Must yield right of way to other aircraft.
- May use visual observer (VO) but not required.
- First-person view camera cannot satisfy "see-and-avoid" requirement but can be used as long as requirement is satisfied in other ways.
- Maximum ground speed of 100 miles/hour (87 knots).
- Minimum weather visibility of 3 miles from control station.
- Maximum altitude of 400 feet above ground level (AGL) or, if higher than 400 feet AGL, remain within 400 feet of a structure.
- Operations in Class B, C, D and E airspace are allowed with the required ATC permission.
- Operations in Class G airspace are allowed without ATC permission.
- No person may act as a remote pilot in command or VO for more than one unmanned aircraft operation at one time.
- No operations from a moving aircraft.
- No operations from a moving vehicle unless the operation is over a sparsely populated area.

71 81 FR 42063. 'Operation and Certification of Small Unmanned Aircraft'(28 June 2016) <www.federalregister.gov/documents/2016/06/28/2016-15079/operation-and-certification-of-small-unmanned-aircraft-systems>.

72 ibid.

- No careless or reckless operations.
- No carriage of hazardous materials.
- Requires preflight inspection by the remote pilot in command.
- A person may not operate a small unmanned aircraft if he or she knows or has reason to know of any physical or mental condition that would interfere with the safe operation of a small UAS.

Remote pilot in command certification and responsibilities

- A person operating a small UAS must either hold a remote pilot airman certificate with a small UAS rating or be under the direct supervision of a person who does hold a remote pilot certificate (remote pilot in command).
- To qualify for a remote pilot certificate, a person must:
  - Demonstrate aeronautical knowledge by passing an initial aeronautical knowledge test at an FAA-approved knowledge testing centre.
- Until international standards are developed, foreign-certificated UAS pilots will be required to obtain an FAA-issued remote pilot certificate with a small UAS rating.
- Ensure that the small unmanned aircraft complies with the existing registration requirements.

Model aircraft

- Part 107 does not apply to model aircraft
- The rule codifies the FAA's enforcement authority in part 101 by prohibiting model aircraft operators from endangering the safety of the NAS

In conjunction with the foregoing FAA rule, the FAA also formed a Drone Advisory Committee (DAC) so that various user stakeholders could meet with the FAA to express their concerns and in the words of the FAA Administrator, assist in the development and implementation of a "*a faster process for innovation to get into the NAS*".[73]

While all of the foregoing activity was taking place, the FAA also issued information regarding the rapidly burgeoning use of UAS and the exponential growth that was expected in coming years. In that regard, the FAA stated that from 2016 to 2021, the number of recreational drones could increase from 1 to 4.5 million while commercial drones could increase from 42,000 to 1 million.[74]

The burgeoning number of UAS together with the federal rule-making designed to integrate UAS into the National Airspace was not universally applauded. As was noted at the first DAC meeting, "*There are over 280 State bills affecting UAS—chaos results when too many local laws are enacted—a strong federal role is needed*".[75] It was also noted by way of explanation that while the FAA has authority to control

73 RTCA, (DAC Meeting Minutes) DAC Meeting Minutes, Paper No: 240-16/DAC-002 (16 September 2016) <www.faa.gov/uas/programs_partnerships/drone_advisory_committee/rtca_dac/media/dac_meeting_minutes_sept_16_2016.pdf>.

74 FAA, 'Aerospace Forecast Fiscal Years 2020–2040' <www.faa.gov/data_research/aviation/aerospace_forecasts/media/FY2020-40_FAA_Aerospace_Forecast.pdf>.

75 DAC Meeting Minutes (n 73) 6.

the airspace, "*the public reasonably expects peace and privacy and UAS conflict with that*".[76] It was then simply stated that local governments want to "set UAS rules".[77]

The concerns about privacy and the right of local governments to establish rules limiting UAS operations is wholly consistent with similar issues arising with respect to manned aviation. However, and as noted earlier, the Supreme Court had long ago held that Federal control over flight operations and the national airspace was exclusive.[78] Nonetheless, and as noted at the DAC meeting, local governments had enacted numerous bills looking to restrict UAS operations. In that context, and as is discussed in Chapter 13, the City of Newton in Massachusetts enacted local regulations "*to prevent nuisances and other disturbances of the enjoyment of both public and private space*".[79] These regulations banned UAS operations below an altitude of 400 feet over private property without the express permission of the owner, beyond the visual line of sight of the operator, over Newton city property or any place where a person has a reasonable expectation of privacy.[80]

A local resident challenged these regulations and argued that Newton did not have the authority to regulate UAS flight in the navigable airspace. The court agreed. In so doing it stated:

> Congress has given the FAA the responsibility of regulating the use of airspace for aircraft navigation and . . . and has specifically directed the FAA to integrate drones into the national airspace system. In furtherance of this duty . . . the FAA requires either that (1) a remote pilot both command and manipulate the flight controls or (2) a visual observer be able to see the drone throughout its flight . . . Second, the FAA allows waiver of the visual observer rule.[81]
>
> The Ordinance limits the methods of piloting a drone beyond that which the FAA has already designated, while also reaching into navigable space. . . .Intervening in the FAA's careful regulation of aircraft safety cannot stand.[82]

The Court's ruling clearly affirmed that the pre-existing aviation regulatory scheme applied to UAS flight. While it would be nice to say that this issue is now settled, a November 2020 ruling by a court in Texas held that a Texas law prohibiting UAV flight over areas where they would be allowed by FAA regulations did not interfere with the FAA's mandate to integrate UAVs into the national airspace and would not be voided.[83] While the Texas court stated that this decision was not in conflict with the ruling by the court in Massachusetts, this conclusion is hard to comprehend. It is even more difficult to square with the prior Supreme Court rulings recognising exclusive federal control of flight in the navigable airspace. How these issues play out in the future will bear careful scrutiny.

76 ibid 5.
77 ibid.
78 *City of Burbank* (n 11) 639.
79 *Singer v. City of Newton*, 284 F. Supp. 3d 125, 128 (D. Mass. 2017).
80 ibid.
81 Id. §§ 107.200, 205.
82 284 F. Supp. 3d 132, 133.
83 *National Press Photographers Association, Texas Press Association, & Joseph Pappalardo v Steven McCraw, in his official capacity as Dir. of Texas Dep't of Pub. Safety, et al*, 2020 WL 7029159 (W.D. Tex., 30 November 2020) 15.

Registration and licencing[84]

Currently, according to the FAA, there are about 1.7 million drones registered with the FAA, of which about 1.2 million are registered recreational drones. The FAA has certified about 200,000 Remote Pilots.[85] The FAA forecasts that the recreational drone fleet will grow by up to 1.59 million units by 2024.[86] With respect to the commercial dronefleet, the FAA projects that by 2024, it will be twice as large as the current number of commercial drones.[87]

All owners of drones weighing more than 0.55 lb (about 250 g) and less than 55 lb (about 25 kg) must register the drone with FAA's small, unmanned aircraft (UA) registry to be able to operate in US airspace. This requirement for registration applies to both recreational and commercial operations. For drones deployed for recreational operations, the owner will be provided with one registration number upon registration, which will apply to all drone units under one ownership, so that the owner is not required to register each drone unit separately. However, for drones deployed for non-recreational purposes, it is mandatory for the owner to register each drone unit separately.

Drones registered under FAA's small UA registry must have an FAA registration number affixed to or marked on the outside surface of the drone. For drones weighing more than 55 lb, the marking requirements are the same as a manned aircraft.

There are no licencing or certification requirements for recreational operations. All non-recreational operations will need to comply with 14 C.F.R. Part 107 (Part 107). Part 107 contains the FAA's rules and operating limitations for commercial operations of drones registered under FAA's small UA registry. Operators of drones for commercial operations under Part 107 must obtain a remote pilot certificate and comply with the operational rules for drones weighing less than 55 lb discussed earlier.

At the time of writing, there is no codified set of operating standards and regulations specifically for drones weighing 55 lb or more. Hence, to operate such drones for commercial operations, operators must either obtain an airworthiness certificate or an exemption from the FAA under 49 U.S.C. section 44807. The exemption under 49 U.S.C. section 44807 is usually granted by FAA if the proposed operation is in the public interest and it would not adversely affect safety. To date, this exemption has been granted predominantly in the context of commercial agriculture-related services.

Unlike some other national regulations where there is a blanket ban on cargo-carrying drone operations, the US stands apart by allowing transportation of property for compensation or hire under Part 107, albeit on a fairly limited scope. The following conditions must be met:

(i) drones, including its payload and cargo, must weigh less than 55 lb total;
(ii) operation is conducted with VLOS and not from a moving vehicle or aircraft; and
(iii) operation occurs wholly within the bounds of a state.

84 FAA, 'Register Your Drone' <www.faa.gov/uas/getting_started/register_drone/>.

85 FAA, 'UAS by the Numbers'<www.faa.gov/uas/resources/by_the_numbers/>.

86 FAA, 'Aerospace Forecast Fiscal Years 2020–2040' <www.faa.gov/data_research/aviation/aerospace_forecasts/media/FY2020-40_FAA_Aerospace_Forecast.pdf>.

87 ibid 52.

For operations involving the transportation of property beyond the scope of Part 107 set out earlier, the operator is required to obtain an air carrier certificate under 14 C.F.R. Part 135. This is the same Part that also applies to traditional manned air carrier operations.

Where to next?

As noted at the outset of this chapter, this discussion provides an overview of how the law regarding UAVs has developed in primarily in the United States as a foundation for further analysis of how future regulatory constructs will develop and to identify the factors likely to influence this process. In this regard, it has been demonstrated that from the outset of manned flight, unmanned flight has been closely tied to the same although trailing a bit behind in its development. During this development, users of this new technology have advocated for a regulatory construct that encourages expanded use while those concerned about privacy, interference with property rights and loss of local control have advocated for restrictive regulation.

In the US, the Federal government has decided that all flight operations must be regulated exclusively at the Federal level in order to insure uniformity. This has not, however, stopped local interests and governments from enacting local laws in this area. To date, the United States Supreme Court has rejected all these attempts at local regulation regarding manned flight. Nonetheless and even though the US Congress has mandated the Federal government to integrate UAS into the existing regulatory system, local governments have continued to push back by enacting restrictive UAS laws. One Federal court has voided these laws while another has allowed them to stand.

It is a virtual certainty that appellate courts will likely have to rule on these issues and at some point, so will the US Supreme Court. While it does appear likely that the Supreme Court will continue to recognise Federal supremacy in this area, the underlying issue of how to create a regulatory structure that balances local interest concerns against the many beneficial uses that this technology provides is still a work in progress.

The Federal government clearly recognises that a harmonious regulatory structure that takes into account all the concerns of both local and industry stakeholders is a goal worth pursuing. Thus, as noted previously, the Federal government created the Drone Advisory Committee to listen to the view of industry and user stakeholders. Concurrently, it created the "Unmanned Aircraft System (UAS) Integration Pilot Program (IPP)" to bring state, local and tribal governments together with private sector entities, such as UAS operators or manufacturers, "*to test and evaluate the integration of civil and public drone operations into our national airspace system*".[88]

One of the key issues to be addressed by the IPP are security concerns related to criminal and/or reckless misuse of this new technology.[89] Policing and security issues are dealt with in Chapters 4 and 7 but suffice it to say that given the increasing number of drones, their small size and potential use in just about any location, it would be impossible to police criminal or reckless misuse without the assistance of local

88 FAA, 'UAS Integration Pilot Program, Program Overview' (30 October 2020)<www.faa.gov/uas/programs_partnerships/integration_pilot_program/>.

89 ibid.

authorities. That assistance will almost certainly require some regulatory carve out for local interests and while it is hoped that a template for same will be mutually developed by the IPP, that remains very much uncertain given the political divisions that are likely to arise.

Concluding comments

Given the expense and expertise required to draft an effective regulatory framework and the number of stakeholders and users needed to justify embarking on this process, it is not surprising that the US is one of the few nations to have moved this process as far along as it has. Although the International Civil Aviation Organization (ICAO) has taken some steps to promulgate fairly basic model regulations,[90] it has also noted that these regulations were based on US and Australian regulations and that "States may also consider UAS regulation that other States have developed/adopted and assess their suitability".[91]

It is believed that it will take a considerable amount of time to craft a more mature regulatory system that will provide a detailed regulatory structure for all the enforcement, training, product certification and expanded use issues that will ultimately be needed. It is expected that this process will be informed by the experience that will come from the observations and information gleaned by the FAA's IPP and DAC programmes as well as the decisions rendered by courts resolving various legal challenges. It will also be informed by whether the weight of public opinion sees more value than harm arising from UAS operations as their use continues to grow in the coming years.

90 See, 'ICAO Model UAS Regulations' (23 June 2020) <www.icao.int/safety/UA/UAID/Documents/Final%20Model%20UAS%20Regulations2%20-%20Parts%20101%20and%20102.pdf>.

91 ibid 1.

16 National regulatory structure and responses

Spain

Gema Díaz Rafael, Enrique Navarro and Diego Olmedo

Introduction

Spain started down a legislative path to regulate the operation of unmanned aircraft in 2014. In that year, a Royal Decree[1] was adopted and converted into Law which focussed exclusively on remotely operated aircraft (ROA)—drones. After a further three-year wait, in 2017 another Royal Decree, 1036/2017, was adopted, extending the regulatory framework.[2]

The European Commission has laid new foundations for European UAS regulation commencing 31 December 2020 by promulgating two delegated regulations on the systems of unmanned aircraft, drones or UAS and on their rules and procedures for use. These are the Delegated Regulation (EU) 2019/945 of the Commission of 12 March 2019 and Implementing Regulation (EU) 2019/947 of the Commission of 24 May 2019.

These Regulations create a common and uniform regulatory framework for all EU Member States based on the "*operational risk*" of the UAS use, with which all EU Member States must comply from 31 December 2020.[3] This means that any regulatory provisions contained in Royal Decree 1036/2017 which are contrary to the EU Regulations will cease to apply at this date. By contrast, other requirements imposed by the Community Regulations but not provided for in the Royal Decree will have to be developed in Spain by the national legislators.

In the next section of this chapter, the new Community legal system which will apply to unmanned aircraft systems (UAS) is examined and consideration given to how it impacts the legislation currently in force in Spain, and how it will have to be developed in order to address new types of operations.

This chapter will examine the legal framework for UAS and potential liability relating to their use and operation under the Spanish legal system.

1 Royal Decree 552/2014 of 27 June 2014.

2 Royal Decree 1036/2017 of 15 December 2017 governing the civilian use of aircraft piloted by remote control and modifying Royal Decree 552/2014 of 27 June 2014 which develops the regulation of air space and common operational provisions for the services and proceedings of air navigation, and Royal Decree 57/2002, of 18 January 2002, approving the Regulation of Air Traffic.BOE [Spanish Official Journal] n° 316 of 29 December 2017.

3 The deadline having been extended because of the COVID-19 pandemic.

The new community regulatory framework

Delegated Regulation 2019/945 and Implementing Regulation 2019/947 are considered in detail in Chapter 14. Accordingly, at this juncture, subject to one caveat, only a broad overview of these Regulations is provided in this chapter. The caveat is that more detailed consideration is provided where the intersection of the EU Regulations and Spanish Law requires more comprehensive discussion.

The EU Regulations[4] are interesting in that they seek to address not just safety issues, but wider concerns around privacy, security and data protection.[5] They also go further by considering product safety and design requirements.[6] For smaller drones, this will be done by use of the well-known CE marking,[7] which will also identify the class of UAS, and be supported by consumer safety information to be supplied with the UAS. The class will allow operators to easily identify the type of UAS they are permitted to operate.

The Regulations were enacted to replace most of the existing domestic or national provisions on drone operations in EU Member States, to in effect create a homogenisation of drone-related legislation across the EU reducing the variety of operational requirements, obligations and restrictions between Member States. They also encourage drone operators to freely circulate within the EU without further registration or paperwork required.

Despite the harmonisation of rules, Member States will be free to define "zones" within their respective airspace to restrict drone operations. Hence, the flight zones will still be designated and regulated by respective national legislation. A system of organisation of airspace is provided for which permits UAS to operate safely in all types of situations, with the intention being that drones will be integrated perfectly with city life and other air traffic.[8]

In order to do this, it will be necessary to define the geographical areas in which UAS operations will be permitted, prohibited or restricted. This information will be provided digitally and, in a form, common to all countries in the European Union in accordance with the terms of Article 15 of the Implementing Regulation.

Any registrations or authorisations required under the harmonised rules will also be implemented at the national level.

The system of regulation is based upon the registration of operators enabling identification in the event of an incident and for data to be collected to track UAS use

4 Commission Implementing Regulation (EU) 2019/947 of 24 May 2019 on the rules and procedures for the operation of unmanned aircraft [2019] OJ L152/45; and Commission Delegated Regulation (EU) 2019/945 of 12 March 2019 on unmanned aircraft systems and on third-country operators of unmanned aircraft systems [2019] OJ L152/1.

5 See the General Data Protection Regulation 2016/679 and detailed discussion in Chapter 10. Council Regulation (EU) 2016/679 of 27 April 2016 on the protection of natural persons with regard to the processing of personal data and on the free movement of such data, and repealing Directive 95/46/EC (General Data Protection Regulation) OJ L119/1 (GDPR).

6 See below re Design.

7 CE marking is an administrative marking that indicates that a product has been assessed by the manufacturer and that it is in conformity with EU health, safety, and environmental protection requirements.<https://europa.eu/youreurope/business/product-requirements/labels-markings/ce-marking/index_en.htm>.

8 Mikko Huttunen, 'The U-Space Concept' (2019) 44(1) Air & Space Law 69–89.

and aid in the development of standards and regulations. The operator will need to be registered with the country of operations' national civil aviation authority as well as displaying a sticker on the UA showing this and uploading it to the UA's remote identification system.[9]

The EU Regulations seek to target the heaviest regulatory burden at the areas of highest perceived risk while maintaining a relatively light touch approach to those operations considered lower risk. It does this by the separation of operations into three categories:

- i Open—low-risk operations not requiring authorisation or declaration before flight;
- ii Specific—medium-risk operation requiring authorisation by the competent authority pre-flight, taking into account the mitigation measures identified in an operational risk assessment, or a pre-flight declaration for certain standard scenarios,[10] or when the operator holds a light UAS operator certificate with the appropriate privileges, or under the auspices of a model aircraft club/association; and
- iii Certified—high-risk operation requiring a certification process consisting of: (i) the certification of the UAS; (ii) a licenced remote pilot; and (iii) an operator approved by the competent authority.[11]

Therefore, depending on their characteristics and the potential risk which they may pose, unmanned aircraft are classified into these categories. Depending on the category, doors will be opened or closed to the pilot to operate more or less easily in different operational scenarios. It will also determine whether or not certain requirements have been complied with, such as registration of the unmanned aircraft and the holding of compulsory third-party liability insurance.

Operators of unmanned aircraft, whether they are natural persons or legal entities whose business includes the operation of unmanned aircraft, as well as any person owning an unmanned aircraft for personal (recreational) use, must register the unmanned aircraft with the competent national aviation authority. This information will be disseminated in an "*interoperable register of operators*" at community level, in accordance with the terms of Article 14 of Implementation Regulation 2019/347.

In addition to the data relating to its identification (name, age and address), particular attention should be paid to the requirement to share information, on the one hand in relation to the *number of the insurance policy* covering the UAS if EU or national law so requires; and on the other hand, the *declaration* by legal entities to the effect that "all staff participating directly in operations are appropriately qualified to carry out their tasks and the UAS will be piloted exclusively by remote pilots with the appropriate level of competence".

These two additional requirements, together with the identification, focus on the identification of the active agents in the event of liability to third parties for damage or the commission of an administrative offence in respect of their obligations relating to safety, data protection, or breaches of basic rights.

9 EU Regulation 2019/947 Article 14.
10 EU Regulation 2019/947, Annex.
11 EU Regulation 2019/947, Article 3.

Operators must register in the Member State in which they reside if they are natural persons, or in which they have their headquarters if they are legal entities, but they may only be registered in one Member State.

It is clear that, in one way or another, the different EU Member States will have to adapt their corresponding legislative systems to the provisions of both these Community Regulations, and that the required adjustments will impact both aviation and wider areas of law. For example, in Spain the concept of an aircraft contained in Article 150 of the *Spanish Air Navigation Aviation Law* will have to be adapted to the new form of unmanned aircraft in accordance with the definitions set out in the Regulations. Furthermore, Spain has yet to decide whether to amend local law to accommodate Article 9.3 of Implementation Regulation 2019/947 that permits Member States to reduce the minimum age of operators from 16 years to 12 years. It will also be necessary to adapt the system of notification of accidents and incidents for unmanned aircraft which may operate in Spanish airspace in accordance with the new categories of unmanned aircraft and existing types of operation.

Finally, in certain circumstances regard may also need to be had to other Community directives and national laws; for example, unmanned aircraft designed as children's "toys" need to comply with different rules, such as those governing the safety of toys.[12]

System of liability within the Spanish legal system

In the majority of cases, for example, in the event of surface damage as a consequence of an accident or incident, or injury caused to people, liability is determined in accordance with the content of Article 1902 of the Spanish Civil Code. So, who might be liable? With three new categories of operation, this may vary, and it will be essential to determine, in the first place, in which category an operation is carried out and with which type of unmanned aircraft.

In the "Open" category of very low risk drone operations, the owner of the unmanned aircraft will normally also be the operator registered with the authorities and the pilot in charge of flying it. As operations start to pose more significant aviation risks to persons overflown or involves sharing the airspace, the operation migrates to the "Specific" operation category. In this context the risks need to be mitigated by additional operational limitations or higher capability of the involved equipment or personnel.[13] Accordingly such operations will likely involve more than simply the owner, but also a pilot, who may be an employee or commercial contractor and must have the expertise and qualifications required by the authorities. When the aviation risks rise to a level akin to normal manned aviation the operation would be positioned in the category of "Certified" operations and additional licencing of

12 See, for example, *RD nº 1205/2011, of 26th August, governing the safety of toys* applies to the manufacture, distribution, import and control of toys in order to ensure an adequate level of safety, but neither refers to RPAS as toys nor excludes them. It only excludes toy [motor] vehicles equipped with combustion engines, and RPAS or unmanned aircraft have electric motors.

13 See, for example, EASA, 'Concept of Operations for Drones, A Risk-based Approach to Regulation of Unmanned Aircraft'<www.easa.europa.eu/sites/default/files/dfu/204696_EASA_concept_drone_brochure_web.pdf>.

pilots and operator approvals would be required.[14] These operations and the aircraft involved therein would be treated in the classic aviation manner.

Both Law no. 18/2014, of 15 October 2014, approving urgent measures, and RD1036/2017 impose an obligation on operators of RPAS to have in place a policy of insurance or other financial guarantee to cover their liability to third parties. The new Implementation Regulation (EU) 2019/947 requires drone operators to have insurance for any drone with a weight above 20 kg and most Member States mandate third-party insurance to operate a lighter drone.[15] As part of the changes introduced by the Regulations there are different considerations to take into account having regard to the risk-based approach which has been introduced, versus the prior less complicated delineation between commercial versus recreational uses. Accordingly, as is discussed in Chapter 22, there are many issues facing insurers and national regulators in determining levels of cover and premiums, especially for specified and certified operations. Similarly, at a national level, maximum levels of liability are established depending on the unmanned aircraft being operated, but these limits will have to be revised in accordance with the new regulatory framework.[16]

There are also challenges in the quantification of losses. A minor injury to a person is, of course, not the same thing as a serious injury or even death. Clearly, in the latter case, there is not the slightest doubt that the maximum limit would apply, but this limit cannot be said to be applicable in the case of a minor injury.

Examining the situation in Spain, the legislation says nothing about how to adjust the level of injury caused by an unmanned aircraft in individual cases, and there is also no case law from the High Court on which any such adjustment could be based. However, there is a Law which would allow injuries to be assessed and quantified fairly—from the most minor lesions through to life-changing injuries. This is *Law 35/2015, of 22nd September 2015,* which reforms the system of valuation of damage and injury caused to persons as a result of road traffic accidents.[17] Although this law focusses on providing a remedy for injuries caused in road traffic accidents, it does also provide a response to and an outcome for injuries caused in other areas and is used in Spain as the reference law for the assessment of physical injury caused by incidents of any kind. This law is used by legal professionals in cases in which the litigation involves a personal grievance or injury and it is repeatedly applied to work-related accidents, medical negligence, criminal injuries and also in the event of air accidents where losses of this nature occur.

The wording of the law establishes *a system of full reparation of damage* caused to the victim according to the level of prejudice suffered, taking into account, amongst other things, the age, employment and family circumstances of the victim, and the number of days over which she/he has been affected, and awarding compensation which is proportional and fair.

14 ibid.

15 EU regulation 2019/947 Article 14 (2) (d) <www.easa.europa.eu/the-agency/faqs/drones-uas>.

16 Currently, the minimum covers required for national aircraft weighing less than 20 kg maximum take-off mass (MTOW) are contained in Royal Decree 37/2001 of 19 January 2001. Under this law, for example, if a Spanish drone of less than 500 kg gross weight causes damage to third parties (personal injury and/or asset damage), the maximum amount of the payment order would be 220,000 DEG.

17 BOE [OJ] nº 228, of 23rd September 2015.

This law, which is very useful in the area of personal civil liability to third parties, requires a twofold interpretation: on the one hand, especially in cases of very serious injury, the assessment must be carried out by a medical practitioner who is a specialist in the assessment of personal injury, who will evaluate all the information provided by the victim as well as making an evaluation of the victim himself/herself and, with that information, will assess the amount which should be awarded to the victim on the basis of the assessment. In addition, it will be for the lawyer to interpret the law from a legal perspective, on the basis of the expert medical report, and to reflect the scope of the indemnity payable to the victim in actual figures.

It is because of this twofold—medico-legal—interpretation that this form of quantification of damages has been accepted in Spain as the most accurate in cases of injury, and it is understood that a fair and equitable indemnity will be obtained by applying this method.

Compensation for asset damage under Spanish Law is based on the cost of restitution of the asset. There must be an actual loss which is capable of being indemnified, and that loss must be proved by the party relying on it. Where the damaged asset is beyond repair the restitution is based on its market value which is subject to the age of the asset, its condition and the law of supply and demand. The market value of an asset will be determined or assessed by an expert following an appropriate investigation of the market and after verifying the age and condition of the asset. Therefore, although there is still no precedent for asset damage caused by unmanned aircraft, there is no shortage of precedent in other contexts.

Liability of the manufacturer[18]

Although a failure to comply with air navigation obligations or the actions of the pilot could give rise to liability in the event of an accident or incident involving unmanned aircraft, mechanical problems, or issues with the design and manufacture could contribute to the occurrence of an accident, or the accident may derive from contributory negligence on the part of both the operator and the manufacturer.

To that end, as stated earlier, both the ICAO and the community legislators are making enormous efforts to establish uniform international and community safety standards from the point of manufacture through to distribution, commissioning and operation. However, because of continual advances and development in the technology relating to this type of aircraft and the active involvement of amateur builders, issues with defects in both design[19] and manufacture[20] may arise. In such cases, reference will have to be made to the content of both Community and national legislation governing manufacturers.

Curiously, civil liability insurance for manufacturers, especially in the aviation sector, is not subject to any international regulation which establishes it as compulsory, as is the case in the Spanish system,[21] although manufacturers take out policies of civil

18 Generally, see discussion in Chapter 12, Product Liability.

19 For example, incorrect choice of materials which may result in a lack of resistance or errors in the determination of maintenance tasks associated with the unmanned aircraft caused by poor design.

20 This may include errors in the construction or assembly of the unmanned aircraft or any of its components.

21 Maria Castell I Marques, 'Drones recreativos. Normativa aplicable, responsabilidad civil y protección de datos [Recreational Drones, Applicable Regulations, Civil Liability and Data Protection]'(January–March 2019) VI(1) Revista de Derecho Civil [Civil Law Review].

liability insurance for defective products in order to be able to respond to any losses which they may cause. The system of liability is established by *Directive 85/374/EEC on liability for damage caused by defective products*[22] which provides that:

> a product is considered to be any moveable asset, including an asset which is joined to or incorporated into another moveable or immovable asset.

The scope of protection extends to both personal injury to any person and material damage caused to objects other than the defective product itself, that is to say, the unmanned aircraft itself, provided that the damaged asset was intended for private consumption or use.

The manufacturer could be considered as the responsible person in a wider sense because, in the majority of cases, the same legal entity is responsible for both the manufacture and assembly and for the mass sale of its product. Manufacturers of unmanned aircraft may argue the exemptions set out in Article 140.1. *General para la Defensa de los Consumidores y Usuarios* (General Act for the Protection of Consumers and Users) hereafter LGDCU, which basically state that it could not have known the defective nature of the product in accordance with the scientific and technical state of the art existing at the time it was marketed and that the defect was due to the product being prepared in accordance with the existing mandatory rules.

Article 143, LGDCU, provides a statute of limitations of three years for actions for the liability of the manufacturer for defective products and a time limit for the extinction of liability of ten years from the date on which the product which caused the damage was put into circulation.[23]

Liability deriving from data protection law[24]

Although both Spanish and Community data protection law is fully applicable to unmanned aircraft, it is not an easy task for an operator or an individual to know how to process it and, because it is such a technical and specialised task, will certainly give rise to doubt and anxiety.

Any attempt to work through such an analysis may give rise to a host of questions. For example: (i) does an operator of an unmanned aircraft, whether she/he is a private individual or a professional, know how to treat any personal data which she/he may obtain as a result of their operation? (ii) can she/he carry out video surveillance exercises? (iii) do Community Regulations 2019/945 and 2019/947 provide for any considerations to be taken into account or do they merely refer to the General Data Protection Regulation (GDPR)?[25] (iv) is this sufficient, or would it have been necessary to provide a specific process for unmanned aircraft? (v) what are the current

22 Transposed into the Spanish legislative system by Law 22/1994, of 6th July 1994 governing civil liability for damage caused by defective products.

23 See Simon Whittaker (ed), *The Development of Product Liability* (vol 1, CUP 2014)248.

24 Generally, see discussion in Chapter 10 Data Protection, Privacy and Big Data.

25 Council Regulation (EU) 2016/679 of 27 April 2016 on the protection of natural persons with regard to the processing of personal data and on the free movement of such data, and repealing Directive 95/46/EC (General Data Protection Regulation) OJ L119/1 (GDPR).<https://eur-lex.europa.eu/legal-content/EN/TXT/PDF/?uri=CELEX:32016R0679&from=EN>.

legal arrangements in Spain? (vi) will the new legislation currently in preparation envisage any express reference to this or will it continue to apply the content of RD 1036/2017? (vii) if an operator accidentally processes personal data inappropriately, what are the legal consequences or what penalties could be applied? and (viii) what are the arrangements for the use of unmanned aircraft by public authorities?

In order to facilitate the task of determining how the Spanish and Community data protection law may apply, the Spanish Data Protection Agency (AEPD) published a guide entitled "Drones and Data Protection"[26] which has been advertised to drone operators and other affected groups. Attention should also be paid to another Report published by AEPD entitled "Guide to the Use of Video Cameras for Security and Other Purposes" that examines the legal structure applicable to "drones" and determines the characteristics, requirements and circumstances which might arise in respect of data processing carried out by unmanned aircraft.[27]

First, it is important to bear in mind what should be understood by "*personal data*". According to the wording of the *General Data Protection Regulation (GDPR)* and *Organic Law 3/2018, of 5th December 2018 governing the Protection of Personal Data and the Guarantee of Digital Rights (LOPDGDD)*, this will be "any information about a natural person who is either identified or identifiable". Starting from this premise and in relation to unmanned aircraft, with regard to the processing of personal data, operations can be divided into two categories:

a) *Operations which do not include the processing of personal data*, for example, inspection of infrastructures, inspection of terrains, topographic surveys or other video or photographic services, but which may: (i) not carry any risk of processing of personal data or (ii) carry a risk of deliberate or accidental processing of personal data.
b) *Operations which inherently include processing of personal data*, such as video surveillance or the recording of events.

The first of these types of operation involve recreational flights in which the use of the images taken is limited to domestic purposes. For example, while on holiday, a drone is flown to record a video as a souvenir. In order to comply with data protection regulations, if the person(s) taking the video want to submit the video to Instagram or another social network, there is a requirement that they assure themselves that the video does not contain any images of or data relating to people, dwellings, vehicles or other objects by which people can be identified and, if such data is present, edit the video in order to anonymise it, either by pixilation or blurring.

In the second type of operation, there is a risk of processing personal data as collateral or accidentally, despite the fact that the objective is not to capture such personal data. The images usually captured are of people in the background, and vehicles and dwellings which are beyond the visual range of the pilot. In such cases, a series

26 Agencia Española Protección Datos (AEPD), 'Drones and Data Protection' <www.aepd.es/sites/default/files/2019-12/guia-drones-en.pdf>.

27 ibid. Specifically, it asked whether it is necessary to manage the drone like a video surveillance camera and therefore to release it with the corresponding file or whether it is only necessary to carry out a data protection impact assessment.

of recommendations are in place which should be followed in order to minimise the presence of people and objects.[28]

The objective of the third type of operation—used for surveillance and recording events—is, in fact, to process personal data. From a data protection perspective, processing of personal data is inherent in this type of operation, and therefore both aviation regulations governing the use of unmanned aircraft and the personal privacy regulations establish an obligation to take the necessary measures to ensure compliance with those regulations.

With regard to the latter type of operation, in accordance with the provisions of Organic Law *4/1997, of 4th August 1997, governing the use of video cameras by the Security Forces*, the security forces are granted exclusive powers to install fixed or mobile video cameras in public places, although Article 42.1 of *Law 5/2014, of 4th April governing Private Security* also allows video surveillance services to be provided by security guards by means of fixed or mobile cameras or video cameras.

On the basis of what has been mentioned earlier, the Law does not permit the installation of fixed or mobile video surveillance cameras in public places, and this prohibition would extend to capturing images of people on a public highway by means of data capturing systems installed in an unmanned aircraft. However, provided that compliance with the principles of limitation of the purpose and minimisation of data under Article 5.1 GDPR is guaranteed, video surveillance may be carried out in private areas or premises (also complying with restrictions on airspace and aviation). Amongst other things, this means complying with the *right to information [notification]* contained in Article 13 GDPR, Article 30 relating to the *recording of processing activities* and the adoption of the corresponding security measures in accordance with the *risk analysis* envisaged in Article 32, GDPR.

With regard to the *right to information [notification]*, operators of unmanned aircraft must find the most appropriate means of notifying affected persons in advance,[29] including giving a clear indication of who is responsible and the purposes of the processing, as well as providing clear and specific information about rights of access to the data.

With regard to the *data protection impact assessment (EIPD),* the study must serve to enable those responsible and operators of unmanned aircraft to disclose the risks to privacy associated with the use of the technology and the procedure for the processing of data which it is intended to carry out. An assessment must be made of whether the processing of personal data is *lawful, necessary and proportionate* and must cover *transparency and security* aspects, as well as document the steps to be taken to minimise any risks which appear during the course of the impact assessment.

In any event, in accordance with Article 5.1, GDPR, functions which are not for surveillance purposes but which do record data, must process personal data in a *lawful, faithful and transparent* manner, be collected for *specific, clear and legitimate purposes*, and the data captured must not subsequently be processed in a manner which is not compatible with those purposes (*limitation of purpose*) and must be appropriate,

28 For example, carrying out flights at times when there are fewer people or by controlling access to the area, reducing the capturing of images to the absolute minimum necessary, reducing the resolution of the image in order to avoid identification, increase the distance from sensitive data or persons, not capturing identifiers of mobile devices, avoiding the unnecessary storage of personal information.

29 Through web pages or in their customer contracts.

relevant and limited to what is necessary in relation to the purposes for which it is processed (*minimisation of data*).

This means that any operation of an unmanned aircraft involving data processing must, in the first instance, comply with the aviation law applicable to the sector, otherwise, data capture and processing during air operations will be deemed not to comply with the *principle of lawfulness* contained in the GDPR and will be subject to the *system of offences and penalties in data protection matters* and the corresponding system in *aviation matters* as well as other, additional, systems (privacy, for example).

The "instigator" and the "operative" of data processing

Under the terms of Article 26 (f) of Royal Decree 1036/2017, the Instigator of data processing is the person who decides on the intended purpose of the images in accordance with the provisions of Article 4.7, GDPR.

In the case of the operation of unmanned aircraft, an example would be the recording of an event, such as a wedding or a private party using a drone. Usually, the editing or processing of the images would be entrusted to a third party, that is, an audio-visual producer who would enter into a contract with an unmanned aircraft pilot to make the recording. The operator of the unmanned aircraft will act as the "operative" for the processing of personal data and must ensure that the relationship with the videographer is regulated by a contract so that she/he can act in accordance with its terms. The "instigator" will be the person who decides on the purpose of the data processing, that is, the person who commissions the filming, whilst the "operative" will be the person who processes the data in accordance with the guidelines and instructions framed in the contractual relationship. If the operator of the unmanned aircraft is the instigator, she/he must comply with the terms of the GDPR. Only with the "express consent" of the persons being recorded and whose images will be published will it be possible to make use of these images.

In cases of video surveillance work carried out using unmanned aircraft, the operator of the aircraft will also act as the "operative" for the processing of personal data and must also ensure that his relationship with the "instigator" is governed by a contract or other legal deed by which he is bound to the instigator and acts on his instructions. He will select the most appropriate technology for the purpose of the operation and will take appropriate measures in relation to privacy, avoiding subsequent compiling and processing of unnecessary data.

Both the instigator and the operative must take the technical and organisational measures necessary to ensure an adequate level of protection against risks to personal rights and freedoms and to prevent unauthorised use of the data captured during the transmission phase, and any unnecessary personal data must be eliminated or anonymised as soon as possible after capture.

Penalties

Offences against the GDPR and the *Organic Law 3/2018 of December 5, governing the Protection of Personal Data and the Guarantee of Digital Rights (LOPD)* may result in the application of penalties in addition to those which may apply in aviation and privacy matters.

Under the terms of Article 83, GDPR, fines of 10 million euros or in the case of an undertaking, up to 2% of total annual global turnover for the previous financial year, whichever is higher, may be imposed for offences such as *failure to take appropriate safety measures* or failing to appoint a data protection officer where necessary; and fines of up to EUR 20 million or in the case of an undertaking, up to 4% of total annual global turnover for the previous financial year, whichever is higher, for offences such as *breaching the rights of affected persons or failure to comply with the basic principles of data processing.*

These fines will be imposed by the Spanish Data Protection Agency (AEPD) as the controlling authority, which will examine[30] the individual circumstances of each case and adjust the penalties accordingly.

To that end, an analysis will be made in order to ascertain whether it is necessary to carry out an "*impact assessment*" on data protection in accordance with the provisions of Article 35.4, GDPR. In the event that an impact assessment is not necessary, but there is a risk to data protection, a risk analysis will have to be carried out in order to be able to take the necessary measures to avoid and mitigate those risks and their consequences as far as possible.

In addition to the terms of the GDPR, the LOPD sets out three types of offence: *very serious* offences, which are deemed to be a material breach of the regulations; *serious* offences, which are deemed to be a substantial violation; and *minor* offences, which are merely infringements of form.

Very serious offences (attracting fines between EUR 300,506.25 and EUR 601,012.10) would include the processing of personal data in breach of the principles and guarantees contained in the GDPR and the failure to notify an affected person of the fact that his/her personal data has been processed; *serious* offences (with fines between EUR 60,101.21 and EUR 300,506.25) include failure to take appropriate technical and organisational measures to ensure an appropriate level of safety against the risks of [data] processing, and *minor* offences (with fines between EUR 601.01 and EUR 60,101.21) include failure to comply with the principle of transparency or the rights of the affected person to information by failing to provide all the required information.

Instigators and operatives of data processing and their representatives in countries outside the EU may also be responsible persons as set out in Article 70, LOPD "Responsible Parties".

Liability deriving from breaches of basic rights: the right to privacy and the inviolability of the home

The right to privacy

On the basis of the content of Article 12 of the Universal Declaration of Human Rights and Article 17 of the International Covenant on Civil and Political Rights[31] as well as the European Convention on the Protection of Human Rights and Fundamental

30 For illustrative purposes, the GDPR sets out a list of factors which establish degrees, including: the nature, seriousness and duration of the offence, the degree of intent or negligence, any means used by the instigator or the operative to try to mitigate the damage and loss and the category of the data affected.

31 Both articles state that: "no person shall be subject to arbitrary intrusion into his/her private life, family, home or correspondence, or to any attack on his/her honour or reputation. Every person is entitled to the protection of the law against such intrusion or attack.

Freedoms,[32] Article 18.1 of the Spanish Constitution[33] enshrines the fundamental right to personal privacy and self-image. This fundamental right may be unlawfully interfered with as a consequence of frames or photographs being taken from an unmanned aircraft.

"Privacy" should be understood as the space in which an individual is protected from any interference or intrusion from outside which that person has not authorised. This concept has been evolving over time since, years ago, privacy meant only the privacy of the home or correspondence. Now, however, it can be defined in relation to all the technologies used for recording and the capturing of images. This right must be respected by the public authorities (under the terms of Article 11 LOPJ [law governing judicial procedure], they may not collect information for legal proceedings which would be in breach of this right) or any individual (who may be guilty of the offence set out in Article 197 CP [Criminal Code]).

The protection of these rights in the event of the capture and processing of personal data and images from unmanned aircraft does not fall into a specific legal structure, for which reason the provisions of the *Spanish Criminal Code* and *Organic Law 1/1982, of 5th May 1982 governing civil protection of the right to personal and family integrity and privacy and to self-image (LOPH)*[34] apply.

In this respect, Article 7.5, LOPH, considers an "*unlawful interference*" to be the capture, reproduction or publication by means of a photograph, film or any other processing of images of people in places or at moments in or outside of their private lives, unless those people hold public office or exercise a public profession and the image is captured during the course of a public activity in a public place (Article 8.2).

Both the Spanish Constitutional Court and the Supreme Court have given a number of different judgments to the effect that this is not an absolute right and is therefore subject to evaluation and proportionality in order to assess the lawfulness or otherwise of the interference, taking into account not only laws, but also social customs and individual circumstances.

In accordance with Supreme Court case law, an assessment must be made of whether the image of the person was captured merely incidentally and whether it was in the nature of an adjunct. According to the Judgment of the Supreme Court (First Division) of 22 February 2006, this is the case when:

> the image is not a principal element, because the presence [of the person] is not necessary, nor does it have any particular relationship with the object of the capture or projection, and there is nothing unworthy or embarrassing for the affected person.

32 Article 8 of the Convention provides that:

> 1. Every person is entitled to the respect of his/her private and family life, home and correspondence. 2. Public authorities may not interfere in the exercise of this right unless such interference is provided for by Law and constitutes a measure which, in a democratic society, may be necessary for the purposes of national security, public safety, the economic health of the country or the defence of good order and the prevention of crime, the protection of health or morals or the protection of the rights and freedoms of others.

33 BOE [OJ] nº 311, of 29th December 1978.

34 BOE[OJ]nº 115, of 14th May 1982.

To the extent that an unlawful interference has occurred, a claim may be made against the perpetrator for an *indemnity* for moral damages, the quantum of which will depend on the circumstances of the case and the seriousness of the actual injury, as established in Article 9.3, LOPH, as well as the adoption of all necessary measures to prevent subsequent interferences (Article 9.2, LOPH).

Generally speaking, the pilot of an unmanned aircraft will be the perpetrator of the breach of the fundamental right, but she/he may also be the victim. This will be the case, for example, if the unmanned aircraft captures his/her image (in private places or at moments in or outside of his/her private life) and the image is published on a web page belonging to a hacker in the course of a cyber attack. In the event that she/he is not the owner of the image, the provider of the data hosting or storage services will also be liable on the basis of the system of liability established by *Law 34/2002, of 11th July 2002 governing information service providers and electronic trading (LSSICE)*. This will be the case if she/he does not withdraw the content or prevent access to it, despite the knowledge that the information stored is in breach of the rights of an indemnifiable third party (Article 16.1, LSSICE). According to the academic opinion of the Supreme Court, indicative knowledge arising out of facts or circumstances is sufficient.

Inviolability of the home

Perhaps one of the most highlighted violations is that of the observation of the interior of a residential property by means of an unmanned aircraft. This could be interpreted as a breach of the inviolability of the home as envisaged by Article 18.2 of our *Magna Carta*. As early as 2016, in a Judgment dated 20 April 2016, the Supreme Court (Second Division) announced that "constitutional protection against intrusion into the home must start, now more than ever, both at the physical entrance and by "*virtual intrusion*", which will occur if a technical device for recording or taking images or approximations of images is used, irrespective of whether or not the occupant himself/herself has taken steps to prevent viewing from outside.

The principle contained in Organic Law *LO13/2015, of 5th October 2015 modifying the Law of Criminal Procedure in order to strengthen the procedural guarantees and regulations governing the means of investigation using technology* should also be borne in mind. This introduces two articles relating to the "use of technical devices for the capturing of images, tracking and tracing".

Article 588 d) a) authorises the capture of images by the police in *public places or spaces* "by any technical means", which must be understood also to include unmanned aircraft and, in the event of wishing to use *enclosed or residential spaces* Article 588 d) a) permits the recording of direct verbal communications and, where appropriate, the obtaining of photographs with authorisation from a court [warrant], where this is generated by the person investigated, on the public highway or other open space, at home or in any other enclosed spaces.

The essential distinction to make here is whether such media are used in *open spaces* or *enclosed* or *residential spaces*. In the former case, the Supreme Court permits the use of GPS tracking devices without the need for authorisation by a court, which means that, by applying this criterion, tracking may be carried out by unmanned aircraft. The Constitutional Court has not made any judgment to the contrary.

With regard to the latter case, that is to say, in *enclosed or residential spaces,* the response is more complicated, to the extent that the Constitutional Court has held that the content of the rule of inviolability of the home is ample and establishes an extensive series of guarantees and powers, including those of closing it against all forms of intrusion, including by mechanical, electronic or other similar methods which may be carried out without the need to penetrate the home directly. In such cases, authorisation must be sought from a court in order to use unmanned aircraft in enclosed or residential spaces, and such authorisation will be given provided that the requirements set out in the Article have been met.

No judgments have been given to date in matters relating to unmanned aircraft. The only judgment at the time of writing is that of the Supreme Court on 20 April 2016 (number 329/2016)[35] which provides an analysis of the constitutional protection provided by Article 18.2 CE and refers to the fact that the defence of the home must refer not only to the physical invasion of the dwelling, but also [the intrusion] by electronic, optical or recording equipment capable of collecting images and provide a better picture than would be obtained by a purely visual inspection. It makes express reference (Second F.J.) to the fact that:

> the technological revolution makes sophisticated intrusive devices available, so that a functional interpretation of Art. 18.2 CE is required. The existence of drones which are remotely controlled so as to allow intrusion into homes is merely one of many imaginable examples.

The use of drones by members of the security forces

Unmanned aircraft may be used by the Security Forces, including the Police (CID), for criminal investigation work as a technological investigation device.

The recording of sound and images by the Security Forces during the course of an investigation must be carried out in accordance with the legal provisions to the extent that the invasion of people's privacy is protected by the rules governing the violation of fundamental rights to privacy, self-image and data protection.

The legal rules relating to the processing of images and personal data by the Security Forces are set out in *LO 4/2015 of 30th March 2015 governing the protection of citizens,* Article 22 of which provides that the governing authority and, if appropriate, the Security Forces, may record persons, places and objects by means of legally authorised fixed or mobile video surveillance cameras, in accordance with current legislation. In this respect, although it is not expressly stated, mobile cameras would have to be understood to include unmanned aircraft.

Equally, as stated earlier, Articles 588 d) a) and 588 c) Law of Criminal Procedure permit the use of technical devices for image capture, tracking and tracing, such devices also being understood to include unmanned aircraft. The question now arises of the evidential value of photographs or recordings made in this way. Can they be regarded as electronic evidence? It would be necessary to make a distinction between the aircraft itself and the electronic material which has to be properly safeguarded from the time it is captured by the unmanned aircraft until it is evaluated in court.

System of penalties

In the event that unmanned aircraft are used in contravention of the regulations and so that they pose a risk to safety, penalties can be applied which, depending on the

35 Judgment of the Supreme Court (Second Division) n° 329/2016, of 20th April 2016.

seriousness of the circumstances, may be a fine of up to EUR 225,000 in accordance with the terms of Articles 32.2, 42b, 44 and 55.1 of Law 21/2003 of 7 July 2003 governing Air Safety (LSA).

Article 7.1 of RD 1036/2017 provides that failure to comply with the provisions of the Royal Decree and its developing regulations will constitute an administrative offence under civil aviation in accordance with the provisions of the Spanish Air Safety Law 21/2003 of 7 July 2003. Administrative liability does not protect the offender from potential criminal liability under Article 53, LSA. As stated earlier, it would be appropriate to review this law in order to include types of infringements into which the new acts or omissions which may be committed by the use of unmanned aircraft could be subsumed.

With regard to existing case law in this sector, particular attention should be paid to the *Judgment of 7/7/2017 given by the Central Contentious Administrative Court nº 1* in relation to "viewings of flights over the internet which does not prove or guarantee the identity of the perpetrator of the aviation offence". The Court overrode a penalty of EUR 13,000 imposed by AESA on a drone operator because it attributed offences to it of overflying a crowd of people and flying at night, thereby failing to comply with the requirements for capturing audio-visual recordings from the air.

The court held that:

> in order to ensure the certainty of the evidence, the viewing of such videos and capturing of films must, as a minimum, be certified by an authorised official with powers of certification, such certification to contain a reference to the equipment used in order to capture the image, the PC and software used to process the data, and incorporate the technical certificates for verification which will prove that they were in perfect working order, the date of capture of links and screenshots, the content and storage of the information, as well as the technical procedures guaranteeing the reliability and authenticity of the [images/recordings] captured.

Environmental liability

Noise pollution

The operation of an unmanned aircraft will always involve "noise emissions", which may be inconvenient or cause nuisance to people and living creatures. Exceeding or violating what could be considered to be "normal" noise levels would entail a number of risks and losses which may be difficult to remedy. In such circumstances, it would be necessary for the law to establish noise levels applicable to unmanned aircraft, and to obtain an undertaking from manufacturers and operators that this would be binding and to comply with it. Compliance would have to be part of the monitoring and supervisory activities of the aviation authorities, and any victims of a breach of fundamental rights would have to be able to seek the protection of the Constitutional Court.

The *Aviation and Environmental Protection Committee (CAEP)* of theICAO has dedicated a great deal of effort to the reduction of the impact of aviation on the environment, and has focussed for years on the impact of aircraft noise. As a result, it has established maximum levels of exposure to noise during take-off and landing operations and has set timetables for air operators to modernise and replace their aircraft with quieter ones. New types of aircraft, which include unmanned aircraft and those which fall into the category of *urban air mobility,* are currently the subject of joint studies with each of the Member States.[36]

For unmanned aircraft, the legislator has already regulated the maximum noise levels to be adhered to by the type of craft operating in the "Open category", and any contraventions by pilots and operators of unmanned aircraft may result in the imposition of fines and penalties and civil liability for any damage and loss incurred.

Limitations on sound power

Delegated Regulation (EU) 2019/945 provides that, in order to provide citizens with a *high level of environmental protection*, it is necessary to limit noise emissions from unmanned aircraft to the minimum possible. Limits on sound power have therefore been established for aircraft which operate in the "open" category, and those limits will be reviewed in each of the transition periods defined in Regulation (EU) 2019/347.

On the basis of what should be understood by a *Level of Sound Power*,[37] two levels have been established: the *measured sound power level* and the *guaranteed sound power level.*

The *measured sound power level* is the level determined on the basis of the detailed measurements set out in *Part 13 of the Appendix to Regulation 2019/945*. These measured values can be determined on the basis of a single unmanned aircraft which is representative of the type of equipment or based on the actual average of various different types of unmanned aircraft.

The *guaranteed sound power level* is the level determined in accordance with the requirements set out in Part 13 of the Appendix, which includes the uncertainties arising out of the variation in production and measurement processes and in respect of which the manufacturer or its authorised representative in the Community will confirm that, according to the technical instruments used and referred to in the technical documentation [the level] will not be exceeded.

In this way, manufacturers and operators of aircraft in Category C1 (between 250 and 900 kg MTOW) and C2 (between 900 and 4000 kg) must respect the maximum levels of sound power specified in Part 15 of the Appendix to the Delegated Regulation which will be reviewed at two and four years from the entry into force of the Implementing Regulation. The levels are established in a descending scale (from 85 dB[38] at the date of entry into force of the Regulation, to 83 dB at two years from that date and 81 dB at four years from that date).

Compliance with these sound power levels must be integrated into the geographical UAS areas in which the operation of unmanned aircraft will be allowed, prohibited or restricted, or in which access will only be granted to certain types of aircraft.

36 See, for example, ICAO Assembly Resolution A40-17, Consolidated statement of continuing ICAO policies and practices relating to environmental protection- General provisions, noise and local air quality; ICAO, 'Report of the Executive Committee on Agenda Item 15' (2 October 2019) A40-WP/625.

37 Level of sound power contemplated in decibels, in relation to 1 pW, as defined in regulation UNE-EN ISO 3744:2010.

38 In relation to the levels of noise of unmanned aircraft, readers may wish to review the study by Airborne Drones, 'Drones Noise Levels' (13 January 2020) <www.airbornedrones.co/drone-noise-levels/>.

System of penalties

Exceeding the levels of sound power may result in the opening of a sanctioning file by the Spanish National Air Safety Agency on the basis of the content of Article 47 of Spanish Air Safety Law (LSA) relating to *infringements of air traffic discipline in matters of noise.*

Being considered for all intents and purposes as "aircraft", exceeding the defined levels may be regarded as an administrative offence contrary to the content of Article 47.2.3ª which provides that "exceeding the maximum noise levels defined in the trajectories and points established in the said processes" will be considered as a serious offence; although it would be necessary for any future development of the regulations to contemplate the inclusion of specific types of administrative offence for this type of aircraft, and therefore the variation of the LSA, at national or domestic level.

On the other hand, it is important to point out that, in accordance with *Law 37/2003, of 17th November 2003*, governing *Noise*,[39] aircraft are considered as "*noise emitters*" (Article 12), and unmanned aircraft should also be considered as such. Consequently, public administrations, city councils and autonomous communities may, within their powers of inspection and sanctioning, open and deal with penalty files relating to noise pollution. The law establishes the following as *very serious offences:"the production of noise pollution above the limit values set out in areas of special noise protection and areas of special noise status"* (Article 28.2.a) or "*exceeding limit values which may be applicable where serious damage or deterioration to the environment has been caused or the health or safety of persons has been placed at serious risk*" (Article 28.2.b). The causing of "damage" or "serious deterioration to the health or safety of persons" will determine which offence would be considered as very serious and subject to fines of between EUR 12,001 and EUR 300,000.

Protection of the constitutional right to physical and moral integrity: risk or damage to health

The exceeding of sound power levels by unmanned aircraft may also cause a breach of the fundamental right to *life, physical and moral integrity* under Article 15; to *personal and family privacy* under Article 18.1, and to the *inviolability of the home* under Article 18.2 of the Spanish Constitution.

As early as 2008, the Spanish Supreme Court made a decision in relation to the noise produced by aircraft in its well-known Judgment of 13 October 2008[40] concerning a noise incident caused by the overflying of a suburb of Madrid and the potential effect of this on or the breach of those fundamental rights.

The fundamental right to personal integrity incorporates the right that *no damage or injury shall be done to the health of persons,* although the Constitutional Court has held that not all cases of risk or damage to health imply a breach of this fundamental right, but only risk or damage which generates "*a real and serious danger to the person*" or "*the relevant risk prevents the effect on the right to physical integrity from*

39 BOE [OJ] nº 276, of 18th November 2003.

40 Judgment of the Supreme Court, Contentious-Administrative Division, Section Seven, relating to cassation appeal nº 1553/2006 against the Judgment of 31st January 2006 of the High Court of Madrid (contentious-administrative division, Section 9).

being recognised". Therefore, as a permanent source of disturbance to the quality of life,[41] noise affects personal and family integrity and that effect may also extend to the inviolability of the home; consequently, the fundamental rights in question may be considered to have been breached if the noise is *constant, persistent or prolonged*. Along the same lines, to the extent that the operation of unmanned aircraft generates a sound footprint, the potential for such effects and/or breaches should be taken into account.

Without prejudice to the right of the victim to *put a stop to that situation*, the Spanish courts recognise *financial indemnities* as compensation for *losses suffered*. In its Judgment of 29 May 2003,[42] relating to noise pollution, the Spanish Supreme Court acknowledged that:

> in order to ensure that its protection is not merely theoretical, the full and effective restoration of the fundamental right breached certainly requires the payment of an indemnity for the loss and damage incurred as a result of that breach.

Clearly, taking *health as a fundamental human need* into account, there is a close relationship between the protection of fundamental rights and the protection of the environment.

Environmental damage

As well as noise emissions, unmanned aircraft may have a contaminating effect as a consequence of the system of charging of the batteries they use.

The majority of the batteries used in such craft are made of a lithium polymer,[43] known as *LiPo Batteries*. This type of battery is characterised by a short life cycle and is usually used in electric cars and industrial machinery. As a planetary resource, it is in short supply, and massive extraction is likely to present an environmental problem.

Another hazard associated with the use of these batteries is that they tend to explode or catch fire if they are damaged or overheat, so that operators of unmanned aircraft are required to exercise meticulous control over the use, storage and disposal of such batteries.[44] In commercial aviation, the transport of such materials in civilian aircraft has already been banned, unless it is being transported as hazardous goods under loading operations.

Lastly, the content of *Law 26/2007 of 23rd October 2007 governing Environmental Responsibility*[45] which harmonises Spanish legislation with *Directive 2004/35/EC*

41 According to the European Environmental Agency (EEA), 16,600 deaths are caused annually by noise in the EU, and noise pollution is one of the principal environmental health concerns in Europe. The EEA has explained that "exposure to noise from transport and industry can cause anxiety, stress, disrupted sleep patterns and the consequent risk of hypertension and cardio-vascular illness"<www.eea.europa.eu/airs/2018/environment-and-health/environmental-noise>.

42 Judgment of the Supreme Court, Third Contentious-Administrative Division of 29 May 2003, Appeal N° 7877/1999.

43 The main deposits of Lithium are found in South America, Bolivia being the largest country supplier.

44 One author has indicated that, in the event of an accident involving an unmanned aircraft, chemicals contained in the circuits may be spilled. See Geoffrey Christopher Rap, 'Unmanned Aerial Exposure: Civil Liability Concerns Arising from Domestic Law Enforcement Employment of Unmanned Aerial Systems' (2009) 85(3) North Dakota Law Review 631.

45 BOE [OJ] n° 25, of 24th October 2007.

on environmental responsibility, as amended by Law 11/2014 of 3rd July 2014 should not be forgotten. This law governs the responsibility of operators to anticipate, avoid and repair any environmental damage, in accordance with Article 45 of the Spanish Constitution,[46] and establishes a definition of "environmental damage" as "damage to wildlife species and their habitat".

Studies[47] have already found that noise emissions from unmanned aircraft could have a detrimental effect on animals and wildlife,[48] and in the near future, if operators of unmanned aircraft fail to respect the regulations and operational limitations imposed by the competent aviation authorities, we may have to face the fact that activists will bring environmental actions based on this law, without prejudice to the criminal and administrative penalties which may cut across personal and property rights.[49]

46 Raul Canosa Usera, 'Existe un verdadero derecho constitucional a disfrutar del medio ambiente' [Is There a True Constitutional Law Which Benefits the Environment?] (2006) 7(1) Anuario de Derecho Humanos. Nueva Época (Human Rights Annual. New Era])151–215.

47 See, for example, E Bennitt, H LA Bartlam-Brooks, TY Hubel and others,'Terrestrial Mammalian Wildlife Responses to Unmanned Aerial Systems Approaches' (2019)9:2142 Scientific Reports<https://doi.org/10.1038/s41598-019-38610-x>.

48 ibid. There is evidence of increased stress among animals and their reactions to the presence of such equipment in their habitat.

49 Leyva Morote and Juan Fernando,'Régimen de Responsabilidad y Mecanismos Jurídicos para la reparación del daño ambiental[System of Liability and Legal Mechanisms for the Repair of Environmental Damage]'(2016)19 Observatorio Medioambiental [Environmental Observer] <https://doi.org/10.5209/OBMD.54163>.

17 National regulatory structure and responses

United Kingdom

Chris Morrison and Alan Kells

Introduction

Prior to 31 January 2020, the United Kingdom's (UK) drone laws could primarily be found in the Air Navigation Order 2016[2] (ANO). Interestingly, on the day the UK left the European Union (EU) it adopted most of the two EU Regulations on drones, known as the Implementing Regulation on the rules and procedures for the operation of unmanned aircraft,[3] and the Delegated Regulation on unmanned aircraft systems and on third-country operators of unmanned aircraft.[4] The adoption of these Regulations alters features of the legislative landscape for operators, owners and remote pilots, by amongst other things, reducing the age requirements for remote pilots, removing the requirement for all commercial operations to have a *permission* from the Civil Aviation Authority (CAA) and creating new criminal offences, all of which will be explored in this chapter. In line with the terminology in the Regulations, we will refer to drones as Unmanned Aircraft Systems[5] (UAS) and Unmanned Aircraft[6] (UA) when discussing this legislation.

Responsibility for regulation in the United Kingdom is split between various organisations, including the CAA, Health and Safety Executive (HSE), Police and Air Accident Investigation Branch (AAIB). In general terms, the respective remits are as follows:

- CAA—responsibility for the safe use of the unmanned vehicle "*in flight*".[7]
- AAIB—the investigation of any accidents or serious incidents when "*in flight*".
- HSE—responsible for health and safety *at work* when the drone is not "*in flight*".
- Police—normally first responders where used dangerously or a nuisance.

2 SI 2016/765.

3 Commission Implementing Regulation (EU) 2019/947 of 24 May 2019 on the procedures and rules for the operation of unmanned aircraft (2019) OJ L152/45.

4 Commission Delegated Regulation (EU) 2019/945 of 12 March 2019 on unmanned aircraft systems and on third-country operators of unmanned aircraft systems (2019) OJ L152/1.

5 "an unmanned aircraft and the equipment to control it remotely", Air Navigation Order 2016 (ANO), sch 1.

6 "any aircraft operating or designed to operate autonomously or to be piloted remotely without a pilot on board", ibid.

7 See ANO, art 3(b)—"from the moment when it first moves for the purpose of taking off, until the moment when it next comes to rest after landing".

The two key regulators for businesses when the UAS is being used are the CAA and HSE. The Memorandum of Understanding between the HSE and CAA confirms the HSE's responsibility for work *on the ground* and the CAA's *in flight*.[8]

Air Navigation Order 2016 (ANO)[9]

Until 31 December 2020, UAS operations in the UK were regulated under the ANO, which was amended several times between 2016 and 2020. On 31 December 2020, the EU Regulations came into force in the UK,[10] and this was also the date the UK left the EU. Perhaps this is unsurprising given the CAA's contribution to the European Union Aviation Safety Agency (EASA)[11] efforts, and hopefully an indication that this will be an area of continued cooperation in this developing field. The remaining provisions of the ANO relating to UAS along with the Regulations will be regulated and enforced by the CAA.

As a result of the changes certain ANO provisions in relation to UAS operations which do not conflict with the EU Regulations are retained, and others have been amended, or removed, to comply with them. Criminal offences have been introduced for failing to comply with the specified provisions of the Regulations. The Regulations themselves have been amended as they apply in the UK to remove references to EU institutions (such as the EASA) and the EU wide operational authorisation provided by the Regulations, by way of the Unmanned Aircraft (Amendment) (EU Exit) Regulations 2020.[12]

Operational requirements

Delegated Regulation 2019/945 and Implementing Regulation 2019/947 are considered in detail in Chapter 14 which sets out the various operational categories and associated requirements. This detail is not repeated here and discussion is limited to particular impacts upon UK owners, operators and remote pilots.

Registration

The UK was an early adopter of the requirement for anyone responsible for a UA (weighing 250 g–20 kg without fuel) to register from 30 November 2019 as an operator and obtain an Operator ID from the Drone and Model Aircraft Registration and Education Service. The clear benefits to registration from a legal and manufacturing/design perspective have been considered in previous chapters. The UA itself had to be

8 UK Civil Aviation Authority, 'Memorandum of Understanding between the Health and Safety Executive, Health and Safety Executive Northern Ireland and the Civil Aviation Authority for Aviation Industry Enforcement Activities' (Memorandum of Understanding, December 2016) <www.caa.co.uk/Our-work/About-us/The-CAA,-HSE-and-HSENI/>.

9 SI 2016/765.

10 The Air Navigation (Amendment) Order 2020, SI 2020/1555; The Air Navigation (Amendment) Order 2019, SI 2019/261; The Air Navigation (Amendment) (No. 2) Order 2018, SI 2018/1160; The Air Navigation (Amendment) Order 2018, 2018/623; and The Air Navigation (Amendment) Order 2017, SI 2017/1112.

11 See discussion in Chapter 14.

12 SI 2020/1593.

labelled with the operator's registration number allowing identification in the event of an incident. This continues to be a requirement. Under the Regulations operators of UA of 250 g and above[13] will need to be registered with the CAA, as well as displaying a sticker on the UA showing the registration and uploading it to the UAS's remote identification system.[14] Other than in limited circumstances there is no requirement to register where the UA weighs less than 250 g, consistent with the risk-based approach adopted by other states and recommended by transnational organisations.

It is a criminal offence for the UAS "operator"[15] (which may be an individual or organisation and need not be the remote pilot) to operate the UAS without registering with the CAA,[16] along with an offence targeted at the owners of Certified UAS if they "cause or permit" the UAS to be flown without being registered with the CAA.[17]

Pre-existing registrations in force at the time of the Brexit transition will continue to operate until the expiration date of the registration. The same applies to a pre-existing Operator ID and Flyer ID for existing operators and remote pilots.[18]

Categories

As set out in Chapter 14, the Regulations separate operations into three distinct categories based on the perceived risk of the operation, targeting the heaviest regulatory burden at the areas of highest perceived risk (heavier UAS, BVLOS, near/over people, etc.) while maintaining a relatively light touch approach to those operations considered lower risk. Chapter 14 provides a detailed description of the three categories, Open, Specific and Certified. It should be noted that the UK has not adopted the declaration of a standard scenario as a route for operating under the Specific category.

Age requirements

The Regulations set out minimum age requirements for remote pilots and operators. This reduces the minimum age for remote pilots to obtain a "*Flyer ID*" from the CAA in the Open category from 16 to 12,[19] and in the Specific category from 16 to 14,[20] or younger if authorised within the framework of a model aircraft club or organisation.[21]

The minimum age for an operator to obtain an "*Operator ID*" from the CAA is set at 18.[22]

13 Or which can in an impact transfer to a human energy above 80 J; or is equipped with a sensor capable of capturing personal data, which is not a "toy" for the purposes of the European Parliament and the Council of 18 June 2009 on the safety of toys (2009) OJ L 170/1; The Toys (Safety) Regulations 2011, reg 4.

14 Commission Implementing Regulation (EU) 2019/947 of 24 May 2019 on the procedures and rules for the operation of unmanned aircraft (2019) OJ L152/45, art 14.

15 "any person operating or intending to operate one or more UAS" ANO as amended, sch 1 para 1.

16 ANO, arts 265A(5)(a) Open, 265A(6)(a) Specific, 265A(7)(a) Certified.

17 ANO, art 265C.

18 Air Navigation (Amendment) Order 2020, SI 2020/1555, art 13.

19 ANO, art 265D(1).

20 ibid art 265D(2)(a).

21 ibid art 265D(2)(b).

22 ibid art 265D(6).

Insurance

The EU Regulations require any operator using a UA above 20 kg to have insurance in place.[23] States are able to require insurance for lighter UA. The UK has done so. There is an exemption in the Regulations for "*model aircraft with an MTOM of less than 20 kg*".[24] The UK has interpreted the exemption as one where the UA is used "*for sport or recreational purposes only*",[25] making insurance a requirement for all commercial operations regardless of the weight of the UA. It is not mandated for recreational users but is recommended.

Insurance must be in place for "*each and every flight*"[26] where it is required. This could be per flight, weekly, monthly or an annual policy so long as it is valid for the duration of the flight.

Commercial operations

Prior to 31 December 2020, a distinction was drawn between commercial and non-commercial operations. Any commercial operation (that was "*any flight by a small unmanned aircraft . . . in return for remuneration or other valuable consideration*")[27] required approval from the CAA.[28] The CAA offered two types of permissions to commercial operators—a *Standard Permission* and *Non-Standard Permission*. The former permitted commercial operations and, subject to the application, could also allow operations within a congested area. The application process required evidence of remote pilot competency and the submission of an Operations Manual[29] setting out how flights would be conducted. The latter was used for other types of operations and was targeted at those seen as higher risk. Applicants for a *Non-Standard Permission* were required to submit an Operating Safety Case, in addition to the *Standard* requirements.

If a commercial operator is able to operate within the confines of the Open category, this application process will no longer be required. It is anticipated quite a significant number of commercial operations will still be required to apply to the CAA, for either an authorisation, LUC or certification, due to the nature of their operations or size of UA involved. In light of this, the requirements previously required by the CAA to secure a commercial permission are useful guides as to what will be required going forward under the Specific or Certified categories, with the key focus being the risks presented by the operation and mitigation measures in place.

23 Commission Implementing Regulation (EU) 2019/947 of 24 May 2019 on the procedures and rules for the operation of unmanned aircraft (2019) OJ L152/45, art14(2)(d). Discussed in detail in Chapter 22.

24 Regulation (EC) No 785/2004 of the European Parliament and of the Council of 21 April 2004 on insurance requirements for air carriers and aircraft operators (2004) OJ L 138/1, art 2(b).

25 UK Civil Aviation Authority, 'CAP722: Unmanned Aircraft System Operations in UK Airspace—Guidance' (Guidance, 5 November 2020) <www.caa.co.uk/Commercial-industry/Aircraft/Unmanned-aircraft/Small-drones/Permissions-and-exemptions-for-commercial-work-involving-small-unmanned-aircraft-and-drones/>, s 1.4.

26 Regulation (EC) No 785/2004 of the European Parliament and of the Council of 21 April 2004 on insurance requirements for air carriers and aircraft operators (2004) OJ L 138/1, art 4(2).

27 ANO (pre-31 December 2020), art 7. Amended in light of the removal of the distinction between commercial and non-commercial operations under the EU Regulations.

28 ANO (pre-31 December 2020), art 94(5).

29 A template Operations Manual is available on the CAA website—UK Civil Aviation Authority, 'CAP 722A—Unmanned Aircraft System Operations in UK Airspace—Operating Safety Cases' (Document, July 2019) <http://publicapps.caa.co.uk/docs/33/CAP722A-UASOSC.pdf>.

Offences

The Regulations will be enforced in the UK by imposing criminal sanctions for failing to comply. A detailed consideration of each offence is beyond the scope of this chapter. In the following, we set out some of the key considerations, offences and penalties to be aware of. Specific offences have been introduced for remote pilots and operators for failing to operate within the parameters of the Regulations, which can result in financial penalties being imposed provided there are no injuries (if there are injuries, imprisonable offences will be possible).

As with any regulatory criminal prosecution, whilst under investigation the prospective defendant should be given an opportunity to give its account (whether by interview under caution or serving written submissions) prior to an enforcement decision being taken. Once a prosecution is brought a defendant will have the opportunity of challenging the case brought against them by pleading *not guilty* challenging prosecution evidence and calling evidence in their own defence.

The new offences created are all summary only offences meaning they will be dealt with in the Magistrates Court. Of note is that the Regulations create an offence for both operators and remote pilots where there is no limit on the fine which may be imposed for flights where the category requirements for the flight are not met.[30]

Operators

The following offences for operators have been introduced from 31 December 2020:

- i *Causing or permitting* a UAS to be flown without meeting the requirements of the relevant category of operations[31]
  - a It is worth noting the phrase *causing or permitting* which is relatively common in the criminal law.
- ii Contravening a "*relevant requirement*" of the Implementing Regulation[32]
  - a A "*relevant requirement*" includes, but is not limited to:[33]
    - i Registration—both being registered and displaying as required;
    - ii Reporting safety occurrences;
    - iii Remote pilot—designation and competency; and
    - iv Specific and Certified—having an operations manual and record keeping.

Remote pilots

Similar offences exist for the remote pilot:

- i Flying a UAS without:[34]
  - a Open—*reasonably* holding the view the operating requirements are met.

30 ANO, arts 265A(2), 265B(2), 265F(1).
31 ANO, arts 265A(1), 265A(2).
32 Commission Implementing Regulation (EU) 2019/947 of 24 May 2019 on the procedures and rules for the operation of unmanned aircraft (2019) OJ L152/45.
33 ANO, arts 265A(5) for Open; and ANO arts 265A(6), 265A(7), 265A(9) for Specific.
34 ANO, arts 265B(1), 265B(2).

 b Specific and Certified—the operating requirements of the category being met.

ii Contravening a "*relevant requirement*" of the Implementing Regulation[35]

 a A "*relevant requirement*" includes but is not limited to:[36]

 i Open

 1 Flight—maximum operating height.
 2 Pilot—competent for the category, carrying proof, fitness to fly.
 3 UAS—safety checks, MTOM check.

 ii Specific (authorisation/LUC)

 1 Pilot—competent for the category, carrying proof, fitness to fly.
 2 Flight—compliance with operator's procedures and operating limitations/conditions, avoid risk of collision.

 iii Specific (model aircraft club/association)

 1 Failing to comply with any condition imposed in the authorisation.

There is a distinction in the offences at point (i) between the offences for the Open and other categories. The higher risk categories make it an offence simply to contravene the requirements, whereas in respect of the Open category it is an offence for the remote pilot to fly a UAS where they do not *reasonably hold the view* the category operating requirements are met. The benefit of this is that it is unlikely to criminalise recreational pilots who make an honest mistake but hold those (likely commercial) operators posing a greater risk to others to a higher standard. However, the Open category remote pilot will still have to be able to demonstrate the reasonableness of their view if there are any issues. Use of an app such as Drone Assist is likely to be one such way. This was developed by the National Airport Transport Service to assist operators with compliance around restricted airspace, which provides a map of commercial air traffic and other potential hazards, which enables details of a UA's flight to be shared with other operators.[37] A further helpful guide for operators and remote pilots is the Drone Code, published by the CAA and NATS.[38]

Tethered aircraft[39]

The amendments to the ANO establish a set or regulations for tethered unmanned aircraft that are less than 1 kg in mass. The reasoning for this is that tethered aircraft with a MTOM of under 1 kg are not covered by the Regulations. As such, the requirements for such aircraft needed to be covered by an amendment to the ANO.

The aircraft covered will have (i) a MTOM of less than 1 kg and (ii) "*is flown within limits imposed by a restraining device which attaches the aircraft to the surface*

35 Commission Implementing Regulation (EU) 2019/947 of 24 May 2019 on the procedures and rules for the operation of unmanned aircraft (2019) OJ L152/45.
36 ANO, arts 265B(5), 265B(6) for Open; and ANO, arts 265B(7), 265B(8) for Specific.
37 Drone Safe, 'Safety Apps' (*Drone Safe UK*) <https://dronesafe.uk/safety-apps/>.
38 Drone Safe, 'Drone code' (*Drone Safe UK*) <https://dronesafe.uk/drone-code/>.
39 ANO, art 265E.

or to a person on the surface".[40] The CAA confirms the overall effect of the provision is that it "*'equalises' the operation of tethered small unmanned aircraft with the equivalent Open category 'untethered' unmanned aircraft*".[41]

The requirements of A1 will apply to tethered aircraft weighing less than 250 g,[42] and A3 to those weighing 250 g–1 kg.[43] Any flight outside of the category requirements,[44] dropping of material or carriage of dangerous goods,[45] or tether in excess of 25 m[46] requires CAA authorisation.

As in the case of UAS covered by the Regulations, criminal penalties apply for breaches.[47]

Penalties[48]

The fine levels remain the same as their equivalent offences previously contained within the ANO. An unlimited fine[49] can be imposed for operations outside of the category operating requirements. Lesser maximum penalties can be imposed for the other new offences.[50] These vary from up to £2,500 for operational/in flight offences such as failing to report safety occurrences by an operator. Those seen as administrative offences carry a penalty of up to £1,000, such as an operator failing to display its registration number on the UA. For the more minor offences, up to £500 will be payable, such as a remote pilot neglecting to carry proof of competency.

There is also scope for the court to order the forfeiture of the UAS. Prosecutions have taken place in UK courts for breaching the previous ANO rules, including the prosecution of a recreational operator who lost control of his UA resulting in it flying close to a road bridge and nuclear submarine facility,[51] and for flying close to a police helicopter,[52] both cases resulting in financial penalties for the operators.

As with any regulator, the CAA will approach decisions on prosecution on a risk related basis, likely with initial, more minor infringements resulting in guidance being provided, but raising to potential prosecution where the breaches are more serious and place people or property at risk.

The fines involved, while significant for individuals, are unlikely to break the bank for commercial operators. The key issues there are reputational—a business is unlikely to achieve a reputation for excellence in a dynamic field with a conviction able to be seen

40 ANO, sch 1.

41 UK Civil Aviation Authority, 'CAP2013: Air Navigation Order 2020 Amendment—Guidance for Unmanned Aircraft System Users' (Guidance, 17 December 2020) <https://publicapps.caa.co.uk/modalapplication.aspx?catid=1&pagetype=65&appid=11&mode=detail&id=9958>.

42 ANO, art 265E(2).

43 ibid.

44 ibid art 265E(3).

45 ibid art 265E(5)(a).

46 ibid art 265E(5)(b).

47 ibid art 265E(7).

48 ibid art 265F; UK Civil Aviation Authority (n 41).

49 In England and Wales, the statutory maximum will apply in Scotland and Northern Ireland.

50 Levels 2, 3 and 4 on the Standard Scale as at the date of publication.

51 Charles Arthur, 'UK's First Drone Conviction Will Bankrupt Me, Says Cumbrian Man' *The Guardian* (London, 3 April 2014) <www.theguardian.com/world/2014/apr/02/uk-first-drone-conviction>.

52 UK Civil Aviation Authority, 'Police and AA Welcome Successful Drone Prosecution after Police Helicopter Incident' (*UK Civil Aviation Authority*, 16 November 2018) <www.caa.co.uk/News/Police-and-CAA-welcome-successful-drone-prosecution-after-police-helicopter-incident/?catid=157>.

by competitors and potential clients alike.[53] Perhaps more importantly it will be difficult for an organisation to grow and potentially move into higher risk work requiring CAA approval, if that organisation has a conviction—it is difficult to convince a regulator you are a safe operator if you have convictions for breaching safety regulations.

Privacy

An ever present issue in the modern world is privacy and data protection. With UAS equipped with devices that inevitably capture personal data (whether inadvertently or otherwise) and notwithstanding any permission from the CAA, any operator, particularly a commercial one, will need to consider the impact of the *General Data Protection Regulation* and the obligations and limitations it places on data *processors* and *controllers*.[54]

This concern feeds into one of the triggers for registration. Any operator flying a UAS "*equipped with a sensor able to capture personal data unless it* [is a '*toy*']",[55] even if it weighs less than 250 g will need to register. However, it is worth noting that CAA guidance records that "*images or other data solely for the use of controlling or monitoring the aircraft*" do not trigger this particular registration requirement.[56]

Health and Safety Executive (HSE)

Where the UAS is used at work, health and safety at work legislation will apply. When not *in flight* this falls within the purview of the health and safety regulator, the HSE.[57] As such, when UAS are used commercially, operators must consider their day-to-day health and safety duties towards employees and non-employees under workplace health and safety legislation. While the technology is new, the familiar health and safety obligations apply when used at work:

- Activities need to be risk assessed;
- Appropriate equipment should be selected and maintained;
- Those operating need to be trained in its safe use; and
- That use will need to be monitored to ensure it is done safely.

To comply with the requirements the operator will need to consider the equipment, available information and the conditions it will be used in. For example, the working environment for a drone being used to inspect an oil platform in the North Sea will be different to photographing an event. Consideration should be given to the operating environment and its impact on the durability of the equipment. Those operating will need to be trained in its use. It is worth considering whether the CAA requirements are sufficient in light of the technology and proposed work environment.

53 The CAA publishes details of successful prosecutions on its website.

54 See discussion in Chapter 10.

55 Commission Implementing Regulation (EU) 2019/947 of 24 May 2019 on the procedures and rules for the operation of unmanned aircraft (2019) OJ L152/45, art 14(5)(a)(ii); "Toy": as defined by of the European Parliament and the Council of 18 June 2009 on the safety of toys (2009) OJ L 170/1; The Toys (Safety) Regulations 2011, reg 4.

56 UK Civil Aviation Authority (n 25) s 1.3.

57 For Northern Ireland this will be the HSENI.

As UAS operations become more common, it will be interesting to see if this segregation can be maintained in practice. Where an incident results in alleged breaches both *in flight* and *on the ground* which regulator will take the lead? A similar conundrum is discussed in Chapter 5, in which the interface between "aviation" and "maritime" with regard to the use of drones is examined in some detail and serious questions are posed as to the ability of classic "aviation" regulators, in their current form, to assess, understand in a timely fashion and appropriately regulate drones usage in the maritime and offshore oil and gas sectors and the concept of certain joint regulatory oversight as between "aviation" and "maritime" is mooted.

Brexit

The big question hanging over many issues in the UK, including drone regulation, is Brexit. In the run up to the UK leaving the EU on 31 December 2020 there was a wholesale adoption of EU laws (including adopting the EU Regulations on the date the UK left) in many areas to enable people and businesses to continue to comply with the laws in place for (in some instances) many years which emanated from the EU. The UK had been operating under these requirements for so long that it was simply a case of adopting them into UK law so that the existing standards and rules in place at the exit date remained the law of the land.

In respect of drones, the rules remain consistent with the EU. Given the UK's involvement in the development of drone regulations and with the EASA, this is unsurprising; however, it is unclear whether that will remain the case. The question remains what happens in the future? Is the adoption by the UK of the EU Regulations on the leave date an indication of future cooperation in this area? Given the difficulties regulators around the world have had keeping up with the constantly developing technology, this is an area one would expect, or at least hope, to see continued cooperation and knowledge sharing.

The legislation confirms pre-existing registrations, permissions (as previously required for commercial operations) and competencies will continue to be recognised (within the UK),[58] and the CAA has also confirmed that where EU aviation law was accompanied by guidance or specifications those requirements will be adopted from 1 January 2021.[59]

Other notable changes include:

EASA—The UK has left the EASA, along with other EU institutions[60]; however, it would not be unreasonable to assume that the organisations will continue to influence each other's approach in the future.

Registration—operators (or certified UAS) registered in the UK will not benefit from the EU wide recognition. The UK and EU states will each consider the other "*Third country*" for the purposes of the Regulations.[61] Any UK operator or remote pilot wishing to operate in a EU state will need to register in an EU

58 The Air Navigation (Amendment) Order 2020, SI 2020/1555, art 13.

59 UK Civil Aviation Authority, 'UK Regulations' (*UK Civil Aviation Authority*) <https://info.caa.co.uk/uk-regulations/>.

60 UK Civil Aviation Authority, 'Drones' (*UK Civil Aviation Authority*) <https://info.caa.co.uk/uk-eu-transition/drones/>.

61 Commission Delegated Regulation (EU) 2019/945 of 12 March 2019 on unmanned aircraft systems and on third-country operators of unmanned aircraft systems (2019) OJ L152/1, art 41.

state and comply with the competency requirements of that state. The same applies to EU operators and remote pilots intending to operate in the UK who will have to comply with UK requirements. The CAA has indicated that the UK system is being developed to meet EU requirements[62]; therefore, reciprocal recognition of registrations is a development to be monitored.

Design—within the UK the CE mark will be replaced by a UKCA (UK Conformity Assessed) mark.[63] CE markings will continue to be recognised until 1 January 2022.

Specified category—the UK has elected not to adopt the *standard scenarios* method of permitting operations in this category. These have not yet been developed. It will be interesting to see if the UK adopts a similar permissioning regime when these are introduced in the EU.

Concluding comments

The UK has been at the forefront of aviation regulation throughout its development and expectations are that it will remain so. While the UK has left the EASA, it is expected that at least initially regulations will continue to mirror those of the EU and that the close neighbours, with many years of technical cooperation behind them, will continue to influence one another's development. That has to be a positive given the challenges faced by regulators to ensure safety in a constantly developing field.

The Regulations provide a clear benefit for commercial operators who can bring their operations into the lower risk Open category, by reducing regulatory burdens and removing the need to obtain permission for commercial operations. While this will be beneficial for those operators who can work within the Open category, for those operating in the Specific and Certified categories, risk mitigation measures demonstrating operations can take place safely remain key for approval. As with any new technology, this will remain the case for the foreseeable future.

The potential for criminal penalties underlines the need for operators and remote pilots to take their safety obligations seriously. On the one hand, nobody wishes to see the criminalisation of people for honest mistakes, but criminal offences for breaching requirements and operating unsafely were in force prior to the Regulations. To date, there have been few drone prosecutions brought by the CAA, with advice and guidance being the preferred option, which we expect to continue for minor breaches, especially during the period the new Regulations bed in.

This remains a dynamic and interesting time in this area which presents opportunities and challenges to government, business and regulators alike. It is one where the law and lawmakers will have to endeavour to keep pace with the technology, but that provides considerable scope for improvements in numerous areas, including transport, logistics and the environment. Given the hesitation around any new technology, the key take-away for any operator—safety first.

62 UK Civil Aviation Authority (n 60).

63 Other than in Northern Ireland where a CE or UKNI mark will be required.
See Department for Business, Energy & Industrial Strategy, 'Guidance—Using the UKCA Marking' (*GOV.UK*, 21 December 2020) <www.gov.uk/guidance/using-the-ukca-marking>.

18 National regulatory structure and responses

Australia

Anthony A. Tarr, James M. Cooper, Maurice Thompson, Yuen Gi Ko and Christopher Pettersen

Introduction

The Australian Civil Aviation Safety Authority ("CASA") has been at the forefront of UAS regulation development and in 2002 Australia was the first State to publish regulations for drones; being Civil Aviation Safety Regulation Part 101.[1] Being the forerunner and with little civil operational experience to draw on from other countries, the initial Australian regulations provided limited detail relating to pilot qualifications, risk management, and airworthiness operational approval processes. Effectively, the regulation only provided a basis for CASA oversight with minimal guidance to industry.[2]

Accordingly, Australia's initial foray into this area of regulation could be described as very much a work in progress, but more recent initiatives have as their principal objectives an updated regulatory framework in Australia that will achieve uniformity, integrate drones' use into the national airspace system and at the same time, achieve the highest possible level of safety. For example, the Senate Standing Committees on Rural and Regional Affairs and Transport produced a Report in 2018 with 10 major recommendations in relation to current and future regulatory requirements that impact on the safe commercial and recreational use of Remotely Piloted Aircraft Systems (RPAS), Unmanned Aerial Systems (UAS) and associated systems.[3] These recommendations are very instructive in the Australian context and more broadly in other jurisdictions considering enhanced or "next-generation" regulatory frameworks. Accordingly, these recommendations are recorded as follows:

1 The Civil Aviation Safety Authority draw on the growing body of international empirical research and collision testing on remotely piloted aircraft systems below 2 kg to immediately reform Part 101 of the Civil Aviation Safety Regulations 1998.[4]

2 The Australian Government introduce a mandatory registration regime for all remotely piloted aircraft systems (RPAS) weighing more than 250 g. As part of

1 Ron I C Bartsch, *Aviation Law in Australia* (5th edn, Thomson-Reuters 2019) 29.

2 ibid 30.

3 Australian Senate Inquiry Committee, 'Regulatory Requirements that Impact on the Safe Use of Remotely Piloted Aircraft Systems, Unmanned Aerial Systems and Associated Systems' (31 July 2018).Hereafter referred to as "Australian Senate Inquiry Report".

4 ibid para 8.10.

registration requirements, RPAS operators should be required to successfully complete a basic competence test regarding the safe use of RPAS and demonstrate an understanding of the penalties for non-compliance with the rules.[5]

3 The Australian Government develops a tiered education programme whereby remotely piloted aircraft system (RPAS) users progressively unlock RPAS capabilities upon completion of each level of training. Three tiers are proposed as follows:

- purchase of the RPAS—mandatory registration requires user to demonstrate knowledge the basic rules for flying RPAS, and the penalties for non-compliance (as described in Recommendation 2);
- recreational use of RPAS—second tier requires user to demonstrate an advanced understanding of aviation rules and safety before unlocking additional capabilities; and
- commercial use of RPAS—final tier requires user to demonstrate comprehensive aviation knowledge before obtaining commercial operator licence and unlocking full RPAS capability.[6]

4 The Civil Aviation Safety Authority, in cooperation with the Australian Federal Police and other relevant authorities, prohibit the use of remotely piloted aircraft systems in the airspace above significant public buildings, critical infrastructure and other vulnerable areas.[7]

5 The Department of Infrastructure, Regional Development and Cities, in cooperation with the Civil Aviation Safety Authority, work with manufacturers of remotely piloted aircraft systems (RPAS) to develop future solutions to RPAS safety, including the implementation of technical restrictions on altitude and distance for "off-the-shelf" RPAS.[8]

6 The Department of Infrastructure, Regional Development and Cities, in cooperation with the Civil Aviation Safety Authority, develop appropriate airworthiness standards for remotely piloted aircraft of all sizes and operations. At a minimum, fail-safe functions such as "return to home" and safe landing functionality, and forced flight termination, should be mandated.[9]

7 The Australian Government develops import controls to enforce airworthiness standards for foreign manufactured remotely piloted aircraft systems.[10]

8 The Department of Infrastructure, Regional Development and Cities, in collaboration with the Civil Aviation Safety Authority, develop a whole-of-government policy for remotely piloted aircraft safety in Australia, and establish appropriate coordination and implementation mechanisms with relevant departments and agencies to implement the policy.

As part of a whole-of-government policy approach, the committee further recommends that the Australian Government explore cost-effective models to

5 ibid para 8.12.
6 ibid para 8.26.
7 ibid para 8.29.
8 ibid para 8.31.
9 ibid para 8.37.
10 ibid para 8.38.

develop and administer new regulatory initiatives for remotely piloted aircraft systems, including a mandatory registration regime and tiered education programme. The harmonisation of state and territory privacy laws should also be considered.[11]

9 As part of a whole-of-government approach to remotely piloted aircraft systems (RPAS) safety, the Civil Aviation Safety Authority work with Airservices Australia and other relevant agencies to implement a comprehensive research and data gathering regime. Information should be collated and centralised in a way that allows for the examination of RPAS registrations, operations, trends and incidents, to provide an evidence base on which to assess the efficacy of current regulations, and to inform the development of future policy and regulations.[12]

10 Following the development of a whole-of-government policy approach to RPAS safety, including the establishment of a national registration system, the Civil Aviation Safety Authority (CASA) work with state and territory enforcement bodies to implement a nationally consistent enforcement regime for remotely piloted aircraft systems. Under this regime, enforcement bodies would be delegated powers to provide on-the-spot fines and report infringements of the regulations directly to CASA.[13]

The Australian Senate Inquiry Report[14] was critical of regulations introduced in 2016,[15] which had (controversially) relaxed regulatory requirements for drones weighing less than 2 kg. This approach, formally entrenched in the *Civil Aviation Legislation Amendment (Part 101) Regulation 2016* (Cth),[16] was designed to balance innovation in this space and to encourage domestic growth.

The Committee criticised those changes on the basis that even small drones are capable of causing considerable damage to rotorcraft and aircraft. Instead, as per their second recommendation the Committee advocated a mandatory registration regime[17] for all drones weighing more than 250 g, together with a tiered education/training programme. Such a compulsory registration regime in Australia would align Australia's regulations with those currently in force in jurisdictions across the world, including the USA and UK where drones over 250 g are required to be registered prior to flight. Registration requirements of all drones would allow enforcement agencies to identify the operator and owner of any drone involved in a near-miss incident or collision and to monitor and penalise unlawful activity.

The committee, in their recommendations mentioned earlier, also recognised that more should be done to ensure that all drone users, whether recreational or commercial, undertake some form of mandatory education and training before flying their drones.[18] The committee was alarmed by numerous reports of reckless drone

11 ibid paras 8.44, 8.45.
12 ibid para 8.50.
13 ibid para 8.64.
14 ibid paras 4.1–4.18.
15 See *Civil Aviation Legislation Amendment (Part 101) Regulation 2016* (Cth); Civil Aviation Safety Authority, 'Commercial Unmanned Flight—Remotely Piloted Aircraft under 2kg' <https://www.casa.gov.au/standard-page/commercial-unmanned-flight-remotely-pilotedaircraft-under-2kg>.
16 Made under the *Civil Aviation Act 1988* (Cth).
17 Australian Senate Inquiry Committee (n 3) paras 8.11–8.20.
18 ibid paras 8.21–8.26.

operations which had hindered emergency operations, flown close to commercial aircrafts, or intruded upon restricted airspace. Accordingly, the committee recommended that drone users be required to undertake mandatory education and training so all operators understand the rules which will ultimately reduce the risks to public safety.

Even more recently, in September 2020, the Department of Infrastructure, Transport, Regional Development and Communications published a Paper entitled "Emerging Aviation Technologies National Aviation Policy Issues Paper",[19] described as being the "first step towards development of a national policy for the management of drones and other emerging aviation technologies".[20] This Paper identifies opportunities and risks associated with these technologies; outlines some of the current approaches for managing these issues; and proposes an approach to policy development. The proposed approach to policy development covers airspace integration, safety, security, noise, environment, privacy, safe and efficient electric take-off and landing vehicles, infrastructure, technology trials and central coordination.[21] These are all important issues and are integral to the development of a comprehensive national policy that will allow Australia to benefit from the considerable opportunities provided by emerging aviation technologies.

The following paragraphs provide an overview of Australia's regulatory framework for drones, a consideration of key recommendations of, and responses to, the Australian Senate Inquiry Report, and an overview of the Emerging Aviation Technologies Paper.

Regulatory framework

The Department of Infrastructure, Transport, Regional Development and Communications explains that there are, broadly speaking, three safety mechanisms/layers currently provided for in Australian legislation. These are: the use of operating conditions, such as the Standard Operating Conditions (SOC), Part 101 of the CASR and legislative instruments; licence requirements for certain drone operators; and approved access to certain types of operations such as within controlled airspace or BVLOS.[22]

Safety

CASA has developed a range of rule categories to support the safe operation of drones in a range of different circumstances and situations. These categories set out a range of operating rules and requirements, with considerable attention paid to operations such as flights over populous areas (crowds and public gatherings), in an urban environment, in unsegregated airspace, in close proximity to airports and helipads, and with operations beyond visual line of sight only permitted in limited instances by the

19 Australian Government Department of Infrastructure, Transport, Regional Development and Communications, 'Emerging Aviation Technologies, National Aviation Policy Issues Paper' (September 2020).

20 ibid.

21 ibid 7; See also, Julie-Anne Tarr, Maurice Thompson and Anthony Tarr, 'Regulation, Risk and Insurance of Drones: An Urgent Global Accountability Imperative' (2019) 8 *Journal of Business Law* 559; Julie-Anne Tarr and others, 'Drones in Australia—Rapidly Evolving Regulatory and Insurance Challenges' (2019) 30 Insurance Law Journal 135.

22 Australian Senate Inquiry Committee (n 3) 25.

granting of approvals or exemptions by aviation regulatory authorities and then only on a case-by-case basis.

For example, Part 101 of *Civil Aviation Safety Regulations 1998* (Cth)[23] requires that all RPA not be operated to create a hazard to other aircraft, persons or property,[24] and that they not be operated over a "populous area" such as beaches, parks and sporting fields.[25] Other standard operating conditions include: fly during the day[26] and keep the UA within visual line of sight[27]; never fly higher than 120 m (400 ft) above the ground[28]; keep the UA at least 30 m away from other people[29]; keep the UA at least 5.5 km away from controlled airspace[30]; never fly over or near an area affecting public safety or where emergency operations are underway (without prior approval). This could include, for example, a situation involving police operations, firefighting efforts or a traffic accident[31]; and only fly one UA at a time.[32]

There are also dedicated rules around drone operations for payment, and rules that enable the use of drones on a person's own land. Drone operations outside of the rule categories must be approved by CASA. CASA's operational regulatory approach utilises the Specific Operations Risk Assessment (SORA) tool developed by the Joint Authority on Rulemaking for Unmanned Systems (JARUS).[33]

Part 101 of the *Civil Aviation Safety Regulations 1998* (Cth) (CASR) and the subsequent development of a supporting Manual of Standards (MOS) for commercial operations, is facilitating the effective regulatory oversight of maintaining aviation safety standards while allowing the continued use of drones.[34] This is supported by the Airspace Regulations 2007 which ensures the management of Australian-administered airspace to provide for the safety of all users of all airspace.[35]

23 Made under the *Civil Aviation Act 1988* (Cth).

24 *Civil Aviation Safety Regulations 1998* (Cth), regs 101.055, 101.280; Generally see Australian Government Civil Aviation Authority, 'CASR Part 101—Unmanned Aircraft and Rockets' (*Australian Government Civil Aviation Authority*, 6 October 2020) <www.casa.gov.au/standard-page/casr-part-101-unmanned-aircraft-and-rocket-operations>.

25 *Civil Aviation Safety Regulations 1998* (Cth), eg. regs 101.250, 101.280. Populous area is defined in the regulations as "an area (that) has a sufficient density of population for some aspect of the operation, or some event that might happen during the operation (in particular, a fault in, or failure of, the aircraft . . .) to pose an unreasonable risk to the life, safety or property of somebody who is in the area but is not connected with the operation", *Civil Aviation Safety Regulations 1998* (Cth) reg 101.025.

26 ibid reg 101.095.

27 ibid reg 101.073.

28 ibid reg 101.085.

29 ibid reg 101.245.

30 ibid reg 101.075.

31 ibid reg 101.238.

32 ibid reg 101.300(5). Note that these general operational constraints commonly are augmented by more specific, often state-based legislation; for example, the *National Parks and Wildlife Regulation 2009* (NSW) sets out minimum approach distances for drones in relation to marine mammals such as whales and dolphins.

33 ibid.

34 Explanatory Statement, Civil Aviation Safety regulations 1998 (Cth) part 101.

35 Australian Government Department of Infrastructure, Transport, Regional Development and Communications (n 19) 26.

Registration and licencing

In response to an Australian Senate Committee Inquiry report,[36] a suite of significant amendments to Australia's drone regulations were made on 25 July 2019 by the *Civil Aviation Safety Amendment (Remotely Piloted Aircraft and Model Aircraft—Registration and Accreditation) Regulations 2019* (Cth).[37] These regulations amend Parts 11, 47 and 101 of the *Civil Aviation Safety Regulations 1998* (Cth) and reverse many of the changes introduced by the 2016 Regulations.[38]

The key change introduced by the 2019 Regulations was in requiring that drones be registered[39] with the Civil Aviation Safety Authority. Addressing problems arising out of the use and deployment of drones in areas such as safety and privacy is exacerbated by the burgeoning numbers of drones, many of which are unregistered or unlicenced, and, more dauntingly, the fact that substantial numbers of drones are operated with limited or no training. In Australia at present, not only is there uncertainty in relation to the number of drones purchased but not licenced or registered,[40] but homemade, reverse engineered and 3D-printed drone production fall outside official figures.[41]

The scheme is intended to be phased in sequentially, commencing with registration for commercial drones followed by registration of recreational drones. The commencement dates for implementation of the registration scheme have been considerably delayed from the original dates,[42] with the current date for commercial drones being 28 January 2021, while recreational drones' registration is foreshadowed to begin in March 2022 and be required to be completed by 30 May 2022.[43]

36 Australian Senate Inquiry Committee (n 3).

37 Amending Part 11, Part 47 and Part 101 of the *Civil Aviation Safety Regulations 1998* (Cth).

38 *Civil Aviation Legislation Amendment (Part 101) Regulation 2016* (Cth). Generally, see Julie-Anne Tarr, Anthony Tarr and Kirsty Paynter, 'Transport, Drones and Regulatory Challenges: Risk Accountability Meets COVID Fast Tracking of a Critical Industry' (2020) 48 Australian Business Law Review 202.

39 The registration and accreditation requirements apply (with certain exceptions) to: drones more than 250 grams operated recreationally, and; all drones operated commercially regardless of weight. Drones weighing 250 g or less and those only flown indoors will not need to be registered. See Australian Government Civil Aviation Safety Authority, 'New Rules for Drone Registration and Accreditation' (*Australian Government Civil Aviation Safety Authority*, 31 July 2019) <www.casa.gov.au/news-article/new-rules-drone-registration-and-accreditation>.

40 See, for example, House of Representatives Standing Committee on Social Policy and Legal Affairs, 'Eyes in the Sky, Inquiry into Drones and the Regulation of Air Safety and Privacy' (July 2014) para 2.4: "RPA sales and imports are unregulated, so it is difficult to estimate the number of RPAs that are currently being used in Australia".

41 J Michelle, 'Top 10 3D Printed Drones' (*3D natives*, 10 December 2018) <www.3dnatives.com/en/top-3d-printed-drones-101220185/>; Evidence to the Australian Transport Safety Bureau Committee, 29 August 2017, 19 (Mr Greg Hood); Also see: DJI, Submission 60 to the Senate Standing Committee on Rural and Regional Affairs and Transport, 'Regulatory Requirements that Impact on the Safe Use of Remotely Piloted Aircraft Systems, Unmanned Aerial Systems and Associated Systems' (2016) 2–3.

42 November 2019 (commercial drones) and March 2020 (recreational drones); *Civil Aviation Safety Amendment (Remotely Piloted Aircraft and Model Aircraft—Registration and Accreditation) Regulations 2019* (Cth); Australian Government Civil Aviation Safety Authority (n 39).

43 See *Civil Aviation Safety Amendment (Remotely Piloted Aircraft and Model Aircraft—Registration and Accreditation) Regulations (No. 2) 2019* (Cth); Shane Carmody, 'Remotely Piloted Aircraft Registration and Accreditation—Further Assistance for Industry' (*Australian Government Civil Aviation Safety Authority*, 1 April 2020) <www.casa.gov.au/about-us/news-article/remotely-piloted-aircraft-registration-and-accreditation-%E2%80%93-further-assistance-industry>;Australian Government

Moreover, the rules require all drone flyers to either have a remote pilot licence or have completed a short online safety quiz. The type of licence and certificate required to be held by the pilot or operator of the drone is dependent on the weight of the drone being operated. There are, however, exemptions to the licencing and certificate requirements such as if the drone is being operated within standard operating conditions (**SOC**), or if the drone is operating under Exempt Operations.[44]

Registration will be through an online "myCASA" portal and last for 12 months. To complete drone registration, the registrant will need to be at least 16 years old, provide proof of identity, an aviation reference number (ARN) and details of the drone—including the make, model, serial number, weight and type of drone.[45] The ARN can be acquired online.

A person flying a drone that weighs more than 250 g must be accredited to show an understanding of the drone safety rules. The accreditation will consist of a short video followed by a quiz to test the applicant's knowledge. That too can be completed online through the "myCASA" portal. The test will be free, with the results being valid for three years, and provide accreditation for flying and supervising others.[46] To apply, the applicant must be at least 16 years old, have a "myCASA" account, provide proof of identity, and have an ARN.

A remote pilot licence (RePL) is required to fly remotely piloted aircraft (RPA) in circumstances that need specialist training. In particular, a RePL is required to fly a drone larger than 2 kg for commercial operations, outside the drone safety rules (standard operating conditions) and for a remotely piloted aircraft operator's certificate (ReOC) holder.[47]

CASA, in foreshadowing these changes, stated that they would help to crack down on people misusing the new technologies and assist in terms of complaints or reports of drones being flown improperly or against the safety rules.[48] There is no doubt that a mandatory drone registration scheme could assist in deterring unsafe or unlawful operation of drones and make it easier to identify those who offend the Regulations. Moreover, contact details provided by registered operators could also be used by CASA to convey important safety information and advisory material regarding the safe use of drones.

These changes are broadly in harmony with requirements, already implemented or forthcoming, in the United States, the United Kingdom and Europe.[49]

Civil Aviation Safety Authority, 'Registration and Accreditation' (*Australian Government Civil Aviation Safety Authority*)<www.casa.gov.au/knowyourdrone/registration-and-accreditation>.

44 Exempt Operations are operations on private property for certain purposes including aerial spotting, aerial photography, agricultural operations, aerial communications retransmission, carriage of cargo or similar activities where such purposes are not remunerated and are within standard operating conditions.

45 Australian Government Civil Aviation Safety Authority, 'Drone Registration' (*Australian Government Civil Aviation Safety Authority*, 2 October 2020) <www.casa.gov.au/drones/register>.

46 Children younger than 16 must be supervised by an accredited adult (aged 18 or older). See, Australian Government Civil Aviation Safety Authority, 'Registration and Accreditation' (Australian Government Civil Aviation Safety Authority) <www.casa.gov.au/knowyourdrone/registration-and-accreditation>.

47 A person who wants to fly for commercial purposes, must also either hold a ReOC or work for a ReOC holder.

48 See Australian Government Civil Aviation Safety Authority, 'Drones' (*Australian Government Civil Aviation Safety Authority*, 30 September 2020) <wwww.casa.gov.au/drones>.

49 See discussion in Chapters 13–17.

Noise, environmental and privacy[50]

The regulatory framework applicable to noise, privacy and environmental issues across Australia may be categorised as a complex mix of responsibility between Federal and State and, in certain respects, local authorities. For example, in relation to the noise impact of aircraft, aviation-specific legislation[51] as well as environmental legislation such as the *Environmental Protection and Biodiversity Conservation Act 1999* (Cth) (EPBC Act) applies at a Federal level. In addition, State and territory governments have general responsibility for ground-based noise impact (under environmental protection or nuisance laws) in their jurisdictions and State level regulation can have multiple layers within it, for example, NSW has the *Environmental Planning and Assessment Act 1979* (NSW) and the *Protection of the Environment (Operations) Act 1997* (NSW). This state legislation also empowers public authorities, such as local councils, to develop further environmental planning instruments known as local environmental plans.[52]

Similarly, there is a mix of responsibility for environmental regulation across Australia. As noted previously, the Commonwealth administers the EPBC Act while each state and territory administers its own legislation. Managing environmental impacts, covering both wildlife and cultural sites, can take the form of location or event-based regulations. These can be created by both the Australian Government and state and territory governments. However, the triggers for assessments under environmental laws (such as the EPBC Act) are unclear with regard to the applicability for drone and electric vertical take-off and landing (eVTOL) operations.[53]

The Emerging Aviation Technologies Paper[54] observes that protection of privacy is considered one of the most contentious issues that communities around the world will need to manage as drone use increases.[55] Managing public perception of privacy and trust in technology is critical to the ability to embed and harness the benefits of technology and innovation.[56] Privacy legislation at the Commonwealth level, and in most States and Territories, supports this right in relation to protecting personal information about individuals,[57] and legal action may be grounded in breach of confidence, trespass or negligence.[58] Other regulations that may be seen to support the right to

50 It is beyond the scope and word limitations for this Chapter to address these matters other than in a very general way but see discussion in Chapter 9. See also Australian Government Department of Infrastructure, Transport, Regional Development and Communications (n 19) 34–47.

51 *Air Navigation (Aircraft Noise) Regulations 2018* (Cth), administered by the Department of Infrastructure, Transport, Regional Development and Communications.

52 Australian Government Department of Infrastructure, Transport, Regional Development and Communications (n 19) 41.

53 ibid.

54 ibid 43.

55 Ronald Ian Charles Bartsch, 'Unmanned and Uncontrolled' (Master's thesis, The University of Sydney 2015) <https://ses.library.usyd.edu.au/handle/2123/14844>.

56 Lisa M Pytlik Zillig and others, 'A Drone by Any other Name' (2018) 37(1) IEEE Technology and Society Magazine 80 <https://ieeexplore.ieee.org/ document/8307142>.

57 Australia is a signatory to the International Covenant on Civil and Political Rights. This recognises a right to protection from unlawful or arbitrary interference with privacy.

58 See discussion in Chapter 9. See also Australian Law Reform Commission, *Serious Invasions of Privacy in the Digital Era* (ALRC Report 123, 2014); and Des Butler, 'A Tort of Invasion of Privacy in Australia' (2005) 29(2) Melbourne University Law Review 339.

privacy in Australia includes Commonwealth, State and Territory legislation that concerns trespass, nuisance and/or surveillance issues.[59]

Emerging Aviation Technologies Paper[60]

The Department of Infrastructure, Transport, Regional Development and Communications provides a succinct and very useful summation of the proposed approach to the development of a national policy for the management of drones and other emerging aviation technologies. It merits recording in full as follows:

1 Airspace integration. The Australian Government, in partnership with industry, will develop a UTM system that would support a combination of centralised government services and industry-provided services that will facilitate fair and competitive access to airspace and mitigate a wide range of risks and impacts.
2 Safety. The Civil Aviation Safety Authority will maintain its commitment to the primacy of safety, while taking a responsive, modern and evidence-based approach to safety regulation and the certification of new aviation technology that provides scope for innovation and flexibility, having regard to the inherent risks of the operating environment, other airspace users and the travelling public.
3 Security. The Australian Government will lead the development of a proportionate and evidence-based approach to managing security risks associated with drones and eVTOL vehicles, which is adaptable to changing circumstances and technologies while ensuring a secure operating environment.
4 Noise. The Department of Infrastructure, Transport, Regional Development and Communications will develop and manage a national regulatory approach to noise management that encourages quieter operations consistent with local community considerations.
5 Environment. The Australian Government will lead the development of a consistent, balanced and proportionate approach to manage the impacts on wildlife and the environment, including the enjoyment of nature areas and cultural sites.
6 Privacy. The Australian Government will lead the development of a nationally consistent approach for managing privacy concerns that balances the impacts on privacy with the needs of drone and eVTOL operations.
7 Electric vertical take-off and landing vehicles. The Australian Government will work with all relevant stakeholders to develop measures for safe, efficient, considerate and reliable eVTOL operations in a competitive market that supports safe, efficient and equitable access for all airspace users.
8 Infrastructure. The Australian Government will lead the development of a coordinated and informed approach to infrastructure planning, investment, requirements and approvals.
9 Technology trials. The Australian Government will develop an approach that fosters partnerships between government and industry to promote shared outcomes

59 See, for example, *Privacy Act 1988* (Cth).
60 Australian Government Department of Infrastructure, Transport, Regional Development and Communications (n 19).

and learning with the goal to support the commencement of future commercial operations.

10 Central coordination. The Department of Infrastructure, Transport, Regional Development and Communications will coordinate an ongoing whole-of-government policy approach to manage future challenges associated with emerging aviation technologies to ensure a consistent and coordinated approach to regulation across issues and jurisdictions.

This approach and the matters emphasised closely correspond to the views expressed by the European Commission[61] in their communication dated 9 December 2020. The Emerging Aviation Technologies Paper and the Commission[62] emphasise the need for coordination, the need to develop and to validate new technologies, and commit to put in place favourable conditions for the development of new technologies and services, and all necessary legislative tools for their validation. These are all important issues and are integral to the development of a comprehensive national policy that will allow Australia to benefit from the considerable opportunities provided by emerging aviation technologies.

However, it may be argued that a national policy that omits a considered assessment and effective implementation of compulsory liability insurance is ignoring a vital dimension in managing the risks and impacts associated with the use and deployment of drones and other emerging aviation technologies.[63] The Emerging Aviation Technology Issues Paper devotes less than half a page of its 62 pages to insurance. This commentary is as follows:

> Most commercial drone operators make the business decision to hold insurance to cover for any damage or injury caused as part of managing the risk of their operations. Recreational users that are members of some drone organizations carry insurance as part of their membership. The requirement to hold insurance is often a condition of engagement by organizations procuring drone-based services. There are a range of models in other sectors where third-party insurance has been mandated, such as for vehicles. However, it remains to be seen whether this would be an appropriate mechanism for drones, especially considering the disparate risk profiles of operations across the drone sector. Aviation traditionally has operated free from mandated compulsory third-party insurance for damage to property or injury, although many industry operators hold insurance policies to cover a range of scenarios as a part of their risk management processes. Any decision to implement an insurance scheme for drone operators will need to be informed by relevant drone accident data, be proportionate to the risk profile of operations,

61 The Commission to the European Parliament, The Council, The European Economic and Social Committee and the Committee of the Regions, 'Sustainable and Smart Mobility Strategy—Putting European Transport on Track for the Future' (Communication) COM (2020) 789 final.

62 ibid paras 64–66.

63 Clyde & Co, Maurice Thompson, Dr Anthony Tarr and Professor Julie-Anne Tarr, Submission No 6 to the Director Airspace and Emerging Technologies, Department of Infrastructure Transport, Regional Development and Communications, 'National Aviation Policy Issues Paper on Emerging Aviation Technologies' (22 October 2020).

be consistent with a holistic approach to regulation and complement the suite of various approaches available to manage risks.[64]

At the outset, it should be noted that the regulatory and community concerns raised are not directed at responsible commercial or recreational drone users who obtain appropriate insurance to manage the risks of their drone operations. That said, there are only limited insurance options available for commercial operators at present, with options ranging from inadequate to well considered and acceptable, with a great deal of room for improvement in general on matters concerning risk differentials with different usage in different environments.[65] In short, it would be a mistake to consider that all commercial drone users in Australia have adequate liability insurance for drones related risks and it may be contended that there will need to be serious developments in this space before comfort levels can be achieved like those the Paper has assumed already exist. In any event, the concerns raised, as in the case of uninsured and/or unlicenced motor vehicles, are directed at those individuals and operators who do not adhere to appropriate standards and behaviour. Furthermore, the laissez-faire approach evident in the commentary from the Paper is in direct contrast to the approach adopted in other jurisdictions such as the European Union where public liability insurance to protect against legal liability for third-party property damage or injury whilst using a drone is mandatory.[66] In addition, the International Civil Aviation Organization ICAO UAS Toolkit,[67] described by ICAO, as a helpful tool to assist States in realising effective UAS operational guidance and safe domestic operations, chapter 2.8 states: "The operator shall have adequate insurance in the event of an incident or accident. Some States require a minimum third-party liability insurance to be in effect for all UAS operations". Accordingly, the authors of this chapter contend that any proactive approach to drone management and regulation must consider compulsory third-party liability insurance and other liability issues as integral parts of any regulatory framework.[68]

Concluding comments

The regulation of drones in Australia has, to date, been predominantly concerned with safety. Given the risks to persons and property this is a perfectly legitimate and supportable preoccupation. However, the extensive and increasing use of drones also raises very serious privacy issues and concerns around data collection and use especially given the intrusive potential of drones equipped with cameras and surveillance capability, which are now readily available to the public. The Australian Senate

64 Australian Government Department of Infrastructure, Transport, Regional Development and Communications (n 19) 25; See also, Tarr, Thompson and Tarr (n 21); Tarr and others (n 21).

65 As discussed in Chapters 20 and 21.

66 Commission Implementing Regulation (EU) 2019/947 of 24 May 2019 on the procedures and rules for the operation of unmanned aircraft (2019) OJ L152/45; Commission Delegated Regulation (EU) 2019/945 of 12 March 2019 on unmanned aircraft systems and on third-country operators of unmanned aircraft systems (2019) OJ L152/1; see discussion in Chapter 22.

67 International Civil Aviation Organization, 'UAS Toolkit: Development of UAS Regulation' (*International Civil Aviation Organization*) <www.icao.int/safety/UA/UASToolkit/Pages/Narrative-Regulation.aspx>.

68 See detailed discussion in Chapter 22.

Inquiry Report and Emerging Aviation Technologies Paper show increasing concern for and intent to address these issues.

In Australia there is a lack of national consistency with regard to state and federal privacy and surveillance legislation,[69] and this inconsistency coupled with the growth of local council by-laws relating to RPAS operations, has made compliance for RPAS operators extremely challenging.[70] It is beyond the scope and length of this chapter to explore in any detail the labyrinthian detail of these privacy and surveillance laws, but it is noted that concern as to their inconsistency is not new. For example, the 2014 House of Representatives report titled *Eyes in the sky: Inquiry into drones and the regulation of air safety and privacy*[71] made a recommendation with regard to the harmonisation of surveillance laws but the Australian Government responded that it is "appropriate that states and territories continue to modify their own surveillance device laws, if necessary".[72]

However, it is encouraging that in the Emerging Aviation Technologies Paper the Australian Government has acknowledged that it will lead the development of a nationally consistent approach for managing privacy concerns that balances the impacts on privacy with the needs of drone and eVTOL operations. The Australian Competition and Consumer Commission (ACCC) in a report[73] released in June 2019 highlights how innovation and rapid technological change has transformed the ability and incentive of entities to collect, use and disclose the personal information of Australian consumers in the digital economy. These changes are accompanied by the growing awareness and concern of Australian consumers regarding privacy and data protection. Drones and their surveillance and data collection capacities fall within this general frame of reference.

The authors of this chapter respectfully concur in the conclusions of the Australian Senate Inquiry Committee[74] that in order for Australia to balance the important challenges of ensuring public and aviation safety, and encouraging innovation, a nationwide enforcement regime, including powers to issue on-the-spot-fines and report infringements, a coordinated "whole of government policy, must be created".[75] The Commonwealth Department of Infrastructure, Transport, Cities and Regional Development currently has carriage of this whole-of-government framework to manage drones and as a first step in this process, the Department is working with Commonwealth

69 Australian Senate Inquiry Committee; Australian Government Department of Infrastructure, Transport, Regional Development and Communications (n 19), paras 7.34–7.36. Along with privacy legislation such as the *Privacy Act 1988* (Cth), surveillance devices legislation, which governs the use of optical surveillance devices and data surveillance tracking devices, has been enacted in five jurisdictions—New South Wales, Victoria, Western Australia, South Australia and the Northern Territory. Yet, these laws create further confusion about the permissible use of RPAS.

70 Australian Government Department of Infrastructure, Transport, Regional Development and Communications (n 19), paras 7.34–7.36; Australian Senate Inquiry Committee; Professor Des Butler, Submission No 18 to the Senate Standing Committee on Rural and Regional Affairs and Transport, 'Regulatory Requirements that Impact on the Safe Use of Remotely Piloted Aircraft Systems, Unmanned Aerial Systems and Associated Systems' (2016) 3.

71 House of Representatives Standing Committee on Social Policy and Legal Affairs (n 40) 48.

72 Australian Government, 'Australian Government response to the Standing Committee on Social Policy and Legal Affairs Report—Eyes in the Sky: Inquiry into Drones and the Regulation of Air Safety and Privacy' (December 2016) 9.

73 Australian Competition & Consumer Commission, 'Digital Platforms Inquiry—Final Report' (Report, June 2019) <www.accc.gov.au/publications/digital-platforms-inquiry-final-report>.

74 Australian Senate Inquiry Committee (n 3) chapter 8.

75 ibid paras 8.39–8.50.

agencies, State Government and industry to develop a national whole-of-government policy position. It is expected that this will form the basis of future work to put in place a range of measures to manage drones that will facilitate innovation from the drone sector, while ensuring adequate controls to address the range of risks and impacts.

Australia, via the work of the Civil Aviation Safety Authority (CASA), has for many years been one of the global leaders in relation to the regulation of drones. However, CASA is constrained in its capacity to regulate drones due to the scope of the Commonwealth's constitutional "aviation" powers with respect to purely intrastate services,[76] and in relation to commercial aspects of aviation. The problem of constitutional limitations over the subject of aviation has plagued successive Australian federal parliaments for almost a century and it is recommended that the question of constitutional reform should be revisited.[77] Such reform, by vesting exclusive civil aviation regulatory authority in the Commonwealth, would address a range of problems being brought into focus in relation to drones, as well as other issues, such as the risk of subjecting air operators to a multitude of non-uniform laws.[78]

Existing regulations now include a registration requirement, as well as education and awareness training, but there is a need for additional enforcement and compliance measures, and technology-based solutions, as part of a "whole-of-government" approach. Ideally there needs to be a drones-specific legal framework covering the breadth of issues commonly arising from drones use—safety, privacy, damage to people or property, and cybersecurity, among others.[79]

The Civil Aviation Safety Authority (CASA) in their submission to the Australian Senate Inquiry, highlights "an increase in the operation of RPA without regard to safety, particularly within restricted airspace, including 'the risk of a catastrophic collision with a passenger aircraft'".[80] Injury to persons and property damage are, of course, very real concerns arising out of the use of drones,[81] and these concerns will become more acute as the use of drones expands to include routine freight delivery and point to point transport for people in high-density-population environments. Furthermore, the increasing use of drones in these contexts also gives rise to very real privacy and noise concerns.[82] Also, increasing investment in infrastructure to support drone use will be needed.[83]

76 See discussion in Chapter 13 and also, for example, *Airlines of NSW v New South Wales (No 1) (Airlines of NSW Case (No 1)* (1964) 113 CLR 1; *Airlines of New South Wales Pty Ltd v New South Wales (No 2)*(1965) 113 CLR 54; *Work Health Authority v Outback Ballooning Pty Ltd* [2019] HCA 2.

77 See, for example, the *Constitution Alteration (Aviation) Bill 1936* (Cth), providing for the insertion in section 51 of the Constitution the words "Air Navigation and Aircraft". The proposed changes were put to the vote in a referendum and was supported by a majority of voters but failed to obtain majorities in four States.

78 Norton White, 'Judicial Decisions Requiring Urgent Legislative Attention' (Briefing Paper, 18 February 2019) comment that the decision in *Work Health Authority v Outback Ballooning Pty Ltd* [2019] HCA 2, is 'likely to add to costs for air operators who will be required to comply with up to 9 sets of safety laws (that may not be consistent) and deal with safety regulators in each State and Territory in addition to CASA'. See <www.aph.gov.au/DocumentStore.ashx?id=cbc1a90a-7031-48fc-adba-31d54d50078a>.

79 See Tarr, Thompson and Tarr (n 21); Tarr, and others (n 21).

80 See Explanatory Statement, Civil Aviation Safety Amendment (Remotely Piloted Aircraft and Model Aircraft—Registration and Accreditation) Regulations 2019(Cth) 6.

81 See, for example, Pam Stewart, 'Drone Danger: Remedies for Damage by Civilian Remotely Piloted Aircraft to Persons or Property on the Ground in Australia' (2016) 23 Torts Law Journal 290.

82 See, for example, Matthew R Koerner, 'Drones and the Fourth Amendment: Redefining Expectations of Privacy' (2015) 64 Duke Law Journal 1129; Tarr, Thompson and Tarr (n 21).

83 New South Wales Government, 'Transport for NSW: Future Transport Strategy 2056' (March 2018) 66.

19 Technology challenges inherent in safety regulation

Julie-Anne Tarr, Nick Sharpe and Patrick Slomski

Introduction

Drone technology stands as a leading disruptor for the 21st century. Although still in its infancy, use in commercial, industrial, and humanitarian assistance support environments as well as in numerous other capacities has already provided considerable economic and public benefits to society. To date, however, government regulation around safe and successful integration of drones into airspace has been predominantly reactive, focussing piecemeal on discrete issues such as registration, restricting flight zones, electronic tracking frameworks and training requisites. Coordination at international, national and regional levels as to an agreed unified vision with clear guiding principles is required urgently for several reasons. Protection of public safety and rights is, of course, paramount in this context but supporting innovation while building capacity for uses and functionality not yet viable (or recognised) are core to value capture over the coming century around this critical industry.

Sheer rapidity of technological evolution in this space, however, poses in itself a critical challenge to regulators for multiple reasons. As outlined in the 2020 European Commission position paper on sustainable future mobility strategies,[1] an agile regulatory framework capable of accommodating and encouraging game changing mobility technologies, including drones, is much needed to pave the way for sustainable technologies in the years and decades to come.[2]

Time to reflect is not however a luxury for which the operational properties of this sector provide. Addressing drone risks beyond property losses – that is of physical injury to third parties, such as mid-air collisions with passenger airplanes, unwitting crash landings into rush hour traffic or flying debris fall out injuries to school children - requires more urgent resolution than the time windows afforded historically to frame regulation around earlier transportation developments.[3] Predecessors in this respect— airplanes, automobiles, trains—evolved in a more measured way through use of costly prototypes. Initial circulation and uses were therefore necessarily far more circumscribed by cost and infrastructure constraints. Conversely, with drones,

1 European Commission, 'Communication from the Commission to the European Parliament, The Council, The European Economic and Social Committee and the Committee of the Regions: Sustainable and Smart Mobility Strategy—Putting European Transport on Track for the Future', Brussels COM (2020) 789 final <https://ec.europa.eu/transport/sites/transport/files/legislation/com20200789.pdf>.

2 ibid paras 64–72.

3 See discussion in Chapters 7, 8 and 9.

regulators have had dynamics demanding immediacy thrust upon them. Not only are drones comparatively cheap and easy to procure as well as largely lacking licencing and tracking requirements but, as remote units, they potentially lack direct accountability if nexus to an operator (with sufficient assets or insurance) cannot be established. Losses flowing from malfunctions therefore stand to be costly to those directly involved, those impacted and to the State both in terms of the injury costs inflicted on innocent third parties by judgment proof defendants and around the transactions costs inherent in recovery.

Just as World War I fast tracked aviation innovation and commercialisation, COVID 19 has jump started public receptiveness to the value of integrating this technology—slating home to regulators the pressing need to provide secure oversight. Although broader frameworks capable of capturing what this industry will become largely remain green field territory, the multijurisdictional regulatory flurries that came with the start of the 2021 calendar year,[4] as set out in other chapters,[5] reflects emerging middle ground around the respective positions of policymakers, business leaders and other stakeholders. Significant leaps in this scalability vs safety tug of war around drone use include Federal Aviation Authority (FAA) authorisations for night uses, deliveries over heavily populated corridors, introduction of digital radio broadcast tracking requirements, and blueprints for protecting people and moving vehicles on the ground from errant drone harm. As many high value applications remain years off in development, facilitating value capture requires effective signposting for stakeholders – government officials, regulators, members of the UAS/Drone industries, designers, corporate adopters, investors – of the variables that support or detract from particular lines of development.

As history illustrates, building international consensus around uniform frameworks of any kind is challenging. Forging a regulatory framework for an industry both nascent and polycentric in its evolution is not surprisingly daunting. The following sections outline some of the key areas of technological development effective regulation must be capable of meeting.

Scalability versus security—BVLOS as a foundation

For drones to operate effectively they must encompass (i) a system capable of operating safely when in complex airspace and (ii) capacity to conduct a task which either reduces first-party risk to life or has demonstrable commercial benefits (speed/cost/time). Drone "scalability" rests on resolution over coming years of both technical and regulatory limitations. Variables, including battery life, payload weight capabilities, size, weight, communication systems and protective/risk mitigation technology are expected to change significantly. In turn, this will enable safety requirements to be loosened that currently limit the vast preponderance of drone uses to line of sight operations.[6]

4 Commission Implementing Regulation (EU) 2019/947 of 24 May 2019 on the rules and procedures for the operation of unmanned aircraft [2019] OJ L152/45; and Commission Delegated Regulation (EU) 2019/945 of 12 March 2019 on unmanned aircraft systems and on third-country operators of unmanned aircraft systems [2019] OJ L152/1.

5 See Chapters 13–18.

6 See the 2019 FAA UAS Symposium (3–5 June 2019) Baltimore, MD <www.faa.gov/uas/resources/events_calendar/archive/2019_uas_symposium/ 3-5 June 2019>.

Requiring direct visual line of sight between a drone and its operator—VLOS—retains pilot control over flight paths in relation to other aircraft, people, obstacles, protected environmental spaces and for collision avoidance purposes. As in the case of other aviation operations, the pilot is responsible for delivering safe outcomes by ensuring all operations are compliant with relevant legislation and safety requirements.

Commercial scalability and greater capture of the real potential value drones offer, however, requires that drones be able to operate beyond the visual line of sight of operators in order to cover greater distances and, going forward, discharge multiple stops if not tasks, as part of a "run". Beyond visual line of sight (BVLOS) is therefore increasingly the subject of regulatory reform attention with numerous countries now permitting, subject to strict pre-requisites, drones flying beyond a controller's visual range. As risks increase significantly when pilot/drone visual connectivity is not present, approvals for waivers require operators show risk mitigations essential to ensuring the safety of all proximate aircraft, people or property. Given the complexities BVLOS flight dynamics present, it is not surprising successful certifications[7] are limited with Israel (2017), the US (2018) and Australia (2019) being early adopters. Until broader risk mitigation and infrastructure rules can be more standardly agreed this is not likely to change.

In moving from VLOS to BVLOS requirement, complex drone operations and commercial functionalities like deliveries become both more viable and more cost effective. Benefits include greater distance coverage, greater data collection with fewer deployments, cost effectiveness against traditional methods such as manned helicopters and airplanes, capacity to replace long-range aerial data collection platforms such as otherwise used in manned aircraft and satellites, lower altitude capacities with higher-resolution data products, and safer outcomes by either providing better coverage of hazardous environments or in enhancing medical care/extractions. Rapid advancement into BVLOS adoption has, however, been limited by the current state of evolution of autonomous systems or full authority autonomous systems[8] necessary for programming these types of operations as well as more broadly by dynamics around operational safety—flight corridors, monitoring, disabling of wayward drones, identification of nefarious intent vehicles, amongst many.

Unlike manned aviation, which relies on human "computers", unmanned drones beyond visual sight lines are controlled by data provided by onboard instruments. Operators remain informed of the position, altitude, speed and direction of the flight trajectory as well as relevant parameters around the aircraft via a telemetry link.

7 Airobotics Drones, 'Airobotics is First to Receive CASA Approval for BVLOS Drone Flights from Remote Operations Center' (22 January2019)<www.airoboticsdrones.com/press-releases/airobotics-is-first-to-receive-casa-approval-for-bvlos-drone-flights-from-remote-operations-center/>.

8 "Artificial intelligence" might be used in this context but technical regulators and the "traditional" aerospace industry tend to use terms such as "autonomous systems" or "full authority autonomous systems". In large part that is due to the fact that "artificial intelligence" has been considered an imprecisely defined and malleable term; and there may be a distinction between decision making systems and learning systems. The UK Civil Aviation Authority adopts the phraseology of *High authority automated systems—those systems that can evaluate data, select a course of action and implement that action without the need for human input. . . .The concept of an "autonomous" UAS is a system that will do everything for itself using high authority automated systems*. See CAP 722 (November 2020) 3.9.1 p 122.

Drones flying BVLOS can, however, also change flight parameters and control sensors to collect data—and will, as artificial intelligence (AI) advances, become increasingly autonomous in relation to decision making as circumstances around them change.[9] Operator training will also change. As these capacities shift, traditional piloting skills will be supplemented by the acquisition of theoretical and practical training knowledge beyond flight rules and navigation such as meteorology, flight performance and planning, and related needs of specific AI systems and drone platform capacities.

Beyond operator training and high-quality AI programming, however, an infrastructure capable of managing UAVs will be essential. Aerial corridor systems will need to be refined well beyond the current regulations that effectively rely on operator capacity to understand and adhere to ceiling caps on flight operations and recognise "no-fly zones". The complexity of this undertaking speaks for itself but, as the US Congress made clear in 2019, it is not a task that can be delayed.[10]

The following sections look at different approaches to addressing safety, security and integration into shared airspace.

Unmanned traffic management (UTM)

Research and development around risk management of use and misuse of drones is essential to both existing drone operations and to future BVLOS adoption. As the Australian Senate Inquiry Committee noted,[11] the integration of Remotely Piloted Aircraft Systems (RPAS)[12] into Australian airspace requires a balance between effective enforcement measures, such as sufficient penalties, registration and restricted flight zones, with that of technology-based solutions.

A potential technology solution that is being considered and studied is the development of an unmanned traffic management system ("UTM"). Various projects are now underway around the world examining how drones flying at low altitudes can be integrated into a shared airspace. This concept was first proposed in 2016 as a way for State aviation authorities and air navigation service providers to "provide real-time information regarding airspace constraints and the intentions of other aircraft available to drone operations and their remote pilots directly or through a UTM service provider".[13] In Australia, Airservices Australia is in the process of developing such a detection system in consultation with industry partners with the aim of

9 See, for example, Cade Metz, 'Police Drones are Starting to Think for Themselves' (*New York Times*, 5 December 2020) <www.nytimes.com/2020/12/05/technology/police-drones.html>.

10 See, for example, Statement of Daniel K Elwell, Deputy Administrator, Federal Aviation Administration, before the Transportation and Infrastructure Subcommittee on Aviation, United States House of Representatives, 'Implementation of the FAA Reauthorization Act 2018' (26 September 2019) <www.transportation.gov/testimony/implementation-faa-reauthorization-act-2018>.

11 Rural and Regional Affairs and Transport Committee, Parliament of Australia, 'Report on the Regulatory Requirements that Impact on the Safe Use of Remotely Piloted Aircraft Systems, Unmanned Aerial Systems and Associated Systems' (Report, 31 July 2018) [6.5]<www.aph.gov.au/Parliamentary_Business/Committees/Senate/Rural_and_Regional_Affairs_and_Transport/Drones/Report> (hereinafter "Australian Senate Inquiry Committee").

12 As noted in Chapter 1, the International Civil Aviation Organization (ICAO) employs the acronym RPAS (standing for Remotely Piloted Aircraft System) or RPA (Remotely Piloted Aircraft).

13 ICAO Report, 'UTM—A Common Framework with Core Principles for Global Harmonization' (3rd edn) 5 <www.icao.int/safety/UA/Documents/UTM%20Framework%20Edition%203.pdf>.

building a flight information management system (FIMS) prototype aimed to facilitate the safe integration of drones with the current air traffic management structure and to mitigate airspace hazards. The FIMS will act as a centralised data platform that will exchange data between the UTM users and the existing air traffic management system ("ATMS") in order to manage airspace risks such as collisions.[14] In Australia, the drone information in the FIMS will be managed by the data in Civil Aviation Safety Authority (CASA) registration system, with registration required of commercial drone users from 28 January 2021.[15]

In the US, the FAA and the National Aeronautics and Space Administration ("NASA") have established a partnership and just completed the second phase in their UTM pilot programme which was established by the *Federal Aviation Administration (FAA) Extension, Safety and Security Act of 2016*.[16] The primary purpose of the pilot programme is to "make it possible for small unmanned aircraft systems, commonly known as "drones" to safely access low-altitude airspace beyond visual line of sight" which is currently prohibited by the Part 107 rules.[17]

In Europe, a similar concept of a UTM system is being explored by the European Organisation for the Safety of Air Navigation (EUROCONTROL) which is looking to integrate drones into a shared airspace below 500 ft across Europe.[18] The CORUS project is an initiative focussed on implementing a uniform UTM system that will facilitate the safe use of drones across borders whilst ensuring that the airspace remains safe for users and the public.[19] The UTM system is linked to the U-space initiative launched in 2016 by the European Commission which is another arm of regulatory framework for drones to enable the safe and efficient operation of drones with UTM and the relevant authorities.[20] It should be noted that full implementation of this concept is expected to begin after 2023 once all the proper rules, documents and technologies can allow drones to be safely integrated seamlessly.[21] The UTM system is just one solution that States are considering around the world to manage air traffic and mitigate drone risks.

Geo-fencing

Geo-fencing is another element of the solutions that are being considered by States as a mechanism to mitigate the risk of drones and can be described as "a virtual barrier which can be used to prevent RPAS from entering restricted airspace".[22] A large proportion of commercially available drones already include geo-fencing capabilities

14 Airservices Australia article 'UTM Commences with Airservices Release of its Requirements for a Flight Information Management System' (26 August 2020) <www.airservicesaustralia.com/utm-drones/>.

15 See CASA, 'Drone Registration' (2021) <www.casa.gov.au/drones/register>.

16 See section 2206 of *Federal Aviation Administration (FAA) Extension, Safety and Security Act of 2016*.

17 NASA, 'UTM 101' (26 June 2020) <www.nasa.gov/aeroresearch/utm-101/>.

18 EUROCONTROL, 'UAS ATM Integration Operational Concept' (27 November 2018) 7.

19 EUROCONTROL, 'Concept of Operations for European UTM Systems' (4 September 2020) <www.eurocontrol.int/project/concept-operations-european-utm-systems>.

20 SESAR, 'A Preliminary Summary of SESAR U-space Research and Innovation Results' (2017–2019)6<www.sesarju.eu/sites/default/files/documents/u-space/U-space%20Drone%20Operations%20Europe.pdf>.

21 ibid.

22 Australian Senate Inquiry Committee (n 11) paras 6.12–6.13.

(software and data contained in the drone that can restrict it from flying in certain areas, such as airports). Geo-fencing could be used to contain drones within a particular area, or to exclude drones from sensitive areas, such as in the airspace of airports, to prevent drone interference with other aircraft activity. "Geo-caging" is also a (to some extent complimentary) term used in some instances describing the prevention through software of the drone leaving a defined volume. It has been used in development test flight programmes and demonstrations in certain jurisdictions.

Following the success of geo-fencing demonstrations held in France to simulate a search and rescue mission, this technology is now expected to be an integral element of UTM (U-space).[23] It should be noted that the responsibility to equip drones with this capability in this case will most likely fall on the manufacturers. In the US, the FAA has encouraged drone manufacturers to include such technology that can assist to reduce the risk of drone incidents which include geo-fencing awareness capabilities. In addition, the FAA has also developed Low Altitude Authorization and Notification Capability (LAANC) where certain commercial drones are granted access through an approval process to fly in low-altitude airspaces near airports.[24]

In Europe, part of the EU Delegated Regulation 2019/945 requires manufacturers to equip drones larger than 250 g with geo-awareness capabilities.[25] "Geo-awareness" is a term used to describe the software that detects a breach, alerts the pilot and provides an opportunity for the pilot to then circumvent the breach. Geo-fencing and geo-awareness is considered to be a foundation service in facilitating the safe and efficient operation of drones.[26]

Although there is much support for the installation of geo-fencing as a way to mitigate the risk of a drone flying near a controlled airspace, concerns remain surrounding the cost of implementing such technology as not all manufacturers have this capability. In addition, concerns also exist around the liability for manufacturers where the geo-fencing system is based on a database that is to be developed by regulatory authorities.[27] Other questions and issues to be addressed include: what happens to a drone once it approaches or reaches a geo-fencing area? Does it fall to the ground? Return to its owner? Is it diverted in some other direction or to another location? Will geo-fencing systems also impact other low-flying aircraft (i.e. piloted aircraft, not drones) in the surrounding area?

The "geo-fencing landscape" will not necessarily be static in the area of drone operation. Geo-fencing software can be installed in the drone itself, but the cost implications of mandating the inclusion of the software in all drones could be prohibitive to some manufacturers or users. There is also the consideration of the need to ensure access by drones of varying type and design to real-time/current geo-fencing data;

23 SESAR, 'U-space Project Successfully Demonstrated Geofencing Technologies' (22 October 2019) <www.sesarju.eu/news/u-space-project-successfully-demonstrated-geofencing-technologies>.

24 Congressional Research Service, 'Protecting Against Rogue Drones' (3 September 2020) <https://fas.org/sgp/crs/homesec/IF11550.pdf>; see also UAS Data Exchange (LAANC) <www.faa.gov/uas/programs_partnerships/data_exchange/>.

25 Commission Delegated Regulation (EU) 2019/945 of 12 March 2019, reg 13 <https://eur-lex.europa.eu/legal-content/EN/TXT/PDF/?uri=CELEX:32019R0945&from=EN>.

26 ACI Europe Airports Council International, 'Drones in the Airport Environment: Concept of Operations & Industry Guidance' (April 2020) <www.skybrary.aero/bookshelf/books/5726.pdf>.

27 Australian Senate Inquiry Committee (n 11) [6.19].

for example, to ensure that temporary exclusion or danger zones are flagged to each drone's system.

Although advances in technology show promise that geo-fencing will be an integral tool to the management of drones in the future, CASA's position at this time is that the geo-fencing technology available does not meet the requisite levels of technical reliability.[28] The UK government stated recently that it was working with drone manufacturers and industry to determine how geo-fencing capabilities may be improved and with the CAA to ensure robust data on airspace restrictions, such as those around airports and other critical national sites, is available in a format that manufacturers and developers can easily use.[29]

Further development in this area is required before it is coined by regulators as "technically reliable" but it is expected to fully integrate with the UTM system to enhance the overall safety of drone operations around aerodromes.[30]

Electronic conspicuity (EC)

Electronic conspicuity is another initiative which will allow the automatic identification of all airspace users, including drones.[31] EC is an umbrella term for technologies that can help airspace users and air traffic services to be more aware of aircraft operating in the same airspace with the ability to "see and be seen", or "detect and be detected". Full adoption of EC solutions in BVLOS operations means that all users operating in a designated block of airspace can be detected electronically. EC solutions may involve multiple elements, including Secondary Surveillance Radar (SSR) transponders[32] or transponders that broadcast the drone's position (ascertained using GPS, for example),[33] installed on the aircraft.

Aircraft equipped with electronic conspicuity equipment can actively signal their presence to other airspace users. Such devices also receive signals which can alert the pilot to other aircraft in the vicinity thus enabling the pilot to see that aircraft and to take action to avoid it. In December 2018, the UK Department of Transport published "Aviation 2050—the future of UK aviation",[34] which proposes that there should be mandatory identification of all aircraft in UK airspace. To this end, the UK government has announced that it will be working with the CAA and other stakeholders, including international partners, on the best way to achieve this objective—taking into consideration the European Union's product standard requirement, expected to come into force in 2022, which will require all drones coming onto the market to be electronically conspicuous.[35]

28 Australian Senate Inquiry Committee (n 11).

29 UK Department of Transport, 'Taking Flight: The Future of Drones in the UK—Government Response' (January 2019) 10.

30 See Chapter 11 for discussion of cyber risks and geo-fencing.

31 See, for example, CAA, 'Electronic Conspicuity Devices'<www.caa.co.uk/General-aviation/Aircraft-ownership-and-maintenance/Electronic-Conspicuity-devices/>.

32 A surveillance radar system which uses transmitters/receivers (interrogators) and transponders. See International Civil Aviation Organization, 'Annex 10—Aeronautical Telecommunications—Volume IV—Surveillance Radar and Collision Avoidance Systems' (5th edn, *International Civil Aviation Organization* 2014).

33 See discussion of Automatic Dependent Surveillance Broadcast (ADS-B) technology in the following.

34 <www.gov.uk/government/consultations/aviation-2050-the-future-of-uk-aviation>.

35 ibid10.

An example of such a system that is being operated and harmonised across the global aviation industry is ADS-B ("Automatic Dependent Surveillance Broadcast").

In the UK it has been recommended that all drones should be fitted with electronic conspicuity technology from 2022 and as an incentive the UK Department of Transport has introduced a rebate scheme available to encourage drone users to adopt the technology.

In Australia, this system has been a requirement for manned aircraft since 2013; however, the possibility to extend this technology to also track unauthorised drones in controlled airspaces is now being examined. States around the world are also looking to harmonise and implement ADS-B technology even with slight differences in technical requirements. For example, the US requires alternative transceiver components not currently used in Australia, but with essentially similar architecture and function.

In an aim to improve drone safety from a drone manufacturer's perspective, DJI, one of the global leaders in drone technology, announced that all new drone models weighing more than 250 g from 1 January 2020 will be equipped with ADS-B capabilities to improve the safety of all operators sharing the airspace.

Currently seen as the answer to unmanned traffic management (UTM), in practice ADS-B comprises three main components:

- A ground-based network to receive the signals from the aircraft.
- An airborne transponder component which transmits (and in some cases can receive) on 978 or 1090 MHz.
- Operational procedures defining the use of the system.

A number of national aviation authorities have been looking into the viability of transponder mandated zones (TMZ) to enable the delivery of UAS operating beyond the visual line of sight (BVLOS). Under UK CAA classification, a TMZ will require all air traffic to carry a pressure-altitude reporting transponder. This stipulation has divided the general aviation community, some of whom have remarked that airspace should become less restrictive. Their concerns are that as the UK tightens up airspace to allow UAS operations, the general aviation aircraft will have to become equipped with more advanced technology to allow them to operate in areas where they have operated previously. These objections have reached ministerial levels, necessitating a delicate balance to be struck for the incorporation of TMZ (where an ADS-B is most useful).

In addition to the volume of aircraft which embody ADS-B, the number of systems which will need to be installed to create the ground-based network is not to be underestimated. Currently, only a handful of companies are capable of providing the network infrastructure. Without national investment at government level, these systems will not be installed to provide the necessary receiving stations needed to feed into a national air traffic picture or allow operation in complex environments such as the very low altitude urban environment.

Although the Australian Senate Inquiry Committee's attention was drawn to ADS-B technology[36] potential concerns were also raised that transponders may cause issues on the air traffic management system whereby air traffic controllers' screens are at

36 Australian Senate Inquiry Committee (n 11) para 6.4.

risk of "being flooded" with ADS-B data.[37] CSIRO[38] expressed further concern that RPAS operating in close proximity to other radio transmitting systems and antennas present "an ongoing safety risk" due to the potential interruption of command signals from the controller.

Radar and traffic collision avoidance systems

Airborne collision avoidance systems such as a traffic collision avoidance system (TCAS) may provide effective protections for aerodromes and controlled airspaces. TCAS is a family of airborne devices that function independently of the ground-based air traffic control (ATC) system and provide collision avoidance protection for a broad spectrum of aircraft types. All TCAS systems provide some degree of collision threat alerting, and a traffic display.[39] Also known as detect and avoid (DAA) or sense and avoid systems, this technology creates the capability to see, sense or detect conflicting traffic or other hazards and prompt the appropriate avoidance action.[40] Considerable research has been invested in drone-based automatic collision avoidance and mass-produced drones with basic functionalities of this are widely available.

These systems are increasingly recognised as critical to integrating unmanned aircraft into the national airspace and, according to Airservices Australia, the installation of DAA systems would eventually allow drones to fully integrate into all airspace classes, in harmony with other airspace users.[41]

For example, the inclusion of an air to air (A2A) radar (radio detection and ranging) system would address one of the biggest challenges to full integration of drone systems into airspace; namely, the ability to detect and avoid other air users.[42] All radar systems work in a similar fashion, as they require a radio transmitter aimed in a certain direction and a receiver that detects the echoes off any objects in its radio beam path. A2A radars operate between 8 and 12 GHz, which in NATO terminology corresponds to X and Ku band. Systems which have been available to the open market have been of a size, weight and cost that limit their use to larger platforms only. However, latest technology advances made by companies such as Echodyne, have pioneered small, compact and lightweight A2A radar systems which have been trialled on small quadcopters. The Echodyne Echoflight MESA radar is the size of an A5 notebook and is a true beam steering radar which operates a multichannel system in the K band. At only 817 g and with 120-degree field of view, it is revolutionising the market and offers a true detection system (up to 6 km) which will enable an operator to take avoiding action in the event of converging aircraft.

37 Mr Thomas McRobert, Civil Air Australia,'Committee Hansard' (6 June 2017)22–23.

38 Australian Senate Inquiry Committee (n 11) CSIRO, *Submission 61* p 3.

39 See US Department of Transportation Federal Aviation Administration, 'Introduction to TCAS II' (28 February 2011) Version 7.1 <www.faa.gov/documentlibrary/media/advisory_circular/tcas%20ii%20v7.1%20intro%20booklet.pdf>.

40 Australian Senate Inquiry Committee (n 11) para 6.23.

41 ibid para 6.24.

42 See, for example, Allistair Moses, Matthew J Rutherford and Kimon P Valavanis, 'Radar-Based Detection and Identification for Miniature Air Vehicles' (2011 IEEE International Conference on Control Applications (CCA) Part of 2011 IEEE Multi-Conference on Systems and Control Denver, CO, USA, 28–30 September 2011)<www.ssrrc.dtc.umn.edu/docs/RadarBasedDetection.pdf>.

There are good prospects for the use of drone-based radar for DAA/traffic collision avoidance. Those radar solutions will require assessment in the varying environments in which the drones are to be used. Complex or cluttered environments may impact the effectivity or range of such radar, for example, and considerations arise as to the range of potential conflicts that can be identified such as the use of radar to detect slow moving small drones at airports, and to monitor extensive low altitude airspace volumes in urban environments.

Communication systems

It is widely recognised that the weak link in all UAS operations is the ability to control a system either inside or outside visual range via a communication link. The link between pilot/mission manager and drone is of crucial importance.

A number of considerations arise when selecting frequencies and control types, but of paramount importance is ensuring that the data link is robust and is not subject to interference. A robust connection should consider the following:

- Transmission power to enhance field strength from the ground control station ("GCS")
- Frequency choice (HF, VHF/UHF (inc. GSM), L-S Band, C, X, Ku bands)
- Omni-directional versus beam focussing solutions
- Communications error management
- Frequency interference (common use protocols)
- Atmospheric conditions which impact signal attenuation
- UAS design (placement of antennas)
- System redundancy (secondary or tertiary communications options)
- Encryption or frequency hopping to guard against hostile jamming
- Spread spectrum techniques for segregated channels for command and control (C^2) and payload control and downlink.

Some drone systems currently employ a dual or triple redundant system to provide a backup if the primary link fails. Whilst this is not true in all cases, next-generation systems are starting to offer this as standard for all drone sizes where a blend of 900 MHz for control and 2.4 or 5 GHz for Wi-Fi payload downlink. Larger systems have bespoke communications packages and allow for primary communications using higher frequency bands which are less affected by atmospheric conditions and with the right power configuration have the ability to reach well beyond 175 km. Their backup systems will usually not include sufficient bandwidth for the payload but will allow for all critical flight systems to be controlled by the GCS.

An example of this is the Schiebel S-100 camcopter which operates its primary connection over a directional C-Band data link, which offers sufficient bandwidth for both aircraft control and payload management. Its backup is a UHF omni-directional system, which does not have the same range as the primary link. However, when coupled with a flight home mode, which is pre-programmed into the aircraft prior to launch, it will allow the aircraft to re-establish communications on the secondary (UHF) channel before reaching its terminal stages of flight. Should none of the communications methods work the S-100 has an auto-land function at a dedicated landing site. This is common to most large UAS platforms, as it forms part of the protections and risk mitigations in the safety chain which is assessed prior to approval of flight operations by national aviation authorities.

Satellite communications (SATCOM)

The inclusion of Satellite Communications for BVLOS operations is a significant undertaking in terms of both the equipment required to manage the transmission of data and the need to contract a third-party service provider. Of note, the cost of the system to transmit full motion video and C^2 can range from £300,000 to £1.2m dependent on the frequency band required.

SATCOM is unsuitable for small systems due to the equipment weight and power requirements. Larger systems already have incorporated the systems which offer a global capability from a single ground control station. An example of this is the US MQ-9 Reaper programme, which is often operated from Creech Air Force Base in Nevada, USA.

To put the weight and size of a SATCOM solution into context, the dome at the front of the MQ-9 houses the satellite antenna which is a curved communications dish array. It is situated at the front as its weight counterbalances that of the engine which is at the rear. Next-generation SATCOM antennae arrays are soon to be flat, which will remove the need of the dome and moving parts associated with the current systems. This will offer a lighter, fixed system and therefore is likely to be incorporated into more air vehicles. A current market solution which is to be market ready in Q3 2021 is the AeroMax flat panel antenna from NXTCOMM, which is a fragmented aperture antenna which was developed by the Georgia Tech Research Institute. This advancement will allow for smaller systems to embody SATCOM connectivity, ultimately offering a level of redundancy which should meet the safety factor requirements of civil aviation authorities.

Automatic identification system (AIS)

An element of UTM and enforcement of drone regulations and laws is remote identification of the drone (and its operator). Numerous UTM (including the European U-space) near-term goals relate to remote electronic identification of drones.

AIS is an example of technology used elsewhere, which may assist in achieving this goal. It is an automatic tracking system used by commercial shipping services which transmits callsign, position, heading and speed data on a common frequency. It is becoming more popular with leisure craft, and when coupled with an AIS database which shows vessel length, class and usually a picture, it greatly improves the ability to interrogate maritime targets from information provided by another sensor; for example, radar information which is overlaid with AIS information and cross-cued to an electro optical/infrared camera (i.e. a camera utilising light across visible and infrared wavelengths) should correlate to the database information.

The embodiment of an AIS detection sensor on UAS is commonplace, and systems such as the Owl VHF from Skagmo Electronics is a good example of the unit which measures 75 mm × 45 mm × 20 mm and weighs only 120 g.

Concluding comments

Enabling safe and secure drone operations will require a balance between effective enforcement measures, such as sufficient penalties, registration and restricted flight zones, with that of technology-based solutions, including geo-fencing, ADS-B, traffic collision avoidance systems, and UTM (unmanned traffic management).

The ability of small UAS vehicles to sense traffic in the airspace and maintain a safe separation distance from other vehicles is a fundamental requirement to the integration of drones into airspace. Sense and avoid algorithms are continuing to develop with onboard sense and avoid capability to detect potential conflicts with other aircraft and autonomously manoeuvre to avoid collisions, while remaining within the airspace boundaries of the mission.[43] Event cameras, which are bio-inspired sensors with reaction times of microseconds, are also being developed so that drones can more reliably detect and avoid fast-moving obstacles.[44] Onboard detection and localisation of drones using depth maps is another developing area to further enhance the safety of drones in shared airspace.[45]

Geo-fencing will also continue to improve. NASA is conducting research into Safeguard, which uses geo-fencing technology to establish flight ceilings to ensure a drone flight remains under its allowable maximum altitude. In the event of a boundary violation, Safeguard can prompt a drone to stop and find an alternate route, perform an emergency landing, and if all else fails cut the power completely to disable the vehicle.[46]

In conclusion to this brief overview, it is clear that many of these systems are developing rapidly and may be deployed in the future as regulatory tools to enable multiple drone operations conducted beyond visual line of sight (BVLOS), and to prevent unsafe drone use.

43 See, for example, NASA's tests with ICAROUS, Independent Configurable Architecture for Reliable Operations of Unmanned Systems, M Consiglio, B Duffy, S Balachandran, L Glaab and C Munoz, 'Sense and Avoid Characterization of the Independent Configurable Architecture for Reliable Operations of Unmanned Systems' (Thirteenth USA/Europe Air Traffic Management Research and Development Seminar, ATM 2019).

44 See, for example, D Falanga, K Kleber and D Scaramuzza, 'Dynamic Obstacle Avoidance for Quadrotors with Event Cameras' (18 March 2020)5(40) Science Roboticsaaz 9712<https://doi.org/10.1126/scirobotics.aaz9712>.

45 See, for example, A Carrio and others, 'Onboard Detection and Localization of Drones Using Depth Maps' (19 February 2020)8 IEEE Access 30480–30490<https://doi.org/10.1109/ACCESS.2020.2971938>.

46 N Joseph, 'Crashing into Safe Autonomous Flight' (5 March 2020) <www.nasa.gov/feature/langley/crashing-into-safe-autonomous-flight>.

Part E

Insurance

20 Insurance

General

Anthony A. Tarr, Darryl Smith, Tom Chamberlain, Simon Ritterband and Kirsty Paynter

Introduction

As discussed in the Regulation chapters (Part D), authorities across the globe are grappling with the task of incorporating drone operations into aviation and other regulatory frameworks, while the range of applications for drone use—both commercial and recreational—is ever expanding.

This exponential growth in the use and deployment of drones poses challenges for regulators, and also insurers. Currently, for example, one of the most significant issues from a regulatory perspective is the lack of clarity regarding regulation for recreational drone use, despite the fact that drone use is increasing day by day. The increase in drone use both recreationally and commercially also brings with it a risk of significant damage to people and property—the past few years have seen a number of incidents and also very significant near-misses which, if the risk had eventuated, would have resulted in major losses.

Insurance products often develop and evolve in tandem with government regulations. In many cases insurance is mandated: compulsory third-party insurance is a good example. However, drones are somewhat different. The approach taken by regulators across the globe to mandate insurance cover for drones is not consistent. Some jurisdictions have mandatory minimum insurance requirements,[1] while others recommend that insurance be obtained or have limited requirements[2] or no requirements at all. This suggests that the appetite for drone insurance products has been driven by other factors, such as an understanding by drone operators of the risks of drone operations, and perhaps in more than equal measure by the rapid emergence and investment by insurers in developing innovative products to meet the demand, price the risks accurately and enable organisations to essentially expand, economise and complement their existing business operations using drones. It is clear that insurance has an integral role in protecting the ongoing viability of drone operations.

Given the regulatory uncertainty, the ongoing development of insurance products by insurers has played and will continue to play a significant role in understanding and mitigating the risks associated with drone operations. In this context, as is usually

1 For example, see Regulation (EC) No 785/2004 and new EU Regulations (EC) 2019/947 and 2019/945, effective from 31 December 2020. Discussed in Chapter 22.

2 For example, the Federal Aviation Administration (FAA) and the Civil Aviation Safety Authority (CASA) do not presently require operators of drones in the United States or Australia, respectively, to take-out third-party liability insurance, but such cover is strongly recommended. Discussed in Chapter 22.

the case with other emerging risks, insurance has a role to play in not only responding and providing cover for the risks as they are currently understood (and for which data is available), but also in shaping, refining and predicting the ongoing and future risk environment.

Some of the key risks associated with drone operations are not likely to change. Other risks will emerge. At present, some of the extant risks include first-party damage to the drone and related components, first-party drone loss, third-party liability, including injuries to others, damage to property and nuisance and breach of privacy. There are also costs of expenses incidental to each of those risks when they occur, such as investigation and legal expenses.

Assessment of risks

One of the main considerations in assessing drone risk is loss history. This data is increasing but there are many uninsured drones which have resulted in unreported accidents. Even where there is a mandatory obligation to report drone incidents,[3] many are likely to be unreported. This is because they are either uninsured or the cost to replace the drone outweighs the damage. Drone operators may lose control of a drone which goes on to cause damage which may remain unreported where the drone and the drone operator is unable to be identified. There may also be instances where the owner of the damaged property or injured party simply does not realise the damage sustained was caused by a drone.

As with any emerging technology, there are unforeseen or overlooked risks and the possibility of undesirable misuse of applications or effects which cannot be anticipated at the current time. As Guy Carpenter explains:

> many manufacturers (some of which are emanating out of less regulated markets such as China) may not be adequately covered. This was evident with Chinese drywall manufacturers who did not have adequate coverage for construction defect. The result was that their liability was shifted to the US-based contractors and distributors. Similarly, we see that the emerging risks associated with UAS and drones will involve highly complex liability scenarios that could encompass all aspects of the global UAS/drone manufacturing and service provider supply chain.[4]

From an operational perspective, one of the key risks is that the drone could collide with or crash into an aircraft or another object or the ground.[5] Early on, those

3 In the US, consumer drone accidents are subject to the Code of Federal Regulations, Title 14 Aeronautics and Space, Chapter 1, Subchapter F, Section 107.9 and state that drone accidents need to be reported if it results in serious injury or loss of consciousness to any person, or causes damage to property (other than the drone itself) exceeding USD $500.

4 See report by Guy Carpenter, Marsh & McLennan Companies, 'A Clearer View of Emerging Risks' (Report, September 2015) <www.guycarp.com/content/dam/guycarp/en/documents/dynamic-content/A_Clearer_View_of_Emerging_Risks.pdf>.

5 See, for example, Pam Stewart, 'Drone Danger: Remedies for Damage by Civilian Remotely Piloted Aircraft to Persons or Property on the Ground in Australia' [2016] UTSLRS 24; (2016) 23 Torts Law Journal 290.

risks appeared to be consistent with general aviation risks, and for that reason the first versions of drone insurance policies were adapted from existing aviation policy wordings.[6]

The risks covered by these policies generally include loss of or damage to the hull, that is, the drone itself, and liability to third parties for injury to persons and property damage caused by the operation of the drone. For example, if a drone experienced breakdown mid-air it is easy to see how a crash could damage or destroy the drone itself. However, the drone could also potentially crash into an individual third party (causing fatal or non-fatal injury) or into a third party's property causing damage or destruction to the property.[7] These are some of the fundamental risks that insurers currently envisage insureds seeking cover for in relation to drone operations.

One of the most significant risks from an insurance perspective in relation to the use of drones is the difficulty to account for or predict the circumstances in which a drone may be used. Of course, current policies exist which require drone users to specify the terrain and conditions in which they intend to operate an insured drone, such as the population density of the area and predicted weather conditions[8]; however, the amount of underwriting required to determine the risk level can be significant.

Operational conditions for drones can change rapidly and frequently. In addition, the fact that drones are significantly more autonomous than other aircraft, such as aeroplanes or helicopters, means that the types of terrain in which they operate is difficult to predict with certainty. This is particularly so in congested areas, where rural and urban fringes are only separated by a few kilometres and it is easy for even recreational drone users to cover a number of types of terrains in a single flight.

Further risk to insurers arises from the fact that, as it currently stands, drones are a rapidly developing technology and are accessible to anyone. Accordingly, to use an Australian example:

> The downside of this rapid growth . . . is that there are burgeoning numbers of drones, many of which are unregistered or unlicensed and, more dauntingly, substantial numbers of drones are operated with limited or no training. Regulators and the community at large therefore face what is hardly a minor safety challenge with the CASA submission to the 2018 Senate inquiry highlighting "an increase in the operation of RPA without regard to safety, particularly within restricted airspace, including 'the risk of a catastrophic collision with a passenger aircraft' ".[9]

6 International Underwriting Association Developing Technology Monitoring Group, 'On-Demand and Conquer: Is the Future of Insurance a Pay-As-You-Go One?' (Report, 9 October 2019) 5<http://iual.informz.ca/IUAL/data/images/2019%20Circular%20Attachments/068_IUA%20Developing%20Technology%20Monitoring%20Group%20-%20Interview%203.pdf>.

7 See, for example, Julie-Anne Tarr, Maurice Thompson and Anthony Tarr, 'Regulation, Risk and Insurance of Drones: An Urgent Global Accountability Imperative' (2019) 8 Journal of Business Law 559, 561.

8 International Underwriting Association Developing Technology Monitoring Group (n 6)5.

9 Julie-Anne Tarr, Anthony Tarr, Ron Bartsch and Maurice Thompson, 'Drones in Australia—Rapidly Evolving Regulatory and Insurance Challenges' (2019) 30 Insurance Law Journal 135, 138.

Simon Ritterband[10] comments that:

> Potentially the highest risk profile pilots are the "Sport or recreational" users and they are the ones with the lowest barrier of entry, as a pilot could simply purchase a Drone, register it, and get flying. Even if they are required to pass a theoretical competency test, which could help reiterate flight regulations, new pilots are still more likely to crash due to pilot error.
>
> Those flying for "work" purposes are more likely to operate within a well-structured process and be better trained than those that don't. Excluding "sport and recreational" pilots from the requirement for insurance leaves the theoretically most risky segment of pilots exposed. Particularly if an uninsured pilot has an accident with third-party repercussions which could also severely damage the public perception towards the UAV industry.
>
> Based on the numbers that have been shared by the CAA, out of the circa 150,000 drone operators registered on the CAA drone registration portal, there are over 80,000 (those that don't hold either a Permission for Commercial Operation (PfCO)[11] or are a member of a recognised association/club (e.g. British Model Flying Association membership) that are very likely to be flying with no third-party liability insurance. This illustrates the point that those less trained and uninsured represent the largest segment of the current industry. Working with the CAA and Department for Transport discussions have been put forward along with other drone insurance companies with suggestions on how we might go about looking into mandatory insurance for the recreational flyer.[12]

There are also significant gaps in domestic and international standards relating to airworthiness, manufacturing standards, design and engineering requirements and certification.[13] Anyone could purchase from a retail store or online, a low-cost drone which may not be airworthy in certain weather conditions or may be generally of poor quality and therefore susceptible to breakdown or failure and the potential consequences thereof. This in turn results in a connected insurance risk, in that underwriters need to consider whether an insured drone is capable of safe operation as its owner intends.

Unlike helicopters or aeroplanes, the rapidly evolving nature of drone technology means that insurers cannot easily utilise standard product specifications—particularly in relation to the software used to operate the drone, which might be updated or upgraded numerous times within a normal annual insurance policy period—as an

10 Correspondence from Simon Ritterband to Dr Anthony Tarr, 1 November 2020, see <www.moonrockinsurance.com.> Simon Ritterband, managing director of Moonrock Insurance Solutions, currently sits on a number of government advisory panels along with the Department for Transport (UK), the CAA and other key stakeholders within the industry. He also sits on the British Standards Institute Committee (BSI).

11 Civil Aviation Authority, 'Drone Operators with a Valid CAA Permission for Commercial Work' <www.caa.co.uk/Consumers/Unmanned-aircraft/General-guidance/Drone-operators-with-a-valid-CAA-permission-for-commercial-work.>; PfCO being 'permission for commercial work.'

12 ibid.

13 Julie-Anne Tarr, Maurice Thompson and Anthony Tarr, Regulation, 'Risk and Insurance of Drones: An Urgent Global Accountability Imperative' (2019) 8 Journal of Business Law 559, 562.

indicator of a drone's reliability and performance. Further, both the operator and the mechanical performance of an aeroplane or a helicopter is easier to predict—in both cases the operator is licenced and highly trained, and the craft itself has standard product specifications and extensive safety data.[14]

In addition to first-party risks (i.e. damage to the drone itself), there are also third-party liability risks. There are numerous examples worldwide of incidents or near misses caused by these risks eventuating. These include a highly publicised "near miss" involving champion skier Marcel Hirscher, who narrowly escaped colliding with a drone that crashed just inches behind him in a World Cup slalom race,[15] or when during the 2015 US Open a drone hovering over a stadium crashed into the stands.[16]

Drone crashes have also been reported to have sparked bushfires in Australia and the United States.[17] There are also increasing accounts of manned aircraft, including passenger airliners, recording near misses with drones.[18] While the issues associated with writing third-party liability cover are not new to insurers, the related risks are arguably magnified with respect to drones. At its simplest, this is because it is much more difficult to predict who will operate the drone and how it will be used. A recreational drone, which is insured for photographing landscapes, could quite easily crash into the wrong area of bushland and cause a bushfire. In addition, even in situations where one would expect the use of a drone is tightly controlled (such as the filming of a World Cup slalom race), the fact remains that if an operational error occurs, the consequences of the drone malfunctioning are very difficult to predict. These risks can, of course, be better understood through careful underwriting, as set out in the next section of this chapter.

If anything, these risks are not at the stage yet where they are stabilising. Instead:

> given technological advances, the veritable explosion in their usage, their capacity to carry payloads and their ability to travel vast distances, the potential for injury or damage resulting from drone operations is ever increasing. Their increased deployment through transport and delivery services in high density population areas will further enhance personal injury and property damage risks.[19]

14 See, for example, United States Government Accountability Office, 'Unmanned Aircraft Systems—Measuring Progress and Addressing Potential Privacy Concerns Would Facilitate Integration into the National Airspace System' (Report to Congressional Requesters, GAO-12-981, September 2012) 14 <www.gao.gov/assets/650/648348.pdf>; Andrew J Armstrong, 'Development of a Methodology for Deriving Safety Metrics for UAV Operational Safety Performance Measurement' (Report, Master of Science in Safety Critical Systems Engineering, Department of Computer Science, York University, January 2010)<www-users.cs.york.ac.uk/~mark/projects/aja506_project.pdf>.

15 Tom Chamberlain and Tony Avery, 'Drones—Everything You Need to Know' (Presentation, 10 September 2019) 33 <www.actuaries.org.uk/system/files/field/document/Hot%20Topic%201_Tom%20Chamberlain_Tony%20Avery.pdf>.

16 Allen R. Wolf and Jorge Aviles, 'Drones Create Liability for Property Owners' (2016) 63(1) Risk Management 18.

17 Julie-Anne Tarr, Anthony Tarr, Ron Bartsch and Maurice Thompson, 'Drones in Australia—Rapidly Evolving Regulatory and Insurance Challenges' (2019) 30 Insurance Law Journal 135, 141.

18 Chamberlain and Avery (n 15) 34.

19 Julie-Anne Tarr, Anthony Tarr, Ron Bartsch and Maurice Thompson, 'Drones in Australia—Rapidly Evolving Regulatory and Insurance Challenges' (2019) 30 Insurance Law Journal 135, 139. See also Jacinta Long and Sarah Yau, 'Drone Damage: What Happens If a Drone Hits You?' (Article, Clyde & Co, 13 December 2017)

There is also the risk of significant expense being caused by recreational drone use where there is an accidental incursion into airspace, on numerous occasions and causing significant expense, as set out in the following:

> There are frequent reports of drones causing hazards to aircraft. A few examples will illustrate. Gatwick Airport, the United Kingdom's second largest airport, was brought to a standstill in December 2018 through the illegal operation of drones within the airport's airspace. This disrupted the travel plans of 125,000 people and cost the airlines an estimated US $63 million.[20]

Another key risk in relation to drone operations is that regulatory requirements either carve out or do not clearly cover recreational use and/or quasi-commercial operations, leading to a lack of clarity.

At the same time, to use Australia as an example:

> Recreational take up continues to fuel market growth of drones in Australia and broader use commercially is exploding exponentially as technology improves to meet commercial and security market demands. Uses in the latter respect currently range from policing, border security, surf lifesaving, emergency and hazard management, delivery of humanitarian aid, ship navigation and piloting, with substantial adaptation emerging continually.[21]

Therefore, injury to individuals and property damage are an extant risk arising out of the use of drones[22] and given technological advances, the increase in their usage, and their ability to travel long distances, the potential for damage resulting from drone usage is ever increasing.[23] There is also little doubt that the applications to which drones will be put will evolve as organisations find ways to employ drones to compete with others, or to provide their products and services more efficiently.[24]

Other risks, both from an operation and insurance perspective, include nuisance, privacy issues and concerns around data collection, through the use of drones to collect information through aerial surveillance, which could result in the drone collecting unintended data.[25] This is particularly pertinent to government agencies and law enforcement,[26] whose increasing use of drones gives rise to serious privacy issues

20 Julie-Anne Tarr, Maurice Thompson and Anthony Tarr, Regulation, 'Risk and Insurance of Drones: An Urgent Global Accountability Imperative' (2019) 8 Journal of Business Law 559, 560. See also Maurice Thompson, Patrick Slomski and James Cooper, 'Gatwick Meltdown: drones in a no-go zone, Clyde & Co, 21 December 2018.

21 Julie-Anne Tarr, Anthony Tarr, Ron Bartsch and Maurice Thompson, 'Drones in Australia—Rapidly Evolving Regulatory and Insurance Challenges' (2019) 30 Insurance Law Journal 135, 137–38.

22 Pam Stewart, 'Drone Danger: Remedies for Damage by Civilian Remotely Piloted Aircraft to Persons or Property on the Ground in Australia' (2016) 23(3) Torts Law Journal 290.

23 Jacinta Long and Sarah Yau, 'Drone Damage: What Happens If a Drone Hits You?(Article, *Clyde & Co*, 13 December 2017).

24 Julie-Anne Tarr, Maurice Thompson and Anthony Tarr, 'Regulation, Risk and Insurance of Drones: An Urgent Global Accountability Imperative' (2019) 8 Journal of Business Law 559, 568.

25 ibid 561.

26 Matthew R Koerner, 'Drones and the Fourth Amendment: Redefining Expectations of Privacy' (2015) 64(6) Duke Law Journal 1129, 1131; Laura La Bella, *Drones and Law Enforcement: Inside the World of Drones* (Rosen Publishing 2017) 10.

and concerns around data collection and use. However, these concerns are equally applicable to non-governmental agencies who, for example, may use drones to collect unauthorised data through aerial surveillance of a mining company's resources or of a land developers' properties.[27] This area is, however, well documented (as are the constraints and challenges more broadly around privacy legislation) and will not be considered in depth in this context.[28] It is worth noting that some insurance policies may cover non-intentional breach of privacy claims in relation to drone operations. Further, with the increase in drone usage and in particular with drone use in recreational settings, there is in turn an alteration of the risk profile in traditional forms of insurance policies, such as home and contents, for example, where an uninsured drone crashes into an insured property.[29]

The hazards associated with the operation of drone use are relatively novel and in turn bring with them a degree of uncertainty. This is, among other reasons, a result of the ever-evolving technology and capabilities of drones which make it difficult for insurance underwriters to accurately assess the risk associated with an insured's activity.[30]

Whether it be from a third-party liability perspective or with respect to breaches in privacy and government regulations, the freedom which vast numbers of drone operators have to cover vast areas of terrain using a drone creates uncertainty. In addition, risks also arise for insurers by virtue of the fact that drones have not been developed nor are they used for a specific purpose. For example, automobiles, planes and helicopters are used for relatively confined purposes, such as transport and delivery, whereas drones have a very broad range of applications, and those applications are constantly evolving.

Insurers providing products for new and evolving risks do face challenges in accessing sufficient relevant data around the emerging risks to enable accurate pricing. Nevertheless, insurers have embraced the challenge to provide protection against future uncertainties and uncertain loss. While the precise delineation and evaluation of risk may be a work in progress, there is already a well-developed insurance market, described in the following sections, providing cover for liability arising from the use of a drone.

Insurers' responses

The insurance industry initially adopted an approach to drone insurance using standard aviation wordings on an annual basis, adapting those policies by removing coverages such as passenger liability, but effectively giving users a standard aviation policy at disproportionate cost of issuance.

27 See, for example, Maurice Thompson, Clyde & Co, observes that "companies are at great risk of industrial espionage from drones", quoted in Ben Norris, 'Drones: The Search for Risk-Based Rules' (*Commercial Risk Europe*, 21 May 2019).

28 Julie-Anne Tarr, Anthony Tarr, Ron Bartsch and Maurice Thompson, 'Drones in Australia—Rapidly Evolving Regulatory and Insurance Challenges' (2019) 30 Insurance Law Journal 135, 138–40.

29 Julie-Anne Tarr, Maurice Thompson and Anthony Tarr, 'Regulation, Risk and Insurance of Drones: An Urgent Global Accountability Imperative' (2019) 8 Journal of Business Law 559, 568.

30 ibid 568.

As Tom Chamberlain[31] explained in an interview with the International Underwriting Association of London,[32] this approach was not necessarily optimal for the insurer or the customer:

"From a UK standpoint, we started writing drone policies around 3 years ago and very quickly realised that the approach we were taking was not an efficient one. We were also using our standard aviation wordings on an annual basis, adapting them by removing coverages such as passenger liability, but effectively giving users a standard aviation policy at disproportionate cost of issuance. As you can imagine, this approach is not optimal for the insurer or the customer!

Firstly, from an efficiency point of view, we have experienced general aviation underwriters whose focus should be to underwrite the medium and large accounts business rather than spend an hour on a relatively low value drone policy.

Secondly, for the customer, there must be a better product out there. One that is cost effective and offers you the cover you actually need. Before we considered providing on-demand insurance, we looked at a number of providers who had developed online platforms. However, these were quite vanilla offerings where proposers would fill out a form, answer 10 or 20 questions and be quoted for an annual policy.

This was not really what we wanted to do. Drones are a new technology, with new users, who want to be doing things digitally, independently planning their flights and most importantly, doing things in a safer way. We continued looking around and came across a company that claimed to have unlocked the risk analytics behind drone flights. This company was Flock. The system they proposed, rather than asking 10–20 questions up front that you would need to underwrite a standard annual policy, they would ask just a couple of questions and fill out the rest of the information required with big data. Rather than being able to take a view on the profile received up front; where and when are you going to be flying, they could capture all of that information in real time and price it on the spot. This for us suddenly fit the mould, providing an efficient way of distributing policies. The system helps promote drone safety and has an approach, which enables us to accurately price drone risks using data that we just would not have had access to otherwise.

The company accesses a significant amount of data from a range of sources, including hyper-local weather data, building density and population density in order to assess the risk posed by a drone in the sky. If it has an accident, what is it likely to hit? A building, a car? Alternatively, is it in an empty field and will it hit a tree or a cow? It worked for us in every respect: it ticked the boxes of efficiency, distribution, technology, big data and safety. Indeed, we saw that this was potentially a new and better way of doing insurance and could see the applications of where this technology could scale further into the insurance world".[33]

31 CUO Aviation—Global Project Manager and Senior Business Analyst, Allianz Global Corporate & Specialty, London, UK.

32 International Underwriting Association Developing Technology Monitoring Group (n 6); see also associated media release, International Underwriting Association, 'IUA Publishes On-Demand Insurance Report' (Media Release, 16 October 2019) <www.iua.co.uk/IUA_Member/Press/Press_Releases_2019/IUA_publishes_on-demand_insurance_report.aspx?WebsiteKey=84dca912-b4fb-4a0f-a6e5-47ad899350aa>.

33 International Underwriting Association Developing Technology Monitoring Group (n 6) 5.

On-demand insurance has its own challenges. As Tom Chamberlain explains, underwriting risk assessments in relation to drone coverage requires:

> specifics such as whether the drone was impacted by the wind or if the stick inputs say you pulled a hard left into the tree and crashed! Inconsistencies between the log and the claim report will then become apparent and dealt with accordingly. We make it very clear at the time the policy is incepted what types of information are going to be stored and used when they are submitting a claim, so they are very aware from the outset the levels of controls in place. But you are right, you can spend maybe a fiver for on-demand insurance and get yourself a new drone, whereas if you are getting an annual policy which is costing GBP 1,000, then the temptation to purchase a policy to bring a fraudulent claim is not that great. The difficulty is balancing chasing after fraud with the cost of doing so. The cost of a drone could be GBP 3,000, whereas the cost of chasing a claim is a lot more, but equally we do not want to encourage fraud.[34]

While insurance providers such as Allianz Global Corporate & Specialty in the UK moved to pricing some of their drone coverage policies to an on-demand basis, not all insurers are migrating to pay-as-you-fly policies.

Simon Ritterband, the managing director of Moonrock Insurance Solutions,[35] reports that his company, as one of the very first entrants into the drone insurance market and now with over 2000 pilots/organisations with polices on an annual basis, provide cover even when the drone is not flying for a specific time period. Moonrock's customer research found that its market segment that operated drones preferred annual insurance, whereby they purchase a policy, file the documents and do not have to think about insurance until a claim was necessary or when renewal came around. It also allowed finance directors to attribute a fixed cost and budget accordingly. Simon Ritterband comments further that:

> Pilots that entered into the commercial drone industry 2015/16 were made up predominantly of model flying enthusiasts moving into the drone industry, aviation enthusiasts, and small single operator pilots working in a small market (television and film productions).This was shortly followed by the advancement of camera and LIDAR[36] equipment that allowed surveying and monitoring companies to utilize drones for their requirements.
>
> Over the past 18 months we have seen a shift in our business due to a consolidation of the market, with far more enterprise businesses taking advantage of

34 ibid 14.

35 Correspondence from Simon Ritterband to Dr Anthony Tarr, 1 November 2020, see <www.moonrockinsurance.com> Simon Ritterband currently sits on a number of government advisory panels along with the Department for Transport (UK), the CAA and other key stakeholders within the industry. He also sits on the British Standards Institute Committee (BSI).

36 Lidar (Light Detection and Ranging) is a method for measuring distances by illuminating the target with laser light and measuring the reflection with a sensor. Differences in laser return times and wavelengths can then be used to make digital 3-D representations of the target. It has terrestrial, airborne, and mobile applications. See, for example, National Oceanic and Atmospheric Administration, 'What is Lidar?' (2020) <https://oceanservice.noaa.gov/facts/lidar.html>.

> drones in-house, including bespoke training for pilots specifically for their business needs (wind farm inspection, agriculture etc).
>
> This has allowed Moonrocks' underwriters to create far more bespoke policies taking into account the levels of risk they may face. The blanket one policy fits all approach is becoming less and less a feature of today's insurers in the drone industry.[37]

The commentary mentioned earlier from respected industry participants reflects the evolving and complex environment of drone insurance. Diverse approaches are needed to meet demand in relation to the commercial, quasi-commercial and recreational proliferation of drones, and to meet demand in industries which have expanded their business activities to include drone operations.

Concluding comments

As has been noted previously in this chapter, the challenges in insuring drone use are particularly novel, not only due to the evolving nature of the technology but also because of the unique factors to be considered as part of risk assessment.[38]

The rapid development of drone technology obviously creates challenges for organisations whose businesses are affected, and also for insurers who need to analyse, plan for change and to some extent predict, the future risk landscape.

Insurance underwriting models generally use historical data to predict the future risk landscape. However, drone technology is arguably moving too fast for this to be the only tool that insurance underwriters utilise. There is, however, one key characteristic of drones that will assist with underwriting drone risks in the future, which is data: drones produce a vast amount of real-time data that can be used to analyse risks as they arise. The data that drones capture should make the task of underwriting drone insurance more accurate, and as drone technology improves and the implementation of drones expands, the data available for underwriting will also increase.

Artificial Intelligence (AI) is a significant tool in helping insurers understand the risks in the drone industry. Dr Ernest Earon comments:[39]

> There are millions of drones operating routinely around the world. We don't have the ability to look back over a hundred plus years, as they do for traditional aviation, to help us understand where the risks are. What we do have, though, is tremendously rich data sets that detail all aspects of a drone's operation, including components like batteries.
>
> The information is there if you can extract it. The challenge is the sheer volume of data, and the subtleties of the signals in that. AI helps us see through all the

37 Correspondence from Simon Ritterband to Dr Anthony Tarr (n 35).

38 Julie-Anne Tarr, Maurice Thompson and Anthony Tarr, 'Regulation, Risk and Insurance of Drones: An Urgent Global Accountability Imperative' (2019) 8 Journal of Business Law 559, 568.

39 Miriam McNabb, 'The Connection Between AI and Drone Insurance—Why the Big Players in Insurance are Believers [Deep Dive]' (30 April 2019) <https://dronelife.com/2019/04/30/the-connection-between-ai-and-drone-insurance-why-the-big-players-in-insurance-are-believers-deep-dive/>. Dr Earon, who is quoted in the article, is chair of the data division of the FAA's Unmanned Aircraft Safety Team, Former CTO and co-founder of Precision Hawk.

noise and clutter and variation of the data to see the underlying patterns, behaviours and yes, risks. It would simply not be possible to do this otherwise.

Risk management and mitigation tools are crucial in helping emerging industries scale and set new standards. AI is a critical component but it's not the only one. A combination of expertise in hardware, software, underwriting and machine learning will be crucial—serving as drivers of growth for any business and industry impacted by this rapidly accelerating digital wave.

Risk assessments from the perspective of an insurer are also made more difficult by the fact that not all risks are entirely understood—even using Big Data. This is inherent in any area of technology which is still developing, though the unique challenge applicable to insuring drones is that the infancy of the technology does not limit the associated risks (it simply means they are yet to be discovered). Notwithstanding this, there are clear areas of risk emerging as the most major considerations for insurers, such as third-party damage, and this is something that, with time, greater understanding of drones' technology will allow insurers to underwrite risks with an even higher level of precision.

As set out earlier in this chapter, regulatory authorities are grappling with the task of incorporating drones into regulatory frameworks. Essentially, there is a lag time between the regulation of drone operations when compared to the speed at which the global drone market is growing. And as this market expands, so too will the drone insurance market.

There are a few key drivers for the drone insurance market moving forward. One is the impetus for certain industries to replace or complement existing services or labour using drones, whether that be to enhance profits or to remain competitive. While replacing existing services and labour with drones is likely to lead to insurance cost savings (e.g. in compulsory workers compensation insurance), there are other costs that organisations will need to insure: and the insurance taken out by commercial entities to protect their services and labour is likely to be replaced or substituted—at least in part—by insurance for drone operations. As that replacement or substitution occurs, the global drone insurance market is likely to increase significantly. As we have seen with other insurance products, most notably cyber insurance, insurers will innovate and develop or adapt products to supply this market as it evolves. Another key driver is the proliferation of recreational drones, and the awareness of consumers about the hazards that are present as part of operating a drone. It appears that in the short to medium term much of the drone insurance market will continue to be driven by drone operators, consumers and insurance brokers, rather than by regulatory mandate.

There are a number of insurance policies on the market that provide a range of cover for drone operations. Chapter 21 considers these policies in greater detail as well as other potential underwriter initiatives. Chapter 22 considers compulsory third-party liability insurance.

21 Underwriting drone insurance

Anthony A. Tarr, Darryl Smith, Maurice Thompson, Tom Chamberlain, Antton Peña and Sam Golden[1]

Introduction

The key insurable risks for drones remain first-party loss, including damage to drones and accessories, and third-party liability for personal injury and property damage. However, as set out in the previous chapter, the operation of drones also has some novel risks—some already in existence and some emerging—which include, for example, nuisance, harassment and breach of privacy. In this chapter we examine how some insurers have approached these issues and examine drone insurance policies and underwriting issues that insurers face in more detail.

While aviation insurance policies have been adapted to suit larger drone operations, the recent growth of industries which have expanded their business activities to include some drone operations, together with the proliferation of the recreational drone market and its ongoing expansion, have led to the development of a range of further innovative insurance solutions to meet that demand. In addition to providing add-on or write-back cover within existing lines of insurance to encompass drone operations, insurers have responded by developing bespoke policies and on-demand "pay as you fly" products.

Underwriting drone insurance

As further applications for drones emerge, drone use increases, and drone apps and functionality become more technologically complex, the ongoing challenges for insurance underwriters are obvious. Such is the technological pace of the development of drones that the risk written at the start of the policy year could turn into a substantially different risk by the conclusion of the policy year.

However, as evidenced by some of the insurance policy examples set out in the following, insurers are adapting to these challenges and have—in a relatively short space of time—demonstrated flexibility in responding to unanticipated problems and have developed innovative products which address the requirements of the full suite of drone users. They range from large organisations that specialise in drone operations and need an annual policy for management purposes, through to the flourishing recreational drone market with its "on-demand" expectations.

1 The authors would also like to thank Clyde & Co colleagues Jonathan Liberis and Chris Albertson for their contribution to the chapter.

During the early stages of any emerging risk, insurers need to grapple with whether that risk is already covered or not effectively excluded by existing insurance, notwithstanding the fact that no premium has been taken into account for it. Asbestos is one example of a type of risk where there were large exposures for insurers with no premium paid. Therefore, one key issue that requires consideration at the outset is whether usual forms of exclusions in insurance policies effectively exclude risks arising from the use of drones, or whether that risk is covered (notwithstanding it was not intended to be covered). A similar issue arose when cyber risks began to emerge. The effective exclusion of those risks from existing suites of policies—some of which were excluded by existing exclusions and others which were drafted specifically to excluded cyber risks—effectively prompted the development of the cyber insurance market.

In relation to drones, many policies exclude claims arising from the use of "aircraft"; however, even though the intention appears to be reasonably clear, a number of coverage issues arise. One issue, for example, is whether a drone, which is generally unmanned, is an "aircraft".[2]

In the United States, "the standard General Commercial Liability ("CGL") policy excluded coverage for "'bodily injury' and 'property damage' arising out of ownership, maintenance, use or entrustment to others of any aircraft . . . owned or operated by or rented or loaned to any insured".[3]

In responding to the potential for ambiguity about whether a drone is an "aircraft", "the Insurance Services Office Inc. (ISO), an organisation that develops standard policy forms, has issued several new forms applicable to the standard CGL policy".[4]

These forms of exclusionary endorsements include:

> This insurance does not apply to:
>
> (1) Unmanned Aircraft
>
> Bodily injury or property damage arising out of the ownership, maintenance, use or entrustment to others of any aircraft that is an "unmanned aircraft". Use includes operation and loading or unloading. . .
>
> This Paragraph [(1)] applies even if the claims against any insured allege negligence or other wrongdoing in the supervision, hiring, employment, training or monitoring of others by that insured, if the occurrence which caused the bodily injury or property damage involved the ownership, maintenance, use or entrustment to others of any aircraft that is an unmanned aircraft.
>
> (2) Aircraft (Other Than Unmanned Aircraft), Auto Or Watercraft
>
> Bodily injury or property damage arising out of the ownership, maintenance, use or entrustment to others of any aircraft (other than unmanned aircraft), auto or watercraft owned or operated by or rented or loaned to any insured. Use includes operation and loading or unloading.[5]

2 See Christopher H. Avery, Diana Brown and Joey Robertson, 'Wave of the Future: Three Emerging Technologies and Their Impact on Insurance Coverage' (2019) 29(2) Southern Law Journal 4.

3 ibid.

4 ibid.

5 ibid 5 (relating to "Coverage A").This article also sets out further forms of exclusionary endorsements applicable to other coverage.

As drones become more prolific, a large range of insurance coverage issues are likely to arise in relation to the application of standard policy exclusions where cover for drone operations and risks was not intended to be covered by the insurer. For example, some home and contents insurance policies which are not intended to cover drone-related claims may nonetheless provide cover for damage caused by drone use.[6] Whether or not such cover exists under standard policies is dependent on the wording of that policy,[7] and the application of the exclusion to the particular circumstances of the claim. These coverage issues may also arise with standard motor insurance policies, for example, where an unregistered drone is the cause of damage to a vehicle and the owner of that vehicle is subsequently left responsible for the repairs.[8]

A standard policy's response to a particular claim will depend on the precise wording of the policy exclusion and the circumstances in which the claim arises. It is likely that insurers will need to further adapt and refine standard forms of policy wordings to effectively exclude drone-related claims as future drone risks emerge, or otherwise find that drone-related risks are unintentionally covered.

Similar to the development of any emerging risk (and following a similar course to that taken by the cyber insurance market), as drones have emerged as a significant stand-alone risk, where necessary, insurers will continue to adapt existing policy wordings to effectively exclude drone operations where the intention is not to provide cover, and continue to pave the way for the development of drone insurance as a stand-alone market. As set out further in the following, the stand-alone drone insurance market has made significant inroads, and continues to progress.

Drone insurance

Some standard commercial public liability policies include cover for liability arising from the incidental use of a drone during usual business operations. However, these policies may exclude cover where the primary function of the business is the operation of a drone. Many insurance policies do not cover or exclude commercial or recreational drone operations.

As set out previously, insurers have taken different approaches to underwriting risks associated with drone operations. These approaches include modifying exclusions within existing policies by way of an endorsement that writes back specific cover for drone operations; drafting bespoke policy wordings, and developing products that can be delivered virtually through an app, and on demand.

These approaches, and some specific examples, are considered in more detail in the following.[9] The purpose is to illustrate the approach utilised by insurance underwriters to the unique challenges presented by drones, rather than to examine the merits of each cover.

6 Julie-Anne Tarr, Anthony Tarr, Ron Bartsch and Maurice Thompson, 'Drones in Australia—Rapidly Evolving Regulatory and Insurance Challenge' (2019) 30 ILJ 135 152.

7 ibid.

8 ibid.

9 Any policy wordings considered in this chapter are, of course, subject to change, and subject to all of the underwriting criteria, terms, conditions, exclusions and endorsements. Policy wordings have been considered for illustrative purposes only.

Write-back drone insurance cover

Drones are becoming more frequently used in particular industries, and for organisations within those industries cover is being developed and underwritten based on their existing needs.

This is particularly the case in relation to small to medium enterprises where third-party liability arising from drone applications is an ongoing risk—for example, in the real estate and the entertainment industries, drones are being used more frequently around residential premises and people.

Without drone insurance, the small to medium enterprise faces a potentially significant uninsured liability exposure. Under a usual form of Public and Products or other liability insurance policy, an insured entity obtains cover for Personal Injury or Property Damage caused by an Occurrence in connection with the Insured's Business, subject to the policy's terms, conditions and exclusions. This cover generally excludes claims arising out of the use of aircraft and/or drones specifically.

In this market, underwriters are now providing insurance cover through endorsements which delete the exclusion in its entirety and write back insurance cover for drone operations. However, with regulatory oversight alone arguably insufficient for some insurers to have confidence that risks associated with drone use are fully captured, further assurance around the management and use of the drone operations within a particular environment (e.g. through a particular app or particular drone platform providing flight management software and analytics, which encompasses things such as aviation compliance and drone fleet management) may be the way forward in enabling insurers to have a more readily useable data set to properly understand and underwrite a particular risk.

Bespoke drone insurance

In the large commercial enterprise and professional drone operator space, there is now a relatively broad range of insurance products which provide bespoke insurance cover for drone operations on an annual basis, usually with a detailed underwriting submission required from the insured. As set out in the previous chapter, some commercial enterprises are actively seeking out this cover so that the insurance is "placed on the books" and can be forgotten about until it is needed.

First party

First-party insurance covers are, at first glance, similar to motor and other first-party property policy wordings; however, there are some specific differences to take into account the unique nature of drone operations which draw more from traditional aviation policy wordings. It is clear from the publicly available policy wordings that insurance underwriters have needed to take a deep dive into the drone industry, using both traditional wording from other policies together with bespoke wording to produce workable solutions.

Insurance cover for first-party loss generally includes payment for replacement or repair of the drone or damaged components of the drone while in flight, which is a key risk given the nature of drone operations. Alternatively, payment by the insurer may be made on the agreed value of the drone.

While this cover may appear to be similar to other standard forms of insurance, such as motor or contents insurance, there are further key underwriting and policy wording issues to be taken into account which require close reference to drone manufacturers' specifications and the life expectancy of the drone and its components. The underwriting considerations in this respect, and the policy wordings which follow, are more akin to those in an aviation policy. This is because the item that is insured (i.e. the drone) requires rigorous and consistent maintenance, similar to an aircraft, rather than an item that requires less maintenance, for example, a motor vehicle or a static item within a home.

Cover may be prescribed to fall within particular boundaries relating to flights and/or peripheral activities, and records or logs of flights and maintenance and spare items/accessories may be required. Given the highly fluid nature of drone operations, these requirements are set out in some policies in detail.

Drones are obviously a highly specialised and technical piece of equipment. Some may be easily damaged. Cover may also be provided for the drone and accessories while the drone is in transit, or on the ground (e.g. where the drone is damaged by another object), or while undertaking other activities peripheral to the operation of the drone. Cover for fire, vandalism, theft and other perils may also be provided.

Cover may also be available for certain emergency costs in circumstances where a drone has been forced to land or is at risk of damaging property or putting people in danger. This is an example of a type of cover that has been specifically drafted or adapted to suit the fluid nature and unique risks of drone operations.

As with most policy wordings for first-party property, there is a line between unintended, insured damage, and progressive or cumulative damage caused by wear and tear or by any mechanical or software defect, failure or malfunction relating to the drone's use. There may also simply be deterioration due to age or use, or damage caused during routine maintenance and repair and inspection or repair. The usual first-party property damage exclusions are included to take these issues into account. In short, the damage or loss must be accidental.

Exclusions for progressive or cumulative damage have been adapted to take into account the nature of drone operations and may include mechanical damage caused by progressive or cumulative exposure (rather than a single incident) to corrosive substances or other elements, and deterioration or aging or lack of performance. Some aspects of exclusions are written back if the drone's maintenance complies with the manufacturer's specifications.

In relation to drones used for videography, damage caused by scratching, fogging or misting of camera lenses or damage to photographic film may be excluded unless arising from a single accident or incident.

Finally, consequential or economic loss, and trading losses, may also be excluded.

Third-party liability

As set out in the previous chapter, the risks associated with drone operations are a combination of risks that are known and understood; risks that are unique to drone operations, and risks that are emerging. Cover for third-party liability arising from drone operations generally follows standard forms of other public and products liability policy wordings, with some notable differences to take into account the unique nature of drone-related risks.

Insuring clauses may provide that the insurer will cover bodily injury/accidental bodily injury (including fatal injury), property damage/accidental property damage or other third-party loss arising from the use of the drone. Invasion of privacy/privacy liability and noise liability are other third-party covers that may also be provided.

The causal connection between the drone incident and the cover differs between policy wordings and jurisdictions. Some of the causal links include "caused by" or "arising out of" or must be linked to an "occurrence" as defined or arise out of the ownership or use of the drone.

Reflecting regulatory requirements or developments in different jurisdictions or alternatively on the basis of underwriting certainty, cover may be confined to use by appropriately licenced or authorised operators or people piloting the drone or supporting the drone operations. This may be included as it is required (i.e. mandatory) from a regulatory compliance perspective, or may be included to provide some certainty to underwriters about the experience or qualifications of the persons operating or supporting the use of the drone.

Drones generally carry camera equipment, but more recent commercial developments are likely to see more drones used for carrying payloads (set out in more detail in previous chapters), which raise the risk of items or objects falling from the drone causing injury or property damage. Specific bespoke covers may be either written into policies to cover these types of risks, where the damage or injury is not caused by the drone itself, but from a failure in its payload. Alternatively, these risks may be excluded, depending upon the insurer's risk appetite.

Finally, third-party cover may also take into account the vicarious contractual or legal obligations that the insured may have to other parties where another party—for example, an outsourced provider—is acting on the insured's behalf.

The exclusions applicable to third-party liability may encompass:

- The usual exclusions relating to employer's liability, including injury to employees of the insured during the course of their employment, which would otherwise be covered by compulsory workers compensation insurance; and
- Damage to other property owned by or in the control of the insured.

Conditions

Conditions imposed on the insured vary significantly between jurisdictions, primarily on the basis of local regulatory requirements.

Obligations under bespoke drone insurance policies may require the insured to:

- Use due diligence.
- Comply with regulatory and statutory requirements.
- Comply with regulatory directives about maintenance and inspection.
- Keep maintenance records.
- Maintain logbooks and flight records, in some cases with caps placed on the annual flying time.

- Only use licenced or trained or authorised operators.
- Assess the drone is airworthy prior to flights.

General exclusions

General exclusions contained in many bespoke drone policies (some of which may be written back through purchasing additional covers) are the usual exclusions applicable to liability policies, which include:

- Liability assumed under contract.
- Dishonesty, fraud and known or prior facts and acts or circumstances.
- Liability arising out of noise, pollution or contamination.
- Natural disasters and perils.
- Criminal and civil fines and penalties.
- Computer viruses.

There are also exclusions which relate specifically to drone risks, which include:

- Use at air shows, air races or other heavily populated events.
- Landing or taking off from a location that does not comply with a manufacturer's recommendations or specifications.
- Where the drone is operated by an unauthorised person.
- Flying the drone outside the territorial or specific geographical limits contained in the policy.

Other covers and extensions

Bespoke policies may also have extensions which address specific risks which the drone operator may be exposed to. Some policies contain a broad range of additional covers—similar to some management liability insurance policies—which enable an insured to choose which covers to add. Covers differ from jurisdiction to jurisdiction.

The additional covers, many of which focus on business continuity, may include:

- Alternative hire costs and recovery costs.
- Cyber liability, including loss of assets and extortion, and electronic business interruption.
- Some statutory liabilities.

On-demand drone insurance

In 2017, *The Economist* proclaimed that data had overtaken oil as the world's most valuable resource—with good reason.[10] Data is being generated at an exponential rate, with reports that in 2018 humans created 2.5 quintillion bytes per day—with

10 The Economist, 'The World's Most Valuable Resource is No Longer Oil, But Data' (*The Economist*, 6 May 2017) <www.economist.com/leaders/2017/05/06/the-worlds-most-valuable-resource-is-no-longer-oil-but-data>.

90 per cent of the world's data produced in the last two years alone.[11] Gathering and analysing big data sets has enabled businesses in various markets to draw powerful insights and to launch smarter products to better serve their customers.

Big data has immense implications for the future of the global $4 trillion insurance industry.[12] However, despite the explosion of data from connected devices, application of this data by insurers for individualised risk models is still largely in its infancy.

For enterprises seeking more tailored insurance solutions based on their unique risk profile, there is good news on the horizon. According to McKinsey, by 2030 the insurance market will evolve to contain highly dynamic, usage-based insurance products that are tailored to customer behaviour.[13] McKinsey predicts that insurance will transition from an annual renewal model to a continuous cycle, with products that constantly adapt to individual behavioural patterns.

The future of the insurance industry does not stop at usage-based products but rather broadens into predictive risk mitigation. As model sophistication evolves with the realisation of Big Data, insurers will have the ability to provide transparent steps to mitigating risk and avoiding claim events.[14] Such a shift in the relationship between insurer and customer aligns with the social trends PwC uncovered in their "Insurance 2020" report.[15]

As discussed in Chapter 20, traditionally, insurance premiums have been calculated by using historical claims and policy data to indicate the level of risk associated with a certain industry, and to forecast the likelihood of future claims. Underwriting in this way works with a high degree of reliability in well-established markets where many years' worth of data is available. However, in new or emerging industries that have little claims or policy data, adequately pricing risk using this method presents a challenge for insurers.[16] This lack of claims data in the drone industry (due to its infancy) makes it difficult for insurers to confidently forecast future losses, and therefore to accurately calculate premium prices. This leads to conservative pricing on policies, resulting in many drone operators and enterprises potentially paying substantially more for insurance than their risk actually requires.

It is further contended that a "broad-brush" approach to insurance pricing oversimplifies a diverse industry. No two drone pilots or flights are the same, and neither are their risk profiles. Accordingly, it is argued that the "one-size-fits-all" approach to pricing that many traditional insurers have adopted results in limited or zero visibility into customer activity. As a result, a lack of consideration by insurers of the risks taken at an individual customer level may result in safety conscious drone enterprises

11 Bernard Marr, 'How Much Data Do we Create Every Day? The Mind-Blowing Stats Everyone Should Read' (*Forbes*, 21 May 2018) <www.forbes.com/sites/bernardmarr/2018/05/21/how-much-data-do-we-create-every-day-the-mind-blowing-stats-everyone-should-read/?sh=45bea19460ba>.

12 Swiss Re, 'Global Insurance Premiums Rise by 1.5% in 2017, Driven by Emerging Markets' (6 July 2018) Insurance Law Journal <www.insurancejournal.com/news/international/2018/07/06/494331.htm>.

13 Tanguy Caitlin and others, 'Insurtech—The Threat that Inspires' (1 March 2017) <www.mckinsey.com/industries/financial-services/our-insights/insurtech-the-threat-that-inspires>.

14 Finbarr Toesland, 'Insurance Moves from Reactive to Predictive' (*Raconteur*, 26 April 2018)<www.raconteur.net/finance/insurance/insurance-moves-reactive-predictive/>.

15 PwC, 'Insurance 2020: Turning Change into Opportunity' (Report, January 2012).

16 Deloitte Center for Financial Services, '2019 Insurance Outlook' (Report, *Deloitte*, 2018) <www2.deloitte.com/ro/en/pages/financial-services/articles/2019-insurance-industry-outlook.html>.

overpaying for their insurance. In this context, risk mitigation is neither incentivised nor enabled by insurers.

These arguments and considerations were the genesis to an alternative approach to assessing and pricing drone insurance. By leveraging Big Data to intelligently identify and quantify flight risks, innovative products have been developed for the drone market to provide tailor-made policies based on individual risk profiles. The result is highly personalised, transparent insurance pricing and the ability for insurers to reward drone enterprises for proactive risk mitigation.

In contrast to traditional insurance pricing, "exposure-based" pricing considers risk on a per-event (or in this case, on a per-flight) basis. By combining real-time data with algorithmic risk assessments, it is possible to predict the likelihood ("probability") of a drone flight resulting in a crash, as well as the associated cost ("severity") of that crash. Multiplying the probability of a crash with its associated severity gives the "technical insurance price" (or expected loss) of a single drone flight.

This allows for an unparalleled degree of precision when assessing and pricing drone flight risks. Rather than treating all drone enterprises in the same way and providing them with an annual policy price, an exposure-based pricing approach allows for the risk of each and every flight undertaken by a drone fleet to be quantified and priced individually. The result is a more accurate correlation between risk and price.

As well as more accurate pricing, an insurer with visibility into a drone pilot's real-time exposure is able to provide actionable insights at the precise moment they are required, for example, by encouraging them not to fly in the wind or rain. Insurers are then able to offer more comprehensive "risk management" solutions, rather than just insurance policies.

Case study Flock cover, app-based "pay-as-you-fly" drone insurance[17]

Some very innovative products have been developed for the drone market.

Flock (in conjunction with Allianz) launched Europe's first app-based "pay-as-you-fly" drone insurance in January 2018 which allows drone users to purchase insurance products through a mobile app. The cost of "pay-as-you-fly" cover is based on levels of exposure, which is assessed on a per-flight basis.[18] The app works as follows:

> Users enter their flight details and receive a quote that changes depending on a number of factors, including the time of day, location and flight conditions, in real-time. It can be utilised by both commercial and recreational drone operators.[19]

Through the mobile app, commercial and recreational pilots are able to purchase customised equipment and liability insurance on demand (lasting from 1 to 8 hours).

17 This Case Study was contributed by Antton *Peña* and Sam Golden from Flock.

18 Flock, 'The Future of Insurance for Connected Drone Fleets' (White Paper, *Flock*, 2019)<https://landing.flockcover.com/enterprise-whitepaper>.

19 Interview with Tom Chamberlain Allianz Global Corporate and Specialty, International Underwriting Association Developing Technology Monitoring Group.
'IUA Publishes on Demand Insurance Report' (*IUA*, 16 October 2019) <www.iua.co.uk/IUA_Member/Press/Press_Releases_2019/IUA_publishes_on-demand_insurance_report.aspx?WebsiteKey=84dca912-b4fb-4a0f-a6e5-47ad899350aa>.

The cost of cover is "exposure-based" as the risk is assessed on a per-flight basis and determined by combining real-time data with algorithmic risk assessments.[20]

This pay-as-you-fly product marked a dramatic departure from traditional insurance, using advanced data-driven analytics to quantify, mitigate and insure drone flight risk in real time via Flock's proprietary Risk Intelligence Engine.

Since launch, Flock's Risk Intelligence Engine has analysed and priced risk for more than 500,000 pay-as-you-fly drone flights. By clearly visualising these risks in the Flock Cover app's in-built Flight Planning Tool, thousands of drone pilots have been empowered to proactively optimise towards lower-risk flights.

Flock's analysis shows that on average, pay-as-you-fly pilots will compare 15 different risk-dependent quotes before purchasing a policy (such as by changing the date and time of flight, or altering the flight plan). By comparing Flight Risk Metrics, pilots can identify when and where it is safest to fly. This has resulted in a 4.5-point reduction of the Flight Risk Metric per flight flown, which has helped pilots lower their final quote price by 15%.

Chris Wyard, Head of Underwriting Data, Allianz comments that Flock are utilising geospatial data in a truly pioneering way to significantly enhance traditional risk assessment, and most importantly deliver superior customer outcomes.[21]

A transition towards exposure-based insurance offers a range of benefits for large drone enterprises. In particular:

- Risk mitigation is enabled and rewarded. This data-driven approach allows large drone operators to understand the level of risk they are exposed to and make changes to reduce risk, and insurance costs as a result. This could be everything from identifying high risk equipment to avoiding dangerous weather conditions or identifying areas where pilots need additional training.
- Revenues and insurance costs are aligned.

With an exposure-based insurance policy, flying more frequently (and thereby undertaking a greater degree of in-flight risk) can result in a higher premium price. In quieter periods, however, enterprises are less exposed to in-flight risk, paying lower premiums as a result. This reduces the complexity of financial planning and stabilises an organisation's cash flow. This is particularly important in industries such as agriculture and wind farm surveying where work is incredibly seasonal.

Flock's product suite is powered by a proprietary Risk Intelligence Engine. This engine aggregates large, unstructured data sets from over 25 third-party and proprietary sources, and assesses them algorithmically to produce a quantified output of risk for any drone flight.

This "Flight Risk Metric" (an indexed score between 1 and 100) represents the expected loss (technical premium price) of a single flight, allowing for the precise pricing of drone insurance on a per-flight basis.

Complex interactions between these varied data sets allow for a high degree of pricing complexity and accuracy. For example, a drone with a maximum wind resistance

20 Flock (n 17).
21 ibid.

of 10 m/s will receive a dramatically different Flight Risk Metric when flown in a light breeze compared to a strong gust.

"Pay-as-you-fly" cover was followed in July 2019 by Flock's introduction of its "Enterprise" product to provide scalable exposure-based insurance for connected drone fleets. Flock Enterprise is a first-of-its-kind insurance product, built from the ground up to accommodate the rapid global proliferation of drone fleets. Just as the Flock Cover mobile app allows SMEs to purchase "pay-as-you-fly" drone insurance on a per-flight basis, Flock Enterprise unlocks exposure-based insurance at scale, and allows larger enterprises to pay for insurance only when they use it. This is achieved by leveraging Flock's Risk Intelligence Engine to automatically assess and price risk for each and every drone flight. These individual flight prices are aggregated and paid in arrears at the end of each month.

As a result, drone enterprises can for the first time pinpoint and quantify the risks (and associated insurance costs) of every single flight undertaken in a given month. This offers unparalleled visibility into risk at an individual flight or portfolio level. It also allows insurance premiums to be directly aligned with actual risks undertaken, rewarding enterprises that take proactive steps to actively mitigate risks.

All of this is achieved seamlessly (and with no need to install additional hardware or software) as Flock Enterprise syncs with third-party drone data collection platforms, ingesting the flight data it needs to assess and price flights.

These types of on-demand insurance will undoubtedly play a fundamental role in the future of the insurance industry generally. New research published by the International Underwriting Association (IUA) observes that pay-as-you go models of cover will allow customers to automatically activate policies when and where they need them.[22] This obviously transcends drone's insurance and there is potential for on-demand insurance models to access new markets and customers. As Tom Chamberlain explains:

> In the future insurance will be based around whatever you are doing. You will be in your house and your insurance will be active and when you leave your front door your premium will step up as it is now unoccupied. You will then get into a shared economy car and your phone will interact and automatically trigger your insurance for that journey. Your insurance will follow you as you go and as your activity changes. It will no longer be a manual process and could realistically work for everything you do requiring insurance.[23]

For some, an annual premium for insurance is inflexible. When a risk averse teenage car driver is grouped by age into the same category as their thrill-seeking peer, the risks posed by each may not be properly reflected in the premium. Surrounded by an ever-growing volume of live data, on-demand insurance can estimate the risk posed by a given activity at any time. On-demand requests to insure drones is a practical and cost-effective way to insure. The data which feeds into the quote provided to the consumer can assess the current weather conditions within a few minutes. The local topography in a defined radius such as proximity to schools and hospitals and the traffic levels on surrounding roads is also analysed. This wealth of data on the external environment can provide simple and tailored insurance. Perhaps the most

22 Christopher Avery and others (n 2).
23 Chamberlain (n 18)

innovative and useful benefit of this on-demand app drone insurance is the current advice it can provide. Where, for example, the drone operator is flying too close to an airport, or temporary restricted airspace the app will advise the operator to select a new flight area. This type of insurance can assist the operators to make safe choices when launching and operating their drone and provide safety insurance if an accident does happen. The coverage of these on-demand insurance policies can be modified without any interaction from an agent. As consumer behaviour shifts with the global pandemic, the need for all-digital, flexible insurance solutions are further amplified.[24]

By 2025, millennials will account for a major share of the workforce and with this demographic shift towards a generation who have grown up with technology, the appetite for app-based and on-demand insurance will increase alongside the rise of the sharing economy and merging technology such as AI and blockchain.[25] Recreational drone operators are accustomed to rapid, simplified and smart technology. This amplifies the necessity to reduce complexity and to minimise impediments within the insurance purchase process. A recreational drone user who has purchased a drone and wants to conduct a test flight may be willing to download an app where they can rapidly obtain insurance, but they are likely to be unwilling to submit answers to detailed underwriting questions where the insurer's response is not immediate.

Cost-effective insurance will further promote this model of insurance. These millennials pose an "existential risk" for insurers due to their love for on-demand services and mobile-first products.[26] Similar to the insurance required for a recreational drone being flown at the park once a month, expensive cameras and bicycles are being offered on-demand insurance for the times when the owner actually takes the camera out and uses it for a special occasion or an annual holiday. With consumers reporting a saving of 30% over traditional insurance, there is both an economic value and the ease with which a drone operator can access it.[27]

On-demand insurance is expanding globally. For example, Brazil recently authorised the use of on-demand insurance policies, explaining[28]:

> the market demanded this flexibility of time and, therefore, SUSEP updated the regulation to make it as flexible as possible to encourage more affordable products and to attract more Brazilian consumers to the market.[29]

24 See comments from Trov, 'On-Demand Insurance Arrives in Brazil, Powered by Trov & Sura' (*Trov*, 27 May 2020) <www.prnewswire.com/news-releases/on-demand-insurance-arrives-in-brazil-powered-by-trov-sura-301065986.html>.

25 Julie-Anne Tarr, 'Distributed Ledger Technology, Blockchain and Insurance: Opportunities, Risks and Challenges' (2018) 29(3) Insurance Law Journal 254–68.

26 See quote from Scott Walcheck, CEO and founder of Trov, 'AXA Partners with Silicon Valley Startup Trov to Launch Insurance "as Simple as Tinder" for British Millennials' (22 November 2016) <www.insider.com/axa-insurance-startup-trov-uk-millennials-insurtech-tinder-airbnb-2016-11>.

27 See quote from Larry Dominique, CEO, Groupe PSA, North America, 'We get a 30 percent saving over traditional insurance, so from an operational point of view we are learning to be very efficient', Trov, 'The World Leader in Insurance Technology' (*Trov*, 2020) <www.trov.com/>.

28 See 'Brazil: Insurance on Demand Authorized by Federal Agency Responsible for Control of Insurance Market' (*The Library of Congress, Global Legal Monitor*, 7 October 2019) <www.loc.gov/law/foreign-news/article/brazil-insurance-on-demand-authorized-by-federal-agency-responsible-for-control-of-insurance-market/>.

29 See comments from the Rafael Scherre, President of SUSEP, 'SUSEP Starts to Allow Insurance in Minutes' (29 August 2019) <https://perma.cc/Z669-QRH6>, ibid.

In India, where third-party insurance is mandatory for drone operations, HDFC Ergo General Insurance will offer on demand insurance to customers on a "pay-as-you-fly" concept.[30]

The global roll out of this type of insurance will lead to improvements in both the data and the ease of use. The idea is very appealing to millennials who are used to purchasing things on demand online with speed, convenience and ease. For an "always on user", it makes sense to purchase insurance "just in time" through the app.[31] This type of insurance provides the traditional peace of mind that there will be coverage in the case of an accident and can provide advice to help the operator reduce their exposure to accidents before and during the flight.

The introduction of pay-as-you-go insurance assists in better promoting drone safety and ultimately will enable insurers to more accurately price drone risks using Big Data.[32] This is accomplished by accessing large amounts of information and data from different sources, including weather data, building density and population density, in a way which allows insurers to assess the risk posed by a certain drone in the sky.[33]

Home and contents cover

In relation to recreational operators of drones, the Australian Senate Inquiry Committee[34] noted that the vast majority of recreational RPAS operators are unlikely to be insured to cover damage or injury caused by devices under their control. Some operators will purchase a specialised public liability product for the use of their drone and some others may have recourse to third-party liability cover under their home and contents insurance where damage caused by a drone occurs on the insured property.

The Insurance Information Institute[35] comments that:

> If a drone is damaged in an accident it is most likely covered under a homeowners or renters insurance policy (subject to a deductible). The liability portion of a homeowners or renters policy may provide coverage against lawsuits for bodily injury or property damage that a policyholder causes to other people with a drone. It may also cover privacy issues—for example if a drone inadvertently takes

30 The Economic Times, 'HDCF Ergo Launches Country's First Drone Cover' (*The Economic Times*, India 15 June 2020) <https://economictimes.indiatimes.com/industry/banking/finance/insure/hdfc-ergo-launches-countrys-first-drone-cover/articleshow/76385048.cms>.

31 See, J Sarkar, 'The Rise of Non Insurance'(*TCS Financial Solutions Journal*, no date) "which explains the further benefits of on-demand insurance where mobility via smart phones will drive this capability wherein coverage and claims can be settled with a few clicks of a mobile app" <www.tcs.com/bancs/insurance/the-rise-of-non-insurance>.

32 Interview with Tom Chamberlain Allianz Global Corporate and Specialty, International Underwriting Association Developing Technology Monitoring Group (n 6).
'IUA Publishes on Demand Insurance Report'(*IUA*, 16 October 2019) <www.iua.co.uk/IUA_Member/P r e s s /
Press_Releases_2019/IUA_publishes_on-demand_insurance_report.aspx?WebsiteKey=84dca912-b4fb-4a0f-a6e5-47ad899350aa>.

33 ibid 5.

34 'Regulatory Requirements that Impact on the Safe Use of Remotely Piloted Aircraft Systems, Unmanned Aerial Systems and Associated Systems (Report, 31 July 2018) para 4.21.

35 'Facts and Statistics: Aviation and Drones' <www.iii.org/fact-statistic/facts-statistics-aviation-and-drones>.

pictures or videotapes a neighbour who then sues the policyholder. It will not cover any intentional invasion of privacy. The policy will cover theft of a drone.

Whether a home and contents policy will provide third-party cover for such damage will, of course, depend on the wording of the policy. For example, some commonly available home and contents policies contain express exclusions for legal liability arising out of an accident involving a drone and most home and contents policies exclude cover where the liability relates to commercial endeavor, that is, being used for business purposes.[36] A simple transaction such as a neighbour paying another neighbour to take photos of his/her house could be assessed as business use and could void any insurance.

Other exclusions in home and content policies such as an "aviation" or "aircraft exclusion", with a definition of aircraft included in the policy, or not,[37] and exclusion of injuries to family members, require any insured seeking to rely upon the terms of a home and contents policy to examine that policy very closely. In discussing the importance of third-party liability insurance in relation to drones, the Netherlands government stated:

> Not all types of third-party liability insurance cover damage caused by drones. If your drone causes damage to property or physical harm, the injured party can hold you liable. This is why it is important to make sure that your third-party liability insurance covers drone-related damage. Paying for damage caused to other people can be expensive.[38]

Similar advice is provided by the Swedish Aviation Authority which recommends that homeowners secure third-party liability insurance since a regular home insurance usually does not cover damages caused by drones.[39]

Other personal, non-commercial insurances may also respond in certain circumstances. For example, private health insurance and no-fault medical coverage policies may provide no-fault medical coverage if someone is accidentally injured by the insured's drone. Moreover, comprehensive motor vehicle insurance may, depending upon the policy terms, cover damage caused to the insured motor vehicle if a policyholder's drone crash-lands into his or her car.[40]

Mutual insurance

With emerging risks come new opportunities and potential for innovation. Recent commentary and research on the growing use of drones has highlighted a number of

36 See, for example, *Philadelphia Indemnity Insurance Company v. Hollycal Production Inc* No. 5:18-cv-00768-PA-SP (C.D. Cal., 7December 2018).

37 Aims, 'Drones Key Issues for Insurance' (White Paper, January 2016) 7.

38 Despite the risks identified by the Government of Netherlands, there is no requirement to have drone insurance to fly drones recreationally. See Rules for the recreational use of drones<www.government.nl/topics/drone/rules-pertaining-to-recreational-use-of-drones>.

39 Transport Styrelesenn, 'Drone-Unmanned Aircraft' (*Transport Styrelsen*, September 2020) <www.transportstyrelsen.se/en/aviation/Aircraft/drones-unmanned-aircraft/> This recommendation is for drones weighing less than 20 kgs—such cover is not a requirement for drones weighing less than 20 kg that are used only for shows and recreation.

40 See, for example, 'Facts and Statistics: Aviation and Drones' <www.iii.org/fact-statistic/facts-statistics-aviation-and-drones>.

emerging and established markets which could be targeted by not only drone users themselves, but by the insurers covering such use. There is potential to develop one or more drone mutual insurance schemes and/or specialised insurance products targeting particular markets and/or areas of activity. Such mutuals or specialised products could command an early market advantage with large corporates or government entities in a given sector where drone usage is sophisticated and yet traditional underwriting is slow to embrace the new risk. Such traditional underwriting is currently hampered as a consequence of the regulatory environment significantly lagging behind the development of the technology and usage and the fact that there are no currently recognised safety and operating standards against which traditional underwriters can assess risk in a given sector.

Three examples of markets that could be targeted would be:

(a) "Drones within the Commodities/Resources sector" covering Soft commodities (crop spraying, harvest timing/quality optimisation, crop quality monitoring); Hard commodities (stockpile monitoring, mine shaft/tunnel inspection and transfers, remote mine mapping, industrial espionage re-stockpiles and release of product to market, remote and hazardous locations deliveries, terrain and substrata mapping, remote sampling); Livestock (live export animal monitoring on vessel, livestock marking and movement); Fisheries (remote offshore species detection for trawler shots and long lines, inter-fleet transfers).
(b) "Drones, Local Authorities and Councils" covering the varied and growing exposures of such bodies in relation to Subdivisions (planning, design, drainage, construction monitoring and compliance); Illegal dumping (assessment, remote monitoring, case evidence); Roads (planning, design, dilapidation/condition studies, traffic monitoring, car park design); Parks and Sports Fields (planning, bike paths, parking, light poles, amenities roof inspections, stadium inspections, irrigation design); Roof Inspection (condition of roof sheeting/gutters/facades, solar panel design/inspection/audits; Waterways (flood level and hydrology studies, pollution, weeds and vegetation analysis, erosion); Coastal (sea-level rise assessment/planning, seawall assessment/design, coastal erosion, cliff stability studies); Geotechnical (landslips, slope stability assessment); Thermal (roof insulation assessment, heat maps of leakage/inefficiency); and Town Planning (whole township digital capture, LGA digital transformation).
(c) "Drones in the maritime and offshore oil and gas industries" providing cover in relation to Vessels (vessel hold inspections, autonomous vessels—blue water, brown water and ports, ship to shore transfers, classification surveys, hazardous goods carriage inspections, sulphur emissions testing by drones, "eye in the sky" navigation; Ports (autonomous tugs, autonomous vehicle systems management, drone's pilotage, container yard operations); and Offshore (commissioning/decommissioning accommodation vessel to rig transfers, rig topside and maintenance surveys, saturation diving support, riser and pipeline inspections and maintenance, oil spill detection and monitoring).

Concluding comments

The final Insurance chapter, Chapter 22, considers compulsory third-party liability insurance in relation to drones.

22 Compulsory third-party liability insurance

Julie-Anne Tarr, Maurice Thompson and Anthony A. Tarr

Introduction

Widespread use of drones is now in place around natural resource management, construction, mining, marine, remote exploration works and repair, geological survey, agricultural land management, urban transport and delivery, aerial photography, media and more.[1] Recreational take-up continues to fuel market growth of drones globally and their increasing use in areas like law enforcement, search and rescue and emergency relief is evolving very rapidly. As the Australian Senate Committee of Inquiry[2] stated in 2018 around contemporary forecasts: "(any) list is not exhaustive, as the range of applications continues to grow at a rapid pace. At the same time RPAS have become the fastest growing segment of the civil aviation market".

The global health challenge of the COVID-19 pandemic and the use of drones in managing COVID-19 outbreaks serves to highlight benefits of enhanced drone use and innovation and it is increasingly clear that the use of drones in the transport of people and goods will be one of the key areas fueling market growth of drones globally.[3] As the New South Wales Government observe in their report "Transport for NSW: Future Transport Strategy 2056"[4] the next 40 years will see more technology-led transformation than the past two centuries with rapid innovation bringing increased automation,[5] including the use of drones to support future transport in areas like rapid point-to-point services that could transform emergency services and deliveries.[6]

It is particularly their foreshadowed usage in urban transport and delivery within high-density-population areas by corporations such as Amazon, Google and Uber that gives re-birth to the debate and underlying issues considered by legislators and regulators in relation to the motor vehicle 100 years ago. For example, in 1920 the Attorney General and Commissioner of Insurance in Massachusetts, in describing legislation

1 See detailed discussion in Chapters 2 and 3.

2 Parliament of Australia, Senate Standing Committee on Rural and Regional Affairs and Transport, 'Regulatory Requirements that Impact on the Safe Use of Remotely Piloted Aircraft Systems, Unmanned Aerial Systems and Associated Systems' (31 July 2018) para 1.15. <www.aph.gov.au/Parliamentary_Business/Committees/Senate/Rural_and_Regional_Affairs_and_Transport/Drones/Report>.

3 See J Tarr, A Tarr and K Paynter, 'Transport, Drones and Regulatory Challenges: Risk Accountability Meets COVID Fast Tracking of a Critical Industry' (2020) 48 Australian Business Law Review 202.

4 See Transport for NSW, 'Future Transport Strategy 2056' (2018) New South Wales Government' <https://future.transport.nsw.gov.au/sites/default/files/media/documents/2018/Future_Transport_2056_Strategy.pdf>.

5 ibid 10.

6 ibid 66.

intended to require motor vehicle owners to have liability insurance or evidence of a bond covering the owner's financial responsibility, stated that these requirements were "drawn upon the theory that the State can and ought to require every person who operates an automobile to furnish protection for the public against the injuries which they may cause".[7] This, it is suggested, is precisely the juncture that has been reached with drones.

As is noted earlier, injury to persons and property damage are very real concerns arising out of the use of drones.[8] If a person who sustains injury or property damage is to have a real opportunity to pursue a damages claim against a drone pilot or operator, it is essential that the person at fault is able to be identified and that the person at fault has the capacity to satisfy any damages award or settlement.

Registration and licencing initiatives will make it easier for "onboard" identification of drone owners, pilots, or operators but in the absence of compulsory third-party insurance there is no certainty that damages awards will be satisfied. This problem is compounded where the drone is unlicenced and/or unregistered and the responsible party cannot be identified in so-called "fly and run" incidents.

As discussed in the Regulation chapters (Part D),[9] the rapid growth in the use and deployment of drones creates significant challenges to regulators and the community at large—both practical and regulatory. The issue as to whether third-party liability insurance should be required, or not, fits very solidly within this "challenge" basket. In the following sections, this chapter briefly outlines the current approaches taken to this issue in several jurisdictions and examines the arguments for and against with particular reference to a recent Policy Paper issued in Australia.[10]

Compulsory liability insurance—current status

The ICAO UAS Toolkit,[11] described by ICAO, as a helpful tool to assist States in realising effective UAS operational guidance and safe domestic operations, chapter 2.8 states:

> The operator shall have adequate insurance in the event of an incident or accident. Some States require a minimum third-party liability insurance to be in effect for all UAS operations.

In many jurisdictions, compulsory insurance requirements are already in place. For example, in the European Union, a commercial drone operator was required to have public liability insurance to protect against legal liability for third-party property

7 Quote from article by Ralph H Blanchard, 'Compulsory Motor Vehicle Liability Insurance in Massachusetts' (1936) 3 Law & Contemporary Problems 537.

8 See Chapter 9.

9 Chapters 13–19.

10 Department of Infrastructure, Transport, Regional Development and Communications, 'Emerging Aviation Technologies National Aviation Policy Issues Paper' (September 2020)<www.infrastructure.gov.au/aviation/drones/files/drone-discussion-paper.pdf>. (hereinafter "Emerging Aviation Technologies Paper"). See also Department of Infrastructure, Transport, Regional Development and Communications, Emerging Aviation Technologies National Aviation Policy Statement May 2021 <www.infrastructure.gov.au/aviation/technology/files/national-emerging-aviation-technologies-policy-statement.pdf>

11 <www.icao.int/safety/UA/UASToolkit/Pages/Narrative-Regulation.aspx>.

damage or injury whist using a drone.[12] Regulation (EC) No 785/2004 required all commercial drone operations to carry third-party liability insurance with the minimum third-party insurance requirement being based on the mass of the aircraft on take-off. Recreational drone operators using a drone with a weight above 20 kg were not excluded from the requirement for compulsory insurance and several Member States had mandated third-party insurance in relation to lighter drones.[13] New Drone Regulations 2019/947 and 2019/945, effective 31 December 2020, adopt a risk-based approach with the emphasis on the type of drone and the purpose for which it is being operated, rather than upon whether the application is commercial or non-commercial.

Until the commencement of the new EU Drone Regulations in the United Kingdom on 31 December 2020,[14] anyone who wanted to fly a drone for commercial work in the United Kingdom needed a "Permission for Commercial Operation" (PfCO) from the CAA. It was a condition of each PfCO that the applicant/operator had appropriate insurance coverage that met the requirements of *Regulation (EC) No. 785/2004*. Pilots with permissions for aerial work (under the PfCO) were only required to have a Public Liability cover of minimum of £1m. Simon Ritterband[15] explains:

> (T)his was to ensure that air carriers and air operators had a minimum level of cover to protect the public. This was defined post 9/11 and far before drones would be considered as a risk on the level that they are now. However, as the exponential growth of drones continues, there becomes new needs to ensure the public are fully protected.

The adoption of new European Union Safety Agency regulations[16] will bring different considerations to bear to take into account the risk based approach embraced by EU Regulations 2019/947 and 2019/945.[17] These Regulations which set the framework for the safe operation of drones in European skies (EU and EASA Member States), do not distinguish between leisure or commercial activities, and take into account the weight and specifications of the drone and the operation it is intended to undertake.

12 Regulation (EC) No 785/2004 of the European Parliament and of the Council of 21 April 2004 on insurance requirements for air carriers and aircraft operators. The adequacy of insurance requirements has been considered in the UK, see, for example, Lloyds, 'Drones Take Flight: Key Issues for Insurance, Emerging Risk Report, Innovation Series' (London, 2015) <www.lloyds.com/news-and-insights/risk-reports/library/drones-take-flight/>.

13 <www.easa.europa.eu/faq/116469>.

14 As of June 2020, the CAA has said that 'as part of the Brexit Treaty, the UK is required by international law to implement any elements of EU regulation that come into force and become applicable within the (Brexit) transition period (to 31 December 2020). Therefore, the new drone laws will become applicable within the UK on Thursday, December 31, 2020.'

15 Correspondence from Simon Ritterband to Dr Anthony Tarr, 1 November 2020, see <www.moonrockinsurance.com/>.
Simon Ritterband, managing director of Moonrock Insurance Solutions, currently sits on a number of government advisory panels along with the Department for Transport (UK), the CAA and other key stakeholders within the industry. He also sits on the British Standards Institute Committee (BSI).

16 EU Regulations 2019/947 and 2019/945. See also Commission Delegated Regulation (EU) 2020/1058 of 27 April 2020 amending Delegated Regulation (EU) 2019/945 as regards the introduction of two new unmanned aircraft systems classes<www.easa.europa.eu/document-library/regulations/commission-delegated-regulation-eu-20201058>.

17 <www.easa.europa.eu/domains/civil-drones-rpas>.

As EASA[18] explain:

> EU Regulation 2019/947, which will be fully applicable from December 30, 2020, caters for most types of operation and their levels of risk. It defines three categories of operations: the "open", "specific" and "certified" categories.

The "open" category addresses operations in the lower risk bracket, where safety is ensured provided the drone operator complies with the relevant requirements for its intended operation. This category is subdivided into three further subcategories called A1, A2 and A3. Operational risks in the "open" category are considered low, and therefore no authorisation is required before starting a flight.

The "specific" category covers riskier operations, where safety is ensured by the drone operator obtaining an operational authorisation from the national competent authority before starting the operation. To obtain the authorisation, the drone operator is required to conduct a safety risk assessment, which will determine the requirements necessary for safe operation of the drone(s).

In the "certified" category, the safety risk is so high that certification of the drone operator and the aircraft is required to ensure safety, as well as the licencing of the remote pilot(s).

The recent changes to EASA Regulations will make the determination of the appropriate level of cover and premium payable, more complicated. Simon Ritterband[19] comments:

> In terms of current commercial use, the majority of operations will fall into the Open and Specific categories—although there will no longer be a distinction between the regulation for commercial and non-commercial pilots. Given that all of the operations outlined within the open category would already be covered by insurers, it presents very few issues to the insurer adjusting to the new regulations. The specific category, however, will provide far more scope to drone operators. Without fully understanding the parameters for this category from the CAA it is difficult for insurers to provide a simple solution. It is not possible for insurers to provide a blanket approval for cover of specified operations. Some of the activities that fall into the specified category will be exactly the same activities that insurers already cover. In these cases, again, cover can be provided rather easily and only presents a challenge with ensuring that operators have the appropriate authorisations to complete these activities. The "new" activities are where data needs to be gathered before insurers can comfortably provide cover without further investigation. In the early days, underwriters should find that the activities are acceptable, and a list of acceptable uses can be created. With time and experience they will be able to have a better understanding of the activities and produce lists of acceptable and unacceptable activities/risks. In essence the new regulations allow a new set of activities that can be undertaken by drone operators. Insurers must decide whether they want to provide cover for these or not, and at what price.

Leaving aside the complexities of Brexit,[20] the extent and scope of the EU Regulations in the United Kingdom and elsewhere was already under active consideration. For

18 ibid.
19 ibid (n 15).
20 See discussion Chapter 17.

example, the House of Lords in considering *Regulation (EC) No. 785/2004* recommended that the Commission clarify the scope and applicability of the Regulation and increase the amount of public liability insurance required by commercial RPAS operators.[21] Furthermore, drone owners and insurers in the UK are closely watching to see if insurance will be made mandatory for lighter drones in the wake of *Air Navigation (Amendment) Order 2018* requiring compulsory registration for drones over 250 g.[22]

Compulsory insurance requirements are also in place in Norway[23] Iceland,[24] Costa Rica, Trinidad and Tobago, Brazil, Chile, Columbia, Guyana, Uruguay, Kenya, Nigeria, Rwanda, South Africa, United Arab Emirates, China, Hong Kong, Philippines, Thailand and Liechtenstein.[25] Some brief examples follow.

Consider, for example, Hong Kong where the operation of drones is regulated by Hong Kong's Civil Aviation Department with the overarching regulation a HK drone operator must observe being *Article 48* of the *Air Navigation (Hong Kong) Order (Cap. 448C)*. Under this Order, there are no operator licencing and certification requirements if a drone weighing less than 7 kg is operated for recreational purposes only. However, if the drone weighs more than 7 kg or if the drone is operated for non-recreational purposes, the operator has to submit an application for non-recreational flight to the HK CAD, and also submit proof of operator ability. Drone operators and owners in Hong Kong can be civilly liable for loss or damage caused to persons or property by a drone on a strict liability basis under the Civil Aviation Ordinance.[26] This means that the plaintiff is not required to prove any fault on the part of the owner or operator. Given the existence of that strict liability regime, the Hong Kong Civil Aviation Department requires proof of insurance for all non-recreational operation of drones and for recreational operations where the drone weighs more than 7 kg.[27] Moreover, the Department has proposed that owners of aerial vehicles over 250 g must purchase insurance for third-party liability for injuries and death with the minimum coverage for vehicles between 250 g and 7 kg to be HK$5 million, while those over 7 kg would require cover of HK$10 million.[28]

21 See Civilian Use of Drones in the EU—European Union Committee<https://publications.parliament.uk/pa/ld201415/ldselect/ldeucom/122/12210.htm>.

22 See, for example, UK Department of Transport, 'Impact Assessment: Insurance for Drones' (15 July 2016)<https://assets.publishing.service.gov.uk/government/uploads/system/uploads/attachment_data/file/579509/drones-insurance_ia.pdf>; Kennedys and Insurance POST, 'Taking Flight: The Rising Importance of Drone Insurance'<www.kennedyslaw.com/media/2102/kennedys_droneswhitepaper.pdf>.

23 See section 18, Insurance, 'The operator is responsible for ensuring that it has insurance cover for third-party liability'; cf. Section 11-2 of the Aviation Act<https://luftfartstilsynet.no/en/drones/commercial-use-of-drones/about-dronesrpas/regulations-of-drones/>.

24 See Icelandic Transport Authority</www.icetra.is/aviation/drones/frequently-asked-questions-faq>.

25 Therese Jones, Rand Corporation, 'International Commercial Drone Regulation and Drone Delivery Services' (2017)<www.rand.org/content/dam/rand/pubs/research_reports/RR1700/RR1718z3/RAND_RR1718z3.pdf>.

26 Section 8(2), *Civil Aviation Ordinance*.

27 In China, commercial drones weighing over 250 g can only be flown with a business licence—to obtain the licence the operator must be covered by insurance against liability for third parties on the surface. See, 'The Law Reviews, The Aviation Law Review, Edition 8' (August 2020) <https://thelawreviews.co.uk/edition/the-aviation-law-review-edition-8/1229750/china>and Hogan Lovells, 'China Launches First Operational Rules for Civil Unmanned Aircraft' (21 January 2016) <www.hoganlovells.com/en/blogs/internet-of-things/china-launches-first-operational-rules-for-civil-unmanned-aircraft>.

28 See Civil Aviation Department <www.cad.gov.hk/english/faq.html#uas>.

In 2019, Kenya declared the use of unmanned aircraft illegal and published a public notice warning the public not to use drones or risk facing the penalties. Kenya has since lifted these restrictions, and the use of drones is now (subject to compliance with the regulations) permissible in Kenya. The regulations set out mandatory insurance requirements in respect of third-party risks for the operation of drones unless dispensed with by the regulatory authority based on the category in which the drone belongs.[29]

The operation of drones in South Africa is governed and regulated by the South African Civil Aviation Authority (SACAA) via Part 101 of the *Civil Aviation Regulations 2011*. Drones are required to be registered with the SACAA register and owners are issued with a certificate of registration[30] by the director of SACAA.

There are various approvals that an operator is required to obtain, depending on whether the drone is being operated for purposes of commercial, corporate, non-profit or private operations. "Private operations" are defined as the use of a drone for an individual's personal and private purposes where there is no commercial outcome, interest or gain. An RPAS Operators Certificate (ROC) is required for all drone operations, except private operations and a ROC holder is required to be adequately insured for third-party liability, with a minimum cover of 500,000 Rand per drone.[31] The insurance requirement is necessary as a result of section 8 of the South African *Civil Aviation Act 2009*, which imposes a strict liability regime for material damage or loss caused by a drone. Any resulting damages may be recovered from the registered owner of the drone without proof of negligence or intention or other cause of action.

Another jurisdiction with compulsory insurance is Brazil, where the National Civil Aviation Agency requires insurance coverage for damage to third parties if the RPA has a maximum take-off weight of greater than 250 g.[32]

Where countries have regulated for compulsory insurance when operating a drone, some are even expressing concerns that minimum levels of insurance such as third-party liability cover may not be enough if an accident such as a "hit and fly" occurs.[33]

The Federal Aviation Administration (FAA), the Civil Aviation Safety Authority (CASA) and the Civil Aviation Authority (CAA) NZ do not presently require operators of drones in the United States,[34] Australia and New Zealand, respectively, to take out third-party liability insurance, but such cover is strongly recommended. For example, the Civil Aviation Safety Authority (CASA) does advise all commercial and recreational drone operators in its "Advisory Circular on Remotely piloted aircraft systems—licensing and operations" that[35]:

29 See The Civil Aviation (Unmanned Aircraft Systems) Regulations, 2020, Kenya Subsidiary Legislation, Section 40 <https://kcaa.or.ke/node/493>.

30 Part 101.02.4(1) of the Civil Aviation Regulations 2011 (South Africa).

31 ibid Regulation 101.04.12.

32 See ANAC, 'National Civil Aviation Agency—Brazil'<www.anac.gov.br/en/faq/drones/operations>.

33 See, for example, the Insurance Regulatory and Development Authority of India, 'Report on the Working Group for Insurance of Remotely Piloted Aircraft' (18 September 2020) <www.irdai.gov.in/ADMINCMS/cms/Search_Results.aspx>.

34 Note that State legislatures having varying requirements. For example, the State of Minnesota requires a drone operator to have liability insurance up to USD $ 100,000 per person and USD $ 300,000 per accident. See Minnesota Department of Transportation <www.dot.state.mn.us/aero/drones/index.html>.

35 (July 2018), para 4.8.10.1.

> CASA strongly recommends that operators discuss with an insurer the potential liability for any damage to third parties resulting from RPAS operation [that is, drone operation] and consider taking out suitable insurance.

CASA recommends that commercial operators of drones take out two kinds of insurance:

1 third-party public liability insurance; and
2 first-party property insurance or UAV insurance (being a specialised insurance product for unmanned aerial vehicles).

In addition, CASA may impose a condition on a licenced commercial drone operator to obtain insurance as part of that operator's risk management procedures. For example, it is likely such a condition would be imposed where the pilot seeks permission to operate the drone for commercial purposes at night. In addition, commercial RPAS operators are typically expected to have public liability coverage as part of state and territory business obligations.[36]

In the case of New Zealand, it should be noted that its no-fault accident compensation scheme (ACC scheme) governed by the *Accident Compensation Act 2001* provides compensatory cover for those who suffer a personal injury in New Zealand, regardless of whether the injured party is a New Zealand citizen. The scheme also covers nervous shock or mental injuries that occur as a result of a physical injury. The ACC scheme bars proceedings being brought for damages arising directly or indirectly out of any personal injury covered by the ACC scheme, either by the injured party, or by the Accident Compensation Corporation after it has paid compensation to the injured person. The operation of drones in New Zealand is governed by parts 101 and 102 of the *Civil Aviation Rules*, and failure to comply with these rules will generally be an offence under *the Civil Aviation (Offences) Regulations* 2006. However, liability for injuries or damage caused by drones is not governed by these regulations and will instead be governed by ordinary principles of negligence. The application of New Zealand's ACC scheme means that liability for injuries caused by drones in New Zealand will be limited to damage arising out of a mental injury not covered by the ACC scheme, and exemplary damages. Accordingly, the reason owners and operators of drones are not required to have (only strongly encouraged to have) compulsory third-party liability insurance in New Zealand is because such cover is already to a significant extent there by virtue of the ACC Act.

From this brief survey, it is clear that there is a difference in opinion or approach in relation to compulsory third-party liability insurance. This is not surprising. Inevitably there will be significant variations in drone regulations and insurance requirements from country to country as regulatory authorities struggle to adapt current and prospective laws to new technology and the particular imperatives, social, economic and political, of their jurisdictions.[37]

36 Department of Industry, Innovation and Science, 'Arrange Insurance for Your Business' (10 May 2016) <www.business.gov.au/info/run/insurance-and-workers-compensation/arrange-insurance-for-your-business>.

37 Therese Jones, Rand Corporation, 'International Commercial Drone Regulation and Drone Delivery Services' (2017) <www.rand.org/content/dam/rand/pubs/research_reports/RR1700/RR1718z3/RAND_

Emerging Aviation Technologies Paper[38]

As noted earlier, this section briefly examines the arguments for and against compulsory liability insurance with particular reference to a Policy Paper issued in Australia in September 2020.[39] A consideration of this Paper, it is suggested, puts the issue as to whether third-party liability insurance should be required, or not, into sharp focus.

This Policy Issues Paper[40] is described by the Department of Infrastructure, Transport, Regional Development and Communications as being the "first step towards development of a national policy for the management of drones and other emerging aviation technologies". The Paper identifies opportunities and risks associated with these technologies, outlines some of the current approaches for managing these issues and proposes an approach to policy development. The proposed approach to policy development covers airspace integration, safety, security, noise, environment, privacy, safe and efficient electric take-off and landing of vehicles, infrastructure, technology trials and central coordination.[41] These are all important issues and are integral to the development of a comprehensive national policy that will allow Australia to benefit from the considerable opportunities provided by emerging aviation technologies.

However, very surprisingly, the Paper devotes less than half a page of its 62 pages to insurance. This largely dismissive commentary is as follows:

> Most commercial drone operators make the business decision to hold insurance to cover for any damage or injury caused as part of managing the risk of their operations. Recreational users that are members of some drone organizations carry insurance as part of their membership. The requirement to hold insurance is often a condition of engagement by organisations procuring drone-based services. There are a range of models in other sectors where third-party insurance has been mandated, such as for vehicles. However, it remains to be seen whether this would be an appropriate mechanism for drones, especially considering the disparate risk profiles of operations across the drone sector. Aviation traditionally has operated free from mandated compulsory third-party insurance for damage to property or injury, although many industry operators hold insurance policies to cover a range of scenarios as a part of their risk management processes. Any decision to implement an insurance scheme for drone operators will need to be informed by relevant drone accident data, be proportionate to the risk profile of operations, be consistent with a holistic approach to regulation and complement the suite of various approaches available to manage risks and impacts from the use of drones. International approaches have included an insurance service as an optional industry developed UTM service.[42]

RR1718z3.pdf>. See this Report for a summary of the then current status of the regulatory environment for drone delivery services.

38 Emerging Aviation Technologies Paper (n 10).

39 ibid.

40 ibid.

41 ibid 7. See also, Julie-Anne Tarr, Maurice Thompson and Anthony Tarr, 'Regulation, Risk and Insurance of Drones: An Urgent Global Accountability Imperative' (2019) Journal of Business Law 559; Julie-Anne Tarr, Anthony Tarr, Ron Bartsch and Maurice Thompson, 'Drones in Australia—Rapidly Evolving Regulatory and Insurance Challenges' (2019) 30 Insurance Law Journal 135.

42 Emerging Aviation Technologies Paper (n 10) 25.

This position is ameliorated to some extent by an undertaking in a Policy Statement[43] issued in May 2021 that the "Australian Government will commence a study regarding the necessity and adequacy of insurance requirements to manage risks associated with the use of emerging aviation technologies" and "will consider the risks of damage associated from the use of drones, the broader suite of measures to manage drone safety, and the cost impacts of insurance on the development of the sector." [44]

The Policy Statement further states that this study:

> . . . will aim to assist the industry to make decisions about suitable insurance options within the emerging environment of drone and eVTOL operations, and to consider the appropriateness of any potential mandatory insurance requirements. The Australian Government recognises the potential impact of a mandatory insurance scheme on the continued innovation and operating costs for the diverse range of drone and eVTOL vehicle applications, and that in most cases, decisions about necessary insurance requirements are best handled by operators as part of individual approaches to risk and liability management.[45]

This laissez-faire approach is in direct contrast to the approach adopted in Europe and other jurisdictions described previously and it can be forcefully argued that any national regulatory policy in relation to drones must consider and address the issue of compulsory third-party liability insurance as a vital dimension in managing the risks and impacts associated with their use and deployment.

There is mounting evidence that injury to persons and property damage are very real concerns arising out of the use of RPAS, and that incidents of actual harm are increasing rapidly.[46] The Policy Issues Paper takes a very "wait and see" approach to ground risks by stating:

> There is no single data set for determining the number of incidents occurring domestically or internationally from drones involving ground risks. In Australia, there were 47 reported terrain collisions from drones between January 2016 and June 2017. It is expected that most recreational drone collisions with terrain would go unreported as there is no requirement to report such an incident in many circumstances, particularly as these collisions do not significantly impact safety in most cases. There is limited documentation of injuries in Australia with most documented cases minor in nature. There have been no fatalities in Australia as a result of a drone colliding with a person. With the exception of military uses, there is limited documentation of any international fatalities from drone collisions. Risks to people on the ground can be from a drone flying into a person, or the drone or debris from a drone falling onto a person. These may have different

43 Department of Infrastructure, Transport, Regional Development and Communications, Emerging Aviation Technologies National Aviation Policy Statement, May 2021. <www.infrastructure.gov.au/aviation/technology/files/national-emerging-aviation-technologies-policy-statement.pdf>.

44 ibid 29.

45 ibid 29.

46 See Julie-Anne Tarr, Maurice Thompson and Anthony Tarr, 'Regulation, Risk and Insurance of Drones: An Urgent Global Accountability Imperative' (2019) Journal of Business Law 559.

> consequences and require different mitigations which could vary considerably based on the size and design of the drone.[47]

This statement, with respect, misses the point from an insurance perspective—the key role of insurance is to protect against future uncertainties and uncertain loss. While the precise delineation and evaluation of risk may be a work in progress there is already a well-developed insurance market, described in Chapter 21, providing cover for liability arising from the use of a drone. Insurers providing products for new and evolving risks do face challenges in accessing sufficient relevant data around the emerging risks to enable accurate pricing. However, these products do exist and if a person who sustains injury or property damage is to have a real opportunity to pursue a damages claim against a drone pilot or operator, it is essential that the person at fault is able to be identified, or alternative recourse be available. Furthermore, that the person at fault has the capacity to satisfy any damages award or settlement. A requirement to hold appropriate third-party liability insurance should not, in these authors' submission, have to wait upon an indeterminate number of future catastrophic injuries or fatalities.

Given the increasing sophistication of these aircraft, the veritable explosion in their usage, their capacity to carry payloads and their ability to travel vast distances, the potential for injury or damage resulting from drone operations is ever increasing.[48] Notwithstanding the assertions in the Policy Issues Paper, numerous examples of personal injury and damage to property are already emerging through drone accidents. These are discussed in Chapter 9.

The increasing use of drones also gives rise to very real privacy concerns. As Matthew Koerner observes[49]:

> Drones have gained notoriety as a weapon against foreign terrorist targets; yet, they have also recently made headlines as an instrument for domestic surveillance. With their sophisticated capabilities and continuously decreasing costs, it is not surprising that drones have attracted numerous consumers—most notably, law enforcement.

These privacy concerns extend beyond law enforcement considerations and encompass issues such as the unauthorised collection of data and industrial espionage. Other real drone risks of a non-safety nature include potential damages arising from private law claims (such as trespass, nuisance, invasion of privacy) and possible damage to a company's goodwill or reputation.

These are further liability risks that need to be addressed by insurance.

Finally, the Policy Issues Paper emphasises that in relation to policy and regulation: "it will be essential that responses are coordinated and consistent across Commonwealth and State/Territory governments. . . . to achieve a nationally consistent and coordinated approach moving forward, facilitating industry compliance and interoperability".[50] To this end, it is noted that the Australian National Transport Commission, in their

47 Emerging Aviation Technologies Paper (n 10) 24–25.

48 Jacinta Long and Sarah Yao, Clyde & Co, 'Drone Damage: What Happens If a Drone Hits You?' (Insight, 12 December 2017).

49 Matthew R Koerner, 'Drones and the Fourth Amendment: Redefining Expectations of Privacy' (2015) 64 Duke Law Journal 1129.

50 Emerging Aviation Technologies Paper (n 10) 54.

Report[51] records that the Australian Transport Ministers have agreed that existing motor accident injury schemes should be expanded to cover crashes caused by automated vehicles—an approach already enshrined in the United Kingdom in the *Automated and Electric Vehicles Act 2018* . When considering drones (i.e. automated aerial vehicles) it is not, therefore, too much of a stretch to contemplate that they should be treated similarly to the proposed treatment of automated vehicles, especially when the drone is an aerial taxi, or aerial delivery vehicle operating in a high-density-population area. It is, therefore, not unreasonable that the operator of such a drone should carry appropriate and adequate liability insurance to ensure that members of the public have recourse to compensation for death, injury or property damage.

Accordingly, in the opinion of the authors of this chapter, a national policy that omits a considered and effective implementation of compulsory liability insurance is ignoring a vital dimension in managing the risks and impacts associated with the use and deployment of drones and other emerging aviation technologies.

Implementation options

Where a decision is made to require third-party liability insurance, a potential implementation option would be to replicate the regime, with necessary modifications and adjustments, which generally applies in Australia, the USA and the UK in respect of motor vehicles.

In Australia, for example, all jurisdictions have a range of statutes that supplement or supplant liability based on the general principles of negligence in the aftermath of road accidents. Compulsory Third Party (CTP) insurance schemes for personal injury and National Injury Insurance Schemes (NIIS) are in place in all Australian jurisdictions to provide lifetime care for catastrophic motor vehicle accident personal injuries.[52] As Mark Brady, Tania Leiman and Kieran Tranter explain:[53]

> This approach to motor vehicle accident personal injury contrasts with claims for motor vehicle accident property damage and other loss, where it has generally been left to the general law of negligence to determine driver liability for claims brought in negligence.

Vehicles are required to have CTP insurance. In the event of a motor vehicle accident this insurance covers any compensation claims that may arise and the motor vehicle accident victims are awarded compensation by the CTP insurer of the offending vehicle. Where the vehicle involved in an accident cannot be identified or is on the road illegally without CTP insurance, legislation across most Australian jurisdictions provides recourse for these victims through a Nominal Defendant.[54]

51 'Automated Vehicle Program Approach September' (2020)<www.ntc.gov.au/transport-reform/automated-vehicle-program>.

52 See, for example, Transport Accident Act 1986 (Vic.); Motor Accident Insurance Act 1994 (Qld); Motor Accidents Compensation Act 1999 (NSW); Lifetime Care and Support (Catastrophic Injuries) Act 2014 (ACT); Motor Accidents (Lifetime Care and Support) Act 2016 (NSW); National Injury Insurance Scheme (Qld) Act 2016; Motor Vehicle (Catastrophic Injuries) Act 2016 (WA).

53 'Automated Vehicles and Australian Personal Injury Compensation Schemes' (2017) 24 Torts Law Journal 32, 36.

54 In the UK, the Motor Insurer's Bureau compensates the victims of road accidents caused by uninsured and untraced motorists. Various arrangements apply in the United States including States that maintain

For example, in Queensland the Nominal Defendant is a statutory body established under the *Motor Accident Insurance Act 1994* (Qld) for the purpose of compensating people who are injured as a result of the negligent driving of unidentified and/or uninsured (no Compulsory Third Party (CTP) insurance) motor vehicles. The Nominal Defendant operation is funded by a levy within the CTP insurance premium with the levy being set on the basis of an actuarial assessment of claim trends. With regard to claims involving uninsured motor vehicles, the Nominal Defendant has the right to recover as a debt, the amount paid in settlement of the claim from the owner or driver (or both) of the uninsured motor vehicle.

The South Australian privatisation model is particularly useful as an example of a framework that could be replicated in the drone context. The role of government is to mandate the CTP insurance, approve the standardised policy coverage and approve the insurers authorised to offer the insurance product. The authorised insurers under this competition model then compete on service, price and other policyholder benefits.[55]

The position is similar in the United Kingdom and the United States.[56] For example, pursuant to the *Road Traffic Act 1988* (UK) motorists must carry third-party insurance against liability for injuries to others and for damage to other person's property, resulting from the use of a vehicle on a public road or in other public places; similarly, in the United States most States require the vehicle owner to carry some minimum level of liability insurance, with few exceptions; such as, allowing alternative arrangements such as posting cash bonds (New Hampshire and Mississippi) or paying an uninsured motor vehicle fee to the State (Virginia).

In the European Union, pursuant to a 2009 motor insurance directive, all motor vehicles in the European Union are required to be covered by compulsory third-party liability insurance.[57] The directive prescribes minimum third-party liability insurance cover in EU countries and introduces a mechanism to compensate local victims of accidents caused by vehicles from another EU country. It imposes an obligation upon Member States to create guarantee funds for the compensation of victims of accidents caused by uninsured or untraceable vehicles. The Directive also harmonises cross-border claims settlement and compensation procedures under Articles 19–27; for example, national compensation bodies, claims representatives in other member states, a time limit to make a "reasoned offer" and rules for national information centres to assist claimants seeking compensation. However, civil liability determinations and calculations of awards remain at the discretion of EU member states.

There are, of course, in addition to the approaches described earlier, a diversity of legislative responses globally to the compensation of third parties arising out of the use of motor vehicles. For example, in South Africa the Road Accident Fund (RAF) is a juristic

---

unsatisfied judgment funds to provide compensation to those who cannot collect damages from an uninsured or under-insured driver.

55 See, for example, Premier of South Australia, 'Car Rego Costs Driven Down with Lower CTP Insurance Premiums in Full Competition' (22 May 2019)<https://premier.sa.gov.au/news/car-rego-costs-driven-down-with-lower-ctp-insurance-premiums-in-full-competition>.

56 See also the third-party liability compensation schemes in Canada, Hong Kong, Hungary, Indonesia, India, Italy, Norway, Romania, Russian Federation, Spain and the United Arab Emirates. This is not an exclusive list.

57 Motor insurance—Directive 2009/103/EC relating to insurance against civil liability in respect of the use of motor vehicles, and the enforcement of the obligation to insure against such liability.

person established by an Act of Parliament,[58] responsible for providing appropriate cover to all road users within the borders of South Africa and for rehabilitating and compensating persons injured as a result of motor vehicles. Contributions to the RAF are done by way of a levy on fuel used for road transportation. Moreover, compensation funds are found in other areas, such as compensating consumers in the case of insolvency of tour operators[59] and to protect victims of terrorism[60] or natural catastrophes.[61]

In the particular case of drones, it is suggested that an adaptation, with appropriate modifications, of the relevant compulsory third-party motor vehicle scheme with associated nominal defendant arrangements or of other accident compensation arrangements could provide a tried and extensively tested pathway to resolving problems flowing from unregistered and/or uninsured drones.

The following factors may be considered material:

- The implementation of a compulsory CTP insurance regime in relation to commercial drone operations will resonate with the broader community interest, especially where personal safety is concerned.
- A model analogous to South Australian CTP insurance arrangements reduces the regulatory burden upon national agencies and could align well with registration processes.
- Such a model would deliver revenue to the national governments.
- A differential premium model can be implemented taking into account considerations such as nature and location of the commercial operations, and whether the operator is accredited to the relevant UAS International Standard (UIS) for its operations.
- The benefits of public liability insurance cover extend far beyond individual compensation. Coupled with a robust registration regime, operators with insurance cover would become more visible, accountable, and traceable in the case of an accident or incident.[62]

In conclusion to this brief description, it should be noted that in relation to autonomous vehicles, automated vehicles or driverless cars, the *Automated and Electric Vehicles Act 2018 (UK)* extends compulsory motor vehicle insurance to cover the use of automated vehicles in automated mode. As such, any victim(s) (including the "driver") of an accident caused by a fault in the automated vehicle itself are covered by the compulsory insurance in place on the vehicle. The insurer is initially liable to pay compensation to any victim, including to the driver who legitimately handed over

58 *Road Accident Fund Act*, 1996 (Act No. 56 of 1996).

59 See, for example, in the UK, Atol's air travel trust fund (ATTF) is a tourism industry-funded safety net which provides compensation to customers when tour operators become insolvent. It is funded by a small per-passenger payment from licensed tour operators who book air travel<www.caa.co.uk/ATOL-protection/Air-travel-trust/About-the-Air-Travel-Trust/>.

60 See, for example, in the US, certain U.S. persons who were injured in acts of international state-sponsored terrorism can apply for compensation to the 'US Victims of State Sponsored Terrorism Fund' <www.usvsst.com/>.

61 See, for example 'The Norwegian National Scheme for Natural Damage Assistance' which provides compensation for damage caused by natural perils, in cases where there is no insurance cover available <www.naturskade.no/en/the-norwegian-natural-perils-pool/>.

62 Parliament of Australia, Senate Standing Committees on Rural and Regional Affairs and Transport (n 2) Submission 51..

control to the vehicle. The insurer then has the right to recover costs from the liable party under existing common law and product liability law.[63]

It is not a quantum leap to entertain the notion that accidents involving automated "aerial" vehicles might be similarly dealt with.

Concluding comments

One difficulty facing regulators is to appropriately assess the risk and to introduce a regulatory framework that is commensurate with that risk. The regulatory intervention ideally needs to tread a path that does not stifle innovation and is not so "heavy handed" as to unduly impact commercial and recreational uses of drones.[64] This is no easy task because the rapid development of drone technology in the industry requires active and ongoing regulatory attention, and regulators are still trying to assess the various risks.[65]

Accordingly, it is entirely understandable and supportable, that Governments endeavor to travel a balanced and proportionate path on their regulatory journey, to provide certainty for industry investment, to provide a clear policy and legal framework that actively encourages and facilitates the use of new technology and to mitigate potential risks and impacts on the community and the environment.[66] In a regulator's endeavours to achieve "middle" ground, though, caution should be exercised lest it moves too slowly and fails to keep pace with technological developments and associated risks.

Given how entrenched compulsory third-party motor vehicle insurance is, it makes little sense that insurance in relation to person or property of third parties arising out of the use of drones is optional. Further, not only is there exponential growth in the number and scope of operations of drones, initiatives such as home deliveries and other uses in close proximity to people increase significantly risk to person and property of third parties.

Finally, it should be noted that the benefits of public liability insurance cover extend far beyond individual compensation. Coupled with a robust registration regime, operators with insurance cover would become more visible, accountable, and traceable in the case of an accident or incident. According to one submission to the Australian

63 'Commentary on provisions of Bill/Act' (2018) <www.legislation.gov.uk/ukpga/2018/18/notes/division/6/index.htm>.

64 See, for example, Kyle Bowyer, 'The Robotics Age: Regulatory and Compliance Implications for Businesses and Financial Institutions' (*The European Financial Review*, 21 April 2018) <www.europeanfinancialreview.com/ the-robotics-age-regulatory-and-compliance-implications-for-businesses-and-financial-institutions/> "Regulation needs to strike a balance between controlling risk and stifling growth. Interestingly, the call for regulation often comes from innovators and thinkers such as Elon Musk and Bill Gates and it is becoming increasingly evident that existing laws regulating product liability, consumer rights, property law, intellectual property and tort law, to name but a few, may not be adequate to manage and control the risks associated with rapidly advancing AI (including technologies such as drones)."

65 See Ben Norris, 'Drones: The Search for Risk-based Rules' (*Commercial Risk Europe*, 21 May 2019). In the article, Jeff Ellis from Clyde & Co is quoted as saying: "Regulations are meant to mitigate a risk. But before you figure out what risk mitigation should be, you need to understand the risk itself. So regulators are now trying to assess the risk. As regulators are satisfying themselves via various testbeds, the rules are going to change".

66 Emerging Aviation Technologies Paper (n 10) 4.

Senate Inquiry Committee[67] the possession of an operator's certificate and the associated insurance policy for a business, regularly acts as a deterrent for unsafe flight. In contrast, amateur or recreational operators who have "no skin in the game" may be more inclined to illegally take on jobs or unsafe operations as "they will most likely lose nothing but the fee they got for the job anyway".[68]

67 Mr Ashley Fairfield, *Submission 51*, p 2 in the Australian Senate Inquiry Committee, this submission was referred to in the Parliament of Australia, Senate Standing Committee on Rural and Regional Affairs and Transport (n 2) para 4.22.

68 ibid.

Part F

Conclusion

23 Drones in the future

Julie-Anne Tarr, Maurice Thompson, Anthony A. Tarr and Jeffrey Ellis

Introduction

The world is becoming increasingly connected and autonomous. In the not-too-distant future it will be commonplace to see drones in our skies, driverless cars on our streets, and robots in our homes. These innovative and disruptive technologies present myriad benefits, but also bring a range of new and complex risks.

As Simon Ritterband observes:

> The genie is well and truly out of the bottle. . . .drones are here to stay and with the world in the grip of a pandemic, new and creative ways of facilitating business have brought drones to the forefront. There is a case to be made that the rate of growth within the industry has grown exponentially because of Covid-19.[1]

Widespread use of drones is now in place around mining, remote exploration works and repair, maritime work, geological survey, agricultural land management, urban transport and delivery, aerial photography, media and more. Recreational take-up continues to fuel market growth of drones globally, and their increasing use in areas like law enforcement, search and rescue and emergency relief is evolving very rapidly. The range of applications continues to grow at an astonishing pace and clear evidence of this continuing trend is apparent from significant increases in patent filings, foreshadowing new ideas and further evolution.[2]

For example, from June 2018 to June 2019, Walmart filed for 97 new drone patents with the World Intellectual Property Organization and Amazon filed 54.[3] The patents range from a gas-filled aerial transport and launch system,[4] devices and methods to

1 Managing Director, Moonrock Insurance Solutions; correspondence with the General Editor, Anthony Tarr, 31 October 2020.

2 R Crossan, 'Adopting Drone Technology' (*BDO United Kingdom*, 17 June 2019) <www.bdo.co.uk/en-gb/news/2019/drone-patents-jump>.

3 See M Coulter, 'Walmart Outpaces Amazon in Drone Patent Race' (*Financial Times*, 16 June 2019) <www.ft.com/content/7cd22fb6-8e79-11e9-a24d-b42f641eca37>. According to the report, China was the global leader with around 6,000 applications followed by the US with 2,045, South Korea with 741, Australia with 81, and Canada with 79 .

4 See details of United States Patent Application 20170233053, D High, 'Gas-filled Carrier Aircrafts and Methods Dispersing Unmanned Aircraft Systems in Delivering Products' (*US Patent and Trademark Office*, 17 August 2017) <http://appft1.uspto.gov/netacgi/nph-Parser?Sect1=PTO1&Sect2=HITOFF&d=PG01&p=1&u=/netahtml/PTO/srchnum.html&r=1&f=G&l=50&s1=20170233053>.

detect and handle incorrectly placed items,[5] and package release systems.[6] To help ensure drone package delivery to the correct person, Amazon owns a patent which describes a process whereby the drone may utilise facial recognition techniques to determine whether the photographic image of the customer matches the customer image provided to the delivery service and then recognise both audible cues and visible gestures such as waving arms and pointing to follow delivery instructions.[7] Before the package is even collected, drones can conduct stocktakes, efficiently and safely replacing staff who manually scan barcodes whilst on a forklift for the higher shelves. Warehousing constitutes 30% of the cost of logistics in the United States, and with businesses motivated to reduce these costs,[8] systems have been developed using drones to scan products and pallet barcodes in warehouses.[9] Replacing the crystal ball with artificial intelligence algorithms from Big Data, Amazon was granted a patent for a shipping system designed to cut delivery times by predicting what buyers are going to buy before they buy it—and shipping products in their general direction, or even right to their door, before the sales occur.[10] After the empty supermarket shelves of 2020, drones could assist with timely speculative transport of goods by forecasting demand spikes and lulls.

Drone technology will continue to evolve and the range and sophistication of applications will expand. Regulators and the community at large will be well served to adopt an attitude that is diametrically the opposite to that which confronted Thomas Edison in 1878. When the news got out that Edison was developing the first practical electric light bulb, a British Parliamentary Committee noted that Edison's light bulb was "good enough for our Transatlantic friends . . . but unworthy of the attention of practical or scientific men".[11]

International regulation

Global action to develop a harmonised approach and international coordination in relation to drones are more than worthy objectives—they are essential given the

5 See details of United States Patent Application 10,669,140, D High, 'Shopping Facility Assistance Systems, Devices and Methods to Detect and Handle Incorrectly Placed Items' (*US Patent and Trademark Office*, 2 June 2020) <https://insight.rpxcorp.com/patent/US10669140B2>.

6 See details of United States Patent Application 10,6301,021, Joseph Rinaldi and others, 'Package Release System for Use in Delivery Packages, and Methods of Delivering Packages' (*US Patent and Trademark Office*, 28 May 2019) <http://patft.uspto.gov/netacgi/nph-Parser?Sect1=PTO2&Sect2=HITOFF&p=1&u=%2Fnetahtml%2FPTO%2Fsearch-bool.html&r=3&f=G&l=50&co1=AND&d=PTXT&s1=10301021&OS=10301021&RS=10301021>.

7 See details of United States Patent Application 9,921,579, 'Human Interaction with Unmanned Aerial Vehicles' (*US Patent and Trademark Office*, 20 March 2018) <http://patft.uspto.gov/netacgi/nph-Parser?Sect2=PTO1&Sect2=HITOFF&p=1&u=/netahtml/PTO/search-bool.html&r=1&f=G&l=50&d=PALL&RefSrch=yes&Query=PN/9921579>. This technology would likely stimulate a great deal of privacy concerns for the public and regulators.

8 E Companik, M Gravier and M Theodore Farris II, 'Feasibility of Warehouse Drone Adoption and Implementation' (2018)28(2) *Journal of Transportation Management* 33–50.

9 See DroneScan details</www.dronescan.co/DroneScan> claims to be up to 50 times faster than manual capturing.

10 Greg Bensinger, 'Amazon Wants to Ship Your Package before You Buy It'(*The Wall Street Journal*, 17 January 2014). US patent number 8615472B2.

11 Clinton Nguyen, '7 World-changing Inventions that Were Ridiculed When They Came Out' (*Tech Insider*, 2 August 2016) <www.insider.com/inventions-that-were-ridiculed-2016-8>.

international nature of aviation and the need to accommodate and integrate the international use of drones. The achievement of these objectives is no easy task as the regulation of ever-increasing drone-related operations and activities is proving to be a challenge for national aviation safety authorities around the world, not just domestically but also in a coordinated global sense. It is a challenge that must be embraced and managed.

It is generally accepted that one of the key challenges facing regulators globally in fully realising the potential of drones is their successful integration into the non-segregated airspace without reducing existing capacity and while maintaining safety levels currently imposed and minimising potential dangers to other aircraft, passengers, and other persons and property on the ground.[12]

Organisations such as the International Civil Aviation Organisation (ICAO) and the European Union Aviation Safety Agency (EASA) have vital roles to play in this regard and more broadly. The ICAO Model UAS Regulations Parts 101, 102 and 149, supported by Advisory Circulars, and its publication of Standard and Recommended Practices (SARPs) are potentially of very significant benefit to member states in reducing time and costs associated with the regulation of drones. These Regulations are based upon a review of existing regulations in Member States in a bid to share best practices that can be implemented by countries seeking to improve, or introduce, UAS regulation.

EASA is another transnational organisation attempting to bring some much-needed clarity to unmanned airspace. Established in 2002 with the aim of ensuring safety and environmental protection within the European Union, its goals in relation to UAS include *managing the safe introduction of UAS into the airspace*[13] as well as the admirable goal of simplifying the regulatory sphere by adopting a single regulatory and certification process among Member States.[14] Such a clear transnational policy will be of assistance in aiding the development of both safety and technology as well as simplifying the process for operators across the EU. There is little doubt that embracing an internationally coordinated implementation strategy will enable the potential benefits of this emerging technology to be more quickly realised while at the same time ensuring society is protected from its harmful risks—at least from a safety perspective.[15]

12 See, for example, European Commission, 'Communication from the Commission to the European Parliament, the Council, the European Economic and Social Committee and the Committee of the Regions, Sustainable and Smart Mobility Strategy—Putting European Transport on Track for the Future' COM 789 final (Brussels, 9 December 2020) <https://ec.europa.eu/transport/sites/transport/files/legislation/com20200789.pdf>.

13 European Plan for Aviation Safety (EPAS) 2020–2024 14.1; S Michaelides-Mateou and C Erotokritou, 'Flying into the Future with UAVs: The Jetstream 31 Flight' (2014)39 Air Space Law 111, 129.

14 The UK will be treated as a Member State until 31 December 2020 under the terms of its withdrawal agreement. Following this it will be treated as a Third Country, subject to any subsequent agreement.

15 See Ron Bartsch, *Aviation Law in Australia* (Thomson Reuters 2018), para. 21.95; David Hodgkinson and Rebecca Johnston, 'Guiding Principles for Drones: A Starting Point for International Regulation' (2018) 3 Perth International Law Journal 158, propose a set of guiding principles, which offer a general framework within which the operation of drones can be regulated. They are based on principles of aviation law and international law, as well as best practice principles. Such operation is to ensure the integration of drones into existing airspace both within States and across borders.

National regulation

At a national level, especially within federal jurisdictions, the interplay between national, state and local (council, local authority or municipal) laws can make for a complex interaction.[16] For the sake of consistency and certainty, aviation law is generally within the sole remit of the national government[17] and there are strong arguments that, in relation to commercial aviation using recognised aerodromes, it is (for the most part) clear cut where the boundaries of national and local legislation are drawn.[18] In the United States, for example, the Supremacy Clause of the US Constitution provides that federal laws are supreme and therefore preempt (override) conflicting state and local regulations.[19] Where the federal government has made clear its intention to be the sole regulator of an area, preemption is relatively straightforward. Difficulties arise where the federal government has not expressly preempted an area particularly where there is crossover with areas traditionally left to the states. Similarly, in Australia, the scope of Commonwealth "aviation" powers do not extend to commercial aspects of aviation, nor, from the recent decision of the High Court in *Work Health Authority v Outback Ballooning Pty Ltd*,[20] does the body of Commonwealth civil aviation laws exclude the application of state and territory occupational health and safety laws.[21]

The battle for control between national and local government is nothing new, and while on the one hand it may seem sensible for control of drones, like aviation, to remain with the national government, unlike aviation, drones do not solely operate along agreed flight paths, from specified aerodromes, and are operated by remote pilots with varying degrees of skill and experience. As such, there is an argument that local authorities will be far more familiar with the risks of operating drones in local areas and therefore better able to regulate this. However, the potentially overlapping requirements of different aspects of local and national legislation provide added complexity to the regulatory oversight of operators, particularly those that may cross state boundaries in the course of their operations. Accordingly, there are strong arguments in jurisdictions like the United States and Australia[22] for legislative reform to clarify or "bright-line" jurisdictional boundaries.[23] In that regard, it should be fairly obvious

16 See detailed discussion in Chapter 13.

17 See, for example, the judgment of the High Court of Australia in *Airlines of New South Wales Pty Ltd v New South Wales* [No 2] (1965) 113 CLR 54.

18 ibid.

19 U.S. CONST. art. VI., cl. 2. 118 See, for example, *Mutual Pharmacy Co. v. Bartlett*, 570 U.S. 472, 476, 479–80 (2013) (holding that federal law preempted state law that directly conflicted with federal prohibition on drug manufacturers independently changing product labels). See also *Singer v. City of Newton* No. 17-10071-WGY, 2017 WL 4176477 (D. Mass., 21September 2017), appeal dismissed, No. 17-2045 (1st Cir., 7 December 2017)where a federal district court held that FAA regulations impliedly preempted sections of a Massachusetts city ordinance. Discussed fully in Chapter 13.

20 (2019) HCA 2.

21 Including the *Civil Aviation Act 1988*(Cth).

22 Julie-Anne Tarr, Anthony Tarr, Ron Bartsch and Maurice Thompson, 'Drones in Australia—A Rapidly Evolving Regulatory and Insurance Challenges' (2019) 30 Insurance Law Journal 135, 143.

23 See, for example, L Page, 'Drone Trespass and the Line Separating the National Airspace and Private Property' (2018) 86 George Washington Law Review 1152, 1173–78 where it is recommended that FAA define navigable airspace so that there is a bright-line height minimum describing where the FAA's exclusive jurisdiction ends, where drones must fly above, and where in the airspace states can regulate without the fear of Federal preemption.

that while the national government is in the best position to establish uniform regulatory requirements, it lacks the manpower and local presence to comprehensively enforce same. Local enforcement clearly requires the participation of local governments and police forces. In light of this mutual need, it seems fairly clear that some form of cooperative federalism is needed in this area.

Balanced regulation

Regulatory intervention ideally needs to tread a path that does not stifle innovation and is not so "heavy handed" as to unduly impact commercial and recreational uses of drones.[24] This is no easy task because the rapid development of drone technology in the industry requires active and ongoing regulatory attention, and regulators are still trying to assess the various risks.[25] Sensitivity to this measured approach is very evident in the communication from the European Commission dated 9 December 2020.[26] This document emphasises the necessity to put European transport on track for the future and the importance of a coordinated European approach to connectivity and transport activity to overcome crises such as the COVID-19 pandemic and to strengthen the European Union's strategic autonomy and resilience.[27] Drones are an integral part of the Commission's vision for innovative and sustainable technologies in transport[28] and the Commission commits to facilitating technological development and to establishing an agile regulatory framework to support the deployment of solutions on the market.[29]

This is a very encouraging communication as coordinated action has the potential to drive international standards for drones akin to that for manned aviation and bring enormous benefits in terms of safety, efficiency of operations, uniformity and technological innovations.

So-called Regulatory Sandboxes and Experimentation Clauses allow regulators to review the social and economic viability of new technology, how the technology fits in with current regulations, and what changes need to be made to counter risk effectively. These Sandboxes are identified by the Council of the European Union as tools for an innovation-friendly, future-proof and resilient regulatory framework that masters

24 See, for example, Kyle Bowyer, 'The Robotics Age: Regulatory and Compliance Implications for Businesses and Financial Institutions' (*The European Financial Review*, 21 April 2018) <www.europeanfinancialreview.com/the-robotics-age-regulatory-and-compliance-implications-for-businesses-and-financial-institutions/>. 'Regulation needs to strike a balance between controlling risk and stifling growth. Interestingly, the call for regulation often comes from innovators and thinkers such as Elon Musk and Bill Gates and it is becoming increasingly evident that existing laws regulating product liability, consumer rights, property law, intellectual property and tort law, to name but a few, may not be adequate to manage and control the risks associated with rapidly advancing AI (including technologies such as drones).'

25 See Ben Norris, 'Drones: The Search for Risk-based Rules' (Commercial Risk Europe, 21 May 2019). In the article, Jeff Ellis from Clyde & Co is quoted as saying: 'Regulations are meant to mitigate a risk. But before you figure out what risk mitigation should be, you need to understand the risk itself. So regulators are now trying to assess the risk. As regulators are satisfying themselves via various testbeds, the rules are going to change.'

26 See, for example, European Commission (n 12).

27 ibid paras 1–5.

28 ibid para 66.

29 ibid para 64–65.

disruptive challenges in the digital age.[30] For example, the CAA has launched two challenges (the Future Air Mobility Challenge and the Beyond Visual Line of Sight in Non-Segregated Airspace: Regulatory Sandbox Challenge) to provide pathways for the trial and approval of innovative solutions and to assist in shaping the requirements for future regulations.[31] Similarly, the FAA from October 2020 commenced a new programme called BEYOND to tackle the challenges of UAS integration. The FAA states that "(t)he program will focus on operating under established rules rather than waivers, collecting data to develop performance-based standards, collecting and addressing community feedback and understanding the societal and community benefits, and to streamline the approval processes for UAS integration".[32] Other nations employing regulatory sandboxes for drone experiments include Russia,[33] Japan,[34] Germany[35] and Malawi.[36]

Regulator or regulators

As discussed in Chapter 13, up to this point in time, most aviation laws and regulation has centred around the delivery of aviation services by aviation companies to users of discreet aviation services (e.g. passenger and cargo transit by aviation carriers to consumers of those same aviation services). In the age of drones, however, companies with historically no aviation experience are pivoting their offerings to take advantage of drones' technology and are entering into and impacting the aviation sector. With

30 Council of the European Union 13026/20 on the Council Conclusions on Regulatory sandboxes and experimentation clauses as tools for an innovation-friendly, future-proof and resilient regulatory framework that masters disruptive challenges in the digital age (2020) BETREG 27.

31 The CAA has launched the Future Air Mobility Challenge and the Beyond Visual Line of Sight in Non-Segregated Airspace: Regulatory Sandbox Challenge to provide pathway to seek approval for the trial of an innovative solution and shape the requirements for future regulations. See CAA, 'Regulatory Challenges for Innovation in Aviation' (*CAA*, 2020) <www.caa.co.uk/Our-work/Innovation/Regulatory-challenges-for-innovation-in-aviation/>.

32 The FAA is tackling the remaining challenges of UAS integration with a new program called BEYOND from October 2020. "The program will focus on operating under established rules rather than waivers, collecting data to develop performance-based standards, collecting and addressing community feedback and understanding the societal and community benefits, and to streamline the approval processes for UAS integration." See United States Department of Transportation, 'BEYOND' (*UAS BEYOND*, 2020) <www.faa.gov/uas/programs_partnerships/beyond/>.

33 On 28 January 2021 Federal Law No 258-FZ will come into force in Russia which will result in the creation of regulatory sandboxes, one of which includes drone cargo transportation. See also Damir R Salikov, 'Regulatory Sandboxes in Russia: New Horizons and Challenges' (2020) 1(2) Digital Law Journal<https://doi.org/10.38044/2686-9136-2020-1-2-17-27>, note the authors' discussion of the challenges a drone taxi may bring to legislation.

34 See details Prime Minister's Office of Japan, 'Regulatory Sandbox System' (2018) <www.kantei.go.jp/jp/singi/keizaisaisei/regulatorysandbox.html>.

35 Autonomous floating water drones could offer entirely new ways to shift the transport of freight from overloaded roads to rivers and canals. However, the technology needed is not yet available, and there are no rules to cover its use. Since it will probably be necessary to use public waterways in the course of the project, exemptions from shipping laws are required. The Economics Affair Ministry in Germany is currently planning a regulatory sandbox which permits the development and testing of autonomous electrical watercraft whilst simultaneously aiming to generate insights into the future development of the relevant rules. See Report on this and other related sandboxes, Federal Ministry for Economics and Energy, 'Making Space for Innovation: The Handbook for Regulatory Sandboxes' (July 2019).

36 See, for example, Maryanne Buechner, 'UNICEF's Ascent into the Drone Age' (*UNICEF USA*, 12 June 2018) <www.unicefusa.org/stories/unicefs-ascent-drone-age/34436>.

drones now so heavily used in the maritime, offshore oil and gas, natural resources, mining and transport sectors, among many others, it could be argued that drones should be regulated separately to classic aviation. At the least, consideration could be given to some dual regulatory oversight, of which there are a number of good examples internationally.[37] At the very least there will be a necessity to cross-pollinate and enhance regulatory agencies with knowledge and skills drawn from sectors recognised to be heavy users or potential users of drone technology, in other words, to create "purpose-built" authorities.

Whole-of-government approach

The authors respectfully concur in the conclusions of the Australian Senate Inquiry Committee[38] that in order to balance the important challenges of ensuring public and aviation safety, and encouraging innovation, a nation-wide enforcement regime, including powers to issue on-the-spot-fines and report infringements, as part of a coordinated "whole-of-government" policy, must be created.[39]

The distribution of responsibility across various agencies or departments of government is normal. For example, in the United Kingdom, regulation is split between various organisations, including the Civil Aviation Authority ("CAA"), Health and Safety Executive ("HSE"), Police and Air Accident Investigation Branch ("AAIB"). In Australia, the Commonwealth Department of Infrastructure, Transport, Cities and Regional Development currently has carriage of this whole-of-government framework to manage drones and as a first step in this process, the department is working with Commonwealth agencies, state government and industry to develop a national "whole-of-government" policy position. It is expected that this will form the basis of future work to put in place a range of measures to manage drones that will facilitate innovation from the drone sector, while ensuring adequate controls to address the range of risks and impacts.

Insurance

The drone insurance market is an evolving and complex environment. Challenges in insuring drone use are particularly novel, not only due to the evolving nature of the technology but also because of the unique factors to be considered as part of risk assessment.[40] Risk assessments from the perspective of an insurer are also made more difficult by the fact that not all risks are entirely understood—even using Big Data.

37 For example, offshore oil and gas rigs in Australia are regulated by two authorities: the National Offshore Petroleum Safety and Environmental Management Authority (NOPSEMA) and the Australian Maritime Safety Authority (AMSA), with the jurisdiction between the two grey to say the least, but competently dealt with via an MOU between the two authorities to cooperate in their dealings with such "maritime" and "offshore" assets and services. A similar obvious example is the USA's Federal Aviation Authority (FAA) which entered into an MOU with the Occupational Safety and Health Administration (OSHA) to jointly regulate in respect of airport ramp safety issues.

38 Senate Standing Committees on Rural and Regional Affairs and Transport, 'Regulatory Requirements that Impact on the Safe Use of Remotely Piloted Aircraft Systems, Unmanned Aerial Systems and Associated Systems' (31 July 2018) chapter 8. ISBN 978-1-76010-808-3.

39 ibid paras. 8.39–8.50.

40 Julie-Anne Tarr, Maurice Thompson, and Anthony Tarr, 'Regulation, Risk and Insurance of Drones: An Urgent Global Accountability Imperative' (2019) 8 Journal of Business Law 559–68.

In addition to the development of bespoke policies, insurers are using innovative solutions such as on-demand "pay-as-you-fly" products and providing add-on or write-back cover within existing product lines. Diverse approaches are needed to meet demand in relation to the recreational proliferation of drones, and to meet demand in industries which have expanded their business activities to include drone operations.

Advocates of exposure based on on-demand insurance for drones maintain that the application of traditional insurance pricing methods in the drone industry has led to many drone operators and enterprises paying substantially more for their insurance than their risk actually requires.[41] It is further asserted that this opaque "one-size-fits-all" approach means that proactive risk mitigation is not incentivised or rewarded by insurers, despite the likelihood of fewer claims. Flock's Sam Golden[42] states that:

> Thankfully, the rise of flying robots has coincided with the rise of Big Data. When used intelligently, Big Data can be harnessed to quantify, intelligently price, and mitigate drone flight risks in real-time. As such, insurance is more transparent, with fairer pricing tailored to individual risk profiles. What's more, rich data insights can enable drone operators to fly safer and be rewarded for doing so.
>
> The future of the insurance industry does not stop at usage-based products but rather broadens into predictive risk mitigation. As model sophistication evolves with the realization of Big Data, insurers will have the ability to provide transparent steps to mitigating risk and avoiding claim events.

Not surprisingly, this view of exposure based on on-demand insurance is not accepted by all market participants. For example, Moonrock Insurance Solutions,[43] in conjunction with their underwriters, considers it preferable to offer a full insurance service providing cover even when the drone is not flying for a specific time period, with polices fully loaded with covers for any eventuality. Simon Ritterband observes that from their comparisons the average costs of on-demand insurance are most often higher than an annual policy if you extrapolate out and factor in the frequency of flights and cost per flight. Moreover, he points out that Moonrock is the only insurer in the market to provide no-claims bonuses, and they also offer additional discounts to insureds for additional training courses and audited fly logs.[44]

Accordingly, as was recognised in Chapter 20, the commentary mentioned earlier from respected industry participants reflects the evolving and complex environment of drone insurance. It does seem clear, though, that diverse approaches are needed to meet demand in relation to the recreational proliferation of drones, and to meet demand in industries which have expanded their business activities to include drone operations.

The increasing use of drones in high-density-population areas discharging services like deliveries and operating as taxis will increase the focus upon compulsory third-party liability insurance in jurisdictions that do not at present mandate such cover.

41 Sam Golden, 'The Future of Insurance for Connected Drone Fleets' (Whitepaper, *Flock*, 2019)<https://landing.flockcover.com/enterprise-whitepaper/>.

42 ibid.

43 See <www.moonrockinsurance.com/>.

44 Managing Director, Moonrock Insurance Solutions; correspondence with the General Editor, Anthony Tarr, 12 January 2021.

While it may be expected that the preponderance of commercial and even recreational drone users will voluntarily take out insurance to protect against the risk of potentially large exposures for third-party damage,[45] this expectation will be of no assistance to a party sustaining property damage or personal injury where the drone operator cannot be found or is impecunious and/or uninsured. While registration and licencing initiatives will make it easier for "onboard" identification of drone owners, pilots or operators, in the absence of compulsory third-party insurance there is no certainty that damages awards will be satisfied. This problem is compounded where the drone is unlicenced and/or unregistered and the responsible party cannot be identified.

As is noted in Chapter 22, the extension of existing motor accident injury schemes to cover crashes caused by automated vehicles, an approach already enshrined in the UK in the *Automated and Electric Vehicles Act 2018*, is an obvious pathway forward. When considering drones (i.e. automated aerial vehicles) it is not too much of a stretch to contemplate that they should be treated similarly to the proposed treatment of automated vehicles, especially when the drone is an aerial taxi, or aerial delivery vehicle operating in a high-density-population area. It is, therefore, not unreasonable that the operator of such a drone should carry appropriate and adequate liability insurance to ensure that members of the public have recourse to compensation for death, injury or property damage.

Privacy and Big Data

The use of drones raises a number of privacy issues in light of the extent and scope of data collection via drones. Drones have long been considered as "eyes in the sky"[46] with all but the most basic consumer models routinely equipped with some form of camera for still or video image capture. More advanced surveillance technologies can combine a sophisticated camera drone's high-quality audiovisual recording and storage capabilities with data analytics tools such as facial recognition software, gait analysis and other biometric assessment techniques to identify individuals for targeted observation. The size and manoeuvrability of drones enables them to monitor individuals at a distance and to follow and track targets, potentially without the knowledge of the person that is subject to surveillance. As technologies develop and drones become "smarter", the possibilities for data collection are almost limitless.

While drone operators must abide by the terms of relevant aviation regulations, those rules must be considered in conjunction with prevailing privacy and data protection laws. There are varying levels of maturity in such legislation ranging from comprehensive, principles-based data protection regimes, such as Europe's General Data Protection Regulation (GDPR),[47] to the patchwork of sectoral and state laws

45 See, for example, Australian Department of Infrastructure, Transport, Regional Development and Communications, 'Emerging Aviation Technologies National Aviation Policy Issues Paper' (September 2020) 25<www.infrastructure.gov.au/aviation/drones/files/drone-discussion-paper.pdf>.

46 See, for example, B Schermer, 'An Eye in the Sky: Privacy Aspects of Drones' (*Leiden Law School Blog*, 2013) <https://leidenlawblog.nl/articles/an-eye-in-the-sky-privacy-aspects-of-drones>.

47 Regulation (EU) 2016/679 of the European Parliament and of the Council on the protection of natural persons with regard to the processing of personal data and on the free movement of such data, and repealing Directive 95/46/EC (General Data Protection Regulation) (of 27 April 2016) L 119/1.

in the United States of America.[48] In emerging markets, the situation may be further complicated by the lack of any specific data protection legislation and the potential application of local criminal, media or defamation laws.[49]

Javaan Chahl and Titilayo T. Ogunwa from the University of South Australia[50] foreshadow increasing privacy challenges in the future, with sensor resolution, modes of operation and sensitivity continuing to improve over time with technological advances and inventions:

> So-called active sensors, those that emit energy to penetrate buildings and clothing, could strip away any semblance of privacy. Radars and laser radars fall into this category. There are numerous reasons why such sensors should not be pointed at people, privacy possibly being the least fundamental, compared to risk to eyes and cells from radiation. Active sensors can be detected in most cases, and clear limits on their use can be imposed. A greater difficulty lies with passive sensors, where radiation emitted or reflected by subjects or targets is received by the sensor that emits no radiation itself. Passive sensors cannot be detected easily, and do not affect the subject.
>
> Videos, in the visible optical spectrum as a passive sensor (no illuminator) are even more problematic for privacy, since their presence in public is normally tolerated. It is not clear what capabilities might be possible in the future using photographs and videos that are captured in the present.
>
> Projecting forwards, the ability to diagnose both chronic and acute clinical conditions from fixed video cameras and drone-based video cameras will emerge. These conditions will have implications for employment, insurance, government benefits, mating success, tenancy, finance, vehicle and firearm permits, witness testimony, electability for office and many other aspects of life. Society will need to come to terms with the implications of these developments.

As discussed in Chapter 10, while a number of countries have implemented separate privacy laws and drone regulations, legislators may wish to consider adopting privacy and data protection regulations specifically for drones.[51] A regulation that identifies explicit privacy responsibilities when using drones would provide consistency and certainty for drone operators, insurance companies, courts and individuals.

Such laws would set forth specific privacy principles and requirements tailored to drone usage, and mirror existing gold standards of data protection, such as the GDPR. For example, such laws should prescribe the adoption of data retention procedures

48 See, for example, Nuala O'Connor, 'Reforming the US Approach to Data Protection and Privacy; A Patchwork of Existing Protections' (*Council on Foreign Relations*, 30 January 2018).

49 See, for example, GSMA, 'Data Privacy Frameworks in MENA: Emerging Approaches and Common Principles' (June 2019) <www.gsma.com/mena/wp-content/uploads/2019/07/GSMA-Data-Privacy-in-MENA-Exec-Summary.pdf>.

50 'Pitfalls of mapping the human landscape.' Case note supplied to Dr Anthony Tarr by the authors, 1 January 2021.

51 A recent issues paper by the Office of the Victorian Information Commissioner on the interaction of IoT devices and privacy concluded that "traditional methods used to protect privacy and better inform individuals about how their personal information is collected, used and disclosed are largely incompatible or insufficient for IoT devices. See Office of the Victorian Information Commissioner, 'The Internet of Things and Privacy' (Issues Paper, February 2020).

and procedural protections for accessing data. Many critics of drones have raised concerns that the collection of aerial imagery and videos will enable pervasive surveillance that allows drone operators (whether a governmental agency or a private individual) to know what individuals are doing at different points in time. Such footage may be retained indefinitely, revealing private details of a person's life. Legislators, therefore, should adopt policies and procedures to address the retention of information and not neglect to focus on the information that is collected, how it is stored, and how it is accessed, in addition to the particular technology used to collect the information.[52]

Additionally, legislators could implement transparency and accountability measures requiring government agencies who operate drones to publish on a regular basis "usage logs" which document the activities conducted by the drones and the information collected during such activities on the website of the agency operating the system.[53] Such usage logs would detail who operated the system, when it was operated, where it was operated (including GPS coordinates), and the purposes of the operation,[54] as well as other details in line with existing data protection principles (e.g., the accountability principle of the GDPR). Drone operators could even be obligated to implement specific software and systems to allow for easy access to flight logs, allowing regulators to monitor how such drones are being used and enable them to hold operators accountable.

The FAA recently promulgated a regulation requiring remote identification of drones to help the FAA, law enforcement, and other federal agencies find the control station when a drone appears to be flying in an unsafe manner or where it is not allowed to fly.[55] However, this law is not without its critics as it has potential negative privacy impacts for businesses and consumers.[56]

Privacy laws regulating drones could also allow legislators to clarify what they mean by specific terminology and to specify the places entitled to specific privacy protections.[57] At the moment, conflicting laws and frameworks have caused confusion in certain countries as to the types of activities that are prohibited and the areas that are protected.[58] Legislators could choose to prohibit or limit certain types of surveillance

52 Gregory McNeal, 'Drones and Aerial Surveillance: Considerations for Legislators' The Project on Civilian Robotics Series (*Brookings*, November 2014) <www.brookings.edu/research/drones-and-aerial-surveillance-considerations-for-legislatures/>.

53 ibid.

54 ibid.

55 Expected to be published in January 2021, Final Rule on Remote Identification of Unmanned Aircraft (Part 89) Federal Code of Regulations, 28 December 2020.

56 As governments seek to provide regulatory solutions, they may inadvertently raise other complications. See the response from Wing in relation to the Remote ID legislation on Wing's blog where Wing writes, 'This approach creates barriers to compliance and will have unintended negative privacy impacts for businesses and consumers. Unlike traditional aircraft flying between known airports, commercial drones fly closer to communities and between businesses and homes. While an observer tracking an airplane can't infer much about the individuals or cargo onboard, an observer tracking a drone can infer sensitive information about specific users, including where they visit, spend time, and live, and where customers receive packages from and when.' Wing, 'Broadcast-Only Remote Identification of Drones May Have Unintended Consequences for American Consumers' (*Wing*, 28 December 2020) <https://wing.com/resource-hub/articles/remote-id-rule/>.

57 ibid.

58 See, for example, Senate Rural and Regional Affairs and Transport References Committee, Parliament of Australia, 'Regulatory Requirements that Impact on the Safe Use of Remotely Piloted Aircraft Systems, Unmanned Aerial Systems and Associated Systems' (Report, 31 July 2018) paras. 7.34–7.36<www.

that may impose serious risks to individual privacy. They could also clarify terms such as "surveillance", "reasonable expectations", "private property" and "public place" to avoid inconsistent interpretations by individuals, lawmakers and courts. Legislators may even wish to adopt entirely new terminology that can be easily understood by different parties and avoid misperceptions.

Drone operators should consider the application of relevant privacy legislation and adopt appropriate measures to mitigate the risks associated with data collection by drones. Best practices and techniques from comparable activities such as CCTV deployment can provide helpful parallels, but consideration should be given to the unique characteristics and capabilities of drone systems.

Drone technology and industry collaboration

One of the primary challenges faced by lawmakers both internationally and domestically in regulating drones is the rapid pace of development in drone technology and the diversity of drone use.[59] For the most part, as previously discussed, regulatory emphasis has understandably focussed on operational safety. Less attention and rigour has been applied to design standards which will also serve to improve safety. As has been stated on numerous occasions previously, the speed with which the technology is developing presents difficulties for regulators in nailing down specified design standards. By the time these have been looked at, the technology has developed again. Moreover, one of the main reasons that design standards languish is because regulators do not yet know what such standards look like. In order to achieve a suitable set of design standards, regulators will have to work closely with industry.

The European Commission as discussed in Chapter 14 intends to drive the research and deployment of innovative and sustainable technologies in transport. It stresses the following imperatives:

> (I)n order to make the digital transformation of the transport sector a reality, the EU needs to ensure that the key digital enablers are in place, including electronic components for mobility, network infrastructure, cloud-to-edge resources, data technologies and governance as well as Artificial Intelligence. The EU should further strengthen its industrial capacities related to the digital supply chain. This includes the design and production of components, software platforms and the Internet of Things technology for a further electrification and automation in transport and mobility.[60]

---

aph.gov.au/Parliamentary_Business/Committees/Senate/Rural_and_Regional_Affairs_and_Transport/Drones/Report>. Along with privacy legislation such as the Privacy Act 1988 (Cth), surveillance devices legislation, which governs the use of optical surveillance devices and data surveillance tracking devices, has been enacted in five jurisdictions—New South Wales, Victoria, Western Australia, South Australia and the Northern Territory. Yet, these laws create further confusion about the permissible use of drones <www.aph.gov.au/Parliamentary_Business/Committees/Senate/Rural_and_Regional_Affairs_and_Transport/Drones/Report>.

59 David Hodgkinson and Rebecca Johnston, 'Guiding Principles for Drones: A Starting Point for International Regulation' (2018) 3 Perth International Law Journal 158–64.

60 See, for example, European Commission (n 12) para 67.

The Commission recognises that an enabling environment for such game-changing mobility technologies is key and commits to working towards facilitating testing and trials, and towards making the regulatory environment fit for innovation, to support the deployment of solutions in the market.[61] From an industry perspective, and drawing upon comments related to Artificial Intelligence, the Chief Executive of Alphabet and Google observes that:

> industry must continue to be a helpful and engaged partner to regulators as they grapple with inevitable tensions and trade-offs.[62]

These sentiments and aspirations of regulators and industry are commendable and there is no doubt that thoughtful, agile and responsive regulation developed in close collaboration with industry is to be encouraged and supported.

Drones and product liability

There is an existing and well-developed body of products liability law that provides an effective analytical framework to address claims against manufacturers and others in the chain of distribution of drones. Product liability claims commonly will require determination of complex issues involving allocation of liability for the damage inflicted by drones between and among the owners, designers, manufacturers and distributors.

The increasing attention being paid by regulators and international organisations[63] to the implementation of design specifications and production standards, and to the imposition of obligations upon manufacturers and those responsible for the design and production of drones, will assist considerably in the resolution of product liability claims and issues.

For example, Commission Implementing Regulation (EU) 2019/947 of 24 May 2019 and Commission Delegated Regulation (EU) 2019/945 of 12 March 2019 on Unmanned Aircraft Systems lay new foundations for European UAS regulation which commenced on 31 December 2020. These Regulations impose the heaviest regulatory burden on operations at the areas of highest perceived risk while maintaining a relatively light touch approach to those operations considered lower risk. It does this by the separation of operations into three categories: Open, Specific and Certified. The Specific category of operation—covering medium risk operations—is based on a risk assessment performed by the Operator according to Article 11 of the Implementing Regulation and on an operational authorisation provided by the Competent Authority based on that risk assessment. The European Aviation Safety Agency (EASA) on 17 December 2020 published the accepted rules and methodology for this risk assessment in a document entitled Special Condition Light Unmanned Aircraft Systems—Medium Risk.[64] This Special Condition prescribes detailed airworthiness standards

61 ibid para 64.

62 Sundar Pinchai, 'Why Google Thinks We Need to Regulate' (*Financial Times Opinion Artificial Intelligence*, 20 January 2020) <www.ft.com/content/3467659a-386d-11ea-ac3c-f68c10993b04>.

63 Such as the European Union, the Federal Aviation Administration, International Civil Aviation Organisation (ICAO) and the International Organisation for Standardisation (ISO).

64 This document in EASA's terminology describes the Acceptable Means of Compliance (ACM) and Guidance Material (GM) for the specific category. See <www.easa.europa.eu/sites/default/files/dfu/

covering structures, design and construction, lift/thrust/power system installation, and systems and installation.[65] The obligations are very extensive and are broadly applicable to unmanned aircraft under 600 kg, with most drones currently under certification in EASA anticipated to adopt this certification basis.[66] This level of detail clearly has significant implications for product liability claims and determinations impacting upon matters such as reasonable care, reasonable design and state-of-the-art defences.[67]

The development of a consistent regulatory and operational framework for drones must of necessity consider product liability issues which in turn are closely connected to the development of drone-specific airworthiness standards, including mandated "fail-safe" functions. The Australian Senate Inquiry Committee[68] in 2018 recognised that to allow drones to fully integrate into shared airspace, they must be subject to standards of airworthiness. The committee recommended that airworthiness standards should extend to drones that arrive in the country through foreign imports, similar to model rockets and laser pointers. The committee also recommended that drones should include a number of fail-safe redundancies, such as return-to-home functionality and forced flight termination.

Drones and artificial intelligence

Sam Daley comments that:

> Artificial intelligence and drones are a match made in tech heaven. Pairing the real-time machine learning technology of AI with the exploratory abilities of unmanned drones gives ground-level operators a human-like eye-in-the-sky. More than ever before, drones play key problem-solving roles in a variety of sectors—including defense, agriculture, natural disaster relief, security and construction. With their ability to increase efficiency and improve safety, drones have become important tools for everyone from firefighters to farmers.[69]

Chapters 2–6 of this Book provide numerous examples of drone deployment and operations across industry, agriculture, the maritime sector, mining, healthcare and humanitarian efforts, law enforcement and security, and transport. Any list will not be exhaustive, as the range of applications continues to grow at a rapid pace, with AI fueling their utility and capacity.

---

special_condition_sc_light-uas_medium_risk_01.pdf>.

65 ibid Subparts C, D, E and F.

66 'EASA Publishes Proposed Standards for Certification of Light Drones' (20 July 2020) <www.easa.europa.eu/newsroom-and-events/press-releases/easa-publishes-proposed-standards-certification-light-drones>.

67 See discussion in Chapter 12.

68 Senate Rural and Regional Affairs and Transport References Committee, Parliament of Australia (n 58) 89 [6.50], paras 8.27–8.38.

69 'Fighting Fires and Saving Elephants: How 12 Companies Are Using the AI Drone to Solve Big Problems' (10 March 2019)<https://builtin.com/artificial-intelligence/drones-ai-companies>. See also, John Villasenor, 'Products Liability and Driverless Cars: Issues and Guiding Principles for Legislation' (*Brookings Institution*, 24 April 2014), 7<www.brookings.edu/research/products-liability-law-as-a-way-to-address-ai-harms/>.

Cameron Chell's 2020 prediction is already proving it will come true:

> In five years . . . drones will be able to think for themselves to navigate a course and complete a task. Today, they already can avoid obstacles while setting out on a human-programmed course. In 15 to 20 years there won't be any object that can't think and share data.[70]

For example, flying BVLOS with a waiver, Chula Vista police in California are using drones equipped with many of the same technologies used by self-driving cars to help the drone avoid obstacles. The drones also have the potential to be instructed with the press of a button, to follow a particular person or vehicle on its own.[71] Drones are becoming more "intelligent" with the capacity to build mental maps of their environment, to autonomously pick ripe fruit, to find insect infestations and to map land mines.[72] Drones, robots, self-driving cars and AI-driven systems will work together.[73]

Drone swarming or flocking is another area of development where technological advances continue to amaze and to capture the broader community's attention. For example, drone swarming entered the mainstream commercial vocabulary in 2017 when hundreds of swarming drones joined Lady Gaga in the US Super Bowl half-time entertainment.[74]

Thomas McMullan comments that:

> Instead of being individually directed by a human controller, the basic idea of a drone swarm is that its machines are able to make decisions among themselves. So far the technology has been at an experimental stage, but it is edging closer to becoming a reality.[75]

Recently robotics researchers led by Gábor Vásárhelyi of the Hungarian Academy of Science[76] have achieved drone swarming or flocking in the real world without the use

70 Cameron Chell, 'Draganfly CEO Sees Human AI Implants By 2045 (and Plenty of Drones)' (7 August 2020) <https://draganfly.com/news/draganfly-ceo-sees-human-ai-implants-by-2045/>.

71 See article, Cade Metz, 'Police Drones are Starting to Think for Themselves' (*New York Times*, 5 December 2020)<www.nytimes.com/2020/12/05/technology/police-drones.html>. Further privacy issues are likely to be raised from technological advances such as these.

72 See Cameron Chell, 'Draganfly: Drone Pioneer Looks to Become World's Go-To Provider for "Unique" Data' (*Draganfly*, 4 August 2020) <https://draganfly.com/news/draganfly-drone-pioneer-looks-to-become-worlds-go-to-provider-for-unique-data/>. As well as uncovering mines without having people at risk, Cameron Chell explains "what's really exciting . . . is the amount of data that we collect—the patterns of mines, the number of mines missed in the past, the areas and the regions. Building a database of this type of stuff really helps the AI to be able to uncover more mines."

73 See, for example, John Koetsier, 'Machine-First World? Getting Drones, Robots, Self-Driving Cars, and AI-Driven Systems to Work Together' (*Forbes*, 6 May 2020).

74 Brian Barrett, 'Lady Gaga's Halftime Show Drones Have a Bright Future' (2 May 2017) <www.wired.com/2017/02/lady-gaga-halftime-show-drones/>.

75 'How Swarming Drones Will Change Warfare' (16 March 2019)<www.bbc.com/news/technology-47555588>.

76 Gábor Vásárhelyi, Csaba Virágh, Gergő Somorjai, Tamás Nepusz, Agoston E. Eiben, andTamás Vicsek, 'Optimized Flocking of Autonomous Drones in Confined Environments' (*Science Robotics*, 18 July 2018) 320.

of a central control system. While the new work solves many of the challenges, more work is to be done. Vásárhelyi and his team note:

> Creating a large decentralised outdoor drone swarm with synchronised flocking behaviour using autonomous collision and object avoidance in a bounded area is as yet an unresolved task.[77]

However, the extent of the research being conducted and the innovative solutions being reported suggest that ways forward to deploy drones in swarms, and in other ways and applications, will be developed. For example, Caltech engineers recently reported that they had developed an AI that allows drone swarms to fly through crowded and unmapped environments.[78] They have designed a new machine-learning algorithm to control the movement of several flying robots through cluttered, unmapped spaces, so these drones do not run into environmental obstacles or each other.[79] The machine-learning algorithm has each drone learning how to fly a given space on its own even as it coordinates with other machines.

Swarms of drones have many potential areas of application.[80] For example, in relation to security, survey, monitoring or surveillance functions, a swarm can cover or monitor a large facility or environment much more efficiently than manual surveillance. In disaster management, such as in the case of a wildfire, a swarm of drones, equipped with fire extinguishers or similar, can quickly examine and handle a large area without endangering human lives.[81]

As these drones and autonomous partnerships offload a multitude of laborious tasks from humans, regulators must take on the task of working with industry, companies and society in general to consider all relevant costs and benefits. Advances in AI technology whilst exciting, innovative and transformative will also give regulators a headache when it comes to catching up with advances and grappling with different types of liability, Big Data and privacy issues—not the least when AI and drones are fellow travellers.

77 See Andrew Masterson, 'Autonomous and Cooperating: The Dawn of the Drone Swarm' (18 July 2018) <https://cosmosmagazine.com/technology/autonomous-and-cooperating-the-dawn-of-the-drone-swarm/> discussing the research of Vásárhelyi and his team.

78 Arooj Ahmed, 'Researchers Have Developed an AI Algorithm that Allows Drone Swarms Fly Through Crowded and Unmapped Environments' (*Digital Information World*, 21 July 2020) <www.digitalinformationworld.com/2020/07/researchers-have-developed-an-ai-algorithm-that-allows-drone-swarms-fly-through-crowded-and-unmapped-environments.html>.

79 The new machine-learning algorithm is called GLAS (Global-to-Local Safe Autonomy Synthesis).

80 There are obviously very significant military applications, which are not addressed in this commentary. But see, for example, Thomas McMullen, 'How Swarming Drones Will Change Warfare' (*BBC News*, 16 March 2019)<www.bbc.com/news/technology-47555588>; Dr Spencer Lynn, David Koelle, and Rich Wronski, 'Drone Swarms: A Transformational Technology' (*Aerospace & Defense Technology*, 1 May 2020) <www.aerodefensetech.com/component/content/article/adt/features/articles/36813>.

81 Anam Tahir, Jari Böling, Mohammad-Hashem Haghbayan, Hannu TToivonen, and Juha Plosila, 'Swarms of Unmanned Aerial Vehicles—A Survey' (December 2019) 16 Journal of Industrial Information Integration 100106.

Concluding comments

As *The Economist* noted in a 2017 article it is not just the rate of change but the "unknown unknowns" that further hamper the development of fit for purpose-regulatory frameworks for drones.

> Trying to imagine how drones will evolve, and the uses to which they will be put, is a bit like trying to forecast the evolution of computing in the 1960s or mobile phones in the 1980s. Their potential as business tools was clear at the time, but the technology developed in unexpected ways. The same will surely be true of drones.[82]

The exponential growth in the use and deployment of drones globally and of the technology underpinning their scope and operation dictates that international and national regulations and associated security and commercial arrangements such as insurance will continue to evolve. Therefore, as stated in the Introduction to this book, this edition is a marker or place maker for the status of the evolution at the end of 2020 and subsequent editions will describe the journey as it unfolds.

82 'Why the Wait for Delivery Drones May be Longer than Expected' (*The Economist Technology Quarterly*, 8 June 2017) <www.economist.com/technology-quarterly/2017/06/08/why-the-wait-for-delivery-drones-may-be-longer-than-expected>.

Index